The Economics of Crime

A National Bureau
of Economic Research
Conference Report

The Economics of Crime
Lessons For and From Latin America

Edited by **Rafael Di Tella, Sebastian Edwards, and Ernesto Schargrodsky**

The University of Chicago Press

Chicago and London

RAFAEL DI TELLA is the Joseph C. Wilson Professor of Business Administration at Harvard Business School, a research associate of the National Bureau of Economic Research, and a member of the Canadian Institute for Advanced Research. SEBASTIAN EDWARDS is the Henry Ford II Professor of International Economics at the Anderson Graduate School of Management, University of California, Los Angeles, and a research associate of the National Bureau of Economic Research. ERNESTO SCHARGRODSKY is a professor and dean of the business school at Universidad Torcuato Di Tella.

The University of Chicago Press, Chicago 60637
The University of Chicago Press, Ltd., London
© 2010 by the National Bureau of Economic Research
All rights reserved. Published 2010
Printed in the United States of America

19 18 17 16 15 14 13 12 11 10   1 2 3 4 5
ISBN-13: 978-0-226-15374-2 (cloth)
ISBN-10: 0-226-15374-6 (cloth)

Library of Congress Cataloging-in-Publication Data

The economics of crime : lessons for and from Latin America / edited
  by Rafael Di Tella, Sebastian Edwards, and Ernesto Schargrodsky.
      p. cm. — (National Bureau of Economic Research conference report)
    Papers presented at the conference "Crime, Institutions, and Policies,"
  organized by the Inter-American Seminar on Economics of the National
  Bureau of Economic Research and Laboratorio de Investigaciones sobre
  Crimen, Instituciones y Políticas of Universidad Torcuato Di Tella, held in
  Buenos Aires, Argentina, Nov. 29–30, 2007.
    Includes bibliographical references and index.
    ISBN-13: 978-0-226-15374-2 (hardcover : alk. paper)
    ISBN-10: 0-226-15374-6 (hardcover : alk. paper)
    ISBN-13: 978-0-226-79185-2 (pbk. : alk. paper)
    ISBN-10: 0-226-79185-8 (pbk. : alk. paper) 1. Crime—Economic aspects—
  Latin America—Congresses. 2. Crime prevention—Economic aspects—Latin
  America—Congresses. I. Di Tella, Rafael. II. Edwards, Sebastian, 1953–
  III. Schargrodsky, Ernesto. IV. National Bureau of Economic Research.
  V. Universidad Torcuato di Tella. Laboratorio de Investigaciones sobre
  Crimen, Instituciones y Políticas. VI. Series: National Bureau of Economic
  Research conference report.
  HV6810.5.E26 2009
  364.98—dc22

                                                                2009052687

Relation of the Directors to the
Work and Publications of the
National Bureau of Economic Research

1. The object of the NBER is to ascertain and present to the economics profession, and to the public more generally, important economic facts and their interpretation in a scientific manner without policy recommendations. The Board of Directors is charged with the responsibility of ensuring that the work of the NBER is carried on in strict conformity with this object.

2. The President shall establish an internal review process to ensure that book manuscripts proposed for publication DO NOT contain policy recommendations. This shall apply both to the proceedings of conferences and to manuscripts by a single author or by one or more co-authors but shall not apply to authors of comments at NBER conferences who are not NBER affiliates.

3. No book manuscript reporting research shall be published by the NBER until the President has sent to each member of the Board a notice that a manuscript is recommended for publication and that in the President's opinion it is suitable for publication in accordance with the above principles of the NBER. Such notification will include a table of contents and an abstract or summary of the manuscript's content, a list of contributors if applicable, and a response form for use by Directors who desire a copy of the manuscript for review. Each manuscript shall contain a summary drawing attention to the nature and treatment of the problem studied and the main conclusions reached.

4. No volume shall be published until forty-five days have elapsed from the above notification of intention to publish it. During this period a copy shall be sent to any Director requesting it, and if any Director objects to publication on the grounds that the manuscript contains policy recommendations, the objection will be presented to the author(s) or editor(s). In case of dispute, all members of the Board shall be notified, and the President shall appoint an ad hoc committee of the Board to decide the matter; thirty days additional shall be granted for this purpose.

5. The President shall present annually to the Board a report describing the internal manuscript review process, any objections made by Directors before publication or by anyone after publication, any disputes about such matters, and how they were handled.

6. Publications of the NBER issued for informational purposes concerning the work of the Bureau, or issued to inform the public of the activities at the Bureau, including but not limited to the NBER Digest and Reporter, shall be consistent with the object stated in paragraph 1. They shall contain a specific disclaimer noting that they have not passed through the review procedures required in this resolution. The Executive Committee of the Board is charged with the review of all such publications from time to time.

7. NBER working papers and manuscripts distributed on the Bureau's web site are not deemed to be publications for the purpose of this resolution, but they shall be consistent with the object stated in paragraph 1. Working papers shall contain a specific disclaimer noting that they have not passed through the review procedures required in this resolution. The NBER's web site shall contain a similar disclaimer. The President shall establish an internal review process to ensure that the working papers and the web site do not contain policy recommendations, and shall report annually to the Board on this process and any concerns raised in connection with it.

8. Unless otherwise determined by the Board or exempted by the terms of paragraphs 6 and 7, a copy of this resolution shall be printed in each NBER publication as described in paragraph 2 above.

Contents

Acknowledgments

This book compiles the papers presented at the conference "Crime, Institutions, and Policies," co-organized by the Inter-American Seminar on Economics of the National Bureau of Economic Research (NBER) and LICIP (Laboratorio de Investigaciones sobre Crimen, Instituciones y Políticas) of Universidad Torcuato Di Tella in Buenos Aires, Argentina, on November 29–30, 2007. We are extremely grateful to the Tinker Foundation for generously supporting the activities at the LICIP, including the organization of this conference, as well as to the Inter-American Development Bank and Fernando de Santibañes. We thank David Pervin and two anonymous reviewers for very helpful comments. Luciana Esquerro, Juan Marcos Wlasiuk, Cecilia de Mendoza, and David Lenis provided excellent research assistance.

Introduction

Rafael Di Tella, Sebastian Edwards,
and Ernesto Schargrodsky

Forty years since the publication of Gary Becker's seminal paper on crime and punishment, law and economics is now an important field of research in economics (Becker 1968). Its influence on policies, however, has varied across countries and over time. In the United States, for example, there is considerable interest in informing policies with academic research, as symbolized by the influence of Richard Posner, one of the leading scholars in the law and economics field and a judge on the United States Court of Appeals for the Seventh Circuit in Chicago. In other regions of the world, scholarly work on crime has a reduced influence on practice, which might be seen as paradoxical given that Americans are often viewed as particularly inclined to be practical.[1] One possible explanation for this is the strength and vitality of American-based academic research in the area of criminology.[2] Latin America, with its very high (and variable) crime rates, and small body of academic work seems to offer challenges and opportunities for the field. Indeed, the extreme macroeconomic dislocations and social inequities of the region present challenges to the application and generalization of research

Rafael Di Tella is the Joseph C. Wilson Professor of Business Administration at Harvard Business School, a research associate of the National Bureau of Economic Research, and a member of the Canadian Institute for Advanced Research. Sebastian Edwards is the Henry Ford II Professor of International Economics at the Anderson Graduate School of Management, University of California, Los Angeles, and a research associate of the National Bureau of Economic Research. Ernesto Schargrodsky is a professor and dean of the business school at Universidad Torcuato Di Tella.

1. On America's anti-intellectual bias, see Hofstadter (1963).

2. The influence of Becker's work is also present in the field of criminology, which obviously has a broader focus than law and economics and that has been as, or more, influential on practice. Note that work by economists has been influential, even though it could be considerably improved by better data and a closer attention to the progress made by research by criminologists. For an interesting review, see Bushway and Reuter (2008).

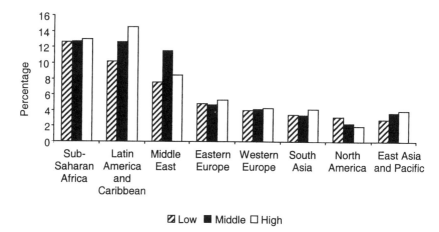

Fig. I.1   People who were assaulted or mugged, last twelve months, by income level
Source: From Di Tella, MacCulloch, and Nopo (2008).

on crime, but at the same time offer many opportunities given the strength of the dynamics involved and the extent of institutional experimentation. This book is an attempt at bringing the economics of crime to Latin America. It does so by presenting studies grounded in the economic approach to studying behavior pioneered by Becker that are either focused on Latin America, or that are focused on topics that are deemed particularly relevant for Latin America.

Latin America has one of the highest crime rates in the world. Ominously, during the last two decades these crime rates have been growing in several countries, making the problem of crime often the primary concern of citizens in the region. The passivity of the State, real or perceived, in the face of growing crime rates has increased skepticism about its ability (and willingness) to combat crime, while at the same time putting the spotlight on the possibility of police corruption and increasing the demand for a more punitive approach. Although comparing crime data across countries is often difficult (given the institutional differences in recording crime, as well as differences in the political economy of reporting and in the efficiency of public agencies), several pieces of evidence suggest crime is high in the region. Homicide rates in Latin America, for example, are more than double the world average (see Prillaman [2003]). The Gallup World Poll, which offers comparable survey data on victimization, suggests crime rates in Latin America are much higher than in the rest of the world, while confidence in the police is lowest. See figures I.1 and I.2 (from Di Tella, MacCulloch, and Nopo [2008]). The Latinbarometer survey offers more details and suggests that for 2007, 38 percent of Latin America's households report having been victims of a crime during the previous twelve months, 6 percentage points

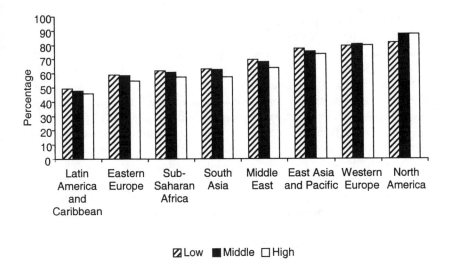

Low   Middle   High

Fig. I.2   People who have confidence in local police force, by income level
Source: From Di Tella, MacCulloch, and Nopo (2008).

higher than the previous year, and 9 points higher than in 1995.[3] These high levels of crime and violence impose significant costs on these societies. Londoño and Guerrero (1999) estimate that the costs of violence in Latin America in 1997 amounted to 14.2 percent of the region's gross domestic product, while Burki and Perry (1998) argue that Latin America's per capita income would be 25 percent higher if it had a crime rate similar to the rest of the world. There may also be high distributional costs of crime. Prillaman (2003) considers crime in Latin America as the primary obstacle for development of the region, affecting democratic consolidation, reducing economic growth, and undermining social capital. According to the Latinbarometer opinion polls, public safety is either the main concern of the population or the second most important concern behind unemployment (it is the main problem in almost half of the countries of the region including Argentina, Colombia, Brazil, and Venezuela).

These high levels of crime and the population's concern over this issue do not appear to have been accompanied by a significant investment in learning more about this problem and about the effectiveness of the policies destined to tackle it. Absent anything like a consensus over which set of practical policies might be more effective in reducing crime, the small body of available work by economists has singled out social polarization, unemployment, and inequality as the main causes of the high levels of crime in Latin America (see, for example, Fajnzylber, Lederman, and Loayza [2000], and Gaviria and Pages [2002]). However, this lack of systematic knowledge has

3. See www.latinobarometro.org.

not stopped the adoption of numerous reforms concerning criminal policy, including changes in the duration of prison sentences, reforms in the codes of procedure, changes in the criminal responsibility age for juvenile offenders, modifications on patrol schemes conducted by the police, numerous purges in the police force, and changes in the prison systems, to name a few.[4] In this context, it is unsurprising that policies have changed back and forth, with several episodes of political overreaction in both directions, from emphasis on the protection of the defendant's human rights—"garantismo"—to more punitive stances—"mano dura." Needless to say, these policies have not been scientifically evaluated and its utilization or interruption has been based on intuitions, opinions, or ideological prejudices, rather than on rigorous studies. Of course, on some aspects of these policies there may never be full agreement, but what is striking is how little information is used in the formation of ideologies about how best to control crime.[5]

Formal policy evaluations are often difficult because of problems with data availability. Victimization surveys are scarce, incomplete, and infrequent. Without reliable victimization surveys, the only source of data have been the crime statistics issued by the governments. However, these statistics in many countries are not publicly available, lack periodicity and detail, and suffer when there is little trust in the police forces. The gap between official data on crime and victimization surveys has been found to be nonrandom, but dependent on socioeconomic levels and corruption perceptions (Soares 2004). Moreover, the importance of crime as a concern of potential voters has sometimes induced political manipulation in the content and timing of release of criminal statistics.[6]

It is possible to argue (optimistically) that the different approaches to fighting crime observed across developed countries, such as France and the United States, arise because of their different ideological traditions (e.g., a more punitive approach might be based on different beliefs about the role of luck versus effort in the determination of legal income, as in Di Tella and Dubra [2008]). However, it is difficult to make the case that the strange panoply of crime-fighting initiatives observed in Latin America arises because of

---

4. In some occasions, these variations introduce "natural" experiments allowing policy evaluation. See Galiani, Rossi, and Schargrodsky (2010) for a study of the effect of conscription on criminal involvement, and Di Tella and Schargrodsky (2004) for an example involving the effect of police on crime.

5. To provide one example, in 1999 the Congress of the Province of Buenos Aires, Argentina, imposed mandatory pretrial detention for people with no fixed residence, if minors intervened in the commission of the crime, and if the crime was committed by various authors (among other conditions). These changes contributed to a dramatic increase in the number of people "preventively" in prison, which reached 85 percent of the prison population of the province. In May 2005, the National Supreme Court of Justice demanded that the Province of Buenos Aires weaken its "preventive prison" laws. No study has been conducted on the effects of these changes in policy (see *Clarín*, August 5, 1999, and October 31, 1999; and *La Nación*, May 4, 2005).

6. This lack of uniform and periodic series has forced researchers to only rely on homicide statistics collected by the World Health Organization from national health registries for international comparisons.

these societies' peculiar preferences and beliefs. A more plausible account simply emphasizes the fact that there is not an informed debate about these issues, in part because there is not enough knowledge about the topic as applied to Latin America (and perhaps more broadly) and in part because of the lack of a tradition of serious data collection and policy evaluation in these societies.

In summary, lack of reliable data and the absence of supporting scientific work have characterized the public debate on safety policies in Latin America. In other areas, such as macroeconomic volatility, Latin America has made progress thanks (at least in part) to academic efforts that lead to a consensus around fiscal responsibility.[7] The book and the conference where these articles were presented are part of an attempt to improve the quality of current debates by bringing recent developments of the economics of crime to Latin America. The book is organized in three sections.

Overview: Latin American Exceptionalism?

The overview chapter (chapter 1, by Soares and Naritomi), presents a survey of the problem of crime in Latin America. It takes a very broad and appropriately reductionist approach to analyze the determinants of the high crime levels, focusing on the negative social conditions in the region, including inequality and poverty, and poor policy design, such as relatively low police presence. They make the case that, to some extent, crime rates in Latin America are not exceptionally high if we take into account these (very coarse) indicators of social and policy conditions. In other words, Soares and Naritomi are not surprised by the high crime rates because a lot of the variation in crime rates in the region is accounted for by variation in what their model specifies as the causes of crime. Their estimates suggest that a large fraction of the high violence levels can be explained by three factors: high inequality, low incarceration rates, and small police forces. Correcting some of these would bring violence in Latin America to, approximately, international levels. This is an important chapter because it suggests that a useful activity for economists might be as simple as to remind policymakers that somewhere in society somebody will keep track of the big, aggregate trends which, for example, trace back the high rates of crime in the region to police forces that are relatively small. Of course, crime and violence in Latin America have a complicated origin, with many subtle mechanisms at play, not all of them easily quantifiable, but the economists' reductionist approach allows us to understand the broad trends that serve as context.[8]

---

7. To give just one example, out of the first eighty-seven papers published in *Economía*, the flagship journal of the Latin American and the Caribbean Economic Association (LACEA), thirty-four were on macroeconomic topics (excluding trade) and one was on crime (Fajnzylber, Lederman, and Loayza 2000).

8. On some of these hard to measure, complex crime dynamics and their collective representation, see the contributions gathered in Isla (2007).

The Economics of Crime Meets Latin America

The second part of the book includes six chapters on the economics of crime in Latin America. The history of the region's growth (or lack thereof) suggests how poverty traps can arise in high crime settings, with crime being both a cause and a consequence of underdevelopment. The first three chapters illustrate three channels through which crime might generate poverty: by reducing investment, by introducing assets losses, and by reducing the value of assets remaining in the control of households. Of course there are many other possible channels, some of them potentially large in size.[9] But these chapters illustrate what we believe is a key characteristic of crime in developing countries in general (and Latin America in particular): it introduces a very high cost to society. In contrast to crime in developed nations, where at least the perception (we are unaware of the existence of convincing estimates) is one of second-order costs, in Latin America crime takes up so many resources directly or indirectly that it represents a first-order impediment to development.[10] The remaining three chapters in the section illustrate how crime might be affected, in turn, by features of underdeveloped economies (related to education, inequality, and demographic trends). Again, while there are many factors that can affect crime, these chapters emphasize three features in which Latin American countries present conditions that are extremely unfavorable relative to other regions and illustrate the general point that socioeconomic conditions in Latin America, together with the poor policy responses, make high crime and poverty traps quite likely.

A poverty trap may emerge with high costs of crime, and this can be expected in weak institutional environments. Thus, a hypothetical high level of crime in the United States has lower costs than the same crime rate in a poor country. This in turn makes high crime more likely to generate traps in poor countries. What are these high costs? A naïve view of the costs of crime would consider crime as just a transfer of a good from one person to another. If the criminal is poorer than the victim, there is even the presumption that crime might improve the distribution of income. Sensible people will disagree with this view on several grounds. The most obvious is that the transfer is not a lump sum but entails costly distortions in behavior, typically because the unpleasantness of crime exceeds the monetary value of the loss. Second, income gained in an illegal manner is not similarly valued by society (by definition), so the gain to the criminal is discounted while the loss to the victim is real (see chapter 3). And finally, the idea that

9. More broadly, there is a negative correlation between crime and the level of economic activity (see, for example, Cook and Zarkin [1985]).

10. Given that institutional details are important in understanding crime dynamics, we were fortunate to have available three pieces on broadly the same issue (the first three chapters on the costs of crime) in the context of the same country (Colombia).

the rich are the primary victims of crime seems counterfactual. And if they are not, one would need to know why this is the case and if this is the result of investments by the rich that should also be counted in the social cost of crime (see chapter 5).

One way that crime represents a cost to society is by reducing investment. Although this seems hard to measure, as so many things affect both investment and crime, the idea is intuitive and illustrated by the many Latin Americans who have acquired human capital traveling abroad but fear returning home, fueling the "brain drain." Chapter 2 by Pshisva and Suarez propose an approach focused on a particularly salient crime: kidnappings. Exploiting variation in kidnappings that target firm managers in different regions of Colombia, they find that firms invest less when kidnappings directly target them, while there is no effect when there are other forms of violent crime that do not explicitly target firms—homicides, guerrilla attacks, and general kidnappings. The estimated effect on one firm is larger for kidnappings suffered by other firms in the same industry. Investment at firms with substantial foreign ownership is particularly sensitive to kidnappings of foreign managers and owners.

Chapter 3, by Gaviria, Medina, Morales, and Núñez, tackles the difficult problem of estimating the full cost of crime. Given that these costs typically exceed the value of the lost property, researchers have developed general measures that are typically of two types: either a global measure that is based on an evaluation of well-being (e.g., happiness) or a measure that uses prices that incorporate all the available information (e.g., from a market equilibrium).[11] Chapter 3 follows the latter approach and is based on hedonic price models, where disamenities like crime are built into real estate market prices. They exploit the fact that households in the city of Bogotá are willing to pay considerable amounts to avoid violent crime. In the highest socioeconomic level, households pay up to 7.2 percent of their house values in order to prevent average homicide rates from increasing one standard deviation. The results suggest that security ends up creating an urban private market that effectively auctions security to the highest bidders. These segmented markets imply significantly different levels of access to public goods among the rich and poor.

Chapter 4 by Ibáñez and Moya contributes to the study of the costs of crime and violence by pointing out that in some cases the amount of insecurity is so high that households are displaced, inducing considerable asset losses. They do so again in the Colombian context, where a conflict of political origin has degenerated in a situation where the state no longer has exclusive control of violence in the area, which is what effectively happens in some impoverished urban areas in Latin America. They collect both qualitative and quantitative evidence on the processes of asset losses and asset

11. Cook and Ludwig (2006) is an example of some of the dimensions that are relevant to welfare evaluations in the area of crime (in their particular case, gun ownership).

reaccumulation following an initial shock. They document that full recovery of the assets is relatively rare: 75 percent of households do not recover their asset values, becoming locked in low income trajectories.

Chapter 5 by Di Tella, Galiani, and Schargrodsky focuses on the impact of a given increase in crime across different income groups. Interestingly, the research literature has not reached anything like a consensus on this issue, in part because, typically, only a small fraction of the population is victimized so that empirical tests often lack the statistical power to detect differences across groups (see, for example, Levitt [1999]). A second difficulty is that crime-avoiding activities vary across income groups. Thus, a lower victimization rate in one group may not reflect a lower burden of crime, but rather a higher investment in avoiding crime. Di Tella, Galiani, and Schargrodsky take advantage of a dramatic increase in crime rates in Argentina during the late 1990s to document several interesting patterns. First, the increase in victimization experienced by the poor is larger than the increase endured by the rich. The difference appears large: low-income people have experienced increases in victimization rates that are almost 50 percent higher than those suffered by high-income people. Second, for home robberies, where the rich can protect themselves (by hiring private security, for example), they find significantly larger increases in victimization rates among the poor. In contrast, for robberies on the street, where the rich can only mimic the poor, they find similar increases in victimization for both income groups. The data also offer direct evidence on pecuniary and nonpecuniary protection activities by both the rich and poor, ranging from the avoidance of dark places to the hiring of private security, with a clear association between changes in protection and mimicking and changes in crime victimization. The evidence is consistent with crime being displaced when potential victims protect themselves (a negative externality from the rich to the poor). Obviously there may be large potential gains from effective, centralized crime control policies (both within and across countries, as the problem is particularly acute when we cross legal jurisdictions), so this is a pressing question for future research.

Chapters 6 and 7 are more directly focused on the determinants of crime. Chapter 6, by De Mello and Schneider, analyzes the role of demography and policy interventions in explaining the large drop in homicides experienced by São Paulo, Brazil, in recent years. They attribute a positive role to several policy interventions including the creation of municipal police forces, the implementation of dry laws, gun control policies, the use of crime geo-referencing and criminal identification systems, and increases in incarceration. However, they argue that these factors cannot really account for the geographic and dynamic crime patterns. Instead, they explain that demographic changes fit well with the pattern of increase and reduction in homicides in São Paulo and other areas of Brazil. This chapter illustrates a different approach to the study of crime, one that relies on estimating the role of long-run underlying trends to calculate the proportion of current crime rates that can be attributed to forces beyond the immediate control

Table I.1   **Latin America's prisons**

Country	Prison population	Growth in incarceration (%)	Inmates per 100,000 inhabitants	Jail occupancy level (%)	Prisoners without sentence (%)
Argentina	60,621	188	154	97.7	53.8
Bolivia	7,310	35	79	165.5	74.4
Brazil	422,590	269	220	149.4	34.3
Chile	45,843	118	276	155	22.5
Colombia	63,648	90	135	130.6	34.9
Costa Rica	8,246	146	181	97.7	14.2
Ecuador	11,358	42	86	146.3	44.4
El Salvador	12,113	126	179	240.8	35.9
Honduras	11,589	103	161	140.4	63.5
Mexico	212,841	148	193	132.5	40.9
Nicaragua	6,060	80	107	132.7	21.4
Panama	11,345	156	339	137.3	58.6
Paraguay	6,037	103	95	116.3	69.5
Peru	39,684	152	141	187.3	63.9
Uruguay	6,947	129	193	146.2	63.1
Venezuela	19,853	−14	74	117.4	61.6

Notes: The second column shows the prison population growth rate between the first and last year of available data, which are: Argentina (1992 and 2006); Bolivia (1996 and 2005); Brazil (1992 and 2007); Chile (1992 and 2007); Colombia (1992 and 2007); Costa Rica (1992 and 2007); Ecuador (1992 and 2004); El Salvador (1992 and 2005); Honduras (1992 and 2005); Mexico (1992 and 2007); Nicaragua (1992 and 2006); Panama (1992 and 2007); Peru (1992 and 2007); Uruguay (1992 and 2006); and Venezuela (1993 and 2005).

of policymakers. The approach produces remarkable results, so the chapter spends considerable effort in understanding whether the magnitudes involved are empirically plausible. Given the large demographic changes in Latin America and the huge interest in learning from the successful São Paulo experience, the analysis appears particularly relevant for the region.

Chapter 7 by Alzúa, Rodriguez, and Villa focuses on the role of prisons. This is an area where there are perhaps some of the biggest institutional differences between Latin America and developed countries and there is huge need for more research (Coyle 2004). Indeed, the poor prison conditions in Latin America suggest the possibility that they increase the likelihood of recidivism for released prisoners (see table I.1 for background information; see Isla and Miguez [2003] for an account of prisons in Argentina; and Di Tella and Schargrodsky [2009] for an evaluation of electronic monitoring as a substitute for prison). Alzúa, Rodriguez, and Villar study one aspect that is important, namely in-prison conflict and the role of educational programs. This appears important in practice as several basic education and vocational training programs are in place in prisons in the region and a large proportion of criminals have low educational attainment. The authors gather data on prisons in Argentina, noting that lack of incentives leads to few teachers being willing to work in prison educational programs, limiting their supply. This feature allows the authors to provide an ambitious attempt at estimating the causal effect of education on violence. The authors show that participation in formal education programs lead to decreases in participation in violent conflicts and in-prison misbehavior. These are bad outcomes per se, but they are also potentially connected to ulterior recidivism. And, of course, increased educational attainment is potentially linked to better opportunities in the legal labor market upon release.

International Evidence

In the final section we include five chapters that study questions in the crime literature that can be expected to be particularly relevant in Latin America, even though they may use data from outside the region (mainly the United States and Europe). The chapters were selected with two criteria in mind. First, they illustrate the broad range of approaches that have been fruitful in the study of crime in developed countries and that could be used to contribute to a better methodological analysis of the high crime rates in the region and the policies useful to reduce it. Second, they are related to topics that are expected to be important to policymakers in the region. While the estimates presented are not tested for validity in Latin America (further research will have to return to this issue), they have the property of dealing with issues and dynamics that can be expected to be general in nature.

The five chapters are focused on three areas that are central to economics and that are particularly relevant to crime: markets (chapter 8), industrial organization (chapter 9), and incentives (chapters 10, 11, and 12). The first chapter (chapter 8, by Dills, Miron, and Summers) focuses on illegal markets for drugs. Given the importance of drugs in Latin America, and given the study of markets is an area where economists can be expected to have substantive comparative expertise (as emphasized in Bushway and Reuter [2008]), the chapter sets the stage for one class of possible contributions to the study of crime in Latin America. It provocatively starts by presenting a pessimistic view of the state of knowledge in the field, arguing that the broad trends in crime over the last forty years suggest that few things have worked. According to Dills, Miron, and Summers, the picture is grim because even the most successful theories (ranging from arrest rates to gun laws), which find some support in recent US data, fail when evaluated over a longer horizon or with cross-country data. In contrast the authors focus on what happens to supply and demand when an artificial law prevents market clearing, connecting drug prohibition and violent crime. It leads naturally to a demand for further work along (at least) two lines. First, as the authors emphasize, a large part of the problem arises because government prohibition policies affect the nature and amount of dispute resolution that takes place through legal (noncriminal) means, reminding us that the full cost of sending a transaction into the shadow economy must include the cost of enforcing informal contracts. Second, and given that part of the demand for drugs arises in the United States, the chapter indirectly raises the possibility that policies might impose large negative externalities across countries (with very different levels of income—on this important issue, see also chapter 5 by Di Tella, Galiani, and Schargrodsky, and chapter 10 by Draca, Machin, and Witt).

The second chapter (chapter 9 by O'Flaherty and Sethi) focuses on the industrial organization of violence. One of the hallmarks of the economics of crime is that it has produced a considerable body of work assigning rational motives to criminals but less work where the focus of the analysis is the use of rational strategies by these actors (to achieve their objectives). This is paradoxical as it is much more difficult to believe that criminals make a rational, informed choice when they decide to become criminals than when, later on, and conditional on having become criminals and having obtained a certain amount of information through firsthand experience on the functioning of the police and of potential victims, decide on a particular approach to commit a crime. A possible explanation is that, given their secret nature, we have relatively little information on the details of these criminal organizations and their strategies. One approach that has received some attention has been to go inside gangs and other criminal organizations to gather some of these data (see, for example, the well-known work of Levitt and Venkatesh [2000] and Venkatesh [2002]; for an alternative research strategy, see Akerlof and Yellen [1994]).[12] An alternative research approach is to deduce aspects of these criminal strategies through the type of criminal acts they undertake. This is broadly the approach undertaken by O'Flaherty and Sethi, who study in detail a significant increase in murders in Newark, New Jersey, where changes in violence played a central role. Using a careful combination of theory and empirics, the authors study the role of strategic complementarities, preemptive killings, and investment in weapon lethality to explain the basic trends in the data. A basic finding is that areas with high murder respond more to changes in fundamentals such as the arrest rate, the conviction rate, and a shrinking police force, than those with low murder rates.

The last three chapters (chapters 10, 11, and 12) deal broadly with applications of the theory of incentives to the problem of crime, including how crime might be displaced by increasing the probability of apprehension through increased police presence (keeping sentences constant) in chapter 10, the effects of severe sentencing (chapter 11), and the incentives to report crimes as punishment varies (chapter 12). In the first of these (chapter 10),

---

12. In some types of criminal activities (for example, with "victimless" crimes) surveys have been used productively. See Gertler, Shah, and Bertozzi (2005) for an example using Mexican data.

Draca, Machin, and Witt study a thorny potential problem in the successful implementation of policies that reduce crime, namely the problem of (geographical or temporal) displacement. Their approach takes advantage of the large (34 percent) increase in police deployment in central London for the six weeks following the terrorist attacks of July 2005 to circumvent the problem caused by the simultaneous determination of police allocation and common crime. During this period, sentencing does not change so this exercise only looks at variation in crime following variation in the probability of detection. Despite having a credible identification strategy and an impressive data to study the problem, the authors fail to find evidence of large amounts of crime being displaced, either to the geographically contiguous areas or to the period after the six weeks of increased police presence. Although it is natural to assume that an extra visible police (in uniform) in a fixed location has little effect on overall crime as it might geographically or temporally displace crime, the results in this chapter suggest that an increased police force, smartly deployed, might in fact reduce total crime, echoing the arguments made for Latin America by Soares and Naritomi in chapter 1, using aggregate data.

Chapter 11 by Mocan and Gittings also focuses on incentives, turning their attention to variation in sentencing. Their focus is on the death penalty and its potential effect scaring off criminals and deterring future crimes. Even though in Latin America there is no formal death penalty, the estimates are of some interest given that it is possible that changes in the death penalty are salient and might well be the main way tougher sentences are communicated to potential offenders. And, of course, people incarcerated are sometimes killed, or become infected with life-threatening illnesses such as HIV-AIDS, which might play a role similar to that of an informal death penalty (see, for example, Katz, Levitt, and Shustorovich [2003], who proxy prison conditions in the United States through the risk of death in prison and find a deterrence effect; for a discussion of prison HIV and prisons as well as overcrowding in Latin America see, for example, Schifter [2002] and Carranza [2001]; Isla and Miguez [2003] offer a rich description of prison conditions in Argentina).[13] Mocan and Gitting estimate a large number of models linking crime (murder rates) and outcomes related to the death penalty (executions, commutations, and removals). They take a cautious

---

13. There are some famous cases of prison slayings. For example, in October 1992, Sao Paulo police were sent in to stop a rebellion at Carandiru, one of the country's most notorious prisons, and shot dead more than 100 inmates. See, for example, "Inside Latin America's worst prison," *BBC News*, Tuesday, 15 December, 1998. The same article reports the existence of routine death threats and that the director of Carandiru claims to be unable to control the prison "Of course I don't have control of the situation. It would be ridiculous to say I did. The prison has 7,500 inmates and only about 1,000 prison officers, divided into four shifts." In 2007 in Argentina, approximately 1 percent of total homicides took place inside of jails or prisons (from the Ministry of Justice's web page, accessed on June 23, 2009).

approach, allowing several possible objections to the main results, and still obtain a negative effect of punitiveness on crime. Changing the measurement of the main variables, and excluding various U.S. states from the analysis allows the authors to show the robustness of the result. Given that most murderers do not face capital punishment, the interpretation of the estimated effects within a rational model is not direct (although it is possible that the existence of the death penalty is taken as a summary indicator of the punitiveness of the state's legal system). Note also that the results are in contrast to previous research that finds no effects of the death penalty on crime (including Katz, Levitt, and Shustorovich [2003], although they use a somewhat different sample). Ultimately, it is worth pointing out that the death penalty is a hotly debated topic in the United States, with both sides being somewhat impermeable to "scientific" arguments. This is probably for good reason, as it is obviously hard to provide moral justifications for sentencing based on general deterrence. But the chapter does remind us that scientific exercises can help us gain some understanding of the models we use to predict crime changes more broadly.

The final chapter (chapter 12) by Iyengar is an excellent example of how incentives are pervasive in the analysis of crime and how even carefully designed policies can go wrong when these are not accounted for at every step of the crime-punishment link. Mandatory arrest following reports of domestic violence was implemented in the United States through state level laws following the results of the Minnesota Domestic Violence Experiment (MDVE). This experiment randomly assigned a police response of arrest or nonarrest (such as counseling) to domestic violence calls, and showed that arresting the suspect resulted in less future violence. In contrast to these predictions, Iyengar shows that the subsequent passing of mandatory arrest laws in several U.S. states coincided with increases in the gap between intimate partner homicide and other kinds of homicide. Interestingly, such gaps did not emerge in states with recommended arrest laws. Iyengar suggests that this may be because abuse victims may be less likely to contact the police in the face of a mandatory arrest law, resulting in fewer police interventions and escalating domestic violence. To explain the difference in results, Iyengar points out that the Minnesota experiment was implemented conditional on the reporting of incidents, and that the public was not aware that randomization in the treatment was involved. The chapter is relevant for the Latin American region both because of the focus on domestic violence (a common problem), and because of the emphasis on the incentives to report criminal acts. It also points out a class of potential difficulties in the implementation of randomized studies in the area of crime.

Although crime rates in Latin America are extremely high and have been growing in many countries in the last two decades, there are cities within the region that have experienced a different dynamic (see chapter 1). For example, Bogotá, which in 1994 had the highest homicide rate among capital cities in Latin America, in 2008 has a homicide rate substantially lower than that of Caracas, Rio de Janeiro, and Washington, DC, and similar to that of Lima and Mexico City. The city of São Paulo, which imitated some of the Bogotá policies, experienced on December 7, 2007 (a week after our conference) its first day without a homicide since the 1950s. Part of their strategies seems to have been simply an investment in the capacity of the state to attack these problems, which resulted in a combination of more intense and effective repressive measures together with social support programs. Research is needed to better understand these experiences, as well as the conditions that led to the worsening performance in other areas of the region. In this book we hope to contribute toward this enterprise.

References

Akerlof, G., and J. Yellen. 1994. Gang behavior, law enforcement, and community values. In *Values and public policy,* ed. H. Aaron, T. Mann, and T. Taylor, 173–6. Washington, DC: Brookings Institution.

Becker, G. 1968. Crime and punishment: An economic approach. *Journal of Political Economy* 76 (2): 169–217.

Bushway, S., and P. Reuter. 2008. Economists' contribution to the study of crime and the criminal justice system. *Crime and Justice: A Review of Research* 37 (1): 389–451.

Burki, J., and G. Perry. 1998. *Beyond the Washington Consensus: Institutions matter.* Washington, DC: World Bank.

Carranza, E. 2001. Prison overcrowding in Latin America and the Caribbean: Situation and possible responses. Paper presented at the International Seminar on Central Issues in Crime Prevention and Criminal Justice. December 14–15, Helsinki, Finland.

Cook, P., and J. Ludwig. 2006. The social costs of gun ownership. *Journal of Public Economics* 90.1–2 (January): 379–91.

Cook, P., and G. Zarkin. 1985. Crime and the business cycle. *Journal of Legal Studies* 14 (1): 115–28.

Coyle, A. 2004. Prison reform efforts around the world: The role of prison administrators. *Pace Law Review* 24 (2): 825–32.

Di Tella, R., and J. Dubra. 2008. Crime and punishment in the "American Dream." *Journal of Public Economics* 92 (7): 1564–84.

Di Tella, R., R. MacCulloch, and H. Nopo. 2008. Happiness and beliefs in criminal environments. InterAmerican Development Bank, Working Paper no. 662, December.

Di Tella, R., and E. Schargrodsky. 2004. Do police reduce crime? Estimates using the allocation of police forces after a terrorist attack. *American Economic Review* 94 (1): 115–33.

———. 2009. Criminal recidivism after prison and electronic monitoring. Working Paper no. 15602. Cambridge, MA: National Bureau of Economic Research, December.

Fajnzylber, P., D. Lederman, and N. Loayza. 2000. Crime and victimization: An economic perspective. *Economia* 1 (1): 219–302.

Galiani, S., M. Rossi, and E. Schargrodsky. 2010. Conscription and crime: Evidence from the Argentine draft lottery. Working Paper. Universidad Torcuato Di Tella.

Gaviria, A., and C. Pages. 2002. Patterns of crime victimization in Latin American cities. *Journal of Development Economics* 67 (1): 181–203.

Gertler, P., M. Shah, and S. Bertozzi. 2005. Risky business: The market for unprotected commercial sex. *Journal of Political Economy* 113 (3): 518–50.

Hofstadter, R. 1963. *Anti-intellectualism in American life.* New York: Knopf.

Isla, A. 2007. *En los Márgenes de la Ley: Inseguridad y Violencia en el Cono Sur.* Compilador, Editorial Paidos.

Isla, A., and D. Miguez. 2003. *Heridas urbanas.* Editorial de las Ciencias.

Katz, L., S. Levitt, and E. Shustorovich. 2003. Prison conditions, capital punishment, and deterrence. *American Law and Economics Review* 5 (2): 318–43.

Levitt, S. 1999. The changing relationship between income and crime victimization. *FRBNY Economic Policy Review* (September): 87–99.

Levitt, S., and S. Venkatesh. 2000. An economic analysis of a drug-selling gang's finances. *Quarterly Journal of Economics* 115 (3): 755–89.

Londoño, J. L., and R. Guerrero. 1999. *Violencia en América Latina: Epidemiología y Costos.* Inter-American Development Bank.

Prillaman, W. C. 2003. *Crime, democracy, and development in Latin America.* Center for Strategic and International Studies, Policy Papers on the Americas, Volume XIV, Study 6.

Schifter, J. 2002. HIV in Latin American prisons. *AIDS Link* 71 (January): 10–15.

Soares, R. 2004. Crime reporting as a measure of institutional development. *Economic Development and Cultural Change* 52 (4): 851–71.

Venkatesh, S. A. 2002. *American project: The rise and fall of a modern ghetto.* Cambridge, MA: Harvard University Press.

I

Overview: Latin American Exceptionalism?

Understanding High Crime Rates in Latin America
The Role of Social and Policy Factors

Rodrigo R. Soares and Joana Naritomi

1.1 Introduction

Latin America has been traditionally seen as a particularly violent region of the world. This perception is not new, even though it may have been enhanced over the last decades with the escalation of violence in countries such as Brazil, Colombia, and Venezuela (see Aguirre [2000]). Still, despite the fact that several candidate explanations have been put forth, there is no consensus regarding the reasons behind this phenomenon.

Table 1.1 presents mortality rates due to violence[1] and statistics related to various dimensions of development for regions of the world (comprising seventy-three countries for which mortality by cause of death is available

Rodrigo R. Soares is associate professor of economics at Pontifical Catholic University of Rio de Janeiro, and a faculty research fellow of the National Bureau of Economic Research. Joana Naritomi is a graduate student in Political Economy and Government at Harvard University.

This manuscript was originally prepared for the conference "Confronting Crime and Violence in Latin America: Crafting a Public Policy Agenda," organized by the Instituto Fernando Henrique Cardoso (iFHC) at the John F. Kennedy School of Government, Harvard University, July 2007. The authors gratefully acknowledge financial support from the iFHC. The chapter benefited from comments from Alejandro Gaviria, Ana Maria Ibáñez, Norman Loayza, Ernesto Schargrodsky, and seminar participants at the iFHC Conference on Crime and Violence in Latin America, the 2007 NBER Inter-American Seminar on Economics (Buenos Aires, Argentina), the 2007 Meeting of the Brazilian Econometric Society (Recife, Brazil), and the 2008 Global Development Conference (Brisbane, Australia).

1. Mortality due to violence is defined as the number of deaths caused by homicides and injuries purposely inflicted by other persons, plus other violent deaths, according to the International Classification of Diseases (ICD). Later on, we restrict our analysis to the category that is most closely related to common crimes, the homicide rate.

Table 1.1   Homicide rates and development variables, world regions, average for the 1990s

Region	Mortality due to violence (per 100,000)	Exp. years of life lost	Life exp.	GDP per capita	Avg. schooling (pop. above 15
Latin America and Caribbean	21.8	0.6	71.4	7,708	6.6
North America	6.5	0.2	76.1	25,672	11.6
Western Europe	4.0	0.1	76.2	19,532	8.7
Former Communist	17.2	0.4	68.9	6,009	8.9
Western Pacific	7.8	0.2	76.0	17,839	9.4

Notes: Regional numbers are unweighted country averages. The only African country included in the WHO cause-specific mortality data is Mauritius, and the only Eastern Mediterranean country is Kuwait. Therefore, these regions are not included in this table. Mortality due to violence and life expectancy calculated based on data from the WHO, income per capita from the Penn World Table (PWT) 6.1, and average schooling from the Barro and Lee data set. Mortality due to violence is homicide and injury purposely inflicted by other persons plus other violent deaths, from the International Classification of Diseases (ICD).

from the World Health Organization [WHO]). The occurrence of deaths due to violence is much more common in Latin America than in any other region: it is roughly 200 percent higher than in North America and in the Western Pacific, 450 percent higher than in Western Europe, and 30 percent higher than in the Former Communist block. The region is also significantly poorer and less educated than the developed countries, but statistical analyses have failed to establish an unequivocal and quantitatively significant link between these variables and crime. In addition, Latin America enjoys higher levels of income and life expectancy than most of the Former Communist block, but still displays substantially higher violence levels.

Crime and violence have many potential welfare implications. The loss in life expectancy at birth due to violence in violent societies can be higher than one year and sometimes even above two (as in Colombia in the 1990s). Recent estimates have shown that increases in mortality represent a quantitatively significant welfare loss, be it directly from the reduced welfare due to a shorter life span, or from the indirect effects of a shorter planning horizon on investments in physical and human capital (see Murphy and Topel [2003] and Lorentzen, McMillan, and Wacziarg [2008] for example). In addition, material costs, including both direct costs and expenditures on criminal justice and crime prevention, add up to a significant fraction of overall production across different regions of the world (Bourguignon 1999). Finally, loss of human capital and productivity of those deceased, incapacitated, and incarcerated add yet another layer to the social inefficiencies generated by crime.

The economic relevance of this phenomenon has been widely recognized in recent years, both in the research community and in the public debate. Today, the causes and consequences of crime are common themes in economic research. They are also among the main topics in the popular media in Latin America, and often bring the region to the headlines in the major media outlets worldwide (see, for example, *The Economist* [2006] and *The Washington Post* [2007]). In reality, crime and violence have been identified as the second most important public policy issue in the region, ranking first for countries such as Argentina, El Salvador, and Venezuela (Latinobarómetro 2006).

There are many possible explanations for the differences in violence observed across regions of the world and the particularly high levels observed in Latin America. These range from distinct definitions of crimes and different reporting rates (percentage of the total number of crimes actually reported to the police), to real differences in the incidence of crime due to inequality, degree of repression, effectiveness of the government, and age composition of the population. The goal of this chapter is to discuss the pattern, causes, and consequence of the high crime rates observed in Latin America. We argue that crime in the region represents a significant welfare loss and a potentially serious hindrance to growth. We then conduct a preliminary assessment of the relative strength of the alternative hypotheses raised in the literature.

In pursuing this goal, we take the rational choice perspective typical from the economic theory of crime. In this setup, criminals respond to economic incentives in the same way that legal workers do (Becker 1968; Stigler 1970). In Stigler's words, "[the criminal] seeks income, and for him the usual rules of occupational choice will hold" (530). Particularly important from our point of view is the fact that the relative attractiveness of criminal activities is intimately related to variables that undergo significant changes during the process of economic development, such as income distribution, institutional development, government effectiveness, and demographic composition of the population. We ask how the economic and social landscape of a society affects the incentives of its citizens to engage in criminal behavior, and confront it with the actions that the government takes to reduce the incidence of crime and violence. From this interaction of forces—the supply of potential criminals faced with the repressive measures imposed by the State—an equilibrium level of crime and violence emerges. We therefore concentrate our discussion on the dimension of crime that is economically motivated and is subject to a cost benefit analysis on the part of the perpetrator.[2]

Our analysis shows that, despite being extremely high, the incidence of crime in Latin America is not much different from what should be expected

---

2. Random acts of violence or violence among family members, which sometimes are regarded as the result of loss of control over one's self, are outside the scope of our analysis. Though these represent a significant fraction of the violent acts registered in different regions of the world, we do not believe that they are responsible for most of the differences observed across regions or countries.

based on socioeconomic and public policy characteristics of its countries. Estimates from the empirical literature suggest that most of its seemingly excessively high violence can be explained by three factors: high inequality, low incarceration rates, and small police forces. In addition, country-specific experiences in the recent past have been heterogeneous in many respects. There are examples of countries that maintained reasonably low violence levels throughout the last decades and also of countries that, starting with very high violence, were able to achieve levels comparable to that of some developed countries. Still, some other countries went through the last thirty years experiencing increasingly high and seemingly uncontrollable crime rates. As a whole, the evidence suggests that it is possible to have an effective policy toward violence reduction, and that this goal has indeed been attained by certain local governments in the region.

The position of some Latin American countries as major producers of drugs or as routes for the international drug traffic has important implications for organized crime and sometimes also for the institutional stability of its states (see, for example, Keefer, Loayza, and Soares [2010]). Here, we deliberately leave this dimension out of the discussion and try not to look at Latin America as being particular. Instead, we look at the more ordinary factors and policies thought to be related to the incidence of crime and ask what they can tell us.

There are numerous experiences of high and low, increasing and decreasing crime rates not accompanied by systematic differences in drug activity. Similarly, there are various other consuming and producing centers around the world that do not display remotely similar crime rates. In Latin America itself, there are today various successful experiences of local crime control that did not confront directly the broader issue of drug production and trafficking. Though drugs may be very important fuels for violence and institutional instability in particular countries (such as Colombia in the 1980s and 1990s) and particular regions of certain countries, we do not believe that they are a major factor determining the high levels of violence observed in Latin America, or explaining the bulk of the distribution of crime in the region. Our analysis suggests that one can go a very long way toward understanding the incidence of common crime and violence in Latin America without resorting to the role of drugs.

The remainder of the chapter is structured as follows. Section 1.2 discusses the welfare implications of crime and violence. Section 1.3 summarizes the main issues in the measurement and comparison of crime rates across countries. Section 1.4 presents the pattern of crime in Latin America, both across countries and through time. Section 1.5 analyzes some candidate explanations for the levels of violence observed in the region. Section 1.6 conducts a preliminary assessment of the relative importance of these candidate explanations based on estimates available from the empirical literature. Section 1.7 discusses the strategy and institutional context of some successful experiences of violence reduction in Latin America. Finally, section 1.8 concludes the chapter.

1.2   Welfare Implications

Crime and violence are a burden to society in several dimensions. There are straightforward consequences to the quality of life, such as reduction in life span, widespread feeling of insecurity, and change in behavior through reduced time on the streets. There is also the social waste from the value of goods lost and destroyed, the public and private expenditures on prevention, and the costs related to criminal justice and prison systems. In addition, and far less straightforward, crime has important nonmonetary welfare consequences, possibly reducing productivity and shortening planning horizons on investments in physical and human capital. It is therefore deleterious to welfare in different ways, and possibly an actual hindrance to development.

From this perspective, the Latin American situation is particularly worrisome. The region fell behind in terms of growth in the last twenty years and is remarkably violent by international standards. According to the International Crime Victimization Survey (ICVS), about 44 percent of Latin Americans are victims of some type of crime every year (average for the 1990s). During the last decade, the region had systematically the highest rate of deaths due to violence in the world: 21.8 per 100,000 inhabitants. This position has given Latin America headlines in major international media outlets and has made it infamous throughout the world. A recent example is a report stating that 729 Israeli and Palestinian minors were killed as a result of violence between 2002 and 2006, while 1,857 minors were reported murdered in Rio de Janeiro, Brazil, during the same period (*The Washington Post* 2007).

Measuring the magnitude of the negative consequences of crime, however, is a difficult task. There are multiple dimensions that one should take into account, and there is no unified framework in the literature to tackle the problem. The material costs of crime and violence, including both direct costs and expenditures on criminal justice and crime prevention, have been estimated to add up to a significant fraction of production across different regions of the world. This number is thought to be around 2.1 percent of the gross domestic product (GDP) per year for the United States, and 3.6 percent for Latin America (see, for example, Bourguignon [1999] and Londoño and Guerrero [1999]). Considering monetary costs related to property crime, the number rises to 2.6 percent for the United States and 5.1 percent for Latin America (Bourguignon 1999). There is, however, debate in the literature on whether this is actually a social cost, rather than a transfer of resources between members of society. Glaeser (1999) argues that, since generally the goods are valued less by the criminals than by the people who lose them, it should indeed be considered a social loss. The value should equal, in equilibrium, the opportunity cost of criminal's time—that is, the time spent on crime instead of legal activities—and this does correspond to a welfare loss.

On top of material costs, one of the most important direct consequences of crime is the increase in injury and mortality rates. Economists have recently developed tools that allow the estimation of the social cost from reductions in life expectancy and have shown that these can be quantitatively very important. In the case of violence, this has been shown to represent a substantial welfare loss, of the same order of magnitude of direct material costs of crime. Based on a willingness to pay approach, Soares (2006) estimates that one year of life expectancy lost to violence is associated on average with a yearly social cost of 3.8 percent of the GDP. This estimate still leaves out the costs due to injury and reduced health, for which there are no trustworthy economic-based estimates available.

The nonmonetary dimension reinforces the severity of the Latin American scenario. In the 1990s, individuals born in Latin America had life expectancies on average 0.6 year lower because of violence (see table 1.1). This number was at least two times higher than the loss in life expectancy for any other region, except for the former Communist countries. It reached its peak in Colombia, where 2.2 expected years of life were lost because of violence. To put these numbers in perspective, reductions in life expectancy due to violence represented social losses analogous to a permanent decline of 9.7 percent of yearly income for Colombia, as compared to only 0.9 percent for the United States (Soares 2006).

Figure 1.1 shows the discounted present social value of violence reduction as a share of GDP for several countries, as estimated by Soares (2006), ordered from highest to lowest. From the nine frontrunners, eight are Latin American: Colombia, with an astounding 281 percent, followed by the Philippines (280 percent), Venezuela (95 percent), Chile (86 percent), El Salvador (73 percent), Belize (71 percent), Suriname (67 percent), Mexico (67 percent), and Brazil (65 percent). The eleven remaining countries that complete the top twenty in figure 1.1 are all Latin American and Caribbean or former Communist. In the other extreme of the distribution, the ten lowest values are all Western European countries, plus Japan.

Mortality due to violence in high-violence areas is a particularly perverse phenomenon due to its concentration at prime ages. Figure 1.2, panels A and B show the age profile of mortality by violence for selected countries. In addition to illustrating the extent of difference between the various countries, the figure also highlights that violent countries such as Brazil, Colombia, and Russia have the vast majority of mortality due to violence concentrated between ages fifteen and forty.

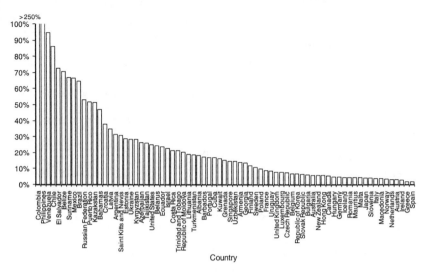

Fig. 1.1   Present value of social cost of violence from reduced life expectancy (percent of GDP), 1990s
Source: Soares (2006).

The nonmonetary dimension of the costs of crime, together with its specific age profile, induces also indirect economic consequences. These are effects from changes in behavior induced by reductions in the length of productive life, such as decreased investments in human capital and health, reduced savings and investments in physical capital, and, therefore, reduced long-run growth.

Shorter life horizons reduce the incentives for individuals to take actions that generate long-term benefits and short-term costs, such as investing in education and saving for the future.[3] One of the main channels linking mortality to growth is fertility (Lorentzen, McMillan, and Wacziarg 2008). There is a positive relationship between mortality and fertility, and a negative relationship between these two variables and investments in human capital. In countries with a high HIV prevalence, for example, parents have on average two more children when compared with countries with low HIV prevalence (Kalemli-Ozcan 2006). This connection leads to a negative correlation between adult mortality and investment in human and physical capital, and it can be a source of poverty traps.

Finally, there are intangible costs in the labor market and negative effects to business climate. According to Londoño and Guerrero (1999), intan-

---

3. Even for those who do go to school, a violent environment can be harmful to human capital accumulation. According to Severnini (2007), conditioning on individual characteristics, students attending more violent schools perform significantly worse in a Brazilian national exam.

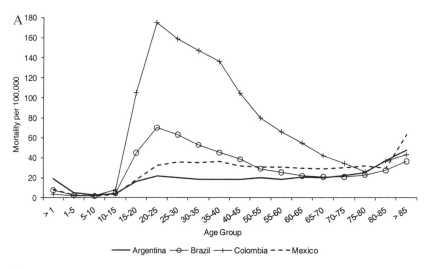

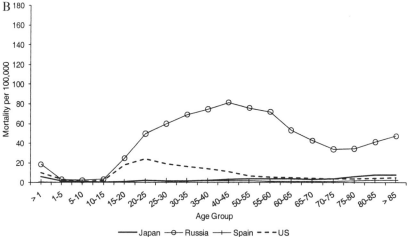

Fig. 1.2   **Mortality due to violence by age group: _A_, Selected Latin American countries, 1990s; _B_, selected comparison countries, 1990s**
Source: Soares (2006).

gible costs of crime—deterioration of productivity, consumption, and labor force—constitute the major part of Latin American's estimated cost of violence, corresponding to 7.1 percent of the region's GDP. Nevertheless, these dimensions are conceptually less clear and difficult to estimate in a convincing way. Still, it is important to highlight the impact of crime on institutional stability and business environment, particularly where there is a significant presence of organized crime. Gaviria and Vélez (2002) argue that crime has a perverse effect on economic efficiency, reducing investment

Table 1.2   Social cost of violence, Latin America and United States, 1990s

	Latin America	United States
Mortality due to violence (per 100,000)	21.8	10.2
GDP per capita	7,708	28,517
Social cost of crime and violence (yearly cost as % GDP)		
Welfare loss from mortality increase	1.98	0.85
Public security expenditures	1.10	0.50
Justice system expenditures	0.50	1.30
Private expenditures on prevention	1.40	0.60
Opportunity cost of incarceration	0.10	0.60
Monetary costs (medical, etc.)	0.60	0.20
Reduced growth	0.11	0.04
Total	5.79	4.09

Notes: Homicide and life expectancy data from the WHO, income per capita from the PWT 6.1. Social cost from mortality due to violence calculated in Soares (2006). Costs from expenditures on public security, justice system, and private prevention for Latin America from Lodoño and Guerrero (1999). For the United States, numbers on public security and justice system from Levitt (1997). Remaining numbers on private expenditures, opportunity, and monetary costs from Bourguignon (1999). Impact on growth based on instrumental variable (IV) estimates of the effect of adult mortality on growth presented in Lorentzen, McMillan, and Wacziarg (2008, table 10, column [1]), using mortality due to violence from the WHO and population fractions from the World Development Indicators (WDI) (estimate presented as the yearly cost in terms of current GDP corresponding to the loss in growth induced by the higher mortality due to violence).

and employment in poor urban Colombian communities. In Brazil, more than 50 percent of managers rank crime as a major business constraint (World Bank 2006b).

The perverse effects of crime are therefore multidimensional and the magnitude of its costs depends on what is taken into account. In any case, costs of crime and violence represent a significant share of aggregate production, and particularly so in Latin America, where crime rates have been high for most of the last decades. In order to illustrate this point, we draw on the literature discussed before and gather in table 1.2 a set of estimates related to various dimensions of the costs of crime and violence. These are the dimensions over which there is not much theoretical controversy and for which comparable estimates exist for the United States and Latin America.

As can be seen, costs of violence as a proportion of GDP are substantially higher in Latin America when compared to the United States. Most of the difference comes from costs related to increased mortality and public and private security expenditures. Overall, costs of violence in the region would be even higher, around 13 percent of GDP, if the intangible dimensions suggested by Londoño and Guerrero (1999) were included in the calculations.

Regardless, it seems indisputable that violence and crime represent a very serious public policy issue in the region. The remainder of this chapter tries to understand the reasons behind this state of affairs. We start by addressing the issue of comparison of crime rates across countries, and then describe the pattern and evolution of violence in the recent past. Following, we ask what factors could lie behind the observed pattern and investigate whether there seems to be effective policies to fight crime available for the governments in the region.

1.3   The Measurement of Crime

Any international comparison of crime has to deal inevitably with the issue of measurement error in crime rates. This problem can be illustrated by the pattern of results common in the first generations of papers on the topic. Early empirical studies on the determinants of cross-regional differences in crime rates were mainly concentrated on the analysis of the effects of inequality and development on crime. Detailed reviews of the criminology literature are presented in Patterson (1991) and Fowles and Merva (1996). The statistical approaches used in the different studies and their respective conclusions were as diverse as they could possibly be. The major part of the evidence regarded U.S. studies, with the units changing from neighborhoods and cities to counties and metropolitan areas. Results on inequality in this case varied between positive and nonsignificant from crime to crime and from study to study, leaving no clearly identifiable pattern. In relation to development, U.S. studies most often indicated a negative effect of income level (or positive effect of poverty level) on crime rates, although nonsignificant and even positive results were sometimes present. The international evidence, surprisingly, suggested a conclusion strikingly different from this one. While the few inequality studies left no clear answer, the evidence on development seemed to be overwhelming: virtually all the international evidence from the criminology literature suggested that development and crime rates were positively and significantly correlated.

The empirical literature from economics has challenged this consensus and raised concerns regarding the problem of underreporting in official crime statistics (Fajnzylber, Lederman, and Loayza 2002a, 2002b, Soares 2004a, 2004b). Previously, this result was regarded almost as a stylized fact by criminologists and sociologists used to the international comparisons of crime rates. Burnham (1990, 44), for example, claims that "evidence as exists seems to suggest that development is indeed probably criminogenic." Along the same lines, Stack's (1984, 236) empirical specification includes "level of economic development, a factor found to be related positively to property crime rates in the previous cross-national research."

But recent evidence has shown that these results have an explanation far more simple than the industrialization-induced social disintegration usually suggested in the sociological literature. One major statistical problem is systematically overlooked in most cross-national studies: the nonrandomness of the reporting error (see, for example, Krohn and Wellford [1977], Krohn [1978], and Stack [1984]). Official data is known to greatly underestimate actual crime rates, and this can constitute a serious problem if the degree of underestimation is correlated with the characteristics of the country.

The rate of crime reporting is the fraction of the total number of crimes that is actually reported to the police. We draw on Soares (2004a) and construct this variable by crossing data from official crime records (United Nations Survey of Crime Trends and Operations of Criminal Justice Systems [UNCS]) with data from victimization surveys (ICVS).

The International Crime Victim Survey (ICVS) is a survey conducted by a group of international research institutes under the coordination of the United Nations Interregional Crime and Justice Research Institute (UNICRI). It contains data for selected countries, irregularly distributed over the years 1989, 1992, and/or 1996/7. Since it is an independent standardized victimization survey, the ICVS should be free from the systematic bias introduced by the problem of underreporting and, therefore, should give an unbiased estimate of the "true" crime rate and of its variation across countries. The other data set used is the UNCS, which is a data set created by the United Nations with information related to several crime and justice-related variables, based on official records. Several countries and years are irregularly covered in the period between 1971 and 1994.

We concentrate on the three types of crimes that can be compared across the victimization survey (ICVS) and the official records survey (UNCS): thefts, burglaries, and contact crimes (robberies, sexual incidents, and threats/assaults). See the discussion in Soares (2004b) for a detailed account of the comparability of the two data sets.

Table 1.3 presents descriptive statistics for crime rates obtained from victimization surveys and from official records (sample composed by forty-five countries). The numbers are extremely different. Comparing the cross-country averages from the ICVS with the ones from the UNCS, we have the following numbers: according to the official records, 2.1 percent for thefts, 0.7 percent for burglaries, and 0.3 percent for contact crimes; according to the victim survey, 25.1 percent for thefts, 6.7 percent for burglaries, and 7.7 percent for contact crimes. Implicitly, this means that the fraction of the total number of crimes reported to the police varies widely across countries and across different types of crime. In reality, this statistic ranges from virtually zero (as for thefts in Egypt or India) to virtually one (as for burglaries in Austria and Finland). Soares (2004a) shows that this variation is strongly related to income per capita. Figures 1.3, 1.4, and 1.5 reproduce this result and illustrate the strong positive correlation between reporting rates of, respectively, thefts, burglaries, and contact crimes and income. Income per

Table 1.3   Official and victimization crime statistics, cross-section of countries, 1990s

	Official Data			Victim Survey Data		
	Theft	Burglary	Contact	Theft	Burglary	Contact
Mean	2.07	0.67	0.25	25.08	6.68	7.65
Standard deviation	2.23	0.72	0.31	6.84	3.74	3.68
Max	7.73	2.74	1.64	41.80	17.40	21.00
Min	0.01	0.01	0.00	11.60	0.80	2.00

Source: Table 3 from Soares (2004a).

Notes: Data is number of crimes as a percentage of population. Official data is taken from the UNCS data set and victim survey data from the ICVS. For comparability between the two data sets, statistics for the official data are calculated from country averages, from 1989 to the last year available. The ICVS data are averages for all the surveys in which the country was included (1989, 1992, and/or 1996/1997).

capita alone explains 65 percent of the cross-country variation in reporting rates for thefts, 54 percent for burglaries, and 45 percent for contact crimes. Soares (2004a) also shows that this correlation is responsible for the criminologists' erroneous conclusion that development and crime rates are positively related.

This result suggests that the positive link between crime and development, usually cited in the criminology literature but regarded with suspicion by economists, does not exist. More generally, it suggests that care must be exercised when comparing official crime rates across countries, since reporting depends on various characteristics that may also be related to the incidence of crime itself. In particular, Soares (2004b) shows that crime reporting is strongly related to institutional stability, police presence, and perceived corruption.

Table 1.4 presents pair-wise correlations between various variables[4] measured as averages for the 1990s and the three reporting rates discussed before. Reporting rates for different crimes are strongly correlated with each other (correlation coefficient significant and above 0.6 in all cases). Time of democratic stability, degree of urbanization, and average schooling are also positively and significantly related to the rate of crime reporting for the three types of crimes. Number of policemen per capita is positively correlated with reporting rates, but coefficients are not significant. Finally, corruption has an extremely high negative and significant correlation with the reporting rates of all types of crime.

Since most of these variables are correlated with overall development, it is difficult to tell precisely what this pattern of correlations reveals. In a

4. Number of policemen per 100,000 inhabitants from the UNCS; time of democratic stability from Beck et al. (2001); percentage of the population living in urban areas from the World Development Indicators; average years of schooling in population aged fifteen and above from the Barro and Lee data set; and indicator constructed from the financial risk associated with corruption, as estimated by the International Country Risk Guide.

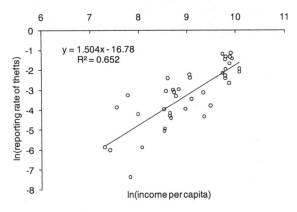

Fig. 1.3   Income per capita and reporting rate of thefts, cross-section of countries, 1990s

Source: Soares (2004b).

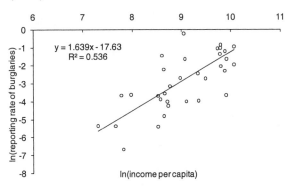

Fig. 1.4   Income per capita and reporting rate of burglaries, cross-section of countries, 1990s

Source: Soares (2004b).

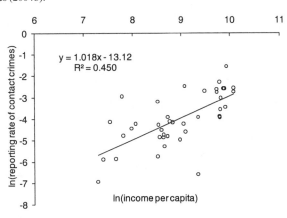

Fig. 1.5   Income per capita and reporting rate of contact crimes, cross-section of countries, 1990s

Source: Soares (2004b).

Table 1.4   Correlation between reporting rate and development, cross-section of countries, 1990s

	ln(report theft)	ln(report burgl)	ln(report cont)	ln(police)	Time democ stability	Urban	Education
ln(report theft)	1						
ln(report burgl)	0.72 (0.00)	1					
ln(report cont)	0.72 (0.00)	0.62 (0.00)	1				
ln(police)	0.30 (0.08)	0.18 (0.34)	0.25 (0.13)	1			
Time democ stability	0.64 (0.00)	0.58 (0.00)	0.61 (0.00)	0.12 (0.50)	1		
Urban	0.67 (0.00)	0.52 (0.00)	0.53 (0.00)	0.24 (0.16)	0.49 (0.00)	1	
Education	0.61 (0.00)	0.49 (0.00)	0.39 (0.02)	0.18 (0.29)	0.37 (0.02)	0.67 (0.00)	1
Corruption	-0.61 (0.00)	-0.68 (0.00)	-0.63 (0.00)	-0.11 (0.52)	-0.70 (0.00)	-0.52 (0.00)	-0.65 (0.00)

Source: Table 3 from Soares (2004b).

Notes: Numbers in parentheses are *p*-values. Variables are natural logs of reporting rates for, respectively, thefts, burglaries, and contact crimes, natural log of number of policemen as percent of population, time of democratic stability, percent of population living in urban areas, average schooling in the population aged fifteen and above, and International Country Risk Guide (ICRG) corruption index.

multivariate setting, Soares (2004b) shows that the most robust correlation is that between reporting rates and measures of institutional development. We reproduce his basic result in table 1.5. The table shows that, in a multivariate setting, the reporting rates of crime tend to be strongly related to institutional development—be it measured as time of democratic stability or as incidence of corruption—and also to police presence. Therefore, comparisons of crime rates across regions, or within a region through time, should bear in mind that differences or changes in the level of institutional development may compromise the meaningful use of official crime statistics.

Still, as of today, victimization data are very irregularly distributed over countries and years, and have limited coverage in terms of the developing world. So, for practical purposes, they cannot be used to give an encompassing picture of the state and evolution of crime rates across different areas of the globe. The alternative is to use the crime data less likely to be contaminated by the reporting bias, namely, homicide rates obtained from sources based on death certificates. It is likely that the elasticity of the reporting rate in relation to development is much smaller for homicides than for other types of crime. In addition, death certificates always have to be filed. Therefore, in this case, reporting does not depend directly on the willingness of citizens, and the record keeping has automatic mechanisms that work outside of the police and judicial structures.

For the reasons outlined, we concentrate most of our analysis of the causes and consequences of crime in Latin America on the number of homicides per 100,000 inhabitants. In the next section, we lay out a broad picture of the pattern and recent evolution of crime in Latin America, using both the scant data available from victimization surveys and time series of homicide rates.

1.4   Crime Patterns in Latin America

Table 1.1 showed that, by international standards, Latin America has an exceptionally high number of deaths due to violence. Tables 1.6 and 1.7 show that high crime in the region is not restricted to homicides and other types of violence that culminate in death. The tables present numbers from victimization surveys (ICVS) for world regions and individual countries, respectively. Excluding Africa, burglary rates are at least 40 percent higher in Latin America than in any other region of the world, while theft rates are at least 30 percent higher and contact crimes rates are at least 70 percent higher. When compared to Africa, Latin America has lower burglary rates by 1 percentage point, virtually identical theft rates, and contact crime rates 3.6 percentage points higher, while overall crime rates are 4 percentage points higher. High crime rates in Latin America span different types of crime and clearly dominate the levels observed in any other region.

Table 1.5 Reporting rate regressions—Cross-section of countries, 1990s

	ln(report theft)		ln(report burgl)		ln(report cont)	
	1	2	1	2	1	2
Police	1.4439**	1.4856**	1.2543**	1.5436**	0.1431	0.1559
	(0.2612)	(0.3114)	(0.5999)	(0.5053)	(0.1772)	(0.1869)
Time democ stability	0.0389**	0.0196**	0.0279**	0.0045	0.0280**	0.0066
	(0.0059)	(0.0076)	(0.0135)	(0.0129)	(0.0070)	(0.0094)
Urban	-0.0083	0.0044	0.0048	-0.0085	0.0062	0.0222
	(0.0114)	(0.0124)	(0.0252)	(0.0194)	(0.0130)	(0.0137)
Education	0.0204	-0.0535	0.0762	-0.2071	0.0109	-0.0796
	(0.0792)	(0.1067)	(0.1761)	(0.1716)	(0.0965)	(0.1181)
Corruption		-0.5826**		-1.2849**		-0.5020**
		(0.2150)		(0.3758)		(0.2367)
Const	-1.7850*	-0.5721	-2.6520	3.6299	-4.9126**	-3.7837**
	(0.9647)	(1.6521)	(2.0824)	(2.7438)	(0.7616)	(1.2783)
F	26.25	20.85	4.45	8.64	6.99	6.09
Number of observations	33.00	33.00	30.00	30.00	35.00	35.00

Source: Table 4 from Soares (2004b).

Notes: Standard errors in parentheses. Robust regression with iteratively reweighted least squares used to deal with outliers. Dependent variables are natural logarithms of reporting rates for, respectively, thefts, burglaries, and contact crimes. Independent variables are natural log of number of policemen as percent of population, time of democratic stability, percent of population living in urban areas, average schooling in the population aged fifteen and above, and ICRG corruption index.

**Significant at the 5 percent level.
*Significant at the 10 percent level.

Table 1.6   **Crime rates (%) from victimization surveys (ICVS), world regions, average for the 1990s**

Region	Burglary	Thefts	Contact crimes	Any crime
Latin America	11.8	16.9	15.0	43.6
Africa	12.9	16.6	11.4	39.6
Asia	3.6	11.1	4.3	18.9
Former Communist	6.8	12.9	7.0	31.7
North America	8.0	10.1	8.7	34.0
Oceania	8.4	9.4	8.3	33.4
Western Europe	4.2	9.5	5.8	28.1

Notes: Regional numbers are unweighted country averages. Source is ICVS (1989, 1992, and 1996/1997). "Burglaries" include attempted burglaries. "Thefts" are bicycle or motorcycle and other personal thefts, including pickpocketing. "Contact crimes" are robberies, sexual incidents, and/or threats/assaults. "Any crime" includes all previous categories plus theft of car/joyriding, theft from car, and car vandalism. Numbers based on major cities from each respective country.

Still, there are marked differences in country-specific experiences within Latin America itself. In the victimization data set, a very narrow set of countries is available (Argentina, Bolivia, Brazil, Colombia, Costa Rica, and Paraguay), but still victimization rates ranges from 4.6 percent to 14.4 percent for burglary, 11.8 percent to 20.2 percent for thefts, and 11 percent to 21 percent for contact crimes. Costa Rica, for example, has relatively low crime and low mortality due to violence, while Colombia has high marks in both statistics.

Heterogeneity across countries also manifests itself in the dynamics of crime rates through time. In order to take a closer look at the evolution of crime rates over the last few decades, we concentrate on homicide rates, the only trustworthy statistic available for a longer time span. We choose a restricted group composed of some of the main countries in the region. This group will also guide our analysis in the later discussion about the candidate explanations for the high crime rates observed in Latin America. The selected countries are: Argentina, Brazil, Chile, Colombia, Costa Rica, Mexico, and Venezuela. The choice of these specific countries makes our discussion a little more focused and concrete, and allows the investigation of certain types of phenomenon for which data are not immediately and widely available.

Figure 1.6, panels A and B plot the homicide rates for Argentina, Brazil, Chile, Colombia, Costa Rica, Mexico, and Venezuela for the period between 1979 and 2006. Homicide data are from cause of death statistics from mortality records (either from the World Health Organization, from the Pan American Health Organization, or from national health authorities). Panel A presents the data for countries within this group that display exception-

Table 1.7   **Crime rates (%) from victimization surveys (ICVS), countries, average for the 1990s**

Country	Burglary	Thefts	Contact crimes	Any crime
Albania	6.0	15.9	5.6	27.1
Argentina	10.5	20.2	14.5	50.7
Australia	7.8	8.1	8.0	30.7
Austria	1.1	12.3	5.8	27.0
Belarus	2.9	8.8	6.2	21.1
Belgium	5.2	4.8	4.7	22.5
Bolivia	13.8	19.2	12.0	40.1
Brazil	4.6	11.8	20.5	41.0
Bulgaria	10.8	12.3	8.3	38.4
Canada	7.5	10.6	7.7	33.0
China	2.5	15.9	4.9	21.6
Colombia	14.1	19.9	21.0	53.7
Costa Rica	14.3	14.3	11.3	39.7
Croatia	2.3	6.1	5.4	20.2
Czech Republic	6.8	17.3	6.2	37.5
Egypt	6.9	9.6	8.3	27.0
England and Wales	6.8	7.8	6.4	31.1
Estonia	11.8	13.6	11.2	39.7
Finland	0.9	10.3	7.6	25.1
France	6.1	11.1	4.7	28.1
Fyr Macedonia	3.5	8.1	3.6	21.6
Georgia	8.2	10.3	8.5	33.4
Germany (W)	3.3	9.4	6.7	29.3
Hungary	4.1	8.3	2.4	24.7
India	3.2	11.1	4.5	19.7
Indonesia	5.4	8.2	3.7	17.2
Italy	5.5	10.4	4.6	31.4
Kyrgyzstan	6.8	12.5	7.5	27.4
Latvia	8.8	15.0	5.9	33.4
Lithuania	9.0	11.2	5.7	33.1
Malta	0.8	4.0	3.4	23.3
Mongolia	13.7	23.4	9.3	43.1
Netherlands	7.8	18.6	8.6	38.4
New Zealand	9.0	10.7	8.5	36.0
North Ireland	4.1	5.7	6.3	24.4
Norway	4.9	6.6	6.8	26.1
Paraguay	13.4	16.0	10.9	36.3
Philippines	3.3	9.0	4.0	16.9
Poland	5.3	13.4	7.6	33.1
Rumania	3.1	13.4	7.9	29.4
Russia	6.1	14.1	9.6	35.0
Scotland	5.0	6.1	5.4	28.3
Slovakia	8.4	15.1	4.0	35.9
Slovenia	5.3	8.9	6.5	30.3
South Africa	9.5	10.0	13.8	35.7
Spain	5.3	7.1	7.2	31.9
Sweden	4.1	16.9	6.5	30.6

Table 1.7   (continued)

Country	Burglary	Thefts	Contact crimes	Any crime
Switzerland	2.7	11.2	2.0	23.6
Tanzania	12.1	18.0	6.8	37.6
Tunisia	10.1	16.5	9.4	35.9
Uganda	21.5	21.7	13.2	53.9
Ukraine	7.8	21.6	9.2	38.2
United States	8.4	9.5	9.6	35.0
Yugoslavia (F.R.)	5.4	8.9	8.5	32.3
Zimbabwe	17.4	23.8	16.9	47.5

Source: ICVS (1989, 1992, and 1996/1997).
Notes: "Burglaries" include attempted burglaries. "Thefts" are bicycle or motorcycle and other personal thefts, including pickpocketing. "Contact crimes" are robberies, sexual incidents, and/or threats/assaults. "Any crime" includes all previous categories plus theft of car/ joyriding, theft from car, and car vandalism. Numbers based on major cities from each respective country.

ally high crime rates during the period, while panel B presents the data for those with lower rates.

The first group includes Brazil, Colombia, and Venezuela, with homicide rates ranging from twenty to above sixty per 100,000 by the beginning of the 2000s. Among these, the Colombian case is the most striking, with an already high rate rising from thirty in the early 1980s to eighty-two in the early 1990s, and then falling to reach a still very high level by the end of the 1990s. Starting in 2002, Colombia then experiences successive reductions in homicide rates, which persist until today, reaching forty per 100,000 in 2006.

The sheer scale of the magnitude and of the changes observed in Colombia dwarves the experiences of other countries, but also in these cases changes have been substantial. In the case of Brazil, the homicide rate rises almost monotonically in the period, increasing by more than 200 percent of its initial value by 2003. In that year, the rate peaks at twenty-nine per 100,000 inhabitants and starts a timid declining trend leading to a level of 26.8 in 2006. Venezuela starts the period at levels similar to those of Brazil, and experiences more or less stable homicide rates until the mid-1990s, when it also starts registering major increases, surpassing Brazil by the early 2000s. Venezuela almost triples its homicide rate in the short period of time between 1998 and 2006.

Panel B of figure 1.6 presents the experiences of Argentina, Chile, Costa Rica, and Mexico, all of which display much lower homicide rates than those registered in the countries from figure 1.6, panel A. Argentina experiences a timid but almost monotonic increase since 1979, with the homicide rate roughly doubling between 1979 and 2003, when it peaks at 7.3 and starts declining to reach 5 in 2006. Chile, on its turn, experiences extremely low homicide rates for the entire period, despite a discrete but stable increase

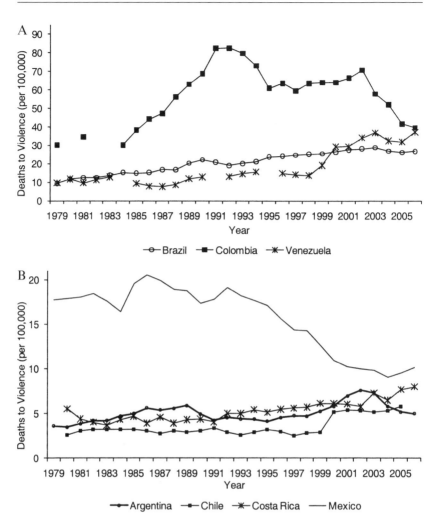

Fig. 1.6   Homicide rate, selected Latin American countries: *A*, higher crime rates; *B*, lower crime rates

Source: WHO, PAHO, and DATASUS.

around the year 2000 (when the rates jump from a historical plateau around three to a new level above five). Similarly, Costa Rica oscillates, but maintains low homicide through most of the period. In the last years of the series, a more sustained increase in crime seems to take place, reaching a rate of eight per 100,000 in 2006. Though relatively high by international standards, homicide rates for Argentina, Chile, and Costa Rica are comparable to those observed in most of the developed world, and are well below the average levels registered in Latin America.

Among the countries in the two figures, the Mexican experience is quite peculiar. Mexico starts with very high homicide rates—eighteen per 100,000—and, after almost twenty years of sustained reductions, reaches only 50 percent of the initial value by 2004.[5] This sustained reduction is then followed by mild increases between 2004 and 2006, from 9.1 to 10.2. Based on media reports, these increases seem to have taken off in the last few years, with the intensified presence and extreme violence of drug cartels along the U.S. border (see, for example, *The New York Times* [2009]). The Mexican experience is both reassuring and worrisome. It portrays, at the same time, a concrete history of long-term reduction in violence, but also shows that gains can always be threatened and reversed.

An important point raised before can be illustrated by the experiences of these countries. Everywhere, but particularly in violent places, homicides are disproportionately concentrated on the young population. Figure 1.7, panels A and B, present the same statistic presented in figure 1.6 but restricted to the age group between fifteen and twenty-four. The figures display similar patterns to the ones discussed previously, but for two distinguishing features. First, in the case of figure 1.7, panel A, the scale is almost twice that observed in figure 1.6, panel A. Second, in figure 1.7, panel B, the incidence of mortality by violence is generally higher than that observed in figure 1.6, panel B, but the difference is not so stark. So, for example, by the end of the 1990s the homicide rate in the age group between fifteen and twenty-four was more than 74 percent higher than that of the general population for Brazil, Colombia, and Venezuela. The same number for Costa Rica was 25 percent. The general point about these figures is that violence falls disproportionately on the young, and particularly so in high violence societies. Figure 1.7, panel A also highlights that changes in violence tend to be more extreme when one looks at younger fractions of the population, as compared to the entire population distribution. The same thing is true about the male population. If we restricted the homicide rate to the male population between fifteen and twenty-four years of age, we would end up with numbers almost two times higher than those observed in figure 1.7, panel A.

This section highlighted that the high crime rates observed in Latin America span various different types of crime and do not seem to be an artifact of the particular statistics used. Nevertheless, it also showed that country-specific experiences in the region have been different in many respects. The question remains, therefore, why some countries have been successful in maintaining low levels of violence or reducing violence to levels observed in the developed world, while others have seen increasing crime rates and

---

5. For the total number of deaths due to violence, results are much more extreme and positive for Chile and Mexico, with the total mortality rate due to violence falling from 40 to 7 in Chile, and from 28 to 13 in Mexico. For the other countries, patterns are very similar to those observed for the homicide rates, just with higher levels.

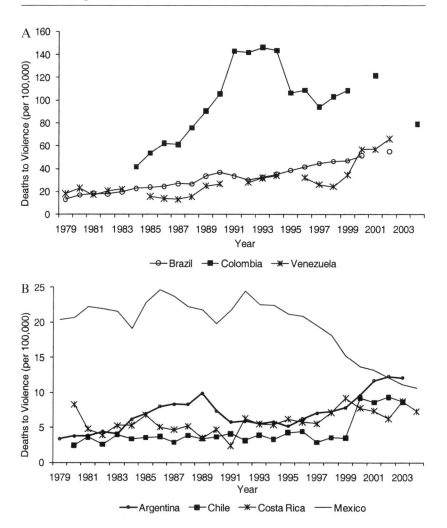

Fig. 1.7   Homicide rate between 15 and 24, selected Latin American countries; *A*, higher crime rates; *B*, lower crime rates
Source: WHO, PAHO, and DATASUS.

seemingly uncontrollable trends. In the next sections, we explore some possible explanations.

1.5   Candidate Explanations

In this section, we concentrate on the group of seven countries enumerated before and conduct an informal assessment of the merit of some hypotheses raised in the literature as potential explanations for the crime rates observed in Latin America. These hypotheses can be broadly classified into two categories: (a) those related to social and economic conditions conducive to an environment where criminal activities are more attractive to a larger fraction of the population; and (b) those related to government actions targeted at repression of criminal activities.

The first group includes economic and demographic conditions that put a large fraction of the population at the margin of choosing whether or not to engage in criminal and violent activities. Economic conditions typically identified are related to growth and inequality. According to the economic theory of crime, the likelihood that individuals will engage in criminal activities increases with the potential gains of crime and falls with its opportunity cost (see, for example, the early treatment of the topic in Ehrlich [1973]). The potential gains from criminal activities are related to the wealth of potential targets, while its opportunity costs are given by the gains from legal activities (low-skill wages in the labor market or returns to micro-entrepreneurship). A poor economic performance in the short run reduces legal opportunities in the economy, without necessarily affecting significantly its stock of wealth, therefore increasing the attractiveness of criminal behavior. Inequality, on its turn, leads to a situation where a significant fraction of the population is endowed with wealth and high income, therefore constituting potential criminal targets, while another fraction has very low income, and thus low opportunity cost of engaging in criminal activities. Sociological theories of relative deprivation also link economic inequality to higher crime.

For these reasons, economic growth and income inequality are variables thought to be important determinants of the incidence of crime. In general, the statistical evidence does support this relationship and recent studies have been able to find systematic correlations between these two variables and various measures of crime rates (see, for example, Bourguignon, Núñez, and Sanchez [2003]; Fajnzylber, Lederman, and Loayza [2002a, 2002b]; and Soares [2004a]). In particular, inequality seems to be a variable closely related to the incidence of crime and violence, both in theory and in the data, and it has been one of the main focuses of both theoretical and empirical work (see papers just cited and Ehrlich [1973], for example).

Demographic factors are associated with the age structure of the population and socioeconomic conditions. A traditional literature from criminology argues that both perpetrators and victims of criminal and violent activities are, in the majority of cases, young. For example, according to the Brazilian 2007 "Map of Violence," the increase in homicide rates in Brazil over the last decades is due exclusively to the increase in the homicide rate among young people: it soared from 30 in the 1980s to 51.7 in 2004, while the rate in other age groups fell slightly, from 21.3 to 20.8 (Waiselfisz 2007). The relationship between age distribution and crime is well established at the individual level in the empirical literature, despite the evidence that its role in explaining aggregate variations in U.S. crime rates in the recent past is rather limited (Levitt 1999). The particularly intense susceptibility of the young to fall into a trajectory of crime and illegality is most likely related to its weak attachment to the labor market and lower risk aversion, and maybe also to stronger peer effects (Grogger 1998). In any case, evidence seems to suggest that this may have been an important factor in the recent experience of some Latin American countries (de Mello and Schneider 2009).

Recently, a more sophisticated version of this argument was developed, claiming that not only the size of a cohort is important, but specifically the number of births of lower quality within a given cohort (unwanted births, births to broken homes under disadvantaged socioeconomic conditions, etc.). This is the logic underlying the idea that the legalization of abortion in the United States was one of the main reasons behind the reduction in crime rates observed in the 1990s (Donohue and Levitt 2001). A similar argument has been applied to the context of developing countries, specifically to the case of Brazil, to suggest that the increase in crime rates starting in the end of the twentieth century was the result of reductions in child mortality rates in the low socioeconomic strata twenty years beforehand (Hartung 2006).

The other relevant dimension in the determination of crime rates is related to the strength and effectiveness of the repressive policies adopted by the government. Policies to curb the incidence of crime include incarceration of offenders and harsher penalties for criminals, large police forces, effective judicial systems, and, overall, respect to the law and a clean and efficient government apparatus. Careful statistical analyses have confirmed beyond doubt the crime-reducing role of police presence and incarceration of criminals (for example, Levitt [1996, 1997, and 2002], and Di Tella and Schargrodsky [2004]). Data availability and the nature of the statistical problem have precluded more detailed evaluation of some of the other dimensions.

In order to evaluate whether these factors seem to have some merit in explaining the incidence of crime in Latin America, we take a closer look at some variables that try to capture the various dimensions discussed before. Data on some of these issues are very scarce in the cross-country context, so we restrict the analysis to the seven Latin American countries enumerated before (Argentina, Brazil, Chile, Colombia, Costa Rica, Mexico, and Venezuela) and to a set of six reference countries. These reference countries are chosen so as to include: two of the most developed countries in the world, the first with low and the second with reasonably high crime rates (Japan and the United States, respectively); an Eastern country that had a similar level of development to that of Latin America until the recent past (South Korea); an European country of similar cultural background (Spain); and low and high crime countries from other cultural traditions (Sweden and Russia, respectively).

For this set of thirteen countries, we look for variables representing the different economic, demographic, and policy factors discussed previously. For the economic and demographic factors, we choose the following variables: growth rate of income per capita between 1980 and 2000 to represent recent economic performance; Gini index to measure income inequality; birth rate in 1980 to represent the size of the entering cohort twenty years prior to 2000; and share of the population between fifteen and twenty-nine years to capture the relative size of the group most likely to engage in criminal activities. In relation to the policy dimensions, we choose the following variables: number of policemen per capita, number of judges per capita, incarceration rate, and a variable indicating the level of institutional development and rule of law in the country (rule of law).[6] The definitions and sources of all the variables are presented in the notes to the following table.

Table 1.8 presents the homicide rate and the eight variables described in the last paragraph for the set of thirteen countries chosen for this closer inspection. The average homicide rate for the selected Latin American countries, which equals 21.5, is much higher than that observed in any country in the comparison group but Russia. Japan, Korea, Spain, and Sweden have all extremely low homicide rates (all below 2), while the United States has a rate (5.9) comparable to the lowest Latin American numbers.

A clear pattern immediately emerges from this table. First, in relation to the economic variables, the selected Latin American countries display particularly poor economic performances and exceptionally high inequality levels. The average growth rate of income per capita between 1980 and 2000 for the countries in the region is only 0.7 percent, less than half that of the lowest growth rate observed in the comparison group, apart from that of Russia, which faced the collapse of communism during this time interval, so its performance does not seem to constitute a particularly appealing comparison in what refers to economic growth. In relation to inequality, the lowest level observed among the selected Latin American countries (45.8 for Venezuela) is higher than the highest level observed in the comparison group (42.5 for Russia). On average, the Gini index is almost 20 points (54 percent) higher in the region than in the comparison group.

The demographic variables also work in the same direction, though maybe not with such extreme differences. Birth rates in the region in 1980, as well as the share of the population between ages fifteen and twenty-nine in 2000, indicate the presence of a large fraction of the population in age groups particularly prone to criminal involvement and victimization. The birth rate in 1980 for the Latin American countries included in the table was 24.9, in contrast to 20.9 in the comparison group, while the shares of the young population in 2000 were, respectively, 27 percent and 22 percent. At the same time, Latin America experienced very fast and intense declines in child mortality

6. The rule of law index is defined as the extent to which agents have confidence in and abide by the rules of society, and in particular the quality of contract enforcement, the police, and the courts, as well as the likelihood of crime and violence. The index is a standardized measure with range between –2.5 (weakest institutions) and 2.5 (strongest institutions). For more detailed description, see Kaufmann, Kraay, and Mastruzzi (2006).

Table 1.8   Mortality due to violence and candidate determinants of crime, selected Latin American and comparison countries

Country	Homicides (per 100,000) 2000	Avg. growth income p.c. (%) 1980–2000	Gini index 2000	Birth rate (per 1,000) 1980	% Population 15–29 2000	Rule of law 2000	Police (per 100,000) 2000	Judges (per 100,000) 2000	Incarceration (per 100,000) 2001
Argentina	5.83	0.2	52.3	24.1	26	0.1	558	4.7	109
Brazil	26.08	0.6	61.2	30.7	28	-0.2	286	9.3	133
Chile	5.15	2.9	56.9	22.8	24	1.2	195	3.6	225
Colombia	70.21	1.1	57.4	31.0	27	-0.7	216	9.4	126
Costa Rica	6.13	0.1	50.1	31.2	27	0.7	39	15.3	157
Mexico	10.96	0.6	55.6	13.5	30	-0.5	451	.	164
Venezuela	26.20	-1.0	45.8	20.7	27	-0.9	15	2.6	59
Avg. for selected Latin American countries	21.5	0.7	54.2	24.9	27	-0.04	252	7.5	139
Japan	0.6	2.4	31.9	34.0	20	1.7	182	2.4	51
Korea	1.7	5.8	36.9	15.9	26	0.5	192	3.4	133
Russia	28.1	-1.2	42.5	15.2	23	-1.0	1,222	46.7	638
Spain	1.0	2.4	31.5	11.6	23	1.3	286	8.4	117
Sweden	1.0	1.5	29.2	15.9	18	1.9	181	19.2	68
United States	5.9	2.3	39.4	32.9	20	1.8	325	11.0	685
Avg. for comparison group	6.4	2.2	35.2	20.9	22	1.0	398	15.2	282

Notes: Growth rate from Penn World Tables 6.1 (real gross domestic income adjusted for terms of trade —rgdptt; the number for Russia is from the World Development Indicators gdp p.c. in 1995 US$). Gini index from WIDER-UN, birth rate from the World Development Indicators, population between 15–29 from the World Health Organization, rule of law index (range: −2.5; +2.5) from the Government Matters V data set (World Bank). Police rate is total police personnel in 2000 from the United Nations Survey on Trends and the Operations of Criminal Justice (1998 for Argentina; 2001 for Mexico, Venezuela, and United States; 1994 for Russia; for Brazil, data from the Ministry of Justice for 2003). Judges refer to magistrates and judges (number of professional judges and magistrates in 2000 from the United Nations Survey on Trends and the Operations of Criminal Justice; 1997 for Argentina; 2001 for United States; for Brazil, 2005 data from Ordem dos Advogados do Brasil—OAB). Incarceration rate is the official records of total prison population from the International Centre of Prison Studies (2002 for Costa Rica and 2000 for Venezuela). Blank cell (.) indicates no relevant data found for Mexico.

rates between 1960 and 1990, opening space for an argument in the reverse direction of that developed by Donohue and Levitt (2001), as suggested by Hartung (2006). In this sense, the frequency of individuals from extreme socioeconomic conditions and fragile household environments is likely to have increased in the distribution of adolescents and young adults.

The previous paragraphs paint a picture of a large fraction of the population in Latin America in age groups prone to involvement in criminal activities, at the same time when economic conditions—low growth and high inequality—make criminal activities particularly attractive. The other side of this equation is the set of repressive policies put in place by the government, and the effectiveness of these policies. The balance between these two forces determines the final incidence of crime and violence in a given society.

Overall, the group of Latin American countries under analysis has very timid repressive policies when compared to the reference group. The average number of policemen per 100,000 inhabitants is 252, as opposed to 398 in the comparison group, while the number of judges is 7.5 in comparison to 15.2, and the incarceration rate is 139 in comparison to 282. In addition, if the index of rule of law captures the efficiency of government policies, it is likely that these instruments are less effective in Latin America than in countries in the comparison group: the average of the index, which varies between –2.5 and +2.5, is –0.4 for the selected Latin American countries and +1.0 for the comparison group.

The differences are even more striking when we contrast the Latin American average to the most violent countries in the comparison group. These are Russia and the United States, which react to the high violence levels by enforcing a very strict set of repressive policies: the number of policemen per 100,000 inhabitants is 1,222 in Russia and 325 in the United States, while the number of judges is forty-seven and eleven, and the incarceration rate is 638 and 685, respectively. In comparison, Brazil Colombia, and Venezuela, the most violent among the selected Latin American countries, have modest levels for these three variables, roughly comparable to or below that of Spain, a country with extremely low incidence of crime. In reality, the most intense use of repressive policies in Latin America is observed precisely among those countries that have enjoyed reasonably controlled levels of violence: the highest numbers of policemen per 100,000 inhabitants are observed in Argentina and Mexico, while the highest number of judges is in Costa Rica, and the highest incarceration rate is in Chile.

The superficial inspection of the numbers from table 1.8 seems to suggest that the high crime rates observed in Latin America are not that surprising after all. Economic and demographic factors are conducive to an environment where a large fraction of the population is at the margin of choosing whether or not to engage in criminal activities. Differences in inequality are particularly striking in this respect. The average Gini index among our seven

Latin American countries is almost twenty points higher than that in the comparison group. At the same time, policies toward the repression of crime are weak and likely ineffective. Most noticeable in this case is the very low number of policemen per 100,000 inhabitants and the incarceration rate, the latter being less than half of that observed in the comparison group.

In the remaining sections, we discuss the scope for successful policy interventions targeted at reducing crime in the region. First, based on the statistical estimates available from the literature, we ask how much one can hope to achieve with the use of the policy instruments available and, over the long run, with changes in socioeconomic conditions. Following, we briefly analyze some specific experiences of localized interventions that have been successful at reducing crime and violence.

1.6   The Scope for Action

The previous section argued that several factors identified as potentially important seem to contribute to the high crime rates observed in Latin America. In this section, we draw on estimates from the empirical literature and ask how much the dimensions discussed before can explain, given what is known quantitatively from the evidence available. In doing so, we are constrained to work only with those variables that map well-established estimates from the empirical literature. For natural reasons, these are also the variables that typically attract most attention.

In what follows, we concentrate on the effects of incarceration rates, number of policemen per 100,000 inhabitants, fraction of the population aged between fifteen and twenty-nine, inequality, and economic growth. Regarding the other variables appearing in table 1.8, there are no widely accepted estimates available in the literature.

In relation to public safety policies, theory argues that increases in prison population can reduce crime through either deterrence or incapacitation effects. Levitt (1996) estimates that violent crime in the United States would be 70 percent higher if the number of prisoners had remained constant over the last decades. He argues that incarcerating one additional prisoner reduces the number of crimes by approximately fifteen per year, a number in close accordance with the level of criminal activity reported by the median prisoner in surveys. His estimates suggest that a 1 percent increase in the incarceration rate reduces the number of violent crimes by –0.379 percent. Levitt (1997, 2002) also argues that increases in police are very effective in reducing violent crime, even though the effect on property crime may be substantially smaller. In this case, the average estimate suggests that a 1 percent increase in the number of policemen per capita is associated with a reduction of –0.435 percent in the incidence of violent crimes.

Estimates for the effect of demographic composition are available from Levitt (1999). He shows that, in the case of the United States, changes in age structure explain 20 percent of the increase in murder rates observed between 1960 and 1980, and 40 percent of the reduction observed between 1980 and 1995. His counterfactual exercise implies an average response of homicides of 0.41 percent per each 1 percent increase in the fraction of young people in the population.

Inequality is probably the single most widely studied factor in the cross-country literature on crime rates. It has been consistently identified as one of the main economic determinants of crime and violence, through its effects on the costs and benefits of criminal activities and on social cohesion (see, among others, Bourguignon [1999]; Fajnzylber, Lederman, and Loayza [2002a, 2002b]; Bourguignon, Núñez, and Sanchez [2003]; and Soares [2004a]). A widely cited study by Fajnzylber, Lederman, and Loayza (2002b) shows that increases in income inequality and reductions in the level of economic activity are significantly related to increases in crime rates. Their statistical model implies that a 1 percentage point increase in the Gini index is associated with a 1.5 percent increase in homicide rates, and that a 1 percentage point increase in the growth rate of income per capita is associated with a decline of 2.4 percent.

Though these various estimates are from different types of data and different sources, not necessarily applicable to the Latin American reality, we use them as benchmarks to guide the discussion on the potential for crime reduction in the region, along the dimensions discussed in the previous section. The question being addressed is whether, given the numbers most commonly cited in the literature, changes in factors typically identified as associated with crime would lead to substantial reductions in crime rates in Latin America. If the answer is yes it means that, at first sight, the Latin American case would not be exceptional and standard policies would be the obvious first choice to tackle the problem. On the other hand, if the answer is no, it would seem that still unidentified characteristics of the region would be responsible for the high crime rates observed, and nonorthodox policies might be called for.

Table 1.9 presents the estimates of the effects on crime of the explanatory variables discussed in the last paragraphs. It also presents counterfactual calculations of the average homicide rate that would be observed in the selected Latin American countries if the different explanatory variables were set to the levels observed in the comparison group. We present the partial impact of each explanatory variable (each one being changed separately), as well as the cumulative impact (various variables being change simultaneously, cumulative from top to bottom).

Maybe the most striking result from this table is the fact that, given the numbers observed and the estimates available from the literature, the high violence levels observed in Latin America are not surprising at all. This fact was already alluded to in the previous section, but it becomes clearer in the simple quantitative exercise from table 1.9. If the average incarceration rates,

Table 1.9   Estimates of the effects of explanatory variables on homicides and differential in crime explained by each variable

Variable	Study	Data	Response of crime to explanatory variable	Mortality to violence in LA if avg. were set to: avg. of comparison [viol.: 21.5 against 6.4]		Mortality to violence in LA if avg. were set to: avg. of comp. w.o. Russia [viol.: 21.5 against 2.1]	
				Partial	Cumulative	Partial	Cumulative
Incarceration rate	Levitt (1996)	United States	−0.379% per 1% change	13.1	13.1	17.3	17.3
Police	Levitt (2002)	United States	−0.435% per 1% change	16.1	9.8	22.2	17.8
Fraction of young population	Levitt (1999)	United States	0.41% per 1% change	19.8	9.0	19.7	16.3
inequality (Gini)	Fajnzylber, Lederman, and Loayza (2002b)	Cross-country	1.5% per unit change	15.4	6.4	14.9	11.3
Growth (income p.c.)	Fajnzylber, Lederman, and Loayza (2002b)	Cross-country	−2.4% per percentage point change	20.7	6.3	20.4	10.7

Notes: For Levitt (1996, 2002), the estimates are elasticities for violent crime. For Levitt (1999) the crime variable is homicide rate and we calculate the average elasticity from the decomposition exercises performed. For Fajnzylber, Lederman, and Loayza (2002b), the estimates are semi-elasticities for homicide rates (ln of the homicide rate on the dependent variable). LA = Latin America.

number of policemen per capita, fraction of young population, inequality, and growth in the selected Latin American countries were set to the averages observed in the comparison group, mortality by violence in Latin America would drop from 21.5 to 6.3. Since Russia is somewhat of an outlier within the comparison group in terms of the harshness of its repressive policies and its crime rates, we also present an alternative scenario where the variables in Latin America are set to the average of the comparison group excluding Russia. In this scenario, the homicide rate in Latin America would fall to 10.7. In any case, the homicide rate falls between 50 percent and 66 percent in the counterfactual exercises, when the explanatory variables are set to the levels observed in the comparison group (including and excluding Russia, respectively).

In the first scenario, homicide rates are actually reduced to a level almost identical to that observed in the comparison group, while in the second scenario it still remains substantially above it, despite attaining quite reasonable levels (equivalent to those observed in the United States during the 1990s, for example). In words, the violence levels observed in Latin America do not seem to be unusually high, given the socioeconomic conditions observed in the region, the repressive policies adopted by its governments, and what is known from the empirical literature about the relationship between these variables and crime. Fajnzylber, Lederman, and Loayza (1998) also reached similar conclusions in an entirely different setting, applying dynamic panel data techniques with a cross-country data set.

Separately, the quantitative roles of inequality, incarceration rates, and police seem to be the most important ones, while age composition and economic growth seem to have only modest effects. According to the counterfactual scenarios, changing the level of inequality to that observed in the comparison group would lead to a reduction of 28 percent in homicide rates, while the similar number for incarceration rates and police presence would be, respectively, 39 percent and 25 percent.

While incarceration rates and number of policemen are policy variables directly under the control of the government, inequality is an outcome variable that typically changes slowly through time (Deininger and Squire 1996). There are various reasons why reduction in inequality is desirable for its own sake, and it should indeed be seen as a valid policy goal. But it is generally not an instrument subject to immediate control of the government, so it should not be seen as a tool within a short- or medium-term strategy for reducing crime.

Given this evidence, a stronger set of measures in relation to incarceration and policing seems to be the most obvious immediate policy choice available. Still, to the extent that income inequality is related to inequality in the provision of public goods and to lack of access to a wide range of basic services by a large fraction of the population, preventive social policies may also be effective. It is difficult to map this idea quantitatively on the empirical estimates of the effect of inequality on crime, but it seems reasonable to assume that, for example, better provision of basic health and education, leading in the medium run to individuals with better opportunities in the legal market, could also lead to reductions in the incidence of crime. The combination of these two perspectives would suggest crime fighting strategies based on the two dimensions identified before: increased intensity and effectiveness of repressive policies, coupled with improvements in the socioeconomic environment and better access to public goods. As the next section illustrates, successful experiences of crime reduction in the region have adopted strategies along these lines.

The discussion in this section brings implicit the idea that the effectiveness of the penal system and of the police force in Latin America, when expanded, would be similar to that of the countries from which the estimates in table 1.9 were generated. This is obviously not necessarily, and not likely, the case. In reality, the effectiveness of any given intervention will depend on the way it is conducted from an operational perspective, and on the institutional context in which it is implemented. In the next section, we discuss the strategy and institutional context of some successful experiences of crime reduction within Latin America.

1.7   Success Experiences

In this section, we take a closer look at two specific experiences of successful crime reduction in Latin America. Local governments have played a key role in the recent past as agents of effective policy changes. In particular, the impressive achievements of Bogotá, Colombia, became an example to many other cities in the region. São Paulo, the largest city in Brazil, followed some of Colombia's capital footsteps, and results are also promising.

1.7.1   Bogotá

Bogotá became a landmark for crime prevention in Latin America. Its policy strategy was inspired by the Development Security and Peace Program (DESPAZ), initially designed for the equally violent city of Cali. This program was launched in mid-1994, when Rodrigo Guerrero was the mayor of Cali, aiming at both fighting and preventing violence through a public health approach. The program was abandoned after Guerrero left office in 1994, but by then it had already been incorporated into a broader public security plan for Bogotá, under the mayoral administration of Antanas Mockus (for a detailed description, see Mockus [2005]).

In 1994, Bogotá had the highest homicide rate among capital cities in Latin America. Today, it has a homicide rate substantially lower than that of Caracas, Rio de Janeiro, and Washington, DC, similar to that of Lima and Mexico City, and still above that of Buenos Aires, Miami, Panama City, and Santiago (Stanford Project on Urban Ecology and Violence 2007).

The public health approach started with the development of a reliable information system aiming at monitoring the characteristics and demographics of cases of intentional and unintentional deaths or injuries, as well as of certain types of other crimes. This was achieved through the creation of an observatory of violence and crime. A package incorporating several different measures along various dimensions was then implemented (Concha-Eastman 2005). This package included the following measures: limited hours for alcohol sales in bars, voluntary disarmament, improved police equipment targeted at faster response, and local projects to improve police performance and manage small conflicts. Local projects comprised conflict resolution initiatives, family police stations, and the Houses of Justice (Casas de Justicia), centers in popular neighborhoods where individuals could access the services of lawyers, social workers, psychologists, and in some cases judges.

The Colombian interventions were based on the idea of integrated municipal programs, combining public health, reclaiming of public space, and criminal justice improvements. These were materialized on crime and violence information systems, improving access to justice, control of alcohol consumption and traffic accidents, assistance to vulnerable groups such as at-risk youth, the "citizen culture" program, and the recovery of public spaces such as parks and bicycle paths. In addition, there were efforts to strengthen the police force, as well as judicial reform. Much media attention was given to the "Ley Zanahoria," imposing a 1:00 AM curfew on alcohol sales, and on the rush hour restrictions on private cars.

As a result, there was a significant reduction in crime rates in Bogotá, in reality much more extreme than initially anticipated. The homicide rate, which was around 80 per 100,000 in 1993, declined to 21 in 2004. In Cali, significant reductions in crime were also observed when DESPAZ was implemented, but as the program was abandoned the change was reversed. In the case of Bogotá, on the other hand, the Peñalosa administration (starting in 1998) persisted in pursuing the Mockus policies, also incorporating an impressive public space recovery program (Concha-Eastman 2005; World Bank 2006a).

1.7.2   São Paulo

On December 7, 2007, the city of São Paulo experienced twenty-four hours without a homicide. This was the first time the city went through an entire day without a single murder since the 1950s (Veja 2007). This remarkable event was the culmination of years of consistent and successful policies in the fight against violent crime.

Following the experience of Bogotá, several cities in the metropolitan area of São Paulo implemented different combinations of the measures included in the Colombian package. Policies included dry-laws, programs of voluntary disarmament, social programs, increases in incarceration rates, and changes in police organization and operation. Against the Brazilian national trend of increasing homicide rates, there was a continuous decline in homicide rates starting in 1999.

Though the particular role played by the different factors remains an open question, reorganization of the police force, stronger social support, and increased incarceration rates seem to have been important (de Mello and Schneider, chapter 6, this volume). These included a change in attitude toward a more quantitative approach to crime fighting and prevention, emphasizing empirical diagnosis of the pattern and distribution of crime, adoption of standardized procedures for police actions, and constant monitoring and evaluation of actions and use of resources. One of the first steps was the creation of InfoCrim, a system of criminal information designed to map criminal data in different police districts to enable a more organized and efficient use of resources. The change in policies also marked a shift to a more systematic involvement of the municipal and federal administrations on the fight against crime, as opposed to the more traditional model, which relied mostly on the state government (Kahn 2007). Some credit is also given to dry laws, which are estimated to have been responsible for a reduction in homicides of more than 10 percent (Biderman, de Mello, and Schneider 2009).

Diadema, a city in the metropolitan area of São Paulo, also achieved considerable success by coordinating the initiatives from various political and social actors and focusing on community cooperation within high-risk areas (World Bank 2006). The municipality implemented monthly town meetings between the mayor, the city council, military and civil police chiefs, business, and religious and community leaders. At the same time, knowledge on violence reduction approaches and contacts with experts were established. As in the city of São Paulo itself, policies also included dry-laws, modern information systems to monitor the evolution of crime through time and space, and, in addition, creation of a task force to work with parents, students, and teachers on violence prevention, particularly targeting school violence. The number of homicides in the case of Diadema was reduced by roughly 70 percent between 1999 and 2005 (data from the Secretary of Public Safety of the state of São Paulo). In the city of São Paulo itself, the number of intentional homicides was reduced by 79 percent. In the entire state, intentional homicides fell from thirty-six to eleven, a 69 percent reduction. In contrast, the most recent numbers for Rio de Janeiro and Brazil as a whole indicate homicide rates of, respectively, 39 and 22 per 100,000.

Still, as Biderman, de Mello, and Schneider (2009) highlight, the specific timing and coverage of the various interventions do not seem to be able to account for the chronology and magnitude of the reduction in homicide rates. Though evidence clearly indicates that several of these policies were indeed effective in reducing crime, they seem to have benefited from a particularly susceptible social environment. As the authors argue, changes in the age distribution of the São Paulo population seem to have provided the fertile ground on which the policy interventions thrived. Precisely in the end of the 1990s, and reflecting a particular stage of the demographic transition, the fraction of the population composed of young people started a consistent decline. The interaction of the demographic change with the wide host of policies adopted seems to provide a reasonable explanation for the remarkable performance of the homicide rates in the state of São Paulo.

If São Paulo's government achieves its goal of ten homicides (both intentional and nonintentional) per 100,000 inhabitants, the state will reach what the World Health Organization recognizes as an acceptable level of mortality due to homicides.

1.8 Concluding Remarks

This chapter argues that the high crime rates observed in Latin America seem to be consistent with the socioeconomic characteristics of its countries and with the policies implemented by governments in the region. There seems to be no basis for the claim that the patterns observed are due to unusual and exceptional characteristics faced by its countries. On the contrary, three factors widely recognized as being major determinants of the incidence of crime—inequality, police presence, and incarceration rates—account for most of the seemingly exceptionally high crime rates. This interpretation is further supported by successful experiences of crime reduction in some areas that would rank among the most violent in the region just a few decades ago. Among others, Bogotá and São Paulo have sustained steady declines in crime rates, particularly homicide, following the consistent and continued implementation of policies combining the use of more intense and effective repressive measures with social support programs.

References

Aguirre, C. 2000. Crime and punishment in Latin American history: A bibliographical essay. In *Reconstructing criminality in Latin America*. ed. C. A. Aguirre and R. Buffington, Wilmington, DE: Scholarly Resources.

Beck, T., G. Clark, A. Groff, P. Keefer, and P. Walsh. 2001. New tools in comparative political economy. *World Bank Economic Review* 15 (1): 165–76.

Becker, G. 1968. Crime and punishment: An economic approach. *Journal of Political Economy* 76 (2): 169–217.

Biderman, C., J. M. P. de Mello, and A. A. Schneider. 2009. Dry law and homicides: Evidence from the São Paulo metropolitan area. *Economic Journal,* forthcoming.

Bourguignon, F. 1999. Crime, violence, and inequitable development. In *Annual World Bank conference on development economics 1999/2000,* ed. B. Pleskovic and J. Stiglitz, 199–220. Washington, DC: World Bank.

Bourguignon, F., J. Núñez, and F. Sanchez. 2003. A structural model of crime and inequality in Colombia. *Journal of the European Economic Association* 1 (2–3): 440–49.

Burnham, R. W. 1990. Crime, development and contemporary criminology. In *Essays on crime and development,* ed. U. Zvekic, 43–55. Rome: United Nations Crime and Justice Research Institute (UNICRI).

Concha-Eastman, A. 2005. Ten years of a successful violence reduction program in Bogotá, Colombia. Paper presented at the National Conference, "Preventing Violence: From Global Perspectives to National Action." 10–11 March, Liverpool.

Deininger, K., and L. Squire. 1996. A new data set measuring income inequality. *The World Bank Economic Review* 10 (3): 565–91.

Di Tella, R., and E. Schargrodsky. 2004. Do police reduce crime? Estimates using the allocation of police forces after a terrorist attack. *American Economic Review* 94 (1): 115–33.

Donohue, J. J., III, and S. D. Levitt. 2001. The impact of legalized abortion on crime. *Quarterly Journal of Economics* 116 (2): 379–420.

Ehrlich, I. 1973. Participation in illegitimate activities: A theoretical and empirical investigation. *Journal of Political Economy* 81 (3): 521–65.

Fajnzylber, P., D. Lederman, and N. V. Loayza. 1998. *Determinants of crime rates in Latin America and the world: An empirical assessment.* Washington, DC: World Bank.

———. 2002a. Inequality and violent crime. *Journal of Law and Economics* 45 (1): 1–40.

———. 2002b. What causes violent crime? *European Economic Review* 46 (7): 1323–57.

Fowles, R., and M. Merva. 1996. Wage inequality and criminal activity: An extreme bounds analysis for the United States, 1975–90. *Criminology* 34 (2): 163–82.

Gaviria, A., and C. Eduardo Vélez. 2002. Who bears the burden of crime and violence in Colombia? In *Colombia poverty report,* vol. 2, chapter 4, 146–61. Washington, DC: World Bank.

Glaeser, E. L. 1999. An overview of crime and punishment. Unpublished Manuscript. Harvard University.

Grogger, J. 1998. Market wages and youth crime. *Journal of Labor Economics* 16 (4): 756–91.

Hartung, G. C. 2006. Fatores demográficos como determinantes da criminalidade. EPGE-FGV. Unpublished Manuscript.

Kahn, T. 2007. Por que a criminalidade está em queda em São Paulo? Unpublished Manuscript. Secretaria de Segurança Pública de São Paulo.

Kalemli-Ozcan, S. 2006. AIDS, "reversal" of the demographic transition and economic development: Evidence from Africa. NBER Working Paper no. 12181. Cambridge, MA: National Bureau of Economic Research, May.

Kauffman, D., A. Kraay, and M. Mastruzzi. 2006. Governance matters V: Governance indicators for 1996–2005. World Bank Policy Research Department Working Paper no. 4012.

Keefer, P., N. V. Loayza, and R. R. Soares. 2010. Drug prohibition and developing countries: Uncertain benefits, certain costs. In *Innocent bystanders: Developing countries and the war on drugs,* ed. P. Keefer and N. Loayza, Cambridge: Cambridge University Press, forthcoming.

Krohn, M. 1978. A Durkheimian analysis of international crime rates. *Social Forces* 57 (2): 654–70.

Krohn, M., and C. F. Wellford. 1977. A static and dynamic analysis of crime and the primary dimensions of nations. *International Journal of Criminology and Penology* 5:1–16.

Latinobarómetro. 2006. *Latinobarómetro report 2006.* Santiago de Chile.

Levitt, S. D. 1996. The effect of prison population size on crime rates: Evidence from prison overcrowding litigation. *Quarterly Journal of Economics* 111 (2): 319–51.

———. 1997. Using electoral cycles in police hiring to estimate the effect of police on crime. *American Economic Review* 87 (3): 270–90.

———. 1999. The limited role of changing age structure in explaining aggregate crime rates. *Criminology* 37 (3): 581–98.

———. 2002. Using electoral cycles in police hiring to estimate the effect of police on crime: Reply. *American Economic Review* 92 (4): 1244–50.

Londoño, J. L., and R. Guerrero. 1999. Violencia en América Latina—Epidemiología y Costos. Inter-American Development Bank, Documento de Trabajo R-375.

Lorentzen, P., J. McMillan, e R. Wacziarg. 2008. Death and development. *Journal of Economic Growth* 13 (2): 81–124.

Mockus, A. 2005. Advancing against violence in Bogotá: Creating civic agency and "Cultural Change." Unpublished Manuscript. Universidad Nacional de Colombia.

Murphy, K. M., and R. H. Topel. 2003. *Measuring the gains from medical research: An economic approach.* Chicago: University of Chicago Press.

New York Times. 2009. In drug war, Mexico fights cartel and itself. March 29.

Patterson, E. 1991. Poverty, income inequality, and community crime rates. *Criminology* 29 (4): 755–76.

Severnini, E. R. 2007. A relação entre violência nas escolas e proficiência dos alunos. PUC-Rio. Unpublished Manuscript.

Soares, R. R. 2004a. Crime reporting as a measure of institutional development. *Economic Development and Cultural Change* 52 (4): 851–71.

———. 2004b. Development, crime, and punishment: Accounting for the international differences in crime rates. *Journal of Development Economics* 73 (1): 155–84.

———. 2006. The welfare cost of violence across countries. *Journal of Health Economics* 25 (5): 821–46.

Stack, S. 1984. Income inequality and property crime: A cross-national analysis of relative deprivation theory. *Criminology* 22 (2): 229–57.

Stanford Project on Urban Ecology and Violence. 2007. *Case Studies: Curbing violence in the urban space: The transformation of Bogota.* Palo Alto, CA: Stanford University.

Stigler, G. 1970. The optimum enforcement of laws. *Journal of Political Economy* 78 (3): 526–36.

The Economist. 2006. Crime and (maybe) punishment: President Uribe faces conflicting pressures as he tries to strike a balance between peace and justice. August 24.

Veja. 2007. Sexta-feira santa: Pela primeira vez, desde a década de 50, São Paulo tem um dia sem assassinatos. December 29.

Waiselfisz, J. J. 2007. Mapa da Violência dos Municípios Brasileiros. OEI (Organização dos Estados Ibero-Americanos para a Educação, a Ciência e a Cultura).

Washington Post. 2007. In Rio, death comes early: Juveniles are often victims as gangs, police vie for control of slums. April 16.

World Bank. 2006a. Crime, violence and economic development in Brazil: Elements for effective public policy. Report no. 36525, Poverty Reduction and Economic Management Sector Unit, Latin America and the Caribbean Region.

World Bank. 2006b. *The investment climate in Brazil, India, and South Africa: A contribution to the IBSA debate.* Washington, DC: World Bank.

Comment   Alejandro Gaviria

This chapter contradicts a widespread opinion, held by political commentators and policymakers alike, that Latin America is an exceptional region in terms of crime and violence. The chapter shows that homicide rates in Latin America are not much different from what one should have expected given its "crime fundamentals." Three factors, in particular, appear to explain much of Latin America high crime rates: high-income inequality, very low incarceration rates, and small police forces.

This conclusion has a straightforward policy implication. If Latin American high levels of crime and violence are not the consequences of some mysterious social or historical force, but the manifestation of identifiable failures of public policy, then violence is tractable. The findings of this chapter cast many doubts on the defeatism that has characterized the public discourse in Latin America regarding the issues of crime and violence. While I agree with the main findings, as well as with its main message of optimism, I think some clarifications are in order about both the findings and the policy implications.

One first point has to do with the novelty of the main claim made in the chapter, namely, the nonexceptional nature of Latin American violence rates once crime fundamentals are taken into account. A similar finding is reported by Fajnzylber, Lederman, and Loayza (2002) in their study about the cross-country determinants of the homicide rate. These authors estimate a dynamic panel for a sample of countries, and show that, after controlling for the average per capita income, the growth rate, the educational attainment of the adult population, the level of inequality, and the arrest rate, a Latin American dummy variable is nonsignificant. Again, the evidence indicates that mean levels of violence in Latin America are not different from what should be expected given this region's economic, social, and law enforcement characteristics.

It is worth pointing out that Fanyzlber, Lederman, and Loayza (1998) use a different methodology to reach the same conclusion. They do not rely on estimated elasticities to build a simple counterfactual (what would the violence and crime levels in Latin America be had this region had the social and law enforcement characteristics of a typical developed country?). They use instead a regression framework in order to show that, once the main characteristics are controlled for, the actual violence levels observed in Latin America are normal.

My second point has to do with the issue of crime dynamics and (in particular) with the issue of ascending spirals of crime that are common in many places of Latin America. The point is simple: the linear extrapolation

Alejandro Gaviria is professor of economics at the University of the Andes.

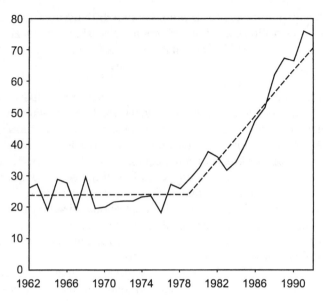

Fig. 1C.1   Homicide rate in Colombia, 1962–1994

used in the chapter is not adequate to account for explosive dynamics of violent crime. Sometimes crime fundamentals are insufficient to comprehend the punctuated evolution of crime and violence. One example suffices to illustrate this point. Figure 1C.1 shows the evolution of the homicide rate in Colombia in the period 1962 to 1994. The homicide rate went from 22 homicides per 100,000 residents in the late seventies to almost 80 in the early nineties.

Gaviria (2000) summarizes the main mechanisms underlying the escalation of homicide rates in Colombia. Crime fundamentals have little to do with it. Inequality did not change much during the period. Incarceration rates and the relative size of police force also remained unchanged. The explosive dynamic was triggered by the cocaine trade and in particular by the emergence of Colombia as the main exporter of cocaine to the United States. However, this is only part of the story. In Colombia, violence fed into itself. Violence made violent crime more appealing by congesting the law enforcement system and hence lowering the probability of punishment. Besides, the interaction of career criminals and local crooks speeds up the diffusion of criminal know-how and criminal technology. Finally, the daily contact of youth with criminal adults and criminal peers resulted in the erosion of morals and hence in a greater predisposition toward crime. As a result, a specific crime shock was greatly amplified.

This example is relevant because it shows that large deviations from the level of violence dictated by crime fundamentals are quite possible. In the same vein, the Colombian case indicates that an understanding of crime waves requires a thorough description of the mechanisms though which violence begets violence. This point is not a minor one since, as mentioned earlier, crime waves are common in many places in Latin America in particular and the world in general.

My third point is almost a mirror image of the previous one. The point is related to the well-known nonlinear prediction bias. The elasticities used in the chapter, based on data from the United States, probably underestimate policy responses in communities with high levels of crime. The case studies presented at the end of the chapter suggest that *normal* elasticities do not apply in the most successful policy interventions. In many cases, the responses went well beyond what should be expected given the estimated elasticities. Successful policies are not only about substantial changes in crime fundamentals. They are mainly about *big* responses to smart policies. In other words, successful policies often imply substantial crime multipliers.

While the simple arithmetic presented in section 1.6 of the chapter suggests that changes in law enforcement variables can by themselves have a substantial effect on crime, the case studies presented in section 1.7 suggest that these changes are most successful if accompanied by interventions in other dimensions: "citizen culture," justice, restrictions on alcohol sales, and so forth. Put differently, the arithmetic of section 1.6 shows that there is ample scope for action, and the examples of section 1.7 show that action is often more complex than simply increasing the size of the police force or raising incarceration rates.

Figure 1C.2 shows the dramatic decline of the homicide rate in the city of Medellin. In 1990, Medellin was the murder capital of the world: the recorded homicide rate was then close to 400 per 100,000 residents. During the early nineties, homicides decreased substantially following the decline of Medellin in the cocaine trade but it still remained very high. Recently, however, the homicide rate plummeted. What happened? More and better policing is a good part of the story. But it is not the whole story. Big libraries and new schools were built in the most violent areas of the city. Public transportation was greatly improved. Educational programs for youth at risk were implemented (Bastidas 2007). While it is difficult to tease out the effects of the different elements of a complex (and an ongoing) strategy, it cannot be argued, in the absence of further evidence, that these other elements do not play an important role.

My last point is also related to the previous one. Any discussion about the fundamental factors that determine the levels of crime and violence cannot avoid the issue of illegal drugs. Fanyzlber, Lederman, and Loayza (1998) show that, after controlling for social and law enforcement characteristics, a dummy variable designating drug-producing countries is significant. Needless to say, illegal drug trade is an important determinant of crime and vio-

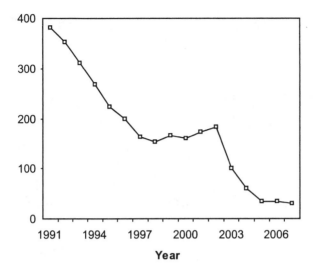

Fig. 1C.2   Homicide rate in the city of Medellin (Colombia), 1990–2007

lence. Drug trafficking *directly* increases violence through their murderous activities. At the same time, drug trafficking *indirectly* increases violence through several channels: congestion of law enforcement, knowledge spill-overs, and cultural change.

Given this, policies aiming at reducing violence in Latin America must necessarily deal with the problem of drugs (and the problem of the drug trade in particular). However, references to this problem are conspicuously absent from the chapter. If the drug trade is widespread, increasing the number of police officers or putting more criminals into prison will not reduce violence, as illustrated by recent events in Mexico. Put succinctly, the drug trade is another crime fundamental.

To conclude, it is important to reiterate the main message of the chapter: Latin American countries are not exceptional in terms of violent crime once fundamentals are taken into account. This fact suggests that there is ample scope for action, that there is much that can be done to reduce violence and crime in the region. In light of the evidence, law enforcement variables are a good place to start. But policies should go beyond the simple recipe of increasing the police force and building more prisons.

Seemingly, a combination of policies is required. At a general level, crime and violence prevention needs to combine different approaches, not only related to criminal justice, but also to public health, conflict resolution, and community-driven development (UNODC and World Bank 2007). As mentioned in the chapter, the combination of repressive measures with social support programs has been quite successful in some Latin American cities. The main challenge faced by academics and policymakers is to understand completely the mechanisms whereby these cities are leaving behind a legacy of violent crime.

References

Bastidas, G. 2007. A drug-runners' stronghold finds a new life. *New York Times,* August, 12.

Gaviria, A. 2000. Increasing returns and the evolution of violent crime: The case of Colombia. *Journal of Development Economics* 61 (1): 1–25.

Fajnzylber, P., D. Lederman, and N. Loayza. 1998. *Determinants of crime rates in Latin America and the world: An empirical assessment.* Washington, DC: World Bank. Available at: www.worldbank.org/laccrime.

———. 2002. What causes violent crime? *European Economic Review* 46:1323–57.

United Nations Office on Drugs and Crime and World Bank. 2007. *Crime violence and development: Trends, costs and policy options in the Caribbean.* Washington, DC: World Bank.

II

The Economics of Crime Meets Latin America

Capital Crimes
Kidnappings and Corporate
Investment in Colombia

Rony Pshisva and Gustavo A. Suarez

2.1 Introduction

Recent cross-country studies suggest that crime hinders economic activity. For example, using survey data for Latin America, Gaviria (2002) finds that firms located in countries where managers report that crime is an obstacle to doing business exhibit lower sales growth. Similarly, Barro (1991) and Alesina and Perotti (1996) find that politically unstable countries grow more slowly and invest less. Developing countries are simultaneously burdened by high crime rates and deficits in economic and social infrastructure, including health and education. Hence, understanding the effect of crime on economic activity is central for debating priorities and strategies for development policy. In addition, high rates of violent crime in developing countries may help researchers explain the puzzling result that capital does not appear to flow from rich countries to poor countries (Lucas 1990).

Rony Pshisva is director of investment banking at Protego Mexico. Gustavo A. Suarez is an economist in the Division of Research and Statistics at the Board of Governors of the Federal Reserve System.

A previous version of this chapter circulated with the title "Captive markets: The impact of kidnappings on corporate investment in Colombia." For generous advice and encouragement, we are grateful to Andrei Shleifer, Jeremy Stein, Larry Katz, and Martin Feldstein. For very useful comments, we are indebted to Alberto Abadie, Philippe Aghion, Pedro Aspe, Antonio Cabrales, Rafael Di Tella, Juan Carlos Echeverry, Carola Frydman, Arturo Galindo, Alejandro Gaviria, Ed Glaeser, Borja Larrain, Nellie Liang, Rodolfo Martell, Adriana Lleras-Muney, Marcelo Moreira, Emily Oster, Jorge Restrepo, Jim Robinson, Raven Saks, Jeremy Tobacman, Piedad Urdinola, Eric Werker, and John Womack. We benefited from the suggestions of seminar participants at Harvard, IESE, the Second Latin American Finance Network, UPF, Purdue, Notre Dame, and the Federal Reserve Board. Ana Maria Diaz, Marcela Eslava, Leopoldo Fergusson, Enrique Lopez, Mercedes Parra, Esperanza Sanabria, and Fabio Sanchez generously shared their data sets. Paola Cuevas provided excellent research assistance. All remaining errors are our own. The views in this chapter do reflect those of the Federal Reserve System.

Negative correlations between crime and investment in cross-country studies may be explained by omitted variables. Importantly, poor economic conditions may simultaneously deter investment and increase incentives to commit crimes. Instead of exploiting variation across countries, this chapter uses variation of crime rates over time within regions in Colombia to understand the relationship between kidnappings and corporate investment rates.

Colombia provides a useful setting for studying the economic consequences of violent crime, because it has experienced high levels of crime in recent decades. The combination of guerrillas, paramilitaries, and drug trafficking has given Colombia the highest per capita rates of homicides and kidnappings in the world since the early 1990s. Furthermore, there has been substantial variation in criminal activity both over time and across regions. The total number of kidnappings in Colombia almost tripled from 1996 to 2000.[1] In 2002, Medellin, the second largest city, reported almost four times the number of homicides per capita of Bogota, the largest city.[2]

Our data set combines detailed information about crime rates across thirty-two regions in Colombia with financial-statement data for an unbalanced panel of roughly 11,000 firms from 1997 to 2003. Using detailed data on the victims of kidnappings allows us to isolate crimes that affect firm managers and owners from widespread forms of crime that victimize the entire population. By comparing the effect of firm-related kidnappings with the effect of broader forms of violent crime, we are able to isolate the relationship between firm-related kidnappings and investment that is not explained by omitted variables that affect all forms of violent crime.

Our main result is that firms invest less when kidnappings directly target firm owners or managers in the region where the firms are headquartered. By contrast, forms of crime that victimize the entire population but that do not explicitly target firm owners or managers are statistically unrelated with corporate investment. These results are not driven by the subset of firms whose managers and owners are actually kidnapped. On the contrary, the negative relationship between firm-related kidnappings and firm investment is explained by the firms that are headquartered in the same region as the firms whose managers and owners are actually victimized. In addition, we find that firms with substantial shares of foreign ownership appear to be more sensitive to the kidnappings of foreign managers and foreign owners. Similarly, firm investment in a given industry is strongly negatively correlated with kidnappings of firm owners and managers within the industry but is unrelated with kidnappings in other industries.

Focusing on firm-level data within a country allow us to exploit firm characteristics to address concerns that unobserved poor demand conditions

1. In section 2.3 we discuss a data set on kidnappings in Colombia (FONDELIBERTAD).
2. Colombia's National Police.

explain a negative correlation between investment and crime. In particular, we compare the effect of kidnappings on firms that sell on local markets and the effects on firms that rely on exports. If omitted poor demand conditions explained the negative correlation between kidnappings and corporate investment, we should expect stronger effects for firms selling in local markets. By contrast, we find similar effects in firms that sell in local markets and those that sell mostly in foreign markets, providing evidence against an explanation of the negative correlation between corporate investment and crime based on omitted demand variables.

The results in this chapter complement recent studies that exploit variation of crime rates within countries. In particular, Abadie and Gardeazabal (2003) show that terrorism reduces firms' returns in the Basque Country using event-study methodologies. Our findings complement their study, because we focus on firm-related crime and not on general forms of crime.

The rest of the chapter is organized as follows. Section 2.2 illustrates the link between kidnappings and investment using a stylized cross-country regression. Section 2.3 provides a brief historical background of Colombia and explains the data set. Section 2.4 outlines the empirical strategy, and section 2.5 reports our main results. Section 2.6 compares alternative explanations for the negative effect of firm-related kidnappings on investment, and section 2.7 concludes.

2.2 Preliminary Evidence From Cross-Country Data

As motivation for our subsequent analysis using data from Colombian firms, this section reports the results of simple cross-country regressions linking the rate of kidnappings by international terrorists with aggregate investment. The rate of kidnappings by international terrorists is both closely related to the measures of violent crime we analyze for the Colombian case and available for a large panel of countries. Other cross-country studies have studied the relationship between more general forms of crime and economic activity (Fajnzylber, Lederman, and Loayza 2002; Gaviria 2002), but none have explicitly focused on kidnappings.

We measure investment as either Gross Capital Formation or net Foreign Direct Investment, both scaled by gross domestic product (GDP). We use an unbalanced panel of 196 countries with annual observations from 1968 to 2002 to estimate pooled ordinary least squares (OLS) regressions with country- and year-fixed effects:

(1) $\text{Investment}_{i,t} = \alpha + \beta \times \text{Kidnappings}_{i,t} + \gamma \times \text{GDP per capita}_{i,t-5}$
$$+ \delta_i + \eta_t + \varepsilon_{i,t},$$

where i indexes countries and t indexes years. Investment, GDP, and population data are taken from the World Bank's World Development Indicators. Finally, $Kidnappings_{i,t}$ is the number of kidnappings per 100,000 population perpetrated by international terrorists, reported in the ITERATE data set.[3]

As a check on the influence of outliers, the regressions reported in this section exclude two country-year observations with net foreign direct investment larger than GDP and one observation with gross capital formation larger than GDP. Similarly, the regressions reported in this section drop two country-year observations with kidnappings rates larger than one per 100,000 people. Results are similar when we keep these observations. Our results are also robust to controlling for indexes of creditor rights protection as in La Porta et al. (1998)[4] and replacing kidnapping rates with their one-year lag.

Table 2.1 reports the results of estimating equation (1) using our two alternative measures of investment. The dependent variable in columns (1) and (2) is gross capital formation, while the dependent variable in columns (3) and (4) is net foreign direct investment. Columns (1) and (3) report the results of an OLS regression of investment on kidnappings and a constant with no other controls, while columns (2) and (4) add country- and year-fixed effects and lagged GDP.

The results in table 2.1 suggest that those countries where kidnappings are more frequent also tend to accumulate domestic capital more slowly and attract less foreign direct investment. The evidence summarized in table 2.1 is suggestive, but raises questions. For example, the relationship between kidnappings and investment may be explained by omitted variables, as poor economic conditions may simultaneously depress investment and motivate criminal activity. Credit conditions are tighter during recessions, as creditors anticipate more frequent defaults, and firms themselves, expecting lower sales, are reluctant to conduct capital expansions. Meanwhile, recessions reduce employment opportunities in legal activities and accentuate income disparities, perhaps stimulating criminal activity. In addition, cross-country regressions, like equation (1), cannot distinguish whether the negative relation between investment and violent crime is mainly concentrated on those households or firms that are direct victims of violent events, or whether the effects are more widely spread.

The limitations of cross-country studies provide a major motivation for studying the link between violent crime and investment using more disaggregated data. The rest of this chapter discusses the relationship between violent crime and investment in the context of a large panel of firms located in Colombia.

---

3. The acronym ITERATE stands for "International Terrorism: Attributes of Terrorist Events." Mickolus et al. (2003) describe the data set in detail.
4. The cost of including creditor right indexes is a sample reduction.

Table 2.1   Cross-country evidence

Dependent variable	Net FDI$_{i,t}$ (% of GDP) (1)	Net FDI$_{i,t}$ (% of GDP) (2)	Gross Capital Formation$_{i,t}$ (% of GDP) (3)	Gross Capital Formation$_{i,t}$ (% of GDP) (4)
Kidnappings per 100,000 people$_{i,t-1}$	−14.104**	−17.709*	−38.989**	−17.198**
	(6.621)	(10.208)	(17.480)	(8.263)
log(GDP per capita)$_{i,t-5}$		0.213		−0.309
		(0.648)		(1.262)
Constant	2.223***	−0.039	23.056***	25.330***
	(0.192)	(4.699)	(0.479)	(9.325)
Country fixed effects?	No	Yes	No	Yes
Year fixed effects?	No	Yes	No	Yes
Observations	3,688	3,688	4,019	4,019
Number of countries	160	160	172	172
R^2	0.001	0.350	0.003	0.551

Notes: Standard errors (in parentheses) are adjusted for country clustering. This table reports the ordinary least squares (OLS) estimate of the effect of kidnappings on investment in an unbalanced panel of 196 countries from 1968 to 2002, corresponding to equation (1) in the text. The dependent variable in columns (1) and (2) is net Foreign Direct Investment (FDI) scaled by GDP, and the dependent variable in columns (3) and (4) is Gross Capital Formation scaled by GDP. The variable Kidnappings is obtained from the ITERATE data set; it is defined as the number of kidnappings by international terrorists divided by 100,000 population. The series of Net FDI, Gross Capital Formation, and GDP per capita are from the World Bank's World Development Indicators data set. We exclude country-year observations for which Net FDI (2 observations) or Gross Capital Formation (1 observation) is larger than the GDP. Similarly, we exclude 2 country-year observations for which the rate of kidnappings is larger than one.
***Significant at the 1 percent level.
**Significant at the 5 percent level.
*Significant at the 10 percent level.

2.3   Data on Firms and Crime in Colombia

2.3.1   Violent Crime in Colombia in Historical Perspective

Colombia is highly violent for its level of development. For example, the United Nations reports that the annual rate of homicides in Colombia averaged sixty-three homicides per 100,000 people between 1998 and 2000, the highest rate in the world.[5] By contrast, the average homicide rates in South America and the Organization for Economic Cooperation and Development (OECD) countries were forty-one per 100,000 people and three per 100,000 people, respectively.

As measured by homicide rates, violent crime in Colombia has trended

5. United Nations, Seventh Survey of Crime Trends and Operations of Criminal Justice.

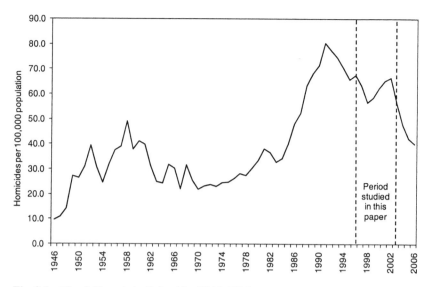

Fig. 2.1   Homicide rate in Colombia, 1946–2005

Sources: National Police, Departmento Administrativo Nacional de Estadística de Colombia (DANE); and Sanchez, Diaz, and Formisano (2003).

up for several decades before the years studied in this chapter. As figure 2.1 illustrates, homicide rates rose sharply in the 1940s, as the two main political parties waged a civil war. Although these political parties agreed on an explicit power-sharing mechanism, higher homicide rates persisted into the 1960s, as some of the peasant resistance groups formed during the civil war evolved into leftist guerrillas like the Revolutionary Armed Forces of Colombia (FARC), one the largest rebel groups currently active (Safford and Palacios 2001). Homicide rates skyrocketed in the 1980s and 1990s, as cocaine production surged (Angrist and Kugler 2008; Bergquist, Peñaranda, and Sanchez 2001). Drug trafficking increased violence, as the government prosecuted drug lords, and different cartels fought for market control. During the last decades of the twentieth century, powerful economic interests— including drug dealers—organized right-wing groups of paramilitaries to protect their businesses from guerrilla extortion.[6]

The dramatic rise in homicides during the 1980s and 1990s parallels increases in other measures of violent crime. As figure 2.2 illustrates, both kidnappings and guerrilla attacks rose steadily throughout the 1990s and peaked in 2000.[7] Kidnappings and guerrilla activity moved together, likely because rebels use hostages to strengthen their political bargaining position

6. Both guerrilla and paramilitaries have been linked with drug trafficking in recent years. See, for example, Streatfeild (2002).

7. Guerrilla attacks (FARC) include bombings, arm-trafficking, massacres, ambushes, piracy, and confrontation with the army or the National Police.

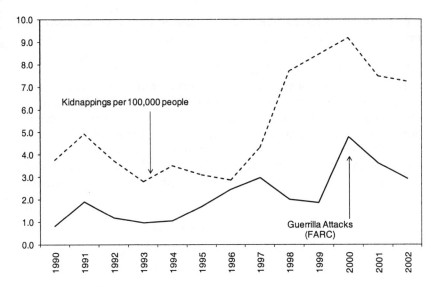

Fig. 2.2   Kidnappings and guerilla attacks, 1990–2002

Sources: National Police, Ministry of Defense, Departamento Administrativo Nacional de Estadística de Colombia (DANE); and Sanchez, Diaz, and Formisano (2003).

and partly finance their operations with monetary ransoms. Paramilitaries, drug cartels, and gangs are also frequently associated with kidnappings. In *News of a Kidnapping,* for instance, Garcia Marquez (1997) reconstructs the story of seven hostages kidnapped in 1989 by the Medellin drug cartel to force the Colombian government into repealing its extradition treaty with the United States. The cartel leaders were keenly interested in securing their trial and imprisonment in Colombia under more favorable terms. After the increase in kidnappings during the 1990s, Colombia became the country with the highest absolute number of kidnappings per year and the highest annual kidnapping rate in the world.[8]

The persistence of high rates of violent crime has motivated several studies measuring the cost of crime and conflict using Colombian data.[9] Using aggregate data, Rubio (1995) shows that increases in crime rates are correlated with lower GDP growth, and Cardenas (2007) argues that the acceleration in criminal activity in the 1990s is partly to blame for Colombia's productivity slowdown. More recently, using household-level data, Barrera and Ibañez (2004) and Rodriguez and Sanchez (2009) study the effects of crime on education. Similarly, exploiting variation in crime rates across

8. In 2003, Kroll, a private security advisor headquartered in New York, estimated that more kidnappings were perpetrated in Colombia (about 4,000 per year) than in other countries. Mexico followed with roughly 3,000 kidnappings per year.

9. Montenegro and Posada (2001) and Riascos and Vargas (2003) survey the literature on the costs of crime and violence in Colombia. For a more recent treatment, see Sanchez (2007).

municipalities, Urdinola (2004) analyzes the effect of violent crime on infant mortality.

2.3.2   Statistics on Kidnappings and Other Types of Crime

The statistics on violent crime in Colombia used in this chapter are aggregated at the level of "department." Colombia is divided into thirty-two departments or semiautonomous administrative units. Colombian departments are similar to states in the United States, but have substantially less legislative autonomy. The FONDELIBERTAD, a governmental organization in Colombia established in 1996, collects detailed information on individual kidnappings reported to the Colombian Ministry of Defense.[10] For each kidnapping event between 1996 and 2002, FONDELIBERTAD reports the date and department in which the kidnapping occurred, the identity of the kidnapper (guerrillas, paramilitaries, common criminals, or not determined), and the number of days in captivity. Importantly for the regression analysis, the data set reports the occupation and nationality of the victim. For most victims with ownership or employment relationships with a firm, the data set reports the name of the firm. In the case of owners, however, the data set does not report the fraction of ownership or whether the victim held stakes in several firms. The data set does not disclose information on monetary ransoms.

The first six columns of table 2.2 summarize the main characteristics of the FONDELIBERTAD data set. As shown in column (1), the data set reports roughly 2,700 kidnappings per year between 1996 and 2002.

The data set attributes 56 percent of overall kidnappings to guerrillas, 14 percent to common criminals, and 5 percent to paramilitaries. (The identity of the kidnappers, is unknown or not disclosed for the rest of the observations.) According to the demands of the kidnappers, FONDELIBERTAD classifies abductions as having either economic or political objectives. Kidnappings for economic reasons typically involve a monetary ransom. Just over half of the kidnappings in the sample are classified as having economic ends, while 10 percent of the kidnappings are classified as having political objectives.[11] As shown in column (2) of table 2.2, only 2 percent of the victims are not Colombian citizens.

Kidnappings and Firms

To focus on the subset of kidnappings that target firms, we define *Kidnappings of Firm Owners* as those where victims own at least part of the firm; and

---

10. The term FONDELIBERTAD is short for Fondo Nacional para la Defensa de la Libertad Personal (National Fund for the Protection of Individual Liberty). In addition to collecting statistics on kidnappings, FONDELIBERTAD provides legal and psychological assistance to affected families, and advises government policies on kidnappings. Publicly available FONDELIBERTAD data on kidnappings after 2003 has been less detailed.

11. The demands of the kidnappers are unknown for roughly a third of the observations.

Table 2.2   **Kidnappings, homicides, and guerrilla attacks by year**

Year	Total kidnappings (1)	Kidnappings of foreigners (2)	Kidnappings of firm management (3)	Kidnapping of firm owners (4)
1996	1,091	41	193	1
1997	1,671	31	205	0
1998	3,023	43	371	32
1999	3,349	57	470	77
2000	3,697	42	n.a.	n.a.
2001	3,050	49	168	60
2002	2,986	31	163	43
Total	18,867	294	1,570	213

Year	Kidnappings of government employees (5)	Kidnappings of Army and National Police (6)	Total homicides (7)	Total guerrilla attacks (8)
1996	23	24	26,130	934
1997	442	38	24,828	1,146
1998	280	266	22,673	790
1999	98	168	23,820	736
2000	n.a.	n.a.	25,859	1,931
2001	84	68	27,356	1,471
2002	112	57	28,363	1,210
Total	1,039	621	179,029	8,218

Notes: This table reports, by year, the total number of kidnappings, homicides, and guerrilla attacks in Colombia from 1996 to 2002. Data on homicides and guerrilla attacks are from the National Police/ Ministry of Defense. Guerrilla attacks considers only attacks perpetrated by FARC. Data on kidnappings are obtained from FONDELIBERTAD. Total kidnappings are all kidnappings reported in the FONDELIBERTAD data set. Government employees include local and national government, except the Army and National Police. Kidnappings of firm management victimize CEOs, presidents, vice presidents, board members, and division managers. Kidnappings of firm owners include those victims who own at least part of the firm.

Kidnappings of Firm Management as those where victims are board members, chief executive officers (CEOs), presidents, vice presidents, or division managers. Table 2.2 reports that just under 10 percent of the kidnappings in the FONDELIBERTAD data set targeted firm management (column [3]), and about 1 percent targeted owners (column [4]).

To compare the effects of kidnappings that target firms to other types of kidnappings, we consider two additional categories. We define government employees as individuals who worked for the local or national government or candidates running for public office at the time of the kidnapping. We group members of the Army and National Police in a separate category, even though they are also government employees. Columns (5) and (6) of table 2.2 report, respectively, that 5 percent of the victims in the FONDELIBERTAD data set were government employees and that 3 percent of the victims served in the Army or the National Police.

Finally, a large fraction of the victims in the data set are under eighteen (about 10 percent), self-employed workers (about 45 percent), and members of not-for-profit organizations such as religious communities and Nongovernmental Organizations (NGOs) (about 5 percent). Occupation is unknown for 12 percent of the observations in the data set.

Other Types of Crime

To isolate the effect of kidnappings on investment from the effect of overall violence, we consider variables other than kidnappings that reflect common crime activity or the armed conflict between government and rebels. Based on reports from Colombia's National Police and Army, the National Planning Department (DNP in Spanish) compiles a data set on different types of crime by department since 1995. We focus on two of the most common types of violent crime in Colombia: guerrilla attacks and homicides.

As a limitation to our analysis, the data on kidnappings are more detailed than the data on guerrilla attacks and homicides. The FONDELIBERTAD data set on kidnappings allows us to identify the victim and his or her occupation (and hence, whether he or she works for a firm). By contrast, the DNP data set on guerrilla attacks and homicides contains no information about individual victims within departments.

Guerrilla attacks in the DNP data set include arm trafficking, massacres, bombings, ambushes, piracy, and confrontations with the army or the National Police. We restrict attention to attacks by FARC for two reasons. First, by the number of combatants and terrorist attacks, FARC is the largest rebel group in Colombia. Second, while other rebel groups operate only in a handful of departments, FARC is widely spread throughout the country. Homicides reported by DNP include all kinds of violent deaths and not only killings related with the armed conflict. Columns (7) and (8) of table 2.2 report the number of terrorist attacks and homicides from 1996 through 2002.

The maps in figure 2.3 illustrate the distribution of kidnappings, homicides, and guerrilla attacks per capita across departments in Colombia.[12] The FARC are somewhat more likely to attack departments with a large fraction of rural population in the southeast of the country or departments with abundant natural resources (like oil-rich Arauca along the Venezuelan border). By contrast, homicides and kidnappings are more evenly distrib-

12. We exclude one department from the statistical analysis—the islands of San Andres and Providencia—because there is no information on crime and other regional characteristics. Additionally, we treat the metropolitan area of Bogota—known as the Capital District—as a separate department, because it concentrates roughly one-fifth of Colombia's population. Data on population are described in the appendix, table 2A.1.

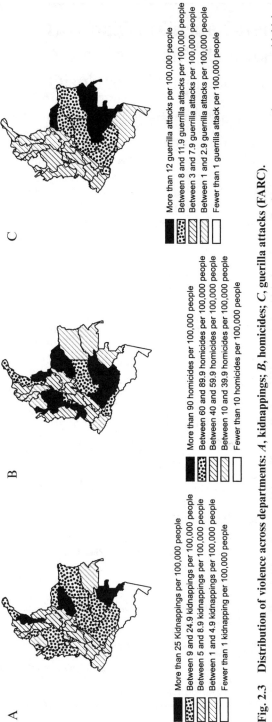

A

B

C

More than 12 guerrilla attacks per 100,000 people
Between 8 and 11.9 guerrilla attacks per 100,000 people
Between 3 and 7.9 guerrilla attacks per 100,000 people
Between 1 and 2.9 guerrilla attacks per 100,000 people
Fewer than 1 guerrilla attack per 100,000 people

More than 90 homicides per 100,000 people
Between 60 and 89.9 homicides per 100,000 people
Between 40 and 59.9 homicides per 100,000 people
Between 10 and 39.9 homicides per 100,000 people
Fewer than 10 homicides per 100,000 people

More than 25 Kidnappings per 100,000 people
Between 9 and 24.9 kidnappings per 100,000 people
Between 5 and 8.9 kidnappings per 100,000 people
Between 1 and 4.9 kidnappings per 100,000 people
Fewer than 1 kidnapping per 100,000 people

Fig. 2.3   Distribution of violence across departments: *A*, kidnappings; *B*, homicides; *C*, guerilla attacks (FARC).

Notes: Panel A shows the distribution of average kidnapping rates (1996–2002) across Colombia's departments. Darker areas represent departments with higher kidnapping rates. Panel B shows the distribution of average homicide rates (1996–2002) across Colombia's departments. Darker areas represent departments with higher homicide rates. Panel C shows the distribution of average guerrilla attacks per capita (1996–2002) across Colombia's departments. Darker areas represent departments with higher guerrilla attacks per capita.

uted across departments than guerrilla attacks.[13] However, kidnappings, homicides, and guerrilla attacks are highly correlated across regions.

2.3.3   Firms

We combined balance sheet and income statement data for publicly-traded firms that report to the Superintendencia Financiera and for privately-owned firms in Colombia that report to the Superintendencia de Sociedades. The Superintendencia Financiera is a government agency that oversees and regulates both banking and securities markets,[14] while the Superintendencia de Sociedades oversees incorporated firms and regulates liquidation and bankruptcy. Combining these two data sets yields an unbalanced panel of almost 11,000 firms with annual observations between 1996 and 2003 (roughly 44,000 firm-year observations).

Prior to 2000, reporting of financial statements to the Superintendencia de Valores was mandatory for all firms incorporated in Colombia. After 2000 only firms with assets above an inflation-indexed threshold are required to report, but a substantial number of firms below the threshold continued to voluntarily report after 2000.[15]

Table 2.3 summarizes the distribution of firms over time and across industries coded in the International Standard Industrial Classification (ISIC). As it is the case in most developing countries, only a small fraction of firms in Colombia are publicly traded (panel A). Roughly half of the observations in the sample are from the manufacturing sector or from the wholesale and retail trade sector (panel B).[16]

Table 2.4 summarizes the characteristics of the firms in the sample.[17] The average firm-year observation has real assets of $7.7 million, while the median firm has real assets of $2.3 million. As it is the case for firm data in other developing and industrialized countries, the sample is skewed toward smaller firms. Investment, defined as the change in net Property, Plant, and Equipment (PPE), scaled by assets is –0.3 percent for the average observation and –0.5 percent for the median. Since our definition of investment

---

13. Collier and Hoeffler (2004) argue that the quest for social justice is not the only cause behind rebellions: in fact, many rebellions pursue the capture of rents. Diaz and Sanchez (2004) study the importance of these two types of causes for the location of FARC in Colombia.

14. The financial reports from publicly-traded firms that we use in this chapter were originally collected by the Superintendencia de Valores, which merged with the Superintendencia Bancaria in 2005 to form the Superintendencia Financiera.

15. The dollar equivalent of the 2003 threshold was about $2 million. The results in this chapter are robust to excluding firms with asset values below the threshold during the entire sample.

16. The results in the following sections are robust to excluding firms in heavily regulated industries (financial intermediation and utilities).

17. Nominal variables are deflated using the Producer Price Index (PPI). Appendix table 2A.1 describes all variables used in this section. Total Assets are translated to U.S. dollars using the exchange rate in 1999, which is the base year of the PPI.

Table 2.3   **Distribution of firms**

Panel A: Distribution by year of firms in sample

	Privately-held firms	Publicly-traded firms	Total
1997	6,700	115	6,815
1998	7,153	67	7,220
1999	6,870	73	6,943
2000	7,139	75	7,214
2001	4,767	77	4,844
2002	4,448	94	4,542
2003	6,648	79	6,727
Total	43,725	580	44,305

Panel B: Distribution by industry (firm-year observations)

Agriculture, hunting, and forestry	3,892
Fishing	126
Mining and quarrying	859
Manufacturing	12,233
Electricity, gas, and water supply	67
Construction	4,391
Wholesale and retail trade	11,540
Hotels and restaurants	766
Transport, storage, and communications	2,122
Financial intermediation	2,237
Real estate, renting, and business activities	4,936
Public administration and defense	0
Education	73
Health and social work	161
Other community, social, and personal service activities	883
Private households with employed persons	19
Extra-territorial organizations and bodies	0
Total	44,305

Notes: Panel A reports the distribution by year of firms in the sample. Data on private firms are collected by the Superintendencia de Sociedades in Colombia; data on public firms are obtained from the Superintendencia Financiera. Panel B reports the distribution of firm-year observations by industry sector, according to the International Standard Industry Classification (ISIC).

captures capital expenditures net of depreciation, investment is not censored at zero.[18] Negative investment for the median and the average observation partly reflects the downturn experienced by the Colombian economy during most of the sample, which overlaps with the emerging market crisis of 1998. The ratio of net income to total assets (return on assets, or ROA), a measure of profitability, is 0.1 percent for the average observation and 1.5 percent for the median. Finally, table 2.4 also reports that foreign firms account for

18. We have no data on gross PPE or capital expenditures in the database.

Table 2.4   Descriptive statistics: Firms' characteristics

	Mean	Median	Standard deviation	Firm-year observations
Total assets (millions of dollars)	7.700	2.308	19.693	44,305
Investment/TA (%)	−0.337	−0.516	16.928	44,305
Return on assets (%)	0.114	1.555	12.175	44,305
Real cash/TA (%)	6.639	2.696	10.262	44,305
Foreign ownership (Yes = 1, No = 0)	0.173	0.000	0.340	33,600

Notes: This table reports descriptive statistics for the firm variables used in the empirical analysis, corresponding to the sample summarized in table 2.3. "Investment" is the change in Property, Plant, and Equipment, and "TA" denotes Total Assets. "Return on Assets" is the ratio of net income to total assets. The dummy variable Foreign Ownership equals 1 if foreigners own at least 50 percent of the firm.

roughly 17 percent of the sample. Firms are classified as foreign if more than 50 percent of its shares are held by foreigners.

The map in figure 2.4 depicts the geographic distribution of the firms in the sample in 2003 and illustrates the high concentration of economic activity. Most firms were headquartered in the northern (or Caribbean) departments or in the central (or Andean) departments. Just a bit over half of the sample was headquartered in Bogota, D.C., and about one-quarter of the sample was headquartered in the departments of Antioquia and Valle del Cauca, mainly in their capital cities (Medellin and Cali, respectively).[19] However, roughly one-fifth of the sample was distributed in twenty-one departments other than Bogota, Antioquia, and Valle del Cauca. Only a small fraction of firms was headquartered in the northwestern department of Choco (close to the border with Panama) or in the southeastern departments (close the borders with Brazil and Peru), as their territory is largely tropical rain forest.

2.4   Empirical Strategy

To measure the relationship between kidnappings and firm investment, our empirical strategy exploits two sources of variation. First, we consider changes over time in kidnapping rates measured at the department level. Second, we compare the effect of kidnappings that target firm-related individuals with the effect of other types of kidnappings (and also to other types of crime).

To estimate the effect of the kidnappings rate of department j on the investment of all firms located in that department, we control for char-

19. Our results are similar when we exclude firms located in Bogota, D.C.

Total: 6,727 firms

■	More than 1,000 firms (1 department: Bogota, D.C. 3,809)
▦	Between 200 and 999 firms (3 departments: Atlantico, 292, Valle del Cauca, 782, Antioquia, 975)
▨	Between 50 and 199 firms (7 departments)
▨	Between 1 and 99 firms (12 departments)
☐	Departments with no firms (9 departments)

Fig. 2.4   Geographic distribution of firms in Colombia, 2003
Note: Figure 2.4 shows the distribution of firms across Colombia's departments in 2003. Darker areas represent departments with more firms.

acteristics of department *j* that may affect both investment decisions and incentives to kidnap. Additionally, we control for firm characteristics that predict investment behavior.

In the traditional "crime and punishment" approach, individuals decide to commit crimes after weighting the costs and benefits of criminal behavior (Becker 1968; Glaeser 1999). For example, adverse economic conditions reduce the opportunity cost of criminal activities. Supportive of this prediction, Fajnzylber, Lederman, and Loayza (2002) find that crime rates are countercyclical and Miguel, Satyanath, and Sergenti (2004) show that negative exogenous shocks to economic growth increase the likelihood of civil conflict in a sample of African countries.[20] Hence, economic conditions in department *j* may determine not only the investment decisions of firms in department *j*, but also the incentives of kidnappers in department *j*. In our statistical analysis, we control for GDP per capita, poverty levels, public infrastructure, and primary school enrollment.[21]

We include homicides and guerrilla attacks in our regressions because we do not want to confound the effect of kidnappings with the effect of the overall civil conflict. To the extent that omitted variables affect all types of

20. Recent studies challenge the conventional view that poverty generates terrorism. For example, Abadie (2006) finds that terrorist risk is not significantly higher in poor countries, after controlling for country characteristics (including political freedom).
21. Appendix table 2A.1 describes department-specific variables.

crime in a similar way, we identify the effect of crime on firm investment from the differential effect of crime specifically targeted against firms.[22]

Empirical studies of corporate investment typically find that firms with higher holdings of liquid assets (or cash) and more favorable investment opportunities (or Tobin's Q) invest more (Fazzari, Hubbard, and Petersen 1988; Stein 2003). In line with these standard results, we control for cash balances scaled by assets and approximate investment opportunities by using net income scaled by assets. Unfortunately, forward-looking proxies for investment opportunities, such as price-to-book ratios, are available only for the small subset of publicly-traded firms in the sample.

We measure the impact of kidnappings on firm investment using the following pooled OLS regression:

$$
(2) \qquad \frac{\text{Investment}_{i,t}}{\text{TA}_{i,t-1}} = \alpha + \beta_1 \times \text{Kidnappings}_{j,t-1} + \beta_2 \\
\times \text{Guerrilla Attacks}_{j,t-1} + \beta_3 \times \text{Homicides}_{j,t-1} \\
+ \delta X_{i,t-1} + \gamma Z_{j,t-1} + \phi_i + \eta_t + \lambda_k + \mu_j + \varepsilon_{i,t},
$$

where i indexes firms, j indexes departments, t indexes years, and k indexes industries. Investment is defined as the change in property, plant, and equipment; and TA denotes total assets. *Kidnappings, Guerrilla Attacks,* and *Homicides* are measured at the department level and scaled by 100,000 people, and $X_{i,t}$ denotes the vector of firm-specific controls: log of total assets, cash holdings scaled by total assets, and net income scaled by total assets. Similarly, $Z_{j,t}$, represents the vector of department controls: income per capita, primary school enrollment, a poverty index,[23] and the extension of roads in 1995. Variables ϕ_i, η_t, λ_k, and μ_j represent firm, year, industry, and department fixed effects, respectively. Finally, standard errors are clustered by department.[24]

We assume that lagged crime rates are good predictors of future crime rates (and hence, future conditions that are potentially relevant for investment). In fact, univariate time series analysis that we do not report here suggests that the rates of kidnappings, homicides, and guerrilla attacks are autoregressive and stationary processes. Furthermore, crime rates in subsequent years are positively correlated.[25]

---

22. Recent developments in the economics of crime suggest that social interactions explain an important component of the variance of crime both across cities and over time (Glaeser, Sacerdote, and Scheinkman 1996; Glaeser and Sacerdote 1999). In a framework where social interactions are important, the incentives to kidnap may depend on the intensity of other types of crime in the same time and place.

23. The index is Necesidades Basicas Insatifechas (NBI) and reflects crowded or substandard housing conditions, school-age children not attending school, and/or lower education of the head of the household.

24. Results are robust to clustering by year-department.

25. Results are robust to using contemporary kidnappings as opposed to lagged kidnappings and to instrument contemporary kidnappings with lagged kidnappings.

2.5 Results

2.5.1 Kidnappings That Target Firms

Table 2.5 reports OLS estimates of equation (2) using alternative types of kidnapping rates as explanatory variables. The first three regressions in the table consider kidnappings whose victims are not directly linked to firms, and the last two regressions consider kidnappings whose victims are firm managers or owners.

Table 2.5   **Kidnappings and firm investment**

| | Dependent variable: Investment_t / Total assets_{t-1} | | | | |
	(1)	(2)	(3)	(4)	(5)
Total kidnappings per 100,000 pop.$_{t-1}$	0.027 (0.078)				
Kidnappings of government employees per 100,000 pop.$_{t-1}$		0.575 (0.691)			
Kidnappings of Army and National Police per 100,000 pop.$_{t-1}$			−0.570 (0.592)		
Kidnappings of firm management per 100,000 pop.$_{t-1}$				−1.332** (0.496)	
Kidnappings of firm owners per 100,000 pop.$_{t-1}$					−4.105* (2.068)
Homicides per 100,000 pop.$_{t-1}$	−0.004 (0.008)	0.000 (0.008)	0.000 (0.010)	0.004 (0.010)	0.004 (0.009)
Guerrilla attacks per 100,000 pop.$_{t-1}$	−0.065 (0.115)	−0.210 (0.259)	−0.216 (0.247)	−0.199 (0.251)	−0.219 (0.241)
Observations	44,305	39,461	39,461	39,461	39,461
Number of firms	10,957	10,877	10,877	10,877	10,877
R^2	0.994	0.995	0.995	0.995	0.995

Notes: This table reports OLS estimates of the effect on investment of kidnappings, homicides, and guerrilla attacks. The results correspond to equation (2) in the text. The dependent variable is the change in Property, Plant, and Equipment scaled by lagged assets. Regressions include lagged firm controls (log assets, cash holdings scaled by assets, and ROA); lagged department controls (GDP per capita, primary school enrollment, a poverty index, and the extension of roads in 1995); and fixed effects (by year, industry, department, and firm). The rates of kidnappings, homicides, and guerrilla attacks are measured at the department level and are scaled by 100,000 population. The sample is an unbalanced panel of firms located in Colombia with annual observations from 1996 to 2003. Total kidnappings are all kidnappings reported in the FONDELIBERTAD data set. Government employees include local and national government, except the Army and the National Police. Firm management includes board members, CEOs, presidents, vice presidents, and division managers. Firm owners are victims who own at least part of the firm. Guerrilla attacks includes FARC attacks reported by the National Police/Ministry of Defense. Standard errors (in parentheses) are adjusted for department clustering.

***Significant at the 1 percent level.

**Significant at the 5 percent level.

*Significant at the 10 percent level.

Kidnappings that target firm owners or managers have a statistically significant negative relationship with corporate investment. To illustrate the economic magnitude of the relationship of firm-related kidnappings, note that a one-standard deviation decrease within a department in the rate of kidnappings victimizing firm management is associated with an average increase of about 1.7 percentage points in investment rates ($= -1.332 \times 1.30$).[26] This is a sizeable effect, as the average investment rate in the sample is about -0.3 percent of total assets. Similarly noticeable magnitudes arise when we rank regions into quartiles based on the rate of kidnappings of firm management and then compare firm investment in the most dangerous quartile with firm investment in the least dangerous quartile.[27]

By contrast, kidnappings whose victims are not directly related to firms have a statistically insignificant relationship with corporate investment. In particular, kidnappings that target government employees, or the Army and National Police are unrelated to investment. Although a few of these coefficients are large, they are imprecisely estimated. In addition, the coefficient on total kidnappings is also not statistically significant.

In sum, while kidnappings that target firm owners or managers have a statistically significant relationship with firm investment, other—more general—types of violent crime that do not target firms directly have no significant relationship with investment. This finding alleviates concerns that our results with firm-related kidnappings may be explained by unobserved variables that drive both overall criminal activity and investment.[28] The identifying assumption in equation (2) is that unobserved variables have no differential effect across different types of crime. For example, if economic conditions that are not captured by GDP affect both criminal activity and corporate investment, we assume that all types of crime are equally affected by such economic conditions.[29]

2.5.2   Firms Directly Affected

A finding that firms directly attacked by kidnappings are forced to cut back on investment would be, to some extent, unsurprising. After all, kidnappings of employees disrupt production and firms may be forced to pay ransoms. However, we find a more surprising—and perhaps more interesting—result: the negative effects of firm-related kidnappings on investment

---

26. Appendix table 2A.2 reports summary statistics of the series of kidnappings, homicides, and guerrilla attacks.

27. Comparing firms in the most violent quartile with firms the least dangerous quartile is equivalent to comparing firms in Antioquia (where the infamous Medellin drug cartel operated in the 1980s and 1990s) with firms in Bogota, D.C.

28. For example, we are unable to observe attitudes toward crime, the effectiveness of local courts and local police, which are likely to affect incentives of both firms and kidnappers.

29. As an illustration, we assume kidnappings of government employees and kidnappings of managers are equally countercyclical.

decisions go beyond the subset of firms directly affected; firms that face a high risk of kidnappings reduce investment even when their own employees are not victims of kidnappings. Potentially, the indirect effect is more harmful for aggregate industrial activity than the direct effect, because it spills over to a larger group of firms.

Of all the kidnappings in the FONDELIBERTAD data set, we classify 1,570 as targeting a firm manager or owner (table 2.2). Of this sample of firm-related kidnappings, we are able to identify the specific firm involved and match it to our sample for roughly 600 firm-year observations, less than 1 percent of the sample. Table 2.6 reports the results of separately estimating equation (2) for two groups of firms: (a) firms whose managers or owners were themselves victims of kidnappings, and (b) the rest of the sample.

Importantly, kidnappings of firm owners and managers have a significant impact on firms that have not been directly affected. The impact on the subset of victimized firms is larger in magnitude but not statistically significant, perhaps because the estimation is based on a considerably smaller sample. The evidence in table 2.6 suggests that the negative relationship between corporate investment and kidnappings of firm owners and managers and investment is not explained by the inclusion of firms whose employees are victims of kidnappings.

2.5.3   Kidnappings in the Same Industry and Kidnappings in Other Industries

If firm managers and owners make investment decisions based on their perceived conditional probability of being kidnapped, the most relevant kidnappings for a firm manager working on a given industry will likely be those occurring in the same line of business. Firms within a given industry are generally better informed about competitive conditions within their own industry, and well-organized industry groups typically promote the sharing of information about common problems or challenges. To test this conjecture, we estimate the following regression:

$$(3) \quad \frac{\text{Investment}_{i,t}}{\text{TA}_{i,t-1}} = \alpha + \beta_1 \times \text{Kidnappings Same Industry}_{j,k,t-1} + \beta_2 \\ \times \text{Kidnappings Other Industries}_{j,k,t-1} + \delta X_{i,t-1} \\ + \pi \tilde{Z}_{j,t-1} + \phi_i + \eta_t + \lambda_k + \mu_j + \varepsilon_{i,t},$$

where X, ϕ, η, λ, and μ are defined as in equation (2). For notational convenience, the vector of department controls is expanded to include homicides and guerrilla attacks and relabeled $\tilde{Z}$. *Kidnappings Same Industry*$_{j,k,t}$ represents the number of kidnappings of firm managers or owners in industry k in departments other than j. *Kidnappings Other Industries*$_{j,k,t}$ represents the number of kidnappings of firm managers or owners in all industries other

Table 2.6   **Direct and indirect effects**

Panel A: Firms directly affected by kidnappings

Dependent variable: Investment$_t$ / Total assets$_{t-1}$

	(1)	(2)
Kidnappings of firms' top management per 100,000 pop.$_{t-1}$	−10.645	
	(7.476)	
Kidnappings of firms' owners per 100,000 pop.$_{t-1}$		−15.944
		(23.580)
Homicides per 100,000 pop.$_{t-1}$	0.072	0.046
	(0.056)	(0.054)
Guerrilla attacks per 100,000 pop.$_{t-1}$	−0.973	−1.229
	(0.592)	(0.718)
Observations	628	628
Number of firms	150	150
R^2	0.275	0.273

Panel B: Firms not directly affected by kidnappings

Dependent variable: Investment$_t$ / Total assets$_{t-1}$

	(1)	(2)
Kidnappings of firms' top management per 100,000 pop.$_{t-1}$	−1.186**	
	(0.461)	
Kidnappings of firms' owners per 100,000 pop.$_{t-1}$		−3.942*
		(1.960)
Homicides per 100,000 pop.$_{t-1}$	0.002	0.002
	(0.010)	(0.009)
Guerrilla attacks per 100,000 pop.$_{t-1}$	−0.170	−0.188
	(0.246)	(0.236)
Observations	38,833	38,833
Number of firms	10,727	10,727
R^2	0.995	0.995

Notes: This table reports OLS estimates of the effect of kidnappings on investment, corresponding to equation (2) in the text. The dependent variable is the change in Property, Plant, and Equipment scaled by lagged assets. Regressions include lagged firm-specific controls (log assets, cash holdings scaled by assets, and ROA); lagged department controls (GDP per capita, primary school enrollment, a poverty index, the extension of roads in 1995, lagged FARC attacks per 100,000, and lagged homicides per 100,000); and fixed effects (by year, industry, department, and firm). Kidnapping rates are measured at the department level and are scaled by 100,000 population. For each type of kidnappings, we present results for two subsamples: (1) firms whose management or owners were subject to kidnappings reported in the FONDELIBERTAD data set (panel A); and (2) firms whose employees and owners were not subject to kidnappings reported in the FONDELIBERTAD data set (panel B). The total sample is an unbalanced panel of firms in Colombia with annual observations from 1996 to 2003. Standard errors (in parentheses) are adjusted for department clustering.

***Significant at the 1 percent level.
**Significant at the 5 percent level.
*Significant at the 10 percent level.

than k and in all departments other than j, scaled by the number of industries.[30] More formally:

$$\text{Kidnappings Same Industry}_{j,k,t} = \sum_{\text{department} \neq j} \text{Firm-Related Kidnappings}_{\text{department},k,t}$$

$$\text{Kidnappings Other Industries}_{j,k,t} = \frac{1}{(\text{Number of industries}_t)} \times \sum_{\substack{\text{department} \neq j \\ \text{industry} \neq k}} \text{Firm-Related Kidnappings}_{\text{department,industry},t}$$

Panel A in table 2.7 reports the results of estimating equation (3) by OLS. Only firm-related kidnappings within an industry have a statistically significant negative relationship with the investment of firms in that industry. The magnitude of the coefficients is not comparable to those in previous tables, because kidnappings are not scaled by 100,000 population, as we aggregate kidnappings over industries and not over geographical units.

The result that own-industry kidnappings have larger effects than kidnappings in other industries is consistent with various explanations. First, rational and fully informed CEOs make corporate decisions based on the conditional probability of being kidnapped; hence, when other managers in the same industry are kidnapped, CEOs perceive a larger probability of victimization. Alternatively, less than fully informed CEOs are more likely to share information (or have a common source of information) with CEOs in the same industry; hence, they only revise the probability of kidnappings upwards when the victim is someone they know or someone they can identify themselves with.

2.5.4   Foreign Firms and Kidnappings of Foreign Citizens

Kidnappings of foreign owners or foreign managers are likely to be more relevant for foreign firms. To test this hypothesis, we estimate the following regression:

$$(4) \qquad \frac{\text{Investment}_{i,t}}{\text{TA}_{i,t-1}} = \alpha + \beta_1 \times \text{Kidnappings Foreigners}_{j,t-1} + \beta_2 \\ \times \text{Kidnappings Foreigners}_{j,t-1} \\ \times \text{Foreign Ownership}_{i,t} + \beta_3 \\ \times \text{Foreign Ownership}_{i,t} + \delta X_{i,t-1} + \pi \tilde{Z}_{j,t-1} \\ + \phi_i + \eta_t + \lambda_k + \mu_j + \varepsilon_{i,t},$$

where *Kidnappings Foreigners* is the rate of firm-related kidnappings with non-Colombian victims scaled by 100,000 population, and firm-related kid-

---

30. Industrial activity tends to cluster by regions. Hence, to avoid confusing the effect of kidnappings in the same department with the effect of kidnappings in the same industry, we exclude observations in the same department in the definitions of own-industry kidnappings and other-industry kidnappings.

Table 2.7　　　　　　**Industry and nationality effects**

Panel A: Kidnappings in the same industry vs. kidnappings in other industries

Dependent variable: Investment$_t$/Total assets$_{t-1}$

Firm-related kidnappings in the same industry$_{t-1}$	−0.036**
	(0.017)
Firm-related kidnappings in other industries$_{t-1}$	−0.001
	(0.001)
Homicides per 100,000 pop.$_{t-1}$	0.001
	(0.011)
Guerrilla attacks per 100,000 pop.$_{t-1}$	−0.208
	(0.265)
Observations	39,379
Number of firms	10,874
R^2	0.995

Panel B: Firm-related kidnappings of Colombians and foreign citizens

Dependent variable: Investment$_t$/Total assets$_{t-1}$

Firm-related kidnappings of non-Colombians per 100,000 pop.$_{t-1}$	−1.854
	(4.295)
Foreign ownership	0.645
	(0.578)
Firm-related kidnappings of non-Colombians per 100,000 pop.$_{t-1}$ $\times$ (foreign ownership)	−6.795**
Non-Colombians per 100,000$_{t-1}$	(3.149)
Homicides per 100,000 pop.$_{t-1}$	0.003
	(0.011)
Guerrilla attacks per 100,000 pop.$_{t-1}$	−0.238
	(0.250)
Observations	33,600
Number of firms	8,455
R^2	0.316

Notes: Panel A of this table reports OLS estimates of the effect on investment of own-industry and other industries kidnappings, corresponding to equation (3) in the text. The sample is an unbalanced panel of firms in Colombia with annual observations from 1996 to 2003. The dependent variable is the change in Property, Plant, and Equipment scaled by lagged assets. Regressions include lagged firm-specific controls (log assets, cash holdings scaled by assets, and ROA); lagged department controls (GDP per capita, primary school enrollment, a poverty index, the extension of roads in 1995, FARC attacks per 100,000, and homicides per 100,000); and fixed effects (by year, industry, department, and firm). For each two-digit ISIC industry code department and year, the variable Firm-related kidnappings in the same industry is the sum of kidnappings of firm management or firm owners in that industry code but in other departments. Firm-related kidnappings in other industries is defined as the sum of kidnappings of firm management and firm owners over all other departments and all other industries divided by the total number of industries. Kidnapping rates are not scaled by 100,000 population. Panel B reports OLS estimates of the effect on investment of firm-related kidnappings of non-Colombians. Victims of firm-related kidnappings are firm owners or firm management. The estimates correspond to equation (4) in the text. The dummy variable Foreign ownership equals 1 if foreigners own at least 50 percent of the firm. Kidnapping rates are measured at the department level and are scaled by 100,000 population. Standard errors (in parentheses) are adjusted for department clustering.

***Significant at the 1 percent level.

**Significant at the 5 percent level.

*Significant at the 10 percent level.

nappings are defined as those victimizing firm management or firm owners. *Foreign Ownership* is a dummy variable that equals 1 for firms with more than 50 percent of foreign ownership. The definition of all other variables follows equation (3).

Panel B of table 2.7 reports OLS estimates of the coefficient on kidnappings of foreign owners or managers and its interaction with the foreign ownership indicator in equation (4). The estimate reported in panel B suggests that foreign firms are significantly more sensitive to kidnappings of foreign citizens than Colombian firms are. The large standard error for the estimate of the marginal effect of foreign kidnappings for firms with foreign ownership reflects the relatively small number of firms with substantial foreign ownership (table 2.4).

2.5.5   Limitations of the Analysis

The estimates of the relationship between firm-related kidnappings and firm investment reported in this section may be biased due to sample selection. An important investment decision of firms is whether to continue operating at all. In fact, shutting down the firm is the extreme form of disinvestment. Unfortunately, we are not able to properly identify firm exit, and our sample consists of active firms. If surviving firms invest more than exiting firms and firms exit more frequently from violent regions, our estimates of the effect of firm-related kidnappings on investment are biased toward zero. The importance of entry and exit decisions is hard to assess with our data, because Superintendencia de Sociedades exempted some smaller firms from mandatory reporting in 2000. Thus, not all firms that stopped reporting in 2000 shut down.

As a second important limitation of our analysis, we are only able to observe a link between individuals and firms for owners and managers. We are not able to identify kidnappings that victimize relatives of firm owners and managers. The effect of this limitation may be nonnegligible, as 10 percent of victims in the FONDELIBERTAD data set are children or teenagers (who might be related to firm managers) or owners.

In addition, our estimates of the relationship between investment and firm-related kidnappings may be biased because of nonrandom allocation of kidnappings across regions and firms. For example, if kidnappers target owners or managers of firms with larger cash holdings, and firms are likely to use them to pay ransoms, we should expect the estimates of the coefficient on firm-related kidnappings to be biased toward zero, since cash-abundant firms tend to invest more than financially constrained firms. However, it seems plausible that kidnappers target individuals based on their own wealth, rather than based on financial information of the firm they work for or they own. Unfortunately, we cannot determine with the available information whether firms really use their own cash to pay ransoms for their managers or owners.

Although most kidnappings in Colombia pursue economic objectives, guerillas, paramilitaries, and drug lords have exploited kidnappings for political reasons too. In the early 1990s, for example, drug dealers kidnapped the relatives of the Colombian political and business elite with the purpose of pressing the government to revoke an extradition treaty with the United States (Garcia Marquez 1997; Bowden 2002). More recently, businessmen, majors, soldiers, and even presidential candidates have been abducted to negotiate the release of imprisoned FARC rebels.

Since crime rates are far higher in Colombia than in most other countries, it may be argued that the evidence presented here is not representative of the effect of crime on investment. Colombia is, however, similar in various dimensions to other countries that experience high crime rates. For example, according to the United Nations, four out of the ten most violent countries in terms of per capita homicides are Latin American.[31] In addition, the average GDP per capita of the ten most violent places is, in year 2000 U.S. dollars, 7,340, while the average GDP per capita of Colombia is 6,340.[32] As many developing countries experience high rates of violent crime, the findings in this section suggest that crime may explain why capital does not flow to poor countries.

2.6   Potential Channels

This section uses firm and industry characteristics to evaluate the evidence for three mechanisms through which crime may deter investment. First, kidnappings may reduce demand for goods and services: during violent periods, households may decide to consume fewer goods or services if consuming them is dangerous (for example, dining out or going to a shopping center), or even to migrate to safer regions. Firms that expect demand to decrease may, as a consequence, invest less. We call this mechanism the *demand channel.*

Second, firms that face a high probability of being victimized by kidnappings may face tighter financial constraints, if financial institutions are reluctant to finance firms when money can be diverted to unproductive activities, like paying ransoms. In addition, banks will deliberately stay out of a region during violent times to protect their owners and employees. In developing countries, where capital markets are not fully developed, banks provide most of the external finance raised by firms. We call this hypothesis the *credit constraints channel.*

Finally, kidnappings may increase the cost of doing business: firms in regions with high kidnapping rates face higher security costs, such as body-guards, armored cars, and intelligence services. Private security firms in

31. United Nations, *Seventh Survey of Crime Trends and Operations of Criminal Justice.* It covers the period 1998 to 2000. The countries with the ten highest rates of homicides are, in order: Colombia, South Africa, Jamaica, Venezuela, Russia, Mexico, Lithuania, Estonia, Latvia, and Belarus.
32. World Bank, *World Development Indicators, 2002.*

Mexico, for instance, estimate that large firms spend between 20,000 and 30,000 dollars per month to protect their executives from kidnappings. We call this hypothesis the *cost channel.*

2.6.1   Demand Channel

The results in section 2.5 hint that the mechanism through which kidnappings reduce investment is likely not a fall in demand, because the baseline regressions control for GDP at the department level. The additional evidence in this section is also inconsistent with the demand channel. In particular, we compare the response of firms that depend on Colombian markets with the response of firms that sell to foreign markets.

If kidnappings reduce investment through a decrease in local consumption, investment by firms that have access to alternative markets should be less sensitive to firm-related kidnappings than investment by firms that sell in local markets only. Firms that sell in foreign markets may be able to shift production to foreign markets when local demand falls.

Table 2.8 compares the effect of firm-related kidnappings on firms that operate in industries that differ in their ability to sell in foreign markets. More formally, we estimate by OLS the following equation:

$$(5) \qquad \frac{\text{Investment}_{i,t}}{\text{TA}_{i,t-1}} = \alpha + \beta_1 \times \text{Kidnappings}_{j,t-1} + \beta_2 \\ \times \text{Industry Tradability}_k + \beta_3 \\ \times \text{Kidnappings}_{j,t-1} \times \text{Industry Tradability}_k \\ + \delta X_{i,t-1} + \pi Z_{j,t-1} + \phi_i + \eta_t + \lambda_k + \mu_j + \varepsilon_{i,t},$$

where *Industry Tradability* is the fraction of exports in total sales for each four-digit ISIC industry code.[33] All other definitions follow equation (3). The interaction terms between industry tradability and kidnappings of firm owners and managers are statistically insignificant, which is hard to reconcile with the demand channel. More important, the absence of a differential effect for firms that depend exclusively on local markets alleviates the concern that our results may be driven by omitted demand variables.

2.6.2   Credit Constraints Channel

Since the markets for corporate bonds and equity in Colombia are thin, the most common form of external financing in Colombia is bank debt. Banks may be reluctant to lend to firms headquartered in regions with high rates of violent crime. If kidnappings that target firms reduce investment through a tightening in credit constraints, firms should contract less bank debt when kidnapping rates go up. To test this hypothesis, we estimate the following equation:

---

33. For each four-digit ISIC industry code, we average the tradability measure from 1991 to 1995 (before the first year in our sample). Appendix table 2A.1 provides additional details.

Table 2.8   **Firm-related kidnappings and industry tradability**

Dependent variable: Investment$_i$/Total assets$_{t-1}$

	(2)	(4)
Kidnappings of firms' top and middle management per 100,000 pop.$_{t-1}$	−1.776* (0.880)	
Kidnappings of firms' top and middle management per 100,000 pop.$_{t-1}$ × (industry tradability)	0.043 (0.060)	
Kidnappings of firms' owners per 100,000 pop.$_{t-1}$		−3.976* (1.957)
Kidnappings of firms' owners per 100,000 pop.$_{t-1}$ × (industry tradability)		−0.023 (0.093)
Industry tradability	−0.146** (0.068)	−0.134** (0.058)
Homicides per 100,000 pop.$_{t-1}$	0.003 (0.011)	0.002 (0.010)
Guerrilla attacks per 100,000 pop.$_{t-1}$	−0.218 (0.266)	−0.236 (0.254)
Observations	39,190	39,190
Number of firms	10,874	10,874
R^2	0.995	0.995

Notes: This table reports the effect on investment of the interaction between firm-related kidnappings and industry tradability. The results correspond to equation (5) in the text. The sample is an unbalanced panel of firms in Colombia with annual observations from 1996 to 2003. The dependent variable is the change in Property, Plant, and Equipment scaled by lagged assets. Regressions include lagged firm controls (log assets, cash holdings scaled by assets, and ROA); lagged department controls (GDP per capita, primary school enrollment, a poverty index, the extension of roads in 1995, guerrilla attacks per 100,000, and homicides per 100,000); and fixed effects (by year, industry, department, and firm). We define Industry tradability as the fraction of exports in total sales at the industry level; this measure of tradability is an average from 1991 to 1995. Kidnappings are measured at the department level and scaled by 100,000 population. Firm management includes board members, CEOs, presidents, vice presidents, and division managers. Firm owners are victims who own at least part of the firm. Standard errors (in parentheses) are adjusted for department clustering.

***Significant at the 1 percent level.
**Significant at the 5 percent level.
*Significant at the 10 percent level.

$$(6) \quad \frac{\Delta \text{ Bank Debt}_{i,t}}{\text{TA}_{i,t-1}} = \alpha + \beta_1 \times \text{Kidnappings}_{j,t-1} + \theta \widetilde{X}_{i,t-1} + \pi \widetilde{Z}_{j,t-1} + \phi_i + \eta_t + \lambda_k + \mu_j + \varepsilon_{i,t},$$

where the vector of firm controls has been expanded to include property, plant, and equipment scaled by total assets, and all other definitions follow equation (3).[34] The credit constraints channel predicts that the coefficient associated with kidnappings is negative. Table 2.9 reports the results of esti-

34. The regression follows the specification of Rajan and Zingales (1995) in their study of capital structure of firms located in industrialized countries.

Table 2.9   **The effect of violence on firm borrowing**

Dependent variable: (Bank debt$_t$ – bank debt$_{t-1}$)/Total assets$_{t-1}$

	(1)	(2)
Kidnappings of firms' top and middle management per 100,000 pop.$_{t-1}$	–1.669 (1.561)	
Kidnappings of firms' owners per 100,000 pop.$_{t-1}$		–3.974 (5.107)
Homicides per 100,000 pop.$_{t-1}$	0.017 (0.012)	0.025 (0.018)
Guerrilla attacks per 100,000 pop.$_{t-1}$	0.083 (0.091)	0.058 (0.101)
Observations	32,894	32,894
Number of firms	10,854	10,854
R^2	0.467	0.467

Notes: This table reports OLS estimates of the effect on firm borrowing of kidnappings, homicides, and guerrilla (FARC) attacks. The dependent variable is the change in bank debt scaled by lagged assets. Regressions include lagged firm-specific controls (log sales, cash holdings scaled by total assets, ROA, and PPE scaled by total assets), lagged department controls (GDP per capita, primary school enrollment, a poverty index, and the extension of roads in 1995), and fixed effects (by year, industry, department, and firm). Kidnappings, homicides, and guerrilla attacks are measured at the department level and scaled by 100,000 population. The sample is an unbalanced panel of firms located in Colombia with annual observations from 1996 to 2003. Firm management includes board members, CEOs, presidents, vice presidents, and division managers. Firm owners are victims who own at least part of the firm. *Guerilla attacks* includes FARC attacks reported by the National Police/Ministry of Defense. Standard errors (in parentheses) are adjusted for department clustering.

mating equation (6) by OLS. The dependent variable in the regression is the change in bank debt scaled by assets. The coefficients associated with kidnappings of firm owners and firm managers are negative but statistically insignificant, providing rather weak evidence that firms contract less debt when kidnappings target firms.

2.6.3   Cost Channel

If kidnappings increase security costs, firms that face high kidnapping rates should report larger administrative expenses. Table 2.10 summarizes the results of running a regression similar to equation (2), with administrative expenses scaled by assets as dependent variable. We use the same regional controls as in equation (2). We use similar firm-specific controls as in equation (2), but return on assets is replaced by sales over assets.[35] Finally, as a proxy for industry concentration, we add the Herfindahl index on sales for each two-digit ISIC code.

The coefficients associated with the kidnapping rates of firm owners and firm managers are statistically indistinguishable from zero, suggesting that

35. Administrative costs likely depend on gross revenue and not on net income.

Table 2.10   The effect of violence on firms' costs

Dependent variable: Administrative expenses$_t$ / Total assets$_{t-1}$

	(1)	(2)
Kidnappings of firms' top and middle management per 100,000 pop.$_{t-1}$	−0.021 (0.021)	
Kidnappings of firms' owners per 100,000 pop.$_{t-1}$		−0.002 (0.064)
Homicides per 100,000 pop.$_{t-1}$	0.0002 (0.0001)	0.0002 (0.0002)
Guerrilla attacks per 100,000 pop.$_{t-1}$	0.002 (0.001)	0.002 (0.001)
Observations	39,818	39,818
Number of firms	10,854	10,854
R^2	0.714	0.714

Notes: This table reports OLS estimates of the effect on firms' administrative costs of kidnappings, homicides, and guerrilla (FARC) attacks. The dependent variable is administrative expenses scaled by assets. Regressions include firm-specific controls (log assets, cash holdings scaled by assets, and sales scaled by assets); department controls (GDP per capita, primary school enrollment, a poverty index, and the extension of roads in 1995); industry controls (Herfindahl index on sales); and fixed effects (by year, industry, department, and firm). Kidnappings, homicides, and guerrilla attacks are measured by department and are scaled by 100,000 population. The sample is an unbalanced panel of firms located in Colombia (annual observations from 1996 to 2003). Firm management includes board members, CEOs, presidents, vice presidents, and division managers. Firm owners are victims who own at least part of the firm. Guerilla attacks includes FARC attacks reported by the National Police/Ministry of Defense. Standard errors (in parentheses) are adjusted for department clustering.

the effect of kidnappings on investment is not likely explained by increased administrative costs. Our evidence on the cost channel is not conclusive, because we cannot observe what fraction of administrative costs corresponds to payments on private security.

2.6.4   Discussion

The evidence in this chapter is consistent with the hypothesis that firms are reluctant to invest when their owners and managers are afraid of becoming victims of kidnappings. A number of different mechanisms may explain the negative effect of firm-related kidnappings on corporate investment. The fact that administrative costs and bank debt are not negatively affected by kidnappings of firm owners and firm managers provides no evidence for mechanisms operating through credit or through costs of protection. Very importantly, the evidence in this section suggests that firm-related kidnappings have no differential effect on the investment of firms that depend on sales to local markets, thus buttressing our identification strategy. If omitted demand variables explained the negative correlation between firm-related kidnappings and corporate investment, one should expect a more negative correlation for firms that sell their products in local markets.

2.7 Conclusions

In this chapter, we exploit variation in different forms of crime within regions in Colombia to measure the negative effect of violent crime on investment under identifying assumptions that are less restrictive than those typically used in cross-country studies. First, unobserved institutional characteristics and crime reporting standards vary more widely across countries than within countries. Second, we are able to observe different types of crime and identify whether firms are directly attacked by crimes. To the extent that omitted variables affect all types of crime in a similar way, we are able to compare the effect of firm-related crimes on investment with the effect of more general forms of crime that do not necessarily target firms. Finally, we exploit cross-sectional differences in firm characteristics to address plausible omitted variables stories. In particular, we use the industry's export share to identify firms that depend exclusively on Colombian demand and firms that sell in foreign markets. Under the assumption that foreign markets are less affected by kidnappings in Colombia, the differential effect of firm-related kidnappings on firms that depend on Colombian demand signals the importance of omitted demand variables.

We find that kidnappings that directly target firm managers or firm owners have a statistically and economically significant negative effect on firm-level investment. By contrast, general forms of crime—such as overall homicides and kidnappings—do not have a significant effect on investment. This second finding suggests that the negative effect of firm-related kidnappings on investment is not driven by omitted variables common to all forms of crime. We also find that firm-related kidnappings affect industries that sell in Colombian markets as well as industries that sell in foreign markets, alleviating the concern that unobservable demand variables explain our basic result. The distribution of violence and kidnappings in Colombia is not truly random. Therefore, the causal effect of violent crime on investment is not fully identified in our empirical strategy.

This chapter presents evidence suggesting that firm-related kidnappings reduce investment, because managers operate under the distraction of fear. Individuals are not only scared because of the probability of expropriation, but also because of threats to their personal security. We provide evidence suggesting that the mechanism is unlikely to operate through demand conditions, credit constraints, or administrative costs.

Recent empirical studies show that institutions that protect property rights foster investment and long-run economic growth (Besley 1995; Acemoglu, Johnson, and Robinson 2001; Easterly and Levine 1997, 2003). One of the most important issues for institutional design and policy reform is to understand what specific aspects of property rights are relevant for economic development (Acemoglu and Johnson 2005). The empirical challenge, therefore, is to dismantle the black box of property rights. Similarly, the results in this chapter suggest that crime may have significant effects on investment. However, crime threatens both property rights and personal security. Our findings suggest that both the security of property rights and personal security are important concerns for investors. The challenge for future research, therefore, is to understand what forms and aspects of crime are particularly relevant for economic activity and investment.

Appendix

Table 2A.1   Department and industry variables: Data description

Variable name	Description	Years covered	Level of aggregation	Source
Poverty index	Necesidades Básicas Insatisfechas (Unfulfilled Basic Needs). Reflects crowded or substandard housing conditions, school-age children not attending school, and/or less than primary education of the head of the household.	1990–2002	Municipality	DANE, CEDE
GDP per capita	Real GDP divided by population. The GDP is measured in constant Colombian pesos of 1994.	1990–2001	Department	DANE
Paved roads in 1995	Paved roads (hundreds of squared kilometers) in 1995.	1995	Municipality	DANE, CEDE
Primary school enrollment	Students enrolled in primary school divided by population between 6 and 12 years.	1993–2002	Municipality	DANE, CEDE
Population	Estimated total population, based on the 1993 census and annual population projections.	1990–2003	Municipality	DANE
Producer price index	Countrywide producer price index.	1990–2003	Countrywide	DANE
Industry tradability	Industry's exports divided by industry's sales. Exports and sales are measured in current Colombian pesos.	1991–1998	4-digit ISIC code	DANE

Notes: This table summarizes department, municipality, and industry variables that are used in the empirical analysis, but are not explained in the main body of the text. All series are annual, except for paved roads, which is observed only for 1995. The DANE is the National Administrative Department of Statistics (Departamento Administrativo Nacional de Estadística) and CEDE is the Center for Research on Economic Development (Centro para Estudios Sobre el Desarrollo Economico) at Universidad de Los Andes.

Table 2A.2   Kidnappings by year and department

Panel A: Average rates by department, 1996–2002 (per 100,000 pop.)

Department	Total kidnappings	Kidnappings of top and middle management	Kidnapping of firm owners	Kidnappings of government employees	Kidnappings of army and national police	Kidnappings of foreigners	Total homicides	Total guerrilla attacks
Antioquia	9.30	1.05	0.09	0.52	0.27	0.10	126.87	3.33
Atlántico	1.02	0.14	0.00	0.01	0.01	0.01	30.22	0.03
Bogotá, D.C.	1.68	0.21	0.05	0.01	0.00	0.06	39.64	0.06
Bolívar	6.44	0.37	0.09	1.03	0.09	0.06	24.04	1.78
Boyacá	4.04	0.21	0.05	0.12	0.11	0.04	20.30	2.21
Caldas	4.20	0.36	0.04	0.05	0.06	0.06	88.10	1.16
Caquetá	14.24	0.67	0.03	1.27	3.22	0.15	107.33	11.52
Cauca	5.40	0.29	0.07	0.82	0.18	0.16	43.02	6.43
Cesar	25.92	1.48	0.06	1.22	0.47	0.16	71.03	2.98
Córdoba	1.64	0.10	0.01	0.04	0.02	0.00	27.79	0.55
Cundinamarca	8.17	0.73	0.15	0.36	0.07	0.20	40.22	6.02
Chocó	12.30	1.15	0.29	0.70	0.71	0.45	50.42	5.40
Huila	5.96	0.57	0.12	0.36	0.20	0.01	51.87	4.51
Guajira	13.78	1.48	0.24	1.00	0.21	0.52	61.11	4.77
Magdalena	8.87	0.64	0.08	0.15	0.06	0.13	49.73	2.54
Meta	16.29	1.51	0.35	0.83	1.00	0.17	65.60	11.01
Nariño	3.06	0.11	0.02	0.85	0.31	0.03	29.64	4.19
N. de Santander	8.25	0.89	0.11	0.81	0.41	0.26	90.54	1.59
Quindío	1.61	0.16	0.02	0.03	0.03	0.00	65.43	1.88
Risaralda	4.16	0.46	0.07	0.25	0.03	0.04	99.06	2.52
Santander	8.31	0.76	0.10	0.57	0.16	0.11	46.46	2.92
Sucre	9.37	0.77	0.05	0.37	0.16	0.05	31.42	2.75
Tolima	7.38	0.74	0.16	0.34	0.31	0.04	52.48	3.54

	Total kidnappings	Kidnappings of top and middle management	Kidnapping of firms' owners	Kidnappings of government employees	Kidnappings of army and national police	Kidnappings of foreigners	Total homicides	Total guerrilla attacks
Valle del C.	4.06	0.48	0.11	0.13	0.02	0.12	92.77	1.19
Arauca	12.88	1.09	0.07	1.44	0.25	0.70	104.81	21.78
Casanare	29.20	3.14	0.30	0.69	0.20	0.18	99.36	9.81
Putumayo	5.72	0.17	0.04	0.59	0.66	0.03	65.12	10.45
Amazonas	0.58	0.00	0.00	0.22	0.00	0.00	9.32	1.99
Guainía	3.08	0.80	0.00	0.00	0.00	0.00	16.44	35.86
Guaviare	17.31	0.00	0.00	0.00	10.04	0.00	115.76	31.02
Vaupés	35.82	0.00	0.00	0.53	12.90	0.00	23.32	31.86
Vichada	10.99	3.34	0.00	1.59	1.59	0.14	23.50	9.95
Colombia	6.39	0.58	0.08	0.39	0.22	0.10	62.89	2.88

Panel B: Means and standard deviation, 1996–2002

	Total kidnappings	Kidnappings of top and middle management	Kidnapping of firms' owners	Kidnappings of government employees	Kidnappings of army and national police	Kidnappings of foreigners	Total homicides	Total guerrilla attacks
Observations	224	192	192	192	192	224	224	224
Mean	8.95	0.39	0.04	0.29	0.71	0.13	58.21	7.43
Std. deviation	20.24	1.44	0.10	0.68	6.49	0.27	35.78	15.09
Std. deviation within department	18.21	1.30	0.09	0.59	4.65	0.22	15.55	11.85

Notes: Panel A reports average rates (per 100,000 pop.) of homicides, guerrilla attacks, and kidnappings by department in Colombia from 1996 to 2002. Panel B reports the mean and standard deviation of these variables in a panel of all thirty-two departments from 1996 to 2002. Data on homicides and guerrilla attacks were obtained from the National Police/Ministry of Defense. Guerrilla attacks include only attacks perpetrated by the Revolutionary Armed Forces of Colombia (FARC). Data on kidnappings were obtained from the FONDELIBERTAD data set. Total Kidnappings are all kidnappings reported in the FONDELIBERTAD data set; Government employees include local and national government employees (judiciary, legislative, and executive branches), except the Army and National Police. Firm-related kidnappings correspond to kidnappings of firms' employees, owners, or contractors; Top management includes CEOs, presidents, vice presidents, and board members; Top and middle management includes division managers and supervisors plus Top management. Annual population is projected by DANE.

References

Abadie, A. 2006. Poverty, political freedom, and the roots of terrorism. *American Economic Review Papers and Proceedings* 96 (2): 50–6.

Abadie, A., and J. Gardeazabal. 2003. The economic costs of conflict: A case study of the Basque Country. *American Economic Review* 93 (1): 113–32.

Acemoglu, D., and S. Johnson. 2005. Unbundling institutions. *Journal of Political Economy* 113 (5): 949–95.

Acemoglu, D., S. Johnson, and J. Robinson. 2001. The colonial origins of comparative development: An empirical investigation. *American Economic Review* 91 (5): 1369–1401.

Alesina, A., and R. Perotti. 1996. Income distribution, political instability and investment. *European Economic Review* 40 (6): 1203–28.

Angrist, J., and A. Kugler. 2008. Rural windfall or a new resource curse? Coca, income, and civil conflict in Colombia. *Review of Economics and Statistics* 90 (2): 191–215.

Barrera, F., and A. M. Ibañez. 2004. Does violence reduce investment in education? A theoretical and empirical approach. CEDE-Universidad de los Andes, Colombia. Working Paper.

Barro, R. J. Economic growth in a cross section of countries. *Quarterly Journal of Economics* 106 (2): 407–43.

Becker, G. S. 1968. Crime and punishment: An economic approach. *Journal of Political Economy* 76:169–217.

Bergquist, C., R. Peñaranda, and G. Sanchez, eds. 2001. *Violence in Colombia: 1990–2000: Waging war and negotiating peace.* Wilmington, DE: Scholarly Resources Inc.

Besley, T. 1995. Property rights and investment incentives: Theory and evidence from Ghana. *Journal of Political Economy* 103 (5): 903–37.

Bowden, M. 2002. *Killing Pablo: The hunt for the world's greatest outlaw.* New York: Penguin Books.

Cardenas, M. 2007. Economic growth in Colombia: A reversal of "fortune"? *Ensayos sobre política económica* 25:220–59.

Collier, P., and A. Hoeffler. 2004. Greed and grievance in Civil War. *Oxford Economic Papers* 56 (4): 563–95.

Diaz, A. M. and F. Sanchez. 2004. Geografía de los cultivos ilícitos y conflicto armado en Colombia. CEDE-Universidad de los Andes, Colombia. Working Paper.

Easterly, W., and R. Levine. 1997. Africa's growth tragedy: Policies and ethnic divisions. *Quarterly Journal of Economics* 112 (4): 1203–50.

———. 2003. Tropics, germs, and crops: How endowments influence economic development. *Journal of Monetary Economics* 50 (1): 3–39.

Fajnzylber, P., D. Lederman, and N. Loayza. 2002. What causes violent crime? *European Economic Review* 46:1323–57.

Fazzari, S. M., R. G. Hubbard, and B. C. Petersen. 1988. Financing constraints and corporate investment. *Brooking Papers on Economic Activity* 1:141–95.

Garcia Marquez, G. 1997. *News of a kidnapping,* New York: Penguin Books.

Gaviria, A. 2002. Assessing the effects of corruption and crime on firm performance: Evidence from Latin America. *Emerging Markets Review* 3:245–68.

Glaeser, E. L. 1999. An overview of crime and punishment. Mimeo, World Bank.

Glaeser, E. L., and B. I. Sacerdote. 1999. Why is there more crime in cities? *Journal of Political Economy* 107 (S6): S225–58.

Glaeser, E. L., B. I. Sacerdote, and J. A. Scheinkman. 1996. Crime and social interactions. *Quarterly Journal of Economics* 111 (2): 507–48.

La Porta, R., F. Lopez-de-Silanes, A. Shleifer, and R. W. Vishny. 1998. Law and finance. *Journal of Political Economy* 106 (6): 1113–55.

Lucas, R. E., Jr. 1990. Why doesn't capital flow from rich to poor countries? *American Economic Review* 80 (2): 92–6.

Mickolus, E. F., T. Sandler, J. M. Murdock, and P. A. Flemming. 2003. *International terrorism: Attributes of terrorist events (ITERATE) data code book.* Ann Arbor, MI: Inter-University Consortium for Political and Social Research.

Miguel, E., S. Satyanath, and E. Sergenti. 2004. Economic shocks and civil conflict: An instrumental variables approach. *Journal of Political Economy* 112 (4): 725–53.

Montenegro, A., and C. Esteban Posada. 2001. *La violencia en Colombia.* Bogotá, Colombia: Alfaomega.

Rajan, R. G., and L. Zingales. 1995. What do we know about capital structure? Some evidence from international data. *Journal of Finance* 50 (5): 1421–60.

Riascos, A. J., and J. F. Vargas. 2003. Violence and growth in Colombia: A brief review of the literature. Mimeo, Royal Holloway College, University of London.

Rodriguez, C., and F. Sanchez. 2009. Armed conflict exposure, human capital investment, and child labor: Evidence from Colombia. CEDE-Universidad de los Andes, Colombia. Working Paper.

Rubio, M. 1995. Crimen y crecimiento en Colombia. *Coyuntura Economica* 25 (1): 101–04.

Safford, F., and M. Palacios. 2001. *Colombia: Fragmented land. Divided society.* New York: Oxford University Press.

Sanchez, F. 2007. *Las cuentas de la violencia.* Bogota, Colombia: Norma.

Sanchez, F., A. M. Diaz, and M. Formisano. 2003. Conflicto, violencia y actividad criminal en Colombia: Un Análisis Espacial. CEDE-Universidad de los Andes, Colombia. Working Paper.

Stein, J. C. 2003. Agency, information, and corporate investment. In *Handbook of the economics of finance,* vol. 1A, ed. G. M. Constantinides, M. Harris, and R. Stulz, 109–63. Amsterdam: Elsevier.

Streatfeild, D. 2002. *Cocaine: An unauthorized biography.* New York: St. Martin's Press.

Urdinola, P. 2004. The hidden cost of violence: Infant mortality in Colombia. Mimeo, University of California at Berkeley.

Comment   Juan Pantano

Summary

In this original and captivating piece, Pshisva and Suarez identify the causal impact of regional kidnapping rates on corporate investment. They find that a one standard deviation decrease in the rate of management-targeted kidnapping within a Colombian department is, on average, associated with an increase of 1.7 percentage points in department-level corporate investment rates. However, the investigation of potential causal mechanisms

Juan Pantano is assistant professor of economics at Washington University in St. Louis.

responsible for this effect turns out to be somewhat inconclusive, with non-significant findings across a range of hypotheses. The study pursues a disaggregated analysis by exploiting firm-level data, a noble endeavor I sympathize with. On one hand, as the authors emphasize, this strategy provides a tighter perspective, relative to what can be learned from cross-country analyses. On the other hand, the results may be idiosyncratic to the Colombian case, and this may cast doubts about what we can learn, in general, about the relationship between kidnapping and investment. In this brief comment, I will first describe the strengths and then highlight some concerns about the study. I will then conclude by sharing some thoughts that this innovative study stimulates.

Strengths

Rather than exploiting a clear source of exogenous variation in the kidnapping rates, the authors come up with an empirical strategy that leverages the rich firm-level microdata to test the causality of the measured association between kidnapping and investment. In particular, the tradability of the firm's product becomes a key ingredient of a clever test, which attempts to rule out the "omitted demand conditions" threat to identification. The authors find that the effect of kidnapping on investment is not smaller for firms who sell abroad, as it should, if poor unobserved local demand conditions were spuriously generating their findings. Importantly, they also show that results are not mechanically driven by the firms whose management fell victim of a kidnapping. Rather, the results hold, more generally, across firms not directly affected by kidnappings but headquartered in the same region.[1]

Concerns

The basic identification strategy is somewhat risky. Indeed, a case can be made that omitted demand conditions could, perhaps, have differential effects across the different types of crime. Moreover, not all types of crime are included in the model to begin with. For example, the property crime rate can affect investment and it is likely to be correlated with kidnappings as well as other crimes. Are kidnappings picking up the effect of other types of crime on investment? Presumably the data from DNP should provide information on property crimes as well as data on guerrilla attacks and homicides. If the data is available, it should be used to test whether it is really kidnappings that drives investment down.

---

1. Given the small number of observations in table 2.6, panel A, it would be interesting to see the results in a specification that pools the data in panels A and B but includes an indicator for whether the firm's management has been kidnapped and an interaction of this indicator with the kidnapping rate at the department level.

In addition to the potential selection problem induced by firms' entry and exit, which the authors acknowledge, there might be another problem if results are being generated by firms' location decisions regarding their investment plans. In such a case the real cost of kidnapping is not the decline in investment (which may not occur at all), but rather the efficiency loss introduced by distorting the optimal geographic allocation across departments of investments that happen anyway.

The test that exploits tradability is without doubt very clever, but results should be interpreted with caution if firms that do not export abroad can nevertheless sell their excess supply in other Colombian regions when facing declines in local demand.

Kidnappings are substantially underreported everywhere. The magnitude of the problem, then, is substantially larger than official figures indicate. The hope is, of course, that the level of underreporting does not vary systematically across regions over time.

What We Want to Know

The reading of Pshisva and Suarez's chapter answers some very important questions and stimulates many others. To mention just a few:

Are firms paying ransom for their kidnapped employees? This seems key to understanding the relationship between management kidnapping and corporate investment. As the authors recognize, however, the available data does not allow them to address this issue.

Are cash abundant firms (who are more likely to invest), still abundant in cash after costly investments are undertaken? Do firms or individuals undertake costly, irreversible investments to make their liquid assets more illiquid, thus becoming less attractive targets to kidnappers? This type of strategic avoidance behavior thus generates a countervailing effect in which the kidnapping rate actually increases investment.

Pshisva and Suarez point out that more than half of the kidnappings in the sample were perpetrated by guerrillas. A natural question is, then, whether corporate investment responds more to kidnappings by guerrillas than it does to those by ordinary criminals? In other words, what is the impact of the guerrilla-perpetrated management-targeted kidnapping rate? Suppose that the overall kidnapping rate is driven by the guerrilla kidnapping rate and that because kidnappings are complex operations, the guerrilla kidnapping rate is a measure of the influence or "ability to operate" that guerrilla groups have in the region. Is it possible that this influence of guerrilla groups, whose political goal is not compatible with private property rights, is the fundamental driver of corporate investment declines? In other words, kidnappings may just proxy for the level of influence that anti-capitalist sentiment has in a given region. It should come as no surprise that investment and, more generally, capital accumulation declines when the regional power of groups that stand against private property increases.

Does personal investment follow the same pattern as corporate investment?

What Can We Learn?

Extrapolation to Other Contexts

While kidnapping rates are up worldwide, Colombia's kidnapping rate has gone down substantially since 2002, some suggest, as a result of Uribe's "Politica de Seguridad Democrática." Fortunately, given this substantial decline, perhaps the results are of no direct relevance for Colombia today. However, we sure can still learn from the Colombia's study. Studies replicating Pshisva and Suarez's strategy should be conducted in other countries facing increasing kidnapping rates. However, it should be kept in mind that the identification of an average impact at the subnational level does not directly translate into an impact at the national level. Among other things, geographic reallocation within departments across Colombia is likely governed by different incentives and mechanisms than those governing reallocation of investment (if any) into countries outside Colombia.

Policy Issues

The lack of causal mechanisms explaining the findings and other data limitations provide no firm ground for strong policy recommendations. There are, however, several questions within the kidnapping policy domain that still require answers. To mention just a few: (a) criminalization of ransom payment; (b) subsidization of unobservable security measures that help track the victim (for example, the possibilities of replicating in the kidnapping context the successful experience of Lo Jack in deterring car theft should be explored carefully); (c) should corporations design their security budgets to prevent the kidnapping of their management, insure against it, or both? (d) What should be the appropriate legal status of kidnapping insurance? Hopefully, future studies will build upon the lead of Pshisva and Suarez and help to shed more light on some of these important questions.

3

The Cost of Avoiding Crime
The Case of Bogotá

Alejandro Gaviria, Carlos Medina, Leonardo Morales,
and Jairo Núñez

3.1 Introduction

Quantifying the costs of crime and violence is a useful exercise because
it contributes to the quality of the public discussion about a fundamental
problem, and because it helps policymakers both prioritize and design cost-
effective policies to diminish the adverse effects of crime. Estimates of the
cost of violence are usually based on health care expenditures and losses
to national economies coming from (among other things) days away from
work, law enforcement expenditures, and unrealized investments.[1]

Nonetheless, these estimations do not usually consider the cost posed by
crime and violence to households within cities, in terms of both the different
risks they face and the coping mechanisms used by them. Specifically, within
a city, the variation of crime and violence rates across neighborhoods provides a market that is serviced by security agencies created for that purpose.
Households often end up paying for security in the form of higher property
and rental values.

There are two relevant issues concerning the *market* for neighborhood

Alejandro Gaviria is professor of economics at the University of the Andes. Carlos Medina
is a researcher at Banco de la Repùblica, the central bank of Colombia. Leonardo Morales is a
researcher at Banco de la Repùblica, the central bank of Colombia. Jairo Núñez is professor
of social policy at Javeriana University.

We thank Alfredo Canavese and the editors for detailed comments of a previous version, and
Carlos Esteban Posada, and seminar participants of the Conference on Crime, Institutions, and
Policies of the NBER-LICIP Inter-American Seminar on Economics, and the Seminario de
Economía at Bogotá and Medellín of the Banco de la República de Colombia for comments.
The opinions expressed here are those of the authors and not of the Banco de la República de
Colombia nor of its Board.

1. Other economic and personal costs are much less quantifiable, like the ones coming from
the pain and suffering of victims of violence.

safety (the amenity under consideration in this chapter) that one should consider. First, one must quantify the cost of this amenity to households. Second, one must identify the impossibility of most households to meet this cost. Even though many households are willing to pay to avoid crime, just a few are actually able to, thus making neighborhood safety (a supposedly pure public good) subject to private markets, and therefore to exclusion.

In this chapter, we study the aforementioned issues for the city of Bogotá, Colombia. We find that households living in the highest socioeconomic stratum (stratum 6) are paying up to 7.2 percent of their house values in order to prevent average homicide rates from increasing in one standard deviation. For their part, households in stratum 5 are paying up to 2.4 percent of their house values to prevent homicide rates from increasing. These results indicate the willingness to pay for security by households in Bogotá, and, additionally, show the emergence of urban private markets for security. These markets imply different levels of access to public goods among the population, and actually, the exclusion of the poorest.

We now proceed to describe the levels of crime in Colombia and some previous work on the topic. Then we describe our data and present the empirical methodology and identification strategy. Finally, we present the results and offer some general conclusions.

3.2   Crime in Colombia and Previous Work

Figure 3.1 shows that in the late 1990s the homicide rate in Colombia was one of the highest in the Latin American and the Caribbean (LAC) region.[2] The Colombian rate was about six times as high as the average rate worldwide and about three times as high as the average rate in the American continent taken as a whole. As of 2002, the homicide rate in the city of Bogotá was similar to that of other large Latin American cities, but it was lower than that of the most violent cities in Colombia, namely Medellín and Cali. In recent years, the homicide rate in Bogotá has fallen precipitously, from a rate of nearly 80 deaths per 100,000 people in 1993, to a rate of 20 per 100,000 in 2007 (Llorente and Rivas 2005).

A wide selection of literature deals with the overall cost of crime and violence (see Cohen and Rubio [2007] for a recent review). For the case of the United States, Krug et al. (2002) argue that the overall cost due to gunshot wounds is close to $130 billion, whereas the costs caused by stab wounds are close to $50 billion. For the United Kingdom, Atkinson, Healey, and Maurato (2005) find that common, moderate, and serious assaults cost about £5,300, £31,000, and £36,000 per average victim household per year, respectively.

Among the studies seeking to estimate households' willingness to pay for security, Cohen et al. (2004) use a contingent valuation methodology to find

---

2. Numbers shown in figure 3.1 correspond to the late 1990s for the case of countries (top graph) and to 2002 for the case cities (bottom graph).

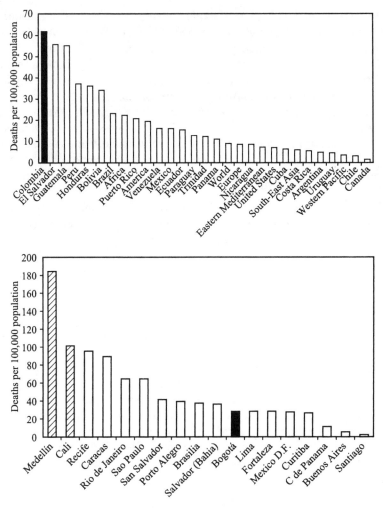

Fig. 3.1   Homicide rates in LAC countries and cities
Sources: Krug et al. (2002); Gaviria and Pages (2002); and Llorente and Rivas (2005).

that a typical American household is willing to pay between $100 and $150 per year for a crime prevention program that reduces specific crimes by 10 percent. The said amount increases according to the severity of crime: $104 for burglaries and $146 for murders. Previously, Cook and Ludwig (2000) and Ludwig and Cook (2001) argued that the average household is willing to pay as much as $200 per year in order to reduce gun violence caused by criminals and juvenile delinquents by 30 percent.

While studies that estimate hedonic price models have often included crime variables in the empirical estimations, the identification of causal effects of these variables has not been an explicit goal in most of the literature.

Whereas Roback (1982) does not find a statistically significant coefficient of crime rates on log earnings, Gyourko and Tracy (1991) do find significant effects. Neither of them addresses explicitly the issue of causality.

For Colombia, the only previous attempt to quantify distributional effects of crime variables is that of Gaviria and Vélez (2001). These authors find that rich households are more likely to be victims of property crime and kidnapping, and are therefore much more willing to modify their behavior for fear of crime: they feel unsafe, and will heavily invest in crime avoidance. The poorest are more likely to be victims of homicides and domestic violence. Other studies have focused on the overall economic cost caused by violence in Colombia. Trujillo and Badel (1998) estimate, for the early nineties, the gross cost of urban criminality and armed conflict in Colombia at 4.3 percent of gross domestic product (GDP). Badel (1999) estimate, for the mid-nineties, the gross direct cost of violence and armed conflict at 4.5 percent of GDP. Londoño and Guerrero (2000) estimate the *direct* cost of violence on health (medical attention and lost years of life) and material losses (public and private security and justice) at 4.9 percent of GDP for a subset of Latin American and Caribbean (LAC) countries, and 11.4 percent of GDP in the case of Colombia. Furthermore, Londoño and Guerrero (2000) also estimate the *indirect* costs of violence (i.e., the effect on productivity, investment, work, and consumption) in 9.2 percent of GDP for the same sample of LAC countries, and 13.3 percent of GDP for Colombia. These authors did not quantify the willingness of households to pay in order to avoid urban violence, as we do in this chapter.

Quite a few previous studies investigate the spatial patterns of crime in Colombia in general and in Bogotá in particular. Núñez and Sánchez (2001) find statistically significant spatial correlation between assaults, auto thefts, and residential and commercial robberies. Similarly, Llorente et al. (2001) illustrate meticulously the spatial segregation of homicides in Bogotá, and, additionally, study its dynamics, finding that homicides are spatially very persistent; they take place mostly around the same areas of the city with different degrees of intensity.

In what follows, we use the previous studies and provide some additional elements that, we believe, support the estimation strategy used in the calculation of the effects of homicide rates on house values and rents. We describe the data used in the estimation before proceeding to present the methodology and the results of the empirical model.

3.3   Data

We use data at the household level taken from the 2003 *Encuesta de Calidad de Vida/ECV (Survey on Quality of Life).*[3] The ECV is carried out at

---

3. This section builds heavily on Medina, Morales, and Núñez (2008).

Stratum

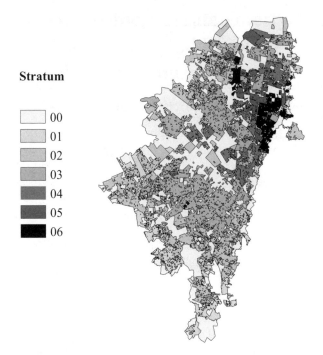

☐	00
☐	01
☐	02
☐	03
■	04
■	05
■	06

Map 3.1   Socioeconomic strata in Bogotá

approximately five-year intervals by Colombia's Administrative Department of National Statistics, DANE.[4] The 2003 ECV (a Living Standards Measurement Study [LSMS] survey) has detailed information about living conditions of households in Bogotá, with more than 12,000 households interviewed in all nineteen subcity urban areas known as localidades.[5] The ECV was purportedly designed to compute employment and unemployment rates at the level of the locality. Within each locality, households were randomly selected. In each locality, households from each of the six different strata used in Colombia for targeting social programs were included.[6] Map 3.1 illustrates the location of the richest and the poorest households in the

4. The survey was collected between June 6 and July 23 of 2003. Household members eighteen and older were directly interviewed.

5. See Medina, Morales, and Núñez (2008) for a detailed description of the spatial data.

6. Urban areas in Colombia are split into six socioeconomic strata: stratum 1 has the lowest socioeconomic levels and stratum 6, the highest. The strata are used to target public service subsidies and other social programs (Medina, Morales, and Núñez 2008). To estimate in which socioeconomic stratum each house is classified, the local governments take into account dwelling characteristics as well as neighborhood amenities. Based on this information, they aggregate neighborhoods into clusters of strata. The methodology allows houses in a cluster to belong to a stratum different to that of its cluster if characteristics are very different to those of its cluster.

city: the former are located mostly in the northeast, and the latter mostly in the south and on the city's periphery.

We also use data from the 1993 Population Census in order to collect information at the census sector level. This information allows us to split Bogotá into more than 500 sectors, with an average population of about 12,000 inhabitants per sector (see divisions in map 3.2).[7]

Table 3.1 presents all variables used in the estimation. Most households in Bogotá are located in socioeconomic strata 2 or 3 (75 percent), and approximately 6 percent in strata 5 and 6, or in stratum 1, respectively. Coverage of public utility services is very high in the city, with nearly 100 percent in electricity, and nearly 90 percent in fixed phone lines. We possess cadastral data for nearly 70 percent of the households. Our variables related to crime include common thefts, aggravated assaults, residential and commercial robberies, auto thefts, and homicides.[8] Figure 3.2 presents the distribution of the crime variables across census sectors. The figure shows that almost all distributions and, in particular, those corresponding to common thefts (*object* thefts herein) and homicides are rather skewed. Figure 3.2 also presents the spatial distribution of the Police Centers of Immediate Attention, the CAIs. This distribution has the same shape as the distribution of the crime and violence variables.

Cadastral data will be made available here on property values for close to 8,900 houses in Bogotá. In addition, we are able to provide the owners' reported values for households claiming home ownership. Reported rent prices are available for houses with tenant households ("how much do you pay"?) and for those living in their own house ("how much would you pay if the house were rented"?) Figure 3.3 presents the distribution of property values. The distribution of property values obtained using only cadastral data is similar to the one obtained when reported rent values are used to complement cadastral data.

Other variables related to quality of life, like the index of quality of life (ICV), the index of Unsatisfied Basic Needs (NBI), the Misery Index, and the Gini coefficient of education (which measures inequality in the distribution of the years of schooling in each census sector), are highly correlated with the socioeconomic strata—positively in the case of ICV, negatively in the case of NBI and the Misery Index.[9] Inequality in the distribution of education is higher in the poorest neighborhoods, which also suffer from higher

---

7. Figures of the 2005 Colombia Population Census have not yet been made available.

8. For the purpose of this study, we understand homicide as the activity by which one person kills another (Art. 323 Penal Code); attacks against life, as harming a person's body or health (Art. 332 Penal Code); and objects theft, as the act of expropriating someone else's goods for one's own benefit (Art. 349 Penal Code).

9. See details of the definition of the ICV in DNP (1997). The NBI index measures the share of households in a specific census sector that has at least one basic need unsatisfied: adequate housing, basic public utility services (water, sewage, and electricity), economic dependency, and/ or primary school dropouts. The Misery Index is estimated as the share of households with at least two unsatisfied basic needs.

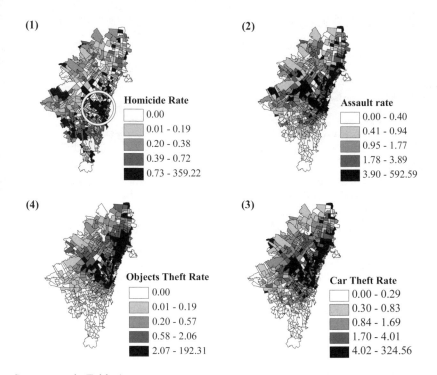

See sources in Table 1.

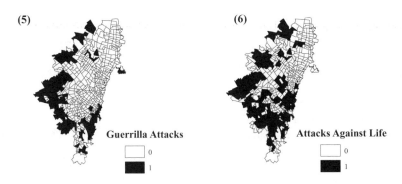

Map 3.2   Quintiles of variables related to crime across census sectors in Bogotá
Source: Medina et al. (2007).
Note: See sources in table 3.1.

Table 3.1   **Descriptive statistic**

Variable	N	Mean	Standard deviation
Stratum 2	12,744	0.325	0.468
Stratum 3	12,744	0.434	0.496
Stratum 4	12,744	0.116	0.320
Stratum 5	12,744	0.030	0.170
Stratum 6	12,744	0.032	0.175
Cadastral house value (as opposed to reported)	12,871	0.690	0.463
Number of rooms	12,771	3.37	1.52
Number of bathrooms	12,760	1.558	0.842
House with piped gas service	12,771	0.656	0.475
House with telephone	12,771	0.877	0.329
Good quality of electricity	12,746	0.899	0.302
Good quality of garbage collection	12,750	0.891	0.312
Water available 24 hrs. a day	12,678	0.982	0.133
Water available every day of the week	12,771	0.967	0.178
Good quality of phone line	12,871	0.731	0.444
House with garden	12,771	0.419	0.493
House with courtyard	12,771	0.046	0.210
House with garage	12,771	0.285	0.451
House with terrace	12,771	0.217	0.412
Parks in neighborhood	12,771	0.131	0.338
The house has suffered because of a natural disaster	12,771	0.046	0.209
House in area vulnerable to natural disasters	12,771	0.070	0.255
Factories in neighborhood	12,771	0.119	0.324
Garbage collector in neighborhood	12,771	0.030	0.172
Marketplaces in neighborhood	12,771	0.070	0.255
Airport in neighborhood	12,771	0.037	0.188
Terminals of ground transportation in neighborhood	12,771	0.033	0.178
House close to open sewers	12,771	0.103	0.304
House close to high tension lines of electricity transmission	12,771	0.018	0.132
You feel safe in your neighborhood	12,771	0.680	0.466
Provision of water is inside the house	12,771	0.973	0.163
The kitchen is an individual room	12,771	0.960	0.195
Shower bath	12,771	0.974	0.160
House[a]	12,771	0.378	0.485
Wall material is any of: brick, block, stone, polished wood	12,771	0.978	0.146
Floor material is any of: marmol, parque, lacquered wood	12,771	0.084	0.277
Floor material is any of: carpet	12,771	0.133	0.339
Floor material is any of: floor tile, vinyl, tablet, wood	12,771	0.595	0.491
Floor material is any of: coarse wood, table, plank	12,771	0.054	0.227
Floor material is any of: cement, gravilla, earth, sand	12,771	0.134	0.341
House with toilet connected to the public sewage	12,771	0.989	0.103
House with potable water service	12,771	0.985	0.120
Number of infantile shelters	[e]12,771	0.070	0.352
Number of asylums	[e]12,771	0.140	0.456
Number of convents	[e]12,771	0.260	0.888
Objects theft rate	[e]12,861	0.869	6.088
Assaults rate	[e]12,861	3.24	22.13
Residential and commercial assault rate	[e]12,861	2.99	9.23
Cars theft rate	[e]12,861	2.48	12.53
Crime rate	[e]12,120	0.538	0.668
Land use	[e]12,861	0.002	0.017
Attacks of FARC, ELN, or other groups[b]	[e]12,871	0.232	0.422
Share of women heads of households	[e]12,861	0.275	0.051
Labor force unemployment rate	[e]12,871	3.89	1.01
Illiteracy rate	[e]12,861	0.030	0.021

Table 3.1 (continued)

Variable	N	Mean	Standard deviation
Average education	[e]12,861	8.365	1.896
Index of quality of life[c]	[e]12,871	82.12	7.09
Gini of education	[e]12,861	0.051	0.013
Number of CAIS[d]	[e]12,861	0.474	9.894
Medical centers	[e]12,861	0.281	1.476
Private hospitals	[e]12,861	0.243	1.384
Police headquarters	[e]12,861	0.241	17.64
Local security funds	[e]12,861	6.95	60.45
Public hospitals	[e]12,861	0.572	19.630
Religious centers	[e]12,861	1.12	3.45
Social welfare centers	[e]12,861	2.30	7.39
Cultural centers	[e]12,861	2.91	11.48
Prisons	[e]12,861	0.032	0.966
Attacks against life	[e]12,861	0.844	18.082
Attacks against wealth	[e]12,861	1.30	22.17
Bars	[e]12,861	1.179	18.727
Brothels	[e]12,861	0.630	17.689
Casinos/places for bets	[e]12,861	0.288	17.659
Places selling drugs/narcotics	[e]12,861	0.879	20.300
People 0–4 years old	[e]12,771	1,183	980
People 5–9 years old	[e]12,771	1,156	929
People 10–14 years old	[e]12,771	1,168	910
People 15–19 years old	[e]12,771	1,092	793
People 20–24 years old	[e]12,771	1,211	890
People 25–29 years old	[e]12,771	1,217	898
People 30–34 years old	[e]12,771	1,132	814
People 35–39 years old	[e]12,771	898	638
People 40–44 years old	[e]12,771	696	499
People 45–49 years old	[e]12,771	506	352
People 50–54 years old	[e]12,771	413	270
People 55–59 years old	[e]12,771	299	186
People 60+ years old	[e]12,771	700	415
Unsatisfied Basic Needs (NBI): Dependency	[e]12,771	37.01	43.36
Accumulation	[e]12,771	418.35	410.15
Dropouts	[e]12,771	6.04	9.18
Public utility services	[e]12,771	37.71	76.72
Housing in	[e]12,771	69.09	97.20
NBI in municipality where born	[e]12,871	26.86	17.34
NBI in municipality where born	[e]12,871	0.097	0.296
Born in urban area	12,771	0.753	0.431
Share of women in household	12,771	0.535	0.268
Household with children	12,771	0.716	0.451
Age of mother minus age of oldest children	12,771	17.13	12.77
Logarithm of rent values	12,669	12.44	0.771
Logarithm of cadastral house values	8,879	17.48	0.777
Logarithm of cadastral or reported house values	10,845	17.50	0.792

Sources: Encuesta de Calidad de Vida 2003, Real State Appraisal of Bogotá, National Police-DIJIN 2000, Paz Pública (2000). Colombian 1993 Population Census.

[a]Dummy variable equal to 1 if house, zero otherwise (apartment, etc.).

[b]Dummy variable equal to 1 if there have been attacks in census sector by FARC, ELN, or other such illegal armed groups.

[c]A-Theoretical estimation of QoL (see methodology in DNP [1997]).

[d]Centros de Atencion Inmediata, CAIS: Centers of Immediate Police Attention.

[e]At the census sector level.

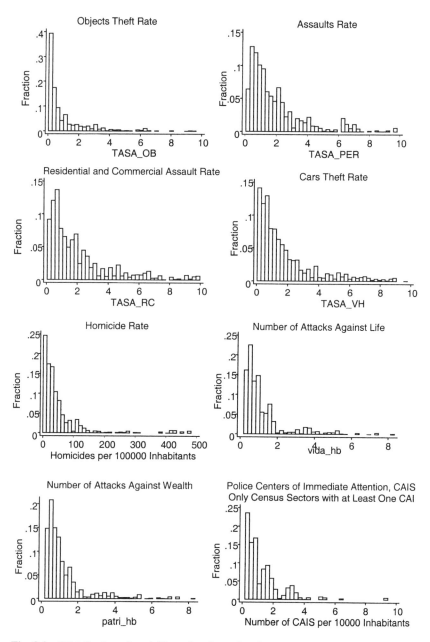

Fig. 3.2 Distribution of variables related to crime by census sector (Bogotá)

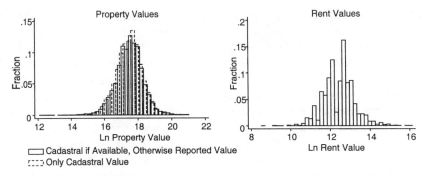

Fig. 3.3   Property and rent values

rates of violent crime as well as from higher incidence of attacks both by guerrillas and other groups (see map 3.2).[10]

We can now illustrate graphically the spatial correlation between quality-of-life indicators and crime variables. Map 3.2 illustrates the spatial patterns of crime variables at the census sector level (quintiles are also used). The circled area, which comprises downtown Bogotá, is the area with the highest homicide rate in the city. If we compare maps 3.1 with map 3.2, it becomes apparent that the highest assault, car, and object theft rates correspond to the highest stratum neighborhoods. On the contrary, homicides, guerrilla attacks, and attacks against life are all much more common in the periphery of the city, which is also much poorer. Spatial correlations suggested by the overlapping of the maps are consistent with the survey data described by Gaviria and Vélez (2001).

3.4   Empirical Analysis

In this section, we present the empirical strategy and the estimation of the effect of crime and violence upon house values and rental prices. We estimate a hedonic regression model of the logarithm of house values on a battery of both household and *amenity* variables. The specification used takes the following form:

(1) $$\ln(P_{ij}) = \alpha_0 + \alpha_1 H_i + \alpha_2 A_j + u_{ij},$$

where P_{ij} is either the value of the house (cadastral or reported by household) or the corresponding rental price (also reported by household), H_i is a vector

---

10. See Fajnzylber, Lederman, and Loayza (1998, 2000, 2002a, 2002b). These authors find a positive relation between income inequality and the homicide and robbery rates. A review of this regularity for Latin American and Caribbean Countries can be found in Heinemann and Verner (2006). For the Colombian case, Sanchez and Núñez (2002) find that inequality in land distribution is positively related to the homicide rate, although it explains just a small fraction of the cross-sectional variation in the homicide rate.

of household characteristics, and A_j is a vector of amenities in census sector j. As customary in the literature, the model assumes that house values incorporate amenities, including access and quality of public goods and services (roads, parks and other green space, transport, security, etc.). In equilibrium, amenities would be capitalized into house values and rents.[11]

Table 3.2 presents the results of estimating equation (1), using three different dependent variables. The first dependent variable takes the cadastral value of a house, if it is available, and takes the value reported by the household if it is not. In this case, we have up to 10,290 households in our sample. The second variable is restricted to the available cadastral values (8,435 observations). Finally, the third variable equals the rental values reported by households (12,024 observations). Each set of results contains both ordinary least squares (OLS) and instrumental variables (IV) results. For all regressions, we estimate robust standard errors, correcting for clustering at the census sector level.

We focus first on the OLS estimates. Overall, the reported estimates have the expected signs. As shown, property values increase for houses located in higher socioeconomic strata, for houses with better characteristics, including the number of rooms, the number of bathrooms, the availability of piped gas, the presence of parks in the neighborhood, the absence of open sewers, and so on. In the first panel, where cadastral values are used if available, and reported values otherwise, we include a dummy variable equal to 1 if cadastral values are used, and to zero otherwise. The estimated coefficient on the dummy implies that cadastral values are on average 10.6 percent lower than the reported commercial values.

Regarding crime variables, the common theft rate (*object* theft) is negatively related to house value. This variable is significant only when rent values are used (panel 3). Homicides rates are negatively related to house values. Attacks by the Revolutionary Armed Forces of Colombia (FARC) or National Liberation Army (ELN) guerrillas and other illegal armed groups are also negatively related to house rental values but the coefficients are hardly significant. On the other hand, residential and commercial assaults and car thefts are unrelated to house values. Finally, property crimes (attacks against wealth) are positively related to house values.

Although we expect all crime variables to be negatively related to house values and rents, there are several sources of endogeneity that can bias the results. On the one hand, if some types of crime occur more often in better neighborhoods—as it is generally the case with property crime—omitted characteristics might be positively correlated with this type of crime. For example, the coefficient of auto theft may be picking up some unobserved

11. See Rosen (1974, 1979, 2002); Thaler and Rosen (1976); Blomquist, Berger, and Hoehn (1988); Roback (1982, 1988); and Gyourko, Kahn, and Tracy (1999), among others. Thaler and Rosen (1976) develop a model that estimates the premium workers' demand for working in riskier occupations.

Table 3.2 Hedonic regression for Bogotá

Variable	Homicide rate (1st stage)		Ln house price[a] OLS		Ln house price[a] 2SLS		Ln house price[b] OLS		Ln house price[b] 2SLS		Ln house rent OLS		Ln house rent 2SLS	
	Coefficient	t	Coefficient	t	Coefficient	t	Coefficient	t	Coefficient	t	Coefficient	t	Coefficient	t
Stratum 2	0.0461	0.53	0.1449	2.83	0.1419	2.58	0.1722	3.06	0.1721	2.84	0.0197	0.62	0.0342	1.01
Stratum 3	0.0826	0.70	0.3047	4.56	0.2980	4.08	0.3087	4.18	0.3061	3.80	0.1105	3.05	0.1362	3.25
Stratum 4	0.2040	1.24	0.3822	4.18	0.3630	3.16	0.3518	3.43	0.3411	2.65	0.2078	4.32	0.2711	3.81
Stratum 5	0.1735	0.91	0.4643	3.78	0.4469	3.22	0.3599	2.59	0.3481	2.22	0.4267	7.09	0.4803	6.45
Stratum 6	0.0469	0.20	0.6254	4.21	0.6206	4.12	0.5027	3.11	0.5011	3.05	0.7254	9.63	0.7390	9.70
Cadastral house value (as opposed to reported)	0.0148	0.65	-0.1066	-5.00	-0.1078	-4.92	0.0000	0.00	0.0000	0.00	-0.0297	-2.67	-0.0251	-2.14
Number of rooms	-0.0013	-0.16	0.0116	1.67	0.0116	1.66	0.0083	1.13	0.0083	1.12	0.1395	24.80	0.1394	24.73
Number of bathrooms	0.0037	0.24	0.2011	12.83	0.2007	12.57	0.1968	11.66	0.1965	11.46	0.1290	11.63	0.1301	11.50
House with piped gas service	-0.0300	-1.00	-0.0046	-0.26	-0.0015	-0.08	-0.0047	-0.24	-0.0026	-0.11	0.0459	3.97	0.0363	2.41
House with telephone	-0.0541	-1.76	-0.1483	-4.89	-0.1430	-3.79	-0.1522	-4.79	-0.1494	-3.75	0.2016	11.35	0.1839	7.40
Good quality of electricity	0.0027	0.16	-0.0197	-1.00	-0.0197	-0.99	-0.0220	-0.97	-0.0224	-0.99	-0.0285	-1.96	-0.0277	-1.91
Good quality of garbage collection	0.0081	0.26	0.0371	1.95	0.0366	1.90	0.0320	1.70	0.0319	1.66	-0.0136	-0.96	-0.0111	-0.78
Water available 24 hrs. a day	0.0098	0.21	0.1238	2.83	0.1218	2.78	0.1526	2.99	0.1512	2.92	0.0223	0.61	0.0255	0.69
Water available every day of the week	0.0126	0.16	0.0318	0.77	0.0311	0.76	0.0398	0.87	0.0401	0.89	-0.0065	-0.29	-0.0022	-0.10
Good quality of phone line	0.0074	0.49	0.0301	2.13	0.0292	2.03	0.0242	1.56	0.0236	1.50	0.0174	1.40	0.0199	1.55
House with garden	-0.0017	-0.07	0.1391	8.23	0.1389	8.23	0.1383	7.67	0.1381	7.67	-0.0055	-0.50	-0.0061	-0.55
House with courtyard	-0.1146	-3.68	0.1441	3.77	0.1551	3.09	0.1610	3.61	0.1661	2.78	-0.0236	-0.81	-0.0598	-1.55
House with garage	-0.0546	-2.17	0.0742	3.84	0.0793	2.92	0.0681	3.38	0.0705	2.40	0.1023	7.11	0.0851	4.05
House with terrace	-0.0221	-0.90	0.1328	7.86	0.1352	7.20	0.1118	6.24	0.1134	5.54	0.0380	3.14	0.0311	2.27
Parks in neighborhood	0.0172	0.47	-0.1084	-3.54	-0.1107	-3.56	-0.1731	-4.75	-0.1763	-4.73	0.0284	1.56	0.0335	1.81
The house has suffered because of a natural disaster	-0.0836	-1.47	0.0916	1.92	0.0994	1.87	0.0293	0.57	0.0345	0.59	0.0180	0.56	-0.0080	-0.21

(continued)

Table 3.2 (continued)

Variable	Homicide rate (1st stage)		Ln house price[a] OLS		Ln house price[a] 2SLS		Ln house price[b] OLS		Ln house price[b] 2SLS		Ln house rent OLS		Ln house rent 2SLS	
	Coefficient	t	Coefficient	t	Coefficient	t	Coefficient	t	Coefficient	t	Coefficient	t	Coefficient	t
Airport in neighborhood	-0.1967	2.52	-0.0485	1.13	-0.0282	0.36	-0.0609	1.26	-0.0473	0.54	0.0640	2.45	0.0023	0.04
Terminals of ground transportation in neighborhood	0.0012	0.02	-0.0103	0.26	-0.0101	0.26	-0.0708	1.54	-0.0725	1.58	0.0541	1.98	0.0546	2.00
House close to open sewers	-0.0642	1.80	-0.0516	2.01	-0.0455	1.38	-0.0489	1.67	-0.0452	1.17	-0.0034	0.21	-0.0234	1.04
House close to high tension lines of electricity transmission	0.0069	0.09	0.0667	1.35	0.0667	1.35	0.0861	1.54	0.0871	1.56	-0.0222	0.64	-0.0195	0.56
You feel safe in your neighborhood	-0.0675	4.44	-0.0076	0.58	-0.0005	0.02	-0.0119	0.86	-0.0077	0.27	-0.0189	2.00	-0.0401	1.93
Provision of water is inside the house	0.0367	0.68	0.0085	0.12	0.0033	0.05	0.0086	0.11	0.0049	0.06	0.2043	3.51	0.2159	3.62
The kitchen is a individual room	0.0561	0.92	0.1194	2.73	0.1123	2.24	0.1043	2.19	0.0991	1.82	0.1254	4.49	0.1444	4.36
Shower bath	-0.0551	1.49	0.0318	0.63	0.0356	0.61	0.0107	0.20	0.0131	0.21	0.0921	2.29	0.0749	1.74
House[c]	0.0166	0.59	-0.1797	8.23	-0.1808	8.29	-0.1953	8.36	-0.1958	8.35	0.0583	4.46	0.0632	4.67
Walls material is any of: brick, block, stone, polished wood	0.0599	1.07	0.1004	1.41	0.0925	1.27	0.0908	1.01	0.0841	0.92	0.1432	3.61	0.1626	3.82
Floor material is any of: marmol, parque, lacquered wood														
Floor material is carpet	0.0268	0.77	-0.2370	7.68	-0.2408	7.58	-0.2397	6.57	-0.2427	6.48	0.0097	0.49	0.0177	0.85
Floor material is any of: floor tile, vinyl, tablet, wood	0.0330	0.86	-0.0290	1.06	-0.0334	1.12	-0.0134	0.44	-0.0166	0.50	-0.0167	0.98	-0.0063	0.33
Floor material is any of: coarse wood, table, plank	0.1531	2.47	0.0487	1.21	0.0307	0.45	0.0638	1.47	0.0519	0.69	-0.0835	3.07	-0.0355	0.72

Floor material is any of: cement, gravilla, earth, sand[g]	-0.0218	-0.60	-0.2331	-5.99	-0.2318	-5.84	-0.2084	-4.84	-0.2078	-4.72	-0.1473	-5.65	-0.1538	-5.68
House with toilet connected to the public sewage	0.0886	0.69	-0.1361	-1.09	-0.1489	-1.16	-0.1925	-1.24	-0.2009	-1.26	0.0742	0.74	0.1015	0.99
House with potable water service	0.1759	1.22	0.2373	2.13	0.2212	1.72	0.3368	2.41	0.3253	2.06	-0.0368	-0.55	0.0188	0.22
Number of infantile shelters[g]	0.0073	0.12	-0.0594	-1.75	-0.0600	-1.76	-0.0994	-1.96	-0.0992	-1.97	0.0019	0.09	0.0042	0.21
Number of asylums[g]	-0.0107	-0.18	0.0009	0.03	0.0019	0.07	0.0116	0.37	0.0123	0.39	0.0209	1.25	0.0175	1.05
Number of conventos[g]	-0.0459	-1.35	-0.0035	-0.25	0.0014	0.07	0.0072	0.40	0.0108	0.43	-0.0057	-0.78	-0.0201	-1.41
Objects theft rate[g]	-0.0991	-1.21	-0.0281	-1.37	-0.0182	-0.47	-0.0141	-0.66	-0.0081	-0.18	-0.0252	-3.10	-0.0562	-1.96
Assaults rate[g]	0.0913	3.95	-0.0053	-0.71	-0.0147	-0.46	-0.0035	-0.46	-0.0095	-0.27	0.0035	1.17	0.0322	1.29
Residential and commercial assault rate[g]	0.0693	1.51	0.0129	1.00	0.0062	0.24	0.0127	0.90	0.0089	0.30	0.0020	0.45	0.0236	1.20
Cars theft rate[g]	-0.0721	-2.75	-0.0017	-0.23	0.0056	0.21	-0.0064	-0.70	-0.0019	-0.06	0.0030	0.88	-0.0197	-0.99
Homicide rate (deaths per 10,000,000 people)[g]			-0.0470	-1.70	0.0555	0.17	-0.0411	-1.45	0.0224	0.06	-0.0115	-1.43	-0.3253	-1.18
Land use[g]	-0.5262	-0.44	-0.0725	-0.15	-0.0094	-0.02	-0.1376	-0.28	-0.0813	-0.16	-0.2480	-0.61	-0.4099	-0.95
Attacks of FARC, ELN, or other groups[d,g]	-0.0237	-0.31	-0.0461	-1.26	-0.0441	-1.15	-0.0366	-0.91	-0.0362	-0.87	-0.0324	-1.60	-0.0400	-1.91
Share of women heads of households[g]	-0.2071	-0.21	-2.2102	-5.45	-2.1998	-5.33	-2.4374	-5.40	-2.4475	-5.33	-0.1445	-0.60	-0.2130	-0.84
Labor force unemployment rate[g]	0.0296	0.57	-0.1002	-4.75	-0.1037	-4.40	-0.1260	-5.84	-0.1288	-5.33	-0.0161	-1.61	-0.0069	-0.50
Illiteracy rate[g]	-5.7389	-1.80	0.0479	0.03	0.6566	0.27	-0.3278	-0.20	0.1107	0.04	1.2972	1.69	-0.5061	-0.29
Average education[g]	-0.3234	-2.73	-0.0380	-0.96	-0.0050	-0.04	-0.0497	-1.10	-0.0282	-0.21	0.0983	4.95	-0.0035	-0.04
Index of quality of life[e,g]	0.0565	2.11	0.0442	4.75	0.0384	1.80	0.0440	4.14	0.0399	1.67	0.0076	1.42	0.0253	1.52
Gini of education[g]	11.0243	1.44	0.2304	0.09	-0.9956	-0.22	-1.8934	-0.63	-2.8396	-0.55	2.8591	1.70	6.3087	1.73
Number of CAIS[f,g]	0.0065	0.14	0.0014	0.10	0.0004	0.03	0.0037	0.27	0.0028	0.20	0.0127	2.10	0.0147	2.30
Medical centers[g]	-0.0655	-2.95	-0.0109	-1.10	-0.0044	-0.18	-0.0131	-1.26	-0.0091	-0.34	-0.0037	-0.87	-0.0243	-1.35
Private hospitals[g]	0.0654	1.89	0.0048	0.30	-0.0017	-0.06	0.0114	0.58	0.0076	0.24	0.0092	1.53	0.0297	1.57
Police headquarters[g]	0.0688	0.58	0.0543	1.04	0.0481	0.91	0.0818	1.50	0.0778	1.40	0.0313	2.48	0.0529	2.36
Local security funds[g]	-0.0064	-1.80	0.0018	1.41	0.0025	1.06	0.0018	1.26	0.0022	0.81	0.0010	1.61	-0.0010	-0.53
Public hospitals[g]	0.0405	0.71	0.0008	0.06	-0.0036	-0.19	-0.0056	-0.41	-0.0093	-0.47	0.0016	0.20	0.0142	1.02
Religious centers[g]	0.0288	0.76	0.0171	1.56	0.0145	0.93	0.0195	1.65	0.0178	1.05	0.0021	0.45	0.0112	1.22
Social welfare centers[g]	0.0266	1.67	0.0084	1.41	0.0054	0.50	0.0110	1.55	0.0091	0.73	-0.0010	-0.40	0.0074	0.97

(continued)

Table 3.2   (continued)

Variable	Homicide rate (1st stage) Coefficient	t	Ln house price[a] OLS Coefficient	t	Ln house price[a] 2SLS Coefficient	t	Ln house price[b] OLS Coefficient	t	Ln house price[b] 2SLS Coefficient	t	Ln house rent OLS Coefficient	t	Ln house rent 2SLS Coefficient	t
Attacks against life[g]	0.0425	0.80	-0.0460	2.60	-0.0508	2.24	-0.0606	3.23	-0.0637	2.61	-0.0067	0.72	0.0068	0.45
Brothels[g]	-0.1068	1.98	0.0024	0.13	0.0133	0.35	0.0148	0.77	0.0215	0.50	-0.0179	1.64	-0.0515	1.70
Casinos/places for bets[g]	0.0310	0.53	-0.0034	0.18	-0.0080	0.37	-0.0192	1.02	-0.0232	1.05	-0.0033	0.30	0.0066	0.50
Places selling drugs/narcotics[g]	-0.0593	1.15	-0.0198	1.16	-0.0135	0.53	-0.0207	1.16	-0.0162	0.58	-0.0002	0.02	-0.0187	1.02
People 10–14 years old[g]	-0.0012	2.86	-0.0004	1.73	-0.0002	0.59	-0.0004	1.85	-0.0003	0.69	0.0000	0.12	-0.0004	1.13
People 15–19 years old[g]	0.0004	0.67	0.0000	0.15	-0.0001	0.28	0.0000	0.15	-0.0001	0.25	-0.0004	2.68	-0.0003	1.54
People 20–24 years old[g]	0.0000	0.07	-0.0001	0.46	-0.0001	0.45	-0.0001	0.22	-0.0001	0.21	0.0001	0.58	0.0001	0.67
People 25–29 years old[g]	-0.0005	1.21	-0.0001	0.26	0.0000	0.06	-0.0002	0.64	-0.0001	0.41	0.0000	0.43	-0.0001	0.65
People 30–34 years old[g]	0.0004	1.00	0.0002	0.91	0.0002	0.61	0.0003	1.01	0.0002	0.72	-0.0001	0.58	0.0001	0.44
People 35–39 years old[g]	0.0000	0.05	-0.0004	1.62	-0.0004	1.60	-0.0004	1.50	-0.0004	1.50	-0.0001	1.03	-0.0001	0.99
People 40–44 years old[g]	0.0010	1.23	0.0004	1.18	0.0003	0.58	0.0004	1.19	0.0003	0.65	0.0003	1.76	0.0006	1.79
People 45–49 years old[g]	-0.0004	0.44	0.0002	0.51	0.0002	0.59	0.0001	0.34	0.0002	0.42	0.0002	1.42	0.0001	0.59
People 50–54 years old[g]	0.0005	0.52	-0.0001	0.19	-0.0001	0.29	0.0000	0.10	-0.0001	0.17	0.0000	0.02	0.0002	0.64
People 55–59 years old[g]	0.0005	0.54	-0.0003	0.88	-0.0004	0.94	-0.0002	0.51	-0.0002	0.52	-0.0001	0.44	0.0001	0.20
People 60+ years old[g]	-0.0004	1.79	0.0005	5.08	0.0005	3.07	0.0005	4.35	0.0005	2.71	0.0001	2.21	0.0000	0.12
Unsatisfied Basic Needs (NBI): Dependency[g]	-0.0008	0.33	0.0012	0.94	0.0013	0.96	0.0013	0.96	0.0013	0.95	0.0010	1.79	0.0008	1.20
Accumulation[g]	0.0007	2.27	0.0006	4.44	0.0006	2.11	0.0007	3.95	0.0006	1.98	0.0001	0.74	0.0003	1.35
Dropouts[g]	0.0176	2.32	-0.0022	0.77	-0.0039	0.63	-0.0015	0.50	-0.0025	0.36	-0.0016	1.07	0.0040	0.80
Public utility services[g]	0.0006	1.79	-0.0002	0.81	-0.0002	0.77	0.0000	0.14	-0.0001	0.21	-0.0002	1.68	0.0000	0.13
Housing in[g]	-0.0001	0.14	0.0003	1.25	0.0003	1.26	0.0005	1.57	0.0005	1.57	-0.0001	0.53	-0.0001	0.70
NBI in Municipality where were born[g]	0.0010	1.60	0.0008	1.85	0.0007	1.43	0.0011	2.24	0.0011	1.81	-0.0006	2.07	-0.0003	0.81
NBI in Municipality where were born[g]	0.0353	1.74	0.0468	2.21	0.0431	1.87	0.0531	2.23	0.0507	1.97	0.0155	0.90	0.0260	1.31
Born in urban area	0.0219	1.22	-0.0078	0.51	-0.0104	0.61	-0.0067	0.42	-0.0083	0.45	-0.0056	0.48	0.0016	0.12
Household with children	0.0673	2.60												

Age of mother minus age of oldest children	-0.0020	-2.52											
Constant	-2.5129	-1.32	14.2025	19.87	14.4826	13.33	14.4844	18.14	14.6996	12.12	9.3414	23.29	8.5617	10.37
Number of observations	12,120		10,290		10,290		8,435		8,435		12,024		12,024	
R^2	0.557		0.578		0.577		0.586		0.585		0.683		0.683	

Sources: Encuesta de Calidad de Vida 2003, Real State Appraisal of Bogotá, National Police-DIJIN 2000, Paz Pública (2000). Colombian 1993 Population Census.

Notes: All regressions include dummy variable of father's and mother's education levels and their interactions. The *t*-statistics computed based on robust standard errors corrected by clustering at the census sector level.

[a] Cadastral values if available; otherwise, the value reported by households surveyed.

[b] Only includes households for which cadastral values are available.

[c] Dummy variable equal to one if house, 0 otherwise (apartment, etc.).

[d] Dummy variable equal to one if there have been attacks in census sector by FARC, ELN, or other groups.

[e] A-Theoretical estimation of QoL (see methodology in DNP [1997]).

[f] Centros de Atención Inmediata, CAIS: Centers of Immediate Police Attention.

[g] At the census sector level.

characteristics that make houses more expensive but also increase the probability of the crime in question. On the other hand, some crimes, like homicides or aggravated assaults, take place more often in poor neighborhoods because wealthier households are more likely to have much better security and the security measures (not always observed) should be already capitalized in house values and rents.

We estimate equation (1) interacting the crime variables included in table 3.2 with the socioeconomic strata. Since households differ from one another according to the socioeconomic strata in which they are located, we expect to take into account these differences and thus attenuate the omitted bias problem.[12] Households differ not only in material well-being but also in their perceptions about crime and safety. Results are presented in table 3.3 for the crime-related variables. Once we include the interactions, the *object* theft rate reveals a pattern of negative capitalization as one moves from the lower to the higher strata. The higher the stratum, the higher the negative effect of theft upon house values. Other variables (assaults, residential and commercial assaults, and attacks by FARC, ELN, and other groups) show no discernable relationship to house or rent values.

As shown in table 3.2, households who report that they feel safe in their neighborhoods pay less rent for their houses. This finding is replicated once interactions are included, especially for the higher strata. This result should be interpreted cautiously, however, because it might be conditioned by differences of perception between the wealthier and the poorer households: if the wealthier homes are located in safer neighborhoods and yet their owners feel more unsafe than the poorer do, the coefficient would be capturing these differences in perception rather than the effect of greater security on capitalized house values.

The variable that measures the number of Centers of Immediate Attention (CAIs)—an indicator of police presence—which previously appeared positively related to house rents but not to house values, become positively and significantly related to house values when interactions are included in the specification.

Even though we already possess a formidable amount of data for control purposes, we are well aware of the desirability of obtaining a much more complete database, one with longitudinal information on which we could exploit the dramatic decrease in the homicide rate that took place during

---

12. The variables "Cadastral"; "You feel safe in Neighborhood"; "Land use"; "Attacks of FARC, ELN, or other groups"; "Number of medical centers"; "Number of private hospitals"; "Number of police headquarters"; "Number of local security funds"; "Number of public hospitals"; "Number of religious centers"; "Number of social welfare centers"; "Number of cultural centers"; "Number of prisons"; "Number of attacks against life"; "Number of attacks against wealth"; "Number of bars"; "Number of brothels"; "Number of casinos/places for bets"; "Number of places selling drugs/narcotics"; "Number of people by age range"; and the dummy variables of father's and mother's education levels and their interactions, are not interacted with the socioeconomic strata.

Table 3.3 **Hedonic regression for Bogotá (Instrument: Age difference between mother and oldest child)**

Variable	Homicide rate (1st stage) Coefficient	t	Ln house price[a] OLS Coefficient	t	Ln house price[a] 2SLS Coefficient	t	Ln house price[b] OLS Coefficient	t	Ln house price[b] 2SLS Coefficient	t	Ln house rent OLS Coefficient	t	Ln house rent 2SLS Coefficient	t
Cadastral value	0.0146	0.69	-0.1135	-5.54	-0.1147	-5.51	0.0433	0.87	0.0423	0.83	-0.0232	-2.15	-0.0221	-1.95
You feel safe in your neighborhood	-0.0250	-0.68	0.0541	1.21	0.0565	1.23					-0.0095	-0.35	-0.0130	-0.47
[c]Stratum 2	-0.0277	-0.73	-0.0411	-0.80	-0.0361	-0.70	-0.0167	-0.30	-0.0177	-0.31	-0.0181	-0.54	-0.0215	-0.62
[c]Stratum 3	-0.0398	-0.97	-0.0629	-1.32	-0.0686	-1.39	-0.0632	-1.20	-0.0780	-1.41	-0.0160	-0.53	-0.0186	-0.58
[c]Stratum 4	-0.0022	-0.04	-0.0732	-1.48	-0.0749	-1.50	-0.0637	-1.15	-0.0714	-1.27	-0.0256	-0.67	-0.0281	-0.74
[c]Stratum 5	0.0538	1.23	-0.1112	-1.57	-0.1088	-1.47	-0.1210	-1.77	-0.1122	-1.53	0.0382	0.82	0.0439	0.90
[c]Stratum 6	0.0430	0.95	-0.0809	-0.91	-0.0618	-0.71	-0.0738	-1.12	-0.0510	-0.75	-0.0867	-1.50	-0.0755	-1.27
Objects theft rate	[g]-0.5349	-3.57	0.0891	1.02	0.0910	0.39	0.0669	0.69	-0.0311	-0.12	-0.0695	-1.77	-0.1229	-0.72
[c]Stratum 2	0.5236	1.73	-0.0541	-0.34	-0.0744	-0.29	-0.0198	-0.12	0.0507	0.18	0.0202	0.31	0.0733	0.43
[c]Stratum 3	0.4175	1.75	-0.0645	-0.72	-0.0738	-0.38	-0.0440	-0.44	0.0225	0.10	0.0545	1.36	0.0950	0.70
[c]Stratum 4	0.5246	3.38	-0.1225	-1.36	-0.1245	-0.54	-0.1114	-1.13	-0.0083	-0.03	0.0677	1.56	0.1174	0.69
[c]Stratum 5	0.5335	3.23	-0.1667	-1.56	-0.1688	-0.72	-0.1063	-0.93	-0.0058	-0.02	0.0608	1.15	0.1131	0.65
[c]Stratum 6	0.4705	4.06	-0.1566	-1.72	-0.0905	-0.43	-0.0364	-0.32	0.0016	0.01	0.0074	0.16	0.0927	0.60
Assaults rate	[g]0.0332	1.65	-0.0174	-0.93	-0.0211	-0.93	-0.0120	-0.59	-0.0119	-0.47	0.0061	0.75	0.0102	0.74
[c]Stratum 2	0.0141	0.23	0.0106	0.39	0.0025	0.09	-0.0006	-0.02	-0.0055	-0.20	0.0029	0.29	0.0066	0.53
[c]Stratum 3	0.1020	2.70	-0.0135	-0.67	0.0006	0.01	-0.0196	-0.86	0.0173	0.34	-0.0111	-1.22	-0.0019	-0.06
[c]Stratum 4	-0.0150	-0.45	0.0021	0.10	0.0069	0.33	-0.0188	-0.82	-0.0146	-0.63	-0.0119	-0.95	-0.0161	-1.18
[c]Stratum 5	-0.0152	-0.45	0.0035	0.13	0.0079	0.33	0.0210	0.80	0.0280	1.09	0.0045	0.26	0.0000	0.00
[c]Stratum 6	-0.0367	-1.28	0.0023	0.10	0.0109	0.41	0.0131	0.54	-0.0013	-0.04	-0.0033	-0.22	-0.0050	-0.23
Residential and commercial assault rate	[g]0.2908	5.96	0.0358	0.58	-0.0194	-0.13	0.0262	0.41	0.0210	0.13	-0.0093	-0.53	0.0253	0.27
[c]Stratum 2	0.0164	0.16	0.0414	0.60	0.0134	0.13	0.0478	0.68	0.0217	0.20	0.0239	0.94	0.0372	0.91
[c]Stratum 3	-0.2549	-3.18	-0.0275	-0.44	0.0297	0.22	-0.0094	-0.15	0.0060	0.04	0.0202	1.06	-0.0111	-0.13
[c]Stratum 4	-0.2107	-4.12	0.0156	0.26	0.0706	0.59	0.0420	0.67	0.0700	0.54	0.0254	1.29	-0.0049	-0.07
[c]Stratum 5	-0.2774	-5.14	0.0192	0.28	0.0775	0.54	0.0011	0.02	0.0109	0.07	-0.0052	-0.21	-0.0385	-0.42
[c]Stratum 6	-0.2890	-4.29	-0.0487	-0.69	-0.1159	-0.76	-0.0803	-0.90	-0.0716	-0.42	0.0287	0.82	-0.0647	-0.63
Cars theft rate	[g]-0.0655	-3.14	-0.0006	-0.04	0.0202	0.54	0.0109	0.47	0.0225	0.56	0.0125	1.32	0.0036	0.15
[c]Stratum 2	-0.1964	-2.94	-0.0398	-1.09	0.0060	0.07	-0.0453	-1.13	-0.0331	-0.35	-0.0184	-0.98	-0.0497	-0.77
[c]Stratum 3	-0.0098	-0.27	0.0083	0.43	-0.0189	-0.68	-0.0083	-0.34	-0.0413	-1.44	-0.0084	-0.83	-0.0067	-0.46
[c]Stratum 4	0.0229	0.72	-0.0003	-0.01	-0.0218	-0.76	-0.0042	-0.16	-0.0275	-0.91	-0.0155	-1.20	-0.0088	-0.52
[c]Stratum 5	0.0048	0.08	-0.0094	-0.30	-0.0348	-1.05	-0.0437	-1.26	-0.0735	-2.08	-0.0028	-0.14	0.0017	0.08
[c]Stratum 6	0.1320	2.77	0.0602	2.12	0.1769	2.31	0.0359	0.97	0.1053	1.29	-0.0334		0.0422	0.77
Homicide rate	[g]		-0.1541	-2.57	0.0261	0.06	-0.1335	-1.93	-0.1050	-0.21	0.0061	0.20	-0.1157	-0.36
[c]Stratum 2			0.1281	1.71	0.1469	0.64	0.1141	1.34	0.1106	0.44	0.0160	0.47	-0.0054	-0.06
[c]Stratum 3			0.1249	1.99	-0.1129	-0.65	0.1084	1.53	-0.1752	-0.92	-0.0198	-0.63	0.0031	0.04
[c]Stratum 4			0.0452	0.47	-0.1160	-0.58	0.0422	0.40	-0.2800	-1.33	-0.0395	-0.76	0.0517	0.51
[c]Stratum 5			-0.1817	-0.85	-0.4501	-2.14	-0.1569	-0.76	-0.3674	-1.60	-0.0673	-0.37	-0.0956	-0.55
[c]Stratum 6			0.7461	2.64	-1.1070	-2.63	0.0634	0.19	-0.7913	-1.91	0.9072	4.25	0.2016	0.78

(continued)

Table 3.3 (continued)

Variable	Homicide rate (1st stage) Coefficient	t	Ln house price[a] OLS Coefficient	t	Ln house price[a] 2SLS Coefficient	t	Ln house price[b] OLS Coefficient	t	Ln house price[b] 2SLS Coefficient	t	Ln house rent OLS Coefficient	t	Ln house rent 2SLS Coefficient	t
Attacks of FARC, ELN, or other groups[d]	[g]-0.0443	-0.60	-0.0064	-0.19	-0.0027	-0.07	0.0175	0.46	0.0098	0.23	-0.0171	-0.85	-0.0213	-0.89
Number of CAIS[f]	0.0528	0.33	-0.1519	-1.88	-0.1384	-1.57	-0.1614	-1.42	-0.0931	-0.73	0.0093	0.18	0.0151	0.28
[c]Stratum 2	0.0052	0.03	0.1831	2.06	0.1647	1.74	0.1965	1.61	0.1349	1.00	0.0204	0.38	0.0222	0.40
[c]Stratum 3	-0.0588	-0.34	0.1732	2.12	0.1607	1.80	0.1784	1.56	0.1093	0.85	0.0024	0.04	-0.0042	-0.07
[c]Stratum 4	-0.1729	-0.91	0.1726	1.94	0.1558	1.32	0.1852	1.53	0.0799	0.54	-0.0128	-0.22	-0.0235	-0.31
[c]Stratum 5	-0.0201	-0.11	0.1765	1.83	0.1676	1.77	0.1629	1.29	0.0923	0.68	-0.0201	-0.33	-0.0136	-0.22
[c]Stratum 6	-0.0615	-0.35	0.3128	3.46	0.3226	3.29	0.2461	1.79	0.1667	1.15	0.0995	1.61	0.1040	1.68
Number of police headquarters	0.0661	0.61	0.0731	1.54	0.0793	1.51	0.0896	1.57	0.1153	1.85	0.0380	2.99	0.0363	1.43
Number of local security funds	[g]-0.0037	-1.05	0.0019	1.42	0.0016	0.85	0.0023	1.50	0.0013	0.60	0.0007	1.06	0.0003	0.19
Number of prisons	[e]0.2143	0.80	0.0230	0.82	0.0165	0.18	0.0246	0.73	0.0734	0.73	0.0060	0.28	0.0221	0.31
Number of attacks against life	[g]-0.0041	0.08	-0.0332	-1.95	-0.0349	-2.02	-0.0569	-2.99	-0.0576	-2.98	-0.0076	-0.81	-0.0068	-0.73
Number of attacks against wealth	[e]0.0954	1.63	0.0195	1.20	0.0177	0.43	0.0294	1.62	0.0469	1.02	0.0031	0.37	0.0125	0.41
Number of bars	[g]-0.0093	-0.15	0.0070	0.45	0.0070	0.44	0.0043	0.26	0.0037	0.22	0.0143	1.77	0.0136	1.57
Number of brothels	[g]-0.0817	-1.57	0.0060	0.34	0.0069	0.20	0.0185	0.99	0.0013	0.03	-0.0117	-1.13	-0.0205	-0.78
Number of casinos/places for bets	[e]0.0431	0.70	0.0017	0.09	-0.0042	-0.17	-0.0149	-0.73	-0.0121	-0.45	-0.0061	-0.58	-0.0010	-0.07
Number of places selling drugs/narcotics	[g]-0.0512	-1.09	-0.0330	-2.00	-0.0366	-1.35	-0.0354	-2.03	-0.0487	-1.66	0.0002	0.02	-0.0046	-0.25
Age of mother minus age of oldest child	-0.0017	-2.32												
Constant	4.9914	1.56	13.2273	7.40	12.5977	4.33	13.7531	5.92	14.2756	4.08	9.0278	7.60	9.6076	5.08
Number of observations	12,120		10,290		10,290		8,435		8,435		12,024		12,024	
R²	0.6314		0.6361		0.6357		0.6508		0.6510		0.7017		0.7012	

Sources: Encuesta de Calidad de Vida 2003, Real State Appraisal of Bogotá, National Police-DIJIN 2000, Paz Pública (2000). Colombian 1993 Population Census.

Notes: All regressions include dummy variable of father's and mother's education levels and their interactions. The t-statistics are computed based on robust standard errors corrected by clustering at the census sector level.

a. Cadastral values if available; otherwise, the value reported by households surveyed.
b. Only includes households for which cadastral values are available.
c. Dummy variable equal to one if house, 0 otherwise (apartment, etc.).
d. Attack by guerrilla groups FARC, ELN, or other groups.
e. A-Theoretical estimation of QoL (See methodology in DNP [1997]).
f. Centros de Atención Inmediata, CAIS: Centers of Immediate Police Attention.
g. At the census sector level.

our period of study, and that could allow us to control for time invariant characteristics. In order to account for the endogeneity of our crime variable, we now proceed to present an instrumental variable strategy.

3.4.1 Instrumenting the Crime Rate

In this section, we attempt to identify the capitalization effect of crime on house values and rents by using an instrumental variable approach. As always, finding a good instrument is the key aspect of this approach. In this case, we need a variable that (a) affects the decision of the household to live in a neighborhood with a determined crime rate, and (b) does not affect the value or rent of the house in a direct fashion.

We use as instruments two variables related to the likelihood that the household head (or his spouse) is a teenage mother. Our instrument choice is based on the following rationale: (a) children of teenage mothers are more likely to become criminals; (b) households harboring a teenage mother are more likely to live in neighborhoods with high crime and homicide rates; and (c) house values are not directly affected by teenage mother residence. If the previous rationale is true, then we can argue that our instrument is related to crime or homicide rates but not to the house value or rent.

The first element of our reasoning, namely that children of teenage mothers are more likely to become criminals, is supported by a wealth of evidence. For example, Krug et al. (2002) enumerated, among the many factors associated with violence in youths, the influence of families. These authors enumerate, in turn, parental conflict in early childhood and poor attachment between parents and children among the relevant family variables.[13] Households headed by teenage mothers are likely to be characterized by a family environment that includes all said factors. Furthermore, Krug et al. (2002) mention "a mother who had her first child at an early age" and "a low level of family cohesion" as important risk factors. In the same vein, Donohue and Levitt (2000) provide indirect evidence, for the United States, to the effect that children being born out of unwanted pregnancies are more likely to become criminals, and in particular, violent offenders. Hunt (2003) provides evidence, also for the United States, that children of teenagers are more likely to commit assaults later in their lives.

If children of teenage mothers are more likely to become criminals and their households are more likely to be poor, then it seems reasonable to expect that these households will sort themselves out in neighborhoods where youth crime is high. These high levels of crime tend to reinforce themselves through social interactions (another risk factor cited by Krug et al. 2002). Again, teenage mothers are more likely to inhabit a neighborhood

---

13. Other studies supporting the relationship between teenage motherhood and their children's likelihood to commit crime in the future are Farrington (1998), Morash (1989), and Nagin, Pogarsky, and Farrington (1997).

with high crime and homicide rates. Of course, one could argue that teenage motherhood is related to socioeconomic level. But the point is that teen pregnancies should be related to violent crime rates even after controlling for several socioeconomic status variables.

As proxy variables for teenage mothers in a household or neighborhood, we use the difference between the age of the spouse of the household (or alternatively the age of the head where the household is female-headed) and her oldest coresiding child. This variable is equal to the age of the woman at the time of her first childbearing, when all the children live in their respective households at the moment of the survey; otherwise, the variable in question would be an upper bound of the age at each woman's first childbearing. We also use the share of mothers between age thirteen and nineteen in all populations of that age range in their respective census sector population.[14]

Figure 3.4 shows the distribution of the variables we use as instruments. Nearly 13 percent of households have a child that was born when his or her mother was between thirteen and nineteen years old. The median of the share of young mothers is 0.07, and about 14 percent of young women are mothers. The average age difference between the mother and the oldest children at home is twenty-five, conditional on having at least one child at home; the unconditional mean is 17 (see table 3.1).

Map 3.3 shows the quintiles of the homicide rate, and of the proxy variables used as instruments: the age difference between the oldest child and his or her mother, and the share of teenage mothers in the relevant census sector (quintiles are also used). As expected, the age difference variable is negatively correlated to the share of teenage mothers in the census sector. There is a high spatial correlation between the age difference and the share of teenage mothers in the census sector, and between these two variables and the quintiles of the homicide rate.

To assess the existence of spatial correlation we compute local Moran I_i estimates by census sector for the three variables shown in map 3.3.[15] When

---

14. Note that if women were exactly half the population in each census sector, the share of mothers between age thirteen and nineteen on total number of women in that age range would be twice as large.

15. The *local Moran index* is used to identify spatial clusters and it is defined as

$$I_i = \frac{Z_i}{\sum_i Z_i^2/N} \sum_{j \in J_i} W_{ij} Z_j.$$

Where $Z = [I - E(I)]/[V(I)]1/2 \sim N(0,1)$, and is the *Moran index*

$$I = \frac{N}{S_0} \frac{\sum_{ij}^N W_{ij}(x_i - \overline{x})(x_j - \overline{x})}{\sum_{i=1}^N (x_i - \overline{x})^2},$$

where x_i is the variable of interest on which we are interested to test spatial correlation, W_{ij} is a matrix of weights, and $S_0 = \sum_i \sum_j W_{ij}$. Matrix W will be defined depending of the variable of interest, using immediate neighbors with their respective neighbors. Positive (negative) values of the I_i index imply the existence of similar (different) values of the phenomenon of interest around area i.

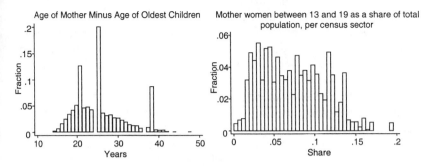

Fig. 3.4   Relative frequencies of instrumental variables

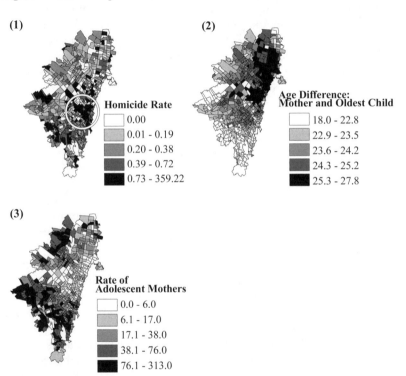

Map 3.3   Quintiles of key variables at the census sector level

constructing the local Moran estimates, we compare the homicide rates at each census sector with those of its neighbors and with those of the neighbors of its neighbors.[16]

According to the results (not reported), there are only a few clusters with high homicide rates in the city, most of them located in downtown Bogotá

16. See Ansellin (1988) and Moran (1948).

(around the circled area shown in map 3.3). On the other hand, we find that there is a wide area in the north of the city that exhibits a very low homicide rate. Finally, we find evidence that allows us to confirm that the southern part of the city is characterized by clusters of women having children at a much younger age and also by a high incidence of teen pregnancies. The opposite is true for the northeastern area of the city.

We also assess the spatial covariance between our instrumental variables and the homicide rate at the census sector level. Our results (not reported) show that our instrumental variables are significantly correlated to the homicide rate in the south and northeast of the city. Results at the northeast of the city are evident: we find clusters of low homicide rates with high (low) age differences (share of teen mothers), meaning that the homicide rate is negatively (positively) spatially correlated to our first (second) instrument. At the south of the city, we find some clusters of higher homicide rates with low (high) age differences (share of teen mothers), meaning that the homicide rate is spatially correlated to our instruments in some census sectors.

The global spatial autocorrelation is 0.044 (p-value: 0.0302) between the share of teen mothers and the homicide rate, and –0.0254 (p-value: 0.2101) between the age difference and the homicide rate.[17] Finally, it is worth stressing that our choice of instruments is based on the assumption that individuals commit a good part of their crimes in the neighborhoods where they live (i.e., we assume that in a particular neighborhood the residence of criminals is associated with the incidence of crimes).

In short, we find that, in the city of Bogotá, our instrumental variables are spatially correlated with the homicide rate. Since households are spatially segregated according to these variables, we expect them to be correlated with the homicide rate in the census sector. On the other hand, we do not expect the instruments to affect house values directly, since they constitute neither relevant house characteristics nor amenities people care about when deciding where to live. In other words, we assume that the teenage pregnancies in the neighborhood are not likely to be capitalized into house values or rents.

Tables 3.2 and 3.3 present the results of the instrumental variables estimation. Table 3.2 presents the estimation results of a specification that does not incorporate interactions, whereas table 3.3 presents the results of a specification that incorporates interactions between the crime variables and the strata. We will focus on table 3.3. The first column presents the first stage results. These results indicate that our instrument (the age difference) is

---

17. Our $W(\cdot)$ is built using the closest neighbors and their closest neighbors. Results for the share of teen mothers are very robust to the $W(\cdot)$ chosen, although those for the age difference are more sensible. When we perform simple averages among the four closest neighbors the spatial correlations become –0.0526 (p-value: 0.0132) and –0.0310 (p-value: 0.1375) for the spatial correlations between the homicide rate and the share of teen mothers and age difference variables, respectively.

statistically significant, and has the expected negative sign. When we use the combination of cadastral and rental values as the dependent variable, we find that the coefficient of the interactions between the homicide rate and strata 3 and 6 are positive in the OLS regression, whereas the coefficients of the interactions between the homicide rate and strata 5 and 6 are significant and negative in the IV regression. When we use only cadastral data as the dependent variable, we find that the coefficient of the interaction between the homicide rate and stratum 6 becomes significant, and negative. When rental values are used, the results are more erratic, and neither of the interactions is significant in the IV regression.

Table 3.4 summarizes the results of the IV estimations. The upper panel of table 3.4 shows that the elasticity of house values to the homicide rate for houses located in socioeconomic stratum 6 is about –0.90 percent. Put differently, if the homicide rate in stratum 6 were to increase by one standard deviation—an increase of 7.3 times the mean value—house values would fall between 5.8 percent and 7.0 percent. In the case of stratum 5, the elasticity is between –0.23 percent and –0.26 percent, which implies a decrease of between 2.3 percent and 2.5 percent in the value of the house if homicides increase by one standard deviation.

The other crime variables (common theft, assaults, residential and commercial assault rates, attacks by guerilla groups, and attacks against wealth) are not significant in the IV estimation. The car theft variable is negative and significant only for its interaction with stratum 5. Finally, "attempts on a person's life" is negative and statistically significant in almost all specifications.

Finally, table 3.5 presents the results of instrumenting the homicide rate with the share of teenage mothers in the census sector. The first column presents the first stage results, and the other columns the second stage results. The first column shows that the instrument variable is statistically significant, and has the expected positive sign.

Turning now to the effects of the homicide rate on property values, we find that in the IV regression the coefficients of the interactions between the homicide rate and strata 5 and 6 are significant, and negative, when we use either house value. When we use only cadastral values, the coefficients of the interactions with strata 3 to 6 are all significant.

The IV results imply that the elasticity of the house value to homicide rate in socioeconomic stratum 6 is between –0.8 percent and –0.95 percent. That is, if the homicide rate in stratum 6 were to increase by one standard deviation, house values would fall between 5.8 percent and 6.9 percent. In the case of strata 3, 4, and 5, the elasticites are –6.9 percent, –0.72 percent, and –0.26 percent, respectively, which imply a fall of 13.5 percent, 4.4 percent, and 2.5 percent in house values after an increase of one standard deviation in homicide rates. Moving a household formerly living in a particular stratum, from an average neighborhood in that stratum, to one with a homicide

Table 3.4 Summary results of the effects of the homicide rate on house values

			Instrument: Age difference			
Variable	Coefficient	Elasticity	D homicide rate (1st dev)/Homicide rate	D House value/ house value	D House value/monthly hhold per capita income	Amount (USD)[a]
Homicide rate	0.02608	0.0104	1.31	0.014	1.15	112
Results with house values coming from cadastral or self-reported data						
Homicide rate interacted with:						
Stratum 5	−0.45010	−0.0023	9.81	−0.023	−1.49	−1,015
Stratum 6	−1.10701	−0.0096	7.29	−0.070	−3.35	−4,884
Results with house values coming only from cadastral data						
Homicide rate	−0.10497	−0.0420	1.31	−0.055	−4.67	−456
Homicide rate interacted with:						
Stratum 5	−0.36745	−0.0026	9.81	−0.025	−1.59	−1,086
Stratum 6	−0.79130	−0.0080	7.29	−0.058	−2.55	−3,714

Instrument: Share of teenage mothers

Results with house values coming from cadastral or self reported data

Homicide rate	0.11250	0.0450	1.31	0.059	4.96	484
Homicide rate interacted with:						
Stratum 3	-0.25556	-0.0354	1.95	-0.069	-7.70	-1,280
Stratum 4	-0.17383	-0.0011	6.19	-0.007	-0.48	-199
Stratum 5	-0.64121	-0.0029	9.81	-0.028	-1.85	-1,266
Stratum 6	-1.17334	-0.0095	7.29	-0.069	-3.29	-4,793

Results with house values coming only from cadastral data

Homicide rate	-0.10497	-0.0420	1.31	-0.055	-4.63	-452
Homicide rate interacted with:						
Stratum 3	-0.17516	-0.0693	1.95	-0.135	-15.08	-2,507
Stratum 4	-0.28005	-0.0072	6.19	-0.044	-3.02	-1,248
Stratum 5	-0.36745	-0.0026	9.81	-0.025	-1.66	-1,131
Stratum 6	-0.79130	-0.0080	7.29	-0.058	-2.78	-4,049

aThe amount is a once and for all change in the house value due to moving from an average neighborhood to one with a homicide rate one standard deviation higher. The dollar amount estimated was based on the exchange rate in December 2003 ($2,778.2/USD).

Table 3.5 Hedonic regression for Bogotá (Instrument: Share of teenage mothers in census sector)

Variable	Homicide rate Coefficient	t	Ln house price[a] OLS Coefficient	t	Ln house price[a] 2SLS Coefficient	t	Ln house price[b] OLS Coefficient	t	Ln house price[b] 2SLS Coefficient	t	Ln house rent OLS Coefficient	t	Ln house rent 2SLS Coefficient	t
Cadastral value	0.0152	0.73	-0.114	-5.54	-0.112	-5.40	0.043	0.87	0.042	0.85	-0.0232	-2.15	-0.0234	-2.17
You feel safe in your neighborhood	-0.022	-0.55	0.054	1.21	0.057	1.29					-0.009	-0.35	-0.007	-0.26
[s]Stratum 2	-0.020	-0.49	-0.041	-0.80	-0.040	-0.79	-0.017	-0.30	-0.011	-0.19	-0.018	-0.54	-0.020	-0.59
[s]Stratum 3	-0.038	-0.85	-0.063	-1.32	-0.072	-1.52	-0.063	-1.20	-0.068	-1.29	-0.016	-0.53	-0.017	-0.57
[s]Stratum 4	-0.0003	-0.01	-0.073	-1.48	-0.074	-1.51	-0.064	-1.15	-0.065	-1.17	0.026	0.67	0.025	0.67
[s]Stratum 5	0.048	1.01	-0.111	-1.57	-0.109	-1.57	-0.121	-1.77	-0.118	-1.71	0.038	0.82	0.035	0.75
[s]Stratum 6	0.042	0.86	-0.081	-0.91	-0.062	-0.72	-0.074	-1.12	-0.048	-0.74	-0.087	-1.50	-0.084	-1.45
Objects theft rate	[g]-0.542	-3.53	0.089	1.02	0.109	0.88	0.067	0.69	0.103	0.78	-0.069	-1.77	-0.059	-0.98
[s]Stratum 2	0.661	2.15	-0.054	-0.34	-0.084	-0.46	-0.020	-0.12	-0.074	-0.39	0.020	0.31	0.009	0.11
[s]Stratum 3	0.432	1.83	-0.065	-0.72	-0.096	-0.83	-0.044	-0.44	-0.093	-0.74	0.054	1.36	0.044	0.80
[s]Stratum 4	0.539	3.41	-0.123	-1.36	-0.145	-1.16	-0.111	-1.13	-0.142	-1.06	0.068	1.56	0.054	0.88
[s]Stratum 5	0.552	3.30	-0.167	-1.56	-0.188	-1.41	-0.106	-0.93	-0.142	-1.01	0.061	1.15	0.048	0.71
[s]Stratum 6	0.503	4.09	-0.157	-1.72	-0.106	-0.87	-0.036	-0.32	-0.135	-0.95	0.007	0.16	0.035	0.53
Assaults rate	[g]0.031	1.37	-0.017	-0.93	-0.027	-1.61	-0.012	-0.59	-0.025	-1.34	0.006	0.75	0.004	0.39
[s]Stratum 2	0.027	0.49	0.011	0.39	0.014	0.56	-0.001	-0.02	0.002	0.08	0.003	0.29	0.004	0.34
[s]Stratum 3	0.094	2.53	-0.014	-0.67	0.014	0.56	-0.020	-0.86	0.010	0.38	-0.011	-1.22	-0.010	-0.78
[s]Stratum 4	-0.014	-0.42	0.002	0.10	0.012	0.61	-0.019	-0.82	-0.007	-0.33	-0.012	-0.95	-0.012	-0.92
[s]Stratum 5	-0.018	-0.53	0.003	0.13	0.009	0.42	0.021	0.80	0.030	1.30	0.005	0.26	0.003	0.16
[s]Stratum 6	-0.031	-1.06	0.002	0.10	0.018	0.80	0.013	0.54	0.010	0.43	-0.003	-0.22	0.002	0.09
Residential and commercial assault rate	[g]0.298	5.20	0.036	0.58	-0.049	-0.53	0.026	0.41	-0.084	-0.90	-0.009	-0.53	-0.016	-0.49
[s]Stratum 2	-0.0397	-0.40	0.041	0.60	0.081	0.80	0.048	0.68	0.097	0.94	0.024	0.94	0.017	0.48
[s]Stratum 3	-0.258	-3.04	-0.027	-0.44	0.061	0.68	-0.009	-0.15	0.105	1.17	0.020	1.06	0.026	0.83
[s]Stratum 4	-0.213	-3.71	0.016	0.26	0.099	1.19	0.042	0.67	0.160	1.88	0.025	1.29	0.027	0.88
[s]Stratum 5	-0.300	-4.91	0.019	0.28	0.108	1.15	0.001	0.02	0.116	1.23	-0.005	-0.21	0.002	0.07
[s]Stratum 6	-0.319	-4.34	-0.049	-0.69	-0.087	-0.86	-0.080	-0.90	0.040	0.36	0.029	0.82	-0.022	-0.42
Cars theft rate	[g]-0.072	-3.03	-0.001	-0.04	0.033	1.32	0.011	0.47	0.054	2.12	0.013	1.32	0.013	1.05
[s]Stratum 2	-0.207	-3.12	-0.040	-1.09	-0.038	-0.61	-0.045	-1.13	-0.037	-0.59	-0.018	-0.98	-0.009	-0.29
[s]Stratum 3	0.003	0.08	0.008	0.43	-0.036	-1.42	-0.008	-0.34	-0.061	-2.36	-0.008	-0.83	-0.008	-0.67
[s]Stratum 4	0.024	0.75	0.000	-0.01	-0.034	-1.36	-0.004	-0.16	-0.049	-1.93	-0.016	-1.20	-0.013	-0.92
[s]Stratum 5	0.017	0.28	-0.009	-0.30	-0.044	-1.44	-0.044	-1.26	-0.089	-2.76	-0.003	-0.14	0.000	0.02
[s]Stratum 6	0.149	3.18	0.060	2.12	0.162	2.77	0.036	0.97	0.073	1.32	-0.033	-1.43	0.024	0.66

Variable	(1) coef	(1) t	(2) coef	(2) t	(3) coef	(3) t	(4) coef	(4) t	(5) coef	(5) t	(6) coef	(6) t	(7) coef	(7) t
Homicide rate [g]			-0.154	-2.57	0.112	0.60	-0.134	-1.93	0.238	1.16	0.006	0.20	0.041	0.23
[g]Stratum 2			0.128	1.71	-0.044	-0.22	0.114	1.34	-0.119	-0.53	0.016	0.47	0.019	
[g]Stratum 3			0.125	1.99	-0.256	-1.72	0.108	1.53	-0.373	-2.23	-0.020	-0.63	-0.042	-0.60
[g]Stratum 4			0.045	0.47	-0.174	-0.98	0.042	0.40	-0.415	-2.18	-0.039	-0.76	0.016	0.17
[g]Stratum 5			-0.182	-0.85	-0.641	-3.22	-0.157	-0.76	-0.648	-2.84	-0.067	-0.37	-0.178	-1.00
[g]Stratum 6			0.746	2.64	-1.173	-2.73	0.063	0.19	-1.174	-2.67	0.907	4.25	0.178	0.71
Attacks of FARC, ELN, or other groups	[g]-0.016	-0.21	-0.0064	-0.19	-0.0042	-0.12	0.0175	0.46	0.0184	0.47	-0.0171	-0.85	-0.0137	-0.68
Number of CAIS[f]	0.019	0.11	-0.1519	-1.88	-0.1408	-1.55	-0.1614	-1.42	-0.0760	-0.53	0.0093	0.18	-0.0121	-0.23
[g]Stratum 2	0.027	0.16	0.1831	2.06	0.1715	1.74	0.1965	1.61	0.1098	0.74	0.0204	0.38	0.0409	0.77
[g]Stratum 3	-0.039	-0.21	0.1732	2.12	0.1628	1.78	0.1784	1.56	0.0927	0.64	0.0024	0.04	0.0241	0.46
[g]Stratum 4	-0.141	-0.70	0.1726	1.94	0.1621	1.61	0.1852	1.53	0.0882	0.59	-0.0128	-0.22	0.0184	0.32
[g]Stratum 5	0.039	0.20	0.1765	1.83	0.1859	1.88	0.1629	1.29	0.0907	0.61	-0.0201	-0.33	0.0157	0.25
[g]Stratum 6	0.009	0.05	0.3128	3.46	0.3217	3.21	0.2461	1.79	0.1377	0.87	0.0995	1.61	0.1316	2.24
Number of police headquarters	0.047	0.48	0.0731	1.54	0.0768	1.70	0.0896	1.57	0.1017	1.88	0.0380	2.99	0.0275	1.84
Local security funds	[g]-0.004	-1.01	0.0019	1.42	0.0014	0.97	0.0023	1.50	0.0018	1.16	0.0007	1.06	0.0007	0.97
Prisons	[g]0.213	0.79	0.0230	0.82	0.0238	0.51	0.0246	0.73	0.0405	0.82	0.0060	0.28	-0.0042	-0.15
Attacks against life	[g]0.002	0.03	-0.0332	-1.95	-0.0335	-1.93	-0.0569	-2.99	-0.0572	-2.96	-0.0076	-0.81	-0.0079	-0.85
Attacks against wealth	[g]0.089	1.50	0.0195	1.20	0.0200	0.93	0.0294	1.62	0.0291	1.26	0.0031	0.37	0.0015	0.14
Bars	[g]0.003	0.04	0.0070	0.45	0.0091	0.59	0.0043	0.26	0.0079	0.48	0.0143	1.77	0.0150	1.82
Brothels	[g]-0.083	-1.60	0.0060	0.34	0.0014	0.06	0.0185	0.99	0.0123	0.50	-0.0117	-1.13	-0.0107	-0.86
Casinos/places for bets	[g]0.043	0.72	0.0017	0.09	-0.0033	-0.16	-0.0149	-0.73	-0.0205	-0.96	-0.0061	-0.58	-0.0078	-0.71
Places selling drugs/narcotics	[g]-0.050	-1.09	-0.0330	-2.00	-0.0393	-2.38	-0.0354	-2.03	-0.0408	-2.39	0.0002	0.02	0.0008	0.08
Share of teenage mothers in census sector	5.892	2.43												
Constant	5.725	1.44	13.2273	7.40	12.1418	5.68	13.7531	5.92	12.2925	4.59	8.9398	7.32	9.5284	7.17
Number of observations	12,111		10,290		10,281		8,435		8,428		12,024		12,015	
R²	0.6382		0.6361		0.6348		0.6508		0.6499		0.7017		0.7011	

Sources: Encuesta de Calidad de Vida 2003, Real State Appraisal of Bogotá, National Police-DIJIN 2000, Paz Pública (2000). Colombian 1993 Population Census.

Notes: All regressions include dummy variable of father and mother's education levels and their interactions. The t-statistics are computed based on robust standard errors corrected by clustering at the census sector level.

[a] Cadastral values if available; otherwise, the value reported by households surveyed.

[b] Only includes households for which cadastral values are available.

[c] Dummy variable equal to one if house, zero otherwise (apartment, etc.).

[d] Attacks by guerrilla groups FARC, ELN, or other groups.

[e] A-Theoretical estimation of QoL. (See methodology in DNP [1997]).

[f] Centros de Atención Inmediata, CAIS: Centers of Immediate Police Attention.

[g] At the census sector level.

rate one standard deviation higher in the same stratum, would allow it to move to a house whose value would be lower in a magnitude equivalent to between 2.5 and 3.4 times its monthly per capita income, or saving for once between $3,700 and $4,900. The same figure for a stratum 5 household would be between 1.5 and 1.85 of its monthly per capita income, or between $1,015 and $1,266. Results for the other variables were very similar to those obtained when the age difference was the instrument of choice.

3.5   Conclusion

In this chapter, we use hedonic price models to estimate the value households located in the city of Bogotá (Colombia) are willing to pay to avoid crime, and in particular, to avoid high homicides rates. We find that households living in the highest socioeconomic stratum (stratum 6) are willing to pay up to 7.0 percent of their house values to avoid an increase of the homicide rate in one standard deviation. Households in stratum 5 are willing to pay up to 2.8 percent of their house values, and those in stratum 4 up to 4.4 percent.

The results reveal the willingness to pay for security by households in Bogotá, and, additionally, reveal the emergence of urban private markets that auction security. These markets imply different levels of access to public goods among the population, and, in fact, the exclusion of the poorest. We find, as well, evidence of negative capitalization of aggravated assaults, and of positive capitalization of the presence of police authority in the form of Centers of Immediate Attention (CAIs).

References

Ansellin, L. 1988. Spatial econometrics methods and models. University of California, Santa Barbara: Kluwer Academic Publishers.

Atkinson, G., A. Healey, and S. Mourato. 2005. Valuing the costs of violent crime: A stated preference approach. *Oxford Economic Papers* 57 (4): 559–85.

Badel, M. 1999. La violencia de los años noventa en Colombia: Su evolución en las grandes ciudades y costos económicos directos. Informe de Consultoría DNP-UPRU, Santafé de Bogotá D.C.

Blomquist, G. C., Berger, M. C., and J. P. Hoehn. 1988. New estimates of quality of life in urban areas. *American Economic Review* 78 (1): 89–107.

Cohen, M., R. Rust, S. Steen, and S. T. Tidd. 2004. Willingness to pay for crime control programs. *Criminology* 42 (1): 86–106.

Cohen, M., and M. Rubio. 2007. Violence and crime in Latin America. Solution paper, Copenhagen Consensus and InterAmerican Development Bank. San José, Costa Rica.

Cook, P. J., and J. Ludwig. 2000. *Gun violence: The real costs.* New York: Oxford University Press.

Departamento Nacional de Planeación (DNP). 1997. Índice de condiciones de vida urbano-rural. Misión Social.

Donohue, J. J., and S. D. Levitt. 2000. The impact of legalized abortion on crime. NBER Working Paper no. 8004. Cambridge, MA: National Bureau of Economic Research, November.

Fajnzylber, P., D. Lederman, and N. Loayza. 1998. Determinants of crime rates in Latin America and the world: An empirical assessment. Washington, DC: World Bank.

———. 2000. Crime and victimization: An economic perspective. *Economia* 1 (1): 219–78.

———. 2002a. Inequality and violent crime. *Journal of Law and Economics* 45 (April): 1–40.

———. 2002b. What causes violent crime? *European Economic Review* 46 (7): 1323–357.

Farrington, D. P. 1998. Predictors, causes, and correlates of male youth violence. In *Youth violence,* ed. M. Tonry and M. H. Moore, 421–75. Chicago: University of Chicago Press.

Gavira, A., and C. E. Vélez. 2001. Who bears the burden of crime in Colombia? Informes de investigacíon no. 003776. Fedesarrollo, Bogotá, Colombia.

Gyourko, J., M. Kahn, and J. Tracy. 1999. Quality of life and environmental comparisons. In *Handbook of regional and urban economics, volume 3,* ed. P. Cheshire and E. Mills, 1413–54. New York: North-Holland.

Gyourko, J., and J. Tracy. 1991. The structure of local public finance and the quality of life. *The Journal of Political Economy* 99 (4): 774–806.

Heinemann, A., and D. Verner. 2006. Crime and violence in development: A literature review of Latin American and Caribbean. World Bank Policy Research Working Paper no. 4041, October.

Hunt, J. 2003. Teen births keep American crime high. NBER Working Paper no. 9632. Cambridge, MA: National Bureau of Economic Research, April.

Krug, E. G., L. L. Dahlberg, J. A. Mercy, A. B. Zwi, and R. Lozano. 2002. *World report on violence and health.* Geneva: World Health Organization.

Llorente, M. V., R. Escobedo, C. Echandía, and M. Rubio. 2001. Violencia homicida en Bogotá: Más que intolerancia. Documento CEDE, Universidad de los Andes no. 2001-04.

Llorente, M. V., and A. Rivas. 2005. La Caída del Crimen en Bogotá: Una Década de Políticas de Seguridad Ciudadana. Serie *Documentos de Buenas Prácticas SDS/SOC.*

Londoño, J. L., and R. Guerrero. 2000. *Violencia en América Latina: Epidemiología y costos.* Inter-American Development Bank.

Ludwig, J., and P. J. Cook. 2001. The benefits of reducing gun violence: Evidence from contingent-valuation survey data. *Journal of Risk and Uncertainty* 22 (3): 207–26.

Medina, C., L. Morales, and J. Núñez. 2008. Quality of life in urban neighborhoods: The case of Bogotá. Borradores de Economía no. 536, November. Banco de la Republica de Colombia.

Moran, P. 1948. The interpretation of statistical maps. *Journal of the Royal Statistical Society* B 10: 243–51.

Morash, M., and L. Rucker. 1989. An exploratory study of the connection of mother's age at childbearing to her children's delinquency in four data sets. *Crime and Delinquency* 35 (January): 45–93.

Nagin, D. S., G. Pogarsky, and D. P. Farrington. 1997. Adolescent mothers and the criminal behavior of their children. *Law and Society Review* 31 (11): 137–62.

Núñez, J., and F. Sánchez. 2001. Interrelaciones espaciales en los delitos contra el patrimonio en Bogota. Mimeo.

Paz Pública. 2000. Escenarios del crimen en los barrios y localidades de Bogotá. Investigación "Caracterización de la Violencia Homicida en Bogotá," Documento de Trabajo no. 1. Bogotá: Paz Pública-CEDE-UNIANDES and Alcaldía de Bogotá (Colombian Economics Congress).

Roback, J. 1982. Wages, rents, and the quality of life. *Journal of Political Economy* 90 (6): 1257–78.

———. 1988. Wages, rents, and amenities: Differences among workers and regions. *Economic Inquiry* 26 (January): 23–41.

Rosen, S. 1974. Hedonic prices and implicit markets: Product differentiation in pure competition. *Journal of Political Economy* 82 (January/February): 34–55.

———. 1979. Wage-based indexes of urban quality of life. In *Current issues in urban economics,* ed. P. Mieszkowski and M. Straszheim. Baltimore: Johns Hopkins University Press.

———. 2002. Markets and diversity. *The American Economic Review* 92 (1): 1–15.

Sanchez, F., and J. Núñez. 2000. Determinantes del crimen violento en un país altamente violento: el caso de Colombia. Mimeo, Universidad de los Andes, Bogotá.

Thaler, R., and S. Rosen. 1976. The value of saving a life: Evidence from the labor market. In *Household production and consumption,* ed. N. E. Terleckyj, 265–302. Chicago: University of Chicago Press.

Trujillo, E., and M. E. Badel. 1998. Los Costos Económicos de la Criminalidad y la Violencia en Colombia: 1991–1996. Archivos de Economía, Departmento Nacional de Planeación, Marzo.

Comment   Alfredo Canavese

The chapter by Gaviria, Medina, Morales, and Núñez uses an econometric model with hedonic prices to estimate the value households are willing to pay to avoid crime in Bogotá. They find that households living in the highest socioeconomic stratum are paying up to 7.2 percent of their house values to keep their average homicide rates constant and households living in the next stratum of richest population in the city would be paying up to 2.4 percent of their house values for the same purpose. They write, "The result reveals the willingness to pay for security by households in Bogotá, and additionally, reveals that a supposed pure public good like security ends up propitiating urban private markets that auction security. These markets imply different levels of access to public goods among the population, and actually, the exclusion of the poorest."

The purpose of this comment is to build a very simple model to make

Alfredo Canavese was a professor at the Universidad Torcuato Di Tella. His lectures illuminated several generations of Argentine economists at the Universidad de Buenos Aires and Universidad Torcuato Di Tella.

clear what the authors are measuring. The model will also help to point out that security is not a pure public good and to understand how inconvenient it is to treat it as such.

Let us assume that the representative inhabitant of Bogotá is a quasilinear consumer whose utility function is $u = v(q) + s$ where q is the quantity demanded of housing (an index of square meters plus living equipment) and s is the quantity consumed of all other goods (measured as a quantity of money). The price of housing is p, there is a probability π that a fraction A of q is stolen. The probability π depends negatively on the level (units) of security per square meter bought x, which cost c per unit. The consumer problem, whose income is m, is to find the values of q and x that solve

(1) $$\text{max. } u = v(q) + s$$

(2) $$\text{s.t. } pq + s + \pi(x)Aq + cxq = m.$$

There is a firm producing housing in a perfect competition market. The production cost C depends on the production level. The firm solves

(3) $$\text{max. } B = pq - C(q)$$

for q.

There are several settings in which the relationship between consumer and firm can be studied. First, I will present the Pareto efficient solution, then the private solutions to end with the study of the public good solution.

To find the Pareto efficient levels for q and x the problem

(4) $$\text{max. } u = v(q) + m - pq - \pi(x)Aq - cxq$$

(5) $$\text{s.t. } \overline{B} = pq - C(q)$$

must be solved. It is equivalent to find the solution for

(6) $$\text{max. } u = v(q) + m - \overline{B} - C(q) - \pi(x)Aq - cxq.$$

First-order conditions for equation (6) imply that x and q should satisfy

(7) $$c = -\frac{d\pi}{dx} A$$

and

(8) $$\frac{dv}{dq} - \pi(x)A = \frac{dC}{dq} + cx.$$

Equation (7) can be solved for x and then, introducing that value of x into equation (8), q is found. The Pareto efficient values x^e and q^e result from (7) and (8). As it is usual, they require equalization of marginal cost and marginal revenue—as in equation (7)—and marginal utility and marginal cost—as in equation (8). By the way, equation (8) shows clearly how harmful crime is for society: marginal cost of production for q increases by cx

and marginal utility of consumption decreases by $\pi(x)A$: both supply and demand drop when compared with the case in which crime does not exist.

In the private solution the firm supplies q and also x as amenities (together with q as it is assumed in the chapter). The demand function for q is obtained from

(9) $$\text{max. } u = v(q) + s$$

(10) $$\text{s.t. } pq + s + \pi(x)Aq = m$$

and it is

(11) $$p^d = \frac{dv}{dq} - \pi(x)A,$$

where p^d is the reservation price. The supply function for q comes from the solution for

(12) $$\text{max. } B = pq - C(q) - cxq,$$

and it is

(13) $$p^s = \frac{dC}{dq} + cx$$

where p^s is the supply price. Equations (12) and (13) show that demand and supply for q depend on amenities provided (x). The changes in reservation and supply prices for q when the level of amenities changes are derived from equations (12) and (13) and they are

(14) $$\frac{dp^d}{dx} = -\frac{d\pi}{dx} A$$

and

(15) $$\frac{dp^s}{dx} = c.$$

I understand that the coefficient a_2 of equation (1) of the chapter measures equation (14) and that it represents the main result reported. Equations (14) and (15) show how the level of amenities provided with housing is determined: whenever $-d\pi/dx \, A$ is higher (lower) than c, the change in the level of p^d that consumers are willing to pay for a new unit of security provided as an amenity in housing is higher (lower) than the marginal cost that the firm requires to supply it and so amenities provided with housing increase (decrease); the process stops when the level of amenities provided with housing is such that $c = -d\pi/dx \, A$. Besides, the working of the market forces make $p^d = p^s$ for housing. Equations (7) and (8) are satisfied and the market solution is Pareto efficient. Security supplied as a private good (in the form of amenities) together with housing is efficient.

In the "public good setting" security is supplied by a public agency financed by a tax levied on housing values in such a way that $tpq = cxq$, where t is the tax rate. The Pareto solution in this case must satisfy

(16) $\max. u = v(q) + m - pq - \pi(x)Aq - tpq$

(17)   s.t. $\overline{B} = pq - C(q)$

(18) $tpq = cxq,$

and x^e and q^e solve the problem. But those are not the private solutions. Private solutions are obtained from

(19) $\max. u = v(q) + m - pq - \pi(x)Aq - tpq,$

which requires that

(20) $$\frac{\partial u}{\partial q} = \frac{dv}{dq} - p - \pi(x)A - tp = 0$$

and

(21) $$\frac{\partial u}{\partial x} = -\frac{d\pi}{dx}A = 0$$

for the consumer. The firm solves

(22) $\max. B = pq - C(q)$

and makes $p = dC/dq$. The public agency chooses t to fulfill equation (18). The problem is posed by the demand for x as shown in equation (21). The consumer faces a flat t and so asks for a maximum level of x: that level for which an increase in security supplied no longer reduces the probability of suffering a crime so that $-d\pi/dx = 0$. The problem is illustrated in the following figure. The efficient level for x is also the level that minimizes social cost CS

(23) $\min. CS = cx + \pi(x)A$

because $dCS/dx = c + d\pi/dx\, A = 0$ is satisfied by x^e.

In figure 3C.1, cx, $\pi(x)A$, and its sum CS are drawn. The point for which $d\pi/dx = 0$ implies a much higher demand for security levels than x^e. The private solution for the "public good setting" is not Pareto efficient, even if $tp = cx^e$, because it divorces quantities from prices. On top of that, the consumer feels he gets a lower level of security than that he is paying for.

The use of quasilinear preferences does not allow exploring income and wealth effects that are important in the chapter, but assuming that A is higher for richer people than for poor people, it is possible to understand why dp^d/dx is higher for richer agents.

The important conclusion that can be added to the chapter is that security is not a public good and should not be treated as such. It is a private good

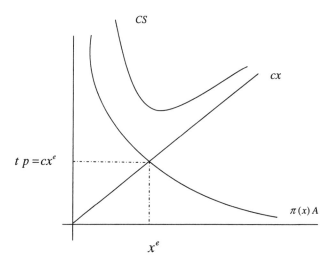

Fig. 3C.1   Market for security

publicly supplied because it has important externalities both positive and negative: a policeman in front of a house discourages crime in the whole block and a private guard in front of the same house displaces crime from it to other houses (perhaps in the same block). But, at the same time, private investment in security by agents belonging to the richer stratum allows public policymakers to displace public security expenditures from richer neighborhoods to poorer ones. The problem is not amenities but public policy. In fact, the chapter supports this conclusion when it says ". . . propitiating urban private markets that auction security. These markets imply different levels of access to *public goods* among the population, and actually, the *exclusion* of the poorest." (Italics are mine.) If exclusion is possible then security is not a public good.

Do Conflicts Create Poverty Traps?
Asset Losses and Recovery for Displaced Households in Colombia

Ana María Ibáñez and Andrés Moya

4.1 Introduction

Internal conflicts may entail large asset losses for certain segments of the civilian population. During internal conflicts, the main victims of war are civilians targeted by armed groups seeking to consolidate territorial strongholds, expand territorial control, and/or seize valuable resources (Azam and Hoefler 2002). Physical assets are destroyed, abandoned, or seized illegally by armed groups (Matowu and Stewart 2001; Brück 2004); financial markets may be disrupted by war activities, and access for particular households may become difficult; also, informal risk-sharing mechanisms are generally undermined. The losses of physical, financial, social, and human capital are therefore substantial.

As a result, internal conflicts may leave a legacy of structural poverty that is difficult to overcome. The recovering of assets after a shock is seldom likely for households located at the lower end of the income distribution, and the negative conditions generated by conflict only serve to aggravate this situation. In addition to the loss of physical assets, victims of conflicts face the possible death of household members, restrictions with respect to financial

Ana María Ibáñez is associate professor of economics at the University of the Andes. Andrés Moya is a PhD student in Agricultural and Resource Economics at the University of California, Davis.

Support from the World Bank, GDN, Microcon, and USAID is gratefully acknowledged. We also express our gratitude to the Colombian Bishop's Conference, Klaus Deininger, Deepa Narayan, Patti Petesch, Pablo Querubin, and Andrea Velásquez. Comments from Martín González Rosada, Sebastian Edwards, Ernesto Schargrodsky, and two anonymous referees, as well as participants in the NBER—LICIP Conference on Crime, Institutions, and Policies, and the 12th LACEA Annual Meeting helped greatly to improve this chapter.

markets, the destruction of social networks, and often insurmountable obstacles to entry into urban labor markets.

The costs of civil conflict often prevail even after peace is achieved. Conflicts congest the law enforcement system, lower the probability of punishment, diffuse criminal knowledge and technology, and erode morals, thus promoting the emergence of criminal and illegal activities (Gaviria 2000). When the conflict ends, criminal violence sometimes soars as the respective destructive technology is now utilized for criminal activities. Guatemala and El Salvador, for example, experienced soaring crime rates after peace agreements were reached (Moser and Winton 2002).

The purpose of this chapter is to analyze how asset losses occur during internal conflicts and the process of asset accumulation following conflict-induced shocks. In order to achieve this objective, we concentrate on a particularly vulnerable group of victims of war—the displaced population in Colombia. Three questions are examined. First, we seek to understand the process and magnitude of asset losses caused by internal conflict. Second, we explore the extent to which the dynamics of the conflict and the purposive targeting by armed units of certain groups within the population determine the magnitude of asset losses caused by forced displacement. Third, we investigate the process of asset recovery by identifying which households are better able to accumulate new assets. In addressing these questions, we rely on the household surveys of 2,322 displaced Colombian households, as well as qualitative studies conducted for the World Bank's "Moving Out of Poverty" Study.

The structure of this chapter is as follows. In the second section, we examine the economic literature for the purposes of understanding how asset holdings shape economic welfare, explaining how households adopt strategies to accumulate and protect assets, and describing how a lack of assets creates poverty traps. The third and fourth sections present the qualitative and quantitative data, and the model and results, respectively. Section five concludes.

4.2   Asset Accumulation Dynamics and Poverty Traps

Standard microeconomic models predict that in the presence of decreasing returns on assets, poor households eventually catch up with wealthier ones in their respective welfare trajectories. Nevertheless, locally increasing returns or exclusionary mechanisms—such as imperfect credit markets—may hinder convergence, and multiple equilibria may arise, restricting some groups to low income trajectories. Where investments are lower due to credit market imperfections, investment indivisibilities, or behavioral components,[1] some economic agents will prove unable to accumulate sufficient

---

1. Mookherjee and Ray (2002) argue that households may not step-up savings due to habit persistence, myopia, or a limited rationality.

asset holdings so as to surpass critical thresholds and thus reach a higher economic trajectory (Galor and Zeira 1993; Durlauf 1992; Mookherjee and Ray 2002; Carter and Barret 2006).

Structural poverty is strongly correlated with initial conditions, such as an insufficient asset base. When returns on small asset holdings are insufficient, income will barely cover subsistence needs, thus leaving a negligible surplus for saving. Although credit is an alternative mechanism for accumulating assets and thus crossing the critical threshold for moving out of poverty, access to credits is often restricted for low income households; this is even more so in developing countries. Sacrificing short-term consumption in order to build up an asset base is also difficult when a household is close to subsistence consumption levels. These constraints may push households into poverty traps, as initial asset inequalities tend to reproduce and deepen themselves over time (Carter and Barret 2006; Zimmermann and Carter 2003; Reardon and Vosti 1995; Rosenzweig and Binswanger 1993).

Aside from determining the ability of households to generate income, assets are an important insurance mechanism for coping with shocks (Little et al. 2006). As a precautionary measure, households often accumulate non-productive assets, which may easily be liquidated when shocks arise (Fafchamps, Udry, and Czukas 1998; Rosenzweig and Wolpin 1993; Corbett 1988). When shocks occur, households rely on nonproductive assets while simultaneously protecting productive assets. The latter are only sold if conditions become extremely harsh, and it becomes absolutely necessary in order to avoid compromising long-term consumption and welfare (Corbett 1988).

Consequently, households usually adopt several strategies to prevent disposing of productive assets during times of crisis. Credit markets often ration out low income households, and insurance mechanisms are generally not sufficient to completely reduce income risks (Townsend 1994; Ligon, Thomas, and Worrall 2001; Foster and Rosenzweig 2001; Fafchamps and Gubert 2007). As a result, households are often compelled to adopt other strategies for protecting assets. A common strategy is to sacrifice short-term consumption in order to avoid the distress sale of assets (Carter and Barret 2006; Hoddinott 2006; Barrett et al. 2004; Zimmermann and Carter 2003). In fact, households tend first to adopt reversible strategies; only as options for mitigating risk become exhausted, strategies that may compromise future consumption—such as forced migration and the sale of land sales—are adopted (Corbett 1988).

Poor households, however, have limited alternatives for protecting assets, which leaves them ill-equipped to cope with shocks, and thus highly prone to falling into poverty traps. In the first place, poor households are near subsistence consumption levels to begin with; reducing consumption in order to build up an asset base hardly constitutes an alternative (Barrett et al. 2004). Additionally, immediate reductions in consumption may imply long-term costs such as school interruption, drops in nutritional status, and reductions in human capital investment, all of which would most likely compromise future consumption (Carter and Barret 2006; Jensen 2000; Jacoby and Skoufias 1997; Foster 1995; Behrman 1988; Corbett 1988). By reducing human capital, depleting physical capital, and/or destroying social capital, shocks may push households into poverty traps. If shocks lead to irreversible asset losses or persist from one period to the next, the negative consequences may become permanent, and income may fall below the critical wealth threshold for several periods (Hoddinott 2006; Dercon 1998).

Longitudinal studies and qualitative evidence show that structural poverty is frequently related to asset deprivation; conversely, the existence of a solid asset base is a strong determinant of upward mobility (Krishna et al. 2006; Adato, Carter, and May 2006; Barrett et al. 2004; Little et al. 2006; Hulme and Shepherd 2003; Barrientos and Shepherd 2003; Sen 2003; Carter and May 1999).

Sociodemographic characteristics, human and social capital, labor markets, and shocks also constitute factors related to structural poverty. By providing support for finding a job, capital for productive activities, and assistance to mitigate crises, social capital facilitates movement out of poverty (Adato, Carter, and May 2006; Barrett et al. 2004; Little et al. 2006). Human capital, paired with access to labor markets, is also an important mechanism for moving ahead, particularly where asset holdings are low. Moreover, investment in human capital allows people to move from low productivity (and low paying) jobs to high productivity ones, thus creating a virtuous cycle (Adato, Carter, and May 2006; Krishna et al. 2006; Barret and McPeak 2006; Barrett et al. 2004; Sen 2003). Lastly, the empirical evidence identifies large shocks as determinants of downward mobility and structural poverty. The death of wage earners, serious illnesses, famines, and civil conflict may push households into structural poverty if the victims are not provided proper aid (Adato, Carter, and May 2006; Hulme and Shepherd 2003; Corbett 1988).

During periods of internal conflict or civil strife, the illegal appropriation, destruction, erosion, and depletion of assets become widespread, generally laying down a legacy of structural poverty for a considerable segment of the population. This in turn may sow the seeds of future conflicts. First, armed groups seize assets from the civilian population for the purposes of financing the war and weakening support among the population for their opponents (Hirshleifer 2001). Added to this, although conflicts may have initially erupted as a consequence of specific grievances, the duration and sustainability of the conflict is greatly determined by the capacity of armed groups to extract rents and appropriate valuable assets from the civilian population. Consequently, the loss of physical capital, especially land, during conflicts can sometimes be substantial (Engel and Ibáñez 2007; Matowu and Stewart 2001; André and Platteau 1998). Second, inasmuch as the civilian population is targeted by armed groups, household disintegration—caused by the death and forced recruitment of household members—becomes widespread; this translates into large losses in human capital. In addition, since some households are forced to migrate from urban to rural areas, returns on their human capital—that is, knowledge related to agricultural production—deteriorates significantly. Third, conflicts severely disrupt formal and informal risk-sharing mechanisms; access to financial markets decreases, informal lending plummets, and links to social networks are weakened. Consequently, the victims of internal conflict are more likely to fall into chronic poverty (Justino and Verwimp 2006).

4.3 Civil Conflict, Crime, and Forced Displacement in Colombia

This section presents a brief history of civil conflict in Colombia, its relation to crime, and a description of the data. Civil conflict in Colombia was triggered toward the end of the early 1960s by the emergence of several left-wing guerrilla groups—the Revolutionary Armed Forces of Colombia (FARC), National Liberation Army (ELN), and People's Revolutionary Army (ERP). Guerrilla-related violence intensified during the late 1970s and early 1980s with the appearance of illegal marijuana and coca drug crops. Illicit drug trade provided rebel groups with massive resources, and has fueled the conflict ever since. These resources also funded the creation of right-wing paramilitary groups with ties to drug barons and land owners, and that in most regions, have contested the power of guerrilla movements. The emergence of paramilitary groups, coupled with the increased resources generated by the illegal drug trade, intensified and prolonged the conflict throughout the country (Gaviria 2000; Thoumi 2002).

Additionally, the conflict generated favorable conditions for the emergence of crime. Gaviria (2000) shows that the conflict, by congesting the law enforcement system, lowering the probability of punishment, diffusing criminal know-how and technology, and generally eroding morals, has promoted the emergence of crime and drug trafficking in Colombia. The appearance of drug trafficking only served to reinforce this trend by further eroding the ability of the Colombian Judicial System to properly function, while bringing about the spreading of crime (Montenegro and Posada 2001).

Intensification of the conflict has caused an escalating trend of attacks against the civilian population and has been the main cause behind forced displacement. Aggression directed at civilians has constituted an explicit and rational strategy for armed groups, as a means of funding their activities and consolidating and expanding their territorial strongholds. Forced displacement, in particular, has become a prevalent strategy for weakening the support of opponents among the population, clearing regions for the growing and trafficking of illegal crops, and expropriating land and resources (Engel and Ibáñez 2007). At the present time, forced displacement affects more than 3.5 million people, a number corresponding to about 7 percent of Colombia's population.

In order to assess how asset loss actually transpires during internal conflicts, as well as the process by which assets are accumulated following the initial shock, we rely on two sources of data. The first one is a household survey of displaced Colombian households conducted in 2004 and 2005. The second one contains qualitative data from the community reports generated by the World Bank's "Moving Out of Poverty" Colombian case study. Both data sources are described in the following paragraphs.

Regarding the first source, the sample of household-level data comprises 2,322 displaced households located in forty-eight municipalities[2] across twenty-one departments. The survey elicits information regarding the forced migration process, socioeconomic conditions before and after displacement, land tenure status, agricultural production, and access to government aid. The migration process is characterized at length through the information collected regarding the armed actors who cause displacement, the triggers behind displacement, and the reasons for choosing a particular reception municipality. Data concerning the socioeconomic conditions before and after displacement were gathered with respect to household composition, health status, access to health services, school enrollment, access to labor markets, labor income, asset ownership, access to formal and informal credits, and the level of participation in formal organizations. Two sections with detailed questions about access to land, the characteristics of plots, land losses, the likelihood of recovering land upon return, and agricultural production were also included.

To achieve these objectives, we constructed a treatment group sample comprised of 769 displaced household beneficiaries of income-generating programs, and a control group comprised of 1,553 displaced household non-beneficiaries of such programs. The control group is representative of the displaced population at large, while the treatment group is representative of those displaced households that are the beneficiaries of income-generating programs.

Given the large mobility of the displaced population and their unwillingness or fear to have their place of residency divulged, constructing a representative sample of it is difficult. In constructing the sample, we could have relied on two data sets of displaced persons. The first data set, Race and Urban Politics Data Set (RUPD), is the official registry of displaced persons and contains all displaced households who are beneficiaries of government assistance. To register in RUPD, displaced households must actively seek out government institutions and legally declare their status, which must then be verified by government authorities. Consequently, the registry suffers from significant underregistration (due to misinformation), arbitrary decision making by public officials, and biases inherent in the registration process (Ibáñez and Velasquez 2009). Moreover, the RUPD data provides little detail

---

2. Municipalities are the smallest administrative units in Colombia. Departments are similar to states in the United States.

concerning the displacement process and household structures. The second data set is the Random Utility Theory (RUT) System, which covers (a) displaced households requesting assistance from any of the 3,764 Catholic parishes scattered throughout the country; and (b) those households included in censuses conducted in certain municipalities by the Catholic Church. The resulting data contained information concerning 32,093 households and nearly 150,000 people.[3] Although the RUT system is not representative of the displaced population as a whole, the detailed questionnaire provides ample information useful for constructing a stratified sample. Consequently, the design for the control sample was based on the RUT sample.

The control sample was divided into two subsamples to correct for RUT bias: (a) 794 RUT households; and (b) 759 non-RUT households. A stratified sample was selected from the RUT sample; enumerators then proceeded to locate the RUT households and administer the survey. Even though the RUT sample covers all of the municipalities that have received displaced persons, only certain households are included in this database, thus allowing for a sample bias. To correct for this bias, for each RUT household surveyed, we tracked and surveyed a non-RUT displaced household in the same neighborhood. Given that the RUT provides rich information for constructing a stratified sample and covers a wide geographical area, we found that this strategy is appropriate for reducing the RUT bias. In fact, a recent survey representative of the displaced population shows that the observable socioeconomic characteristics are indeed similar to those highlighted in our sample (Garay 2008).

The beneficiaries of income-generating programs were surveyed in the same municipalities selected from the RUT and non-RUT samples. Households were randomly selected from a beneficiary list provided by three organizations responsible for implementing these programs. Such programs seek to boost the productive activities of displaced households by offering labor training, courses for small enterprises' management, and seed capital for initiating productive activities. Information about the programs is disseminated through massive information campaigns. The potential beneficiaries, identified during an initial stage, must prove that they are displaced persons and have been recipients of Emergency Humanitarian Aid (EHA).[4] Households with high dependency ratios, female-headed households, and

3. The survey elicits information aimed at identifying the causes of and actors responsible for displacement, household characteristics, land tenure status, access to labor markets, and the level of education before and after displacement, as well as the different needs of displaced persons/households. The questionnaire also seeks to gain information regarding participation in organizations and the willingness of displaced households to return to respective points of origin.

4. Emergency Humanitarian Aid is provided to those displaced households that are registered in the State Official Registry System. This assistance is provided during the first three months of displacement, and covers food aid, cash to cover transportation needs, and housing costs for up to three months.

households with younger heads have priority over other households. Once the potential beneficiaries are selected, program operators visit their homes to verify the declared conditions, as well as to design a preliminary support plan.

After the visits, the pool is further narrowed, and a relatively small group of potential beneficiaries is selected. This group must attend training programs where they learn how to design labor or small enterprise plans; these are then submitted to a committee, which in turn selects the actual group of beneficiaries. Benefits include labor training, small enterprise courses, or a combination of both, as well as psychological support. By the end of the program, labor and enterprise plans should be fully designed. Those beneficiaries who have submitted the former are hired by private firms for short-term practice. During this period, their wages are funded by the implementing organizations; the practice concludes three months later, after which the private firms can decide whether they wish to hire the beneficiaries. Detailed small enterprise plans should include a feasibility analysis, an investment schedule, and a business plan. The beneficiaries of small enterprise training receive a maximum sum of US$500 as seed capital with which to initiate the economic activity designed during the program.

In addition, we used qualitative data from the community reports of the World Bank's "Moving Out of Poverty" study. The purpose of the study was to understand the factors that help or hinder movements out of poverty. Eight case studies were undertaken at return and destination sites for displaced households in Colombia. The community reports allow us to understand the impact of forced displacement, how forced migration imposes asset losses upon displaced households, and the process by which some households are able to recover assets and steadily improve their living conditions at destination sites. By mixing qualitative and quantitative evidence, we are able to identify which households are better able to recover from displacement shock, as well as the dynamics behind this recovery.

4.4   Empirical Analysis

The purpose of this section is to understand how a severe shock, namely internal conflict and forced displacement, causes asset loss, and how households are able to recover from this shock. We adopt both quantitative and qualitative approaches in order to achieve our objective, inclusive of: (a) a detailed description of the losses stemming from forced displacement; (b) qualitative evidence that enables us to understand the complex process by which a displaced population recovers it assets; and (c) ordinary least squares (OLS), instrumental variable (IV), and quartile regressions so as to identify the determinants of asset losses as a consequence of displacement, as well as asset accumulation after displacement.

4.4.1   Qualitative Analysis

This section describes the impact of forced displacement on its victims based on qualitative data from the eight case studies of the World Bank's "Moving Out of Poverty" Colombian case study. We assess the impact of forced displacement on household welfare, examine the process of asset loss, and identify the three different groups of displaced households that emerge after the process of migration and asset loss.

Welfare Impacts of Forced Displacement and the Process of Asset Losses

Civil conflicts impose economic costs even before displacement takes place. In the Colombian case, civil conflict and the presence of armed groups has halted economic production, undervalued assets, and hampered government support. Guerrillas and paramilitaries have increasingly exerted control over the civilian population, its social relations, and productive activities. As a result, towns in conflict zones face fewer economic opportunities, a sudden stop in agricultural production, a drop in daily agricultural wages, and pervasive unemployment. The presence of illegal armed groups also undermines governmental support and erodes social capital in some communities. Access to labor training, technical assistance programs, credits, and support for productive projects has thus basically disappeared. The prospect of renewed violence and the fact that communities become stigmatized as belonging to "conflict zones" increases uncertainty, decreases land value, and leads households to cut back on investment.

Forced displacement, on the other hand, produces substantial losses of physical assets, which translates into vulnerability to poverty. Displaced households lose or abandon their life's work, crops, animals, lands, land improvements, investments, and houses. As a result, such households experience a harsh and sudden decline in living conditions and productive capacity. Moreover, losing land and other physical assets not only hinders a household's capacity to earn income, it also eliminates the possibility of production for self-consumption. A lack of land access entails fewer economic opportunities, impedes the ability of households to cope properly with the shock of displacement, and is generally identified by households as the predominant factor underlying their descent into poverty.

Some households—mainly those that migrated as a preventive measure—were able to sell their assets prior to migrating. Such sales allowed them to mitigate the displacement shock during the first months of settlement, and to enjoy better economic conditions at destination sites. Frequently, however, such sales took place at prices well below market levels. Such distress sales barely covered consumption needs for a few months, and conditions generally worsened significantly once savings were exhausted; thus, while they postponed the erosion of asset bases, they did not prevent it.

Participation in urban labor markets was slow due to the depreciation of human capital, discrimination against displaced persons, and the fragile psychological conditions resulting from being victims of violence. Given that displaced households mostly arrived from rural areas and that their working experience was limited to agricultural activities, the returns from "agricultural human capital" generally decreased in urban areas. Conflict and forced migration may also have caused psychological disorders, which often produce a sense of helplessness, defeat, and irrational fear. People facing such disorders were usually scared to venture out of their homes and search for jobs. Lastly, conflict and forced displacement may have produced household fragmentation as well as resulted in the death or abandonment of household members, individuals often of a productive age. Women often became the heads of households by default, something that further increased households' vulnerability. All these elements constituted obstacles to finding jobs and generating income.

A lack of physical assets, suitable employment opportunities, and risk-sharing mechanisms implied substantial welfare losses for households, which consequently became unable to cope with future shocks. The loss of relatives, connections, and social networks presumably led to fewer opportunities to work, study, and participate in community savings programs. Although some households participated in social networks at destination sites, informal risk-sharing mechanisms nonetheless did not fully insure against risk, as participants' income levels were fairly low and homogenous. The disruption of social networks also generated obstacles for acquiring formal and informal credit. Generally speaking, displaced households were rationed out of formal financial markets, and were thus obliged to apply for usurious credits, credits for which guarantees and references were not required; as a consequence, profits were sucked up by the large cost of the credit. Accumulating assets became virtually impossible because income was barely sufficient to cover subsistence needs and pay off credits.

Three Groups of Displaced Households

The qualitative evidence allows us to distinguish between three groups of displaced households based on the different paths they followed toward asset recovery—households that are chronically poor both before and after displacement; households that could possibly become chronically poor; and households capable of initiating a recovery process, but for which the magnitude of recovery is unclear.

The first group—households that were chronically poor both before and after displacement—were asset-deprived households at the site of origin, and remained poor after displacement due to the difficulty of coping with the conflict-induced shock. These households exhibited low levels of human capital, were unable to find appropriate jobs that matched their agricultural working experience, were fairly isolated from social connections, and had household structures that denoted a high degree of vulnerability to poverty.

The second group is comprised of households falling into poverty following displacement. Prior to displacement, these households were better off and had relatively large asset holdings. Because of conflict and displacement, they suffered considerable asset losses, and the deterioration in the economic welfare of these households was particularly large. Asset losses—inclusive of the loss of physical, social, financial, human, and institutional assets— placed them on low-income trajectories, where the possibility of moving onto high-performance trajectories seemed remote. Since the returns from different kinds of assets complement one another, and households in this group lacked most of them, providing or gaining access to one asset generally did not improve their situation.

The last group is comprised of households capable of achieving successful asset recovery dynamics. These households shared some common characteristics—a combination of higher levels of education and training, contact with and access to social networks at reception sites, savings and micro-credits, and one or more sources of income.

Better educated households and those whose members had suitable working experience were able to engage in economic activities and extract higher rents, in contrast to households made up of members with no formal education or who were previously dedicated to agricultural activities. Labor training programs were critical for households recovering their productive capacity and undertaking new activities; this was particularly the case for women, who felt empowered after participating in training programs.

Human capital alone, although necessary, was not sufficient for recovering from the shock of displacement. Having an additional source of income— whether in the form of savings, credits, or agricultural production—was crucial to the recovery process. Labor training without seed capital or micro-credits proved useless. While labor training did boost confidence and provided knowledge relevant to an unknown occupation, to be effective, it must be complemented with seed capital. Those households that successfully overcame the consequences of displacement were able to allocate savings, resources from asset sales, and seed capital to the recovery of productive capacity—in the form of access to land plots at destination sites, land improvements, and/or the purchasing of livestock—as opposed to the supplying of basic needs. Income-generating programs thus might constitute a factor promoting recovery, inasmuch as they provide resources for recovering productive capabilities. Nonetheless, most beneficiaries of such programs considered that the amount of seed capital provided was insufficient for starting a profitable business. Projects promoting cooperatives or associative income-generating schemes appeared to have a higher impact and a greater likelihood of succeeding than individual projects, inasmuch as they can be potentially larger, and the risk is shared among members. Savings, seed capital, and liquid capital, however, were not sufficient to guarantee successful asset recovery. Households with insufficient assets, low levels of human capital, no social networks, and no labor training faced difficulties in starting small businesses, and ended up depleting these resources without recovering.

The importance of social networks and social capital in facilitating the move out of poverty is manifold. First, social networks provide resources and assistance during the migration process in fulfilling basic needs. Second, social networks at destination municipalities may provide households with employment opportunities as well as much-needed working and business permits; likewise, access to government or nongovernmental organization (NGO) programs. Although social capital is perceived as an instrument for recovery, participation in social networks does not in and of itself guarantee a transition to high-yield activities. Even households that actively participated in formal organizations often remained trapped in low-yield trajectories because access to investment capital was restricted and property rights were not well defined. The qualitative evidence from the "Moving Out of Poverty" study in Colombia provides insights into the virtuous and vicious cycles that characterize the process of asset recovery. These cycles are assessed in greater detail in the following section.

Asset Loss and Asset Accumulation: A Simple Reduced-Form Model for Identifying Determinants

The purpose of this section is to provide evidence concerning the impact of internal conflict upon asset trajectories, and the ability of households to recover from conflict-related shocks. We first examine the process of asset loss stemming from forced displacement and how the dynamics of conflict determine asset losses. Second, we identify the determinants of asset accumulation once those forcefully displaced resettle at their destination points.

The asset dynamics of displaced households are described by two different factors: the value of assets at the municipality of origin that were abandoned following displacement (A_L); and the value of the asset base at the receiving municipality (A_R). Each of these is in turn influenced by other factors. Thus, asset losses are driven by the internal conflict's dynamics in the region of origin, the victimization process households endure prior to displacement, and the strategies households adopt in order to minimize asset loss. Asset accumulation at the point of destination, on the other hand, is determined by the income generation capacity of households, their vulnerability conditions, the level of their participation in programs aimed at supporting displaced households, and the respective settlement process.

We discuss first the determinants of asset losses (A_L). The conflict dynamics that trigger forced migration are strongly linked to asset loss. For example, since armed groups need to fund their operations, the presence of illegal armed groups (P_I) at sites of origin frequently results in asset seizure and abandonment. Conversely, the presence of government forces (P_G) will likely serve to protect households from illegal groups' attacks, and thus reduce the likelihood of their being forced to move and abandon assets.

The victimization profile of a household may determine the extent of asset loss it experiences. When household members are forced to flee hastily in order to save their lives, or after being the victims of violent events (reactive displacement [Re]), the possibility of protecting assets becomes greatly minimalized. On the other hand, when households migrate preventively out of fear that the conflict will escalate in the region, it is easier to plan the migration. In the latter case, then, protecting, selling, or transferring assets to family or friends is more likely; likewise, controlling assets at origin municipalities. Direct attacks sometimes imply the death or disappearance of family members, usually the main breadwinners, who in the case of rural households are frequently male (PP). Since land titles are generally registered to male household heads and informal marital unions are widespread in Colombian rural areas, households that lose the main breadwinner often find it difficult to recover land. Such households may face substantial asset losses.

Attacks on the civil population are not random. Certain groups are deliberately targeted as part of a war strategy. Thus, for instance, community leaders or households with strong social networks (CS_O) are more likely to be targeted by armed groups. Notwithstanding, social networks can be effective mechanisms for some households to control assets and exploit land plots following displacement. Consequently, the impact of social capital on asset loss is uncertain. Landowners and tenants (L) are also attractive targets for armed groups as, once having fled, their abandoned lands can be seized by armed groups. The incentive to attack landowners increases the larger the land plot; on the other hand, large landowners are better able to adopt strategies for protecting their assets. The age structure of a household (S) may also prompt attacks by armed groups—young men constitute potential combatants, and thus are desirable as recruits. Direct attacks undermine a household's ability to protect its assets; thus, households with high levels of social capital, access to land, or with young males, may face large asset losses. An interesting factor concerns the ethnic make-up of the household. Belonging to an ethnic minority (Me), such as an indigenous or Afro-Colombian group, may also determine the extent of asset loss. The effect, however, is difficult to establish a priori. Ethnic minorities suffer direct attacks from armed groups with greater frequency; hence, these households face greater obstacles when trying to control assets at origin sites following displacement. On the other hand, ethnic minorities often possess collective land titles, which may help protect them against illegal land seizures by armed groups.

Households are not necessarily passive victims of armed conflict, and some households adopt strategies aimed at minimizing the extent of asset loss. Relocating within the municipality is sometimes employed, for example, as a means of protecting and/or recovering assets. Households may decide to migrate within the municipality (M) in order to maintain control over their productive assets, continue with productive activities on their land plots, and/or extract rents. Other factors may also play a role; households facing tight budget constraints, for instance, may not be able to migrate outside of the municipality. Since households may decide to migrate within the municipality in order to protect assets, intramunicipal displacement must be considered an endogenous variable. We use instrumental variable estimations to correct for endogeneity. Besides protecting assets, households may decide to migrate within the municipality if friends and families residing at the destination site are able or willing to provide support. Notwithstanding, contacts at destination sites—such as family and friends—do not determine the extent of asset losses. Contacts at destination sites are therefore used as the exclusion variables. In order to protect land plots following displacement, households may decide to register their title in official records (F). Having legal title over land plots may hinder illegal seizure, thus discouraging attacks by armed groups, or helping households protect land once forced displacement has occurred. Notwithstanding, having legal title may prove ineffective in regions where the rule of law and the protection of property rights is lacking, which is usually the case in regions experiencing conflict. In addition, formal land titles may boost the value of land, implying higher asset losses. Human capital, (H), constitutes an element allowing households to devise strategies for protecting assets prior to migration. Better educated individuals may design effective strategies for protecting assets at origin sites, selling them prior to migration, and/or controlling them at destination sites. On the other hand, better educated individuals may constitute effective community leaders, and thus be seen as posing a threat to armed groups seeking to dissolve any civil resistance. Additionally, the uncertainty of losing assets such as land may push certain households to invest more in transferable capital, like education, instead of location-specific assets; for these households then, the loss of physical assets might be lower. Thus, the impact of human capital on asset loss is uncertain.

The determinants of asset loss are defined then by the following reduced form:

$$A_L = A_L(P_I, P_G, R_e, PP, CS_o, L, S, M, F).$$

Asset accumulation at destination sites is driven by factors other than those that determine asset loss. First, the length of settlement in destination sites, (T), may exert a positive or negative influence on asset accumulation. As households become settled for longer periods of time at destination sites, knowledge about the labor market increases and economic opportunities broaden, thus increasing the likelihood of accumulating new assets. As the duration of settlement at the new location increases, however, respective governmental aid programs eventually come to an end, and the short-term benefits of income-generating programs vanish. If the first effect exceeds the second effect—that is, if a household's ability to recover productive capacity offsets the discontinuation of resources from aid programs—the period of settlement will have exerted a positive effect on asset dynamics. Conversely, if the second effect is stronger than the first one, then the period of settlement will have affected asset dynamics negatively.

Human capital, (H), may make adaptation to the conditions at the destination site easier, thus improving asset accumulation following displacement. Higher levels of human capital may be fundamental to competing in urban labor markets and finding alternative sources of income, and thus accumulating new assets. However, human capital is not necessarily a transferable asset. Agricultural experience (Ag) is not useful in urban labor markets, for example, inasmuch as there, the predominant occupations for low-skilled workers are in construction, services, and/or petty trade. In such cases, the resultant depreciation of human capital restricts earning possibilities and, consequently, asset accumulation.

The ability to generate income is crucial for promoting asset accumulation. Income earned in labor markets or through small enterprises, (Y_R), besides covering subsistence needs, may be invested in new productive assets. Some displaced households are still able to control assets in their hometowns and extract rents from production on their land plots. Using rents obtained by exploiting these plots, they are able to accumulate new assets at receiving municipalities. Social networks and social capital at destination municipalities, (CS_R), among other things, help households mitigate shocks, acquire information about aid programs or job opportunities, and gain access to special assistance programs and credits.

A household's structure and its socioeconomic characteristics are also determinants of displaced asset dynamics. Among other factors, income generation and the accumulation of assets depend on a household's structure and the age of the household head. High dependency ratios, (D), imply fewer members who are generating income and members who have greater needs, thus restricting the household's capacity for recovering assets. Female household heads, (J), may face more obstacles than men to accumulating new assets, due to their vulnerability following displacement. Age, (E), may exhibit an inverted u-shape relationship with respect to asset dynamics. Because young displaced persons have less work experience, their incomes tend to be low; this further makes asset recovery difficult. On the other hand, older persons may have difficulties learning new occupations and adapting to changing circumstances. Asset accumulation, consequently, increases with age, but only with diminishing marginal returns. Lastly, belonging to an ethnic minority may have a negative impact on asset accumulation, as these groups face particular vulnerabilities, given their cultural heritage, language barriers, and so forth.

Access to programs targeting displaced households, such as income generation programs G_i, may provide an initial stimulus for recovering productive capacity. Establishing the causal link between access to income-generating programs and asset accumulation, however, is difficult. First, as explained before, access to these programs is conditional on having first received humanitarian aid, such as providing basic needs during the first three months following displacement. Although humanitarian aid does not contribute to asset accumulation, beneficiary households may receive other kinds of support, such that it may promote asset accumulation. Whether this is the case or not is impossible to identify from our data. Thus, the coefficient for income-generating programs may be capturing the impact of other programs as well. Second, since in addition to other factors income-generating programs are not randomly assigned—with households being selected according to the magnitude of their vulnerability and economic conditions—being the beneficiary of such programs constitutes an endogenous variable. To correct for this endogeneity, we employ an instrumental variables approach, based on whether a household was a beneficiary of humanitarian aid. As described before, only those households that had previously received humanitarian aid were potential beneficiaries of income-generating programs; thus, we anticipate that this variable will be a strong predictor of program participation. However, asset accumulation is not determined by a short-term program, which is designed primarily to cover basic needs. The accumulation for asset holdings for household i, then, is defined as:

$$A_R = A_R(T, H, Ag, Y_R, CS_R, D, J, PP, E, Me, G).$$

The reduced-form equations for asset loss stemming from displacement and asset accumulation at destination sites are estimated using the National Survey of Displaced Households (ENHD) described in the previous sections.

4.4.2   Quantitative Analysis: The Determinants of Asset Loss and Asset Accumulation

In order to identify the determinants of asset loss and asset accumulation for displaced households using the models specified in section 4.3.4., we first estimate a group of regressions. Before discussing the determinants of asset dynamics, we discuss here some descriptive statistics, and analyze the magnitude of asset loss stemming from forced displacement. The figures for asset loss are only estimated for the control group.

The displacement process together with household characteristics are

Table 4.1   The displacement process and household characteristics

	Mean (Standard deviation)
Reactive displacement	86.2%
Perception of the presence of illegal armed groups at origin site	89.6%
Perception of the presence of government forces at origin site	50.3%
Intramunicipal displacement	15.2%
Intradepartmental displacement	57.6%
Migration directly to destination	88.9%
Time of settlement at destination site—days	1.345 (1.040)
Ethnic minority	24.2%
Male head of household	62.7%
Household size	5.16 (2.14)
Number of persons between 12 and 17 years of age	0.84 (0.99)
Number of persons between 18 and 65 years of age	2.48 (1.36)
Dependency ratio	0.34 (0.34)
Years of age of household head	42.6 (13.3)
Number of persons between 12 and 17 years of age	0.84 (0.99)
Number of persons between 18 and 65 years of age	2.48 (1.36)

Source: Authors' calculations based on ENHD (2004).

presented in table 4.1. First, the level of violence in the regions of origin is extremely large. More than 86 percent of households displaced reactively;[5] that is, after being victimized in an attack by illegal armed groups. Moreover, while displaced households readily perceive the presence of illegal armed groups (89.6 percent of the time), it is less often the case that they perceive the presence of government forces (50.3 percent of the time), such as provide protection. Second, while some households do prefer to migrate within the general vicinity of their hometown (15.2 percent), most actually end up migrating out of their municipality, directly to their final destination municipality. Third, displaced households are a particularly vulnerable group relative to other groups within the Colombian population. Compared to urban poor households, for instance, displaced households are larger, have a higher

5. A household displaces reactively when it is the victim of a direct treat, following the homicide, forced recruitment or abduction of a household member, or the massacre of some or one household member.

frequency of female heads, have greater dependency ratios, and more often are made up of ethnic minorities.

The length of settlement at destination sites merits a separate discussion. The distribution for length of settlement is spread, with the average length of settlement being 1.345 days, and with a standard deviation of 1,040 days. Such a large time horizon may cause an attrition bias as the sample may only identify those displaced households that remain trapped in poverty, whereas successful households may have moved to other neighborhoods and lost their connection with the church. However, the length of settlement for most households is less than five years: the median is 1,200 days (3.28 years) and the seventy-fifth quartile is 1.759 (4.8 years).[6]

The loss and recovery of housing, physical capital, and land are presented in table 4.2. Nearly half of the sample reports losing their home as a consequence of displacement, with only a few households able to acquire new housing at destination sites. However, close to 18 percent of households' homes were not legally owned prior to displacement, whereas following displacement, there was a greater tendency to own houses—that is, at destination sites. The average monetary housing loss per household is $3,333.[7]

Productive assets, other than those related to land and plot improvement, comprise the greater bulk of asset loss and are difficult to recover following displacement. In fact, productive asset depletion worsens over time following settlement at destination sites. On the other hand, households are able to recover expensive articles with much greater ease, such as electronic appliances and mobile goods (e.g., vehicles).

Land seizure or abandonment is also considerable. Given the predominant proportion of the displaced population that has a rural origin, it is not surprising that nearly 55 percent of displaced households had formal or informal access to land; the average size of land plots is 13.2 hectares, which is not negligible. Given the weak property rights that prevail in Colombian rural areas, recovering land once the conflict ends is a complex process—over 30 percent of displaced households legally owned land, while the remainder had only informal access to it. Moreover, only 12.8 percent still controlled their land plots following displacement, either directly or with the support of family and friends. Consequently, only 25 percent of households are deemed likely to recover land upon their return. If recovering land is difficult, recovering the capital invested to improve land plots or increase agricultural productivity is even more so. Close to one-fifth of land plots had irrigation, the average number of livestock was twenty-nine, and the net present value of foregone agricultural revenue over a lifetime is $15,787 per household.[8]

6. We thank Ernesto Schargrodsky for raising this point.
7. We used the exchange rate for 09/02/2007, which stood at US\$ 1 = COP\$ 2,160.
8. To calculate the net present value of foregone agricultural revenues, we assume that agricultural production ends when the household head dies; we thus use a discount rate of 9.5

ble 4.2	Asset loss and asset recovery: Housing, physical capital, and land		
riable		Mean	Standard error
ousing			
Percentage of households that lost housing at the origin site		46.50%	—
Percentage of households that lost housing at the origin site and recovered it at the reception site		6.40%	—
Percentage of households that did not own housing at the origin site and own housing at the destination site		17.90%	—
Average loss in housing		US $3,333	US $278
hysical assets			
Productive assets (excluding land) at the origin site		US $370	US $42
Other assets at the origin site		US $93	US $5
Percentage of productive assets at the origin site		55.20%	0.02%
Productive assets (excluding land) at the destination site		US $19	US $5
Other assets at the destination site		US $93	US $5
Percentage of productive assets at the destination site		12.80%	0.03%
and			
Land tenure		55.40%	—
Total hectares of land owned		13.2	2.1
Value of total hectares owned		US $3,981	US $417
Percentage of hectares with formal property titles		31.20%	—
Average number of hectares lost		4	0.8
Value of hectares lost		US $972	US $185
Percentage of hectares than can be recovered after return		25.80%	—
Percentage of hectares under family control		12.80%	—
Percentage of land with irrigation		19.00%	—
Number of animals		29.9	2.6
Net present value of agricultural profit loss		US $15,787	US $2,500
Total assets and asset recovery			
Value of assets at origin site (excluding land)		US $7,037	US $278
Value of assets at destination site (excluding land)		US $3,194	US $231
Net loss of assets		US $–3,796	US $32

Source: Authors' calculations based on ENHD (2004).

When physical assets and land are accounted for, the average loss per household is nearly $7,037. The capacity of displaced households to recover from this kind of asset loss is limited. If we measure the recovery of assets as the value of assets at the destination site minus the value of assets at the site of origin, on average, households report a net loss of approximately $3,796 per household.

Displacement shock, aside from significantly decreasing victims' asset holdings, condenses the asset distribution around a lower mean and median. Figure 4.1 depicts the distribution of asset values before and after displacement. Prior to displacement, the mean and median of asset values are larger

percent. According to the World Health Organization (WHO), the life expectancy of women and men in Colombian rural areas is 76.3 and 67.5 years, respectively.

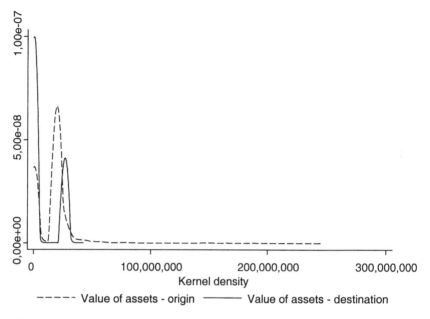

Fig. 4.1   Values of assets at origin and destination sites—kernel density
Source: Authors' calculations based on ENHD (2004).

and the distribution more spread out; asset values at the upper tail of the distribution are more frequent. Following displacement, the distribution condenses significantly, with most households concentrated near zero, and with just a few households having a larger value of assets.

Asset recovery is difficult for most displaced households. Figure 4.2 depicts a quadratic fit between the net change in asset value and the length of settlement for the three groups identified in the qualitative analysis. Group 1 corresponds to the first quartile of the net change in asset value, group 2 to the second and third quartile, and group 3 to the fourth quartile. The majority of displaced households, close to 75 percent of them, reported a negative net change in asset value, while only 25 percent of displaced households were able to recover assets following displacement. Consequently, the median of asset recovery is zero, which indicates a worrisome trend. As identified by the qualitative evidence, group 1 faced large asset losses, which only deepened as time passed; the recuperation of assets was slow for group 2, such that after five years of displacement, asset loss was still higher than asset accumulation; and while group 3 was able to recover from the displacement shock, the stock of assets at destination sites remained constant.

Although in theory households might resort to labor income, credits, and risk-sharing mechanisms in order to recover assets, access to these mechanisms is not widespread among the displaced population. The figures for

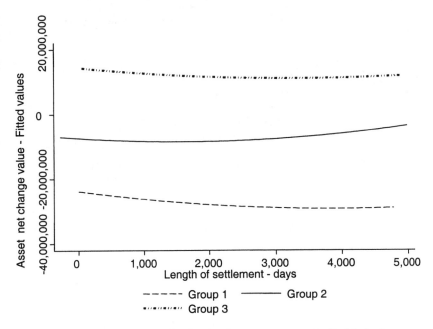

Fig. 4.2   Net change in asset value for the three groups—quadratic fitted value

Source: Authors' calculations based on ENHD (2004).

Note: Asset recovery is measured as the value of assets at destination sites minus asset losses caused by displacement.

financial capital, access to labor markets, and human and social capital before and after displacement are presented in table 4.3. First, the potential access to informal credits drops sharply following displacement (from 17.9 percent to 9.3 percent). Access to formal credit markets at destination sites does increase fivefold relative to access at origin sites, though this is largely because with respect to the latter, access is negligible; thus, at destination sites, only 6.6 percent of households are the beneficiaries of formal credits. Furthermore, credit conditions gradually worsen over time at destination sites—the amounts approved are half those approved at origin sites, and the number of monthly installments eventually declines.

Drops in asset holding returns are not fully compensated by labor income. Unemployment rates for all household members soar following displacement, and the pace at which labor conditions improve is extremely slow—initially, the unemployment rate for household heads during the first three months of settlement at destination sites is 53 percent; after a year, it is 16 percent. Because displaced households face poor labor conditions and are mostly absorbed by informal labor markets, the labor income per equivalent adult corresponds to less than half of labor income prior to displacement.

The depreciation of human capital and low education levels are important

Table 4.3   Financial capital, labor markets, human capital, and social capital

Variable	Mean	Standard deviation
Financial capital—informal credits		
Potential access to informal credits at the origin site	17.90%	—
Access to informal credits at the origin site	8.30%	—
Potential access to informal credits at the destination site	9.30%	—
Access to informal credits at the destination site	6.40%	—
Financial capital—formal credits		
Access to formal credits at the origin site	1.40%	—
Credit amount at the origin site	US $1,481	US $1,019
Number of monthly installments at the origin site	14.5	1
Access to formal credits at the destination site	6.60%	—
Amount of credit at the destination site	US $741	US $185
Number of monthly installments at the destination site	10.4	1.4
Labor markets		
Unemployment level for household heads at the origin site	1.70%	—
Labor income per equivalent adult at the origin site	US $893	US $151
Unemployment level for household heads at the destination site	16.10%	—
Labor income per equivalent adult at the destination site	US $289	US $17
Human capital		
Years of education of household head	5.7	0.1
Dedicated to agricultural activities at the origin site	57.30%	—
Social capital		
Main breadwinner died or abandoned household	8.50%	—
Participation in organizations at the origin site	32.60%	—
Number of organizations per household at the origin site	0.33	0.03
Leadership position at the origin site	7.50%	—
Participation in organizations at the destination site	29.00%	—
Number of organizations per household at the destination site	0.25	0.02
Leadership position at the destination site	4.20%	—

Source: Authors' calculations based on ENHD (2004).

obstacles that displaced households need to overcome when competing in urban markets. Tight labor markets at destination sites may partially hinder the rapid absorption of displaced households. Hence, even after a year of settlement, the unemployment rate for displaced household heads is still greater than that for the urban extreme poor. Low formal human capital (5.7 years) and inadequate previous labor experience with respect to urban jobs (57.3 percent of displaced persons were dedicated to agriculture prior to displacement) may be the main causes driving high unemployment rates.

Informal risk-sharing mechanisms are also severely disrupted. Informal credits, as discussed before, drop significantly. Some families disintegrate on account of the main breadwinner dying or abandoning the household (8.5

percent). While households that participated in organizations prior to displacement often rapidly become engaged at destination sites, the new organizations are usually dramatically different from those to which they previously belonged. Prior to displacement, displaced households were generally members of organizations dedicated to fostering productive activities (e.g., peasant organizations and cooperatives) through the provision of credits, technical assistance, and mediation with formal institutions. At destination sites, households are mostly members of organizations dedicated to charity work—that is, organizations aimed at providing subsistence support rather than promoting productive activities.

Asset Losses

We estimate regressions in order to first identify the determinants of asset loss. Several regressions were estimated to check for the robustness of the results. Table 4.4 presents the results for the OLS, IV, and quartile regressions. Given that certain characteristics of the department of origin may also determine the nature and extent of asset loss, we estimate regressions with and without department[9] controls. Inasmuch as armed groups may adopt different displacement tactics depending upon the war strategies they adopt, we estimate each regression separately for massive and individual displacement. We expect that where the war objective of illegal armed groups is to depopulate territory in order to strengthen territorial control, expelling the population en masse (massive displacement) is more effective. On the other hand, when asset seizure is the objective, the deliberate targeting of particular households (individual displacement) will more likely be adopted. The latter case may adjust better to the model we defined. Lastly, we expect that the beneficiaries of income-generating programs should have unobservable characteristics closely related to their entrepreneurial abilities, characteristics, which if known, might help them design strategies for protecting assets. Consequently, we estimate the regressions separately for the beneficiaries and nonbeneficiaries of income-generating programs. Since the results are robust for the different specifications, we only present the estimations for the complete sample using department controls. However, we discuss the different specifications whenever they account for a significant change in the results.

We estimate OLS regressions and IV regressions in order to instrument for migrating within the municipality. The results for the first stage of the instrumental variable regression are presented in table 4A.1 of the appendix, and correspond nicely with an F-statistic equal to 11.39. Since the process of asset loss appears highly nonlinear, we estimate quartile regressions.

The results reveal conflict dynamics that exert a heavy toll on assets. The fact of reactive displacement and the losing of a male household head are

9. Departments roughly correspond to states in the United States.

Table 4.4 The determinants of asset loss[a]

Variables	GLS — Coefficient (t-statistic)	GLS — Coefficient (t-statistic)	GLS — Coefficient (t-statistic)	IV — Coefficient (t-statistic)	IV — Coefficient (t-statistic)	IV — Coefficient (t-statistic)	Quantile regressions — Coefficient (t-statistic) (0.25)	Quantile regressions — Coefficient (t-statistic) (0.50)	Quantile regressions — Coefficient (t-statistic) (0.75)
Reactive displacement	4,868.60 (3.66)***			3,694.08 (3.06)***	3,433.21 (2.88)***	3,412.77 (2.66)***	233.58 (1.39)	1,238.52 (1.92)*	912.36 (2.11)**
Household head dead or no longer present	6,988.40 (2.03)**			5,930.97 (1.91)*	6,716.26 (2.17)**	6,776.35 (2.66)***	111.54 (0.55)	2,663.29 (3.43)***	261.37 (0.51)
Perception of the presence of illegal armed groups	-4,186.06 (-1.35)			-4,593.06 (-1.54)	-4,592.17 (-1.55)	-4,577.37 (-1.54)	-380.63 (-2.00)**	-1,311.16 (-1.80)*	-321.68 (-0.66)
Perception of the presence of government forces	-2,592.93 (-2.41)**			-3,272.00 (-2.95)***	-3,048.56 (-2.74)***	-2,972.55 (-1.47)	-130.49 (-0.89)	-1,442.21 (-2.57)***	-221.78 (-0.60)
Intramunicipal displacement		-2,460.72 (-1.94)**		-2,809.80 (-2.20)**	-2,805.65 (-2.18)**	-2,041.00 (-0.13)	-280.62 (-1.60)	-503.69 (-0.75)	-180.59 (-0.40)
Household head—average number of organizations at origin site		1,198.87 (1.57)	2,958.11 (3.00)***	1,135.03 (1.50)	1,293.71 (1.75)*	1,272.29 (1.49)	117.61 (1.36)	753.28 (2.36)**	435.36 (2.19)**
Formal land title		12,116.33 (5.18)***		10,380.97 (4.22)***	9,856.80 (4.02)***	9,821.87 (3.86)***	8,013.95 (46.01)***	13,329.46 (19.54)***	5,145.45 (11.12)***
Formal land title*presence of government forces		-310.03 (-0.13)		3,223.03 (1.23)	3,324.42 (1.28)	3,364.14 (1.27)	-3,564.67 (-14.47)***	1,041.35 (1.09)	-239.08 (-0.37)
Total hectares of land		164.99 (3.80)***		163.30 (3.77)***	161.94 (3.75)***	162.12 (3.72)***	36.94 (32.04)***	112.56 (27.89)***	256.36 (100.77)***
Years of schooling for household head			988.99 (2.08)**		836.39 (1.90)*	839.10 (1.88)*	28.55 (1.05)	262.20 (2.50)***	126.89 (1.73)*
Number of persons between 12 and 17 years of age			1,441.24 (2.39)**		930.81 (1.83)*	924.81 (1.81)*	32.28 (0.55)	160.54 (0.72)	157.52 (1.09)
Number of persons between 17 and 65 years of age			1,738.44 (4.21)***		1,249.23 (3.23)***	1,246.08 (3.30)***	104.34 (2.53)***	915.72 (5.46)***	382.85 (3.41)***
Ethnic minority			-313.02 (-0.27)		-935.66 (-0.79)	-968.83 (-0.69)	-109.61 (-0.69)	884.38 (1.44)	103.08 (0.25)
Constant	629.96 (0.21)	-476.68 (-0.77)	-11,106.13 (-3.28)***	474.99 (0.15)	-7,467.33 (-2.05)**	-7,451.34 (-2.05)**	759.00 (2.45)***	-3,250.07 (-2.71)	-2,739.15 (-3.37)***
Observations	2,320	2,318	2,318	2,318	2,318	2,318	2,318	2,318	2,318
R^2	0.0448	0.2067	0.0514	0.217	0.2251	0.2205	0.0403	0.1383	0.1067

Source: Authors' calculations based on ENHD (2004).

Note: Department Controls are included. GLS = general least squares.

[a] Asset losses divided by 1,000.

***Significant at the 1 percent level.

**Significant at the 5 percent level.

*Significant at the 10 percent level.

both statistically significant; the magnitudes of the coefficients are large, and the results are robust for different specifications. Moreover, while it is not significant in the first quartile, the coefficient for reactive displacement becomes larger and statistically significant in the upper quartiles. The coefficient estimates for reactive displacement decrease when additional controls are included, yet this should be expected, inasmuch as violence targets particular groups within the population. The direct and traumatic victimization represented by reactive displacement and by the loss of the main breadwinner imposes asset losses of (Colombian pesos) COP$3.4 million (US$1.574) and $COP6.7 million (US$3,101), respectively.

The strategies adopted by households or by government forces to help mitigate asset loss are not sufficient to offset the impact of the conflict. Although migrating within the municipality and the presence of government forces does reduce asset loss, the combined effect of both variables is only COP$5.8 million (US$2,685), which does not even counteract the loss of the main household breadwinner. In addition, the positive impact of migrating within the municipality is not robust for different specification. When department controls are included, the size of the coefficient halves; this variable then may be capturing some regional effects and not necessarily the effectiveness of intramunicipal displacement. Once the variable is instrumentalized, the statistical significance disappears. The quartile regressions also show no statistical significance for intramunicipal displacement. On the other hand, the effectiveness of government forces is robust for different specifications, even if the impact does not offset either reactive displacement or the loss of the main breadwinner.

Formal titles for land plots, rather than reducing asset loss, seems to actually increase its extent. The coefficient for formality is not only positive and significant, it also shows the largest magnitude (COP$9.8 million [US$4,537]). One possible explanation is that land plots with formal titles are the largest and thus the most attractive ones. However, after controlling for the size of land plots, the size and significance of the coefficients are similar. Another interpretation is that when lawlessness is pervasive, formal titles are not sufficient for protecting assets. To test for this hypothesis, we interact the formality of land titles with the presence of government forces. Again, the size and significance of the coefficients are similar. In addition, quartile regressions show that the impact of formality with respect to land titles is particularly strong for the median quartile, while decreasing for the last one. Land plots with formal titles may be more valuable due to the formality of the land titles. The positive effect of land plot size on asset loss seems to corroborate this hypothesis.

The targeting of particular groups within the population in order to achieve war objectives also imposes large asset losses, though some variables are not statistically significant. First, better educated households face greater asset loss; as indicated by the quartile regressions, the effect increases for the highest quartiles. However, the coefficient for years of schooling is not robust for different specifications of the model. Second, young household members may be forcefully recruited or may act as combatants for opponents groups, and are thus targeted often. These attacks appear to increase the extent of asset loss. This effect is particularly strong for persons between eighteen and sixty-five years of age—having an additional member in this age range increases asset loss by COP$1.2 million (US$555). Third, although the coefficient for participation in formal organizations is positive, it is not statistically significant. However, when the quartile regressions are estimated, participation in organizations implies positive asset loss for the median and third quartile, and the impact is not negligible. For example, for the median quartile, participation in an additional organization increases asset loss by COP$0.75 million (US$347), while the increment in asset loss generated by reactive displacement for the same quartile is COP$1.2 million (US$555). Lastly, apparently, ethnic minorities do not face greater levels of asset loss. When department controls are not included, the extent of asset loss for ethnic minorities is greater, but the effect vanishes after including department controls. Regions where ethnic minorities are located coincide with regions strategically important to illegal armed groups. Thus, ethnic minorities may be attacked simply by virtue of living in strategically valuable regions, and not necessarily because they are ethnic minorities.

The results presented in table 4.4 clearly indicate that conflict-induced shocks impose greater asset losses. The impact of the conflict upon asset loss is hardly offset by strategies adopted to prevent loss or by the protection provided by government forces.

Asset Accumulation

In order to understand the process of asset accumulation, we estimate regressions to identify the determinants of asset accumulation. Several alternative specifications were estimated in order to verify the robustness of the results. First, asset accumulation, besides being determined by households' characteristics, may also depend on regional characteristics as well as the municipality size. Among other things, some regions are more prosperous, their labor markets are more dynamic, and/or they are more willing to receive displaced population. These factors contribute to the displaced population's asset accumulation process. In addition, the size of the urban center may determine how easy or difficult it is to acquire new asset holdings. Although large cities may provide more economic opportunities, adapting to a large and anonymous city may prove hard for rural households, such as are often found among the displaced population. To control for city size, we include controls for Bogotá (the capital city of Colombia), large cities with populations between 700,000 and 3,000,000 people, and medium-sized cities with populations between 100,000 and 699,000 people. We do not control for small cities with less than 100,000 inhabitants. To control for regional heterogeneity, we include department controls. Second, we estimate the determinants of asset accumulation separately for length of settlement, income-generating capacities, and household vulnerability. Finally, we drop outliers from the time of settlement in order to identify whether potential attrition causes an overestimation of poverty traps. Dropping outliers does not, however, change the estimation results.

Instrumental variable regressions and quartile regressions are also estimated. The first stage of the instrumental variable regression is presented in table 4A.2 of the appendix. The first stage fits well, with an *F*-statistic ranging from 8.37 and 10.06. Much as with asset loss, asset accumulation exhibits several nonlinearities, as shown in the figures discussed in section 4.3.4. To deal with these nonlinearities, we estimate quartile regressions.

The results for all the regressions are presented in tables 4.5 and 4.6. The results for the regressions without the controls for city size are not presented; the coefficient estimates are robust for the inclusion of these controls, and the prediction power of the model barely increases. As settlement at destination sites progresses, asset accumulation expands. The coefficient and its significance are similar for the different specifications estimated. We also include interactions for length of settlement and certain household characteristics, such as the fact of having previously been dedicated to agricultural activities or having lost the main breadwinner; the coefficients, however, are not statistically significant and are thus not reported. However, the contribution of length of settlement is not large and even decreases after a while, thus exhibiting the inverted u-shaped relation noted earlier. After controlling for all other variables, a displaced household needs more than eleven years in order to recover the average asset loss stemming from displacement. Furthermore, the effect of length of settlement is weak for households in the first two quartiles of the regression, and only picks up for households located at the upper end of the asset distribution. These results hold even when the outliers for length of settlement are eliminated.

Insertion into labor markets and the capacity to generate income positively contribute to asset accumulation at destination sites. In particular, insertion in labor markets appears as an effective strategy for accumulating assets more effectively; having an unemployed head reduces asset accumulation by COP$1.4 million (US$648). Although the coefficient for unemployment somehow decreases when additional controls are included, the size of the coefficient is still large, and is significant for the different specifications. The negative impact of unemployment is particularly large for households in the upper quartile of the asset distribution.

Human capital variables play an important role with respect to asset accumulation, yet the sign representative of having been previously dedicated to agricultural activities is the opposite of the expected one. Better educated households are able to accumulate more assets, yet the effect is not large given the overall low education levels of the displaced population. One additional year of education for an average displaced household whose head has 5.7 years of schooling increases asset accumulation by COP$0.12 million

Table 4.5   The determinants of asset accumulation

Variables	Coefficient (t-statistic)	Coefficient (t-statistic)	Coefficient (t-statistic)	Coefficient (t-statistic)	Coefficient (t-statistic)	Coefficient (t-statistic)	Coefficient (t-statistic)	Coefficient (t-statistic)
Length of settlement—days	5.9849 (13.52)***	5.0295 (11.15)***					5.4392 (11.98)***	4.3369 (9.29)***
Length of settlement squared	−0.0005 (−7.28)***	−0.0004 (−5.98)***					−0.0005 (−6.53)***	−0.0004 (−4.99)***
Years of schooling—household head			724.5709 (2.22)**	629.3155 (1.99)**			605.5615 (1.93)*	535.1510 (1.73)*
Years of schooling squared			−50.1199 (−2.63)***	−41.8751 (−2.26)**			−44.6176 (−2.44)**	−38.6286 (−2.14)**
Dedicated to agricultural activities—origin site			2,184.0950 (4.26)***	1,510.2020 (3.04)***			1,768.3990 (3.30)***	1,208.7300 (2.29)**
Age—household head			350.1363 (3.36)***	401.6913 (4.02)***			207.5940 (1.96)**	265.0617 (2.57)***
Age squared			−2.8989 (−2.66)***	−3.4527 (−3.30)***			−1.6865 (−1.54)	−2.2781 (−2.13)**
Unemployment at destination—household head			−2,524.0160 (−3.78)***	−1,996.9930 (−3.09)***			−1,010.3210 (−1.56)	−1,046.7110 (−1.65)*
Potential rents—assets at origin site			0.0000 (0.14)	0.0000 (−0.26)			0.0000 (−0.08)	−0.0001 (−0.33)
Contact at destination (family, friend)			−684.2316 (−1.25)	−485.1001 (−0.91)			127.2599 (0.24)	37.4021 (0.07)
HH average number of organizations—destination			−193.7157 (−0.50)	83.3880 (0.22)			−409.2494 (−1.10)	−160.8150 (−0.44)
Beneficiaries of income-generating programs			3,227.1260 (5.49)***	3,391.9620 (5.87)***			1,840.8230 (3.20)***	2,159.8890 (3.74)***
Male household head					2,084.8420 (3.64)***	1,529.4110 (2.76)***	978.1162 (1.69)*	817.0753 (1.43)
Head abandoned or left household					−283.5218 (−0.30)	−394.9613 (−0.43)	470.1106 (−0.52)	−651.4437 (−0.73)
Ethnic minority					−2,464.0960 (−4.00)***	−1,890.5620 (−2.79)***	−2,448.7600 (−4.16)***	−1,828.4010 (−2.80)***
Dependency ratio					−969.9969 (−0.90)	−1,893.3370 (−1.81)*	808.6833 (0.74)	136.8013 (0.13)
Constant	2,191.3410 (3.03)***	−9,588.1870 (−0.86)	−2,931.0320 (−1.02)	−14,954.7900 (−1.27)	9,027.2670 (11.17)***	−1,491.9110 (−0.13)	−5,859.4880 (−1.95)***	−19,492.5800 (−1.69)*
Department controls	No	Yes	No	Yes	No	Yes	No	Yes
Observations	2,332	2,331	2,319	2,318	2,321	2,320	2,319	2,318
R^2	0.1052	0.1851	0.0536	0.1612	0.0256	0.1337	0.1343	0.2067

Source: Authors' calculations based on ENHD (2004).

Note: Controls for municipality size are included (country capital, large city, and medium size city).

***Significant at the 1 percent level.

**Significant at the 5 percent level.

*Significant at the 10 percent level.

Table 4.6   The determinants of asset accumulation

	IV		Quantile regression		
Variables	Coefficient (t-statistic)	Coefficient (t-statistic)	Coefficient (t-statistic) q(0.25)	Coefficient (t-statistic) q(0.50)	Coefficient (t-statistic) q(0.75)
Length of settlement—days	4.9934 (4.86)***	3.0998 (2.05)**	0.1476 (10.47)***	0.4145 (11.98)***	1.0936 (13.19)***
Length of settlement squared	-0.0004 (-3.53)***	-0.0002 (-1.27)	0.0000 (-5.98)***	0.0000 (-7.05)***	-0.0001 (-8.17)***
Years of schooling of household head	517.8523 (1.59)	408.1864 (1.16)	24.8761 (2.61)***	29.9790 (1.20)	2.1582 (0.03)
Years of schooling squared	-41.8577 (-2.46)***	-34.5049 (-1.79)*	-1.3010 (-2.43)**	-1.6385 (-1.12)	-0.5409 (-0.14)
Dedicated to agricultural activities at origin site	1942.9430 (3.30)***	1499.2370 (2.30)**	-27.1154 (-1.58)	3.9144 (0.09)	192.4528 (1.86)*
Age of the household head	172.7377 (1.41)	206.5441 (1.61)	9.6973 (2.87)***	20.7839 (2.49)***	49.5402 (2.44)**
Age squared	-1.1452 (-0.80)	-1.4695 (-0.99)	-0.0973 (-2.83)***	-0.1942 (-2.25)**	-0.4407 (-2.09)**
Unemployment at destination site—household head	-248.5263 (-0.19)	235.8879 (0.16)	-67.8770 (-3.26)***	-98.3382 (-1.91)*	-243.5680 (-1.93)*
Potential rents—assets at origin site	0.0000 (-0.15)	-0.0001 (-0.81)	0.0000 (2.53)***	0.0000 (-0.63)	0.0000 (0.35)
Contact at destination site (family, friend)	314.5051 (0.57)	188.0833 (0.33)	26.4329 (1.58)	9.6449 (0.23)	-15.5832 (-0.15)
Household head—average number organization at destination site	-132.8377 (-0.27)	217.8818 (0.40)	0.0837 (0.01)	8.1493 (0.28)	2.5950 (0.04)
					(continued)

Table 4.6 (continued)

Variables	IV		Quantile regression		
	Coefficient (t-statistic)	Coefficient (t-statistic)	Coefficient (t-statistic) q(0.25)	Coefficient (t-statistic) q(0.50)	Coefficient (t-statistic) q(0.75)
Beneficiaries of income-generating programs	6744.4650	10734.5900	146.6346	284.0821	248.5947
	(0.81)	(1.12)	(7.88)***	(6.08)***	(2.22)***
Male household head	650.9820	165.4665	52.5938	102.0972	162.0971
	(0.82)	(0.18)	(2.83)***	(2.21)**	(1.47)
Head abandoned or left household	-1086.7560	-1727.6980	-48.5975	-58.9054	-127.6213
	(-0.84)	(-1.14)	(-1.70)*	(-0.82)	(-0.72)
Ethnic minority	-2791.1260	-1882.1500	-41.0669	-90.5849	-427.3063
	(-4.42)***	(-2.68)***	(-1.96)**	(-1.72)*	(-3.36)***
Dependency ratio	1341.9860	1333.7860	-14.0638	-150.7804	11.0863
	(0.94)	(0.81)	(0.39)	(-1.74)*	(0.05)
Constant	-7272.8910	-16487.2800	-642.4860	-1576.8250	-3809.1740
	(-2.51)***	(-3.37)***	(-6.39)***	(-6.15)***	(-5.98)***
Department controls	No	Yes	Yes	Yes	Yes
Observations	2,319	2,318	2,318	2,318	2,318
R^2	0.094	0.1058	0.007	0.0824	0.2429

Source: Authors' calculations based on ENHD (2004).

Note: Controls for municipality size are included (country capital, large city, and medium-sized city).

***Significant at the 1 percent level.

**Significant at the 5 percent level.

*Significant at the 10 percent level.

(US$55). The effect of education vanishes, however, for quartile regressions, and is only significant for households in the lowest quartile. On the other hand, the fact of having been previously dedicated to agriculture contributes positively to asset accumulation. This result is opposite our a priori hypothesis, and is robust for all of the different specifications. Presumably, after controlling for other characteristics, this variable may be capturing some unobservable characteristics, such as the entrepreneurial ability of persons who had small agricultural enterprises prior to displacement. Lastly, asset accumulation is higher for households with middle-aged heads. The impact of age is higher as we move up the quartiles.

Assets at origin sites that are still under a household's control—likewise, social capital—do not contribute in any way to asset accumulation. Assets at origin sites are not statistically significant and the coefficient is negligible. Despite being able to control a proportion of their assets at the point of origin, these assets may not be producing rents, or the rents may not be sufficient to expand asset holdings. Social capital—the number of organizations with which household members are affiliated at destination sites, likewise, the number of contacts they have—is not statistically significant for any of the estimated specifications. Therefore, only human capital seems to contribute to asset accumulation at destination sites.

After controlling for other characteristics, the contribution of income-generating programs to asset accumulation is large and significant. Asset holdings for beneficiaries of income-generating programs are COP$2.2 million (US$1018) larger. The coefficient for beneficiaries of income-generating programs, however, is not robust. When additional controls are included, the coefficient decreases significantly. This result is expected, as being the beneficiary of income-generating programs is related to household characteristics. Despite these positive results, the coefficient for participation in income-generating programs loses significance after instrumentalizing for it.

Vulnerable households are less able to recover from asset loss. Male-headed households fare better during the recovery process, and as we move up the quartiles, the significance of a household being male-headed with respect to asset recovery increases. The estimations that include only vulnerability variables show a large and significant positive effect for having a male household head. However, once other controls are incorporated into the estimation, the size of the coefficient reduces. Presumably, female-headed households exhibit particular vulnerable characteristics that reduce asset accumulation. After controlling for these characteristics, the impact of being a male-headed household decreases (COP$1 million [US$462]). On the other hand, asset accumulation does indeed seem difficult for ethnic minorities. Ethnic minorities face poor conditions at destination sites because their connections with their cultural heritage and social networks have been broken; some groups have difficulties speaking in Spanish, and thus have less access to government programs. Thus, the asset holdings of ethnic minorities are COP$2.0 million (US$925) lower. This result is robust for different specification and persists even after controlling for other characteristics.

The displacement shock is certainly large. Conflict and forced migration brings about a depletion of physical, financial, human, and social capital. The erosion of a household's asset base, coupled with restricted access to labor markets, pushes a displaced household into an extremely vulnerable situation and hinders asset accumulation, thus imposing high long-term costs that are not easily overcome. Notably, these consequences persist through time. Indeed, only a small group of households appear to have initiated a moderate accumulation of assets under such conditions. The extent of asset accumulation for displaced households is strongly related to the conditions required for successful productive activities—a longer period of settlement at destination sites, access to credits, to employment, and a less vulnerable household structure. However, since the asset loss due to displacement is substantial, households will not be able to engage in virtuous cycles of asset accumulation. For example, asset loss for a household that reactively displaced and suffered the death of its main breadwinner is COP$10.2 million (US$4,722) higher than for other households. On the other hand, none of the variables determining asset accumulation at destination sites is able to offset this effect.

4.5   Conclusions

A conflict-induced shock imposes heavy asset losses upon a group of victims, in this case, a displaced population. The nature of conflict-related events leading to forced displacement and the resulting consequences strongly determines the magnitude of asset loss. Better-off households with larger asset holdings or that are strongly embedded in social networks pose attractive targets for illegal armed groups. Because their asset holdings prior to displacement are large and the consequences of the attacks are correspondingly extremely costly, such households suffer substantial asset loss. On the other hand, households with a less traumatic victimization profile or that migrate preventively in anticipation that the conflict will escalate tend to face less severe asset loss, and are thus better able to cope with displacement shock.

Regardless of the extent of asset loss caused by forced migration, all displaced households are left with an asset base seemingly insufficient for escaping poverty. Displaced persons cannot be assimilated in the same way that traditional migrants are. Our results show that displaced households do not catch up even after consolidating settlement at destination sites. Displaced households become locked into a low-level economic trajectory; once that happens, leaping forward into a high-return asset level becomes highly unlikely. In this respect, forced displacement has generated a poverty trap for certain segments of the Colombian population. Targeted assistance, such as asset transfers and protections against shocks, is needed to stimulate growth.

Appendix

First-stage regressions for instrumental variable regressions

Table 4A.1   **First stage: Intramunicipal displacement**

Variables	Coefficient (t-statistic)
Reactive displacement	0.0231
	(1.15)
Household head dead or not present	–0.0731
	(–2.96)***
Perception of the presence of illegal armed groups	–0.0229
	(–1.00)
Perception of the presence of government forces	–0.0955
	(–5.51)***
Household—average number of organizations	0.0289
	(2.88)***
Formal land title	0.0442
	(2.09)**
Formal land title*presence of government forces	–0.0506
	(–1.71)*
Total hectares of land	–0.0003
	(–2.05)*
Years of schooling of the household head	–0.0026
	(–0.78)
Number of persons between 12 and 17 years of age	0.0085
	(1.21)
Number of persons between 17 and 65 years of age	0.0042
	(0.80)
Ethnic minority	0.0405
	(2.12)**
Contacts at destination site	0.0636
	(4.18)***
Dedicated to agricultural activities at origin site	0.0201
	(1.38)
Constant	–0.1040
	(–0.32)
Observations	2,318
F-statistic	11.39

***Significant at the 1 percent level.
**Significant at the 5 percent level.
*Significant at the 10 percent level.

Table 4A.2   **First stage: Beneficiaries of income-generating programs**

Variables	Coefficient (*t*-statistic)	Coefficient (*t*-statistic)
Length of settlement—days	0.0001	0.0002
	(6.56)***	(8.54)***
Length of settlement squared	0.0000	0.0000
	(−4.44)***	(−5.90)***
Years of schooling of the household head	0.0145	0.0116
	(1.17)	(0.95)
Years of schooling squared	−0.0005	−0.0004
	(−0.75)	(−0.58)
Dedicated to agricultural activities at origin site	−0.0337	−0.0380
	(−1.58)	(−1.83)*
Age—household head	0.0076	0.0072
	(1.81)*	(1.78)*
Age squared	−0.0001	−0.0001
	(−2.48)***	(−2.32)**
Unemployment at destination site of household head	−0.1341	−0.1278
	(−5.24)***	(−5.14)***
Potential rents—assets at origin site	0.0000	0.0000
	(0.33)	(0.38)
Contact at destination site (family, friend)	−0.0196	−0.0121
	(−0.94)	(−0.59)
Household head—average number organization at destination site	−0.0427	−0.0441
	(−2.91)***	(−3.08)***
Male household head	0.0688	0.0757
	(2.99)***	(3.38)***
Head abandoned or left household	0.1103	0.1226
	(3.04)***	(3.48)***
Ethnic minority	0.0371	−0.0113
	(1.66)*	(−0.44)
Dependency ratio	−0.1161	−0.1298
	(−2.68)***	(−3.09)***
Beneficiary of humanitarian aid	0.0748	0.0685
	(3.00)***	(2.82)***
Constant	0.0259	−0.4391
	0.22	(−0.97)
Department controls	No	Yes
Observations	2,319	2,318
F-statistic	10.06	8.37

Source: Authors' calculations based on ENHD (2004).

Notes: Controls for urbanization structure are included. These include country capital, large city, medium-sized city, and small city.

***Significant at the 1 percent level.

**Significant at the 5 percent level.

*Significant at the 10 percent level.

References

Adato, M., M. R. Carter, and J. May. 2006. Exploring poverty traps and social exclusion in South Africa using qualitative and quantitative data. *Journal of Development Studies* 42 (2): 226–47.

André, C., and J. P. Platteau. 1998. Land relations under unbearable stress: Rwanda caught in the Malthusian trap. *Journal of Economic Behavior and Organization* 34 (1): 1–47.

Azam, J. P., and A. Hoeffler. 2002. Violence against civilians in civil wars: Looting or terror? *Journal of Peace Research* 39 (4): 461–85.

Barrett, C. B., P. P. Marenya, J. McPeak, B. Minten, F. Murithi, W. Oluoch-Kosura, F. Place, J. C. Randrianarisoa, J. Rasambainarivo, and J. Wangila. 2004. *Welfare dynamics in rural Kenya and Madagascar.* BASIS Document, University of Wisconsin-Madison.

Barrett, C. B., and J. G. McPeak. 2006. Poverty traps and safety nets. In *Poverty, inequality and development, essays in honor of Erik Thorbecke,* ed. A. de Janvry and R. Kanbur, 131–54. New York: Springer.

Barrientos, A., and A. Shepherd. 2003. Chronic poverty and social protection. Paper presented at the Chronic Poverty Research Centre (CPRC) Conference on Chronic Poverty, University of Manchester. 7–9 April, Manchester, England.

Brück, T. 2004. Coping strategies in post-war rural Mozambique. Households in Conflict Network (HiCN) Working Paper no. 02.

Carter, M. R., and C. Barrett. 2006. The economics of poverty traps and persistent poverty: An asset based approach. *Journal of Development Studies* 42 (2): 178–99.

Carter, M. R., and J. May. 1999. Poverty, livelihood and class in rural South Africa. *World Development* 27 (1): 1–20.

Corbett, J. 1988. Famine and household coping strategies. *World Development* 16 (9): 1099–1112.

Dercon, S. 1998. Wealth, risk and activity choice: Cattle in Western Tanzania. *Journal of Development Economics* 55:1–42.

Durlauf, S. N. 1992. A theory of persistent income inequality. NBER Working Paper no. 4056. Cambridge, MA: National Bureau of Economic Research, April.

Engel, S., and A. M. Ibáñez. 2007. Displacement due to violence in Colombia: A household level analysis. *Economic Development and Cultural Change* 55 (2): 335–65.

Fafchamps, M., and F. Gubert. 2007. The formation of risk-sharing networks. *Journal of Development Economics* 83 (2): 326–50.

Fafchamps, M., C. Udry, and K. Czukas. 1998. Drought and savings in West Africa: Are livestock a buffer stock? *Journal of Development Economics* 55:273–305.

Foster, A., and M. Rosenzweig. 2001. Imperfect commitment, altruism and the family: Evidence from transfer behavior in low-income rural areas. *Review of Economic and Statistics* 83 (3): 389–407.

Galor, O., and J. Zeira. 1993. Income distribution and macroeconomics. *The Review of Economic Studies* 60 (1): 35–52.

Gaviria, A. 2000. Increasing returns and the evolution of violent crime: The case of Colombia. *Journal of Development Economics* 61 (1): 1–25.

Garay, L. J. 2008. *Proceso Nacional de Verificación de los Derechos de la Población Desplazada.* Primer informe a la Corte Constitucional, Bogotá, Colombia.

Hirshleifer, J. 2001. *The dark side of the force, economic foundations of conflict theory.* Cambridge: Cambridge University Press.

Hoddinott, J. 2006. Shocks and their consequences across and within households in rural Zimbabwe. *Journal of Development Studies* 42 (2): 301–21.

Hulme, D., and A. Shepherd. 2003. Conceptualizing chronic poverty. *World Development* 31 (3): 403–23.

Jacoby, H., and E. Skoufias. 1997. Risk, financial markets, and human capital in a developing country. *Review of Economic Studies* 64 (3): 311–35.

Jensen, R. 2000. Agricultural volatility and investments in children. *American Economic Review* 90 (2): 399–404.

Justino, P., and P. Verwimp. 2006. Poverty dynamics, violent conflict and convergence in Rwanda. HiCN Working Paper no. 16.

Krishna, A., D. Lumonya, M. Markiewicz, F. Mugumya, A. Kafuko, and J. Wegoye. 2006. Escaping poverty and becoming poor in 36 villages of central and western Uganda. *Journal of Development Studies* 42 (2): 346–70.

Ligon, E., J. P. Thomas, and T. Worrall. 2001. Informal insurance arrangements in village economies. *Review of Economic Studies* 69 (1): 209–44.

Little, P. D., M. P. Stone, T. Mogues, A. P. Castro, and W. Negatu. 2006. Moving in place: Drought and poverty dynamics in South Woll, Ethiopia. *Journal of Development Studies* 42 (2): 200–25.

Matowu, J. M., and F. Stewart. 2001. Uganda: The social and economic costs of conflict. In *War and underdevelopment, volume 2: Country experiences,* ed. F. Stewart and V. Fitzgerald, 240–88. New York: Oxford University Press.

Montenegro, A., and C. E. Posada. 2001. *La violencia en Colombia.* Bogotá, Colombia: Alfaomega.

Mookherjee, D., and D. Ray. 2002. Contractual structure and wealth accumulation. *The American Economic Review* 92 (4): 818–49.

Moser, C., and A. Winston. 2002. Violence in the Central-American region: Toward an integrated framework for violence reduction. Working Paper no. 171. Overseas Development Institute, London.

Reardon, T., and S. A. Vosti. 1995. Links between rural poverty and the environment in developing countries: Asset categories and investment poverty. *World Development* 23 (9): 1495–1506.

Rosenzweig, M. R., and H. P. Binswanger. 1993. Wealth, weather risk and the composition of profitability of agricultural investments. *Economic Journal* 103 (416): 56–78.

Rosenzweig, M., and K. I. Wolpin. 1993. Credit market constraints, consumption smoothing and the accumulation of durable production assets in low income countries: Investments in bullocks in India. *Journal of Political Economy* 101 (2): 223–44.

Sen, B. 2003. Drivers of escape and descent: Changing household fortunes in rural Bangladesh. *World Development* 31 (3): 513–34.

Thoumi, F. E. 2002. Illegal drugs in Colombia: From illegal economic boom to social crisis 71. *Annals of the American Academy of Political and Social Science* 582: 102–16.

Townsend, R. M. 1994. Risk and insurance in village India. *Econometrica* 62 (3): 539–91.

Zimmerman, F. J., and M. R. Carter. 2003. Asset smoothing, consumption smoothing and the reproduction of inequality under risk and subsistence constraints. *Journal of Development Economics* 71:233–60.

Comment   Martín González-Rozada

The chapter analyzes the determinants of asset losses due to the internal conflict in Colombia. In particular it focuses on understanding the magnitude of household's asset losses caused by forced displacement by armed groups and the dynamics that eventually helped displaced households to recover their productive ability and asset base. Since there is evidence that after these kinds of conflicts end criminal and illegal activities emerge, establishing how the asset losses occur during internal conflicts and understanding the process of asset accumulation post-conflicts will help to design public action aimed at preventing an increase in criminal violence. The study uses both qualitative and quantitative methodologies to achieve these goals.

The chapter does a very good job in describing the losses stemming from forced displacement and the qualitative methodology used is very well suited for this. This methodology is also used to identify the determinants of asset losses and asset accumulation. On the other hand, the quantitative methodology used to quantify the determinants of asset losses and asset accumulation in the new places deserves a few comments.

The quantitative analysis is based on a constructed sample of displaced households' beneficiaries of income-generating programs (treatment group) and displaced households' nonbeneficiaries of such programs (control group). Even when the authors say that the control group is representative of the displaced population at large there are reasons to think it could be a strong assumption. The control group sample is selected using another sample as a sampling frame (the RUT system). The RUT system covers only 150,000 people of the more than 2.5 million people affected by forced displacement (as reported in the chapter). The RUT system is not representative of the displaced population; however, the design of the control sample is based on it. The RUT system is taken as a sampling frame. From this system, through a stratified sampling procedure, authors select a group of RUT households and add another group of similar size (non-RUT displaced households) obtained from neighborhood households to the RUT households selected in the stratification process. It seems that the whole representativeness of the control group sample depends on the RUT system having all the characteristics of displaced population in Colombia. This feature is not trivial since to be listed in the RUT system the displaced households had to request assistance in a parish of the Catholic Church, or they are included by censuses conducted by the Catholic Church (not in all municipalities). The fact that at most about 6 percent of the displaced people requested assistance from a parish of the Catholic Church seems to indicate

Martín González-Rozada is professor of economics at the Universidad Torcuato Di Tella.

that probably displaced people not listed in the RUT system have dissimilar characteristics. Given the size difference between those displaced people listed and not listed in the RUT system and the potential differences in the characteristics of both groups, one should expect the non-RUT households to be of a larger size than the RUT households. All these features make it difficult to believe that the control group sample is representative of the displaced population. Nevertheless, the chapter points out that there exists "a recent survey representative of the displaced population" that shows similar observable socioeconomic characteristics to those founded in the chapter. I think it should be useful, as a way to improve the robustness of the important results already founded in the chapter, if the authors can address in more detail the aforementioned concerns.

Crime Distribution and Victim Behavior during a Crime Wave

Rafael Di Tella, Sebastian Galiani,
and Ernesto Schargrodsky

5.1 Introduction

Previous research on crime by criminologists, sociologists, and economists has found it hard to estimate the distribution of the burden of a given increase in crime across the different groups in society. One important difficulty is that crime-avoiding activities, such as protection and mimicking of low-victimization types, may differ across groups (particularly across different income groups) or may change over time (see, for example, Cook [1986]; Clarke [1983]; and Bushway and Reuter [2008]). As Levitt (1999) explains:

> ". . . the natural tendency is to calculate the extra burden borne by the poor as a result of higher crime victimization. Such a calculation, however, would ignore the fact that individuals distort their behavior in costly ways (for example, by moving to the suburbs, investing in security systems, or not going out after dark). Any measure of the burden of crime should incorporate not only the costs of those victimized, but also the investment made to avoid victimization. For example, if crime avoidance is a positive function of income (Cullen and Levitt (1999)), then ignoring costs of avoidance will understate the true crime-related burden felt by the rich. (Levitt 1999, 88).

Rafael Di Tella is the Joseph C. Wilson Professor of Business Administration at Harvard Business School, a research associate of the National Bureau of Economic Research, and a member of the Canadian Institute for Advanced Research. Sebastian Galiani is professor of economics at Washington University in St. Louis. Ernesto Schargrodsky is a professor and dean of the business school at Universidad Torcuato Di Tella.

We thank participants at various seminars for helpful comments, the IDB Poverty Reduction and Social Protection Network for financial support, and Maximiliano Appendino, Matias Cattaneo, and Paulo Somaini for excellent research assistance.

Thus, a lower victimization rate in one group may not reflect a lower burden of crime, but rather a higher investment in crime avoidance. Moreover, protection activities by one group can displace crime onto another group. Data on protection, and other crime-avoiding activities required for a proper calculation, however, are not part of the official statistics collected by the police and are rare in victimization surveys and empirical studies (see, for example, Ehrlich [1996], who makes this point explicitly). Another serious difficulty is that only a small fraction of the population is usually victimized, and sharp changes in victimization rates are unusual, making it hard to design tests with sufficient statistical power to detect differential changes across income groups. This is evident, for example, in Levitt (1999), who uses data for the United States.

We study the question of how an increase in crime is distributed across income groups using a crime survey in Argentina where people were asked about their victimization experience, crime-avoiding activities, and income levels. The focus on Argentina is potentially helpful as the country experienced a sharp increase in crime rates during the 1990s (especially during the 2001 crisis), giving salience to the problem of crime. Official statistics, for example, show that the main categories of crime more than doubled (at least) in Buenos Aires during the 1990s, in spite of a reduction in crime-reporting rates. In a relatively short period of time, the main cities of the country experienced striking increases in crime, making crime either the main or one of the main concerns of the population, according to opinion polls. Abundant anecdotal evidence suggests that this crime wave was accompanied by a significant growth in private security protection and other crime-avoiding strategies.

Our results confirm that there was a large, statistically significant increase in crime over the period of analysis. The total victimization rate, which stands for having been a victim of a crime at home or in the street, went up approximately 24 percentage points. We then use this victimization survey to obtain several estimates of interest. First, significant differences are observed across income groups. The poor (i.e., those below our estimate of the median income in the sample) experience an increase in the total victimization rate of 28 percentage points, while the rich (i.e., those above the sample median) experience an increase of 19 percentage points. In other words, the poor have experienced increases in victimization rates that are almost 1.5 times larger than those experienced by high-income people.

We then study whether this could be explained by differential crime avoidance by the rich. One piece of indirect evidence is obtained by studying victimization categories where the cost of changes in behavior (i.e., adaptation) differs. For example, changing behavior to avoid street robbery (for example, by avoiding dark places or by mimicking less attractive targets) costs less money than changing behavior to avoid home robbery (for example, by hiring private security).[1] An important finding is that robberies in the street, where the rich cannot do better than mimic the behavior of the poor, show similar increases in victimization for both income groups. For home robberies, where the rich can protect themselves with expensive protection devices, we find larger increases in victimization rates among the poor. The size of this differential impact is large. In the early 1990s, rich individuals reported victimization rates that are more than double those reported by the poor. But by 2001, high-income respondents reported victimization rates at home that are smaller (in fact, they are only 75 percent of those reported by the poor).

A third finding of the chapter concerns direct evidence on crime-avoidance activities by high- and low-income groups. For mimicking strategies, we consider avoiding the use of jewelry and avoiding dangerous places. For protection strategies, we consider the use of alarm and the hiring of private security. We cannot reject the hypothesis of broadly similar changes in mimicking across high- and low-income groups, but we estimate a significantly larger increase in protection activities by the rich.

Fourth, we then estimate the correlation between victim-adaptation measures and crime victimization in panel regressions. We find a negative correlation between individual private protection measures and home crime victimization rates, controlling for individual and period fixed effects as well as neighborhood specific-period effects. We also offer some tentative arguments that can be used in a causal interpretation.

Finally, the chapter concludes with a short section illustrating one possible use of these estimates to construct an indicator of the burden of crime across income groups. We observe, for example, that street crime allows for mimicking and other low-cost forms of victim adaptation, and that street crime has evolved similarly for rich and poor. Thus, it appears safe to assume that the burden of street crime is similar for both groups under the assumption of negligible mimicking costs. For home robbery, the data paint a different picture. Consider a given increase in victimization at home. On the one hand, high- and low-income groups protect themselves at different rates. Interpreting our estimates of protection on home robbery as causal, we note that the rich are predicted to have avoided almost all of the crime increase (indeed, the difference between the predicted victimization rate and zero is not significant). We note that this is consistent with the observed dynamics of home victimization for the rich (which exhibits no detectable change). On the other hand, and again under a causal interpretation of our estimates, the poor are predicted to have avoided a small part of the increase in crime. We note that this is inconsistent with the observed dynamics of home victimization for the poor, which shows a large increase: the predicted rate of

---

1. The use of personal bodyguards on the street is exceptional.

home robbery for the poor is less than half of what is actually observed. We conjecture that this is the result of a negative externality on the poor, arising from the home protection of the rich.

Although several topics studied in criminology are closely connected to our chapter, previous empirical work on the precise question that we focus on is not large.[2] Some well-known work in criminology has found that victimization rates are higher among high-income groups (see, for example, Shaw and McKay [1942]; Pantazis [2000]; Nilsson and Estrada [2003]; inter alia).[3] It is hard, however, to translate the results of these papers into the differential burden across income groups from a given increase in crime without more information on the adaptation activities of potential victims.[4] A study by Levitt (1999) uses data on crime rates across Chicago neighborhoods as well as data from the U.S. National Crime Victimization Survey over the period 1970 to 1990 to focus on a similar set of issues. He finds that property crime in the United States became more concentrated among the poor during this period by approximately 60 percent. Closer to our purposes is Gaviria and Pages (2002), who study victimization rates for seventeen countries in Latin America between 1996 and 1998, presenting a simple model where potential victims have the possibility of protecting themselves. They show that crime in Latin America tends to affect mostly rich and middle class households living in larger cities. There is relatively less empirical work on victim adaptation by economists, although work by Lott (1998) and Lott and Mustard (1997) has explored the possibility that potential victims protect themselves through concealed handguns, while Cullen and Levitt (1999) study urban flight as a response to high rates of city crime. A related issue is that criminals may respond to victim adaptation; for example, by switching to other areas or other crimes. Hessling (1994) reviews the literature on crime displacement (see also Cornish and Clarke [1987]). Levitt (1999) explains several limitations of previous work, including those emerging from the lack of information on crime avoidance activities.

Section 5.2 briefly describes the theory that illustrates the effect of increases

---

2. To give just one example: Cook (1986) focuses on how adaptation by potential victims can explain the difference between the emotional cost of crime (of which one measure is fear and appears to be higher for women than for men) and actual victimization experience (which is higher for men). See also the discussion on page 20 of Bushway and Reuter (2008).

3. A broader comparison across countries, with somewhat different results, is presented in van Kesteren, Mayhew, and Nieuwbeerta (2000). Note that there is certainly also work aimed at understanding how income distribution (or unemployment rates) are related to crime levels.

4. For reviews of the literature see Land, McCall, and Cohen (1990); Patterson (1991); inter alia. While empirical work on the issue of private protection is rare, theoretical work includes Shavell (1991); de Meza and Gould (1992); and Koo and Png (1994). See also Becker (1965, 1968); Ehrlich (1973); Witte (1980); Freeman (1996); Tauchen, Witte, and Griesinger (1994); Papps and Winkelman (2000); Fajnzylber, Lederman, and Loayza (2000, 2002); Dal Bo and Dal Bo (2004); Mocan, Billups, and Overland (2005); inter alia. Glaeser and Sacerdote (1999) discuss the high crime rates in cities, while Londono, Gaviria, and Guerrero (2000) discuss property crime relative to violent crime in Latin America.

in victimization across income groups when victims can adapt. Section 5.3 describes our data and empirical strategy. Section 5.4 presents our basic set of results, while section 5.5 concludes.

5.2   A Theoretical Illustration of Crime with Victim-Adaptation

When crime increases, high-income citizens can protect themselves through the acquisition of expensive alarms or the hiring of private security devices. If this occurs, it is possible that low-income households suffer the main increase in victimization. We illustrate these ideas using a simple and stylized one-shot game.

Start by assuming a continuum of agents with indexed ability x_i spread over the closed interval [0, 1] with distribution function $G(.)$, assumed to be continuous over the domain of x and strictly concave. One simple way to derive equilibrium crime is to assume that a friction exists in the labor market, so that wages below f cannot be paid legally. This means the fraction $G(f)$ of individuals become criminals to avoid starvation.

Noncriminals earn $w_i = x_i$ and have to decide whether to set up an (observable) security system at cost c, or do nothing in this regard. For simplicity, we assume that the security system is fully effective and that wealth is not observable, so that criminals distribute randomly among unprotected agents.[5] Then, people set up a security system if

$$w_i - c > w_i(1 - p),$$

where p the probability of victimization is equal to

$$p = \frac{G(f)}{G(w^*)},$$

and where the cut-off w^* is defined as

$$\frac{G(f)}{G(w^*)} w^* = c,$$

where agents with $w_i \geq w^*$ hire security systems.[6]

Note that when the predisposition for crime increases—for example, because the friction f becomes larger—the consumption of security systems increases (agents with lower w_i now protect themselves). And because protection is a normal good (and assumed to be effective), increases in crime lead

---

5. The assumption of fully effective protection seems strong, but we note that private security booths are patently observable, while the main companies installing alarm systems also place a sticker on the main entrance with the legend "this house is fitted with an alarm system by company xx." This is in contrast to the car protection system (Lo Jack) studied in Ayres and Levitt (1998).

6. Note that if the security system cost c is too high nobody hires private security, as it may happen for street protection. Also note that we allow thieves to become victims themselves, but we assume they do not hire private security.

the distribution of crime to become concentrated on lower income groups. Indeed, the probability of victimization for the unprotected increases on two accounts. First, the total number of criminals increases. And second, the number of unprotected targets is lower as more citizens hire private security. The concentration of crime increases on the group of poor individuals is all a consequence of crime displacement taking place due to higher investment in protection. In summary, the model yields the following predictions:

- The use of private security devices increases with the number of criminals.
- The use of private security devices concentrates on rich households.
- The poor suffer the main burden of crime increases.

The predictions of this simple model can be compared to our data on the evolution of crime in Argentina during the 1990s. At a relatively low unemployment rate, crime was low. As unemployment rates soared in the mid-1990s, the rich increasingly paid the costs of hiring private protection. This behavioral response allowed the rich to avoid victimization, so that subsequent increases in unemployment continued raising the crime levels experienced by the poor. Crime rises as a result of the increase in the number of criminals (due to, say, higher unemployment), but it concentrates disproportionally in poor neighborhoods as high-income neighborhoods hire private security devices (which constitutes a negative externality on the poor).[7]

5.3   Data and Empirical Strategy

5.3.1   Design and Data Description

Design

A household victimization survey is the main source of information for this study.[8] The target population of the study was the population of the Buenos Aires Metropolitan Area. The questionnaire was performed in 2002 to 200 households in the city of Buenos Aires and 200 households in the suburban Great Buenos Aires through telephone interviews. In addition, 100 street interviews were performed to people that declared not to have a home telephone line. The survey collected information on victimization

---

7. Gaviria and Pages (2002) present a related model of crime protection, but without displacement. Dal Bo and Dal Bo (2004) analyze a general equilibrium model of appropriation, which predicts a positive association between crime and inequality that can naturally be applied to study the changes during a period of economic reforms such as those that occurred in Argentina during the 1990s. Fanzylver et al. (2002) document such a positive correlation.

8. The survey was performed by the opinion poll company Catterberg & Associates for the Inter-American Development Bank (IDB) Poverty Reduction and Social Protection Network.

events, crime reporting, behavioral responses to crime, consumption of private protection, possession of durable goods and assets, and demographic household information. Note that official crime statistics do not typically collect such data, so that their inadequacy (for the purposes of this chapter) goes beyond the usual difficulties arising from victim underreporting or political manipulation.

Although the survey was cross-sectional, it asked households to report retrospective information for the entire decade (1990 to 2001). However, retrospective information is sometimes subject to recall bias. Thus, the survey was designed exploiting several techniques specially developed to minimize this nuisance. First, the information set was restricted to major crime events: armed robberies and forcible entry into homes. The restriction to major events significantly reduces typical recall bias of retrospection, which is mainly associated to "microscopic" events (Aday 1996; Reuband 1994). Moreover, we concentrate on whether the household has been the victim of a crime during a period of time, but not on the number of times this has occurred. We should expect that recall bias has a larger effect on the latter than on the former. Additionally, the retrospective information was asked sacrificing precision about the exact year of occurrence of an event, but gaining confidence by considering longer time periods. Thus, the survey considered three periods: 1990 to 1994 (the first part of the decade with one-digit unemployment rates and strong growth); 1995 to 2000 (the period after the Tequila Crisis, with the unemployment rate around 15 percent—after a peak of 18.3 percent—and a declining economy after 1998); and the final year of 2001 (with an unemployment rate of 18 percent that then reached 21.5 percent in early 2002, together with the default of the external debt, a large devaluation, and political instability). Moreover, the survey used bounded recall procedures to reduce underreporting of crime events that took place in previous periods (see, among others, Aday [1996]; Sudman, Finn, and Lannon 1984). More importantly, our main question is which group has been mostly affected by the increase in crime levels. As this question refers to the relative changes in victimization rates rather than the levels, the results will not be affected by recall bias if this bias affects both groups (rich and poor) similarly (this is the root identification assumption of our chapter).

A final data issue is that the measure of income levels is a delicate matter because some people decline to reveal their income in a survey. Income questions could be particularly sensitive in a survey about private security. Instead of asking directly about income, the survey addressed this problem by asking questions on education level, ocupation, and availability of cars, appliances (personal computer, air conditioner, and automatic washing machine), and credit cards, in order to infer income levels from these variables. The opinion poll company, following the methodology developed by the Argentine Marketing Association (1998), provided us with an index of income level that collapses all the indicators of household education, ocupa-

Table 5.1   Victimization and reporting rates

	Home robbery		Street robbery	
	Victimization	Reporting	Victimization	Reporting
1990–1994	0.08	0.74	0.10	0.51
1995–2000	0.10	0.45	0.28	0.47
2001	0.10	0.43	0.35	0.37

tion, and wealth into a continuous variable. Appendix A shows the details of this methodology. We define a household as rich if its income index is equal or above the median in our sample (which would approximately correspond to the urban middle class), and poor otherwise.

Data

Our research strategy is based on exploiting the salience of crime in Buenos Aires after the sharp increases in crime during the second half of the 1990s and in particular during the year 2001. Table 5.1 shows that 10.2 percent of the households interviewed by the survey suffered a home robbery (forcible entry into their house) during 2001. This percentage was the same for the whole period 1995 to 2000, and 7.9 percent for 1990 to 1994. Only 43.1 percent of these crimes were reported to the police in 2001, but the figure was larger in the previous years (45.1 percent for 1995 to 2000, and 74.4 percent for 1990 to 1994). For robberies outside the home, 34.6 percent of the individuals in our sample declare that at least one member of the household has been robbed during 2001. This percentage was 27.5 percent for 1995 to 2000, and 10.0 percent for 1990 to 1994, suggesting that there was a significant increase in victimization rates (note that the question refers to periods of different length). The reporting rate of this type of crime tends to be lower than for home robberies, but it is also decreasing (36.8 percent for 2001, 46.7 percent for 1995 to 2000, and 51.1 percent for 1990 to 1994).[9]

These reporting rates confirm that, because of victims' tendency to underreport, official figures underestimate crime levels.[10] Indeed, this problem worsens during crime waves, because crime reporting falls as crime increases. Moreover, the rich are significantly more likely to report crimes at home than the poor, although there were no significant differences in the reporting of street crimes across income groups.

Consistent with this evidence of sharp crime increases, table 5A.6 in

9. These crime and reporting rates are consistent with other victimization surveys performed in the Buenos Aires metropolitan area. For example, a survey performed by the Justice Ministry reports that 41 percent of the respondents declared to have suffered a crime during 1999, but only 29 percent of those crimes were reported to the police (Ministerio de Justicia 2000).

10. Soares (2004) shows that the positive links between crime and development arise because of increases in crime reporting.

appendix B shows a growing feeling of insecurity in the population. The exact question asks, "In your neighborhood, would you say that insecurity with respect to one decade ago has increased a lot, some, a little, has not changed at all, or has decreased?" The answers show that 68.8 percent of individuals think that insecurity increased some or a lot over the previous decade. Less than 1 percent of respondents find that insecurity decreased.

Our research strategy requires changes in crime of the magnitude observed in Argentina between 1990 and 2001 for two reasons. First, it gives us some confidence that crime has "salience" as an issue to individual respondents so that the information produced through the administration of surveys has reasonable accuracy and reliability. Second, it is statistically possible to detect differences across groups (in this case following income lines) without extremely large samples.

Finally, to provide some evidence on the potential presence of recall bias affecting our results, we exploit two extra survey questions. The survey asked at the beginning the number of times a member of the household had been robbed on the street during the period 1990 to 1994. At the very end of the questionnaire, the survey then asked again the number of times a member of the household had been robbed on the street during 1990 to 1992, and during 1993 to 1994, something that allows us to control for the consistency of the responses. There is a high level of consistency among respondents. The correlation between the sum of the responses to these two final questions and the previous response for the whole period is 0.9. Additionally, note that our empirical strategy is based on comparisons across income groups, which will not be affected by recall bias as long as this bias is uncorrelated with income levels. The correlation between our income level index and the difference between the original report of crime and the ex-post report is very low (0.02).

5.3.2 Empirical Strategy

In this chapter we test several propositions regarding the relationship between victimization and income. We first study differences in the change in crime rates across income groups. Specifically we test:

$$(1) \qquad \qquad \Delta Crime_{rich} = \Delta Crime_{poor}$$

against the alternative hypothesis of different crime rates for the two groups, and where $\Delta Crime_{group}$ denotes the change in the crime rate for *group* = *rich, poor* from 1990 to 2001 considering the three subperiods 1990 to 1994, 1995 to 2000, and 2001. Given that the periods have differing lengths, the meaning of having the value of 0.1 (which stands for having 10 percent of the respondents victimized) in two different periods means different things. This makes it transparent that we believe that historical victimization rates taken from memory must be taken with care when used to make absolute statements across periods, such as, "the amount of crime has increased" (although it can partially be done). Instead, we are confident in making statements about differences across groups in a given period, where victimization rates are strictly comparable, and also in conducting difference-in-differences analysis, which exploits the differential change in victimatization between groups, and for which the change in the length of periods, and hence the likelihood of the realization of the event of interest, is affected equally for rich and poor.[11]

Another test concerns differences in the way potential victims adapt across the two income groups. A variety of victim strategies are possible. First, victims may actively protect themselves in such a way that it is more costly for criminals to access the bounty and get away with it safely. A typical example is the hiring of a private security guard, but it also includes the use of alarms and locks. A second possibility is that potential victims may change their behavior in order to passively reduce the likelihood of suffering a crime. A typical example is the case of potential victims of crime who avoid certain high-risk activities (walking alone on the street versus walking in groups). Potential victims may also reduce the expected cost of crime by carrying less money or jewels, both because this reduces the cost of any given crime and also because the probability of suffering a crime is lower. In the latter case victim adaptation can take the form of mimicking, whereby members of some group resemble the potential victims of another group with a lower probability of suffering a crime. For example, carrying fewer jewels makes a rich individual (with lots of money in his wallet) resemble a poor individual (with a thin wallet), where the latter are less attractive to criminals.

As a first approach to testing for the existence of victim adaptation, we study different types of crime where some forms of adaptation are not possible. For example, it is extremely hard to use protection to reduce crime on the streets. Although some extremely rich individuals use bodyguards, this is absolutely exceptional in Argentina. The type of adaptation to reduce such crimes is likely to be cheap, such as walking on the part of the street where there is light, so it is likely to be used by both income groups. However, the use of security guards and alarms as protection for crimes at home is feasible, but expensive, and likely to be used more intensively by the rich. In other words, we test

$$(2) \qquad \Delta \text{CrimeType}_{rich} = \Delta \text{CrimeType}_{poor}$$

where $\Delta CrimeType_{group}$ denotes the change in the crime rate of $type = street,$ $home$ and for the $group = rich, poor$ over the relevant time period. The expectation is that the change in street crime becomes similar for both groups when victims adapt. In contrast, since private protection is more likely to

---

11. This is analogous to the widely conducted studies in education that exploit panel data of test scores, where the inherent difficulty of the exam changes from year to year. These analyses also assume that this potential problem is controlled by the inclusion of year fixed-effects in the regression equations. See Lavy (2002); Galiani, Gertler, and Schargrodsky (2008); inter alia.

be purchased by the rich, we expect the change in home crime to be greater for the poor when victims adapt.

We complement this evidence with direct information on activities that denote adaptation:

$$(3) \qquad\qquad \Delta\text{Activity}_{rich} = \Delta\text{Activity}_{poor},$$

where $\Delta Activity_{group}$ denotes the change in the activity for the *group = rich, poor* over the relevant time period. The expectation is that the change in activities that involve protection at home (security guards and alarms), or a reduction in expected crime costs (avoid carrying jewels or credit cards, and avoid dark and dangerous places) are more intensive for rich individuals.

The final empirical exercise of the chapter is to estimate the effect of changes in behavior ($\Delta Activity_{group}$) on crime victimization ($\Delta CrimeType_{group}$). Although individual, period, and neighborhood period effects are included, it should be noted that an obvious difficulty in estimating such a relationship is the possibility of reverse causality. Accordingly, we explore some arguments that can be used in a causal interpretation of the estimates we present.

5.4   Empirical Results

5.4.1   Total Victimization Rates (at Home plus in the Street)

Figure 5.1 shows that approximately 15 percent of our sample declares to have been the victim of crime (either in the street or at home) at least once during the period 1990 to 1994. This goes up to almost 35 percent during 1995 and 2000 and to almost 40 percent during the year 2001. This survey evidence is consistent with the crime increase documented in official statistics and the media. The official statistics reveal that the number of criminal acts reported to the police in the city of Buenos Aires went up from 2,039 per 100,000 people to 6,633 in the year 2001, an increase of 225 percent. Property crime for the same period went up from 1,685 per 100,000 to 4,687, an increase of 178 percent.

More interesting is figure 5.2, where total crime is separated by income group using our index for income levels. The rich start the decade with double the victimization rate than the poor (22 percent versus 11 percent, a difference that is significant at the 1 percent level). By the year 2001, the rates had risen to approximately 40 percent and were statistically indistinguishable. Statistical tests are presented in table 5.2.

The evidence suggests that the poor have been the recipients of most of the increase in crime. The increase in crime for the poor has been approximately 1.5 times that suffered by the rich. The difference-in-differences change of the victimization rates between the first and last period of our study is significant at the 5 percent level. As a comparison note, for the United States,

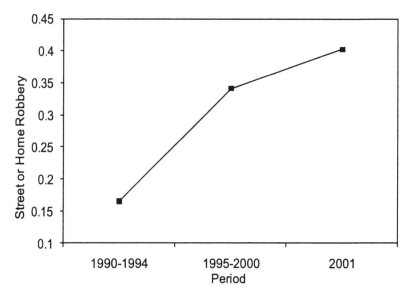

Fig. 5.1 Total victimization rates (street or home robbery)

Levitt (1999) finds that property crime has become more concentrated on the poor over time. The magnitude of our finding is in line with his estimates. He reports that while in the 1970s high-income households were slightly more likely to be burglarized than low-income households, by the 1990s low-income households were 60 percent more likely to be the victims of crime.

5.4.2   Victimization Rates at Home and in the Street

Figures 5.3 and 5.4 separately present the evolution of two different types of crime, at home or in the street, where victim adaptation is likely to differ by income group. Indeed, some of the possible behavioral responses at home involve costly actions (alarm, etc.) whereas those on the street appear to be cheaper (avoid the use of jewelry). Thus, a different response in the two crime categories would be indirect evidence of victim adaptation.

Figure 5.3 studies the evolution of victimization rates for street robberies across income groups. The difference-in-differences analysis for robberies suffered by household members outside the house is presented in table 5.3. For the three periods, high-income households suffered a higher victimization rate than low-income families. The cross-sectional difference seems significant (at the 10 percent level of statistical significance) for the three periods. Moreover, both groups have suffered a significant increase in crime levels. Difference-in-differences tests, however, are never statistically significant at conventional levels, suggesting that the evolution of victimization rates have not differed across income groups.

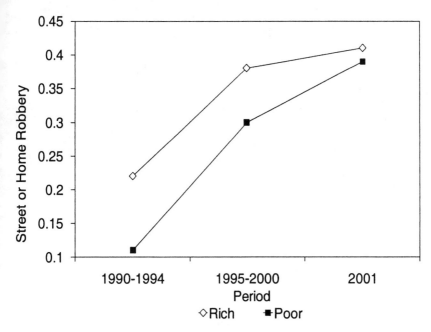

Fig. 5.2 Total victimization rates (street or home robbery), rich vs. poor

Table 5.2　　　　　　**Total victimization rates (street or home robbery)**

Home robbery	1990–1994	1995–2000	2001	[2001]–[1990–1994] Diff-in-diff	[1995–2000]–[1990–1994] Diff-in-diff	[2001]–[1995–2000] Diff-in-diff
Rich	0.22	0.38	0.41			
Poor	0.11	0.30	0.39			
Rich-Poor						
Diff	0.12***	0.09**	0.02	–0.11**	–0.05	–0.07
	(0.03)	(0.04)	(0.04)	(0.05)	(0.05)	(0.06)

Note: Standard errors (SE) are in parentheses.
***Significant at the 1 percent level.
**Significant at the 5 percent level.
*Significant at the 10 percent level.

Figure 5.4 studies victimization at home, while the accompanying table 5.4 presents the associated tests. For the period 1990 to 1994, high-income households suffered a home victimization rate that was more than double that observed by low-income families (11 percent versus 5 percent). After that period, low-income households suffered a significant increase in victim-

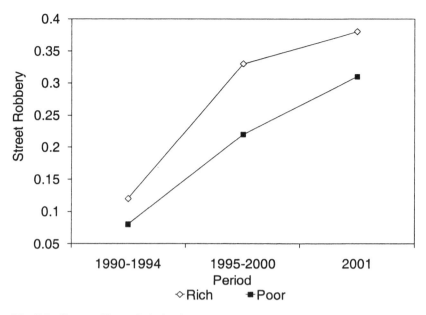

Fig. 5.3   Street robbery victimization rates

Table 5.3   **Street robbery victimization rates**

Home robbery	1990–1994	1995–2000	2001	[2001]–[1990–1994] Diff-in-diff	[1995–2000]–[1990–1994] Diff-in-diff	[2001]–[1995–2000] Diff-in-diff
Rich	0.12	0.33	0.38			
Poor	0.08	0.22	0.31			
Rich-Poor Diff	0.05*	0.11***	0.08*	0.02	0.03	–0.04
	(0.03)	(0.04)	(0.04)	(0.05)	(0.04)	(0.06)

Note: Standard errors (SE) are in parentheses.
***Significant at the 1 percent level.
**Significant at the 5 percent level.
*Significant at the 10 percent level.

ization likelihood, while high-income families show a nonsignificant decline. The cross-sectional difference becomes insignificant in those subsequent periods. Thus, the victimization rate of the low-income households caught up to the high-income rate during the decade. Importantly, the difference-in-differences tests show that the change in the victimization rate of the low-income group is significantly different from the change for the high-income households.

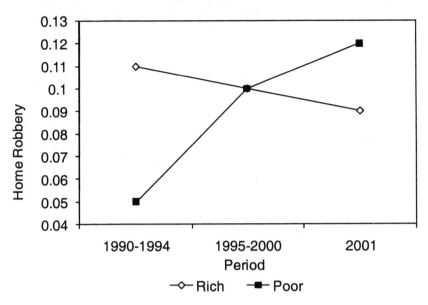

Fig. 5.4   Home robbery victimization rates

Table 5.4		Home robbery victimization rates				
Home robbery	1990– 1994	1995– 2000	2001	[2001]– [1990–1994] Diff-in-diff	[1995–2000]– [1990–1994] Diff-in-diff	[2001]– [1995–2000] Diff-in-diff
Rich	0.11	0.10	0.09			
Poor	0.05	0.10	0.12			
Rich-Poor Diff	0.06*** (0.02)	–0.00 (0.03)	–0.03 (0.03)	–0.09*** (0.04)	–0.06* (0.03)	–0.03 (0.04)

Note: Standard errors (SE) are in parentheses.
***Significant at the 1 percent level.
**Significant at the 5 percent level.
*Significant at the 10 percent level.

5.4.3   Adaptation at Home and in the Street

A possible explanation for these differing crime dynamics by income group is that victims adapt. Figures 5.5 through 5.8, with their corresponding tables, present four possible forms of adaptation. The first two involve costly investments in self-protection devices (hiring private security and buying alarms) while the last two involve a change in behavior that reduces the exposure to crime. Figure 5.5 (and the corresponding table 5.5) focuses on

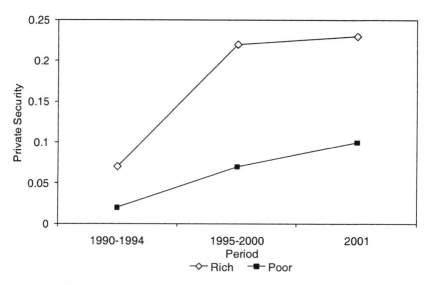

Fig. 5.5   Victim adaptation at home: Hiring private security

Table 5.5   Victim adaptation at home: Hiring private security

Home robbery	1990–1994	1995–2000	2001	[2001]–[1990–1994] Diff-in-diff	[1995–2000]–[1990–1994] Diff-in-diff	[2001]–[1995–2000] Diff-in-diff
Rich	0.07	0.22	0.23			
Poor	0.02	0.07	0.10			
Rich-Poor Diff	0.05***	0.15***	0.13***	0.08***	0.10***	–0.02
	(0.02)	(0.03)	(0.03)	(0.03)	(0.03)	(0.01)

Note: Standard errors (SE) are in parentheses.
***Significant at the 1 percent level.
**Significant at the 5 percent level.
*Significant at the 10 percent level.

the hiring of private security guards, an industry that grew substantially during the 1990s in Argentina and that affects home robbery. The survey reveals that few households hire private security in the early part of the decade (7 percent of the rich versus 2 percent of the poor). By the year 2001, the hiring of private security had grown 16 percentage points among the rich and 8 percentage points for the poor. The difference in these changes in protection is statistically significant at the 1 percent level.

A similar picture of differential adaptation emerges from studying data on installing alarms, a cheaper form of protection at home (see figure 5.6

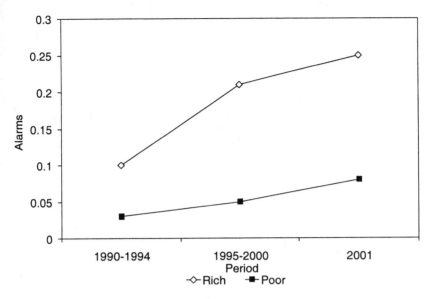

Fig. 5.6   Victim adaptation at home: Alarms

Table 5.6   Victim adaptation at home: Alarms

Home robbery	1990–1994	1995–2000	2001	[2001]–[1990–1994] Diff-in-diff	[1995–2000]–[1990–1994] Diff-in-diff	[2001]–[1995–2000] Diff-in-diff
Rich	0.1	0.21	0.25			
Poor	0.02	0.05	0.08			
Rich-Poor Diff	0.07***	0.16***	0.17***	0.09***	0.09***	0.006
	(0.02)	(0.03)	(0.03)	(0.03)	(0.02)	(0.01)

Note: Standard errors (SE) are in parentheses.
***Significant at the 1 percent level.
**Significant at the 5 percent level.
*Significant at the 10 percent level.

and the corresponding table 5.6). Relatively few respondents declare to have alarms installed in the early part of the sample period (10 percent of the rich versus 2 percent of the poor). By the year 2001, 25 percent of the rich and 8 percent of the poor have alarms. The change for the rich (15 percentage points) is larger than the increase for the poor (6 percentage points) and the changes between groups are statistically different at conventional levels of significance.

There are only a limited variety of strategies that people can employ

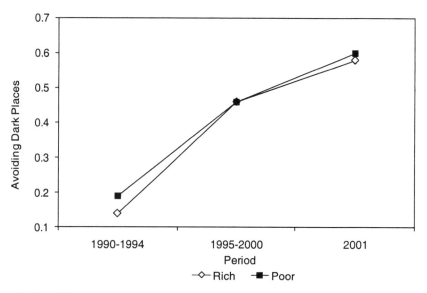

Fig. 5.7   Victim adaptation on the street: Avoiding dark places

Table 5.7   Victim adaptation on the street: Avoiding dark places

Home robbery	1990–1994	1995–2000	2001	[2001]–[1990–1994] Diff-in-diff	[1995–2000]–[1990–1994] Diff-in-diff	[2001]–[1995–2000] Diff-in-diff
Rich	0.14	0.46	0.58			
Poor	0.19	0.46	0.60			
Rich-Poor Diff	–0.06*	0.00	–0.02	0.04	0.06	–0.02
	(0.03)	(0.04)	(0.04)	(0.04)	(0.04)	(0.03)

Note: Standard errors (SE) are in parentheses.
***Significant at the 1 percent level.
**Significant at the 5 percent level.
*Significant at the 10 percent level.

to avoid becoming a victim of a robbery outside their houses.[12] The survey asked on avoiding dark places and avoiding the use of jewels. Figure 5.7 shows that both income groups have adapted by avoiding dark places as crime rates increased. More than 60 percent of the interviewed people

12. In the sample, 173 households declared that one of its members had been robbed outside the house during 2001. Those robberies took place on the street (125), in a car or public transportation (27), at work (3), in a shop or restaurant (15), at a bank or ATM (2), and other places (1).

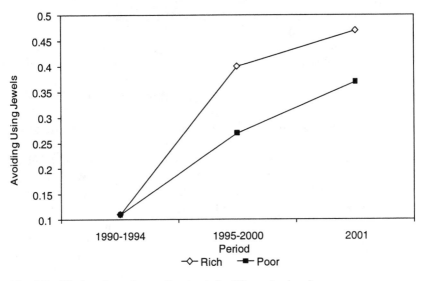

Fig. 5.8   Victim adaptation on the street: Avoiding using jewels

Table 5.8   Victim adaptation on the street: Avoiding using jewels

Home robbery	1990–1994	1995–2000	2001	[2001]–[1990–1994] Diff-in-diff	[1995–2000]–[1990–1994] Diff-in-diff	[2001]–[1995–2000] Diff-in-diff
Rich	0.11	0.40	0.47			
Poor	0.11	0.27	0.37			
Rich-Poor Diff	0.01	0.13***	0.11***	0.10***	0.13***	–0.03
	(0.03)	(0.04)	(0.04)	(0.04)	(0.04)	(0.03)

Note: Standard errors (SE) are in parentheses.
***Significant at the 1 percent level.
**Significant at the 5 percent level.
*Significant at the 10 percent level.

declared to avoid dark places by the year 2001. There do not appear to be differences in the adoption of this strategy between poor and rich individuals, as table 5.7 confirms.

A second measure of adaptation on the street is avoiding using jewels (see fig. 5.8 and table 5.8). Early in the sample period only 11 percent of the sample declared avoiding the use of jewels, a rate that is similar across income groups (although presumably the stock of jewels is larger among the rich). By the year 2001, 47 percent of the rich and 37 percent of the poor declared to purposely avoid using jewels. The difference for the two groups is significant and, more importantly, the differences across income groups in the change in "Avoid using Jewels" are significant.

An alternative explanation for the differing crime dynamics by income group is that public officials might have biases against the poor in the provision of police services (World Bank 2000). The evidence, however, is not consistent with this hypothesis. First note that in Argentina, public police provision is not decentralized at the county level. Although the police told us that they purposely avoid cross-sectional differences,[13] it is still possible that political economy considerations (but not those directly based on local tax collection) can lead to more intense public police deterrence in rich neighborhoods. However, note that such political economy aspects would explain the observed crime dynamics only if the differential deployment of police on rich versus poor areas changes over time. The survey explores the presence of differential public police provision, as it included information on police protection by asking at which frequency police walk or drive in front of people's houses. Table 5A.7 in appendix B presents the survey responses on public police protection, which reveal no differences in the treatment and protection that the poor receive from the police relative to the rich.

5.4.4   The Impact of Victim Adaptation on Home Robbery

Our data allows us to estimate correlations between the adoption of protection measures and victimization at home. Table 5.9 presents the results for having private security and having an alarm. All regressions include household fixed effects, and two estimates are reported for each protection device, one that controls for period fixed effects and one that controls for zone of residence-period fixed effects. In order to conduct this analysis we divide the Buenos Aires metropolitan area into seven zones of residence. The correlation is negative and significant. Both protective devices appear to reduce the likelihood of victimization at home in a given period of time. When entered together in the regression, private security appears to be 20 percent more effective than the use of alarms, but the difference is not significant at conventional levels. The last two columns produce the same results, aggregating the two measures of home protection into an index of security devices at home—that is, the average value of the private security and alarm dummy variables.[14]

---

13. We conducted a series of interviews with key informants, including several officials at the Security Ministry, the chief of the Federal Police during part of the 1990s, a former federal judge, and a former federal prosecutor, among others.

14. An alternative specification following the approach in the literature on technological horizontal spillovers (for a recent example see Smarzynska Javorcik [2004] and the references cited therein) exploits differences in average protection across our seven zones. Accordingly, we added to our baseline model (column [7] of table 5.9) the average level of protection of the rich by zone of residence interacted with a dummy that equals one if the household is classified as rich. The coefficient on the "Aggregate Level of Security Devices at Home" (which is simply the average for the zone) is negative, although only significant at the 10 percent level. The coefficient

Obviously, caution must be exerted when giving these correlations a causal interpretation.[15] However, we note that the obvious sources of confounding effects are controlled for in the models we estimate. One potentially serious issue in relating the adoption of protection measures and victimization is that some people are both more likely to be victimized and also more likely to use security devices irrespective of the causal effect of the latter on the former. This problem, however, does not interfere with our estimates because we are including individual fixed effects in our models. We also believe that our estimates do not reflect a tendency for people to protect themselves in the presence of a crime wave because we are including period fixed effects. Moreover, and perhaps most importantly, the inclusion of zone of residence-period fixed effects also controls for the possibility that our estimates are biased downward because of a tendency for people who live in areas where there is a particularly large increase in crime to protect themselves.[16]

Table 5.10 presents some further evidence that is relevant to provide our estimates with a causal interpretation, by investigating whether exposure to crime in previous periods predicts the adoption of security devices. The negative and insignificant coefficient does not suggest a reverse causality.

5.4.5 One Possible Calculation for the Burden of Crime (Using Home Robbery)

These estimates can be used to approximate the burden of crime suffered by the different groups. Indeed, it is possible to start with the estimated model in column (7) of table 5.9 and note that in this estimated equation the 2001 period fixed effect is equal to 0.04 (t-value = 2.03). This gives us a measure of the overall increase in home victimization for the period 1990 to 2001 in the absence of any adaptation by victims.

We first focus on the implications for the rich. Given that the increase in the "Index of Security Devices at Home" for the period for the high-income group was in fact 0.154, we can conclude (under a causal interpretation of

---

on "Index of Security Devices at Home" is still negative and significant. Indeed, its size is very similar to that reported in the corresponding regression in table 5.9, column (7).

15. For the causal effect of the introduction of fixed and observable police protection, a technology that resembles private security protection, see Di Tella and Schargrodsky (2004). They also discuss potential crime displacement induced by observable security guards. Ayres and Levitt (1998) show positive externalities from the use of unobservable protection devices.

16. Strictly, this analysis is only correct for home victimization because the measures of adaptation refer to the stock (e.g., whether people use alarms or hire private security), whereas our measures of adaptation on the street refer to changes (e.g., to avoid using jewels, not the absolute amount of jewelry that people use). Such changes are not necessarily related to stocks (those that do not have jewels can only trivially "avoid using jewels"). In an attempt to conduct a similar analysis for street victimization, we regressed street victimization on the changes in avoiding using jewels and avoiding dark places, household fixed effects and period (or zone of residence-period) fixed effects. These changes were never statistically significant, neither when entered alone nor when both changes were included together.

Table 5.9   The impact of security devices on home robbery

	(1)	(2)	(3)	(4)	(5)	(6)	(7)	(8)
Private security	-0.124**	-0.112**			-0.118**	-0.103**		
	(0.048)	(0.048)			(0.049)	(0.050)		
Alarm			-0.085*	-0.106**	-0.063	-0.086*		
			(0.052)	(0.052)	(0.052)	(0.053)		
Index of security devices at home							-0.183***	-0.190***
							(0.065)	(0.065)
Period fixed effects	Yes	No	Yes	No	Yes	No	Yes	No
Zone-period fixed effects	No	Yes	No	Yes	No	Yes	No	Yes
Number of observations	1,472	1,471	1,475	1,474	1,457	1,456	1,457	1,456

Notes: The OLS regressions, standard errors in parentheses. All regressions include household fixed effects. The dependent variable is "Victimization at Home."

***Significant at the 1 percent level.

**Significant at the 5 percent level.

*Significant at the 10 percent level.

Table 5.10   **The impact of lagged crime on the acquisition of home security devices**

	(1)	(2)
Lagged home robbery	–0.010	–0.010
	(0.013)	(0.014)
Period fixed effects	Yes	No
Zone-period fixed effects	No	Yes
Number of observations	970	970

Notes: The OLS regressions, standard errors in parentheses. All regressions include household fixed effects. The dependent variable is the "Index of Security Devices at Home."

our estimates in table 5.9) that protection helped the rich reduce crime by 0.028 (0.028 = 0.183 * 0.154) and hence avoid 70 percent of the exogenous increase in crime (0.7 = 0.028/0.04). This means that the rich are predicted to have avoided almost all of the crime increase. A formal test of the hypothesis that the reduction in crime as a result of protection is in fact 0.04 is not rejected at conventional levels of statistical significance [$F(1, 996) = 1.38$]. We note that this is consistent with the observed dynamics of home victimization for the rich: the change in home robbery between 1990 and 2001 for the rich is not statistically significant at conventional levels (see table 5.4). Thus, the evidence is broadly consistent with the hypothesis that the rich homes avoided the Argentine crime wave by increasing their level of protection.

On the other hand, and again under a causal interpretation of our estimates, the poor are predicted to have avoided only a small part of the increase in crime. The increase in the "Index of Security Devices at Home" for the period for the poor was 0.065, so protection helped the poor reduce crime by 0.011 (0.011 = 0.065 * 0.183) and hence avoid 27 percent of the shock in crime (0.27 = 0.011/0.04). We note that the predicted increase of 0.029 (= 0.04 – 0.011) is inconsistent with the observed dynamics of home victimization for the poor because "Home Robbery" for the poor increases by 0.07 (see table 5.4). In other words, the predicted rate of home robbery for the poor is less than half of what is actually observed.

We conjecture that this discrepancy is the result of a negative externality arising from home protection by the rich. Indeed, the excess of crime observed for the poor over the predicted rate is 0.041, which is consistent with the rich avoiding all the increase in crime, which gets diverted to the poor (we do not reject the null hypothesis of full displacement at conventional levels of statistical significance [$F(1, 966) = 0.2$]. Of course, this is just one way to decompose the changes in crime in our sample. But it highlights the main message of our simple model, whereby after a large exogenous increase in crime, the rich protect themselves, avoiding all the effect of crime, while the poor receive more crime than otherwise as a result of the displacement or negative externality generated by the rich.

5.5   Conclusion

An important question in the literature on crime concerns the relative impact among the rich and poor of a given increase in crime. The observed victimization rates for the groups are insufficient to derive the differential welfare burden of crime because individuals change their behavior in costly ways in order to avoid crime (for example, by hiring protection and engaging in mimicking types with lower victimization risk). The extent of such investments to avoid crime is likely to differ across income groups. If the rich have more resources to invest in crime protection, ignoring victim adaptation will obscure the burden of crime suffered by the rich (and the externalities such behavior may impose on the poor). In this chapter we provide several estimates that contribute to evaluate these effects.

We take advantage of a dramatic increase in crime that took place in Argentina during the 1990s using a survey that asked individuals their victimization rates at different points in time and their investment in crime avoidance, both at home and on the street. While our data has some weaknesses (for example, the assumption of similar rates of recollections of victimization episodes across income groups might be questioned), we believe that the importance of the question (which socioeconomic group is most affected by a crime shock) and the paucity of previous results, provide justification for experimenting with a different approach. Moreover, some of the conditions in Argentina during this period (for example, the general salience of crime and the sharp increases in crime rates and in crime-avoiding activities) make it a reasonable place to look for retrospective victimization information. We obtain several findings of interest, including:

1. During the period leading up to the economic crisis of 2001, crime increased more for the poor than for the rich. The increase in the total victimization rate for the poor was 1.5 times the increase in total victimization observed for the rich.

2. Changes in victimization in the street were similar for both income groups. In contrast, the increase in victimization at home was larger for the poor than for the rich. Indeed, whereas in the early part of the decade, victimization at home for the rich was significantly larger than for the poor, in the year 2001 they were similar (if anything it was somewhat larger for the poor). This pattern is suggestive of victim adaptation because the cost of adaptation is lower on the street relative to home.

3. Direct evidence on victim adaptation reveals a different pattern across income groups. The rich are significantly more likely to hire private security and to install alarms than the poor. Adaptation on the street presents a different picture. The rich and the poor report similar increases in the avoidance of dark places. The rich report a larger increase in the avoidance

of using jewels (although we expect them to start out with a higher level of jewelry).

4. We report a negative correlation between victimization at home and the use of alarms or private security, even after controlling for household fixed effects, for period fixed effects, and for the interaction of zones and period fixed effects. We also report that previous experience with victimization at home is not correlated with the adoption of security devices.

5. We illustrate one possible use of these measures to estimate how victims' behavior affects the distribution of the crime burden across income group. We observe that street crime has evolved similarly for rich and poor. Given that victim adaptation on the street (e.g., mimicking) is likely to be cheap, it appears safe to assume a similar burden of street crime for both groups. For victimization at home, and under a causal interpretation of our estimates, we note that the rich are predicted to have avoided almost all of the crime increase. This is indeed consistent with the observed dynamics of home victimization for the rich (which exhibits no detectable change). On the other hand, the poor are predicted to have avoided a small part of the increase in crime. This is inconsistent with the observed dynamics of home victimization for the poor, which exhibits a large increase. Indeed, the predicted rate of home robbery for the poor is less than half of what is actually observed, which is consistent with crime displacement from the rich to the poor. Given the lack of regulation of private protection activities in most of the world, our results highlight the need for the better design of public security policies of further investigating the extent to which victim adaptation induces negative externalities across groups.

Appendix A

Computation of the Income Level Index following Argentine Marketing Association (1998)

The Income Level index (IL) assigns a point average for each household according to three variables. The index can take values between 4 and 100 points. The variables and the maximum values are summarized in table 5A.1.

Assignment of Points for Each Variable

1. Educational level of the household head. The values vary from 0 to 32 points according to table 5A.2.

2. Occupation of the household head. The assigned points range from 4 to 40 according to table 5A.3.

3. Wealth.
   (a) Goods and services. It measures the household capacity of accu-
       mulation of goods and services. The points are assigned accord-
       ing to table 5A.4.
   (b) Automobile: the questions asked are concerned with (a) the num-
       ber of automobiles owned; (b) the branch, model, and age of the
       first automobile, if applies; and (c) the branch, model, and age of
       the second automobile, if applies. Using this information, points
       are assigned separately for each car according to table 5A.5.

Finally, the automobile point assignment must satisfy the following two
rules: (1) if the final number of points is between 1 and 3, then zero is assigned to this category; and (2) if the sum of the points assigned for both
cars together reaches 15 points or more, then 14 is assigned to this category.

Table 5A.1

Variable	Maximum possible value
Education	32
Occupation	40
Wealth	
(a) Goods and services	14
(b) Automobile	14
Total	100

Table 5A.2

Educational level	Points
No studies	0
Primary school incomplete	5
Primary school complete	9
High school incomplete	13
High school complete	17
Vocational school incomplete	19
University incomplete	22
Vocational school complete	27
University complete	31
Postgraduate studies	32

Table 5A.3

Nonemployee	Points	Employee	Points
Do not work		Domestic employee	7
Asset Holder	20	Family worker without fixed income	13
		Nonqualified operator	9
Self-employed		Qualified operator	17
Day laborer	4	Technician/foreman	23
Other nonspecialized job	11	Low hierarchy employee	
Retailer without employees	18	Public sector	12
Technician/specialized worker	24	Private sector	17
Independent professional	30	Middle hierarchy employee	
Other self-employed	17	Public sector	19
		Private sector	24
Employer		High hierarchy employee	
1–5 employees	30	Public sector	26
6–20 employees	36	Private sector	30
21 or more employees	40	Top hierarchy employee	
		Public sector	28
		Private sector	37

Note: Two-thirds of the points of his or her last occupation are assigned to unemployed, retired, or pensioner household heads.

Table 5A.4

Number of the following goods and services owned: PC, air conditioner, credit card, and automatic washing machine	Points
0	0
1	3
2	7
3	11
4	14

Table 5A.5

	Branch/model		
Age	Inferior	Medium	Superior
10 or more years	1.5	2	2.75
Between 6 and 9 years	3.5	6	6.5
Between 3 and 5 years	5.5	7	8.5
Less than 2 years	6.5	8	9.5

Appendix B

Table 5A.6   Perceived insecurity

In your neighborhood, would you say that insecurity with respect to one decade ago has increased a lot, some, a little, has not changed at all, or has decreased?	Rich (%)	Poor (%)
Increased a lot	35.2	38.5
Increased some	29.7	27.1
Increased a little	13.7	8.2
No change	14.8	20.9
Decreased	0.4	1.2
No answer	6.2	4.1

Table 5A.7   Frequency of police patrolling

How often do the police usually patrol your street?	Rich (%)	Poor (%)
Every day	50.4	43.9
Twice or three times a week	10.9	12.7
Once a week	5.5	6.1
At least once a month	4.7	6.6
Less than once a month	2.7	2.9
Never	11.7	16.0
No answer	14.1	11.9

References

Aday, L. 1996. *Designing and conducting health surveys.* New York: Jossey-Bass.
Argentine Marketing Association. 1998. Indice de Nivel Socio Económico Argentino. Unpublished manuscript.
Ayres, I., and S. Levitt. 1998. Measuring positive externalities from unobservable victim precaution: An empirical analysis of Lojack. *Quarterly Journal of Economics* 113 (1): 43–77.
Becker, G. 1965. A theory of the allocation of time. *Economic Journal* 75 (299): 493–517.
———. 1968. Crime and punishment: An economic approach. *Journal of Political Economy* 76 (2): 169–217.
Bushway, S., and P. Reuter. 2008. Economists' contribution to the study of crime and the criminal justice system. *Crime and Justice* 37 (1): 389–451.
Clarke, R. 1983. Situational crime prevention: Its theoretical basis and practical scope. In *Crime and justice: A review of research, volume 4,* ed. M. Tonry and N. Morris, 225–56. Chicago: University of Chicago Press.
Cook, P. 1986. The demand and supply of criminal opportunities. In *Crime and justice: A review of research, volume 7,* ed. M. Tonry and N. Morris, 1–27. Chicago: University of Chicago Press.
Cornish, D., and R. Clarke. 1987. Understanding crime displacement: An application of rational choice theory. *Criminology* 25 (4): 933–47.

Cullen, J., and S. D. Levitt. 1999. Crime, urban flight, and the consequences for cities. *Review of Economics and Statistics* 81 (2): 159–69.

de Meza, D., and J. R. Gould. 1992. The social efficiency of private decisions to enforce property rights. *Journal of Political Economy* 100 (3): 561–80.

Dal Bo, E., and P. Dal Bo. 2004. Workers, warriors and criminals: Social conflict in General Equilibrium. Working Paper no. 2004-11. Brown University, Department of Economics.

Di Tella, R., and E. Schargrodsky. 2004. Do police reduce crime? Estimates using the allocation of police forces after a terrorist attack. *American Economic Review* 94 (1): 115–33.

Ehrlich, I. 1973. Participation in illegitimate activities: A theoretical and empirical investigation. *Journal of Political Economy* 81 (3): 521–65.

———. 1996. Crime, punishment, and the market for offenses. *Journal of Economic Perspectives* 10 (1): 43–67.

Fajnzylber, P., D. Lederman, and N. Loayza. 2000. Crime and victimization: An economic perspective. *Economia* 1 (1): 219–302.

———. 2002. Inequality and violent crime. *Journal of Law and Economics* 45 (1): 1–40.

Freeman, R. 1996. Why do so many young American men commit crimes and what might we do about it? *Journal of Economic Perspectives* 10 (1): 25–42.

Galiani, S., P. Gertler, and E. Schargrodsky. 2008. School decentralization: Helping the good get better, but leaving the poor behind. *Journal of Public Economics* 92 (10–11): 2106–20.

Gaviria, A., and C. Pages. 2002. Patterns of crime victimization in Latin American cities. *Journal of Development Economics* 67 (1): 181–203.

Glaeser, E., and B. Sacerdote. 1999. Why is there more crime in cities? *Journal of Political Economy* 107:S225–58.x

Hessling, R. 1994. Displacement: A review of the empirical literature. In *Crime prevention studies,* III, ed. R. Clarke, 197–230. Monsey, NY: Criminal Justice Press.

Koo, H.-W., and I. Png. 1994. Private security: Deterrent or diversion? *International Review of Law and Economics* 14 (1): 87–101.

Land, K., P. McCall, and L. Cohen. 1990. Structural covariates of homicide rates: Are there any invariances across time and space? *American Journal of Sociology* 95:922–63.

Lavy, V. 2002. Evaluating the effect of teacher's group performance incentives on pupil achievement. *Journal of Political Economy* 110 (6): 1286–1317.

Levitt, S. 1999. The changing relationship between income and crime victimization. *FRBNY Economic Policy Review* 5 (3): 87–99.

Londono, J. L., A. Gaviria, and R. Guerrero. 2000. *Epidemolog_a y costos de la violencia en America Latina.* Washington, DC: Inter-American Development Bank.

Lott, J. 1998. *More guns, less crime.* London: University of Chicago Press.

Lott, J., and D. Mustard. 1997. Crime, deterrence, and right-to-carry concealed handguns. *Journal of Legal Studies* 26 (1): 1–68.

Mocan, N., S. Billups, and J. Overland. 2005. A dynamic model of differential human capital and criminal activity. *Economica* 72 (November): 655–81.

Ministerio de Justicia. 2000. Estudio de Victimización en Centros Urbanos de la Argentina. Unpublished manuscript.

Nilsson, A., and F. Estrada. 2003. Victimization, inequality and welfare during an economic recession: A study of self reported victimization in Sweden 1988–1999. *British Journal of Criminology* 43 (4): 655–72.

Pantazis, C. 2000. Fear of crime, vulnerability and poverty. *British Journal of Criminology* 40 (3): 414–36.

Patterson, E. B. 1991. Poverty, income inequality, and community crime rates. *Criminology* 29:755–76.
Papps, K., and R. Winkelmann. 2000. Unemployment and crime: New evidence for an old question. *New Zealand Economic Papers* 34 (1): 53–72.
Reuband, K. 1994. Reconstructing social change through retrospective questions: Methodological problems and prospects. In *Autobiographical memory and the validity of retrospective reports,* ed. N. Schwartz and S. Sudman, 306–11. New York: Springer-Verlag.
Shavell, S. 1991. Individual precautions to prevent theft: Private vs. socially optimal behavior. *International Review of Law and Economics* 11:123–32.
Shaw, C. R., and H. D. MacKay. 1942. *Juvenile delinquency and urban areas.* Chicago: University of Chicago Press.
Soares, R. 2004. Development, crime, and punishment: Accounting for the international differences in crime rates. *Journal of Development Economics* 73 (1): 155–84.
Smarzynska Javorcik, B. 2004. Does foreign direct investment increase the productivity of domestic firms? In search of spillover effects through backward linkages. *American Economic Review* 94 (3): 605–27.
Sudman, S., A. Finn, and L. Lannon. 1984. The use of bounded recall procedures in single interviews. *Public Opinion Quarterly* 48 (2): 520–24.
Tauchen, H., A. Dryden Witte, and H. Griesinger. 1994. Criminal deterrence: Revisiting the issue with a birth cohort. *Review of Economics and Statistics* 76 (3): 399–412.
Van Kesteren, J., P. Mayhew, and P. Nieuwbeerta. 2000. *Criminal victimization in seventeen industrialized countries.* The Hague, Netherlands: WODC (Research and Documentation Centre).
Witte, A. 1980. Estimating the economic model of crime with individual data. *Quarterly Journal of Economics* 94 (1): 155–67.
World Bank. 2000. *Attacking poverty.* World Development Report 2000/2001. Washington, DC: World Bank.

Comment   Lucas Ronconi

Crime is an important concern for Latin Americans. In Argentina, a recent opinion poll suggests that it is the most important problem (Latinobarometro 2008). However, relatively little research is available. This chapter is an important contribution toward reducing that gap.

The chapter uses a retrospective survey and shows the four following points. First, there was a large increase in victimization (both street and home robbery) from 1990 to 2001 in the Buenos Aires Metropolitan area. Second, the growth in street robbery was similar for both poor and rich households, while home robbery increased mainly among the poor. Third,

Lucas Ronconi is associate researcher at the Center for the Implementation of Public Policies Promoting Equity and Growth (CIPPEC) and executive director of the Research Laboratory on Crime, Institutions and Politics (LICIP) at the Universidad Torcuato Di Tella.

there was a larger expansion in the use of security devices at home (i.e., alarms and private security) among the rich compared to the poor; but both groups present similar changes in behavior aimed at avoiding street robbery. Fourth, households that consume security devices at home are less likely to be victims of home robbery.

Based on this evidence the authors conclude that the larger increase in home robbery experienced by the poor is the result of a negative externality on the poor arising from the home protection of the rich. In other words, the use of security devices at home produces crime displacement across income groups. This is an interesting interpretation. But, is it correct? Does it explain most of the relative variation in victimization across socioeconomic groups? The answer to these questions depends on whether the criminals involved in the crime wave are similar to those who committed crimes in the early 1990s. If they are similar, such as employing the same strategy to select their victims, then the explanation proposed by the authors is more likely to be correct. Those who committed crimes in the 2000s thought about stealing from rich people's houses as in the early 1990s, but decided to steal from poor people because it was too risky to steal from the rich due to the relative change in the use of security devices across socioeconomic groups. But, if the new criminals differ from the previous ones, this interpretation is less likely to be correct. The magnitude of the 2001 crisis and the emergence of a new drug consumed in the Buenos Aires shantytowns, locally known as paco (a cheap and highly addictive smokable cocaine residue), suggests this is a possibility that should be considered. Perhaps the new criminals are less sophisticated and simply steal from their neighbors—who are predominantly lower income—and this difference could be driving the relative increase in home robbery among the poor. Testing the relative merits of these arguments requires information about criminals' characteristics, which is regrettably unavailable in the collected data.

A related point is that, even assuming crime displacement effectively occurs, whether it occurs across or within income groups. The share of rich households with alarms in 2001 was only one-fourth (and a similar percentage hires private security). Why would a criminal who decided not to steal from a rich house due to the security device steal from a poor house when there are so many rich houses unprotected? The chapter does not explore crime displacement within income groups (something that can be easily added), in part because the model assumes that wealth is not observable. But this is an unrealistic assumption when analyzing home robbery.

There are a number of concerns related to the data, although I suspect they are relatively less important. First, only four types of protection strategies are considered, two to avoid home robbery and two to avoid street crime. The chapter does not take into account other strategies such as changes in transportation, in interactions among people, or their extent of activity in public areas. Furthermore, the analyzed strategies are mainly to avoid crime committed by strangers. Different strategies are used to avoid nonstranger crime. Whether the distribution and evolution across income groups of the excluded protection strategies resembles the analyzed ones remains unanswered.

Second, as pointed out by the authors, using a retrospective survey to measure the evolution of victimization and crime-avoiding strategies between the rich and the poor will not affect the results if the recall bias affects both groups similarly. There are some reasons to suspect this assumption does not hold. But more important is the fact that households are characterized as either poor or rich during the whole 1990 to 2001 period based on their education, occupation, and wealth in 2002. Some rich households, such as those with socioeconomic status (SES) slightly above the median in 2002, could actually have been poor in early years, and vice versa. Perhaps the authors should exclude from the analysis those households with SES close to the threshold. Additionally, a more disaggregated measure of income could be used, such as income quintiles, instead of categorizing households as either poor or rich. This will allow testing whether crime shifts occurred from the upper-middle class to the lower-middle class or from the richest class to the poorest, and so forth.

Both measures of victimization use the household as a unit of analysis, ignoring family size. However, the probability that at least a member of the household suffers a street robbery is a positive function of household size. Moreover, the size of the household could evolve differently across SES. If the size of poor households increases faster, then the observed similar growth in street crime between rich and poor households would indicate a relatively larger increase in street crime among rich people. Finally, it would be interesting to have more details about the sample design and to know whether there are differences in response rates across income groups.

There is no question that a panel survey would have been better for exploring this issue, but I commend the authors for using the available data to attempt to inform this important issue.

Assessing São Paulo's Large Drop in Homicides
The Role of Demography and Policy Interventions

João M. P. de Mello and Alexandre Schneider[‡]

6.1 Introduction

The São Paulo Metropolitan Area (SMPA) has received significant attention in the domestic and international media for its sharp swings in homicides during the 1990s and 2000s.[1] After increasing steadily over the 1990s, homicides fell sharply in the 2000s. There were twenty-four homicides per 100,000 inhabitants in 2005 at the SPMA, down from fifty-two in the 1999 peak, and 20 percent *less* than the level in the early 1990s. The dynamics are similar to large American cities, where homicides peaked ten years before. Figure 6.1 summarizes the motivation for this chapter. Although the spotlight was always on the SPMA, homicides movements are similar across the board.[2] One can see considerable cross-city variation in levels, but the dynamics of homicides is remarkably similar across cities.

This chapter assesses the causes behind this large shift in homicides. It is composed of six sections including this introduction. Section 6.2 describes the data sources. Section 6.3 is descriptive and provides an overview of the

João M P De Mello is assistant professor of economics at Pontifical Catholic University in Rio de Janeiro. Alexandre Schneider is secretary of education of the municipality of São Paulo.

‡Mr. Schneider would like to stress that opinions expressed here are solely from the authors, and do not reflect any official position of the Mayorship of São Paulo. The authors would like to thank Rodrigo Soares, Sebastian Edwards, Rafael Di Tella, Ernesto Schargrodsky, Lucas Llach and all participants at the LICIP-NBER "Crime, Institutions and Policies" at the Universidad Torcuato Di Tella in Buenos Aires, Nov-2007. Usual disclaimer applies.

1. In the last three years the British weekly newspaper *The Economist* twice reported on the murder trends in São Paulo (*Protecting citizens from themselves*, Oct 20th 2005, and *Not as violent as you thought*, Aug 21st 2008)

2. Specific graphs for all cities with more than 100,000 inhabitants are available upon request.

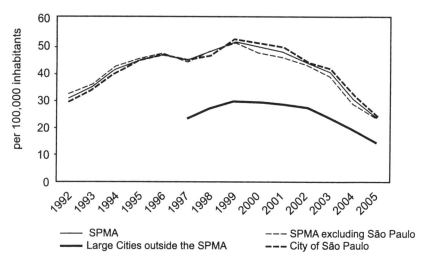

Fig. 6.1   Homicides in the State of São Paulo
Source: Secretaria de Segurança de São Paulo.

evolution of crime not only in São Paulo, but in Brazil in general. We show three important facts. First, the homicide phenomenon is a peculiarity of the 1990s and 2000s. Homicides were flat or only slightly increasing before they surged in the 1990s. Second, crime rates also dropped in other categories, suggesting a common component across crime categories. Finally, homicides follow a similar trend in the rest of Brazil, with a three- to four-year lag, again suggesting a common component across regions. In section 6.4, we assess a long list of suspects. Improvements in policing occurred. The most important are: (a) the adoption of a unified data and intelligence system (INFOCRIM, a version of Compustat); (b) the implementation of a photo database of criminals; (c) and the cracking down on illegal firearms possession. Incarcerated population also increased over the period. Among municipal-level policy measures, several others are worth mentioning: the adoption of "dry laws" (which are restrictions on the recreational sales of alcohol), the creation of municipal police forces, and the adoption of Disque-Denuncia (anonymous hotline to report crimes). See Kahn and Zanetic [2005].[3] Finally, the state of São Paulo cracked down on illegal gun possession, which might have contributed to the reduction in homicides (Goertzel and Kahn 2007).

Homicides dropped more sharply in São Paulo than in the rest of the country, which suggest that the policies helped to reduce homicides. How-

---

3. From 2003, the "Disarmament Act" (Lei do Desarmamento, Lei No. 10.826) is a federal act that increased significant the penal and civil costs of illegal possession and trade of firearms. See http://www.camara.gov.br/internet/infdoc/Publicacoes/html/pdf/Desarmamento.pdf.

ever, they fail to account for the timing of the reversal in the late 1990s because homicides had been dropping for at least a couple of years *before* the first policies were implemented. Consider the dry laws. Their adoption is not nearly as broad as the drop in homicides. In addition, the timing does not match: in all but one city, adoption occurred *after* 2001. Evidence shows that they did cause a nonnegligible reduction in homicides, but they are only a contributing factor, strengthening a trend that was already in place.[4] Another good example is INFOCRIM. The system was first implemented in the city of São Paulo in 2000, then in the rest of the SPMA. Outside the SPMA, implementation started only after 2005.

In section 6.4 we provide evidence on the demographic explanation. In contrast to other candidates, demographics rationalize not only the decline in the 1990s, but also the surge in homicides in the 1990s. Furthermore, and again in contrast with other explanations, demographics explains not only the dynamics of homicide in São Paulo, but also in the rest of the country. Homicides peaked in São Paulo in the late 1990s, just as the population aged fifteen to twenty-four also peaked. In the rest of the country, homicides and the population aged fifteen to twenty-four peaked a few years later.

Section 6.5 concludes the paper with a brief discussion. The case of São Paulo is particularly interesting when compared with the U.S. experience. Zimring (2007) shows that the large shift in crime in late 1980s to early 1990s was not confined to New York (the most publicized case), but occurred across the board in the United States. However, New York stands out. The analogy with São Paulo and Brazil is immediate. In the case of São Paulo, the increase and drop in homicides is widespread *within* the state and throughout the country. Also in line with the American case, several factors help to explain the decline of homicides in the 2000s. However, only demography also rationalizes the decline of homicides in the 2000s *and* the surge in the 1990s. Analogously to New York, the decline in São Paulo has been (so far) more pronounced than in the rest of country. Finally, Zimring (2007) analyzes data from Canada and shows a remarkable similarity between American and Canadian crime trends, suggesting a common component explanation. In Zimring's (2007) own words:

> But what joint causes might have operated in Canada and the United States throughout the 1990s? This uncomfortably open question is of obvious importance to *rethinking* the causes of the U.S. decline . . . What would explain the 30% or so of slow and steady decline over the nine years following 1991 in the United States and Canada? The *only* traditional theory of decline supported by parallel U.S. and Canadian data trends is the *decline of high-risk age groups as a percentage of the population*. But

---

4. By comparing homicide dynamics in adopting and nonadopting municipalities in the SPMA, Biderman, de Mello, and Scheider (2009) estimate that dry laws caused a reduction of roughly 12 percent in homicides.

even if all the decline in youth share of population that occurred both in 1980s and 1990s is counted toward the crime decline that was confined to the 1990s, it would be difficult to find many criminologists who would expect that feature alone to produce a crime decline greater than 10%, and even that 10% should have been spread more evenly across two decades in both countries.

[But *the demographic similarity*] between Canada and the United States over the period 1980 onwards invites, if it does not *demand,* a reconsideration of the magnitude of age structure effects on crime.[5]

We accept Zimring's invitation to reconsider the magnitude of age structure effects. Using data from São Paulo, we recover a very large elasticity of homicides to changes in the size of the fifteen to twenty-four-year-old population. The criminologists' difficulty in considering the demographic explanation is based on the conventional wisdom that age structure effects are small. The similarity between the United States and Canada, and our estimates for São Paulo, demands a reconsideration of the magnitude of elasticities.

6.2   Data

We use several sources of data. The city-level homicide data for the state of São Paulo come from the Secretaria de Segurança Pública de São Paulo (Secretaria), the state-level enforcement authority. Although hospital data is available, we prefer police reports. Geographical location of hospital murder data is tricky at the city level, since the murder victim may be taken to a hospital in another city (is it much less likely that victims will cross state lines).

Data on other crime categories are also from the Secretaria. Crime data in Brazil is limited when compared to the United States and Canada. Reliable police crime data are not available for a long period in Brazil. São Paulo has consistent police report data for some categories since 1984, which allows some backward look at the evolution of crime by categories. For the rest of the country we use hospital data from DATASUS, which have the same consistent categorizations since the mid 1990s.

For states other than São Paulo, no consistent series for crime categories other than murder is available. For São Paulo we have data dating back to 1984. Even for São Paulo, using data from crime categories other than homicide is a tricky business. As Biderman, de Mello, and Schneider (2009) put it, "Most crime statistics suffer from serious underreporting in Brazil, stemming from historical lack of confidence in authorities. Underreporting *per se* does not invalidate the use of other categories, but extra caution must be exercised because reporting imprsoved over the sample period. Institutional

5. Our emphasis.

innovations in the state-level bureaucracy reduced the costs of reporting. Among them are: i) the creation of Poupa-Tempo, whose claque is 'time saver,' which are offices where all bureaucratic errands, including reporting crimes, may be done; ii) Delegacia Eletrônica (electronic police station) for online reporting; and iii) Delegacias da Mulher, police stations specialized in domestic violence." The "sample period" in Biderman, de Mello, and Schneider (2009) is roughly similar to our period of analysis.

State-level murder data come from DATASUS, the hospital database of the National Ministry of Health. Although the data go back quite a long time, the taxonomy of violent deaths changed in 1996.[6] Thus, for estimating the state-level panel model we use data from 1996 onwards in order to keep consistency of observations across time.[7] For depicting national aggregates, when inconsistency is less costly, we use data from 1991. Also from DATA-SUS are data on the age distribution of homicide victims.

Demographics are from the Instituto Brasileiro de Estatística e Geografia (IBGE), the Brazilian equivalent of the Bureau of Statistics. For census years (1991 and 2000), full population counts by age groups are available. For noncensus years in the 1990s, and for all years at the city level, population by age group is projected based on the 1991 and 2000 census, and the population counts of 1996 and 2007.[8]

Data on the age distribution of perpetrators is from the Secretària de Justiça do Estado de São Paulo, the state-level equivalent of a Department of Justice. Finally, we use two victimization surveys for the city of São Paulo, both conducted by the Instituto Futuro Brasil (IFB), a São Paulo-based think tank. One was conducted in 2003 and another in 2008. Results are comparable over time.

6.3 Taking a Wider Look: Other Crimes in São Paulo and Homicides Across the Country

This section provides a wide overview of crime in São Paulo and the rest of the country. A wide view puts the dynamics of homicide in São Paulo into perspective. With data dating from before the mid-1990s we may judge whether the 1990-to-2000 crime shift is in fact a peculiarity. Data from other crime categories, and data from other states, allow us to assess how widespread the movements in crime are.

---

6. From 1996 onwards, the system of morbidity taxonomy has been the 10th International Classification of Diseases (ICD-10), which substituted the previous system (the ICD-9). Differences in classification for deaths by external causes exist and the Brazilian ICD-9 and 10 series are not compatible with each other. More details can be found at the World Health Organization website at http://www.who.int/classifications/icd/en/.

7. Elasticity estimates are similar if the series is extended back to 1991.

8. Results are similar if for the 2000s use projections based on the 2000 census and the 2007 population count.

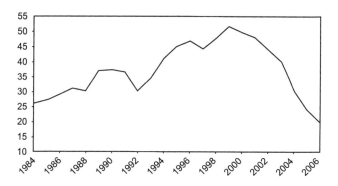

Fig. 6.2   Homicides per 100,000 inhabitants
Source: Secretaria de Segurança Publica de São Paulo (SSP-SP).

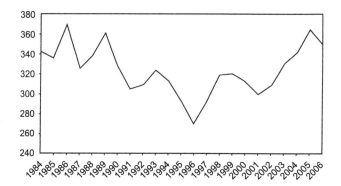

Fig. 6.3   Assault per 100,000 inhabitants
Source: Secretaria de Segurança Publica de São Paulo (SSP-SP).

6.3.1   Looking Backwards and at Other Categories

We start by showing some long trends of several crime categories in SPMA. Data dates back to 1984.[9] Figures 6.2 through 6.5 show four categories: homicides, assault, common robbery and theft, and vehicle robbery and theft. The important distinction between vehicle and common theft (everything but vehicle) is underreporting. While common robberies and thefts are severely underreported, vehicles are quite well measured because of insurance and legal liability reasons (see Biderman, de Mello, and Schneider [2009]).

The big surge in homicides is mainly a phenomenon from the 1990s. Although homicides were picking up since the mid-1980s, neither pace of increase nor the consistency is comparable to the 1990s. Furthermore, the decline in homicides in the 2000s is also an unprecedented phenomenon.

---

9. Data from before the 1990s is only available for the SPMA.

Assaults, if anything, follow a pattern symmetrically opposite to homicides. However, underreporting of assaults changed over time. Consider Disque-Denúncia, an anonymous hotline to report crime. Anecdotal evidence suggests that Disque-Denúncia improved reporting of assaults (see Kahn and Zanetic [2005]). Figure 6.4 shows data from the two victimization surveys conducted in city of São Paulo in 2003 and 2008. Panel a contains information on the victimization. In 2003, 4 percent of respondents declared they had been a victim of assault in the previous eighteen months. In 2008, the figure drops to 2.7 percent, a 33 percent reduction (the difference is statistically significant at the 1 percent level).

Panel b contains information on reporting by victims. In 2003, 29 percent of victims of assault that "called or informed," and 23 percent filed a complaint (which implies a police report is generated). In 2008, these percentages were 34 percent and 27.5 percent, respectively. In summary, victimization data suggest that assaults dropped in the 2000s, in line with the pattern of homicides. For the 1990s, data is inconclusive because of time-varying underreporting.

Figure 6.5 shows data on thefts and robbery. We present two separate categories: vehicle and everything else (common). Vehicle theft and robbery resembles the dynamics of homicide. They surge in the 1990s, reach a peak between 1999 and 2000, and then decline monotonically. Common robberies and thefts also surge in 1990s. In contrast to vehicles, they do not peak in the late 1990s. In fact, data suggest the stabilized at the high late 1990s plateau. Again, however, data is not informative because of improvement in reporting in the 2000s.

In summary, different well-measured crime categories show that crime in general surged in the 1990s and then dropped in the 2000s, suggesting a common component explanation.

6.3.2   The Rest of Brazil

Figure 6.6 shows the evolution of homicide rates in São Paulo vis-à-vis the rest of the country.

Brazil is São Paulo with a three- to four-year lag. The increase of homicides during the 1990s was remarkably similar in São Paulo and in the rest of Brazil. The two series reached a peak in different yet reasonably close moments in time: while homicides in São Paulo peaked around 1999, in Brazil the peak was in 2003. From the peak, homicides dropped much faster in São Paulo, possibly reflecting a peculiarity in terms of policies implemented, or perhaps little time has passed since the peak in the whole country.

Aggregate figures may hide important local heterogeneity that may be incompatible with a common component explanation. Figure 6.7 shows the evolution of homicides in several Brazilian states. Although some heterogeneity exists, the comovement in homicides is remarkable, reinforcing the idea of a common component.[10]

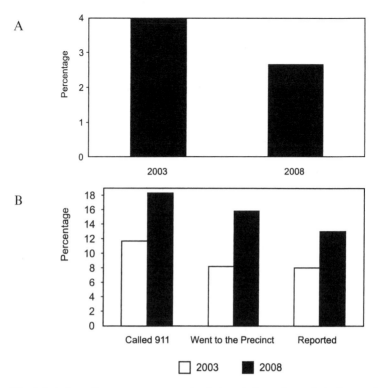

Fig. 6.4 _A_, Assault, percentage reporting being victims of assault in the previous eighteen months; _B_, Percentage reporting assault by categories
Source: Instituto Futuro Brasil (IFB).

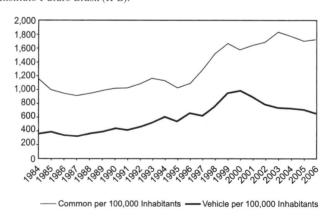

— Common per 100,000 Inhabitants — Vehicle per 100,000 Inhabitants

Fig. 6.5   Robbery and theft
Source: Secretaria de Segurança Publica de São Paulo (SSP-SP).

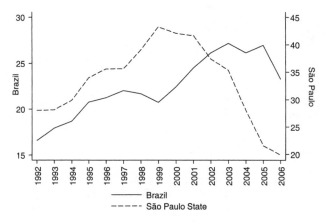

Fig. 6.6   Homicide rates per 100,000 inhabitants, Brazil versus São Paulo from 1992 to 2006.
Source: DATASUS Secretaria de Segurança Publica do Estado de São Paulo.

Consider the state of Rio de Janeiro. It experiences a big surge in homicides in the first half of the 1990s, a (still unexplained) phenomenon that made the state infamous for its violence. Homicides decline afterwards, just to increase again between the late 1990s and early 2000s. After 2002 they start to decline consistently. If one is prepared to consider the early 1990s surge a sporadic event, homicides in Rio follow the same pattern as the aggregate for Brazil (figure 6.6).

All other states depicted in figure 6.7 show a familiar pattern. Homicides increase almost monotonically in the 1990s. In all cases, homicides stabilize in the early- to mid-1990s and then start to decline with different intensity. In summary, data from other states in the country show two things. First, homicides have strong comovement across states, suggesting a common explanation. Second, the decline in the rest of Brazil starts later than in São Paulo.

6.4   Possible Culprits: Police, Guns, Incarceration, Arrests . . .

As a reaction to the surge in crime during the 1990s, São Paulo implemented major policy interventions, both at the municipal and the state level. In this section we consider these policy interventions as explanations for the large shift in homicides in the state of São Paulo.

---

10. We show only the most important states in terms of population. Figures for other states are available upon request.

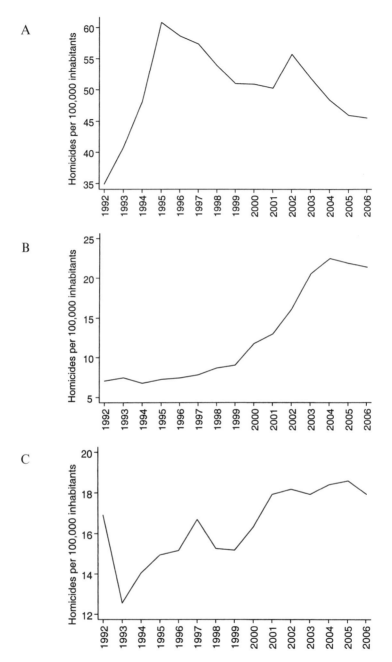

Fig. 6.7 Evolution of homicides across States: *A*, Rio de Janeiro; *B*, Minas Gerais; *C*, Rio Grande do Sul

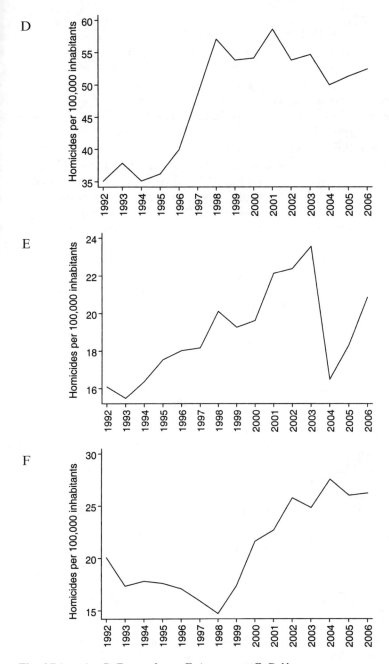

Fig. 6.7 (cont.)   *D*, **Pernambuco;** *E*, **Amazonas;** *F*, **Goiás**
Source: DATASUS and Instituto Brasileiro de Geografia e Estatística (IBGE).

6.4.1   Police and Policing

Anecdotal evidence in press stories suggests that the reduction in crime during the 2000s is a consequence of years of well-conceived and well-executed crime-fighting policies. In this subsection we assess the potential contribution of these policies.

As expected, policy reacted to the rise in homicides during the 1990s. Table 6.1 lists the most relevant police-type policies adopted from the second half of the 1990s through 2007.

Most likely, all policy interventions had an impact on crime. The presence of a Compustat system such as INFOCRIM helps law enforcement. Nevertheless, it is difficult to imagine that interventions can account for the dynamics of homicide in the state of São Paulo. One reason is timing. All policy interventions occurred either exactly when the trend in homicides have been reversed (1999 to 2000), or afterwards. Although INFOCRIM was implemented in 1999, it became fully operational only in 2001, and data has not been used to determine local police force until recently.

Figure 6.8 shows the number of police and arrests. Unfortunately we only had data starting in 2001 on both variables. Nevertheless, the numbers

Table 6.1   **Policy interventions**

Policy	Level	Date
Creation of INFOCRIM, a database system of crime georeferencing	SPMA and large cities	1999[a]
Executive order linking number of police officer to INFOCRIM	SPMA and large cities	2007
Creation of DISQUE-DENÚNCIA, an anonymous crime hotline to denounce crime	State	2000
Creation of FOTOCRIM, a database of pictures of wanted and in prison	State	1999
Effective implementation of FOTOCRIM as an instrument of photograph identification	State	2002
Elaboration of the Plano de Combate aos Homicídios, with emphasis on capturing repeated murderers	State	2001
Creation of Municipal Police Forces	SPMA[b]	1962–2003[c]
"Operação Saturação", a centralized, systematic, and permanent operation in drug-trafficking areas	State	2006

Sources: Kanh and Zanetic (2005) and Biderman, de Mello, and Schneider (2009)

[a]The year 1999 is the inauguration in the city of São Paulo. The INFOCRIM starts to expand to other cities in SPMA in 2002. Other large cities in the state enter the system in 2005. See Biderman, de Mello, and Schneider (2009).

[b]Twenty-six out of the thirty-nine cities that form the SPMA have Municipal Police Forces.

[c]Seven Municipal Police Forces were created after 1998.

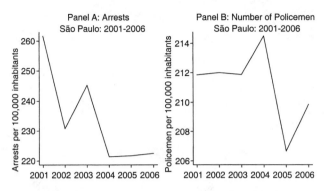

Fig. 6.8   Arrests and number of policemen per 100,000 inhabitants
Source: Secretaria de Segurança Pública do Estado de São Paulo.

are still informative. Panel a includes arrest statistics. From 2001, arrests dropped from 260 to 220 per 100,000 inhabitants, a 15 percent decline. If an increase in severity or in the efficiency of police work explained the decline in crime during the 2000s, one should see the opposite: arrests should be increase over the period. The fact that arrests *decline* in the period most likely reflects reverse causality: declining crime reduces arrests.

Panel b includes the number of policemen. The scale makes the series seemingly volatile. In fact, the number of policemen stayed constant over the period. Thus, a big quantitative increase in police cannot explain the large reduction in crime during the 2000s. Of course, police quality may have improved but most interventions that improved police work occurred only later in the decade, and cannot explain the timing of the shift in homicides (see table 6.1).

6.4.2   Incarceration

Figure 6.9 shows the prison population per 100,000 inhabitants in the state of São Paulo from 1994 through 2006 (period of data availability).

The figure illustrates the difficulty in attributing the dynamics of homicide to incarceration. Incarceration rates rise monotonically, suggesting that, at least for the period of the 1990s, incarceration reacted to crime, and not contrary. Incarceration continues to increase in the 2000s even as crime decline, possibly reflecting an increased toughness in law enforcement. Nevertheless, it is hard to attribute causality. Among other things, incarcerated population increases at a reduced pace in the period from 2004 to 2006, when compared with the 1994 to 2003 period, again suggesting reverse causality.

6.4.3   Municipal Level Interventions

Public security is mainly a state attribution in Brazil. Nevertheless, municipalities also reacted to the surge in crime during the 1990s, enacting laws

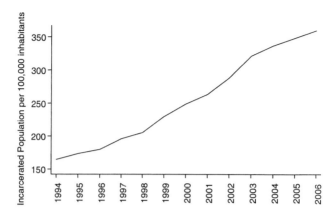

Fig. 6.9   Incarceration rates São Paulo: 1994 to 2006
Source: Secretaria da Administração Penitenciária do Estado de São Paulo.

and implementing crime fighting policies. In this subsection we describe the most important ones.

A most publicized local intervention was the adoption of mandatory night closing hours for bars and restaurants, popularly known as dry laws. In the SPMA, sixteen out of thirty-nine municipalities adopted such restriction on bars' opening hours. Evidence suggests that dry laws did have causal impact on homicides. Biderman, de Mello, and Schneider (2009) find that dry law caused a 10 percent decline in homicides. Although this impact is practically relevant, dry laws cannot rationalize aggregate movements of crime in São Paulo. First, the first city to adopt was Barueri in March of 2001—almost two years after the peak of homicides. Second, the decline in homicides is much deeper than 10 percent. Finally, the breadth of the decline is much ampler than a few cities in the SPMA, as figure 6.1 shows.

Another important local-level policy was the Disque-Denúncia, an anonymous hotline for reporting crimes and suspicious activity. Disque-Denúncia is a state-level policy that started in October 2000. Eight out of the thirty-nine municipalities passed laws mandating that the Disque-Denúncia number should be displayed in public places (schools, hospitals, buses, etc). Evidence suggests that adherence to the Disque-Denúncia program did have an impact on crime (see Kahn and Zanetic [2005]). Again, this impact is not strong enough, wide enough and implementation was not early enough to explain the aggregate dynamics of crime in the state of São Paulo.[11]

Other important municipal policies were the establishment of municipal

---

11. Kahn and Zanetic (2005) point out the big surge in calls in the Santos Metropolitan Region (the second largest in the state) in 2004, when Santos adhered to the system. Homicides in Santos had been declining for four years at that point.

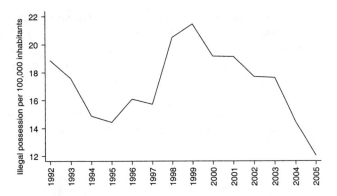

Fig. 6.10   Illegal firearm possession rates São Paulo: 1992 to 2005
Source: Secretaria de Segurança Pública do Estado de São Paulo.

police forces and municipal secretaries of public safety. Again, their timing and breadth are not compatible with being a first order explanation.[12] In summary, municipal interventions contributed to the decline in crime rates but they cannot explain the general aggregate movement in crime in the state of São Paulo.

6.4.3   Gun Control

In December 2003, the federal congress passed a federal law that substantially restricted the legal possession of firearms, and substantially increase the penalties for illegal possession (Lei do Desarmamento). While it is clear that this legislation cannot explain the timing of the shift in homicides, it does suggest that gun control did increase over the period. Anecdotal evidence suggests that starting in 1997 the state of São Paulo cracked down on the illegal possession of firearms, which leads local analysts to attribute the sharp swings in homicides to gun control (see *The Economist* [2005] and Goertzel and Kahn [2007]).

Figure 6.10 has the data on rate of illegal firearm possession over the 1992 to 2005 period (period of data availability).

The time-series pattern of illegal firearm possession seemingly matches the pattern of the homicide data. However, a few subtleties obscure causal interpretation. First is the issue of measurement. Reported illegal firearm possession is a combination of the prevalence of firearms in the population (which one wants to observe) and police enforcement (which one wants to isolate). Consider the increase in illegal possession starting in 1997. This movement is in line with the anecdotal evidence that police cracked down on illegal gun possession (see Goertzel and Kahn [2007]). Thus, the hike in late

---

12. See Kahn and Zanetic (2005) on the timing of secretaries of public safety and municipal police forces.

1990s less is not due to an increase in firearm prevalence but to a tightening in enforcement. Along these lines, if one is prepared to assume away the problem of measurement and consider that the movement in illegal possession in the late 1990s was in fact an increase in prevalence, then one must also assume it was so in the early 1990s. But then it is hard to reconcile the movements in firearm prevalence and homicides. In summary, it seems that movement in guns prevalence played a role in the reduction of violence in the 2000s but it explains neither the increase in violence in the 1990 nor the reversal in the late 1990s.

6.5   The Demographic Explanation

This section shows evidence that the age structure is the main determinant of the aggregate movements in homicides in the state of São Paulo. First, we show that young males aged fifteen to twenty-four are not only the main victims of homicides, but also the main perpetrators. Second, we show that the aggregate time-series patterns of population aged fifteen to twenty-four matches perfectly the time-series pattern of homicides: the age group fifteen to twenty-four increases during the 1990s, reaches a peak in 2000, and the drops. Finally, we use a panel of cities to estimate the elasticity of homicides rates to changes in size of the fifteen- to twenty-four-year-old population. Elasticities are estimated controlling for city and year fixed effects. Thus, results account for all time-invariant city heterogeneity and, more importantly, to all aggregate (common to all cities) shocks to homicides and age structure. The only variation left is how the age structure changed differently in different cities. Thus no spurious pure time-series relationship arises.

6.5.1   The Demographic Hypothesis

At the individual level, criminal involvement and age is one of the most robust relationships in all social sciences, dating back to at least Goring (1913). A very non-exhaustive list of more recent work would include Wilson and Herrnstein (1985), Blumstein (1995) and Cook and Laub (1998).

Despite the individual level evidence, and the pronounced importance of the fifteen to twenty-four cohort in both perpetrating and being victims of homicides, recent literature is ambiguous as to the importance of changes in age structure to explain aggregate crime. Fox (2000) finds that demography explains the major homicide trends from the mid-1960s through the mid-1980s, but account neither for the increase in violence in 1980s nor for the reduction during the 1990s. Holding age-specific murder rates constant, Levitt (1999) finds that changes in age structure explain less than 10 percent of the aggregate time-series variation over the 1960 to 1995 period. Zimring (2007) examines in depth all the explanations for what he calls "the great American crime decline." He shows that demographic trends were favorable in 1990s. Similarly to Levitt (1999), he also shows that, holding either ex-ante

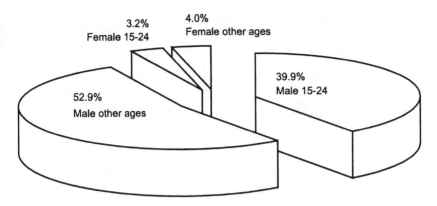

Fig. 6.11   Distribution of homicide victims by age and gender over the 1991 to 2004 period
Source: DATASUS.

or ex-post age-specific homicide rates constant, changes in age structure cannot account for the magnitude of the shift in homicides. However, in both cases, the interpretation of the decomposition hinges crucially on the assumption that age-specific homicide rates do not change with the size of the age group. With Brazilian data, I find that the size of the fourteen to twenty-five age group affects homicide rate for ages fifteen to twenty-four, which invalidate procedures such as Levitt's (1999) (see section 8). For this reason I adopt the strategy of computing elasticities, and use them to predict homicides.

Using hospital data, figure 6.11 shows the age distribution of homicide victims in the period 1991 through and 2006 in the state of São Paulo. Persons aged fifteen to twenty-four represent almost 40 percent of homicide victims. The second most victimized category is twenty-five to thirty-four with roughly 30 percent of victims. If one uses data from the state-level secretary of security, the fifteen to twenty-four age group represents a higher proportion of perpetrators of homicides, around 45 percent in 2003.

In summary, the demographic hypothesis is theoretically plausible for the state of São Paulo. In the subsections we test whether it is empirically relevant.

6.5.2   Time-Series Patterns

Table 6.2 shows some descriptive statistics for SPMA and for all other cities with more 100,000 inhabitant, for three periods: 1991 to 1995, 1996 to 2000, and 2001 to 2005. Two key variables are depicted: homicide rates and percent of male population aged fifteen to twenty-four.

Table 6.2 summarizes the story of this chapter. Homicide rates and the percentage of males between fifteen and twenty-four years old move together

Table 6.2   **Means for three different periods**

	SPMA[a]		Other large cities[b]	
	Homicide rate[c]	Percentage male 15–24	Homicide rate[c]	Percentage male 15–24
1991–1995	41.79	9.37	15.83	9.36
1996–2000	54.66	9.58	25.54	9.58
2001–2005	45.95	9.18	23.87	9.37

Sources: DATASUS and Instituto Brasileiro de Geografia e Economia (IBGE).
[a]Cities in the São Paulo Metropolitan Area.
[b]Cities with more than 100,000 inhabitants in 2000.
[c]Per 100,000 inhabitants.

over time. Suggestively, in large cities outside the SPMA, where the demography varied less, crime also varied less.

To assess how much the demography explains of the time-series pattern of crime we perform two Oxaca-Blinder-type decompositions. The DATASUS data has information on the victims' age, which can be used as proxy for age group specific homicide rates.[13]

Let H_{ta} be the homicide victim rate of age group a in year t. Victims are divided into nine groups, and $t = 1991, 1992, \ldots, 2004$.[14] Let P_{at} be the proportion of the population that, at year t, is the age group a. The overall homicide rate at time t is approximately[15]:

$$H_t = \sum_a P_{ta} H_{ta}.$$

Define H_{ta_τ} as the homicide rate that would prevail in year t if age group specific homicides are kept constant but the demographic distribution changed to that of year τ. In other words:

$$H_{ta_\tau} = \sum_a P_{\tau a} H_{ta}.$$

H_{ta_τ} is used as a rough prediction of what would the homicide rate be in year τ if the demography changed but the level of homicides of year t were kept constant. Figures 6.12 and 6.13 show predicted and actual homicides for the 1984 to 2004, and 1991 to 2004 periods; holding homicide victim rates of 1984 and 1991, respectively.

Visual inspection of figures 6.12 and 6.13 show two facts. First, there

13. Levitt (1999) uses incarceration data, which is generated on the offender side, a better unavailable measure.
14. Groups are zero to four, five to fourteen, fifteen to twenty-four, twenty-five to thirty-four, thirty-five to forty-four, forty-five to fifty-four, fifty-five to sixty-four, sixty-five to seventy-four, and over seventy-five.
15. The "actual" homicide is rate is the sum of homicides over the sum of population.

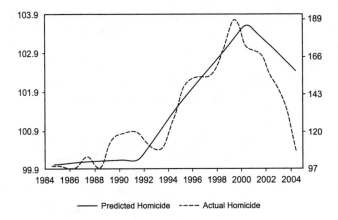

Fig. 6.12   Predicted versus actual, base 100 in 1984
Sources: Fundação SEADE and Secretaria de Segurança Pública de São Paulo.

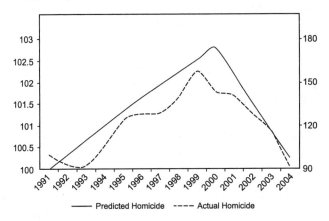

Fig. 6.13   Predicted versus actual, base 100 in 1991
Sources: Fundação SEADE and Secretaria de Segurança Pública de São Paulo.

is a remarkable comovement between the two series. This is true for the whole 1984 to 2004 period, and for the subperiod of 1991 to 2004. Thus, not only changes in the size of the fifteen to twenty-four age group predict homicides *but also changes in the whole age structure of the population.* Second, demographic changes do not pin down the level of homicides, but the decompositions are a qualitative exercise. As Levitt (1999) shows, quantitative interpretation is only warranted when the age-group specific crime rates are not a function of the population in the age-specific groups. Levitt (1999) finds evidence for U.S. data that this assumption is satisfied. With São Paulo data this is not the case. Regressions, whose results we omit, show that age-specific homicides rates are functions of age-specific population. Thus, only the qualitative interpretation of timing of increase and decrease is warranted. As Zimring (2007) shows, a nontrivial difference exists if we use ex-ante or ex-post age-specific homicide rates. If ex-post rates were used, predicted homicides in 1999 would be 30 percent higher than in 1991. This is still short of the 78 percent increase, but it is much closer. In any event, when specific homicide rates are a function of population then qualitative movements are more informative than quantitative ones.

6.5.2   Panel Evidence

Ultimately demography and crime are not randomly determined but are choices of the agents. Consequently, the relationship between demography and homicides may suffer from the usual problems: of reverse causality and omission of common determinants. Additionally, using time series variation alone one cannot dismiss the possibility that the relation arising in figures 6.12 and 6.13, and table 6.2 are a product of a sheer coincidence (although demography and homicides seem related above and beyond the inclusion of a high-order polynomial of time).

Reverse causation seems highly improbable, at least as a first order phenomenon empirically. It is true that homicide victims are concentrated in the male age bracket fifteen to twenty-four. There are, however, too few murders to make a significant difference. For an illustration, at its 1999 peak, the city of São Paulo had 2,418 homicides whose victims were fifteen- to twenty-four-year-old males. Although the number is certainly very high, it amounts to no more than 0.25 percent of the 969,241 young males living in São Paulo that year. Furthermore, reverse causation, in this case, would bias the estimated relationship between demographics and crime towards zero.

Demography has two pillars. One is fertility and mortality, which is largely produced by decisions made several years—if not decades—before. Second is migration, a shorter-term decision. Similarly, crime is a decision made in the present. From the first channel (fertility), there is little chance that demography and crime have a common cause. Migration is more challenging for the estimation strategy, and it is further discussed below.

In this subsection we estimate how demography impacts violent crime using, along with variation over time, how demography evolved in different large cities in the state of São Paulo. Cross-city variation allows us to evaluate the "coincidence" explanation. Let i be a city and t be a year. The estimated model is:

$$(1) \qquad \log(Homicide)_{it} = \beta_0 + \beta_1 \log(Male1524)_{it} + Controls_{it}$$
$$+ \sum_{t=1}^{T} \tau_t \, TIME_t + \sum_{t=1}^{I} \iota_i \, CITY_i + \varepsilon_{it}.$$

Homicides are rates per 100,000 inhabitants, *Male*1524 is the percentage of fifteen to twenty-four year old males. $TIME_t$ is a full set of year dummies, and $CITY_i$ is a full set of city dummies. *Controls*, in some specifications, will include the log of population and the log of the high-school dropout rate. These two controls are quite important for our purposes. First, population will capture migration movements, the component of demography that is a product of current choices of agents. Second, it may be easier to maintain youngsters at school if there fewer of them.

With a panel structure, one can discard *all* pure time-series variation (and all pure cross-city variation), leaving only how demography changed *differently in different cities* as a source of variation to estimate its impact on homicides. Several more layers of coincidence are now necessary to produce the results spuriously. Second, we can account for all time-invariant heterogeneity among cities, which helps identify the effect of demography. The different panels in figure 6.14 illustrate graphically the type of variation explored when estimating equation (1). The proportion of fifteen to twenty-four year-old males and homicide rates are depicted for five large cities statewide.[16]

São Paulo, São José dos Campos and Itapecirica follow the typical pattern: proportion of fifteen to twenty-four year-old males increased until 2000 and fell thereafter, with homicides following the same pattern. However, where the proportion of fifteen to twenty-four year-old males increased less pronouncedly, and fell less pronouncedly (São Paulo), homicides also went up smoothly and fell relatively smoothly. In other cities, such as São José and Itapecirica, the proportion of fifteen to twenty-four year-old males increased smoothly, but then drop steeply, homicides also increase smoothly and then dropped pronouncedly. Finally, consider Suzano and Embu. In the former, the proportion of fifteen to twenty-four year-old males fell throughout the 1997 to 2005 period, and homicides followed the same pattern. On the other, in Embu the proportion of fifteen to twenty-four year-old males increased sharply until 2000, and so did homicides; from 2000 onwards, the proportion of fifteen to twenty-four year-old males fell very subtly, and so did homicides.

Table 6.3 presents several models estimated using only data from the São Paulo Metropolitan Area (SPMA), in which case there is data starting in 1991.

Column (1) presents the simplest possible model, without city or year dummies and with no controls included. A 1 percent increase in the percentage of fifteen to twenty-four year-old males is associated with 3.92 percent increase in homicides. To have a sense of practical importance, between 1996 and 2000, there were 9.58 percent of young males in the SPMA, and 9.18 percent in the 2001 to 2005 period (see table 6.2), which represents a 4.2 percent difference. Therefore, the coefficient implies that 16.37 percent of the reduction in homicides, which actually fell some 16 percent over the period.[17]

---

16. We depict no more than five cities for the sake of consciousness. Several other cities would confirm the pattern.

17. This is an extrapolation of a local interpretation of the log-in-log regression.

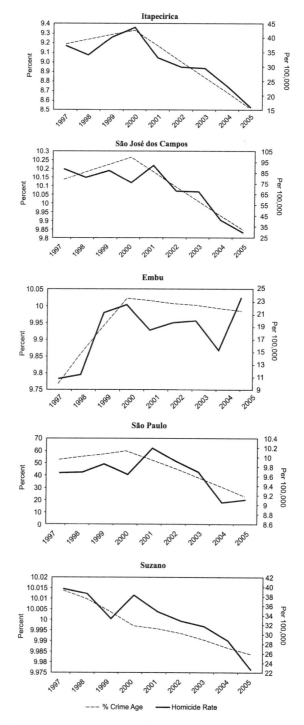

Fig. 6.14   Homicides and percent aged fifteen to twenty-four in different cities

Sources: Fundação SEADE and Secretaria de Segurança Pública de São Paulo.

Table 6.3   Homicide regression, SMPA 1991–2005

	(1)[a]	(2)[a]	(3)[b]	(4)[b]	(5)[b]	(6)[b]	(7)[b]	(8)[b]
Log (crime age)	3.92				2.02		1.71	
	(0.43)***				(0.63)***		(0.70)**	
Log (crime age) $t-1$		4.18	4.95	5.48		2.65		2.37
		(0.46)***	(0.59)***	(0.75)***		(0.77)***		(0.83)***
Log (population)							0.19	0.18
							(0.28)	(0.31)
Log (dropout rate)[c]							0.04	0.03
							(0.06)	(0.06)
Year dummies?	No	No	No	No	Yes	Yes	Yes	Yes
Number of Observations	515	482			515	482	514	481
R^2	0.12	0.13	0.70	0.70	0.76	0.77	0.76	0.77

Sources: Secretaria de Segurança Pública de São Paulo (SSP-SP) and Instituto Brasileiro de Geografia e Economia (IBGE).

Notes: Dependent variable: Log of homicide rate per 100,000 inhabitants. All standard errors are White-Huber heteroskedastic corrected, unless otherwise noted.

[a]OLS regression.

[b]Fixed-effects regression.

[c]High-school dropout rate, moving average over the second and third lags.

***Significant at the 1 percent level.

**Significant at the 5 percent level.

*Significant at the 10 percent level.

Since it is not clear whether current or (recent) past demography matters, homicides are regressed on the lag of *Male*1524 (column [2]). Results are even stronger.

Interestingly, when city-fixed effects are accounted for, the impact of demography is *stronger,* for both contemporaneous and the lag (4.95 percent and 5.48 percent). As expected, including year dummies dampens results, and so does including the two controls. However, we can always reject the null hypothesis of that demography does not cause homicides at reasonable significant levels. The lowest possible estimates arise when the two controls, population and high school dropout rates. Neither population nor dropout rates seem to belong to the equation, but the percentage of fifteen to twenty-four year-old males do. At the lowest estimate, changes in the *Male*1524 imply a reduction of 7.14 percent in homicides from the second half of the 1990s and the first half of the 2000s. Finally, in column (9), the most complete model is estimated using a moving average of $MALE1524$. Results, as expected, are between those in columns (7) and (8). In table 6.4, again using data from the SPMA, several econometric robustness checks are performed. For the sake of conciseness all models are estimated with the moving average of column (9).

Four pairs of regressions are presented, including and not including the controls. All regressions account for city and year fixed effects. The first is a pair of weighted least square regressions, in which the variance is modeled as a decreasing function of population. There are cities of wildly different sizes in the SPMA, and homicides are a relatively rare occurrence, observations from small cities are very noisy. Results are in line with those in column (9) of table 6.3. While in columns (1) and (2) the variance is modeled, in columns (3) and (4) the autocorrelation in modeled as an AR(1) process. Results are stronger.

In dynamic models, if the first lag belongs to the equation, and errors are auto-correlated (which columns [3] and [4] suggest is the case), the first lag is endogenous, and all coefficients are biased. To account for this possibility, we estimate the model by GMM using lags of the regressors as instruments (see Arellano and Bond [1991] for details). Even after including the first lag of homicide, results are once more stronger (columns [7] and [8]).[18]

Finally, the model is estimated with the sample restricted to 1997 onwards, for two reasons. First, by shortening the sample on the time dimension, one reduces the odds that time-varying unobserved heterogeneity across cities is driving results. Second, and more importantly, for 1997 onwards data are

---

18. The model is estimated in first-difference. After estimating the model by the generalized method of moments (GMM), we tested for first and second order autocorrelation on the error term. This is important because if *second* order autocorrelation is still present, coefficients could be biased if the second lag of homicides belongs to the equation. While first order autocorrelation is indeed present, after including the first lag of homicides second order correlation is not present.

Table 6.4   Homicide regression, SMPA 1991–2005

	(1)[c]	(2)[c]	(3)[d]	(4)[d]	(5)[c]	(6)[e]	(7)[f]	(8)[f]
Average log (crime age)[a]	1.87	1.77	2.58	2.40	2.80	2.81	3.28	5.13
	(0.57)***	(0.67)***	(0.97)***	(1.10)**	(0.98)***	(1.07)***	(0.91)***	(1.07)***
Log (population)		0.01		0.01		0.04		−1.62
		(0.21)		(0.40)		(0.47)		(0.59)***
Log (dropout rate)[b]		0.07		0.40		0.07		0.40
		(0.05)		(0.45)		(0.05)		(0.49)
ΔLog(homicide rate)$t-1$					0.28	0.28		
					(0.05)***	(0.05)***		
Year dummies?	Yes	Yes	Yes	Yes	Yes	Yes	Yes	Yes
Number of Observations	481	481	482	481	436	436	317	316
R^2	0.79	0.79	0.76	0.76			0.83	0.83

Sources: Secretaria de Segurança Pública de São Paulo (SSP-SP) and Instituto Brasileiro de Geografia e Economia (IBGE).

Notes: Dependent variable: Log of homicide rate per 100,000 inhabitants. All regressions account for city fixed effects. All standard errors are White-Huber heteroskedastic corrected, unless otherwise noted.

[a]Moving average over current and first lag.

[b]High-school dropout rate, moving average over the second and third lags.

[c]Weighted least squares, weight = population 0.5.

[d]General least squares (GLS) regression, model for the error term: AR(1).

[e]Arellano-Bond general method of moments (GMM) regression, all variables in first-differences.

[f]Year? 1997.

***Significant at the 1 percent level.

**Significant at the 5 percent level.

*Significant at the 10 percent level.

available for cities outside the SPMA. Results are significantly stronger than those with the whole 1991 to 2005 sample. In table 6.5, some of the models presented in tables 6.3 and 6.4 are replicated for a sample of all cities with more than 100,000 inhabitants.[19]

Three important messages arise from the table 6.5. First, when only the 1997 to 2005 period is considered, results are stronger than with the whole 1991 to 2005 period. The inclusion of large cities outside the SPMA does not change results in any significant way. We interpret these results as suggesting two facts. First, the phenomenon is wider than the SPMA. Second, with a shorter time length it is less likely that demography captures time-varying heterogeneity. Finally, confirm previous estimates, population seem to reduce homicides, and some models now suggest that more high-school dropout rates increase homicide as one should expect. The coefficient on population is puzzling in the light of the previous literature on social interaction that would predict crime rates are higher in larger cities (Glaeser, Sacerdote, and Scheinkman 1996). Our results suggest that, perhaps, economically dynamic and safer cities receive an influx of population. Since young males are more prone to moving, unobserved migration movements (imperfectly captured by population) would work towards biasing the impact of young males on homicides *towards zero*.

6.6   Conclusion and Discussion

Using data from São Paulo, we recover very large impact of age structure on homicides. Using the average panel elasticities estimated in tables 6.3 through 6.5 (3.4), we predict *aggregate* homicides using only changes in the *aggregate* proportion of the fifteen- to twenty-four year population. Demography predicts a 22 percent increase in homicides between 1991 and 2000, and a return to the 1991 level in 2004. This matches well the actual movement in homicides.

Aggregate movements in crime in São Paulo and Brazil resemble the case of New York and the rest of the United States ten years earlier. A strong common component across cities drove trends crime in the United States (Zimring 2007). However, in New York, a harbinger, the movements were more pronounced, especially the decline. Analogously, São Paulo antici-pated the rest of the country. Yet another similarity, the decline was particu-larly pronounced in São Paulo, suggesting that the policy reactions outlined in section 6.3 did have an impact. However, only demography explains the decline in 2000s, the timing of reversal *and* the surge in the 1990s. This, along with the common component character of the crime trends, shows

---

19. We do not present all models for the sake of brevity. All other results are in line with those presented.

Table 6.5   Homicide regression, large cities 1997–2005, dependent variable: Log of homicide rate per 100,000 inhabitants

	(1)[a]	(2)[b]	(3)[b]	(4)[b]	(5)[b]	(6)[bc]	(7)[bd]	(8)[be]	(9)[be]	(10)[be]
Log (crime age)	6.06 (0.50)***	6.32 (0.58)***	4.67 (1.01)***	6.37 (1.07)***		5.91 (0.87)***	6.03 (1.24)***	5.80 (1.54)***	3.12 (1.83)*	
Average log (crime age)					7.70 (1.22)***					4.35 (1.77)**
Log(population)				−2.09 (0.59)***	−2.97 (0.70)***	−1.71 (0.51)***	−1.88 (0.68)***	−2.96 (0.82)***	−2.99 (1.10)***	−3.20 (1.05)***
Log(dropout rate)				0.06 (0.06)	0.09 (0.06)	0.06 (0.06)	0.07 (0.05)	0.10 (0.07)	0.14 (0.07)**	0.15 (0.07)**
ΔLog(homicide rate)$_{t-1}$								0.43 (0.08)***	0.48 (0.09)***	0.46 (0.08)***
ΔLog(homicide rate)$_{t-2}$									0.37 (0.07)***	0.36 (0.07)***
Year dummies?	No	No	Yes	Yes	Yes	Yes	Yes	Yes	Yes	Yes
Number of Observations	585	585	585	585	520	436	585	455	390	390
R^2	0.17	0.85	0.86	0.87	0.87	0.88	0.87			

Sources: Secretaria de Segurança Pública de São Paulo (SSP-SP) and Instituto Brasileiro de Geografia e Economia (IBGE).

Notes: All regressions account for city fixed effects. All standard errors are White-Huber heteroskedastic corrected, unless otherwise noted. Average log(crime age) and Dropouts as defined in tables 6.3 and 6.4.

[a]OLS.

[b]City-fixed effects included.

[c]Weighted least squares, weight = population 0.5.

[d]GLS regression, model for the error term: AR(1).

[e]Arellano-Bond GMM regression, all variables in first-differences.

***Significant at the 1 percent level.

**Significant at the 5 percent level.

*Significant at the 10 percent level.

that demography is the key element driving movements in homicide in São Paulo over the last two decades.

Our results are seemingly in contraction to Naritomi and Soares (chap. 1 in this volume), which find only a small role for demography in explaining why crime is high in Latin America. Two facts reconcile the results. First, Naritomi and Soares use age-crime elasticities available in the literature, which perhaps needs revisiting. Second, Naritomi and Soares measure quite a different object: the contribution of different determinants using mainly cross-country differences. We measure the impact of a large shift in one contributing factor over time. Nothing guarantees that the impacts are similar. For example, country A may have 1 percent more young males than B, but many other factors may contribute more to explain differences in crime rates. However, if one changes the amount of young males sharply in one country, the impact of age structure may be much stronger, conditional on other determinants being fairly constant. Thus, our results should not be judged by the yardstick of cross-section estimates (Naritomi and Soares's object) but by the yardstick of identification: is it credible that other things are fairly constant in our data? We claim that it is, especially when panel data is used.

The results in this paper are important per se for criminology science. While there is undisputable evidence that offenders are mostly males between fifteen and twenty-four years old, whether age structure has an aggregate impact is not clear. Levitt (1999), for example, finds a limited role for demography. Our result can reconcile these two seemingly opposing pieces of evidence. Although age structure must mechanically contribute to crime rates, whether it makes an aggregate difference will probably depend on law enforcement, the efficacy of the judicial system, institutional development, educational and labor opportunity for young males, and so forth. Perhaps, in the state of São Paulo, differently from the United States, the environment was ripe for demography to flourish as a cause of homicides.

The results are also important in terms of policy. While it is hard to influence demography in the short-run, suboptimal policy overreaction can be avoided if demography is the driving factor.

References

Arellano, M., and S. Bond. 1991. Some specification tests for panel data: Monte Carlo evidence and an application to employment equations. *The Review of Economic Studies* 58:277–97.
Biderman, C., J. de Mello, and A. Schneider. 2009. Dry Law and homicides: Evidence from the São Paulo metropolitan area. Forthcoming. *Economic Journal.* Available now online at: http://www.3.interscience.wiley.com/journal/122575269/abstract ?CRETRY=1&SRETRY=0.

Blumstein, A. Prisons. 2002. In *Crime,* eds. Wilson, J., and Petersilia, J. San Francisco: ICS Press.

Cook, P., and J. Laub. 1998. The Unprecedented Epidemic in Youth Violence. In *Crime and Justice: A Review of Research,* ed. Tonry, M. Chicago: the University of Chicago Press.

Glaeser, E., B. Sacerdote, and J. Scheinkman. 1996. Crime and social interaction. *The Quarterly Journal of Economics* 111 (May): 507–48.

Goertzel, T., and T. Kahn. 2009. The great São Paulo homicide drop. *Homicide Studies* 13 (4): 398–410.

Goring, C. 1913. *The English Convict.* Montclair: Patterson Smith.

Kahn, T., and A. Zanetic. 2005. O papel dos municípios na segurança pública. *Estudos Criminológicos* 4 (July).

Levitt, S. 1999. The limited role of changing age structure in explaining aggregate crime rates. *Criminology* 37 (3): 581–97.

Wilson, J., and R. Hernstein. 1985. *Crime and human nature.* New York: Simon & Schuster.

Zimring, F. 2007. *The great American crime decline.* Oxford: Oxford University Press.

Comment   Lucas Llach

João De Mello and Alexandre Schneider (henceforth, DMS) present and discuss a remarkable social phenomenon: after increasing significantly over the 1990s, homicide rates in the State of São Paulo, Brazil, roughly halved in the first quinquennium of this century. Readers expecting some sort of magic policy formula to produce this fabulous trend would be disappointed. The authors' explanation for the sudden drop in the number of homicides is as far from policy as one can get: they attribute the decline to long-run demographic trends.

The authors argue that a question of timing discards policing innovations as the most likely explanation of the decline, as the majority of the new policies were implemented after the crime rate began to fall. It should be fair to note, however, that while it is true that crime peaked in 1999, most of the decline occurred after 2001: homicides per 100,000 inhabitants were around fifty in 1999, about forty-five in 2001, and close to twenty in 2006 (figure 6.2). The bulk of the decrease either followed or was contemporaneous with most of the policy innovations listed by the authors in table 6.1.

Also, the authors' interpretation of the decrease in the arrest/population ratio—namely, that arresting became more lax or that it just accompanied the decrease in crime rates—is misleading. While the rate of arrests declined just 15 percent after 2001, homicide rates fell around 55 percent. If homi-

Lucas Llach is professor of history and government at the Universidad Torcuato Di Tella.

cides are a proxy for crime in general, as the authors argue, then the *probability of arrest*—the relevant measure for crime deterrence—increased by around 90 percent (0.85/0.45 = 1.88). Such an increase in deterrence should appear at least as a serious candidate to account for some of the reduction in crime rates.

One of the reasons why the authors think that something deeper than policy changes has been behind the bewildering fall in crime rates in São Paulo is the supposedly similar crime trend elsewhere in Brazil. These similarities, however, are in the eye of the beholder and in the scaling of the graphs. My own impression is that there is something Paulista about São Paulo: the decline in the homicide rate from the previous peak was 53.5 percent (peaked in 1999), compared to around 18.2 percent in Rio (2002), 4.5 percent in Minas (2004), 2.7 percent in Rio Grande (2005), 9.5 percent in Pernambuco (2001), 8.7 percent in Amazonas (2003) and 4.7 percent in Goiás (2004). There is a very large Paulista specificity going on that demands a Paulista explanation.

De Mello and Schneider contend that the homicide rate rose and fell hand in hand with the percentage of young people in São Paulo's population. The share of the population in the "trouble age" (fifteen to twenty-four) reached a maximum around 2000, as the populous cohort born around 1980 turned twenty; as this numerous "trouble cohort" matured, homicide rates declined.

As a first approach to measure the effect of age structure on homicides, DMS present the murder rates that would have prevailed in each year *t* if the age-specific homicide rates of a base year are applied to the age structure of that year *t*. This counterfactual estimate is compared to the actual evolution of homicide rates. The visual effect of this superimposition of curves (figures 6.11 and 6.12) is impressive: actual homicide rates and homicide rates predicted solely by changes in age structure move hand in hand.

The unusual practice of using axes with different scaling for actual and predicted values, however, makes the exercise quite deceptive. A visual correspondence between the trends of predicted and actual homicide rates obtains only when one of the axes (actual rates) varies between 100 and 200 and the other spans only from 100 to 104. With the same age-specific murder rates of 1984, the variation in the age distribution would have accounted for changes in homicide rates from an index of 100 in 1984 to a maximum of around 104 in 1999, and back to around 100 in 2004. The curve of actual homicide rates shows the same inverted U pattern, though with a much wider amplitude. Homicide rates reached almost 190 (1984 = 100) in 1999 and fell to around 150 in 2004.

The bottom line should be that most of the change in overall murder rates has to be accounted for not by variations in age structure but in age-specific crime rates. For the DMS argument to be correct, an increase in the proportion of the "trouble age" group should lead to an increased incidence of crime among youngsters and/or among other age groups. The authors' demographic argument should rest on that peculiar connection, given the weak direct effect of age structure estimated in their counterfactual exercise.

The authors explore econometrically the connections between age and crime across Paulista cities, in panel data exercises covering fifteen years. The estimates come with a steep age elasticity of homicide rates—up to 5 percent in the highest case, implying that a 1 percent increase in the "trouble age" population leads to a 5 percent increase in homicides. Again, such a high number implies a change in age-specific homicide rates as a result of variations in age structure. It is only natural to wonder whether the omission of additional variables is affecting these results. For example, variables related to economic conditions—which are discarded in the abstract but never discussed in the paper—and to security policies—harder to measure—are among the most striking omissions.

While demographic trends can certainly be a source of movement in crime rates in general and homicide rates in particular, changes in age structure normally—for example, in the absence of episodes such as wars or massive migrations—move at low speed. Unless some very powerful externalities and scale effects are at work they are, thus, hardly capable of explaining wide short-run variations in aggregate crime behavior, such as the one observed in São Paulo.

The Quality of Life in Prisons
Do Educational Programs Reduce
In-Prison Conflicts?

María Laura Alzúa, Catherine Rodriguez,
and Edgar Villa

7.1 Introduction

The quality of life in prisons is a relevant component of the effective punishment prisoners face while doing time. For a given sentence, a more violent and conflictive facility makes punishment harsher. Katz, Levitt, and Schustorovich (2003) find evidence that quality of life in prisons, proxied by the number of deaths within a facility, has a deterrent effect on crime and that such effect is higher than the controversial deterrent effect of death penalty. Di Tella and Dubra (2008) build a model where society's beliefs, the level of punishment, and the economic system are jointly determined, giving rise to two different equilibria: one with harsher punishment than the other. The authors show that the severity of punishment is jointly determined with the economic system.[1] From the point of view of a system based on retribution,

María Laura Alzúa is professor of economics at the Universidad Nacional de la Plata and researcher at the Center for Distributional and Labor Studies, CEDLAS.

Catherine Rodriguez is assistant professor and researcher at Universidad de los Andes.

Edgar Villa is professor of economics at Pontífica Universidad Javeriana.

The authors would like to thank Rafael Di Tella, Sebastián Edwards, Ernesto Schargrodsky, and all participants in the Inter-American Seminar on Economics, Seminario Universidad Javeriana, LACEA-LAMES 2008 and Canadian Economic Association 2008 for helpful comments. Ignacio Dussaut provided excellent research assistance. Finally, the authors wish to thank Francisco Scarfo and Hernan Olaetta for their useful help, and the Dirección Nacional de Política Criminal of Argentina for providing the data used in this paper. Even though we made our best effort to incorporate these useful comments all remaining errors are the authors'.

1. They develop a model to explain the empirical fact that countries that believe in the so called "American dream," where effort pays have also harsher punishment. They show beliefs are correlated with the economic system and, too, with the system of punishment. In their model, two equilibria (harsh and soft punishment) arise. Both equilibria have identical fundamentals but different beliefs about the luck relative to effort in the realization of income.

varying prison conditions corresponds to a change in retribution which is not legislated. In this sense, worse prison conditions could be seen as one society's taste for more severe punishment and a legal system which does not encompass such taste. Also, for adherents to the idea of deterrence, the quality of prison life is also relevant, since it may also represent varying degrees of deterrence which are not directly related to the intended punishment.

In Argentina, which is just one example but that may be generalized to other western democracies, the idea of imprisonment is to restrain an individual from ambulatory freedom. This means that in principle, individuals should face the same rights in prisons (i.e., health, education, human and civil rights) than individuals outside them, with the exception of free circulation. For example, if an inmate does not meet the years of education mandated by law, she should be able to get her education while in prison. The same applies to health and the minimum requirements covered by law. In this context, degraded living conditions inside prisons impose a higher punishment that the one mandated by law. While the quality of life inside prison is not completely independent from average prisoners' characteristics[2], it should be the prison authorities' duty to ensure inmates are fulfilling their sentence properly, according to the punishment mandated by law.

The quality of life in prison has many dimensions, ranging from providing prison amenities such as athletic facilities and cable TV in the United States to very basic health and educational services in Latin America. However, the level of conflict within a prison can be considered as a proxy variable for such quality of life. High conflictive jails can be regarded as having a low quality of life and vice-versa. It is true that the level of conflict for a given prison is not independent from the prisoners inside, which varies a lot among facilities. However, at least for the case of Latin American prisons, there are also many circumstances affecting the level of conflict within a prison that are related to their management and administration. For the specific case of Argentina, Isla and Miguez (2003) document the very poor quality in the prison administration system mentioning several factors. Among them, personnel absenteeism is very high, human capital of prison managers and guards is very low. Moreover, prison guards hardly have any skill in conflict resolution techniques and some times they are the ones initiating a conflict and/or perpetuating bitterness among prisoners.

If we believe that sentences mandated by law, either adhering at the idea of retribution or to the deterrence one, reflect society's taste for punishment then, the quality of life in prisons should be guaranteed to surpass some set of minimal standards. We argue that quality of life within prisons can be proxied by in-prison conflict and violent behavior. Therefore to lower in-prison conflicts is one way of enhancing the living standards of prisoners.

---

2. Dangerous prisoners may often cause harm to their peers, lowering the quality of life in prisons.

However, lowering prison conflicts puts some pressure on public expenditure from local and federal governments, which often lack human resources to perform such activities. Moreover, there is an old criminological finding (Schnur 1949) showing a positive relationship between prison conflicts and recidivism, but in the opposite direction of the argument held by Katz, Levitt, and Shustorovich (2003).

Given the motives described above, it seems relevant to study which policies that are already in place can decrease in-prison conflict. Among the activities that are present in most prisons, educational programs are often available to prisoners for several reasons. The main argument to have prison based educational and training programs is that given the high incarceration rate of individuals, from minorities or vulnerable groups, such programs are often justified to facilitate offenders to reintegrate into society successfully. Wilson, Gallagher, and Mackenzie (1999) survey the literature looking at the relationship between educational programs and recidivism. Unfortunately, most of the evidence cannot overcome the selection problem; for example, less conflictive prisoners are more likely to participate and less likely to relapse in the first place. Steurer, Smith, and Tracy (2001) show that participants in prison-based educational programs in three states of the American Union enjoy higher subsequent earnings once they are released from prison. Unfortunately, the study does not address the bias caused from self-selection into educational programs. Tyler and Kling (2006) use panel data in order to control for time invariant unobserved heterogeneity among inmates in the state of Florida and find that General Educational Development (GED) programs offered in prison increase postrelease earnings 15 percent for minorities with respect to nonparticipants, even though these effects fade after three years. They find no significant effect of participating in GED programs.

In terms of experiences in developing countries, Argentina boasts a long tradition in prison-based educational programs, starting in the early 1950s. However, evidence on the effects of such programs is scarce, and neither literature concerning prison conditions in Argentina is abundant. Isla and Miguez (2003) provide anecdotal evidence of life inside prisons for convicted thieves. They state that in Argentine prisons they are often neglected and that there are violent spaces where the quality of life is quite poor. According to the authors, by no means do prisons have any "reforming effect" on inmates. Prisons are portrayed as highly corrupted places, where prison authorities are often the ones inciting violent behavior. Furthermore, given the current state of the prison system, a prison is regarded as a "school of criminals" perpetuating exclusion and marginality.[3] In contrast with this view, Scarfo (2008) provides also anecdotal evidence of schools functioning in prisons in

---

3. Evidence of this is found by Bayer, Hjalmarsson, and Pozen (2009) for juvenile correctionals in the United States.

the province of Buenos Aires, where half of the country's prison population is concentrated. According to the author, schools provide a safe environment within the prison, and classrooms are spaces where penitentiary officers are not allowed while lectures are taking place. Scarfo argues that educational programs within prisons are important as a way to help individuals to reenter society. In a survey of about 200 individual cases of prisoners, it can be observed the very low educational attainment of inmates.[4] Moreover, tests administered prior to this survey show that while more than 92 percent of surveyed individuals state they can read and write, they fail basic reading/writing requirements. Also, 50 percent of respondents stated that they believe they will learn useful things by participating in in-prison educational programs, and 32 percent think they will have a better chance of improving their "conduct." Focus groups among prison students in the province of Buenos Aires reveal a perception that education is regarded as beneficial inside and eventually outside prison since it can improve prisoners' skills.

It is entirely possible that both views can come to be true for different individuals: some could be truly reformed while others can become better criminals. Given these opposite views of in-prison education programs it is quite interesting to evaluate which one holds. For policy considerations one would be interested in finding out if, on average, individuals that participate in education programs tend to engage in less conflicts/violent behavior.

Using census data for sentenced male Argentinean prisoners during 2002 to 2005, this chapter studies the importance of improving the quality of life in prisons for those that participate in educational programs relative to those that do not by observing if there is a reduction in different indicators of conflict/violent behavior. Law 24.660 from 1996 mandates that all prisoners with less than the minimum required education level should participate in education programs. Because of administrative limitations at the province level this mandate is not completely fulfilled for all eligible prisoners. Specifically, on average only 25 percent of eligible prisoners under the mandate of the law actually end up participating. Moreover, this percentage varies widely within and across provinces which gives us a seemingly source of exogenous variation that creates two groups of individuals: those that by law should receive the minimum required education and do so, and those that should but do not. Under a probit estimation procedure we find that participation in education programs for this population significantly reduces conflicts measured by injuries, property damages, sanctions, and severe sanctions within prisons. Specifically, the estimated magnitudes of the effects on injuries lie between 0.1 and 0.3 percentage points; on property damages between 0.1 and 0.8 percentage points; on sanctions between 1.3 and 1.8 percentage points, and for severe sanctions lie between 0.9 and 1.5 percentage points. Acknowledging the possible existence of an omitted self-selection

---

4. This finding is consistent with the survey data we later use in the chapter.

term we use per capita expenditure in education at the province level as an instrument for education participation. We find that participation in education programs reduces on average property damages in a percentage point in a statistically significant way which interpreted relative to the mean percentage of property damages in the sample yields a reduction of 50 percent in these type of conflicts.

The remainder of the chapter is organized as follows: section 7.2 presents the conceptual framework, section 7.3 briefly describes the Argentinean Penal and Educational System for inmates, section 7.4 describes the data used in the chapter while section 7.5 presents the main results. Finally, section 7.6 concludes.

7.2   Conceptual Framework

To estimate the impact of prison education participation on conflictive behavior one needs an exogenous variation in participation at the individual level, since it could be the case that there is self-selection from prisoners to participate in these programs. In this chapter, we exploit a mandatory law of prisoners' education rights in Argentina. Law 24.195 of 1996 states that prisons must guarantee schooling for inmates whose educational attainment is below the compulsory nine years of basic education (complete Educación General Básica EGB).[5] The law mandates that any inmate failing to provide the necessary documentation that proves that he has not completed EGB must attend school while in prison. For higher educational levels, prisons may or may not offer such education. However, there are administrative and financial limitations at the provincial level to fulfill the mandate of this law. This gives us an exogenous variation which creates two groups of individuals: those that by law should receive education EGB and do and those that should and do not.

In this chapter we first study the relation between education participation for these two groups on several conflict behavior measures at the individual level through a simple difference estimator of the form:

$$(1) \qquad \text{conf} = \alpha + \beta\text{edpart} + X\gamma + Z\delta + \text{error},$$

where *conf* denotes a binary measure of conflict/violence at the individual level. *Edpart* is a binary variable for eligible individuals under the law that takes the value one if the individual participates in EGB program and zero otherwise. Finally, the terms X and Z represent individual and prison/province characteristics. If, due to administrative and financial limitations, participation of prisoners in educational programs at the province level is

5. It is worth mentioning that this law has been modified by Law 26.206 of December 2006. However, the period analyzed in this chapter is 2002–2005, and therefore Law 24.195 is the relevant one for us.

randomly assigned (or only depends on controls X and/or Z), a probit estimator gives an unbiased and consistent estimate of β.

If we are willing to assume selection into educational programs takes place based on observable characteristics, we can apply propensity score matching. We obtain local linear propensity score estimates of the average treatment effect that education participation has on conflicts inside prisons where participation is based on all variables included in X and Z.

However, it could be the case that some type of self-selection among prisoners is present in this process. If such effect is not fully captured by X or Z, both the probit and the matching estimator are biased and inconsistent. If in the error term there is something correlated with the education decision, both estimators will be biased. A priori it is difficult to know whether positive or negative selection may emerge. One view is that prisoners truly interested in being reformed might self-select positively into these programs if participation is granted on request. On the other hand, it could be the case that participation in these programs depends on the influence a prisoner has inside the prison. If so, these could actually be the most violent individuals that probably do not view education as a way to reform themselves. Finally, it could also be possible that prison authorities select which prisoners participate either as a reward for good behavior or a precautionary measure by sending the most conflictive prisoners.

Under this scenario the law mandate should be seen as generating only a *partial* exogenous variation of participation in prison education programs. Therefore, to estimate the effect of participation on conflictive behavior one requires a second source of exogenous variation that determines individual participation within the two groups but should not affect directly conflictive behavior. We argue that in Argentina a source of exogenous variation that determines participation in prison education programs is total per capita spending in education at the province level. Even under a self-selection story the final number of prisoners that end up participating will depend on the supply of education inputs—for example, number of available seats in the classroom or availability of teachers for adult education, among others. While prison education is mandated at the national level, it is actually supplied by provincial authorities. Hence, the final supply of in prison education depends on schooling public budgets at the provincial level.

Figures 7.1 to 7.4 provide evidence compatible with our assumption. They show a reduced form relation between mean per capita education expenditure at the provincial level and the corresponding percentage of conflictive interactions within prisons used in this chapter. Conflict or violence at the province level is an average across prison facilities of four in prison measures: (a) property damages, (b) personal injuries, (c) sanctions to prisoners due to inappropriate behavior, and (d), severe sanctions.[6] These figures

---

6. All these measures are described in detail in the data section.

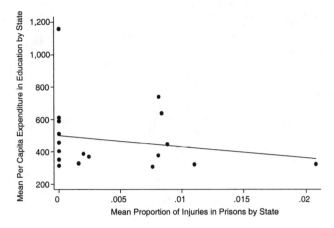

Fig. 7.1   **Injuries in eligible population from 2002 to 2005**

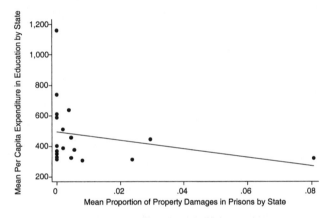

Fig. 7.2   **Property damages in eligible population from 2002 to 2005**

reveal a negative relation between mean per capita expenditure in education and measures of conflict in prisons across provinces. Provinces that have a higher per capita expenditure in education have on average lower in prison conflicts. Our theory is that per capita expenditure in education influence the supply of education for prisoners. To substantiate this we regress conflictive behavior of an individual on his education participation in prison programs and instrument the latter by per capita expenditure in education at the province level.

The exclusion restriction of this two-stage instrumental variable procedure is that, conditional on the controls included in the regression, per capita expenditure in education at the province level is only related with in prison conflict through education participation in prison education programs. Particularly, this restriction will not hold if per capita expenditure in education

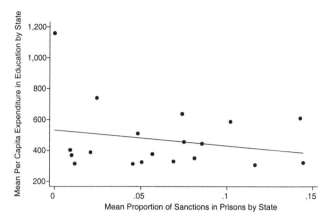

Fig. 7.3   Sanctions in eligible population from 2002 to 2005

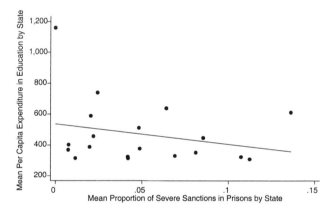

Fig. 7.4   Severe sanctions in eligible population from 2002 to 2005

at the province level is correlated with the attitudes of provincial authorities or civil population toward prisoners' well-being. For instance, provinces that care about in-prison conflicts could allocate a higher amount of resources to the education sector. We believe this is not the case for several reasons. First, while expenditure on education is decentralized, given the way the central government redistributes taxes at the province level, there is very little scope for provincial governments to increase/decrease educational expenditure.[7] Second, the total expenditure in education at the province level should not be influenced by the small or even negligible number of prisoners relative to the aggregate population. Specifically, on average prison population rep-

---

7. Law 24.195 sets the amount that should be spent on education at the national level. Moreover, most of provincial income is not generated by provincial revenues but by national government transfers, circa 80 percent, according to Rivas and Mezzadra (2006). The authors show that there is little correlation between provincial educational needs and transfers and that such transfers are the result of complicated political agreements instead of a set of rules.

resents only 0.001 percent of total population in the province. Last but not least, if there is indeed a correlation between total expenditure in education and preferences of prisoner well-being at the province level it is reasonable to believe that it would be constant through time. All specifications include province fixed effects and dummies indicating changes of government at the province level in order to account for this possibility.

7.3   Prisons and Education in Argentina

7.3.1   The Argentine Penal Legislation

In 1996 the Argentine Congress approved Law 24.660. This law regulates punishment depriving personal freedom for convicted individuals and replaced the previous which dated back to 1958. The goal of this new law is to make inmates acquire the capacity to understand and respect the law, endeavoring their proper reintegration to society. Law 24.660 states that the mandatory treatment of the inmates must be programmed and individually monitored with respect to the norms that regulate life, discipline, and work. Moreover, the penitentiary regime is based on the notion of *progressiveness.* This notion limits the time that inmates stay in closed prisons as well as the time for promotion to the following stage, conditioned on a positive evaluation of the inmates conduct.[8] The progressiveness of the penitentiary regime applied to convicts is characterized by four periods:

1. *Observational period:* during this period, the inmate is evaluated in several dimensions. He or she has medical, psychological and social evaluations, together with a criminological profile. All this information must be properly filed and updated.

2. *Treatment period:* during this period and according to prison facilities, the inmate goes through different phases in order to gradually attenuate the restrictions imposed by the sentence. This may include changes within each prison department or even prison transfers.

3. *Test period:* this period comprises the gradual incorporation of the inmate to less restrictive activities, including the incorporation to the regime of semiliberty.

4. *Parole period:* the inmate leaves the prison for periods up to seventy-two hours in order to carry out different activities: studying, participation in training programs, family visits, work, and so forth.

Each time an inmate enters a prison, he or she must be examined by a doctor, who certificates the inmates' physical and mental health. Also, some basic information about the inmate is gathered on his or her personal file.[9] Once the entry proceedings are finished, and in order to avoid possible con-

---

8. Cfr. Argentine Law 24.660, articles 1–6.
9. Marital and legal status, educational level, and so forth.

flicts among prisoners, inmates are gathered into homogeneous groups taking into account the offenders sex, age, physical and mental health, schooling attainment, criminal record, and the nature of the offence committed.

The *Federal* Penitentiary Service (SPF, for its Spanish abbreviation) is in charge of all federal prisons in Argentina while each *Provincial* Penitentiary Service is in charge of the remaining prisons within each province. All offenders to the federal system are put away in federal prisons; for example, tax evasion, drug trafficking, smuggling, counterfeiting, money laundering (among other felonies) as well as all offences committed in the National Capital City (CABA[10]). All other prisoners must serve time in the provincial penitentiaries. When a sentenced prisoner is sent to prison, the criteria to choose which prison they should be sent to is based on the type of crime committed and distance to their relatives.

7.3.2   Educational Requirements for Inmates

The educational system in Argentina is divided in five periods: (a) initial education (kindergarten) for children between three and five years of age; (b) general education (EGB or Educación General Básica) which is mandatory, lasts for nine years and starts at the age of six; (c) "polimodal" education (high school) which lasts for three years and where students can opt for different specializations (humanities, sciences, etc.) during this cycle;[11] (d) superior education which includes tertiary and university studies; and finally, (e) graduate education.

The penal system is designed to encourage prisoners' good behavior by means of rewarding positive actions and punishing negative ones. The education acquired is oriented so as to make inmates acknowledge her obligations and the norms that govern life in society. In particular, the inmates' right to acquire education must be guaranteed from the moment they enter the prison. Specifically, Law 24.660 states that every prisoner whose educational attainment is below the compulsory nine years (EGB) must receive education while in prison. For other educational levels (polimodal and superior education), prisoners may or may not receive such education.[12]

The system regulating education in Argentina was decentralized in the early nineteen nineties, where the Argentine Congress transferred most primary and secondary schools to provincial governments. Even though in-prison education is supervised by the Ministry of Justice (a national authority) as a result of school decentralization this federal entity has to make individual agreements with each Ministry of Education at the province level.

---

10. Ciudad Autónoma de Buenos Aires.
11. In order to compare it with the United States system, EGB is the sum of elementary education plus two years of high school. On the other hand, polimodal level is equivalent to the last three years of high school in the United States.
12. For example in Buenos Aires, some university degrees can be obtained. The Centro Universitario de Devoto has over 200 university students who are inmmates.

Hence, while all the in-prison education is coordinated at the national level, it has to be supplied by provincial authorities. In this vein, each provincial government must guarantee a functioning school in each prison.

However, there are severe limitations to fulfill the mandate of Law 24.660. The first problem is a chronic shortage of supply of prison educational programs. One important input of such programs is adult education teachers who are scarce across the country. This scarceness is more evident for prisons given that there are no extra incentives for teachers to work in those institutions.[13] Second, even though the facilities that have both remanded and sentenced prisoners should guarantee in prison education to all of them, the Ministry of Justice does not enforce this requirement for the remanded prisoners. So, in practice, education is not really available for all the inmates that should be attending school. Finally, even though there is a protocol for allocating inmates to classes in the case of excess demand, favoring first those who are either illiterate or are about to finish compulsory education, such protocol is generally altered by prison authorities.

7.4 Data

The data used in this chapter comes from The National Statistical System about the Observance of Punishment (SNEEP for its Spanish abbreviation).[14] The system has the objective of periodically gathering statistical information about all sentenced and remanded prisoners in the whole country. Annually, the system collects the data from both federal and provincial prisons. The information is gathered through a specific questionnaire which includes census data of prison population and specifies important events that happened to the prisoner during that year. In the first part of the questionnaire there is information about the inmate's age, sex, nationality, marital status, educational level, working status and training level, place of residence before incarceration, judicial jurisdiction, legal status, where the inmate comes from (direct entry or transferred from another prison), and type of the offence committed. In the second part of the questionnaire there is information about what the inmate did over the past year. There are also questions about the prisoners' activities (work in prison, training attainment, participation in educational programs, sports and recreational activities), and if they received medical attention and visits. Finally, there is also a record about the inmate's conduct, disciplinary sanctions, attempts to escape, security measures,[15] and their status on the progressive system.

Information from the SNEEP is available through out the period 2002 to 2005. Each year, data on all remanded and sentenced prisoners in the

13. There is no wage differential for teaching in prisons.
14. Sistema Nacional de Estadísticas sobre Ejecución de la Pena (SNEEP).
15. Cfr. Penal Code, art. 52.

country is collected, which implies information on approximately 45,000 individuals per year. Unfortunately, the system is not designed to allow the merging of observations in a panel of prisons nor prisoners throughout the period, forcing us to use the data as a pooled cross-section data set. Based on this restriction, the pooled years give us information on 184,374 inmates. However, in this chapter information of only a selected group of prisoners will be used. Specifically, we restrict our information to only prisoners that have received a sentence (43.1 percent of all prisoners) and that are in the observational or treatment period of progressiveness to ensure ourselves that they spend all of their time inside the correctional (72.39 percent of all sentenced prisoners). This selection was done due to several motives. First, the sample is restricted to sentenced prisoners because education is not available for remanded prisoners, in spite of being required by law.[16] Secondly, we only consider sentenced inmates who are not able to leave the prisons because inmates in test or parole treatment may leave the prison for some period of time, and some of them may participate in educational activities outside the prisons, but this information is not available in SNEEP.

Moreover, we further restrict this sample to use only male Argentinean prisoners excluding the relatively few foreigners that are located in provincial prisons since the mandate of the law states that prisons must guarantee schooling for argentine inmates whose educational attainment is below the compulsory nine years of basic education (complete EGB). We also decided to drop all prisoners that report zero as their age (twenty-nine prisoners) and if their reported date of sentence was before 1993 (396 prisoners), after 2005 (1,010 prisoners) or missing (2,734).[17] Hence, our treatment and control groups are those that by law should receive education EGB and do and those that should and do not. Of our restricted sample, 81 percent of them report a level of education lower than EGB leaving us with a final restricted sample of 26,531 prisoners. We find that only 30 percent of the prisoners who should receive mandatory education indeed are participating in an educational program. These 7,829 prisoners will therefore comprise our treatment group while the remaining 18,702 conform our control group.

The main characteristics of the sample can be observed in tables 7.1 and 7.2. The first table presents the number of prisoners in each province that have not completed EGB and hence, according to Law 24.660, should be receiving education while in prison. As it can be appraised, effective partici-

16. The latter do not participate from formal educational programs because they are often transferred among different prisons/regions while waiting for trial—educational curricula is not homogeneous across states—and due to the lack of adult teachers, who are always assigned first to sentenced prisoners.

17. This last restriction was done because Law 24.660 was passed in 1993 and hence only prisoners sentenced after this date should be covered by it. Similarly, if the date of reported sentence was after 2005 or missing it would mean that the prisoners are really still under process or we are not able to determine for certain if he is condemned or his case is still under process.

Table 7.1   Rate of participation in formal education programs of prisoners who
                   should be receiving education

State	Number of prisoners	Mean rate of participation	Standard deviation
Buenos Aires	3,319	0.28	0.45
CABA	364	0.10	0.30
Catamarca	365	0.01	0.10
Chaco	8,005	0.34	0.47
Chubut	932	0.47	0.50
Cordoba	1,318	0.36	0.48
Corrientes	1,378	0.71	0.45
Entre Rios	1,020	0.20	0.40
Formosa	402	0.53	0.50
Jujuy	347	0.27	0.44
La Pampa	548	0.20	0.40
La Rioja	48	0.00	0.00
Mendoza	172	0.12	0.32
Misiones	970	0.12	0.32
Neuquen	613	0.30	0.46
Rio Negro	692	0.30	0.46
Salta	809	0.11	0.31
San Juan	658	0.09	0.29
San Luis	387	0.03	0.17
Santa Cruz	130	0.73	0.45
Santa Fe	3,539	0.22	0.41
Santiago del Estero	89	0.34	0.48
Tierra del Fuego	62	0.15	0.36
Tucuman	364	0.09	0.29
Total	26,531	0.25	0.37

Source: SNEEP. Authors' calculations.

pation rates of inmates in formal education programs is relatively low even though the law states it should be 100 percent. While the average participation rate is 25 percent, it actually varies widely across provinces suggesting different administrative state units have different supply of educational facilities available to inmates. For example, participation is above 50 percent in only three provinces and is below 10 percent in five others. Moreover, as can be observed the standard deviation across years in each province also varies widely. Table 7.2 shows summary statistics of the individual characteristics of the inmates in the selected sample and of the prisons they belong to.

In terms of the information used to measure conflicts (*conf*) four different specifications are used. Two are related to the punishment individuals receive as a result of inappropriate conduct and the other two comprise information of actual violent activities. A first measure of inappropriate behavior is sanctions (sancs) which takes the value one if the inmate received any type of sanction during the period observed. A second measure is severe sanc-

Table 7.2   Characteristics of prisoners and prisons

Characteristic	Number of prisoners	Mean	Standard deviation
Individual characteristics			
Age	26,501	31.22	9.93
Married	26,531	0.11	—
Unemployed when entered prison	26,531	0.31	—
Number of years in prison	23,804	3.68	2.49
Number of crimes committed	26,531	1.32	0.68
Participates in working programs	26,531	0.49	—
Participates in sport activities	26,415	0.86	—
Received visits in the past year	26,531	0.83	—
Tried to escape	26,406	0.09	—
Has a reduction in sentence time	26,026	0.04	—
Recidivist	26,133	0.32	—
Prison characteristics			
Number of inmates	26,531	802.00	609.03
Average age of prisoners	26,531	31.47	2.53
% Assassins	26,531	0.16	0.13
% Rapist	26,531	0.22	0.30
% Thieves	26,531	0.53	0.14
% Inmates with primary education	26,531	0.50	0.17
% Inmates with secondary education	26,531	0.15	0.08
% Inmates with tertiary education	26,531	0.00	0.01
% Inmates who tried to escape	26,531	0.09	0.25

Source: SNEEP. Authors' calculations.
Note: Dashed cells indicate that the standard deviation was very small, and it shows very close to zero.

tions (sevsancs) which takes the value one if the inmate received a severe sanction during the period, where severe sanction means that the inmate was isolated in his chamber for fifteen consecutive days or seven weekends, as well as if the inmate was taken to a higher security facility. It should be noticed that sancs includes sevsancs in the sense that all severe sanctions are sanctions. Our first measure of violent activities is involvement in damaged property (Pd) which takes the value one if the inmate participated in any violent behavior where property damages occurred during the corresponding period. A second measure of violent activity is defined as injuries (Inj) which takes the value one if the inmate participated in any violent behavior that involved injuries or mortal wounds to others during the observed period. The two measures Pd and Inj are disjoint in the sense that property damages does not include acts of violence that ended up in injuries. Furthermore, the survey includes a question which serves to determine if the prisoner had an inappropriate conduct during the observed period. To reduce measurement error on our dependent variables we interact this information with the four measures of conflict giving us measures of conflict for individuals that were actually reported to have an inappropriate conduct.

Table 7.3   **Measures of violence inside prisons**

Characteristic	Number of prisoners	Mean	Standard deviation
Injuries	25,066	0.01	0.08
Damaged property	25,066	0.02	0.13
Sanctions	25,066	0.09	0.28
Severe sanctions	25,066	0.08	0.27

Source: SNEEP. Authors' calculations.

Descriptive statistics of these conflict measures are shown in table 7.3. While 9 percent of the sample faced some sort of sanctions as punishment for inappropriate behavior, 8 percent faced some type of severe sanction. In contrast, only 2 percent of the inmates have participated in violent activities causing property damages, and only 1 percent are reported to be involved in extremely violent episodes causing injuries. Violent indicators somehow misrepresent conflict in prisons, as it can be observed between the differences in the percentage of inmates participating in violent activities vis à vis the ones receiving sanctions. This divergence is caused by the fact that the inmate can appeal to the courts when faced with in-prison violent charges. If he is found not guilty, this information is removed from the inmate's file, whereas prisoner's punishment via sanctions cannot be undone. Hence in the rest of the chapter we use both type of measures.

7.5   Results

7.5.1   Probit Estimates

Recall that we have a pooled cross section data set at the individual level. We use a maximum likelihood approach to estimate β which yields a probit difference estimator under normality of the error term. The corresponding empirical specification of equation (1) is the following:

$$\text{conf}_{ips} = \alpha + \beta \text{edpart}_{ips} + X_{ips}\gamma + Z_{ps}\delta + \eta_t + a_s + u_{ips},$$

where conf_{ips} is the binary measure of conflict of individual i in prison p and province s; edpart_{ips} takes the value one if individual i in prison p and province s participates in an education program under the mandate of Law 24.660 and zero otherwise; X and Z are vectors of individual and prison/province characteristics respectively described in table 7.2, η_t and a_s are time and province fixed effects while u_{ips}, represents the idiosyncratic error.

Table 7.4 reports four different specifications of (2) for each of our conflict measures where all of them include province and time fixed effects. Moreover, in all specifications we present both Huber-White robust standard errors allowing arbitrary patterns of within-province serial correlation and

Table 7.4　Probit estimates (dependent variables: conflict/violent behavior)

Characteristic	Injuries				Property damage			
	I	II	III	IV	I	II	III	IV
Participates in education program	0.029	−0.159	−0.231	−0.227	−0.302	−0.263	−0.221	−0.209
	(0.063)	(0.085)*	(0.092)**	(0.093)**	(0.065)***	(0.078)***	(0.102)**	(0.103)**
	[0.233]	[0.195]	[0.137]*	[0.137]*	[0.328]	[0.312]	[0.170]	[0.169]
Participates in work activities				−0.402				−0.23
				(0.087)***				(0.074)***
				[0.072]***				[0.153]
Number of years in prison		0.031	0.031	0.033		0.025	0.036	0.033
		(0.014)**	(0.014)**	(0.014)**		(0.013)*	(0.015)**	(0.015)**
		[0.011]***	[0.010]***	[0.011]***		[0.025]	[0.026]	[0.029]
Age		−0.037	−0.037	−0.034		−0.059	−0.066	−0.065
		(0.006)***	(0.007)***	(0.007)***		(0.005)***	(0.006)***	(0.006)***
		[0.011]***	[0.009]***	[0.010]***		[0.007]***	[0.006]***	[0.005]***
Married		−0.195	−0.174	−0.163		−0.367	−0.052	−0.051
		(0.181)	(0.186)	(0.187)		(0.137)***	(0.138)	(0.138)
		[0.196]	[0.204]	[0.208]		[0.191]*	[0.125]	[0.127]
Unemployed when entered prison		0.013	0.051	−0.059		−0.117	0.019	−0.102
		(0.075)	(0.077)	(0.085)		(0.062)*	(0.068)	(0.076)
		[0.048]	[0.082]	[0.104]		[0.058]**	[0.066]	[0.112]

	(1)	(2)	(3)	(4)	(5)	(6)
Number of crimes committed	0.078 (0.047)* [0.023]***	0.042 (0.048) [0.026]	0.041 (0.048) [0.026]	0.018 (0.046) [0.055]	-0.023 (0.053) [0.064]	-0.021 (0.054) [0.066]
Participates in sport activities	0.01 (0.092) [0.067]	-0.008 (0.097) [0.078]	-0.004 (0.100) [0.076]	-0.387 (0.063)*** [0.197]**	-0.625 (0.081)*** [0.244]**	-0.623 (0.081)*** [0.247]**
Received visits in the past year	-0.233 (0.095)** [0.100]**	-0.127 (0.097) [0.095]	-0.128 (0.098) [0.093]	-0.445 (0.087)*** [0.172]***	-0.092 (0.090) [0.102]	-0.09 (0.090) [0.102]
Tried to escape	-0.14 (0.167) [0.222]	0.646 (0.215)*** [0.349]*	0.652 (0.215)*** [0.340]*	-0.025 (0.126) [0.233]	0.592 (0.166)*** [0.231]**	0.621 (0.167)*** [0.219]***
Has a reduction in sentence time	-0.101 (0.178) [0.152]	-0.201 (0.184) [0.149]	-0.165 (0.186) [0.151]	-0.73 (0.235)*** [0.151]***	-0.636 (0.264)** [0.186]***	-0.624 (0.264)** [0.191]***
Recidivist	0.177 (0.069)** [0.092]*	0.163 (0.073)** [0.097]*	0.147 (0.074)** [0.102]	0.109 (0.067) [0.089]	0.137 (0.073)* [0.087]	0.133 (0.073)* [0.085]
Prison and state characteristics	No	Yes	Yes	No	Yes	Yes
Observations	20,774	17,754	17,754	19,295	16,553	16,553

(continued)

Table 7.4 (continued)

Characteristics	Sanctions				Severe sanctions			
	I	II	III	IV	I	II	III	IV
Participates in education program	-0.106 (0.026)*** [0.089]	-0.131 (0.031)*** [0.080]*	-0.144 (0.033)*** [0.057]**	-0.128 (0.033)*** [0.056]**	-0.075 (0.027)*** [0.060]	-0.087 (0.031)*** [0.055]	-0.116 (0.034)*** [0.052]**	-0.1 (0.034)*** [0.053]*
Participates in work activities				-0.443 (0.032)*** [0.120]***				-0.417 (0.033)*** [0.118]***
Number of years in prison		0.009 (0.006) [0.010]	0.013 (0.006)** [0.008]	0.018 (0.006)*** [0.009]**		0.006 (0.007) [0.009]	0.01 (0.007) [0.008]	0.015 (0.007)** [0.008]*
Age		-0.046 (0.002)*** [0.006]***	-0.047 (0.002)*** [0.005]***	-0.045 (0.002)*** [0.005]***		-0.047 (0.003)*** [0.006]***	-0.048 (0.003)*** [0.005]***	-0.045 (0.003)*** [0.005]***
Married		-0.139 (0.056)** [0.086]	-0.101 (0.058)* [0.070]	-0.088 (0.058) [0.074]		-0.084 (0.057) [0.083]	-0.062 (0.060) [0.078]	-0.046 (0.060) [0.082]
Unemployed when entered prison		0.04 (0.029) [0.051]	0.075 (0.031)** [0.051]	-0.03 (0.032) [0.059]		0 (0.031) [0.063]	0.039 (0.032) [0.061]	-0.058 (0.034)* [0.061]
Number of crimes committed		0.04 (0.020)** [0.020]**	0.043 (0.021)** [0.021]**	0.044 (0.021)** [0.025]*		0.04 (0.021)* [0.021]*	0.045 (0.022)** [0.024]*	0.047 (0.022)** [0.027]*

	(1)	(2)	(3)	(4)	(5)	(6)	(7)
Participates in sport activities	−0.275	−0.371	−0.369		−0.312	−0.381	−0.382
	(0.036)***	(0.040)***	(0.041)***		(0.037)***	(0.041)***	(0.042)***
	[0.095]***	[0.142]***	[0.139]***		[0.135]**	[0.161]**	[0.157]**
Received visits in the past year	−0.212	−0.118	−0.125		−0.119	−0.031	−0.038
	(0.037)***	(0.038)***	(0.039)***		(0.038)***	(0.040)	(0.040)
	[0.082]**	[0.065]*	[0.069]*		[0.092]	[0.094]	[0.100]
Tried to escape	−0.13	−0.177	−0.134		−0.129	−0.26	−0.217
	(0.057)**	(0.104)*	(0.103)		(0.059)**	(0.110)**	(0.108)**
	[0.147]	[0.388]	[0.385]		[0.132]	[0.377]	[0.373]
Has a reduction in sentence time	−0.15	−0.203	−0.196		−0.084	−0.139	−0.131
	(0.074)**	(0.076)***	(0.076)***		(0.078)	(0.081)*	(0.081)
	[0.305]	[0.254]	[0.256]		[0.279]	[0.219]	[0.202]
Recidivist	0.192	0.2	0.184		0.207	0.218	0.202
	(0.029)***	(0.030)***	(0.030)***		(0.030)***	(0.031)***	(0.031)***
	[0.082]**	[0.085]**	[0.091]**		[0.088]**	[0.089]**	[0.095]**
	[0.140]***				[0.112]**		
Prison and state characteristics	No	Yes	Yes	No	No	Yes	Yes
Observations	24,918	21,582	21,582	24,918	21,582	21,582	21,582

Notes: Robust standard errors in parentheses. Cluster (at province level) standard errors in brackets. All regressions include state and time fixed effects.

***Significant at the 1 percent level.

**Significant at the 5 percent level.

*Significant at the 10 percent level.

clustered standard errors at the province level.[18] The first specification for each measure presents the estimate of β controlling only for province and time fixed effects. For most of the conflict measures the estimate is negative and statistically significant under robust standard errors, suggesting that participation in education programs is related with lower in prison conflict. Nonetheless, all measures are statistically insignificant under clustered standard errors.

These estimates would provide an unbiased and consistent effect of prison education programs if participation was independent of any individual, prison, and province characteristic. This assumption is probably too strong and hence the remaining specifications reported in table 7.4 include in a stepwise fashion additional controls from the X and Z vectors. The second specification includes only prisoners' individual characteristics. As can be observed, the sign, magnitude and statistical significance of education participation is maintained for all conflict measures. The only exception is injuries which is now negative and statistically significant suggesting that participation is correlated with some prisoner characteristics. It is interesting to note that there are some consistent characteristics that are related with conflictive/violent behavior inside prisons. For example, individuals that have spent more time in jail, that are sentenced for a greater number of committed felonies, and that are recidivist are more likely to engage in inappropriate behavior. On the contrary, individuals that are older, married, and practice some sport within the prison are less likely to engage in this type of behavior. Although not reported, the third specification include prison and province characteristics. Among them we find that prisons with a higher number of prisoners, percentage of thieves and rapists are more likely to have more violent interactions. We also find that prisons with a higher percentage of murderers are less likely to have violent interactions between prisoners. This result may be driven by the fact that these are probably high security prisons where prisoners have less freedom and are more monitored. Not surprisingly, after controlling for province fixed effects, poverty and unemployment at the province level do not significantly explain conflict inside prisons.

Even after controlling for all these individual, prison and province characteristics, it might still be the case that there is an unobservable characteristic of the individual or the prison that determines both participation and inappropriate behavior. The survey also provides information of whether the prisoner participates in any type of labor activity inside the prison. It is reasonable to believe that participation in these activities could proxy for the unobservables that determine participation in education programs.

18. Bertrand, Duflon, and Mullaínathan (2004) report that robust standard errors provide good performance in panels where the number of time periods is small such as the one we have. However, cluster standard errors are also reported to allow possible correlation among prisoners within the same province.

Hence, the last specifications of table 7.4 include a dummy variable that gives information if the prisoner participates or not in labor activities. As can be observed, prisoners that participate in labor activities are less likely to engage in conflictive behavior. More importantly, the estimate of education participation does not change significantly which reassures our previous findings. These results are statistically significant under both cluster and robust standard errors, except for property damages which is never significant under the former.

Based on these last specifications we find that participation in education programs reduces on average conflictive/violent behavior. The practical significance of such programs are not negligible. Specifically, participation in education programs reduces injuries and property damages in 0.1 percentage points evaluated at the mean of all control variables. Relative to the mean percentage of these violent behaviors reported in table 7.3 we find that education programs reduce them in 17 percent and 6 percent, respectively. Furthermore, participation in education programs reduce on average sanctions and severe sanctions in 1.3 and 0.9 percentage points (or 15 percent and 11 percent relative to the corresponding sample mean), respectively.

It is important to note that we cannot differentiate the transmission mechanisms through which this effect of education programs takes place. It is perfectly consistent with our results that two different mechanisms are at work. On the one side, education programs could influence the behavior of prisoners through changes in their moral values and psychological attitudes towards violent behavior. On the other side, it could be that the effect found is capturing a reduction in idle time of prisoners. On average, participation in education programs requires three hours per week day (excluding Saturday and Sundays), amounting to fifteen hours per week. Assuming that a prisoner has fourteen hours per day in idle time, participation in education programs represents 15 percent of total time endowment. Given that we find that on average inappropriate behavior is reduced in 15 percent the second story is quite plausible. However, if the effect was entirely driven through this second channel we would expect to observe that after controlling for labor activities (which also demands time) the estimate would have reduced significantly pointwise. We do not observe this which also gives evidence in favor of the first channel.

For policy purposes it might not be so important to distinguish which channel is at work. For behavior within prisons the relevant aspect is that education programs can reduce conflictive and violent behavior which is important per se. For behavior outside the prison, once the sentence term is completed, the evidence in favor of the positive effects of education programs on violent behavior has been established. Schnur (1949) finds that recidivism rates decrease for prisoners with lower measures of misconduct inside prisons. Furthermore, Phipps et al. (1999), Wilson, Gallagher, and Mackenzie (2000); Steuer and Smith (2003); and Tyler and Kling (2006) have

Table 7.5   **Propensity score matching estimates**

Conflict/violence	Number of observations	ATT	Bias	Bootstrap SE	T-statistic
Injuries	6,305	–0.003	0.001	0.002	–1.531
Property damage	6,305	–0.009	0.000	0.003	–3.284
Sanctions	6,305	–0.019	0.000	0.007	–2.734
Severe sanctions	6,305	–0.015	0.001	0.007	–2.257

Notes: All estimates are based on local linear regression matching. ATT = Average effect of Treatment on the Treated.

obtained evidence in favor of positive effects that prison based education may have on recidivism rates and post release income.

7.5.2   Propensity Score Matching Estimates

We also estimate the average treatment effect of participating in education programs for the eligible population using a local linear propensity score matching methodology. To estimate the propensity to participate in these prison based education programs we use all the variables in vectors X and Z. The results reported in table 7.5 show that the average treatment effect for all conflict measures is negative and statistically significant at the 1 percent level except for injuries. Compared to the probit estimates we find that the average treatment effects under this estimation procedure are greater in absolute terms. For the ones that are statistically significant the magnitude of the effect under this estimation procedure is 0.8 percentage points for property damages, 1.8 percentage points for sanctions, and 1.5 percentage points for severe sanctions. Relative to the mean percentage of each conflict measure in the sample these amount to a reduction of 51 percent, 20 percent, and 19 percent, respectively.

7.5.3   IV Estimates

As mentioned in the conceptual framework, the estimates presented above could be biased and inconsistent if some type of self-selection among prisoners is present. If in the error term there is a self-selection term that represents tendency to conflictive behavior, which is not captured by any variable included in X or Z, a positive or a negative selection bias may arise. If prisoners that are less (respectively more) prone to violent behavior are self-selecting themselves into the program a negative (positive) bias arises in the difference estimator. That is the effect previously found would be on average over (under) estimated.

To account for this possibility, we instrument education participation with per capita expenditure in education at the province level. As shown in figures 7.1 to 7.4 there is a negative reduced form relationship between mean

Table 7.6   **IV Probit estimates (dependent variables: Conflict/violent behavior**

Characteristic	Injuries	Property damage	Sanctions	Severe sanctions
Participates in education	−1.556	−2.543	−0.183	−0.047
program	(1.059)	(0.773)***	(0.544)	(0.514)
	[0.918]*	[1.473]*	[0.804]	[0.924]
Observations	17,754	16,553	21,535	21,535
First stage				
State per capita investment	0.003	0.003	0.002	0.002
in education	(0.000)***	(0.000)***	(0.000)***	(0.000)***
	[0.001]***	[0.001]***	[0.001]*	[0.001]*

Notes: Bootstrap standard errors in parentheses. Cluster (at province level) standard errors in brackets. All regressions include state and time fixed effects as well as the controls in model IV of table 7.4.
***Significant at the 1 percent level.
**Significant at the 5 percent level.
*Significant at the 10 percent level.

per capita education expenditure at the province level and our four conflict measures. Our exclusion restriction is that mean per capita education expenditure at the province level directly determines individual participation in prison based education programs but is not correlated with the supposedly omitted self selection term. Evidence that our instrument is relevant for individual participation is provided in the lower panel of table 7.6. For all specifications, the coefficient of mean per capita education expenditure at the province level is positive and statistically significant at the 1 and 10 percent level depending on the standard errors used. Even though not reported, all specifications include controls X and Z as well as time and province fixed effects.

A possible critique to the use of this instrument may be that expenditure in education of a given province is correlated with the province's preferences for the well-being of prisoners and hence directly related with conflict behavior inside prisons. We argue that this is not the case for several reasons. As previously mentioned, there is very little scope for state governments to modify educational expenditures. Furthermore, the number of prisoners relative to the aggregate provincial population is insignificant making it difficult to imagine that expenditure in education decisions could be significantly influenced by the well being of prison population. Evidence compatible with this view is shown in figure 7.5. It presents the trend of mean per capita expenditure in education across provinces which clearly has increased over the period of analysis in all of them. These trends suggest that expenditure decisions could be regarded as exogenous relative to in prison conflict measures. An additional exercise we carried out was to analyze changes in the

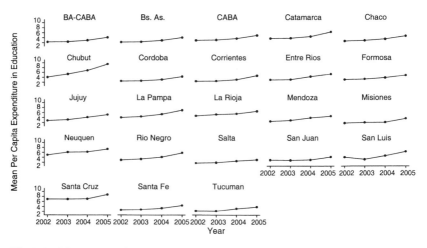

Fig. 7.5   Mean per capita expenditure in education by state
Source: Ministerio de Economía.

growth rate instead of the level of education expenditures. Although results are not shown, we find no significant trend in this case either. Results are available upon request. Finally, all regressions include province fixed effects and control for changes of state governors during 2002 to 2005. These variables allow us to control for constant preferences regarding the well being of prisoners as well as any changes that might occur due to changes in governors. Ultimately we argue that our instrument is capturing how changes in expenditure within provinces influence individual participation in prison education programs.

Table 7.6 presents the difference estimates using our instrumental variable.[19] Relative to our previous finding we observe that the effect of participation in prison education programs has a higher absolute coefficient for all conflict measures. Under our exclusion restriction this implies that the difference estimator presented a positive bias and that prisoners with a higher unobservable violence propensity were self selecting themselves. Alternatively, this is also compatible with the idea that prisons' authorities are selecting their most conflictive prisoners into these programs. Nonetheless, the standard errors also increase and hence only for the property damage measure we are able to reject the null hypothesis using the bootstrap standard errors. Under cluster standard errors we are also able to reject the null for injuries. In practical terms these findings imply that on average individuals that participate relative to those that do not are one percentage point less likely to engage in conflicts where there are property damages or

---

19. All specifications present bootstrap standard errors to account for the first stage estimation.

injuries. Relative to the mean percentage of property damages and injuries in our sample this amounts to a reduction of almost 60 percent and 90 percent, respectively. Notice that this effect is similar to the one found for property damages using the propensity score matching procedure.

7.6 Conclusions

The level of conflicts is a relevant policy variable given its high correlation with the quality of life within a prison. Either adhering to deterrence or retributions views for punishment, if prison conditions are degraded, effective punishment differs from the one mandated by law. This extra punishment, which is not legislated, may indicate a divergence from society's taste for punishment, as indicated by its legal system. Also, maintaining order within a prison is costly and puts pressure on subnational governments' budgets. In this sense, it is important to see if there are any policies which can lower in prison conflict.

Using a census of sentenced male Argentinean prisoners for 2002 to 2005, we estimate the effect that prison based education programs have on in prison conflict behavior. The treatment and control groups are selected based on Law 24.660 from 1996 which mandates that all prisoners with less than the minimum required education level (complete EGB) should participate in educational programs. Under probit and propensity score matching methodologies we find that participation in education programs reduces significantly injuries, property damages, sanctions, and severe sanctions within prisons. Using per capita expenditure in education at the province level as an instrument for participation we find that education programs reduce only property damages in a statistically significant way. The results of IV probit suggest that the probit difference estimator presents a positive selection bias implying that prisoners with a higher innate violence propensity are self selected (or selected by prison authorities) into these programs.

The reduction in conflicts due to education participation is compatible with two transmission mechanisms. On the one side, education programs could change prisoners' moral values and psychological attitudes towards violent behavior. On the other side, it could simply be the result of less idle time. Even though we believe that the first channel is the one at work, for policy purposes it might not be so important to distinguish between both channels. As far as behavior within prisons is concerned, the relevant aspect is that education programs can reduce conflictive and violent behavior which is important per se. For behavior outside the prison, once the sentence term is completed, the evidence in favor of the positive effects of education programs on violent behavior, reduction in recidivism and better labor opportunities has been established.

Even though we are not able to do a cost benefit analysis of education programs inside prisons, the evidence suggests that these should be promoted and extended if they turn out to be financially viable. Future research should comprise a cost benefit analysis not only including the monetary value of conflict reduction inside prisons but also measuring the positive effects education has outside penitentiaries.

References

Bayer, P., R. Hjalmarsson, and D. Pozen. 2009. Building criminal capital behind bars: Peer effects in juvenile corrections. *Quarterly Journal of Economics* 124 (1): 105–47.

Bertrand, M., E. Duflo, and S. Mullainathan. 2004. How much should we trust differences-in-differences estimates? *The Quarterly Journal of Economics* 119 (1): 249–75.

Di Tella, R., and J. Dubra. 2008. Crime and punishment in the "American Dream." *Journal of Public Economics* 92 (7): 1564–84.

Isla, A., and D. Miguez. 2003. Heridas Urbanas. *Editorial de las Ciencias.*

Katz, L., S. Levitt, and E. Shustorovich. 2003. Prison conditions, capital punishment and deterrence. *American Law and Economics Review* 5 (2): 318–43.

Law 24.660. 1996. Ejecución de la Pena Privativa de la Libertad.

Phipps, P., K. Korinek, S. Aos, and R. Lieb. 1999. *Research findings on adult corrections programs.* Washington State Institute for Public Policy.

Rivas, A., and F. Mezzadra. 2006. Coparticipación y equidad educativa: un debate pendiente en el campo de la educación. Documento de Trabajo CIPPEC.

Scarfo, F. 2008. Los Fines de la Educación Básica en Cárceles de la Provincia de Buenos Aires. *Editorial Universitaria de La Plata.*

Schnur, A. C. 1949. Prison conduct and recidivism. *Journal of Criminal Law and Criminology* 40 (1): 1931–51.

Steurer, S., and L. Smith. 2003. *Education reduces crime: Three-state recidivism study.* Elkridge, MD: Correctional Education Association.

Steurer, S., L. Smith, and A. Tracy. 2001. *Three state recidivism study.* Prepared for the Office of Correctional Education, U.S. Department of Education. Lanham, MD: Correctional Education Association.

Tyler, J., and J. Kling. 2006. Prison-based education and re-entry into the mainstream labor market. NBER Working Paper no. 12114. Cambridge, MA: National Bureau of Economic Research, March.

Wilson, D., Gallagher, C., and D. Mackenzie. 2000. A meta-analysis of corrections-based education, vocation, and work programs for adult offenders. *Journal of Research of Crime and Delinquency* 37:347–68.

Comment   Andrés Borenstein

I think this is a very interesting and relevant chapter for policy analysis, either for the Argentine authorities or to extrapolate the experience to other countries.

According to the authors there is a positive and statistically significant relation between the good behavior (or rather, not participating in violent episodes or not being punished) of an inmate and the education he receives in prison. This goes along with intuition but it is good to get the numbers right through the econometrics. The authors work well with the obvious endogeneity problem in such a way that the numbers are robust to take economic and policy conclusions out of them.

The authors recognize a serious difficulty in gathering the data and this, while completely true in the context of the Argentine prison management, may shed some doubts over the good coefficients they report in this chapter. Keeping good quality data in Argentine jails is a kind of sophistication in Argentina, and possibly this is the first analysis of this kind, so administrative staff of the penitentiary system can only get better.

In any case, for the usefulness of this comment we have to assume that the data supporting the coefficients is the best possible set we can get. In this context there are a number of policy implications to bear in mind using these figures.

First and foremost, the Argentine prison system needs more teachers if it wants to fulfill one of its main goals: to provide people with less incentives to engage in crime once they are released, which is not the likeliest outcome nowadays. Getting teachers to work in prison is not easy. There is already a big selection bias in teachers in the public school system, which means that good teachers work in safe and reasonably rich environments; the opposite is also true, naturally with lots of exceptions. Thus, the prison system should consider options to supplement teacher's salaries and make in-prison classrooms more attractive for education workers, be it through salary differentials or other perks. This should be a good investment for the taxpayer, even without counting all the positive externalities that education produces.

Second, the results lead us to think that the policy of making education mandatory to some inmates but not to all is suboptimal. With such good coefficients, lawmakers should not doubt making education widespread. Of course, there are limitations to impose education on remanded prisoners, but any attempt should be valued.

Third, the coefficients are also significant and positive (albeit lower than in

Andrés Borenstein is chief economist at the British Embassy in Buenos Aires, and a professor of economics at Universidad Torcuato di Tella.

education) for other activities such as sports. This may mean that the prison system could invest in sport facilities, coaches; and so forth, producing a similar effect. Given that inmates could prefer sports to classrooms and that it is hard to obtain teachers, this seems like a fairly positive alternative.

A less positive related comment is that perhaps what makes prisoners behave well is keeping them busy. The analogy with teenage children is interesting. If one wants inmates not to take part in Mafia, fighting, or some other misbehaviors, it is good to keep them busy. This would explain why education, sports, or perhaps any other alternative to kill time in prison are good alternatives.

Another factor that might play a role is that penitentiary officers may decide not to punish those receiving education. It is worth bearing in mind that the education level of "jail authorities" is also quite low, so there might be a so-called "respect effect" to those who engage in education.

Overall I think it is a great chapter and also think there is scope for more research, conceivably enlarging the sample and educating the data keepers to ensure an immaculate set where perhaps more conclusions could be drawn.

III

International Evidence

What Do Economists Know about Crime?

Angela K. Dills, Jeffrey A. Miron, and Garrett Summers

8.1 Introduction

Since Gary Becker's (1968) seminal article on the economic model of crime, economists have devoted considerable effort to determining its empirical validity. Much of this research examines deterrence, the idea that policy can reduce crime by raising the expected costs. This literature focuses in particular on arrest and incarceration rates, policing levels, and punishments like the death penalty. Considerable additional research, while not directly focused on deterrence, considers hypotheses derived from economic models and uses statistical techniques commonly employed by economists. Such hypotheses include, among others, the roles of abortion legalization, gun laws, guns, lead, and drug prohibition in causing crime.

In this chapter we evaluate what economists have learned over the past forty years about the major determinants of crime. We consider both the policy variables related to deterrence and the more unconventional factors examined by economists. We rely on two kinds of evidence: an examination of aggregate data over long time periods and across countries, and a critical review of the literature.

Our empirical strategy consists mainly of plots that, one by one, compare crime rates with potential determinants; that is, we examine the univariate,

Angela K. Dills is visiting lecturer in economics at Wellesley College. Jeffrey A. Miron is senior lecturer and director of undergraduate studies in the Department of Economics at Harvard University, and a research associate of the National Bureau of Economic Research. Garrett Summers is an economist in the Office of the Secretary of Defense.

We thank Steve Levitt, John Donohue, Mark Duggan, and John Lott for providing data. Larry Katz, Caroline Hoxby and Sebastian Edwards provided valuable comments on a previous draft.

"noninstrumented," relation between crime and possible explanatory factors. This approach suffers two large defects: the right model of crime is undoubtedly multifactorial, and the raw correlation between crime and a potential determinant can be misleading in the presence of endogeneity.

We nevertheless argue that examining the data in this fashion sheds considerable light on which determinants of crime are empirically important. This approach shows that the raw correlations in the data are frequently the wrong sign relative to standard models or claims. This does not prove a multivariate, "instrumented" analysis would not uncover a different effect, but it suggests this outcome is not especially likely and that any instrument would have to exert a strong impact on the endogenous variable to reverse the raw correlation. We also show, moreover, that a multivariate approach (admittedly, one that is not well-identified) fails to display the "correct" correlations in the vast majority of cases.

Based on this evaluation, we argue that economists know little about the main factors identified in the economics of crime literature as key determinants of crime. This conclusion applies both to policy variables like arrest rates or capital punishment and to indirect factors such as abortion or gun laws. The reason is that even hypotheses that find some support in U.S. data for recent decades are inconsistent with data over longer horizons or across countries. Thus, these hypotheses are less persuasive than a focus on recent U.S. evidence might suggest.

The hypothesis that drug prohibition generates violence, however, is consistent with the long time series and cross-country facts. Previous research has considered this hypothesis; we focus on a broader set of data and show the potentially large role that drug prohibition plays in determining violence. The evidence we present is only suggestive, but it indicates this hypothesis deserves further exploration. This analysis is also consistent with a general perspective in which government policies that affect the amount and nature of dispute resolution play an important role in determining violence.

The chapter proceeds as follows. In section 8.2 we present basic facts about crime over the past century in the United States and other countries. Section 8.3 examines whether individual deterrence variables appear to explain crime. Section 8.4 considers alternative determinants of crime, while Section 8.5 considers the role of drug prohibition, still focusing on explanatory variables one by one. Section 8.6 presents ordinary least squares (OLS) regressions that potentially account for multiple determinants of crime. Section 8.7 concludes.

8.2   Stylized Facts

Recent research on crime typically uses the past several decades of U.S. data. This is in part because data on crime and its possible determinants are

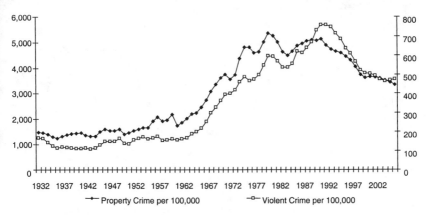

Fig. 8.1   Violent and property crime rates per 100,000: 1932 to 2006
Source: FBI Uniform Crime Reports (UCR) (various years).

more readily available for this period, in part because crime data for other countries are less readily available or difficult to compare to U.S. data. This focus also occurs because crime has fluctuated substantially during the past several decades in the United States, making it an inherently interesting period.

It is nevertheless possible and interesting to consider longer time series and, in some cases, data from other countries. Crime varies substantially across time and space, so a broader perspective can support or refute hypotheses of interest. We begin, therefore, by establishing key facts about crime over the long run and across countries.

Figure 8.1 presents the violent crime and property crime rates in the United States over the period 1932 to 2006. The data are from the FBI's Uniform Crime Reports. All data are in per capita terms.

Violent crime began to rise in the mid-1960s and increased overall until the early 1990s, when it began a persistent decline. The decline was substantial, but even by 2006 violent crime was still well above its level in the 1940s and 1950s. Some of the upward trend might reflect changes in crime reporting, so the measured difference between 2006 and the 1950s may overstate the true change.

Property crime behaves similarly to violent crime. Property crime increased beginning in the mid-1960s and remained substantially higher from the 1970s through the present compared to the 1940s and 1950s. Violent crime and property crime differ somewhat after 1970, with property crime peaking in 1980 rather than in the early 1990s. Property crime did increase during the latter half of the 1980s, but less so than violent crime.

Figure 8.2 presents the murder rate and the homicide rate. The murder rate is from the same source as the violent and property crime rates; the homicide

Fig. 8.2   Vital statistics homicide and UCR murder rate per 100,000: 1900 to 2005
Source: CDC, National Vital Statistics; Eckberg (1995); FBI UCR.

rate is from vital statistics sources and is available for a longer time period.[1] Murder behaves similarly to the overall violent crime rate. The murder rate increased substantially in the 1960s and early 1970s, displayed a marked increase in the 1980s, and a dramatic decline in the 1990s. The murder rate declined between the 1930s and the 1950s, however, while the violent crime rate did not. More importantly, the decline in the murder rate during the 1990s returned to virtually its 1960s level, while violent crime remains well above its 1960s levels. The decline in the murder rate also appears to have abated by the end of the sample. The homicide rate behaves similarly to the murder rate, but the pre-1950s decline is more apparent.[2] In addition, the homicide rate displays a persistent increase over the first three decades of the century and an enormous decline during the 1930s.

What these data show is that U.S. crime exhibited substantial variation well before the 1980s and 1990s, with fluctuations in both directions. The homicide rate does not show an overall upward trend, although this might reflect changing medical technology in the treatment of gun shots and other serious injuries.[3] A convincing explanation of crime can ideally account for all of this variation, not just the past two decades.

We turn next to data for other countries. We focus on vital statistics mea-

---

1. Data for the early years are problematic due to changes in the coverage area and underreporting of homicide, so we employ an adjusted series for 1900–1932 (Eckberg 1995).

2. Deaths resulting from the 9/11 terrorist attacks are recorded as homicides but not as murders.

3. See Harris et al. (2002). This decline in murder would tend to increase reported assaults since some of those assaulted do not die.

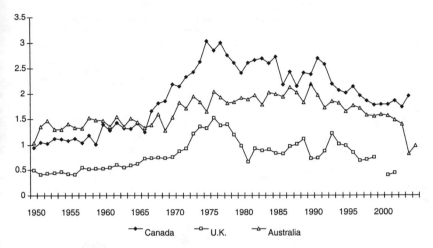

Fig. 8.3   Cross-country homicides per 100,000: 1950 to 2005
Source: World Health Organization (WHO).

sures of the homicide rate, since this series is more accurately and consistently reported than most crime statistics.

Figure 8.3 shows homicide rates for Canada, the United Kingdom and Australia over time. The average level of homicide has been substantially lower in these three countries than in the United States over the same period. Homicide nevertheless displays substantial variation, and this variation is broadly similar to that in the United States. Homicide rates rose during the 1960s and early 1970s but then declined over the remaining part of the sample. This similarity raises doubt about U.S.-specific explanations for the major fluctuations in crime.

Table 8.1 compares homicide rates across countries. Among Organization for Economic Cooperation and Development (OECD) countries, the United States is a major outlier, with a homicide rate in 2001 of 7.06, compared to the OECD average of 1.62. Compared to a broader set of countries, however, the U.S. homicide rate is less unusual. The average for all countries in the sample is 6.28, and nineteen countries have rates in excess of the U.S. rate, sometimes by substantial amounts. The most extreme case is Colombia, where the homicide rate is 62.38.

A convincing account of the determinants of homicide, therefore, should explain not only the fluctuations over recent decades in the United States but also longer term fluctuations in the United States and in other countries. Likewise, a complete account should explain the differences in homicide across countries. In particular, this account should explain why the United States has a higher rate than most similar countries but a lower rate than a broad range of other countries.

Table 8.1   **Homicides per 100,000 population, various countries, around 2001**

United States	7.06				
OECD countries					
Australia	1.57	Hungary	2.43	New Zealand	1.4
Austria	0.95	Iceland	0.70	Norway	0.7
Belgium	1.74	Ireland	1.04	Poland	1.7
Canada	1.49	Italy	0.97	Portugal	1.3
Czech Republic	1.32	Japan	0.58	Slovakia	2.0
Denmark	1.26	Korea	1.59	Spain	1.0
Finland	2.97	Luxembourg	2.04	Sweden	0.9
France	0.83	Mexico	10.10	Switzerland	1.1
Germany	0.68	Netherlands	1.26	United Kingdom	0.4
Greece	1.05				
OECD average	1.62				
Other countries					
Albania	7.17	Croatia	1.96	Romania	3.49
Argentina	6.93	Cuba	5.38	Russian Federation	29.85
Armenia	1.76	Estonia	15.17	Serbia and Montenegro	2.92
Azerbaijan	2.59	Georgia	3.92	Singapore	0.75
Bahamas	20.79	Hong Kong	0.77	Slovenia	0.80
Barbados	10.47	Israel	5.64	Tajikistan	2.47
Belarus	11.23	Kazakhstan	15.52	Macedonia	6.44
Brazil	26.37	Kuwait	1.74	Thailand	5.65
Bulgaria	3.08	Kyrgyzstan	6.72	Trinidad and Tobago	8.52
Cayman Islands	11.51	Latvia	12.31	Turkmenistan	7.07
Chile	9.98	Lithuania	10.23	Ukraine	12.65
China	1.98	Malta	2.29	Uruguay	5.54
Colombia	62.38	Mauritius	2.78	Uzbekistan	3.13
Costa Rica	6.05	Moldova	11.21	Venezuela	26.23
Other average	9.37				

Sources: WHO; most figures constructed from WHO Mortality database. Data for Mauritius and Denmark are for 2000; data for China for 1999; data for Belgium (1997). Some figures constructed from table 1 of WHOSIS: these include Mexico, New Zealand (2000), Argentina, Bahamas (2000), Barbados (2000), Brazil (2000), Cayman Islands (2000), Chile, Colombia (1999), Costa Rica, Cuba, Thailand (2000), Trinidad and Tobago (1998), Turkmenistan (1998), Uruguay (2000), Uzbekistan (2000), and Venezuela (2000). No data were available for a nearby year for Turkey. Population for the Cayman Islands from the *CIA World Factbook*.

8.3   Determinants of Crime: Deterrence Variables

In this section we explore the crime-reducing effect of deterrence variables like the arrest or incarceration rate. These variables are in principle controllable by policy, and they affect crime either by raising the expected cost of crime or by incapacitating criminals. We consider these variables in the context of the stylized facts above.[4]

4. For an early attempt to develop and test the implications of the deterrence model, see Ehrlich (1973). For reviews of the literature and related work on deterrence, see Cameron (1988), Benson, Kim, and Rassmussen (1994), Ehrlich (1996), Nagin (1997), Freeman (1999), and Levitt (2004).

The first variable of interest is arrests per capita, which is a proxy for the probability that a criminal offender is caught by the criminal justice system and subjected to punishment. Other things equal, a higher probability of arrest should imply a lower incidence of crime. The ideal proxy would be arrests per crime, and part of the literature considers this measure. Given the likelihood of measurement error in both crime and arrest counts, however, arrests per crime and crime per capita almost certainly show a strong negative correlation due to "ratio bias," regardless of the true relation. We focus, therefore, on arrests per capita.

Figures 8.4a–8.4c show arrest rates over time for violent crime, property crime, and murder, along with the related crime rate. The first-order fact is that arrest rates and crime correlate positively, contrary to what should occur if the main operative mechanism is that higher arrest probabilities reduce crime. This positive correlation does not prove the arrest probability has no deterrent effect, nor does it imply that higher arrests increase crime. Instead, it likely indicates that a third factor is simultaneously driving both crime and arrests. For example, political economy considerations could cause arrest rates to respond positively to crime rates. Alternatively, the strong positive relation might be a reporting effect, since recording of crime and arrests tends to go together. The fact that the correlation is positive, however, raises doubt as to whether arrests have a major deterrent effect, and it suggests that an appropriate instrument would have to be powerful to overcome the inherent endogeneity in the arrest rate.

A second key deterrence variable is the size of the police force. Though it might seem obvious that police should reduce crime, this implication is not immediate. The standard model of crime identifies the probabilities of arrest and conviction, along with the expected punishment, as the primary deterrence variables. If these are held constant, police *per se* should have no additional impact. In practice, comparing police and crime makes sense for several reasons. Counting the number of police is easier than assessing arrest probabilities, and the probability of arrest is plausibly increasing in the size of the police force. Also, the relation between police and crime does not suffer from ratio bias. Despite the plausibility of the hypothesis, however, a long literature has found it difficult to confirm an effect of police on crime.[5] This is plausibly because jurisdictions with high crime rates tend to hire more police. In principle one can address this by finding an appropriate instrument, but in practice such instruments are rare.[6]

Figure 8.5 plots police personnel and police officers per capita in the United States from 1934 to 2006. The number of police crept upward in the

5. See the discussion in Cameron (1988), Cornwell and Trumbell (1994), or Moody and Marvell (1996).

6. Levitt (1997) attempts to solve the endogeneity problem using the timing of mayoral and gubernatorial election cycles and finds a strong negative impact of police on crime. The results are sensitive, however, to a coding error (McCrary 2002).

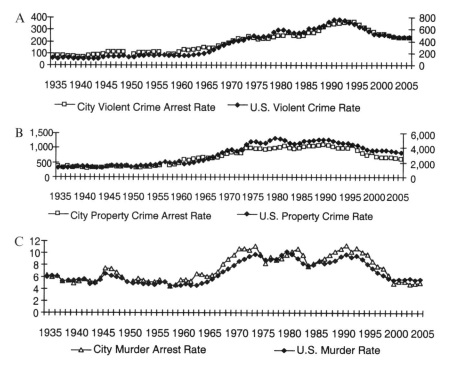

Fig. 8.4   Crime rates and arrest rates in cities with over 2,500 (1935 to 2006): *A*, violent crimes; *B*, property crimes; *C*, murder
Source: FBI UCR (various years).

early part of the period, increased more rapidly in the late 1960s, flattened out in the 1970s, and increased through 1999. The number of police officers increased less rapidly than police employees although a similar peak occurs in 1999. The steady, slight increase in police occurred simultaneously with large fluctuations in crime rates. Police and crime both increase in the 1960s; declines in crime begin years before the decline in police at the turn of the twenty-first century. Thus, the overall correlation between police and crime is the opposite of what is implied by the deterrence hypothesis.

The perverse correlation does not prove deterrence is wrong or that police increase crime. These data, however, make clear the hurdle any structural estimation must overcome: the dominant variation in the data is in the wrong direction, so any instrument would need to be powerful to find a negative effect of police on crime. The perverse correlation also suggests skepticism about the effectiveness of this aspect of the deterrence hypothesis.

A third key deterrence variable is the incarceration rate. Incarceration can affect crime through several channels. First, the threat of incarceration

Fig. 8.5   Police employees per 1,000 and the Index I crime rate, 1934 to 2006
Sources: FBI UCR (various years).

can raise the expected punishment for crime. Second, persons in prison cannot commit crimes against the nonprison population. Both channels imply that greater incarceration leads to less crime. A possibly offsetting effect is that incarceration might make some persons more criminogenic due to lost human capital, peer effects (hardening), or increased criminal capital.[7] Thus, the magnitude and possibly the sign of any incarceration effect can only be determined empirically.

Much of the literature suggests a small, crime-reducing effect of incarceration on net, but some research suggests a zero or even perverse effect.[8] One possible interpretation is that the true effect is negative but reverse causation biases the coefficient toward zero, since a higher crime rate likely implies more incarcerations. As in the arrests and police literature, the key empirical issue is therefore whether an appropriate instrument exists.[9]

Figure 8.6 presents the incarceration rate for the United States from 1925 to 2006. After fluctuating in a relatively narrow range from 1925 to 1970, the incarceration rate began increasing in the early 1970s at a steady rate

7. Chen and Shapiro (2004), for example, provide evidence of a hardening effect.
8. See Johnson and Raphael (2006) for a recent review of the literature. Abrams (2006) provides evidence based on add-on gun laws that incarceration deters crime, while Kessler and Levitt (1999) document both a deterrent and an incapacitation effect based on sentence enhancements. Webster, Doob, and Zimring (2006) critique Kessler and Levitt (1999); Levitt (2006) responds.
9. Levitt (1996) uses lagged judicial decisions to circumvent this problem. This instrument does not satisfy the exclusion restriction, however, if the error term is serially correlated. Also, the first stage *F*-statistics are well below 10 in many cases. Johnson and Raphael (2006), using

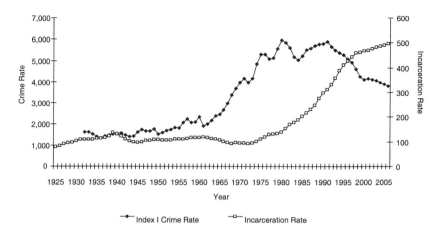

Fig. 8.6   Incarceration rate per 100,000 and Index I crime rate, 1925 to 2006
Sources: Index I Crime Rate—FBI UCR (various years). *Sourcebook of Criminal Justice Statistics.* Available online at www.albany.edu/sourcebook/wk1/t628.wk1.

and has now reached a level almost five times the average rate over the pre-1970 period.[10]

This figure poses a challenge for the view that incarceration reduces crime. Starting around 1990, the incarceration rate climbs while the crime rate falls drastically, which is consistent with the view that incarceration reduces crime. During the early part of the sample, however, crime fluctuated substantially while the incarceration rate did not. In the 1970s and early 1980s, both rates climbed simultaneously, the opposite of what deterrence and incapacitation imply. The average level of the incarceration rate, moreover, is much higher in the past several decades, so even a small causal effect of incarceration in reducing crime implies much lower crime than now observed.

Further evidence on the relation between incarceration and crime comes from cross-country comparisons. Figures 8.7a–8.7c show scatter plots of homicide and incarceration rates for several groups of countries. The first consists of the fifty-eight countries with available data on both incarceration rates and homicide.[11] This figure suggests a positive correlation between incarceration rates and homicide rates, but it is dominated by a few countries that plausibly differ across multiple dimensions from the remaining

---

a different identification scheme, find evidence consistent with Levitt but show the effect of incarceration has become much weaker in recent years.

10. The average incarceration rate from 1925–1969 is 108 prisoners per 100,000. The incarceration rate in 2006 was 497 per 100,000. The average incarceration rate from 1970–2006 is 280.

11. Walmsley (2004) provides incarceration rates for 205 independent countries and dependent territories and reports that 62.5 percent of countries have incarceration rates below 150 per 100,000.

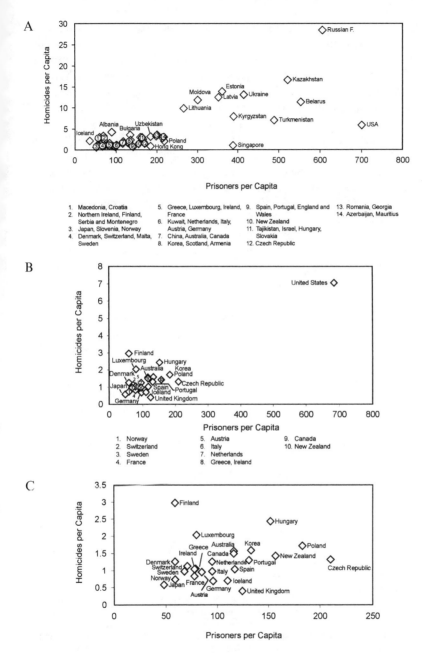

Fig. 8.7 Homicides per capita and prisoners per capita 2001: *A*, fifty-eight countries; *B*, OECD; *C*, OECD excluding the United States

Sources: International prisoners data from OECD Factbook 2007: Economic, Environmental and Social Statistics and Walmsley (2004). Homicides from WHO.

countries. The second figure shows data for the OECD countries. These again suggest a strong positive relation between homicide and incarceration, but the United States is an extreme outlier. The third figure excludes the United States and still shows a significant, positive correlation. Yet again one cannot draw a structural conclusion, but the strong, perverse correlation between homicide and incarceration should make one cautious in accepting the proposition that increased incarceration reduces crime.

A final deterrence variable that economists link to crime, especially homicide, is capital punishment. According to the deterrence model, imposing capital punishment rather than life imprisonment increases the expected cost of crime, thereby reducing crimes like murder. Initial empirical work based on aggregate U.S. data appeared to suggest that capital punishment reduces homicide (Ehrlich 1975, 1977), but subsequent work raised doubts about this conclusion (e.g., Passell and Taylor, 1977).[12] Due to the Supreme Court's reinstatement of the death penalty in 1976 and the subsequent increase in executions during the 1980s and 1990s, as well as renewed political interest in the death penalty, several papers have reexamined the issue using post-moratorium, state-level data. Most of these papers claim to find a significant deterrent effect, but many of the results are not robust to reasonable modifications of the statistical specification.[13] More broadly, Donohue and Wolfers (2005) argue that the evidence does not support a substantial deterrent effect of the death penalty.

We review here the first-order facts related to capital punishment. Figure 8.8 plots the number of executions in the United States against the homicide rate.[14] In some sub-periods the correlation is negative, as implied by deterrence hypothesis, but in other sub-periods the correlation is positive. For example, executions increased rapidly while murder fell during the 1990s, but from 1900 to the early 1960s executions and homicide moved together. During the moratorium period, murder fluctuated considerably even though the number of executions was zero.[15]

---

12. The single most important critique is that the results are highly sensitive to sample period and/or functional form. This is because the last few years of the sample had zero executions. If one excludes these, as seen below, the correlation between executions and homicide is positive. If one includes these in a linear specification, the correlation is still positive. The original Ehrlich paper, however, used the log of executions and assumed a small number of executions to avoid taking the log of zero.

13. See, for example, Dezhbakhsh, Rubin, and Shepherd (2003); Mocan and Gittings (2003); Shepherd (2004); and Dezhbakhsh and Shepherd (2006). Dezhbakhsh, Rubin, and Shepherd and Shepherd fail to use state trends and/or clustered standard errors. Dezahbakhsh and Shepherd's results are sensitive to measuring executions in levels rather than adjusted for population. Mocan and Gittings results are sensitive to the assumed lag between executions and murders. Mocan and Gittings (2006) argue that the theoretically sound assumption about this lag supports an effect of the death penalty, but their case for the assumed lag is not persuasive. Katz, Levitt, and Shustorivich (2003) fail to find an economically or statistically significant effect of the death penalty. Cohen-Cole et al. (2007) find limited evidence for a deterrent effect.

14. For the homicide rate we use vital statistics homicides, adjusted by Eckberg (1995).

15. For 1900–2005 (full sample) the correlation is –0.11, p-value = 0.28; for 1900–1955 it is 0.34, p-value=0.012; and for 1956–2005 it is –0.60, p-value=0.000.

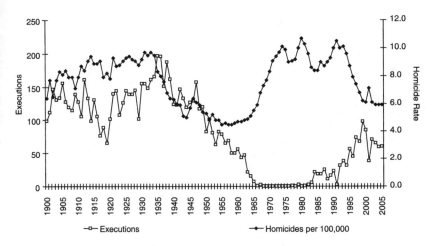

Fig. 8.8 Executions and homicide rate per 100,000: 1900 to 2005

Source: Espy, M. W., and J. O. Smykla. *Executions in the United States, 1608–2002: The Espy file* [Computer file]. 4th ICPSR ed. Compiled by M. Watt Espy and John Ortiz Smykla, University of Alabama. Ann Arbor, MI: Inter-university Consortium for Political and Social Research [producer and distributor], 2004. Vital Statistics Homicides adjusted by Eckberg (1995).

Figure 8.9 graphs similar data for Canada from 1926 through 2005. The first forty years showed substantial variation in the number of executions while the homicide rate remained relatively stable. The correlation for 1926 to 2005 is significantly negative (–0.59, p-value 0.00), consistent with a deterrent effect of capital punishment. For the time period 1926 to 1962, however, the correlation is significantly positive (0.34, p-value = 0.039.)[16] In the last forty years, homicide has fluctuated substantially while the execution rate has been constant at zero. Thus, the overall negative correlation is an artifact of two very different regimes; in one the correlation is perverse, and in the other it is zero.

Figure 8.10 demonstrates a similar result for the United Kingdom. Homicides per capita fluctuated substantially over the past forty years despite an almost complete absence of executions. Thus, the data provide little affirmative evidence that is consistent with the standard deterrence story.

8.3.1 Discussion

The previous results present a challenge to key aspects of the deterrence model of crime. An important feature of this model is the implication that policy can reduce crime by manipulating variables such as arrest rates, policing levels, and so on. The aggregate data do not provide much confirmation for this perspective, at least not in a simplistic, "more X, less crime" kind of way.

16. For the time period 1926–1966, the correlation becomes an insignificant 0.24, p-value = 0.128.

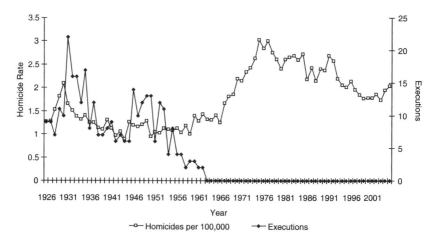

Fig. 8.9   Canada homicides per 100,000 and executions, 1926 to 2005

Sources: Canadian executions: 1926–1960 from *Historical Statistics of Canada;* 1961–1962 from http://geocities.com/richard.clark32@btinternet.com/canada.htm. Extended time series of homicides for Canada also from *Historical Statistics of Canada.* Social Science Federation of Canada and Statistics Canada.

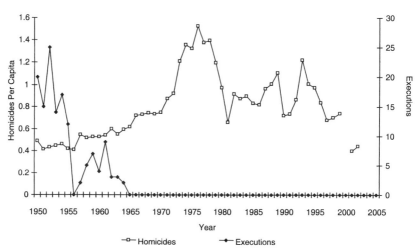

Fig. 8.10   U.K. homicides per capita and executions, 1950 to 2005

Source: U.K. executions from http://www.murderfile.net.

This conclusion in no way suggests that criminals are not rational or that they fail to respond to incentives. On the one hand, the analysis above is too broad brush to support such a specific claim. On the other hand, numerous analyses do find that criminals respond to incentives in roughly rational ways; this research, however, focuses on responses that are local or in response to specific and unambiguous changes or differences in the incentives faced by criminals.[17] So, we do not mean to throw out the baby with the bath water by arguing against the deterrence model at a general level or minimizing its usefulness as an organizing device. We are instead focusing on specific, policy-relevant implications, and we are addressing the naïve, "if we hire more police, or make more arrests, or lock more people up, that will necessarily reduce crime" perspective. This application of the deterrence model is not supported by the data. A key question, then, is why we do not find more evidence of deterrence with respect to these variables.

One possibility is that data limitations make it difficult to test these hypotheses in the settings where they are most relevant. For example, it could be that going from no police force to some police force indeed reduces crime, but the observed variation in the size of modern police forces is over a range where diminishing returns have set in so that additional police have little impact. Thus, our evidence cannot rule out the possibility that adding more police is unlikely to lower crime, but substantially reducing police might increase crime.

A different hypothesis is that most existing analyses, even those using city- or state-level data, are too aggregated with respect to time period, place, type of crime, and type of police effort to uncover a number of effects that might operate in practice. Thus, while putting more police on the street in a specific neighborhood and instructing them to target a particular kind of crime might indeed reduce that kind of crime in that neighborhood, especially in the short term, simply hiring more police who sit behind desks pushing paper is unlikely to reduce any kind of crime.

A third hypothesis is that deterrence variables might have counterproductive effects as well as some beneficial effects. Some expansions of police might increase crime, as we will subsequently discuss, because the police work at enforcing drug prohibition or other counter-productive activities.[18] In the case of capital punishment, the reality might be that criminals pay considerable attention to the expected costs but that executions are rare, so it is approximately rational to ignore the possibility of being executed.[19] Regarding the effect of incarceration via deterrence, it might be that some criminals do not regard prison as worse than life outside or view the negative impacts on their future lives once released as small. Kling (2006), for example, finds that incarceration has minimal impact on post-incarceration employment and earnings.

A different reason the key policy variables in the deterrence model may

17. See, for example, Di Tella and Schargrodsky (2004), Klick and Tabarrok (2005), and Iyengar (2008).
18. For example, Iyengar (2007) finds that laws mandating arrest for reports of domestic violence increase intimate homicides, plausibly because the laws reduce reporting of initial violent acts.
19. In the U.S. in recent years, the number of executions per year has been less than 100 while the number of homicides has been over 20,000.

have small effects on crime is that the underlying behavioral parameters of criminals do not imply a big response. Criminals may be people with high discount rates and/or myopic preferences, in which case the threat of future punishment should play a relatively small role.[20]

Thus, while one interpretation of our deterrence results is that economists do not have the right data to find these effects, an alternative, reasonable interpretation is that increases in the standard deterrence variables have small or perverse effects over the relevant range.

8.4   Alternative Determinants of Crime

Perhaps due to the difficulties in establishing links between policy variables and crime, economists have considered a number of alternative explanations. In this section we examine several that have received significant attention in recent years. Our assessment is that none provides a convincing explanation for a substantial fraction of the variation in crime.

In a provocative paper, Lott and Mustard (1997) (henceforth, LM) argue that laws protecting the right to carry a concealed gun (RTC laws) increase concealed carry and therefore reduce crime by causing criminals to worry their intended targets might be armed. Lott and Mustard also suggest that RTC laws cause criminals to substitute away from crimes against persons, like murder, rape, robbery, and assault, to crimes "against" property, like burglary, larceny, and auto theft. The original LM analysis appeared to find that RTC laws reduce violent crime and increase property crime, consistent with the *a priori* considerations. Subsequent research, however, has raised questions about the LM conclusions, while Lott has defended these conclusions.[21]

We reconsider the LM hypothesis using long-run, aggregate data. Figure 8.11 shows the fraction of the U.S. population living under RTC laws in each year since 1900. The fraction rose steadily and substantially starting in the mid-1980s, yet violent crime does not fall until the 1990s. Despite an enormous change in the fraction of the population living in a state covered by an RTC law, crime has neither skyrocketed nor plummeted over the sample. The homicide rate, in particular, shows no particular trend, and this is a crime category that is most plausibly affected by RTC laws. Thus neither the view that RTC laws increase crime, nor the view that RTC laws decrease crime, receives obvious support from the aggregate data.

In contrast to the hypothesis that gun laws reduce crime, a different litera-

---

20. Lee and McCrary (2005) provide evidence consistent with this view. Lochner (2003) finds that individual beliefs about the probability of arrest are substantially idiosyncratic and not responsive to local neighborhood conditions. These beliefs do adjust in response to individual arrest experience, however, and these beliefs do correlate with criminal behavior.

21. For critiques of the LM analysis, see Black and Nagin (1998), Ayres and Donohue (2003a, 2003b), and Helland and Tabarrok (2004). For responses, see Lott (1998, 2003) and Plassmann and Whitley (2003).

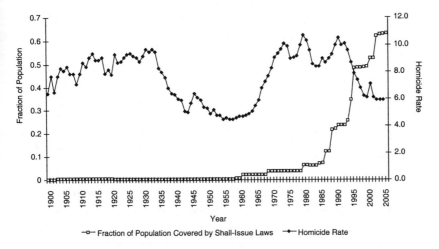

Fig. 8.11   Fraction of U.S. population covered by Shall-Issue Laws and homicide rate, 1900 to 2006

Source: Grossman and Lee (2008) and annual state population estimates from the Census Bureau. Vital Statistics homicides adjusted by Eckberg (1995).

ture considers whether guns themselves cause crime.[22] We again confront this hypothesis with aggregate level data. Figure 8.12 shows the stock of guns over time in conjunction with the violent crime rate. Crime declines numerous times, including a major decline from 1990 onward, despite a large and ever-increasing stock of guns. This makes it implausible that guns per se play a large role in causing crime, although it does not rule out some role.

A different hypothesis that has received enormous attention is that legalization of abortion in the early 1970s caused a substantial fraction of the decline in crime during the 1990s (Donohue and Levitt 2001). The logic is that access to legal abortion allows women to have children in environments less likely to produce future criminals. Thus, cohorts born after legalization should have a lower propensity to commit crime. Further, crime should have begun falling about fifteen years after legalization and continued falling as successive cohorts born after legalization entered their high crime years. Donohue and Levitt (2001), (henceforth DL) provide evidence that appears consistent with their hypothesis, stating in particular that "legalized abortion appears to account for as much as 50 percent of the recent drop in crime" (p. 379). Several authors, however, have disputed the DL conclusion, while DL have responded with evidence that claims to validate their original position.[23]

22. For a recent summary and critique of this literature, see National Research Council (2005).

23. See Joyce (2003, 2009), Lott and Whitley (2007), Foote and Goetz (2008), and Dills and Miron (2006), for critiques, and Donohue and Levitt (2004, 2008) for responses.

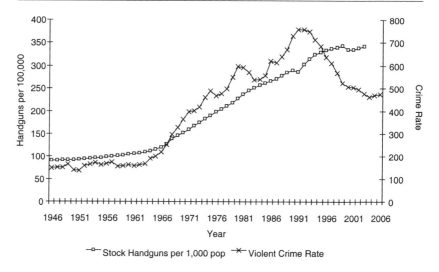

Fig. 8.12   Stock of handguns in the U.S. and the violent crime rate, 1946 to 2006

Sources: Gun data from Kleck (1997, updated with additional data from author). FBI UCR (various years) for the Index Crime Rate.

We revisit this issue using aggregate and cross-country data. Figures 8.13a–8.13c compare the abortion rate in the United States lagged twenty years with the violent crime, property crime, and homicide rates. The figures show visually what we know from history: no legal abortions occurred before 1970, and the legalization in 1970 to 1973 could not have affected crime rates before the late 1980s. Nevertheless, major fluctuations in crime occurred before 1990. This does not mean abortion legalization played no role in the declines in the past two decades, but the magnitude of legalized abortion's impact on crime is likely modest or confined to only the most recent period.[24]

Figure 8.14 shows the homicide rates in a number of other countries that have legalized or substantially liberalized abortion access. The evidence from these countries provides little support for hypothesis that legalizing abortion reduces crime. While the data from some countries are consistent with the DL hypothesis (e.g. Canada, France, Italy), several countries' data show the opposite correlation (e.g. Denmark, Finland, Hungary, Poland). In other cases crime was falling before legalization and does not decline any more quickly (twenty years) after legalization (e.g. Japan, Norway).[25]

24. We note that Donohue and Levitt emphasize the role of abortion legalization in explaining the decline in crime in the 1990s; they do not assert that abortion policy explains the longer time series. They do claim that legalization explains as much as half of the decline in the 1990s. Our view is therefore that if several other substantial declines in crime have occurred, during periods when abortion legalization could not have played a role, this should introduce some caution about the quantitative importance during recent decades.

25. For a related analysis that reaches a similar conclusion, see Kahane, Paton, and Simmons (2008).

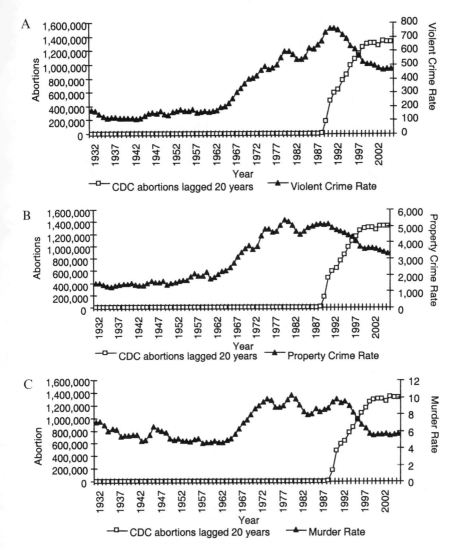

Fig. 8.13 U.S. crime rates and abortions lagged 20 years, 1932 to 2006: *A*, violent crime; *B*, property crime; *C*, murder

Source: CDC abortions' figures from "Abortion Surveillance" (various years), published in various issued of the MMWR.

A final hypothesis recently advanced to explain the variation in homicide rates is exposure to lead through paint or gasoline. According to this hypothesis, this exposure generates aggressive, antisocial behavior and violent tendencies later in life. Reyes (2007) and Nevin (2007) argue that laws restricting the use of lead have reduced this exposure and contributed to the recent decline in violent crime.

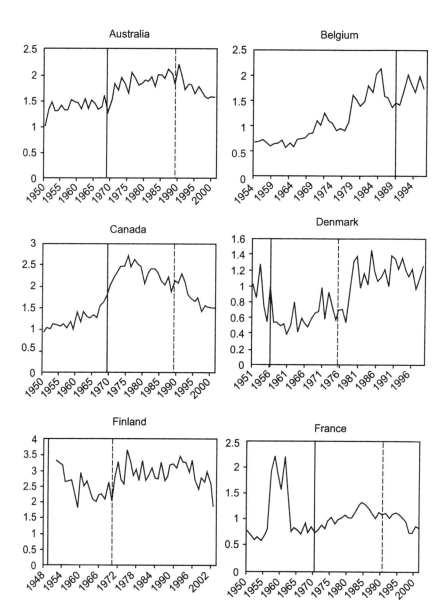

Fig. 8.14   Homicide rate time series and legalization of abortion

Sources: Homicide figures from WHO.

Note: Black vertical line indicates legalization of abortion; red vertical line indicates twenty years later.

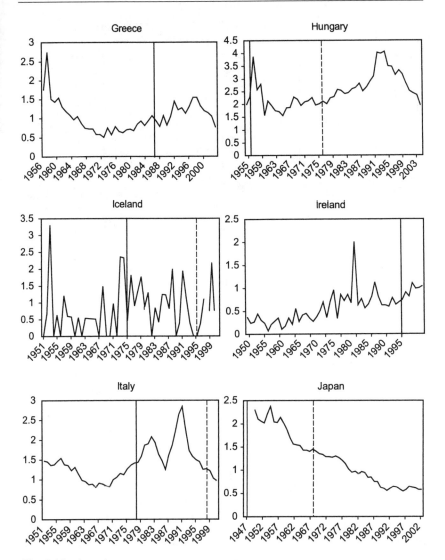

Fig. 8.14   (cont.)

Figure 8.15 plots the U.S. murder rate and a measure of environmental lead exposure lagged twenty years for 1961 through 2005. During some parts of the sample, the correlation is positive, consistent with the Reyes/ Nevin hypothesis, but in other time periods, especially the late 1960s to the mid-1980s, the correlation is negative or zero.[26] Further, lead exposure falls

26. For 1961–1974, the correlation is –0.5762 (p-value = 0.0310). Between 1975 and 1992 the correlation is 0.2181 (p-value = 0.3846) and between 1993 and 2005 the correlation is 0.3331 (p-value = 0.2661).

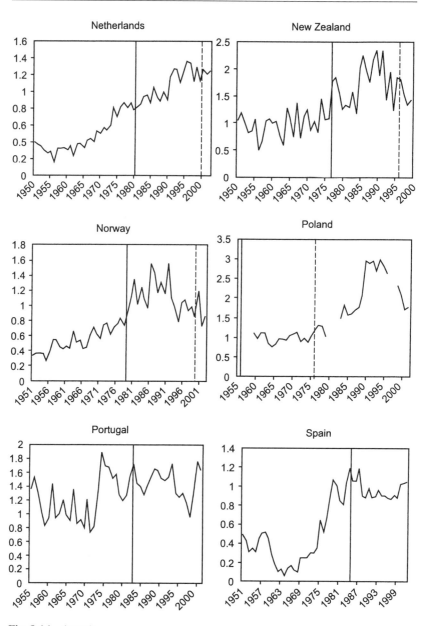

Fig. 8.14   (cont.)

to virtually nil by the end of the sample, yet crime appears to have leveled off. This makes the case for the lead hypothesis highly dependent upon the time period examined.

Figure 8.16 shows alternative measurements of lead exposure based on motor vehicle or motor fuel data. All proxies for lead increased dramati-

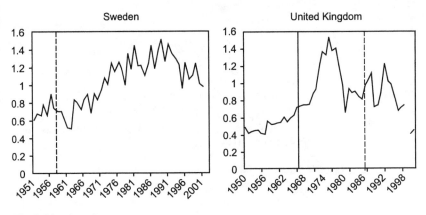

Fig. 8.14 (cont.)

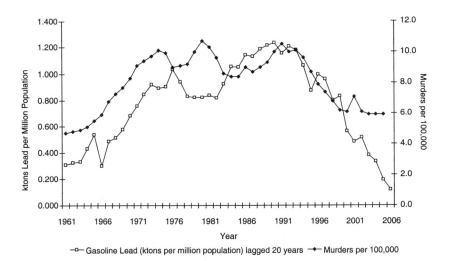

Fig. 8.15 Lead lagged twenty years and murders per 100,000: 1961 to 2006
Sources: Aggregate lead data from Reyes (2007).

cally from around 1910 through 1970. If the lead hypothesis is correct, then crime should have displayed a measurable increase between 1925 and 1985. The U.S. murder rate, however, decreased between the 1930s and 1950s. The murder rate does rise from the 1960s through the mid-1970s, but much unexplained variation remains between the mid-1970s and mid-1980s.

Our bottom line assessment on all these hypotheses is therefore as follows: each may contain an element of truth, and nothing we have done proves they are false. Any claim that these hypotheses explain large components of the fluctuations in crime, however, does not seem consistent with the aggregate data.

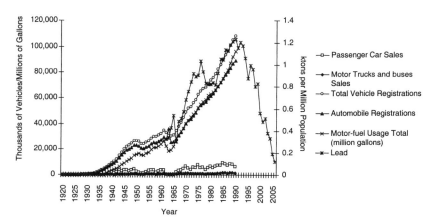

Fig. 8.16   Alternate measures of lead exposure lagged twenty years, 1920 to 2006
Sources: Automobile/fuel usage data are from the Historical Statistics of the United States.

8.5   Drug Prohibition

The previous analysis leaves a puzzle: why has crime fluctuated over the past several decades, and why are crime rates so different across countries? One possibility is that reporting conventions differ over time and place, and this undoubtedly plays a role for many crime categories and perhaps even for the most consistently reported crime series, homicide. The differences across time and space, however, seem too dramatic for this to be the main story.

We believe instead that a different mechanism, in both a general and a specific form, explains much of the variation in crime—especially violent crime—both over time and across countries. This hypothesis is that violence is more common when and where mechanisms for nonviolent dispute resolution are not readily available. This view has two implications.

At a general level, countries with weak systems for defining and enforcing property rights are likely to see elevated violence because market participants cannot use courts or nonviolent adjudication methods backed up by the courts. This is consistent with the fact that many former Soviet republics and some developing economies have high homicide rates. In these countries the rules are not always clear, and the government system for enforcing the rules is not effective. Countries with weak systems for defining and enforcing property rights are plausibly also ones in which property crimes like theft would be common.

At a specific level, the view that violence occurs when alternative dispute resolution mechanisms are not available implies that if government forces a market underground, participants substitute violence for other dispute-resolution mechanisms. The best example is drug prohibition; by forcing drug markets underground, prohibition encourages the use of violence to resolve disputes. In particular, greater enforcement of prohibition makes it harder for suppliers and demanders to circumvent the prohibition legally (for example, by obtaining the prohibited goods through medical channels). Enforcement also reallocates property rights and upsets reputations, so the ability of private parties to establish nonviolent dispute resolution diminishes with greater enforcement, while the number of disputes likely increases. Thus, more enforcement means a larger black market and more scope for violent dispute resolution.[27]

This hypothesis is related to, but partially distinct from, the "crack cocaine" hypothesis advanced in Fryer, et. al. (2005) (FHLM). They suggest that the major upturn in violence in the 1980s and the subsequent decline in the 1990s resulted from crack's introduction and spread. When crack arrived in cities beginning in the early 1980s, the property rights to distribution (e.g., street corners) were not assigned, and since crack dealers could not use advertising or lawsuits to capture market share or property rights, they used violence instead. Over time, according to FHLM, these property rights evolved (*de facto*), so violence subsided.

We agree with this hypothesis as far as it goes, but we argue it is incomplete. First, disputes arise in markets for many reasons beyond the initial assignment of property rights, and these disputes would presumably continue as long as a market operates. Second, the FHLM hypothesis does not explain fluctuations in violence outside the sample of the 1980s and early 1990s, or in other countries.

The "drug enforcement-generates-violence" hypothesis, however, potentially explains differences in crime across a broad range of time and space. Drug and alcohol prohibition enforcement have varied substantially over the past eighty years, which might explain fluctuations in U.S. violence over that time period. Similarly, prohibition enforcement differs across countries in ways that potentially explain differences in violence.

Drug enforcement might also explain variation in crime categories other than murder and assault. An increase in drug prices from increased enforcement may cause income-generating crime such as robbery, larceny, burglary, or auto theft. If increased police effort to enforce drug prohibition comes at the expense of other activities, deterrence for nondrug crimes might decline as enforcement increases. Further, increased incarceration of drug prisoners might overcrowd prisons and cause early release of nondrug prisoners, implying additional nondrug crime. Finally, incarceration of drug prisoners might cause people with generally low criminal proclivity to become more criminogenic.[28]

---

27. See Goldstein (1985), Goldstein et al. (1989) and Miron (2001) for further discussion.
28. An effect might also operate in the other direction; locking up people who commit both drug crime and nondrug crime might lower general crime (Kuziemko and Levitt 2004).

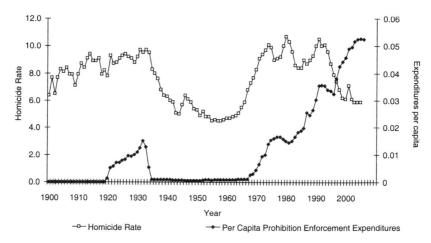

Fig. 8.17   **Expenditures on prohibitions per capita and homicides per 100,000: 1900 to 2006**

Sources: Homicide rate from FBI UCR (various years). Projected prohibition enforcement expenditures based on Miron (1999) with data from the Budget of the United States Government (various years).

Figure 8.17 presents data on expenditure for enforcement of alcohol and drug prohibition over time in the United States.[29] These data are broadly consistent with the view that differences in violence and perhaps other crime as well, result to a significant degree from differences in enforcement of alcohol and drug prohibition. The variations over time correlate well with the murder and homicide rates and, to a lesser degree, with the overall violent and property crime rates.[30] The relatively high rate of homicide in the United States compared to Europe is consistent with the fact that European countries enforce drug prohibition to a far lesser degree (Miron 2001). The relatively high homicide rates in various drug source countries (Colombia, Mexico) is further evidence consistent with the enforcement hypothesis.[31]

29. The data are based on those in Miron (1999).

30. The increases in crime in the 1960s seem to predate the increases in enforcement. One possibility is that the baby boom generation was entering its teens and twenties, which in part caused the increase in both crime and enforcement. In the regressions reported in section 8.6, we control for demographics.

31. Fajnzylber, Lederman, and Loayza (2002) use panel data for a large sample of developed and developing countries to examine the determinants of violent crime. They find some evidence that being a drug producer or having a high drug possession arrest rate is associated with more violence. Grogger and Willis (2000) find that rise in urban crime rates in the 1980s is strongly correlated with the introduction of crack cocaine. Some interpret this as suggesting crack has an independent, psychopharmacological effect in causing crime, but the correlation is more consistent with the FHLM story (since crack remained but crime declined). Goldstein et al. (1989) provide micro evidence that crime during the crack epidemic in New York City in 1988 resulted from disputes related to the drug trade. Dobkin and Nicosia (2009) provide evidence against the view that drug use per se causes crime. Prasad (2009) finds that economic

8.6 An Accounting Exercise

The discussion so far has considered potential crime determinants one by one, and it has relied on raw rather than instrumented correlations. In this section we address the first of these issues by considering regressions of crime rates on a multitude of possible determinants. We make no attempt to address the second issue because we are pessimistic that valid instruments exist at this level of aggregation.[32] Indeed, even finely tuned or clever instruments are often not compelling in practice, either because they have low explanatory power or are not really themselves exogenous.[33] Further, calculating accurate standards error is often difficult in standard panel regressions (Bertrand, Duflo, and Mullainathan 2004).

Table 8.2 shows regressions of various crime rates on measures of arrests, police, incarceration, executions, RTC laws, abortion, lead, and drug and alcohol prohibition enforcement.[34] The regressions also control for several factors that we have not examined explicitly: the age structure, economic conditions, and education. The existing literature provides some confirmation that each of these plays a role, although this evidence is less consistent than one might like.[35] We consider two samples: a shorter one (1961 to 2004) that includes all these variables, and a longer one that includes the variables available for the entire sample of the dependent variable. This is 1932 to 2005 for all four series, plus 1900 to 2005 for homicide.

The results are consistent with the conclusions derived above from the univariate correlations. The arrest rate enters significantly but with the wrong sign. Police per capita never enters significantly and is typically the wrong

---

liberalization in India, which brought much informal activity into the legal sector, was accompanied by a large decrease in violence.

32. Fisher and Nagin (1978) is the classic reference on the difficulty of identifying the crime function.

33. On the problems created by weak instruments, see Staiger and Stock (1997).

34. The regression includes a time trend, logged GNP per capita measured in 1992 dollars from the Bureau of Economic Analysis, the fraction of the population aged fifteen to twenty-four from the Census Bureau, and the fraction of the population with at least a high school diploma from the Census Bureau. Most other factors are lagged one year. These include real prohibition expenditures per capita (from the Office of Management and Budget of the United States), the percent of the population covered by right to carry laws (from Grossman and Lee [2008]) and the Census Bureau), the incarceration rate (from the Sourcebook of Criminal Justice Statistics), the arrest rate (from the FBI's UCR from various years), police employees per capita (from the FBI's UCR), and the stock of handguns per capita (from Kleck, 1997). CDC abortions are included measured in thousands and lagged 20 years. The Reyes (2007) measure of lead exposure in kilotons per million population is included lagged 20 years. In a few cases, a variable was missing data for a limited number of years. We linearly interpolated values for these missing observations. In particular, we interpolated values for police in 1936–1938, 1942, and 1952; for the arrest rates in 1950 and 1957; and the percent high school graduate for 1956, 1957, 1959, 1962, and 1964. We estimate Newey-West standard errors allowing for first order autocorrelation.

35. On the role of the age structure, see Levitt (1999) and De Mello and Schneider (see chapter 6, this volume). For recent evidence on the role of education, see Lochner (2004).

Table 8.2   Multivariate regressions of U.S. crime rates on potential determinants

	Property crime		Violent crimes		Murders		Homicides		
	1961–2004 (1)	1932–2005 (2)	1961–2004 (3)	1932–2005 (4)	1961–2004 (5)	1932–2005 (6)	1961–2004 (7)	1932–2005 (8)	1900–2005 (9)
Trend	0.0317	0.0369	0.0546	0.0448	0.0276	0.0178	0.0248	0.0241	0.0316
	(1.49)	(9.64)	(1.81)	(6.90)	(0.94)	(3.05)	(0.77)	(4.06)	(3.32)
$\ln$(GNP per capita)	0.2625	−0.3541	0.8808	−0.4337	0.7434	−0.1787	0.8491	−0.6114	−1.1302
	(0.52)	(2.83)	(1.45)	(2.01)	(1.41)	(0.98)	(1.48)	(3.52)	(3.16)
% aged 15–24	1.2754	5.6154	−3.7314	4.3692	−5.7484	5.2577	−6.7234	7.9815	5.6972
	(0.51)	(6.07)	(1.44)	(2.85)	(2.09)	(4.76)	(2.30)	(6.75)	(3.86)
Prohibition expenditures per capita$_{t-1}$	3.2995	7.5471	−0.1931	21.6664	9.8620	15.6705	2.7608	14.6486	21.3226
	(0.81)	(1.55)	(0.04)	(2.56)	(2.14)	(2.62)	(0.48)	(2.27)	(3.51)
% covered by right to carry$_{t-1}$	−0.3932	−1.7027	−0.2082	−2.4350	−0.4089	−1.6177	−0.4830	−1.8579	−2.2918
	(1.53)	(5.79)	(0.69)	(4.52)	(1.19)	(3.53)	(1.15)	(2.70)	(4.64)
Incarceration rate$_{t-1}$	−0.0036	−0.0002	−0.0061	−0.0004	−0.0066	−0.0008	−0.0060	−0.0001	
	(2.22)	(0.31)	(3.80)	(0.42)	(3.89)	(0.92)	(3.10)	(0.13)	
Executions per capita$_{t-1}$	−441.6479	−43.7983	−263.9329	80.5164	−531.6189	158.1099	−376.5246	123.3264	
	(1.79)	(0.66)	(0.71)	(0.67)	(1.76)	(1.46)	(1.02)	(1.16)	
Abortion (thousands)$_{t-20}$	0.000304		0.000364		0.000525		0.000624	0.000022	
	(1.69)		(1.83)		(2.76)		(2.65)	(0.08)	
Arrest rate$_{t-1}$	0.0005		0.0030		0.0468		0.0417		
	(2.36)		(3.15)		(3.51)		(2.68)		
Police per capita$_{t-1}$	−0.0168		0.0304		0.0127		0.0835		
	(0.10)		(0.16)		(0.07)		(0.52)		
Guns per capita$_{t-1}$	0.0052		0.0035		0.0068		0.0012		
	(2.47)		(1.54)		(2.46)		(0.27)		
% high school graduate or more	−0.0309		−0.0320		−0.0448		−0.0094		
	(1.27)		(1.33)		(1.92)		(0.34)		
Lead$_{t-20}$	0.1091		0.0707		0.0503		0.0526		
	(1.10)		(0.55)		(0.43)		(0.43)		
Constant	−56.1936	−62.1396	−108.3916	−78.9484	−56.8818	−32.3040	−53.4762	−40.9172	−50.2325
	(1.37)	(9.45)	(1.92)	(7.02)	(1.06)	(3.20)	(0.91)	(3.95)	(3.28)
Observations	44	74	44	74	44	74	44	74	105

Note: Newey-West t-statistics in parentheses.

sign. The execution rate never enters significantly and is sometimes the wrong sign. Greater incarceration does correlate with lower crime in the shorter sample but not in the longer samples, consistent with the graphical evidence above.

Right to carry laws are consistently correlated with lower crime, but the correlation is about as negative for property crime as for violent crime, which is not consistent with the LM hypothesis. Guns are positively correlated with crime for all four crime series, but again the correlation is particularly strong for property crime, which is counterintuitive. Abortion enters with the wrong sign, sometimes significantly. Lead enters positively, consistent with the Reyes/Levin view, but the effect is never significant. It is also largest in magnitude for property crime, which is the opposite of the Reyes result and inconsistent with the view that lead poisoning promotes aggression in particular.

Enforcement of prohibition is associated with greater crime in all but one regression, and most of the coefficients are significant. In particular, for overall violent crime and murder/homicide in the longer samples, the coefficients are consistently positive and significant.

As noted, one should not draw structural conclusions from these regressions, but they are not consistent with the view that standard deterrence variables, as well as other factors recently addressed in the economics of crime literature, are robust determinants of crime. At the same time, they are consistent with the view that drug prohibition enforcement plays an important role, especially for violent crime categories.

8.7 Conclusion

The economic model of crime first posited in 1968 has spurred a large literature that tries to estimate the empirically relevant determinants of crime. This chapter has examined aggregate data for first-order evidence on these determinants; these data, however, provide little confirmation that these determinants have a significant impact on long-run trends or major differences across countries. While this does not mean these theories are wrong, we believe that any estimation finding a strong effect not seen in the aggregate data deserves careful scrutiny.

We do find one theory that is consistent with the aggregate time series and cross-country data on crime: the view that enforcement of drug prohibition encourages violent dispute resolution.

This perspective is also consistent with phenomena beyond those typically labeled crime. Acts of terrorism, civil unrest, and civil war can be thought of as dispute resolution. These activities are more likely when, on the one hand, more disputes exist because of policies that provide the basis for such disputes (e.g., laws mandating one religion or language). These activities are also more likely when, on the other hand, groups that disagree with government policies have few nonviolent mechanisms for expressing their grievances. Thus, an alternative perspective to the deterrence model, at least for much violent crime, is one that examines how policies affect both the amount and nature of dispute resolution.

References

Abrams, D. S. 2006. More guns, more time: Using add-on gun laws to estimate the deterrent effect of incarceration on crime. Ph.D. diss. University of Chicago Law School.

Ayres, I., and J. J. Donohue, III. 2003a. Shooting down the "more guns, less crime" hypothesis. *Stanford Law Review* 55: 1193–1312.

———. 2003b. The latest misfires in support of the "more guns, less crime" hypothesis. *Stanford Law Review* 55: 1371–1398.

Becker, G. S. 1968. Crime and punishment: An economic approach. *Journal of Political Economy* 76 (2): 169–217.

Benson, B. L., I. Kim, and D. W. Rasmussen. 1994. Estimating deterrence effects: A public choice perspective on the economics of crime literature. *Southern Economic Journal* 61 (July): 161–8.

Black, D. A., and D. S. Nagin. 1998. Do right-to-carry laws deter violent crime? *Journal of Legal Studies* 27 (1): 209–19.

Bertrand, M., E. Duflo, and S. Mullainathan. 2004. How much should we trust differences-in-differences estimates? *Quarterly Journal of Economics* 119 (1): 249–75.

Bureau of Justice Statistics, *Sourcebook of Criminal Justice Statistics.* Available online at: http://www.albany.edu/sourcebook/.

Cameron, S. 1988. The economics of crime deterrence: A survey of theory and evidence. *Kyklos* 41 (2): 301–23.

Center for Disease Control (various years). Abortion surveillance. *Morbidity and Mortality Weekly Report.*

Center for Disease Control/National Center for Health Statistics, National Vital Statistics System, Mortality data (http://www.cdc.gov/nchs/datawh/statab/unpubd/mortabs/hist290a.htm).

Chen, M. K., and J. M. Shapiro. 2004. Does prison harden inmates? A discontinuity-based approach. NBER Discussion Paper no. 1450. Cambridge, MA: National Bureau of Economic Research.

Cohen-Cole, E., S. Durlauf, J. Fagan, and D. Nagin. 2007. Model uncertainty and the deterrent effect of capital punishment. Ph.D. diss. manuscript, University of Wisconsin.

Cornwell, C., and W. N. Trumbell. 1994. Estimating the economic model of crime with panel data. *The Review of Economics and Statistics.* 76 (2): 360–6.

Dezhbakhsh, H., P. H. Rubin, and J. M. Shepherd. 2003. Does capital punishment have a deterrent effect? New evidence from postmoratorium panel data. *American Law and Economics Review* 5 (2): 344–76.

Dezhbakhsh, H., and J. M. Shepherd. 2006. The deterrent effect of capital punishment: Evidence from a "judicial experiment." *Economic Inquiry* 44 (3): 512–35.

Di Tella, R., and E. Schargrodsky. 2004. Do police reduce crime? Estimates using the allocation of police forces after a terrorist attack. *The American Economic Review* 94 (1): 115–33.

Dills, A. K., and J. A. Miron. 2006. A comment on Donohue and Levitt's (2006) Reply to Foote and Goetz (2005). Department of Economics, Harvard University. Available at [http://www.economics.harvard.edu/faculty/miron/files/Comment_on _DL_FG.pdf].

Dobkin, C., and N. Nicosia. 2009. The war on drugs: Methamphetamine, public health, and crime. *American Economic Review* 99 (1): 324–49.

Donohue, J. J., III, and S. D. Levitt. 2001. The impact of legalized abortion on crime. *Quarterly Journal of Economics* 116 (2): 379–420.

———— 2004. Further evidence that legalized abortion lowered crime: A reply to joyce. *Journal of Human Resources* 39 (1): 29–49.

———— 2008. Measurement error, legalized abortion, and the decline in crime: A response to Foote and Goetz. *Quarterly Journal of Economics* 123 (1): 425–40.

Donohue, J. J., III, and J. Wolfers. 2005. Uses and abuses of empirical evidence in the death penalty debate. *Stanford Law Review* 58 (December): 791–846.

Eckberg, D. L. 1995. Estimates of early twentieth-century U.S. homicide rates: An econometric forecasting approach. *Demography* 32 (1): 1–16.

Ehrlich, I. 1973. Participation in illegitimate activities: A theoretical and empirical investigation. *Journal of Political Economy* 81 (3): 521–65.

———— 1975. The deterrent effect of capital punishment: A question of life and death. *American Economic Review* 65 (3): 397–417.

———— 1977. Capital punishment and deterrence: Some further thoughts and additional evidence. *Journal of Political Economy* 85 (4): 741–88.

———— 1996. Crime, punishment, and the market for offenses. *Journal of Economic Perspectives* 10 (1): 43–67.

Espy, M. W., and J. O. Smykla. 2004. *Executions in the United States, 1608–2002: The Espy File* [Computer file]. 4th ICPSR ed. Compiled by M. Watt Espy and John Ortiz Smykla, University of Alabama. Ann Arbor, MI: Inter-university Consortium for Political and Social Research [producer and distributor].

Fajinzylber, P., D. Lederman, and N. Loayza. 2002. What causes violent crime? *European Economic Review* 46 (July): 1323–57.

Federal Bureau of Investigation (various years). *Crime in the United States.* Recent issues available at http://www.fbi.gov/ucr/ucr.htm.

Fisher, F. M., and D. Nagin. 1978. On the feasibility of identifying the crime function in a simultaneous model of crime rates and sanction levels. In *Deterrence and incapacitation: Report of the panel on research on deterrent and incapacitative effects, Assembly of behavioral and social sciences,* ed. A. Blumstein et al. Washington, DC: National Research Council, National Academy of Sciences.

Foote, C. L., and C. F. Goetz. 2008. The impact of legalized abortion on crime: A comment. *Quarterly Journal of Economics* 123 (1): 1–48.

Freeman, R. B. 1999. The economics of crime. In *Handbook of labor economics,* eds. Orley Ashenfelter and David Card. Amsterdam: Elsevier.

Fryer, R. G., Jr., P. S. Heaton, S. D. Levitt, and K. M. Murphy. 2005. Measuring the impact of crack cocaine NBER Working Paper no. 11318. Cambridge, MA: National Bureau of Economic Research, May.

Goldstein, P. J. 1985. The drugs/violence nexus: A tripartite conceptual framework. *Journal of Drug Issues* 15 (Fall): 493–506.

Goldstein, P. J., H. H. Brownstein, P. J. Ryan, and P. A. Bellucci. 1989. Crack and homicide in New York City, 1988: A conceptually based event analysis. *Contemporary Drug Problems* 16 (4): 651–87.

Grogger, J. and M. Willis. 2000. The emergence of crack cocaine and the rise in urban crime rates. *Review of Economics and Statistics* 82 (4): 519–29.

Grossman, R. S., and S. A. Lee. 2008. May issue vs. shall issue: Explaining the pattern of concealed carry gun laws, 1960–2001. *Contemporary Economic Policy* 26 (2): 198–206.

Harris, A. R., S. H. Thomas, G. A. Fisher, D. J. Hirsch. 2002. Murder and medicine: The lethality of criminal assault 1960–1999. *Homicide Studies* 6 (2): 128–66.

Helland, E., and A. Tabarrok. 2004. Using placebo laws to test "more guns, less crime." *Advances in Economic Analysis & Policy* 4 (1): 1–7.

Iyengar, R. 2007. Does the certainty of arrest reduce domestic violence? Evidence from mandatory and recommended arrest laws. NBER Working Paper no. 13186. Cambridge, MA: National Bureau of Economics, June.

———. 2008. I'd rather be hanged for a sheep than a lamb: The unintended consequences of "Three-Strikes" Laws. NBER Working Paper no. 13784. Cambridge, MA: National Bureau of Economics, February.

Johnson, R., and S. Raphael. 2006. How much crime reduction does the marginal prisoner buy? Ph. D. diss. Goldman School of Public Policy, University of California, Berkeley.

Joyce, T. 2003. Did legalized abortion lower crime? *Journal of Human Resources* 38 (1): 1–37.

———. 2009. A simple test of abortion and crime. *Review of Economics and Statistics* 91 (1): 112–23.

Kahane, L. H., D. Paton, and R. Simmons. 2008. The abortion-crime link: Evidence from England and Wales. *Economica* 75 (297): 1–21.

Katz, L., S. D. Levitt, and E. Shustorovich. 2003. Prison conditions, capital punishment, and deterrence. *American Law and Economics Review* 5 (2): 318–43.

Kessler, D., and S. D. Levitt. 1999. Using sentence enhancements to distinguish between deterrence and incapacitation. *Journal of Law and Economics* 42 (1, part 2): 343–63.

Kleck, G. 1997. *Targeting guns: Firearms and their control.* Hawthorne, NY: Aldine de Gruyter.

Klick, J., and A. Tabarrok. 2005. Using terror alert levels to estimate the effect of police on crime. *Journal of Law and Economics* 48 (April): 267–80.

Kling, J. R. 2006. Incarceration length, employment, and earnings. NBER Working Paper no. 12003. Cambridge, MA: National Bureau of Economics, February.

Kuziemko, I., and S. D. Levitt. 2004. An empirical analysis of imprisoning drug offenders. *Journal of Public Economics* 88 (August): 2043–66.

Lee, D. S., and J. McCrary. 2005. Crime, punishment, and myopia. NBER Working Paper no. 11491. Cambridge, MA: National Bureau of Economics, July.

Levitt, S. 1996. The effect of prison population size on crime rates: Evidence from prison overcrowding litigation. *Quarterly Journal of Economics* 111 (2): 319–52.

———. 1997. Using electoral cycles in police hiring to estimate the effect of police on crime. *American Economic Review* 87 (3): 270–90.

———. 1999. The limited role of changing age structure in explaining aggregate crime rates. *Criminology* 37 (3): 581–97.

———. 2004. Understanding why crime fell in the 1990s: Four factors that explain the decline and six that do not. *Journal of Economic Perspectives* 18 (1): 163–90.

———. 2006. The case of the critics who missed the point: A reply to Webster et al. *Crime and Public Policy* 5 (3): 449–60.

Lochner, L. 2003. Individual perceptions of the criminal justice system. NBER Working Paper no. 9474. Cambridge, MA: National Bureau of Economic Research, February.

————. 2004. Education, work, and crime: A human capital approach. NBER Working Paper no. 10478. Cambridge, MA: National Bureau of Economic Research, May.

Lott, J. R., Jr. 1998. The concealed-handgun debate. *Journal of Legal Studies* 27 (1): 221–43.

————. 2003. *The bias against guns: Why almost everything you've heard about gun control is wrong.* Washington, DC: Regnery Publishing, Inc.

Lott, J. R., Jr., and D. B. Mustard. 1997. Crime, deterrence, and right-to-carry concealed handguns. *Journal of Legal Studies* 26 (1): 1–68.

Lott, J. R., Jr., and J. Whitley. 2007. Abortion and crime: Unwanted children and out-of-wedlock births. *Economic Inquiry,* 45 (2): 304–24.

McCrary, J. 2002. Using electoral cycles in police hiring to estimate the effect of police on crime: Comment. *American Economic Review* 92 (4): 1236–43.

Miron, J. A. 1999. Violence and the U.S. prohibitions of drugs and alcohol. *American Law and Economics Review* 1 (1): 78–114.

————. 2001. Violence, guns, and drugs: A cross-country analysis. *Journal of Law and Economics* 44 (2, pt. 2): 615–34.

Mocan, H. N., and R. K. Gittings. 2003. Getting off death row: Commuted sentences and the deterrent effect of capital punishment. *Journal of Law and Economics* 46 (2): 453–78.

————. 2006. The impact of incentives on human behavior: Can we make it disappear? The case of the death penalty. NBER Working Paper no. 12631. Cambridge, MA: National Bureau of Economics, October.

Moody, C., and T. B. Marvell. 1996. Police levels, crime rates, and specification problems. *Criminology* 24 (3): 606–46.

Nagin, D. 1997. Criminal deterrence research: A review of the evidence and a research agenda for the outset of the twenty-first century. Ph. D. diss. Carnegie-Mellon University.

National Research Council. 2005. *Firearms and violence: A critical review.* Washington, DC: The National Academies Press.

Nevin, R. 2007. Understanding international crime trends: The legacy of preschool lead exposure. *Environmental Research* 104 (3): 315–36.

Office of Management and Budget (various years), *Budget of the United States Government.* Washington, DC: U.S. Government Printing Office.

Organization for Economic Co-operation and Development. 2007. *OECD Factbook 2007: Economic, Environmental, and Social Statistics.*

Passell, P., and J. B. Taylor. 1977. The deterrent effect of capital punishment: Another view. *American Economic Review* 67 (3): 445–51.

Plassmann, F., and J. Whitley. 2003. Confirming "more guns, less crime." *Stanford Law Review* 55 (1): 1313–69.

Prasad, K. 2009. Economic liberalization and violent crime in India. Ph. D. diss. University of Maryland.

Reyes, J. 2007. Environmental policy as social policy? The impact of childhood lead exposure on crime. *B.E. Journal of Economic Analysis and Policy* 7 (1): Contributions, Article 51.

Shepherd, J. M. 2004. Murders of passion, execution delays, and the deterrence of capital punishment. *Journal of Legal Studies* 33 (2): 283–321.

Social Science Federation of Canada and Statistics Canada. 1983. *Historical statistics of Canada,* second edition, available from Statistics Canada at: http://www.statcan.ca/english/freepub/11-516-XIE/sectiona/toc.htm.

Staiger, D., and J. H. Stock. 1997. Instrumental variables regression with weak instruments. *Econometrica* 65 (3): 557–86.

U.S. Bureau of the Census. 1975. *Historical statistics of the United States: Colonial times to 1970.* Washington, DC: U.S. Government Printing Office.

Walmsley, R. 2004. *World prison population list (Fifth edition).* Home Office Findings 234, available at http://www.homeoffice.gov.uk/rds/pdfs2/r234.pdf.

Webster, C. M., A. N. Doob, and F. E. Zimring. 2006. Proposition 8 and the crime rate in California: The case of the disappearing deterrent effect. *Crime and Public Policy* 5 (3): 417–48.

World Health Organization Mortality Database. Available at: http://www.who.int/healthinfo/morttables/en/index.html.

Comment   Philip J. Cook

The chapter by Dills, Miron, and Summers (hereafter "DMS") grabs attention through provocative claims about economists' ignorance when it comes to "the main factors identified in the economics of crime literature as key determinants of crime." The exception offered to this nihilistic conclusion is a finding that drug prohibition generates violence, a result that has been documented by (among others) one of the authors of this chapter, Miron.

DMS's claim that forty years of empirical research by economists has been unproductive rests less on a careful review of the literature (see, e.g., Cook 1980; Nagin 1998; Levitt and Miles 2007) than on several time-series plots of national crime rates juxtaposed with a potentially causal variable. Two of these causal variables relate to the core issue in the economics of crime—the deterrent effect of the threat of criminal sanctions—and are plausibly important: the arrest rate, and the size of the police force. In my comments I will focus on these two variables. Two other variables, the execution rate and the imprisonment rate, are relevant to deterrence but of less interest. Execution is a very rare sanction in practice and the execution rate tells us very little about the likelihood or severity of punishment for the typical murder (Cook, in press). The imprisonment rate has a theoretically ambiguous relationship to crime.[1]

The method of empirical inquiry by which DMS reach their damning conclusion is, ironically, far less sophisticated than the literature they critique. From the first econometric studies that were published on the effect of sanction threat on crime (Ehrlich 1973; Carr-Hill and Stern 1973; Sjoquist

Philip J. Cook is Senior Associate Dean for Faculty and Research and ITT/Terry Sanford Professor of Public Policy at Sanford School of Public Policy, Duke University, and a research associate of the National Bureau of Economic Research.

1. As demonstrated by Blumstein and Nagin (1978), the relationship between crime and the imprisonment rate is not monotonic. At a low probability, an increase in the probability is likely to generate an increase in the imprisonment rate; at a high probability, an increase in probability may well generate a reduction in the imprisonment rate. The logic is identical to the relationship between price and revenue along a demand curve.

1973), economists have recognized and attempted to address the reasonable supposition that crime rates are determined by many factors, not just the sanction threat level. These pioneers also recognized that variables like the arrest rate and police per capita are simultaneously determined with crime rates, and estimating the deterrent effect requires dealing with a difficult identification problem. Contributors to this field have in recent years developed creative efforts to solve this identification problem, with some success (Levitt and Miles 2007). In any event, the current study is a giant step backward methodologically speaking—back to the early work of criminologists who were computing simple correlations (Gibbs 1968).

Indeed, DSM confess that their approach is problematic, in that it "suffers two large defects: the right model is multifactorial, and the raw correlation between crime and a potential determinant can be misleading in the presence of endogeneity." They justify their naïve approach with the odd claim that their approach "does not prove a multivariate, 'instrumented' analysis would not uncover a different effect, but it suggests this outcome is not especially likely . . ." In other words, a simple bivariate association is enough to tell us the big-picture story with a high degree of confidence. Not so.

Take the case of the variable "police per capita." What DMS seem to be arguing is that if police per capita has an important deterrent effect on crime, then the intertemporal correlation between crime rates and police variable will be negative pretty much regardless of socioeconomic, demographic, cultural, and policy changes that have occurred over the period. That is a particularly strange claim given that we know (and the early econometric studies recognized) that there is another relationship between crime rates and police per capita, that reflects the public demand for public safety. We thus have two relationships, both plausibly strong, that have opposite signs:

Supply of offenses: crime rates negatively related to police per capita.
Demand for safety: police per capita positively related to crime.

There is an obvious analogy here between supply and demand in goods markets. If the observed time series data are generated by shifts in the supply of offenses schedule (due to demographic or cultural change, say), then the data will trace out the positively sloped demand function. So if we in fact observe a positive relationship, that tells us nothing at all about whether the supply of offenses is responsive to the threat embodied in increases in police.

There is also a fundamental problem with DMS's analysis of the arrest rate. The authors use arrests per capita as their proxy for the theoretically correct variable, namely the probability of arrest given crime. What is the logical connection between arrests per capita and the probability of arrest given crime? Over time, arrest per capita will be *positively* correlated with crime rates if, for example, the true probability of arrest (given crime) remains constant.[2] Finding that positive correlation (as do DMS) tells us literally nothing about the subject at hand, which is the deterrent effect of changes in the probability of arrest.

So where do DMS end up? They say they are focusing on the ". . . naïve 'if we hire more police, or make more arrests . . . that will necessarily reduce crime' perspective." They conclude that ". . . while one interpretation of our deterrence results is that economists do not have the right data to find these effects, an alternative, reasonable interpretation is that increases in the standard deterrence variables have small or perverse effects over the relevant range." In my judgment, DMS are 0 for 2: they have not provided a correction to what economists have actually shown (since DMS's method is far more primitive than the norm in the economics literature), and they have not shown that arrest rates and police resources have "small or perverse effects" (since their results are entirely compatible with a strong deterrent effect).

There is much reason to believe that crime rates tend to go down when the probability of punishment increases, other things equal. The review essays cited above include evidence from natural experiments, laboratory experiments, and credible econometric studies. Based on my reading of the evidence, my "naïve" prediction is that if we disbanded the police force the resulting crime surge would be unambiguous.

References

Blumstein, A., and D. Nagin. 1978. On the optimal use of incarceration. *Operations Research* 26 (3): 381–405.

Carr-Hill, R. A., and N. Stern. 1973. An econometric model of the supply and control of recorded offences in England and Wales. *Journal of Public Economics* 2: 289–318.

Cook, P. J. 1980. Research in criminal deterrence: Laying the groundwork for the second decade. In *Crime and justice: An annual review of research Vol. 2,* eds. N. Morris and M. Tonry, 211–68. Chicago: University of Chicago Press.

Cook, P. J. (in press) Potential savings from abolition of the death penalty in North Carolina. *American Law and Economics Review.*

Ehrlich, I. 1973. Participation in illegitimate activities: A theoretical and empirical investigation. *Journal of Political Economy* 81 (3): 521–65.

Gibbs, J. P. 1968. Crime, punishment, and deterrence. *Southwestern Social Science Quarterly* 48 (March): 515–30.

Levitt, S. D., and T. Miles. 2007. The empirical study of criminal punishment. In *The handbook of law and economics,* eds. M. Polinsky and S. Shavell, 453–95. Amsterdam: Elsevier.

Nagin, D. 1998. Criminal deterrence research: A review of the evidence and a research agenda for the outset of the 21st century. In *Crime and justice: An annual review of research,* ed. M. Tonry, 23: 1–42. Chicago: University of Chicago Press.

Sjoquist, D. 1973. Property crime and economic behavior: Some empirical results. *American Economic Review* 63 (3): 439–46.

2. Furthermore, it is easy to show that if crime is highly deterrable with respect to the arrest probability, then arrest per capita is inversely related to the arrest probability.

Peaceable Kingdoms and War Zones
Preemption, Ballistics, and Murder in Newark

Brendan O'Flaherty and Rajiv Sethi

"If I had not put an end to him today, he would have killed me tomorrow."[1]

9.1 Introduction

In 2006, 105 people were murdered in Newark, New Jersey, almost twice as many as were killed in 2000. If murders occurred in Newark at the national rate, there would have been sixteen. Using standard measures of the value of a statistical life, this implies a loss of $445 to $623 million from excess murders in Newark in 2006.[2] The entire cost of running city government was firmly in that range. Furthermore, while the increase in murder can be attributed almost entirely to an increase in gunshot homicides, the overall incidence of shooting incidents did not rise appreciably. What happened was a dramatic increase in *lethality:* far more shootings resulted in victim death.

Brendan O'Flaherty is professor of economics at Columbia University. Rajiv Sethi is professor of economics at Barnard College, Columbia University, and an external professor at the Santa Fe Institute.

The views expressed herein are our own and not necessarily those of the Newark Police Department or of the City of Newark. This work would not have been possible without the assistance of Director Garry McCarthy; Deputy Chief Gus Miniotis; Sgt Henry Gajda; and, especially, Megan Ambrosio of the Newark Police Department, Mayor Cory Booker, and former Business Administrator Bo Kemp of the City of Newark. We also thank Daniel Brehon, Philip Cook, Guillermo Cruces, Jeffrey Fagan, Alejandro Gaviria, Amanda Geller, Mark Kleiman, Glenn Loury, Jens Ludwig, Joao de Mello, Timothy Moore, and Peter Reuter for their comments; Lois Gonzales and Dennis F. Mazone for providing data; and Leora Kelman, Michael Tannenbaum, and Ariel Zucker for excellent research assistance.

1. Grace Doyle of Chicago, July 3, 1899, explaining why she shot her husband Timothy (quoted in Adler 2006, 101).

2. Aldy and Viscusi (2003) is a definitive reference on this topic. Levitt and Venkatesh (2000) estimate that young gang members in Chicago act as if they value their lives at much lower rates—an order of magnitude or two lower. Because these estimates are so far below the norm in this huge literature, perhaps some of the standard assumptions do not hold—the decision makers may not be aware of true probabilities, for instance, or their outside opportunities may

Why are so many people killed in Newark? Why did murders rise so sharply from 2000 to 2006? Why did the increase come about through greater lethality rather than more frequent shooting? What can be done to reduce the killing? And, more generally, what changes in fundamentals trigger changes in lethality and the incidence of murder, and how does the mechanism operate? We address these questions by developing a theoretical model of murder that is relevant not only to Newark, but also to other areas with high and volatile murder rates, including many cities in Latin America.

Murder differs from other serious crimes in several important respects. To begin with, murder is defined in part by a medical condition—clinical death—and random chance plays a major role in determining whether attempts at killing end up becoming murders. Second, murder admits a much wider array of motives than most other crimes, including jealousy, rage, paranoia, vengeance, and greed. Third, even in the absence of any legal sanction for murder, ordinary people under normal circumstances would gain little from taking the life of another. This is clearly not the case for crimes such as robbery or theft.

Fourth, murder is extremely serious. Most individuals value life more than they value large amounts of money and are willing to pay substantial sums to avoid even small increases in the risk of death. The average murder results in welfare losses estimated to be at least 5,000 times as large as the losses from the average robbery (Aldy and Viscusi 2003). Hence, people are willing to take drastic steps to avoid being killed, and these steps may include *the preemptive killing of others*. Our simplest answer then to the question of why people kill so often in Newark is that they kill to avoid being killed. Other motives are present, to be sure, but huge deviations from national norms can be sustained only if a significant proportion of murders are motivated by self-protection. Some Newark streets are sometimes described as a war zone, and in war, too, soldiers kill to save their lives and those of their comrades.

More precisely, the decision to kill is characterized by strategic complementarity: an increase in the likelihood of being killed by someone raises the incentives to kill them first.[3] Under such circumstances it is possible for expectations of high murder rates to become self-fulfilling: murders beget murders. Furthermore, small changes in fundamentals can, under certain circumstances, induce large changes in the equilibrium murder rate. We show how this can happen as a result of a dramatic change in the choice of lethal-

---

not be accurately modeled. Many Newark murder victims resemble the young gang members studied by Levitt and Venkatesh, but many do not.

3. Thus, our story is an example of the social multiplier discussed in Goldin and Katz (2002) and Glaeser, Sacerdote, and Scheinkman (2003). Rasmusen (1996) and Schrag and Scotchmer (1997) also develop models where increases in criminal activity are self-reinforcing, but their analyses deal with crime in general rather than murder in particular and are, therefore, based on different mechanisms (employer stereotypes and judicial errors, respectively). These mechanisms seem better at explaining long-run differences across communities than at explaining rapid changes in a particular community.

ity so that murders increase even as shootings remain relatively stable. We believe that this is what happened in Newark in the early years of this century. While we cannot identify any single trigger, several changes occurred that may have been enough to shift the equilibrium drastically: the prosecutor's office fell into disarray, the number of prisoners decreased, the police department withered, and the corrections department reorganized state prisons in a way that facilitated networking among gang members. Taken together, the impact of these changes was to drive expectations beyond a tipping point, resulting in a cascade of killings motivated in part by self-protection.

Our model is useful prospectively as well. How can Newark's murders be cut? The obvious answer is to improve fundamentals—for instance, by investing in high quality professional police work that increases the probability that murderers will be apprehended and convicted. Once a high murder regime has been entered, however, it cannot be escaped simply by restoring fundamentals to their initial values. According to our analysis, the corrective changes that are required in order shift expectations of murder rates back down to earlier levels may be much greater in magnitude than the changes that triggered the rise in the first place. The analysis also tells us what sorts of public relations efforts to mount and which to avoid. More speculatively, we look at ideas like multiple classes of liquor licenses and other efforts to quarantine the contagion of violence. A clear implication of the model is that murders will decline in a manner that is as sharp and sudden as the increase has been. In fact, it may be the case that such a collapse in the murder rate is already underway: in early 2008, Newark went over forty days without a single murder, the longest recorded spell without a murder in the history of the city.

The idea that two armed individuals may choose to shoot at each other simply out of fear that they may be shot first dates back at least to Schelling (1960). Even when both parties to a potential conflict prefer that no violence occurs, uncertainty about the motives or intentions of others can result in mutual aggression. This process has been modelled formally as a coordination game with incomplete information by Baliga and Sjöström (2004), who identify conditions under which there is a unique (Bayes-Nash) equilibrium in which both players attack with certainty.[4] We build on this work by introducing the possibility that individuals face not just the option of violence but also a choice of lethality, where greater lethality must be purchased at some cost. This allows us to explore how equilibrium levels of lethality and

---

4. This happens because there is some proportion, possibly very small, of individuals for whom aggression is a dominant strategy. The presence of such types places a lower bound on the likelihood of being attacked, which induces some individuals for whom aggression is *not* a dominant strategy to also attack. Applying this reasoning iteratively, one can see that peace may be impossible to support in equilibrium provided the distribution of the costs of aggression does not rise too steeply. Baliga and Sjöström explore the possibility that cheap talk could allow the parties to coordinate on the peaceful outcome. Basu (2006) applies a variant of this model to examine racial conflict, and Baliga, Lucca, and Sjöström (2007) extend it to study the manner in which political institutions affect the likelihood of war.

murder covary with the underlying parameters of interest. For instance, one implication of our model is that a deterioration in fundamentals causes murders to rise more rapidly than shootings, so the ratio of shootings to murders declines.[5] This is consistent with the Newark data.

In related work, Gaviria (2000) tries to understand an episode of sharply increasing murder (in Colombia from the early 1970s to the early 1990s) and uses a model of strategic complementarity to explain why the increase was so sharp. The sources of strategic complementarity are quite different from those considered here: instead of preemptive escalation, Gaviria emphasizes congestion in law enforcement, gun diffusion, and cultural changes. We do not believe that these latter mechanisms were operative to an important degree in Newark and will explain why in the sequel. Along similar lines, Blumstein, Rivara, and Rosenfeld (2000) look at the rise in youth homicide in the United States in the late 1980s and attribute it to changes in the drug market that led to the diffusion of guns. Their model also (implicitly) emphasizes contagion among gun-bearers and potential murderers. Again, we do not think that gun-diffusion was a particularly important part of the Newark story. Our model of preemption, we believe, is more widely relevant in the sense that preemption could have played a significant role in both the Colombian episode and that in the United States in the 1980s.

The plan of the chapter is the following. We begin by describing the time trend of murders in Newark and in the nation as a whole. Newark's time trend is unusual (though not unique) within the nation but not unusual within New Jersey. This tells us that we cannot simply appeal to national trends to explain what is happening—nor do Newark officials have to wait for national trends to right themselves. Section 9.3 is about the mechanics of murder in Newark. Demographically, the rise is confined almost exclusively to African American men but not confined by time or premises. Gunshot wounds are entirely responsible for the rise but not because there were more shootings. The primary story is that shootings became more lethal, and they did so on many dimensions—more multiple shot incidents, more high-caliber weapons, and more just plain accuracy. Section 9.4 presents our model and shows some of the correspondence with Newark data. Section 9.5 reviews some of the existing empirical literature in economics on murder and shows how our model is consistent with this literature. We concentrate on arrest rates, incarceration, and police strength. At first glance, murder appears nowhere near as responsive to fundamentals as our model indicates it should be in many cities, but we show several reasons why many of the papers we review would miss the responsiveness in situations like Newark's.

Next, in section 9.6, we look at the possible changes in fundamentals that could have driven the increase we observe. Upper-bound estimates on the

---

5. In fact, we show that it is theoretically possible for shootings to decline in absolute terms even as murders rise.

three fundamentals account for a large part of the rise in murder in Newark, and we think that strategic complementarity can explain much of the rest. We review witness intimidation and show how it complements the answers we are proposing. We also show why many New Jersey cities experienced the same rise in murder that Newark did at about the same time. On the other hand, we argue that interjurisdictional spillovers and changes in the drug and gun markets and in the macroeconomy explain little of the trend in Newark. Finally, in section 9.7, we turn to policy. We look at the three most famous incidents of murder reduction (Boston, Richmond, and New York City), critically review the literature on whether the associated programs actually caused the reductions, and draw implications for the city of Newark. The second half of section 9.7 presents our tentative recommendations for Newark, and section 9.8 concludes.

9.2 Murder Trends

Figure 9.1 compares the murder rate in Newark since 1977 with the national rate. To make the two series comparable, we set their 2000 values equal to 100. Both series peak in the 1980 and fall until around 2000. (Newark's trough is actually 1997, but the number of murders in 1997 is only two different from the number in 2000.) The fall in Newark murders is more precipitous than the fall in national murders and does not seem to be interrupted by the crack epidemic, unlike the national series. As expected, murders in Newark fluctuate more than the aggregate for the nation as a whole although the two series track each other quite closely until 2000. After that, the picture changes. The national series stays essentially flat, but Newark rises. By 2005, which is approximately the same as 2006, Newark murders have returned to their late-1980s, early-1990s level: below the peak but substantially above the trough. Newark has also sustained this level for several years.

The increase in murders that Newark experienced is not a national phenomenon or even a national urban phenomenon. Among large cities, only a few are like Newark. Figure 9.2 shows the percentage change in murders for the ten largest cities, and all other cities with at least 100,000 African American residents in 2000. The comparison is between the geometric mean of 1998 and 1999 murders and the geometric mean of 2005 and 2006 murders.[6] Clearly, there was no general increase in murder in big cities during this period. Eleven cities experienced decreases, and only four saw a bigger increase than Newark. Hence, one cannot appeal to national phenomena, or even to national urban phenomena, to explain what has been happening there. In particular, explanations appealing to popular music, cell phone

6. We use two years to smooth out some noise, and we use the geometric mean because we are interested in percentage changes. The 1999 data are not available for Baltimore, and the 1998 data are not available for Cincinnati. In these cases, we use just the one available year (our source is the FBI, Uniform Crime Reports).

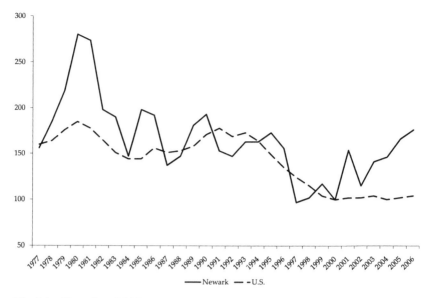

Fig. 9.1 Newark and U.S. murder rates, 1977–2006 (2000 rate = 100)

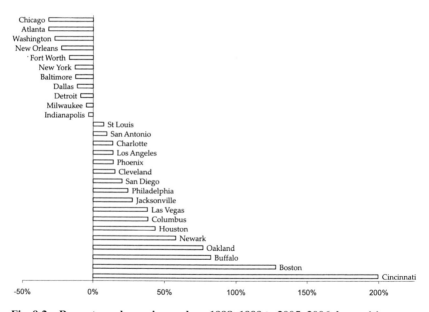

Fig. 9.2 Percentage change in murders, 1998–1999 to 2005–2006, large cities

Table 9.1   **Percentage increase in murders, 1998–1999 to 2005–2006, New Jersey cities**

East Orange	–2.3
Paterson	16.5
Camden	26.7
Newark	57.7
Jersey City	74.4
Elizabeth	100.3
Trenton	115.6
Irvington	155.6

usage, or culture in general are sharply contradicted by figure 9.2. The discordance between Newark and New York City, which is just a few miles away and is part of the same media market, is especially strong.

The rise in murders appears to be a *New Jersey* urban trend, not a national urban trend. Murders in most other New Jersey cities rose as fast as they did in Newark or faster. Murders did not rise quickly in New Jersey outside these cities. Table 9.1 provides the details for all cities with more than 100,000 residents or more than ten murders in most recent years. The numbers involved here are generally subject to a greater proportion of noise than the numbers for the large cities nationally.

The contrast between New Jersey cities and the large cities outside New Jersey is stark. Except for East Orange, where numbers are small and noisy, all cities saw double-digit increases, and four saw increases larger than Newark.[7]

9.3   The Mechanics of Murder in Newark

The modal Newark murder today occurs late at night or early in the morning, with the body discovered on the streets. The weapon is a gun, and the victim is an African American man, usually with some sort of connection to drugs and gangs, but not one that can be readily ascertained or easily articulated. In this section, we show that these are the marginal murders, not just the modal ones, and we argue that they increased mainly because would-be murderers became more lethal in a variety of dimensions. This section is based on Newark Police Department (NPD) homicide and shooting logs and on autopsies by the state medical examiner.

7. New Jersey cities also depart from national trends in other respects. Over the period 1977 to 2006, the national rate dropped from a peak in 1980 to troughs in 2000 and 2004. Camden and Elizabeth had peak years in 1995, well after the national rate and the big cities began to fall, while for Irvington, East Orange, and Trenton, the record high years for murders occurred during the post-2000 upsurge.

Table 9.2   Demographics of murder victims, 2000–2007 (under 12 years of age included in "other")

	Black males			Black females	Hispanic males	Hispanic females	Other
	12–18	19–29	30+				
2000	4	27	9	5	3	2	8
2001	5	33	10	10	12	2	23
2002	2	20	15	6	14	2	8
2003	5	32	22	12	9	0	3
2004	6	43	14	9	19	3	0
2005	10	44	25	6	9	0	4
2006	14	39	30	9	10	0	3
2007	13	40	19	8	6	2	11

9.3.1   Who?

Table 9.2 shows that murder victims in Newark are predominantly African American men, and almost all of the increase in murders has been among this group. (The large number of "other" victims in 2001 primarily reflects incomplete recording.) The overall increase in murder victimization over the period 2000 to 2006 was forty-three, or 107 percent for black males, and four, or 22 percent for everyone else. While murder has increased among all age groups of African American men, the largest increase has been among men over thirty. In contrast with the period studied by Blumstein, Rivara, and Rosenfeld (2000), this is consistent with stories about returning prisoners and inconsistent with stories about wild teenagers.

9.3.2   Why?

The NPD homicide log contains a short description of the motive for many murders (sometimes, of course, nothing is known for sure except that a body was found). Table 9.3 shows how these ascribed motives have evolved as murder has increased.

"Gang" means murders believed to directly further a gang's objectives and not otherwise classified as "drugs" or "disputes." "Disputes" includes murders where the parties are believed to be engaged in a conflict, but the police are unsure about what—it could be drugs, or women, or money owed, or whether the Nets have a stronger backcourt than the Knicks (even if the parties have gang or drug connections). "Disputes" also includes retaliations and murders where the police know what the dispute is about, but it is not drugs or gangs. "Domestic violence" includes traditional spousal murders as well as fatal incidences of child abuse, parent abuse, and fights between unmarried couples, gay or straight, who live together.

Disputes are the second most important motive, and rose considerably. This categorization probably understates their prominence, however,

ble 9.3			Newark murders by motive, 2000–2007				
	Gang	Dispute	Drugs	Domestic violence	Robbery	Unknown	Other	Total
)00	13	3	5	5	2	27	3	58
)01	14	12	7	9	8	41	4	95
)02	14	5	5	4	5	30	4	67
)03	16	10	0	9	4	39	5	83
)04	29	8	12	9	5	19	12	94
)05	24	33	21	4	11	1	4	98
)06	9	36	23	6	11	11	9	105
)07	12	27	29	7	8	15	1	99

because drug, gang, and domestic violence murders are also disputes. Taken together, these categories account for a substantial proportion of murders: 31 to 36 percent over the 2000 to 2003 period, 52 percent in 2004, 80 percent in 2005, 70 percent in 2006, and 76 percent in 2007. They also account for much of the growth in murder, rising by 129 percent if one compares the 2000 to 2001 average to the average in 2005 to 2006. What the large number of murders in the disputes category tell us is that the contentions that end with murder arise over a wide array of matters, not just drugs and gangs. "Disputes" also indicates that most murders happen in a context of *bilateral* animosity: both killer and victim have reason to wish ill for the other, even before the crime occurs.

Studying motives also indicates that murders in Newark do not occur primarily in some simple context like an organized war between two or three well-known gangs. To be sure, gang wars occur, and many victims and perpetrators are members of some sort of gang. But formal gang wars account for only a small proportion of murders. This heterogeneity in motives was also found in Colombia in the 1980s, despite the prominence of drug cartels and paramilitary organizations in accounts of this period. Gaviria summarizes the results of several studies: "Over 80% of all homicides in Colombia are the manifestation of an amorphous violence not directly related to a few major criminal organizations" (2000, 6).

9.3.3   How?

Both the marginal and the modal murder in Newark is accomplished by gunshot. The number of nongunshot homicides shows no trend between 2000 and 2006. Table 9.4 provides the details.

We can examine the reasons why gunshot homicides rose in more detail. Newark police keep detailed records on gun discharge incidents, and so we can investigate how gunshot murders rose. Newark investigators sort gun discharge incidents into three categories. "Shooting-hit" (S_h) is an incident in which a bullet wounds a person, but not fatally. "Shooting-no hit" (S_{nh}) is

Table 9.4   Murders by gunshot wound in Newark, 2000–2007

	Gunshot	Other	Total
2000	41	17	58
2001	57	38	95
2002	49	18	67
2003	39	44	83
2004	74	20	94
2005	85	13	98
2006	91	14	105
2007	84	15	99

an incident in which a bullet is fired at a person, but does not hit him. "Shots fired" (S_f) is an incident in which a gun is fired, and investigators do not know whether the shooter had an intended victim or sought only to send a message of ill will or warning. (Because shooting-no hit is distinguished from shots fired through an assessment of intention by an acknowledged victim or a police officer, many economists might prefer to ignore this distinction because in all these incidents, the shooter does something that increases somebody's probability of death. Accordingly, we perform all analyses in a way that allows readers to choose for themselves how to consider "shots fired.") The record is of *incidents,* not of gun discharges. A single incident may involve many shots. We define "gross gun discharge incidents" as the sum of gun discharge incidents and gunshot homicides (H). Sometimes we will refer to gross gun discharge incidents simply as "shootings" (S).

Our first attempt to understand why gun homicides rose is to decompose the transition from gross gun discharge incidents to gun homicides into several steps of increasing seriousness. By definition:

$$H = S - S_f - S_{nh} - S_h,$$

which yields the following identity:

$$\log H = \log S + \log\left(\frac{S - S_f}{S}\right) + \log\left(\frac{S - S_f - S_{nh}}{S - S_f}\right)$$
$$+ \log\left(\frac{S - S_f - S_{nh} - S_h}{S - S_f - S_{nh}}\right).$$

The second term on the right-hand side we call the *intention ratio* (the proportion of shots with intention to hit someone); the third term the *hit ratio* (the proportion of shots with intention that actually hit); and the third the *kill ratio* (the proportion of shots that hit that killed). Taking changes in these terms over time lets us see how much of the increase in gun homicides was due to more shootings, how much to a higher intention ratio, how much to a higher hit ratio, and how much to a higher kill ratio. Table 9.5 carries out this decomposition.

Table 9.5   **Decomposition of gun homicides in Newark (all magnitudes in natural logs)**

	Shootings	Intention	Hit	Kill	Gun homicides
2000	6.402	−0.451	−0.250	−1.987	3.714
2001	6.337	−0.429	−0.181	−1.684	4.043
2002	6.277	−0.469	−0.156	−1.761	3.892
2003	6.349	−0.378	−0.142	−1.751	4.078
2004	6.486	−0.411	−0.127	−1.644	4.304
2005	6.553	−0.400	−0.146	−1.564	4.443
2006	6.537	−0.357	−0.130	−1.539	4.511
2007	6.308	−.302	−.140	−1.435	4.431
2007–2000	−0.094	0.149	0.110	0.552	0.717
Share (%)	−13	21	15	77	100

Gun homicides increased by more than 70 log points between 2000 and 2007, but shootings actually *decreased* over this period. The rise in homicides cannot, therefore, be attributed simply to more shootings. A higher proportion of shootings had intent to hit someone, and a higher proportion did hit someone, but the major story is that the probability of a murder conditional on a hit rose: 77 percent of the log rise in gun homicides is due to the higher conditional probability of death conditional on being hit by a gunshot. Murders rose mainly because shootings became more deadly, especially shootings where someone was wounded.

Why did shootings become more deadly? Possible answers are (a) potential murderers acquired better weapons with the capacity to fire more frequently, so a higher proportion of gross gun discharge incidents involved multiple shots, (b) potential murderers acquired higher caliber weapons that were more likely to kill when they did not make direct hits, (c) potential murderers acquired more skills, (d) potential murderers exerted more effort in trying to kill their victims (for instance, by standing closer to the victim or driving by more slowly or firing more shots), and (e) emergency medical care became less effective. These reasons have different implications for policy, as we shall see.

We can find out a lot about why shootings became more deadly by combining the information in the NPD shooting and homicide logs with autopsy reports from the state medical examiner. The appendix describes how we do this and the simplifying assumptions that we make. The results (reported in tables 9A.1–9A.3) allow us to attribute the rise in gun homicides above the 1999 to 2003 average to a series of different technical and behavioral changes. They indicate that gunshot homicides increased because of better marksmanship and greater effort, because of higher caliber weapons, because a larger proportion of gross gun discharge incidents involved multiple shots (either because of the presence of semiautomatic weapons or greater willingness of perpetrators to keep firing), and because the number of gross gun discharge incidents increased. Our models are too crude for us to have much confidence in the exact attribution, but each of these factors seems to have made a significant difference. Shootings became more deadly in all dimensions.

Our conclusion that murders in Newark rose in the early twenty-first century because of greater intention to kill is similar to the conclusion that Swersey (1980) arrives at about a rise in murders in Harlem in the early 1970s (see Cook 1983). The phenomenon we are studying is not unique.

For policy and prediction purposes, an important distinction is between irreversible investments—greater skill and better hardware to the extent that resale is difficult—and transitory effort. Irreversible investments make lethality cheaper in the future and, thus, contain the seeds of hysteresis, but transitory effort does not. Our analysis suggests that both irreversible investment and effort contributed to the rise in gun homicide. Hysteresis is going to be a problem in reducing murders but not an insurmountable one. Our next task is to ask why potential murderers in Newark made these investments and undertook this effort. We need a formal model to do this.

9.4   A Model of Preemptive Murder and Endogenous Lethality

In this section, we provide an outline of a model and discuss its properties. For a more complete analysis with formal proofs, we refer the reader to our working paper (O'Flaherty and Sethi 2008).

The model has the following structure. Individuals are heterogeneous with respect to the costs they expect to incur when they commit murder, and these costs are private information. They may arm themselves prior to any dispute or choose to remain unarmed. Two types of weapon are available, with the more lethal weapon also being more costly to procure. Few individuals gain directly from the killing of others, but most would rather kill than be killed. Investments in greater lethality make one safer in the following sense: holding constant the investment made by one's opponent, the likelihood that one is killed is smaller when one's own lethality choice is greater. Investment decisions are characterized by strategic complementarity: greater investments in lethality by others heightens fear and induces individuals to increase their own investments. Multiple equilibria can arise quite naturally in this setting, and small changes in fundamentals can give rise to very sharp (and possibly discontinuous) changes in behavior. At such points of discontinuity, we show that the murder rate and investments in lethality both rise dramatically, while the overall incidence of shooting can decline. This is consistent with the Newark data.

9.4.1   Preliminaries

We have seen that most murders in Newark occur in circumstances where two parties bear some mutual animosity—disputes, gang fights, drug deals gone bad—and each may gain from the other's death. (Ex post, certainly, the victim would have been better off had he killed his murderer first.) For ease of exposition, we assume that the parties to the conflict are ex ante identical (their characteristics drawn from the same probability distribution) although our results do not depend on this assumption of symmetry.

We use the term "interaction" to describe a dispute between two individuals that could potentially result in murder. This term should be interpreted broadly. It could be a fleeting exchange of fire lasting just a few seconds, or an extended feud, with the parties trying to ambush each other at opportune moments. Thus, a single interaction may spawn numerous unilateral gross gun discharge incidents over a period of many months. Indeed, victims almost never have guns in their possession when the police arrive. Sometimes the guns have been stolen after their death, but, in many cases, the victims had access to guns but were not carrying them when they were attacked.

Two types of weapon are available, one more lethal than the other. We define the lethality of a weapon to be the probability that its use in a single shooting incident will kill its target when the target is unarmed. Let α and β denote the two available levels of lethality, with $\beta > \alpha > 0$. Individuals may endow themselves with either one of these weapons or remain unarmed. The cost of acquiring the more lethal weapon is $c > 0$, and the less lethal weapon is assumed for simplicity to be costless.

"Two types of weapon" should not be interpreted literally as an assumption about hardware. The assumption is that there are two ways to try to kill someone, and the more lethal one is more expensive in some way. Thus, the contrast could be between standard guns and semiautomatics that permit more shots in an incident; between small caliber guns and large caliber guns; between being untrained and being a skilled marksman; between firing while driving by at high speed and shooting point blank on the sidewalk; or between making little effort with haphazard fire and cool, concentrated, and close mayhem. The previous section suggested that murderers in Newark raised lethality by making all of these adjustments.

The probability that an individual is killed in any given interaction depends not only on the lethality of his opponent's weapon, but also on the lethality of his own. We assume that at most one individual is killed in any given interaction, and let $p(x, y)$ denote the probability that a player using lethality $x \in \{0, \alpha, \beta\}$ is killed when his opponent uses lethality $y \in \{0, \alpha, \beta\}$. Then $p(0, y) = y$, and $p(x, 0) = 0$ by definition. A plausible assumption is that $p(x, y)$ is decreasing in its first argument and increasing in its second: other things equal, a player is more likely to be killed if his opponent uses a more lethal weapon or if he himself uses a less lethal one. For instance, an individual who shoots first and misses may face return fire, and possession of a less lethal weapon makes this scenario more likely.

An example of an interaction structure that gives rise to a specific function $p(x, y)$ with these properties is the following. Suppose that each of the two players has at most one opportunity to shoot and that they fire in sequence.

Each player faces probability one-half of being the first to shoot. If the first shooter hits his target, the interaction ends. If not, the targeted individual shoots back, at which point the interaction ends regardless of the outcome. In this case,

(1) $$p(x, y) = \frac{1}{2}y + \frac{1}{2}(1 - x)y = \frac{1}{2}y(2 - x).$$

We shall assume throughout this section that $p(x, y)$ is given by equation (1); a more general treatment of the problem may be found in O'Flaherty and Sethi (2008).

If neither player is killed, their payoffs are each normalized to 0. Otherwise, the victim's payoff is $-\delta$, and the shooter's payoff is $-\gamma$. This latter payoff reflects in part the likelihood of arrest and prosecution and the severity of the subsequent sentence. It also reflects the gains he realizes (other than his own survival) from the other party's death, as well as such factors as mood, anger, and the consumption of alcohol or drugs. Suppose that $\delta > 0$ and is commonly known, but γ is private information, drawn (independently across players) from a probability distribution with full support on the real line. Hence, there are some individuals whose disutility γ from successfully shooting someone is negative, even taking into account the risk of incarceration. The distribution function is denoted $F(\gamma)$, and the corresponding density function is $f(\gamma)$.

If a player with cost γ chooses lethality x and is confronted by someone choosing lethality y, his payoff is

(2) $$\pi_{xy}(\gamma) = -p(x, y)\delta - p(y, x)\gamma.$$

This is the payoff from the interaction itself and does not include the cost c that is incurred if $x = \beta$. Given c, $F(\gamma)$, and $p(x, y)$, equation (2) defines a Bayesian game in which each player chooses an action $x \in \{0, \alpha, \beta\}$ contingent on the value of his (privately observed) cost γ. Let $s(\gamma)$ denote an individual's strategy, which identifies with each value of γ a level of lethality $x \in \{0, \alpha, \beta\}$.

Suppose that a player believes that his opponent will use lethality α with probability λ, and lethality β with probability μ, where $\lambda + \mu \leq 1$. Then the expected payoff from choosing action x is

$$\pi_x(\gamma) = -(1 - \lambda - \mu)\gamma x - \lambda[p(x, \alpha)\delta + p(\alpha, x)\gamma]$$
$$- \mu[p(x, \beta)\delta + p(\beta, x)\gamma].$$

A strategy $s^*(\gamma)$ corresponds to a symmetric Bayes-Nash equilibrium if the beliefs (λ, μ) of the players are correct conditional on the fact that they both adopt $s^*(\gamma)$, and $s^*(\gamma)$ is a best response to those beliefs (taking account of the cost c if lethality β is chosen).

When $p(x, y)$ is given by equation (1), it can be shown that there exists at least one symmetric equilibrium s^* (γ). Furthermore, any such equilibrium has the following partitional structure: the lowest cost individuals choose lethality β, the highest cost individuals remain unarmed, and a set of individuals with intermediate costs choose lethality α. Formally, there exist cost thresholds γ_1 and γ_2 such that $\gamma_1 < \gamma_2$ and s^* (γ) = β for $\gamma < \gamma_1$, s^* (γ) = α for $\gamma \in$ (γ_1, γ_2), and s^* (γ) = 0 for $\gamma > \gamma_2$. In order to see how these thresholds vary with the values of the underlying parameters, let $\omega = \lambda\alpha + \mu\beta$ denote the likelihood of being killed conditional on being unarmed, and let $c' = c/(\beta - \alpha)$ denote the cost of switching from α to β normalized by the resulting increase in lethality. Then the thresholds γ_1 and γ_2 can be expressed as simple functions of ω and c' as follows:

(3)
$$\gamma_1 = \frac{\delta\omega - 2c'}{2 - \omega} \text{ and } \gamma_2 = \frac{\delta\omega}{2 - \omega}.$$

In any interaction, the likelihood of a murder is ω (2 – ω), the expected value of gun discharges is ($\lambda + \mu$) (2 – ω), and the ratio of murders to gun discharges is, therefore, $\omega/(\lambda + \mu)$.

We shall refer to ω as the level of *danger*. One can also think of ω as the level of "tension," to use the term often used by police to describe the situation that prevails before murders. When people are tense, they jump to respond to any provocation or danger, real or imagined. Tension begets murders, and murders, in turn, raise tension. In this sense, our model can be interpreted as an analysis of equilibrium tension.

Because ω is endogenously determined, equation (3) is consistent with the occurrence of multiple equilibria. However, because ω uniquely determines the thresholds γ_1 and γ_2, it also uniquely determines the probabilities λ and μ with which the levels of lethality α and β are used. Hence, there can be at most one equilibrium corresponding to any given value of equilibrium danger ω. We next explore conditions under which multiple equilibria exist.

9.4.2   Multiplicity of Equilibriums

One of the key questions here is the manner in which changes in the distribution of costs $F(\gamma)$ affect the set of equilibria. To this end, we introduce a shift parameter a and write the distribution of costs as $F(\gamma, a)$. We adopt the convention that for any pair a, a' satisfying $a > a'$, we have $F(\gamma, a') > F(\gamma, a)$. That is, a decrease in a shifts the distribution to the left, corresponding to an overall decline in the expected costs of attempted murder (or an increase in the expected gains, not including survival). Such a shift could be induced, for instance, by a decline in the effectiveness of the criminal justice system.

The following example illustrates the possibility that a small decline in a can cause large and discontinuous changes in the level of lethality chosen and in the murder rate.

EXAMPLE 1. Suppose that $\alpha = 0.2$, $\beta = 0.6$, $\delta = 20$, $c = 1$, $p(x, y) = y(2 - x)/2$, and γ is normally distributed with variance 1 and mean a. If $a = 1.03$, there exist three equilibria with levels of danger $\omega = 0.18$, $\omega = 0.23$, and $\omega = 0.60$, respectively. If $a = 1.02$, however, there is a unique equilibrium with $\omega = 0.60$.

This example illustrates that a small shift in the cost distribution can result in a large, discontinuous change in equilibrium danger. Figure 9.3 shows how the entire set of equilibria varies with a over the range [0.9, 1.4] for the specification used in Example 1. (Note that the horizontal axis is reversed.) Suppose that one begins on the lower arm of the equilibrium set, and a declines to the point at which equilibrium becomes unique. Such a decline results in an upward jump in the murder rate that can be very difficult to reverse. Even if the value of a were restored to its original magnitude, the existence of multiple equilibriums when a is large implies that the society may be trapped in a state with a high level of danger, lethality, and killing. Declines in the murder rate, if they are to be sustainable, require swift and substantial reductions in the level of fear.

It is useful to see what happens at the point of discontinuity to the level of danger ω, the murder rate, gross gun discharge incidents, the proportion λ using lethality α, the proportion μ using lethality β, and the proportion $1 - \lambda - \mu$ who remain unarmed. These shifts are depicted in figure 9.4. As the threshold value of a is crossed, the level of danger jumps up discontinuously as both the unarmed and the individuals using lethality α switch to the higher lethality β. The use of the less lethal weapon collapses to practically zero, as does the proportion of the population who choose to remain unarmed. The murder rate rises discontinuously, but total gun discharges *decline*. This is because the higher level of lethality results in lower victim survival and, hence, a reduced likelihood of a retaliatory strike. More generally, the effect of a rise in a on shootings is theoretically ambiguous.

Notice that even before the point of discontinuity is reached, the level of danger and the rate of lethality begin to rise at an increasing rate. As the environment becomes more dangerous, more parties switch to higher lethality, which, in turn, makes the world more dangerous. Danger is increasing not only because there are more violent people, but also because people who were formerly nonviolent are switching to violence. The number of murders also grows more quickly, but the number of gross gun discharge incidents does not increase as rapidly as the number of murders. This is because greater lethality makes it more likely that feuds will end quickly. This is consistent with the Newark experience.

9.4.3   The Murder Multiplier

Many analyses of murder (and other crimes) do not take game-theoretic considerations into account. They work with a single-actor decision problem

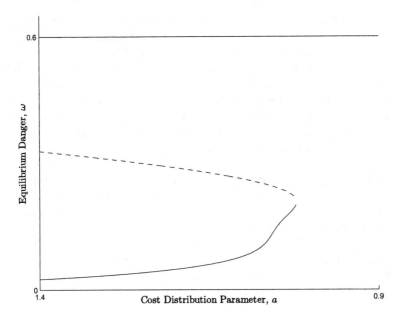

Fig. 9.3   Effects of changes in a on the set of equilibria

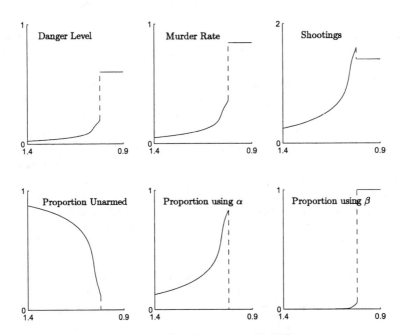

Fig. 9.4   Equilibrium danger, murder, shootings, and lethality

and ask what would make a person viewed in isolation more or less likely to commit murder. To link our approach to that literature, we ask what levels of shooting would prevail if no party had a preemption motive.

This is equivalent to asking what level of lethality would be chosen by an actor who was certain that his opponent was unarmed. Using equation (2), such an individual would choose lethality 0 if $\gamma > 0$, and lethality β if $\gamma < -c'$. If $0 > \gamma > -c'$, then lethality α is chosen. Accordingly, we define autonomous shooting probabilities as follows: $\tilde{\lambda} = F(0) - F(-c')$, and $\tilde{\mu} = F(-c')$. The autonomous level of danger is then $\tilde{\omega} = \alpha\tilde{\lambda} + \beta\tilde{\mu}$.

The analogy is with autonomous expenditure in the simple Keynesian model of goods market equilibrium. In that model, equilibrium expenditure is greater than autonomous expenditure because of strategic complementarity: more autonomous spending by the government, say, induces consumers to spend more, which induces other consumers to spend more, and so on. The ratio of equilibrium to autonomous expenditure is the multiplier. In our model, there is a murder multiplier that also operates through strategic complementarity, and makes equilibrium murders greater than autonomous murders. More precisely, we can prove that the autonomous shooting probability $\tilde{\lambda} + \tilde{\mu}$ is always less than the shooting probability in *any* equilibrium, and if the cost of victimization δ is sufficiently high, then the autonomous level of danger $\tilde{\omega}$ is always less than any equilibrium level of danger. It follows that autonomous murder is less than equilibrium murder.

More formally, consider any equilibrium, and let (λ^*, μ^*) denote the equilibrium rates of use of α and β weapons, respectively, and ω^* the corresponding level of danger. Then it can be shown that (a) $\lambda^* + \mu^* > \tilde{\lambda} + \tilde{\mu}$, and (b) if $\delta \geq c'$, then $\omega^* > \tilde{\omega}$. The condition $\delta \geq c'$ is unrestrictive, requiring only that the cost of murder victimization exceed the unit cost of greater lethality. Moreover, because the murder rate is increasing in the level of danger, equilibrium murders exceed autonomous murders when this condition is met.

Somewhat surprisingly, the preemptive motive can actually reduce murders relative to the decision-theoretic benchmark if δ is sufficiently small. The reason is that the game theoretic equilibrium takes into account the possibility that if one is shot before one can shoot, the lethality of one's weapon becomes irrelevant, and a costly investment in greater lethality is wasted. Possession of a more lethal weapon does make it less likely that one is shot, but when δ is small, this provides a negligible incentive to invest.

9.4.4   Comparative Statics

The preceding example shows that a decline in a can cause the equilibrium set to change in a manner that results in discontinuous increases in lethality and danger. Similar effects can arise as a result of changes in other parameters of the model. Specifically, it can be shown that there exists a strictly increasing function $\varphi : [0, \beta] \rightarrow [0, \beta]$ such $\omega = \varphi(\omega)$ if and only if ω is an

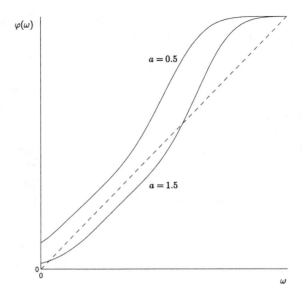

Fig. 9.5   The function $\varphi(\omega)$ for two values of a

equilibrium level of danger. The function $\varphi(\omega)$ is decreasing in a and c and increasing in β and δ.

The function $\varphi(\omega)$ may be viewed as a best response function: if individuals choose optimal strategies based on the belief that the level of danger is ω, then the realized level of danger will be $\varphi(\omega)$. The fact that optimal strategies depend only on ω (and not on the underlying values of λ and μ) makes this case especially tractable. The function $\varphi(\omega)$ is given by

(4) $$\varphi(\omega) = \alpha F\left(\frac{\delta\omega}{2-\omega}\right) + (\beta - \alpha) F\left(\frac{\delta\omega - 2c'}{2-\omega}\right).$$

Note that by definition, the level of autonomous danger is $\tilde{\omega} = \varphi(0)$.

As an example, suppose that γ is normally distributed with mean a and variance 1, and all parameter values are as in Example 1. Figure 9.5 shows $\varphi(\omega)$ for two different values of a. When $a = 1.5$, there are three equilibria. Declines in a (which correspond to a shift to the left in the cost function) shift $\varphi(\omega)$ upward. At some value of a, the equilibrium set contracts in size, and there is a unique equilibrium with a high level of danger.

In general, any change in the primitives of the model that causes the function $\varphi(\omega)$ to shift upward can result in the kind of effect identified in figure 9.5, with discontinuous changes in equilibrium danger and the lethality and extent of weapon use. A discontinuous rise in equilibrium danger can be triggered by (a) a shift to the left in the net penalty distribution $F(\gamma)$, (b) a decline in the cost of high lethality c, (c) an increase in the disutility of victimization δ, or (d) an increase in the highest level of feasible lethality β. These effects are all intuitive in sign, given the importance of the preemptive motive for murder. In each case, a small parameter shift can give rise to a cascade of expectations resulting in sharp increases in danger. While the initial (disequilibrium) effect of the change may be small, individual responses to the change induce even greater responses from others.

The effect on equilibrium danger of increases in α are ambiguous. On the one hand, murders increase because those choosing lethality α are more likely to strike their targets. On the other hand, the narrowing of the gap between β and α raises the effective price of lethality c' and induces fewer individuals to adopt the more lethal weapon. Hence, somewhat paradoxically, a rise in the lethality of some weapons, holding constant the lethality of others, can result in reduced equilibrium danger.

To summarize, the sharp increase in murder rates could have been triggered by one or more of the following: the availability of weapons of greater lethality or lower cost, a greater aversion to being victimized (which encourages preemptive first strikes), or a general decline in the expected penalties faced by offenders. The key point is that a small change in any of these parameters can give rise to sharp, discontinuous changes in murder rates due to the cascading effect of expectations coupled with the preemptive motive for killing.

9.4.5   Peaceable Kingdoms and War Zones

In most of the United States most of the time, murder is a rare event. A non-Hispanic white woman was about 3.7 times as likely to die from an unintentional fall in 2002 as to be murdered (Minino et al. 2006, table 9). How can we account for this fact in our model? The basic reasons why murder is rare most of the time are that the autonomous level of murder is low and that at the autonomous level of murder, few people are on the margin. For most people most of the time, there is not much to be gained from murdering someone, compared with the psychic and legal penalties that are likely to follow. If $\tilde{\omega} = \varphi(0)$ is very small and the $\varphi(\omega)$ curve is very flat, then there will be a stable internal equilibrium very close to 0 (see figure 9.5).

Note that from equation (4), we have

$$\varphi'(\omega) = \frac{2}{(2 - \omega)^2} \left[\alpha\delta f(\gamma_1) + (\beta - \alpha)(\delta - c')f(\gamma_2)\right].$$

If $f(\gamma_1)$ and $f(\gamma_2)$ are both very small because almost no one is on the margin between becoming armed and remaining unarmed, then the $\varphi(\omega)$ curve will be very flat, and there will be a stable equilibrium very close to $\tilde{\omega}$. This depends both on the intercept $\tilde{\omega}$ and the slope $\varphi'(\omega)$ being small. The first depends on $F(0)$ and $F(-c')$ being small; the second on $f(0)$ and $f(-c')$ and the density function in their respective neighborhoods being small. Both conditions are probably often met for many modern American communities. We call such communities *peaceable kingdoms*. In such communities, comparative statics on $\tilde{\omega}$ are a good approximation to comparative statics on ω^*, and the standard single-actor analysis is not especially misleading. Thus, in most times and places, ignoring preemption is not a serious error.

When the level of danger is great, even at a stable internal equilibrium, the multiplier is large, and comparative statics are different from comparative statics on $\tilde{\omega}$. Effects usually work in the same direction, but they are magnified. We call communities with a lot of danger and a large multiplier *war zones.*

We can show, in fact, that even at stable internal equilibria, as danger grows, the effects of parameter changes grow infinitely large, even before a discontinuous jump to a new equilibrium. To see this, we introduce a shift parameter q and write the best response function as $\varphi(\omega, q)$. Assume that the derivative $\varphi_2(\omega, q)$ is positive and bounded away from 0 for all ω and q. Define

$$\hat{\omega}(q) = \inf \{\omega \mid \omega = \varphi(\omega, q)\}.$$

This is the lowest level of danger consistent with equilibrium for any given q. Suppose that for all q in some closed set $[\bar{q}, \hat{q}]$, we have $\hat{\omega}(q) < \beta$, and $\hat{\omega}(q)$ has a discontinuity at $\hat{q}$. Then $\lim_{q \to \hat{q}^-} \hat{\omega}'(q) = \infty$. Hence, small changes in underlying parameters can give rise to very large effects on equilibrium danger (and, hence, equilibrium murder) in places that are very violent. War zones are like this, and peaceable kingdoms are not.

9.4.6   Dynamics

What happens when this game is played repeatedly? A fully developed intertemporal model is clearly beyond the scope of this chapter, but we can point in some general directions. If the cost required to produce lethality is an irreversible investment, then lethality produced in one period reduces the cost of lethality in subsequent periods. Lower cost of lethality in subsequent periods implies more murders in subsequent periods. So if irreversible investments are what produce lethality, murders today increase murders tomorrow, ceteris paribus. Examples of irreversible investments include skilled marksmanship and the transaction costs involved in acquiring guns.[8]

This prediction is based on a model of myopic decision making, but the basic conclusion should be robust. Consider a rational expectations world and a surprise change in fundamentals in period t that increases equilibrium murder and lethality. The murder shock raises irreversible investments in period t, and so raises murder in period $t + 1$, no matter what period $t + 1$ fundamentals are. Seen from period $t - 1$, expected murders are higher in

---

8. The relevant cost of using a gun one already owns is the opportunity cost, the money one could make selling or renting it to someone else. But because illegal gun markets have huge transaction costs, this is usually well below the acquisition cost. See Cook et al. (2005).

period $t + 1$ than if the period t shock had never occurred. That is, expected $t + 1$ murders conditional on a positive murder shock in period t are greater than unconditional expected $t + 1$ murders. Comparing two communities with the same fundamentals and different histories, the community with more murders in the past will have more murders today.

Selection of agents may also affect intertemporal dynamics. Suppose that net murder costs γ are positively correlated over time within individuals: people with low net costs today are likely to have low net costs tomorrow. Within any population, those with higher γ are more likely to be murdered. Under weak conditions, the distribution of γ tomorrow will be stochastically dominated by the distribution today. The population will grow more dangerous over time as less dangerous individuals are weeded out. On the other hand, incarceration could work in the opposite direction.

9.5   Prediction Biases

Criminologists and economists have produced an impressive empirical literature on homicide. This literature can help us understand what set off the rise in Newark murders and what policies are likely to reverse this trend. The general message of this literature is that fundamentals and incentives matter: police, arrest rates, and incarceration usually reduce murder. Not every paper finds that every incentive matters, but many find that these standard variables reduce murder. Murder is not unpredictable.

Our model of preemptive murder, however, indicates that some of the estimates of the size of these effects are likely to be too low for Newark in this decade. There are two general reasons. First, responses to policies are likely to be greater in situations where the level of danger is high than in situations where the level of danger is low. An equation fitted on a data set in which most communities have small murder rates will find much smaller average responses than prevail in communities where danger is high. Studies that report on average responsiveness are likely to underestimate the size of responses in places like Newark. We call this problem *nonlinearity prediction bias.*

Second, studies that define narrowly the type of murders that a particular policy is supposed to affect may underestimate the policy's effect for two reasons. They may miss murders outside the narrow circle that they draw that were really affected by the policy, and, worse, they may use these murders that should be inside the circle as a comparison group. For example, suppose we want to study a particular policy targeted at husbands who kill their wives. What happens if we look only at murders committed by husbands? Our preemption model tells us that there is a first-order bias in this research strategy because if husbands become less likely to kill wives, wives will be less likely to kill husbands. The proper procedure looks at both kinds of spousal murders. The problem is exacerbated if the study uses murders of husbands by wives as a control group. We call this problem *narrow-estimation bias.*

We begin with the arrest rate because it is the most traditional deterrence variable and possibly a major part of the Newark story. Levitt (1998) uses panel data for fifty-nine large cities for 1970 to 1992 to find the effect of arrest rates on various crimes. For most crimes, he finds significant effects. But for murder, although some of his equations have significant coefficients, his final preferred conclusion has murder arrests associated with a tiny, insignificant rise in murders.

More recent papers show larger effects. Corman and Mocan (2005) use monthly data for New York City for the period 1974 to 1999. They used lagged arrests to avoid endogeneity problems and find significant negative effects comparable to an elasticity of –0.4. In an earlier paper, Corman and Mocan (2000) use data for a slightly different period but still find approximately the same elasticity.

Finally, Dezhbaksh, Rubin, and Shepherd (2003) use panel data for 3,054 counties for the period 1977 to 1996. They estimate a system of equations by two-stage least squares (2SLS). The arrest rate is endogenous but enters into the murder equation. They find a large and significant negative effect. Because most counties most of the time are peaceable kingdoms, these estimates are likely to be affected by nonlinearity prediction bias.

The effects of prison population are also included in many studies. Many of these, especially those using state or state-level data found no effect on murder. Zimring and Hawkins (1995) looked at a California time series in the 1980s, and Marvell and Moody (1994) used a panel of states. Katz, Levitt, and Shustorovich (2003) also use state panel data for 1950 to 1990; they do not find a significant effect of prisoners per capita on murder, but they do find that states with more noisome prison conditions, as proxied by prisoner deaths, have fewer murders.

Levitt (1996) is the most famous study of the effect of prison population on crime. With state data, he uses court-ordered releases as an instrument and finds significant effects (fewer prisoners, more crime) for most index crimes, but not for murder. State authorities may have been clever enough to preclude the release of would-be murderers when they faced these orders. More plausibly, remember that in war zones, the threshold γ at which murder is committed is higher than in peaceable kingdoms. (This always holds for the threshold for attempting murder with α-lethality and usually holds for the threshold for attempting murder with β-lethality.) Many marginal prisoners may often be between these two thresholds—they are neither homicidal maniacs (who would stay in prison almost always) nor choirboys (who would not be in prison in the first place). Thus, reductions in prison population would raise murders in war zones but not in peaceable kingdoms. Because most communities are peaceable kingdoms, Levitt's study could have missed the effect in war zones.

On the other hand, researchers using national data have found effects of prison population on murder. Bowker (1981) and Cohen and Land (1987) found modest effects. Devine, Sheley, and Smith (1988) and Marvell and

Moody (1997) use national time series for very long periods and find elasticities greater than one in absolute value. The latter paper argues that ordinary least squares (OLS) is appropriate because murderers are a small part of prison population and shows that murder does not Granger-cause prison population.

Our model suggests a reason why national time series data find large effects for prison population and state-level panels do not. Suppose most states are peaceable kingdoms and a few are not, but a large proportion of murders take place in the few that are not. Prisoners have a minuscule effect in peaceable kingdoms but a large effect in war zones. Then national data, being aggregates, are dominated by the war-zone effects, while the state panels are dominated by the peaceable kingdom effects. (Marvell and Moody [1997] try to explain the difference by interstate migration.)

Corman and Mocan (2005) also look at prison population in their analysis of New York City. Their explanatory variable is total prisoners from New York City, and they find a significant though small coefficient of –.08. Raphael and Stoll (2004) also use state panel data, but they consider prisoner releases and prisoner commitments separately. For murder, they find that the effect of a prisoner release is very close to the effect of a prisoner commitment but opposite in sign. Thus, changes in murder should depend approximately on changes in prison population, however they occur. Their estimates imply that a reduction of 1,000 in prison population, lagged a year, raises murders by between eleven and twenty-eight.

A number of papers also have results about police strength. Levitt (2002) uses a panel of 122 cities from 1975 to 1995. In his most convincing version, he uses firefighters as an instrument for police officers. He finds a significant elasticity of –0.9, which is larger than the elasticity of any other crime except motor vehicle theft. Dezhbaksh, Rubin, and Shepherd (2003) use police expenditures in their 2SLS system and find an indirect effect on murder but do not report the magnitude. On the other hand, Corman and Mocan (2000, 2005) in both of their papers include police strength as an explanatory variable, but it does not have a significant effect on murder in either. Dezhbaksh and Shepherd (2006) also found no significant impact of police expenditures on murder. They used a panel of states for the period 1960 to 2000. Because most police do not work on homicides, these negative results may not be surprising. Levitt believes his instrumental variable picks up cities with a culture that promotes spending on public safety; such a culture may produce large investments in homicide squads and training, even holding the total size of the police force constant. So the instrument may have more information about how much effort is devoted to murder than day-to-day changes in total police strength.

Finally, we should note that Glaeser and Sacerdote (1996) is a paper directly related to ours in that it tries explain the huge intertemporal and interspatial variance of crime rates by appealing to social interactions. They conclude, however, that the amount of social interaction is "almost negligible in murder and rape" although it is much greater for petty property crimes. Our fundamental difference with Glaeser and Sacerdote is how they measure social interactions. Their model has two types of people: those who can be influenced to commit crime by whether their neighbors commit crime and those who cannot. (Influence in their model is contagion or imitation, not self-protection as in our model.) Their measure of social interaction is the proportion of people in the entire population who can be influenced in the average jurisdiction. In a sense, their findings are a confirmation of our assertions about peaceable kingdoms. Perhaps it would be more relevant for murder to measure social interactions by the proportion of people who can be influenced relative to the proportion committing the crime, not the entire population.

9.6   What happened in Newark?

Our story is simple: murders rose in Newark because criminal justice became less effective in several dimensions more or less simultaneously, and this set off a cycle where more people began killing for their own safety. The rise in murders was larger than the empirical literature predicts, but nonlinearity prediction bias could be at work. Several other factors, such as falling conviction rates and state prison segregation policies may also have mattered.

In this section, we will first argue that the model of preemption and increasing lethality that we developed in section 9.4 is consistent with Newark's experience. Then we document the deterioration of criminal justice and discuss how much of an increase in murder this may have caused. Finally, we look at some other possible explanations.

9.6.1   Congruence with the Preemption Model

The obvious testable implication of the preemption model is that the ratio of murders to gross gun discharge incidents should rise as murders rise. Clearly, this has been the case in Newark. Recall that the model predicts greater lethality even if the rise in murders is caused by deteriorating deterrence or a toughening of the population distribution. The type of guns that potential murderers use can change even if the relative price and availability of high quality guns stays the same.

An easy extension of the model to a world where people have many different ways, places, and times to kill each other also generates some testable propositions. First, suppose that agents have many different ways in which they can increase lethality, instead of just one. Then an increase in murder and lethality driven by deterrence deterioration is likely to use all available means of lethality enhancement—partly because of heterogeneity among agents and partly because of diminishing marginal returns. Again, that is what we see happening in Newark.

Second, suppose that agents have many different times and places at which to try to kill their victims. Then we would expect to see the increase in gross gun discharge incidents spread fairly uniformly over times and places—not only because of heterogeneity and diminishing marginal returns, but also because stalking a victim has elements of a zero-sum two-person game where randomization is often part of the optimal equilibrium strategy. Lethality should rise everywhere at more or less the same rate, too. This, too, is consistent with what we see in Newark.

On the other hand, preemption effects work only within a social or business network. If I have no connection with you, I don't gain from killing you, and I don't fear you will kill me. Disputes presume some engagement. Thus, the preemption model is consistent with the rise in murder and lethality being confined to a single demographic group, African American men.

Many other stories about the rise in homicide are not consistent with these facts. For instance, if homicide rose because a particular type of weapon became cheaper or more easily available or better, we would not see an increase in lethality in all dimensions, but we would see a rise across all demographic groups. Worse emergency medicine would also be seen as a rise in murder across all demographic groups.

9.6.2   Arrest Rates

The ratio of arrests for murder to murders declined precipitously in Essex County, falling from 0.811 in 1998 to 0.462 in 2005. Arrests per murder is a crude indicator for the clearance rate because several individuals are sometimes arrested for one murder, because one individual may be arrested for several murders, and because arrests may not occur during the same year in which a murder is recorded. But it is the most widely available measure. Nationally, the ratio is currently close to one.

Table 9.6 shows how the arrest-murder ratio declined in Essex County while it remained fairly stable in the rest of New Jersey, in the aggregate.

What does this fall in arrest rates tell us about changes in murder? From 2000 to 2006, the Essex arrest rate fell 31 percent. If we use Corman and Mocan's –0.4 elasticity, the implication is a 12 percent increase in murders. If we think of the deterrent effect of an arrest as acting with a one-year lag, then the relevant comparison is between 1999 and 2005: a 42 percent decrease in the arrest rate, which implies a 17 percent murder rise. Dezhbaksh, Rubin, and Shepherd (2003) use linear specifications, not logarithmic. Their results imply two to five more murders using the contemporaneous approach, three to seven more using the lagged approach. The tops of these ranges are close to the respective Corman-Mocan implications.

These falling arrest rates may have been exacerbated by falling conviction rates. The Essex prosecutor's office during this period developed a flagrant reputation for failing to win convictions in homicide cases (Kleinknecht and Schuppe 2006). If the conviction rates were falling after 2000, then it would probably have contributed to the rise in murder. But we do not know whether

Table 9.6   Arrest/murder ratio: Essex County and rest of state, 1998–2006

	Essex County	Rest of state
1998	0.811	0.847
1999	0.738	0.933
2000	0.602	0.908
2001	0.592	0.866
2002	0.477	0.872
2003	0.652	0.879
2004	0.463	0.816
2005	0.426	0.801
2006	0.418	0.917

Source: New Jersey State Police.

it was rising or falling. Moreover, econometric studies of conviction rates (as opposed to arrest rates) are rare.

The decrease in arrest rates appears to be a simple case of declining productivity, not the congestion in law enforcement that Gaviria (2000) describes in Colombia and Sah (1991) explains theoretically. (Freeman, Grogger, and Sonstelie [1996] also use a variant of the Sah model to explain interjurisdictional differences in crime.) There were actually fewer murder arrests in Essex County in 2005 than there were in 1999.

Murder, moreover, is only one piece of law enforcement agencies' workload. A rise in murder alone should not overwhelm these agencies because they can redirect resources from other activities. Thus, congestion is a serious problem only if most major crimes rise together (as they did in Colombia). But in Newark, most other crime was falling during this period. Reported robbery and aggravated assault fell by 30 percent between 2000 and 2006, and major property crime fell by a smaller percentage. This fall in other crime does not appear to be the result of improved police performance or enhanced deterrence; resources were not being sucked away from murder to reduce these other crimes. The arrest-offense ratio for these other crimes fell in Essex County even though the number of crimes decreased. Table 9.7 provides the details. In summary, law enforcement agencies were not overwhelmed; the arrest-offense ratio for murder did not fall because of congestion.

9.6.3   Prisoners

After rising steadily from 4,515 in 1994 to a high of 6,241 in 1999, the number of state prisoners originally sentenced from Essex County fell sharply to 4,408 by 2006. The decline was 29.4 percent from January 1999 to January 2006 and 15.4 percent from January 2001 to January 2006. Table 9.8 provides details and comparisons with other counties.

As we saw in the last section, studies differ widely on the effect of pris-

Table 9.7   Change in other serious crime and in arrest rates, 2000 and 2006

	Newark (% change in no. of offences)	Essex County arrest rates	
		2000	2006
Robbery	−31.2	0.214	0.207
Aggravated assault	−30.0	0.577	0.439
Burglary	−28.0	0.147	0.131
Motor vehicle theft	−6.3	0.013	0.006

Source: New Jersey State Police.

Table 9.8   **New Jersey state prison population by county, 1994–2006, selected years (no. of prisoners sentenced from selected counties; population in early January)**

	Essex	Hudson	Union	Passaic	Mercer	Camden
2001	5209	2695	2327	2218	1197	3874
2003	4830	2455	2211	2179	1275	3477
2004	4789	2518	2268	2264	1395	3457
2005	4607	2388	2176	2204	1390	3404
2006	4408	2269	2238	2294	1345	3580
Change 2001–2006 (%)	−15.4	−15.8	−3.8	+3.4	+12.4	−7.6

Source: New Jersey Department of Corrections, Web site and personal communication.

oners on murder. Some studies find no effect, and Corman-Mocan's –0.08 elasticity implies only a 1.2 percent rise in murders. But the results of Devine, Sheley, and Smith (1988) and Marvell and Moody (1997) imply roughly a 20 percent murder increase in Essex County from 2000 to 2005. The results of Raphael and Stoll (2004) are consistent with those of Marvell and Moody and, in fact, imply a slightly larger increase in murder.

9.6.4   Police

According to the Federal Bureau of Investigation (FBI) Uniform Crime Reports, the number of police officers in Newark fell by 8.0 percent from October 31, 2000 to October 31, 2006. (Counting police officers is not an exact science, but this is the data source that Levitt used.) Levitt's (2002) results imply that this fall in police strength should have raised murders in Newark by 7.2 percent. However, several extenuating factors imply that policing in Newark may have contributed more to the rise in murders than Levitt's average indicates. During this period, the physical facilities of the NPD fell into severe disrepair, normal hours of work decreased, and the command structure went through several upheavals.

9.6.5   Accounting for the Increase in Murder

Taking upper bounds of these three ranges implies a predicted 51 percent rise in murders from 2000 to 2006; that is, an increase from fifty-nine to eighty-nine. Actual murders in 2006 were 105. The difference of sixteen is not statistically significant.[9] We might be tempted to say that these three changes—fewer arrests, fewer prisoners, fewer police—account for the whole rise in murders. Such a conclusion would be strained, however. The bottom of the ranges predict only about sixty-seven murders in 2006, not eighty-nine. The Marvell and Moody paper on prison population is much weaker than the Levitt paper on the usual criteria. And the three changes are not necessarily independent so that using them to compound each other is questionable. Instead, we interpret the upper bound accounting exercise as a demonstration that in combination with these three factors the amount of nonlinearity prediction bias does not need to be unreasonably large to account for most of the rise in murder. These three factors and a modest amount of strategic complementarity do a pretty good job of explaining what happened in Newark.

9.6.6   Other New Jersey Cities

A great deal of the change in North Jersey murders can be explained by the three fundamentals of arrests, prisoners, and police. These worsened everywhere but Paterson, and murders rose substantially everywhere but Paterson. The numbers of murders in other cities is so small, however, that noise makes comparisons unreliable.

9.6.7   Witness Intimidation

Witness intimidation is a major problem in Newark that contributes to the low arrest and conviction rates. It also contributes to murder directly because some murders are committed to keep witnesses from testifying. However, there are no measures of witness intimidation, and so it is impossible to tell whether it was increasing or decreasing during the period we are studying.

Witness intimidation has important elements of strategic complementarity. If several witnesses see a crime, and threats are more likely to be carried out if the defendant is acquitted, then the fewer witnesses testify, the greater the cost for any remaining witness to testify. Multiple equilibria are possible, including equilibria with codes of silence. O'Flaherty and Sethi (2010) provide a detailed analysis of witness intimidation.

---

9. The methods developed by Fisz (1955) and Detre and White (1970) indicate that the analog of a t-statistic for the null hypothesis that Poisson variables of 89 and 105 are drawn from the same distribution is slightly less than 1.15. Murders in Newark, however, are a stuttering Poisson process because sometimes multiple murder incidents occur. Considering 89 and 105 as stuttering Poisson variables would reduce the t-statistic further.

9.6.8   Drugs

Many murderers and murder victims are or were engaged in the illicit drug business, either as buyers or sellers or both. The reasons for this association between drugs and murder are well known: legal means of dispute resolution are not available to this business; markets are imperfect, and so deaths of particular individuals can present large and persistent profit opportunities for other individuals; cooperation with law enforcement can be very harmful to an enterprise, and so assassination of those who cooperate can be very profitable; and the marginal penalty for murder is small for many people in this business (the prospect of a life sentence for murder is less intimidating for a person who stands a very good chance of soon being sentenced to twenty years as a drug dealer than it is for someone who has committed no other crimes). Selection may also play a role as naturally vicious people may have a comparative advantage in this industry.

But nothing indicates that changes in illicit drug markets played a major role in the rise in murder in Newark. Generally, two sorts of changes could increase murders. First, an outward shift of the demand curve could increase the quantity of drugs sold and so raise the number of people involved in the industry. Tables 9.9 and 9.10 show no rise in the consumption of illicit drugs, at least up until the middle of the period. (More recent information is unavailable.)

Second, an increase in the difference between retail and wholesale prices would reflect a larger sum of money being allocated to industry employment and to ex post profits. More money would be involved in distributing the same quantity of drugs, and that money could give rise to more murders. Becker, Murphy, and Grossman (2006) argue that greater enforcement efforts increase this difference and Miron (1999, 2001) shows that enforcement efforts Granger-cause murders in a long U.S. time series and in a cross-section of nations. Table 9.11 shows estimated prices for major illicit drugs in New Jersey between 2000 and 2006. In North Jersey, the wholesale-retail markup fell on average. This should have reduced murders. The wholesale-retail markup rose in South Jersey; this may be why murders rose in Camden more than the changes in arrests, prisoners, and police predicted.

The ethnic pattern of the rise in murders in Newark provides weak corroboration for the assertion that drugs did not play a major role in the increase in murders. National data indicate that non-Hispanic blacks, non-Hispanic whites and Hispanics consume illicit drugs at roughly comparable rates, and Hispanics and blacks are both incarcerated at high rates for drug crimes.[10] Thus, changes in the drug business should have increased murders

10. At year-end 2005, 23.7 percent of black prisoners and 22.9 percent of Hispanic prisoners under state jurisdiction were charged with drug crimes. But overall, the rate of per capita imprisonment among Hispanics was around two-fifths of the rate among blacks (Harrison and Beck 2007).

ble 9.9	Prevalence estimates of drug use in New Jersey, 1999–2005 (% of population aged 12 and over)					
	1999	1999–2000	2000–2001	2002–2003	2003–2004	2004–2005
ιst month illicit drug use	7.2	6.1	5.8	7.0	6.9	7.2
ιast year cocaine use	2.1	1.5	1.3	2.2	2.0	2.0

ource: Substance Abuse and Mental Health Services Administration (SAMHSA), National Household ιurvey of Drug Abuse.

Table 9.10	Emergency room mentions of heroin and cocaine, Newark metropolitan area, 1998–2002	
	Heroin	Cocaine
Jan.–June 1998	2,575	1,481
July–Dec. 1998	2,437	1,349
Jan.–June 1999	2,301	1,180
July–Dec. 1999	2,433	1,137
Jan.–June 2000	2,285	1,080
July–Dec. 2000	2,114	1,043
Jan.–June 2001	1,849	1,031
July–Dec. 2001	1,869	384
Jan.–June 2002	1,938	1,023
July–Dec. 2002	1,793	378

Source: Substance Abuse and Mental Health Services Administration (SAMHSA), Drug Abuse Warning Network.

of Hispanics and possibly of whites in Newark, not just blacks. As we have seen, that did not happen.

9.6.9   Guns

Although gun homicides accounted for most of the increase in Newark murders, changes in the price and availability of guns probably did not make a major contribution to the murder rise. More guns and more lethal guns came to Newark because people wanted them and were willing to pay more for them, not because they were cheaper or easier to obtain.

Two strands of argument support this conclusion. First, national trends are different from Newark trends. Although murders by gunshot have been rising in Newark since 2000, they have not been rising nationally. National firearm homicides peaked in 1993 and fell by 47 percent to 1999. Between 1999 and 2006, they rose modestly, by 20 percent, so that 2006 firearm homicides were 37 percent below the peak in 1993. Because the wholesale gun market is national, this trend casts some doubt on a simple story about lower gun prices being responsible for more gunshot murders in Newark.

Table 9.11   Drug prices in New Jersey, first quarter of calendar year, 2000–2006 ($)

	North Jersey						South Jersey					
	Heroin		Cocaine		Crack		Heroin		Cocaine		Crack	
	Kilo	Bag	Kilo	Bag	Kilo	Bag	Kilo	Bag	Kilo	Bag	Kilo	Bag
2000	79	17	37	12	25	16	158	16	29	24	23	10
2001	71	10	26	10	23	14	177	15	27	22	25	16
2002	85	14	27	12	31	22	177	16	29	16	19	7
2003	63	11	25	14	24	22	98	16	27	24	19	10
2004	72	12	23	14	39	12	98	17	28	16	19	10
2005	67	9	25	14	26	14	98	22	25	22	19	14
2006	54	9	19	14	24	14	88	22	22	22	25	14
% change	−32	−47	−49	+17	−4	−12	−44	+37	−224	−8	+9	+40

Source: Drug Enforcement Administration (DEA), Illicit Drug Price Reports.
Notes: Point estimates calculated as geometric means of upper and lower limits of bounds given in original data. Kilo prices are in thousands of dollars.

Table 9.12   **Proportion of suicides by firearm in New Jersey, 1993–2003**

	% of total	% of African American	% of African American male
1998	37	40	43
1999	35	48	51
2000	28	19	22
2001	28	41	46
2002	32	42	44
2003	31	28	37
2004	31	33	40

Source: New Jersey Department of Health and Senior Services.

Indeed, because the rise in gross gunshot discharge incidents is a relatively small part of the story of rising gunshot murders in Newark, the only way gun prices could have had a major impact would be for the price of high-quality guns to fall relative to the price of low-quality guns. But if that were to be happening on the wholesale level, other cities would experience the same rise in deadliness that Newark has experienced, and national gunshot murders would increase. Thus, the gun-diffusion explanations in Gaviria (2000) and Blumstein, Rivara, and Rosenfeld (2000) probably do not apply to Newark.

Second, suicide data do not indicate greater availability of either all guns or better guns in New Jersey. Some researchers have used the proportion of suicides that occur by gunshot as an indicator of the how available guns are in an area (see, for example, Cook and Ludwig 2006). The logic is the following: If guns are easy to acquire, then almost everybody attempting suicide will use a gun. If guns are hard to acquire, then almost nobody attempting suicide will use a gun. So if we observe that a high proportion of suicides are by gun, we can conclude that guns are easy to obtain and vice versa. Similarly, if we observe a rising proportion of suicides by gun, we can conclude that guns are easier to obtain.

Table 9.12 provides information on suicides in New Jersey. There is no evidence of an upward trend although the numbers involved are small. Because the data report on *successful* suicides, a rise in the *quality* of guns, holding everything else equal, would increase the proportion of gunshot suicides. This table is weak evidence against the hypothesis that easier gun availability is driving the rise in gun murders. If guns were easier to obtain, we would expect to see them used more often for suicides as well as for homicides.

On the other hand, in 1998, New Jersey became the first and for most of this period the only state to segregate gang members in a particular prison, East Jersey State. Cook et al. (2005) show that personal networks are crucial to the operation of illegal gun markets. Prison segregation may have improved networks among New Jersey gang members, making it easier for them to obtain high quality guns. This would explain why New Jersey cities (except Paterson) are so different from almost all cities in the rest of the nation. But this argument is entirely speculative.

9.6.10   Unemployment

Between 2000 and 2006, unemployment rose in Newark and then fell back almost to its original level. According to the New Jersey Department of Labor and Workforce Development, the Newark unemployment rate rose modestly over the period, from 8.0 percent in 2000, to 8.5 percent in 2005, and to 8.3 percent in 2006, although it was much higher in some of the intervening years.

Raphael and Winter-Ebmer (2001) is probably the most rigorous study of unemployment effects on crime. They find significant positive effects for most crime: most crimes go up when unemployment goes up. But for murder they find negative effects, which are significant in several specifications with instrumental variables. Cook and Zarkin (1985) also find that murder is procyclical.

Hence, the business cycle did not contribute to the rise in murder in Newark and may even have reduced it.

9.7   Policies to Reduce Murder

No matter why murders rose, making them fall is a worthwhile goal. In this section, we will examine three programs for murder reduction for which claims of efficacy have been made, evaluate them in light of both the empirical literature and our model, and finally make some recommendations about how to reduce murders in Newark.

9.7.1   Programs That May Have Worked

Three murder-reduction programs in the last fifteen years have received considerable attention: Operation Ceasefire in Boston; Project Exile in Richmond, Virginia; and the combination of Compstat and broken windows in New York City. Murders fell substantially while all of these programs were in operation, but nobody knows what would have happened if the programs were not in operation. None of these programs has been subjected to a high quality test like a controlled experiment or a large natural experiment with an independent instrumental variable. Therefore, serious questions have been raised about whether each of these programs actually *caused* the reduction associated with it, and these objections are essentially unanswerable. There just is not enough independent variation. Rosenfeld, Fornango, and Baumer (2005) is a good summary of these programs.

Directed at youth, Operation Ceasefire in Boston involved direct communication with gang members that violence would not be tolerated. Police, youth workers, parole and probation officials, the U.S. attorney, and the local district attorney all told gang members in a series of meetings, "We're here because of the shooting. We're not going to leave until it stops. And until it does, nobody is going to so much as jaywalk, nor make any money, nor have any fun" (Kennedy et al. 2001, 27–28). Posters described what happened to recalcitrant gang members: "They were warned. They didn't listen." The idea was to turn gang pressure into pressure against shooting. Simultaneous efforts were made to trace and interdict crime guns.

Richmond's Project Exile was directed at older offenders, not youth, but also employed an extensive communications strategy. Exile primarily involved sentence enhancements for violent or drug crimes involving guns. The method was federal prosecution because federal crimes carry longer sentences and higher bail, and federal prisons are out of state. These harsh sentences were announced with a media blitz: "An illegal gun will get you five years in federal prison," the billboards and ads said.

New York's strategy was two-pronged, and it is difficult to sort out their independent effects. One prong was strict accountability for police officers through Compstat, and the other was a crackdown on misdemeanors—the "broken windows" strategy named after Wilson and Kelling's (1982) famous article. There was no explicit public relations strategy, but the initiatives received enormous media coverage. The message was that police were getting tough, and the flood of misdemeanor arrests was in part meant to demonstrate to potential offenders that that was in fact the truth.

Thus, a public message was part of all three programs. That the message was public is crucial for our model. To change his behavior substantially, an agent needs to know not only that his payoffs have changed but also that the payoffs of the agents he interacts with have changed too. All three programs tried to accomplish both tasks.

All three programs also tried to punish both shootings and murders. This strategy was not explicitly part of our model, because all that mattered was the expected net cost of given lethality. But because shootings are much more common than murders, certainty may have more deterrent value than severity, and actual punishments are probably needed for credibility, the strategy seems reasonable.

We have already noted that all three programs have received both favorable and unfavorable evaluations, but our model suggests that the unfavorable evaluations of Ceasefire and Exile may be too harsh because of narrow-estimation bias. The consensus among peer-reviewed papers is that broken windows did not reduce murders, but the evidence is inconclusive on Compstat.

In Braga et al. (2001), Kennedy et al. (2001), and Piehl et al. (2003), the Ceasefire research team looked at the time series of youth gun homicides, youth gun assaults, and shots-fired calls in Boston. They found reductions in youth violence in the Boston time series, controlling for a number of trends, including adult homicides, and in comparison with twenty-nine other New

England cities and thirty-nine large U.S. cities. Because youth homicides may have influenced adult homicides, at least some of these tests were too strict, but Ceasefire passed them.

Rosenfeld, Fornango, and Baumer (2005), however, used a national data set of ninety-five large cities and controlled for a wide array of demographic and criminal justice variables, including police strength and incarceration, and found that the Boston decrease in youth gun homicide was not statistically significantly different from the sample average when the age group fifteen to twenty-four was used. With the age group eleven to twenty-four, the decrease was marginally significant. They note (434): "The lack of statistical significance reflects Boston's low youth firearm homicide counts during the intervention period (from 21 in 1996 to 10 in 1999)." Narrow-estimation bias may contribute to the problems of small numbers. Cook and Ludwig (2006) also raise questions about the power of the Ceasefire evaluations.

In contrast, Rosenfeld, Fornango, and Baumer (2005) find a statistically significant decrease in gun homicides when they apply their methods to Project Exile, even though their point estimate of Ceasefire's effect was larger. Richmond had more homicides to work with. Raphael and Ludwig (2003), however, reached the opposite conclusion about Exile.

There are several differences between the two papers, most especially a controversy about how to treat the unusually large number of gun homicides in 1997, the year the intervention began but before much happened. More notable for us is that Raphael and Ludwig (2003) control for juvenile homicides in Richmond when they look at adult homicides in Richmond. We don't know what the effect of using this control is, but it is another example of possible narrow-estimation bias.

Raphael and Ludwig (2003) also argue that the reduction in murders in Richmond was mostly mean-reversion. Our model lets us interpret this argument and the data they present for it quite differently. They show that across cities the change in the natural log of gun homicide rates in the late 1990s, when rates were falling, was negatively correlated with the change between the mid-1990s and the mid-1980s. Cities that had bigger increases in the early decade had bigger decreases in the later quinquennium. Because Richmond had a large increase, mean reversion implies that it should have a big decrease, too. However, general evidence for mean-reversion in homicide rates is scant. Corman and Mocan check for it in New York City monthly data in both of their papers and cannot reject unit roots. The national murder rate time series over the past thirty years is clearly not mean-reverting.

Our model suggests an alternative interpretation for the correlation Raphael and Ludwig (2003) find. Suppose fundamentals change roughly the same way everywhere. Then war zones will have bigger increases in murder than peaceable kingdoms when fundamentals are getting worse and bigger decreases when fundamentals are getting better. If we compare a period when fundamentals are getting better everywhere with a period when fundamentals are getting worse everywhere, the Raphael-Ludwig correlation will hold, even if murder rates are not a mean-reverting process. Thus, the Raphael-Ludwig correlation provides some weak confirmation for our model of murder.

This way of looking at murder rates also suggests another way of interpreting the conclusion from Rosenfeld, Fornango, and Baumer (2005) that Project Exile reduced murder rates significantly while Operation Ceasefire and the New York combination did not. Richmond had a much higher murder rate than either New York or Boston at the start of the interventions. Thus, the same intervention would have produced a bigger effect in Richmond than in the other two cities. Rosenfeld, Fornango, and Baumer (2005) may have found not that Project Exile was more effective but that Richmond was more receptive.

For New York, some papers test broken windows alone and some test the combination of broken windows and Compstat; no work tests Compstat alone. In their study using monthly data from New York City police precincts, Corman and Mocan (2005) include citywide misdemeanor arrests as an explanatory variable. Misdemeanor arrests have no significant effect on murder although they did reduce robbery and motor vehicle theft. Kelling and Sousa (2001) also studied New York City, but only for approximately a decade. They found that violent crime declined more in precincts that had more misdemeanor arrests over the decade, but they did not publish any results about homicide. They also do not control for own arrests or police strength and do not address reverse causation (less violent crime would allow police more time to make misdemeanor arrests). Harcourt and Ludwig (2006) show that neither of these studies could support a finding that misdemeanor arrests reduce crime (they use the Kelling-Sousa and Corman-Mocan approaches on misdemeanor arrests to demonstrate that success of the New York Yankees drives crime in New York)—although, in fact, neither study found that such arrests reduce murder.

The multicity study of Rosenfeld, Fornango, and Baumer (2005) tested broken windows and Compstat jointly by comparing New York's homicide rate decline with the national average, both adjusted for controls. They found that, adjusted for controls, New York's homicide decline was not bigger than the national average (the point estimate was that it was smaller, but insignificantly so).

Thus, while there are some indications that programs that involve public communications and concentrate on shooters as well as killers may have some efficacy, the evidence is not compelling for any particular program. (This is essentially the same conclusion that Levitt [2004] reaches in his review of the 1990s crime decline and that Cook and Ludwig [2006] reach in their review of gun violence.) Of course, the evidence for such traditional variables as arrest rates and police strength is fairly strong.

9.7.2   Implications for Newark

What do these results imply about policies for Newark to pursue? Consider first the effects of making more arrests for murder and convicting more guilty suspects. More resources devoted to these tasks probably have two multiplier effects: more arrests and more convictions make more witnesses come forward, and more witnesses lead to even more arrests and more convictions; more arrests and more convictions lead to fewer people willing to murder for gain; fewer people willing to murder for gain lead to fewer people killing for self-protection.

Expansions of the police department to accomplish this end probably pass cost-benefit tests. Levitt's (2002) elasticity of murder with respect to police strength implies that added police expenditures in general reduce murders at a cost of about $2 million per life in Newark, well below the value of most American statistical lives, though not above the value that Levitt and Venkatesh (2000) conclude that young gang members place on their lives. Expansions concentrated on homicide reduction should do much better, as we have argued in the literature review.

Second, public messages that heighten fear may be counterproductive. Billboards that say, "Stop the killing" tell rational people that a lot of killing is going on and they need to protect themselves; so do repeated assertions that murders are going up everywhere (which is not true). Repeated laments that witnesses never testify tell rational would-be witnesses that testifying is very dangerous.

Of course, public messages cannot be wrong or misleading either; one cannot tell people that drinking Newark water makes bullets bounce off them. Messages suggesting that more apprehensions are being made, or more witnesses are coming forward, or more old cases are being solved could be highly effective provided that they are credible. (It might also be worthwhile to publicize how abysmally inaccurate most Newark shooters are.) For this to work, of course, actual progress would have to be made on the necessary detective work and witness protection.

Raising the cost of holding high quality guns reduces murders with all types of guns and so can have a substantial payoff. How to do this is less obvious. Cook and Ludwig (2006) provide a useful summary of the empirical literature on gun control strategies. They find that directed patrolling against illicit carrying stands the best chance of reducing homicide.

Raising the marginal penalty for murder by reducing penalties for other crimes is a riskier strategy. Shifting police and prosecutorial resources from other crimes accomplishes this implicitly because the marginal penalty for murder depends on the expected punishment for having committed other crimes. If resources are shifted from those crimes that people contemplating murder are likely to have committed, or are likely to commit soon, then the marginal penalty for murder will rise.

Prisoner reentry programs also implicitly reduce penalties for nonmurder crimes and so raise the marginal penalty for murder. If your life is ruined for any crime you commit, then if you have committed any other crime, the marginal penalty for murder is small. (A rigorous statement of this proposition is in O'Flaherty 1998.) Making postprison life better for other crimes makes murder more costly. But this is a long-run effect that may not be of any relevance in the next few years.

Programs that focus on former prisoners have a second possible payoff. For reducing murder, the most crucial place to lower the probability density function of γ is probably slightly above 0—people who would not kill if self-protection were not an issue but who do so readily when self-protection is an issue. In a different atmosphere or with a different crowd, they would not kill, but their willingness to kill in the dangerous environment they find themselves in encourages still more people to arm themselves and kill pre-emptively. If the probability density in neighborhood were to be decreased and moved to slightly higher values of γ, equilibrium murder would fall considerably. Former prisoners are probably heavily concentrated in this crucial range of γ.

How to change γ for this group is not certain, however. Employment is likely to help because it will occupy their time and further many of their aspirations. But, in general and in the aggregate, there is scant evidence that employment reduces murder as Raphael and Winter-Ebmer (2001) and Cook and Zarkin (1985) have shown.

Recreation, broadly conceived, may be more strategic, considering the large number of disputes among Newark's murder motives. The key is finding things that thirty-year-old former prisoners like to do after work and helping them to do these things in an atmosphere without guns and where disputes are settled amicably or with fists. Churches may assist with this, but some effective forms of recreation may not be wholesome enough for churches or even the city to sponsor directly.

Recreational segregation may also reduce murder. Consider a society where the equilibrium number of murders is far above the number of autonomous murders (our picture of Newark today). To make the situation simple, assume $\beta = \alpha$, and so $F(0)$ is the number of autonomous murder attempts. Now split the society in two, with all agents with negative γ in one new society and all those with positive γ in the other new society. Aggregate murder goes down to the autonomous level: the positive-γ society is murder-free, while in the negative-γ society, everyone shoots everyone else—but all of these people were shooting in the original society anyway—and they would be the only people shooting in the original society at the autonomous murder rate. (In the long run, segregation may be even more effective because the negative-γ society will steadily lose population from murder and incarceration, but the population of the positive-γ society will stay the same.)

One way to increase recreational segregation might be to establish different categories of bars and allow some categories greater privileges like later closing hours in return for restrictions like a no-guns policy. Privileges would be lost if a bar were connected to too many shootings. On the other hand, closing down the bloodiest bars promotes the kind of recreational integration that could increase the incidence of homicide. Murderers are going to go someplace, and it is better that they be with each other than that they be forced to associate with people who will as a result become killers in self-protection.

9.8   Conclusion

We have no direct empirical evidence about our primary theoretical contribution—the difference between autonomous and equilibrium murder that arises because of self-protective preemption—although results like those of Raphael and Ludwig (2003) can be interpreted as supportive. Clearly much good empirical work can and should be done in this area. A lot of theoretical work is missing, too—detailed models of segregation and models of witness intimidation have already been cited. In the meanwhile, we have good circumstantial evidence that strategic complementarity is a big part of the explanation for why murder rose in Newark and in other cities in North Jersey.

Substantively, murders can be reduced in Newark. Murders rose because small changes in fundamentals were magnified by a cycle of self-protective preemption (and probably also by a cycle of self-protective witness temerity). Some irreversible investments were made, but the changes in fundamentals needed to reverse the process, while larger than those that started the process, are probably not prohibitively large.

Appendix
How Gunshots Became More Lethal

In this appendix, we look at the ways in which gunshot wounds in Newark became more lethal in the early years of this century. In particular, we will try to infer how much of the change is due to changes in hardware (higher caliber weapons, semiautomatics, etc.) and how much of it is due to greater effort on the part of shooters.

We will combine information from the NPD homicide log, the NPD shooting log, and the record of autopsies maintained by the state regional medical examiner. We obtained the information from the medical examiner because the NPD did not collect reliable information on whether murders involved multiple wounds. Only an autopsy can determine whether multiple wounds are involved (as opposed to "through-and-throughs"—bullets that create wounds on both entering and exiting the decedent's body). An officer on the scene of a crime does not have enough information on this question.

The medical examiner's office, however, does not classify homicides in the same way that the NPD does. For the medical examiner, a homicide is classified in Newark if the death occurs at a Newark hospital. For the NPD, a homicide is classified in Newark if the incident that causes the death occurs in Newark. Newark is a net importer of homicide victims, especially in recent years, as a number of close suburban hospitals have closed. With the cooperation of the medical examiner's office and the NPD, we were able to reconcile the two sets of records and report information on gun homicides where the shooting occurred in Newark.

We classified a homicide as "multiple wounds" if the medical examiner in describing the cause of death used either the phrase "multiple wounds" or the word "wounds." Staff from the medical examiner's office have told us that the phrases are used interchangeably with no particular significance attaching to one as opposed to the other.

Ideally, we would like to know how many shooting incidents involved multiple shots and how many shots they involved because then we could separate the effect of more shots from the effect of increased deadliness of the average single shot. But we do not have such information. The closest we come to it is the number of homicides with multiple wounds, and from that information, we have to infer the number of shooting incidents involving multiple shots. Within the category of multiple wound homicides, moreover, we do not know the number of bullets that hit the victim; we know only that it is greater than one.

Notice that an increase in the number of multiple shot shooting incidents raises the number of murders in two ways, holding the lethality of each shot constant. Obviously it increases the number of multiple-wound murders. Less obviously, it also increases the number of single-wound murders because a shooter who fires twice or three times is more likely to hit his target once than a shooter who fires only once. Thus, drawing inferences about the causes of rising lethality from the data we have will require a highly parametrized model with many assumptions. This has to be a highly stylized exercise.

We make the following assumptions: (a) in any shooting incident, either one shot or two shots are fired; there are never more than two shots fired; (b) throughout a year, all gross gun discharge incidents are homogeneous, except for the number of shots fired; (c) when two shots are fired, the probabilities of hitting are independent, as are the probabilities of being accurate enough to kill if only a single shot hit; (d) if a victim is hit twice, he will die. The fourth assumption biases our results to a finding that multiple shootings lead to many murders and makes the role of multiple shootings more important than if, for instance, we had assumed that only the most accurate shot mattered. This assumption finds some support in Zimring (1972), who found that with the type of guns that are most in use now, almost all multiple wound shootings were fatal. But, of course, medical technology has improved along with gun technology since the 1970s.

These assumptions let us describe the shooting process with three nonlinear equations in three unknown probabilities. These are d, the probability that an assailant fires two shots; h, the probability that a shot hits a victim in such a manner that, if it were the only shot to hit him, it would not be fatal; and m, the probability that a shot hits a victim in such a manner that, if it were the only shot to hit him, it would be fatal. Let μ_2 denote the empirical ratio of multiple wound murders to shootings in a particular year. (We calculate shootings with and without shots fired.) In order for a shooting to be a multiple wound murder, the murderer must shoot twice, and both of those shots must hit the victim. Hence,

$$(A1) \qquad \mu_2 = d(m + h)^2.$$

Let μ_1 denote the empirical ratio of single wound murders to gross gun discharge incidents (with or without shots fired). A single wound murder could occur two different ways. The murderer could shoot once and kill; or he could shoot twice and kill with one shot and miss with the other. Hence,

$$(A2) \qquad \mu_1 = (1 - d)m + 2dm(1 - m - h).$$

Finally, let η denote the empirical ratio of shooting hits to gross gun discharge incidents. A shooting hit could occur two different ways. The assailant could shoot once and hit but not kill; or he could shoot twice, with one shot hitting nonfatally and the other missing. Hence,

$$(A3) \qquad \eta = (1 - d)h + 2dh(1 - m - h).$$

We can solve equations (A1) to (A3) in each year to find the underlying parameters d, m, and h. Table 9A.1 shows the results of this exercise. Both versions (with and without shots fired) tell the same qualitative story. All three parameters generally rise over the period although not monotonically. (The NPD shooting log was just beginning to be kept in 1999, and the unusual results here may be the result of initial reporting difficulties.) The largest percentage increase is in m, the lethality of an individual shot. The probability h that an individual shot wounds nonfatally increases the least in percentage terms, while the multiple-shot proportion d rises by an intermediate percentage.

Two kinds of changes could be driving the rises in d and in m: hardware and software. For m, the hardware change would be higher caliber weapons, and the software change could be better marksmanship and greater effort (approaching closer to the victim, for instance). For d, the hardware change would be weapons like semiautomatics that make it easier to fire more shots and to fire them more quickly, and the software change would be willingness

Table 9A.1   **Estimated parameters of the multiple shooting model**

	Including shots fired			Excluding shots fired		
	m	h	d	m	h	d
1999	0.046	0.480	0.195	0.065	0.487	0.243
2000	0.024	0.421	0.191	0.041	0.715	0.105
2001	0.053	0.442	0.188	0.087	0.730	0.106
2002	0.051	0.441	0.178	0.087	0.757	0.097
2003	0.056	0.506	0.101	0.085	0.771	0.064
2004	0.052	0.477	0.217	0.086	0.780	0.123
2005	0.062	0.461	0.234	0.100	0.748	0.132
2006	0.061	0.496	0.229	0.094	0.767	0.137
2007	0.060	0.506	0.296	0.090	0.751	0.181

to take the time to fire more shots. Our data do not allow inferences about the relative importance of these changes in d, but an auxiliary model can allow us to infer something about the effect of higher caliber weapons in raising m, the single-shot fatality rate.

Assume that all shooters are aiming at the same target, and consider a single shot. If the shooter misses the target by less than w, a physical constant, the victim is wounded (we are assuming no growth in the body mass of victims during this period). If the shooter misses by less than $k < w$, the victim dies. Our key assumption is that k depends on the caliber of the weapon (higher caliber weapons imply a larger kill radius k), and w does not depend on the caliber of the weapon. A high caliber bullet that misses entirely has the same effect as a low caliber weapon that misses entirely. Finally, we assume that where shots actually hit relative to the target is distributed normally with zero mean and variance that depends on the skill and effort of the shooter. Let σ denote the standard deviation of shots in any year, and let Φ denote the standard normal cumulative distribution function. Then we have

(A4)
$$\Phi\left(\frac{k}{\sigma}\right) - \Phi\left(\frac{k}{\sigma}\right) = m,$$

(A5)
$$\Phi\left(\frac{w}{\sigma}\right) - \Phi\left(\frac{k}{\sigma}\right) = \frac{h}{2}.$$

We call k/σ and w/σ the normalized kill and hit radii, respectively. Equation (A4) says that single-shot murders occur when a shot hits within k of the target, and equation (A5) says that nonfatal wounds occur when a shot hits a distance from the target between w and k. Solving equations (A4) and (A5) yields

$$\frac{k}{\sigma} = \Phi^{-1}\left(\frac{1+m}{2}\right)$$

$$\frac{w}{\sigma} = \Phi^{-1}\left(\frac{1+m+h}{2}\right).$$

These values are shown in table 9A.2.

Two conclusions are immediate from this table. First, because the normalized hit radius is growing, either skill or effort or both is growing. Because w is a physical constant, w/σ can rise only if σ falls, and a fall in σ is better marksmanship or greater effort. Second, because the normalized kill radius is growing faster than the normalized hit radius, caliber must be increasing, too. If software were the whole story, then k would be constant and k/σ would fall at the same rate as w/σ). Thus, k is rising, which is due to higher caliber.

Because all the relationships are nonlinear, to understand the relative importance of the changes in the different parameters, we perform a series of counterfactual calculations. In each of these calculations, we keep one parameter constant at its average value for 1999 to 2003 and find out how many murders would have occurred in a later year if all other parameters assumed their actual values. Thus, for instance, to find the effect of more multiple shooting incidents on 2006 murders, we ask how many murders would have occurred in 2006 if d were reduced to its average value for 1999 to 2003 and all other 2006 parameters maintained their actual values. If reducing d to its 1999 to 2003 average value reduces the number of murders in 2006 greatly, then we can say that the rise in d contributed greatly to the rise in murders in 2006. We make these calculations for 2004, 2005, and 2006.

Specifically, we are interested in five sets of counterfactual scenarios:

Table 9A.2   **Estimated parameters of the target missing model**

	Including shots fired		Excluding shots fired	
	k/σ	w/σ	k/σ	w/σ
1999	0.058	0.717	0.081	0.759
2000	0.031	0.591	0.052	1.167
2001	0.066	0.667	0.109	1.332
2002	0.064	0.661	0.109	1.420
2003	0.070	0.776	0.107	1.461
2004	0.066	0.722	0.108	1.498
2005	0.077	0.711	0.126	1.432
2006	0.077	0.767	0.119	1.481
2007	0.076	0.783	0.113	1.408

1. Shootings: How many murders can be attributed to the increase in the number of gross gun discharge incidents? We keep the number of shootings at its 1999 to 2003 average and let the ratio of gun homicides to shootings maintain its actual value in each later year.

2. Multiple-shots: How many murders can be attributed to the increase in the proportion of gross gun discharge incidents that involve multiple shots? We keep d at its 1999 to 2003 value and let all other parameters maintain their actual values in later years. We use equations (A1) to (A3) to find μ_1 and μ_2 and multiply these imputed values by the actual number of gross gun discharge incidents.

3. Single-shot lethality: How many murders can be attributed to the increase in the lethality of a single shot? We keep m at its 1999 to 2003 average value and let all other parameters maintain their actual values in later years.

4. Caliber: How many murders can be attributed to the increase in caliber? Essentially, we hold k constant at its average value of 1999 to 2003 but let σ and all other parameters evolve as they actually did. We call this the constant caliber scenario. Specifically, we calculate the ratio between average k/σ and average w/σ for 1999 to 2003 and then calculate what k/σ would be in each of the years from 2004 through 2006 if w/σ took its actual value, but the ratio between k/σ and w/σ stayed at its average 1999 to 2003 value. From these values of k/σ and w/σ, we calculate m and h for these years and then calculate how many gun homicides would have occurred with these values of m and h.

5. Marksmanship and effort: How many murders can be attributed to the increase in single-shot marksmanship and effort? This is the difference between the number of murders attributed to single-shot lethality and the number attributed to caliber. Essentially, we are taking enough probability mass out of the kill radius to return m to its 1999 to 2003 value and putting enough probability mass in the annulus between the kill and wound radii for h to take its actual value. (Recall that this is only single-shot marksmanship and effort. Effort may also have increased the rate of multiple shootings.)

Table 9A.3 summarizes the results of these calculations. Each entry in the table gives the difference between the number of gun homicides that would have occurred in a particular year under a particular counterfactual scenario and the number that actually occurred. The final line gives the difference between gun homicides in the particular year and average gun homicides in 1999 to 2003; it is the reduction that would have been achieved if nothing had changed. We have included a line "other and interaction" to reflect the fact that we have not experimented with changes in h and that the system is nonlinear so that there is no expectation that the sum of individual effects should equal the total effect. But for the most part, the sum of individual effects comes close to the total effect.

Table 9A.3   **Attribution of increase in gun homicides over 1999–2003 (number of gunshot homicides per year)**

	Including shots fired				Excluding shots fired			
	2004	2005	2006	2007	2004	2005	2006	200˙
Marksmanship and effort	2.6	7.0	9.4	2.5	5.9	8.0	8.9	5.9
Caliber	2.4	6.3	2.7	7.1	0.3	6.3	2.7	2.1
Single-shot lethality	5.0	13.3	12.1	9.6	6.2	14.3	11.6	8.0
Multiple shots	8.5	12.1	4.5	21.6	−0.1	2.9	4.5	15.2
Shootings	12.6	19.5	18.2	0.2	12.3	20.8	22.1	8.8
Other and interaction	−0.3	−5.1	7.0	4.4	7.4	1.8	3.6	3.8
Total change	25.8	39.8	41.8	35.8	25.8	39.8	41.8	35.8

The surprising results on multiple shots when shots fired are excluded are due almost entirely to 1999, which we have noted is not entirely trustworthy. Excluding 1999 and using 2000 to 2003 as the base period instead changes the multiple-shots results to look very similar to the results when shots fired are included.

The outstanding conclusion from table 9A.3 is that everything contributed to the increase in gun homicides. Caliber appears to be the least important, but it still is responsible for as many as six additional homicides in 2005 and nine in 2007. Multiple shots seem to be much more important in 2007 than it was in previous years.

We have some independent confirmation that these estimates are reasonable. For most gun homicides, the NPD learns the caliber of the weapon involved. Generally, higher caliber weapons are more common in more recent years. Zimring (1972) provides old estimates of the relative single-shot lethality of weapons of differing caliber. In an earlier version of this paper, we used somewhat arbitrary extensions of Zimring's conclusions to modern guns and calculated the change in single-shot lethality that the change in composition of guns the NPD was seeing would imply. The estimates were comfortingly similar to the changes in m that our caliber scenario implied.

References

Adler, Jeffrey S. 2006. *First in violence, deepest in dirt: Homicide in Chicago, 1875–1920.* Cambridge, MA: Harvard University Press.
Aldy, Joseph, and Kip Viscusi. 2003. The value of a statistical life: A critical review of market estimates throughout the world. NBER Working Paper no. 9487. Cambridge, MA: National Bureau of Economic Research.
Baliga, Sandeep, David O. Lucca, and Tomas Sjöström. 2007. Domestic political

survival and international conflict: Is democracy good for peace? Northwestern University. Unpublished Manuscript.

Baliga, Sandeep, and Tomas Sjöström. 2004. Arms races and negotiations. *Review of Economic Studies* 71 (2): 351–69.

Basu, Kaushik. 2006. Racial conflict and the malignancy of identity. *Journal of Economic Inequality* 3:221–41.

Becker, Gary, Kevin Murphy, and Michael Grossman. 2006. The market for illegal goods: The case of drugs. *Journal of Political Economy* 114 (1): 38–60.

Blumstein, Alfred, Frederick P. Rivara, and Richard Rosenfeld. 2000. The rise and decline of homicide—and why. *Annual Review of Public Health* 21:505–41.

Bowker, Lee H. 1981. Crime and the use of prisons in the United States: A time-series analysis. *Criminology* 27:206–12.

Braga, Anthony, David M. Kennedy, Elin J. Waring, and Anne M. Piehl. 2001. Problem-oriented policing, youth violence, and deterrence: An evaluation of Boston's Operation Ceasefire. *Journal of Research in Crime and Delinquency* 38: 195–225.

Cohen, Lawrence E., and Kenneth C. Land. 1987. Age structure and crime: Symmetry versus asymmetry and the projection of crime rates through the 1990s. *American Sociological Review* 52:170–83.

Cook, Philip J. 1983. The influence of gun availability on violent crime patterns. *Crime and Justice* 4:49–89.

Cook, Philip J., and Jens Ludwig. 2006. Aiming for evidence-based gun policy. *Journal of Policy Analysis and Management* 25 (3): 691–736.

Cook, Philip J., Jens Ludwig, Sudhir Venkatesh, and Anthony Braga. 2005. Underground gun markets. NBER Working Paper no. 11737. Cambridge, MA: National Bureau of Economic Research.

Cook, Philip J., and Gary A. Zarkin. 1985. Crime and the business cycle. *Journal of Legal Studies* 14 (1): 115–28.

Corman, Hope, and H. Naci Mocan. 2000. A times series analysis of crime, deterrence, and drug abuse in New York City. *American Economic Review* 90 (3): 584–604.

———. 2005. Carrots, sticks, and broken windows. *Journal of Law and Economics* 48 (1): 235–66.

Detre, Katherine, and Colin White. 1970. Note: The comparison of two Poisson-distributed observations. *Biometrics* 26 (4): 851–54.

Devine, Joel A., Joseph F. Sheley, and M. Dwayne Smith. 1988. Macroeconomic and social-control policy influences on crime rate changes 1948–1985. *American Sociological Review* 53:407–20.

Dezhbaksh, Hashem, Paul H. Rubin, and Joanna M. Shepherd. 2003. Does capital punishment have a deterrent effect? New evidence from postmoratorium panel data. *American Law and Economics Review* 5 (1): 344–77.

Dezhbaksh, Hashem, and Joanna M. Shepherd. 2006. The deterrent effect of capital punishment: Evidence from a "judicial experiment." *Economic Inquiry* 44 (3): 512–35.

Fisz, M. 1955. The limit distribution of a random variable which is a difference of two independent Poisson variables. *Colloquium Mathematica* 3:138–46.

Freeman, Scott, Jeffrey Grogger and Jon Sonstelie. 1996. The spatial concentration of crime. *Journal of Urban Economics* 40 (2): 216–31.

Gaviria, Alejandro. 2000. Increasing returns and the evolution of violent crime: The case of Colombia. *Journal of Development Economics* 61:1–25.

Glaeser, Edward L., and Bruce Sacerdote. 1996. Crime and social interactions. *Quarterly Journal of Economics* 111 (2): 507–48.

Glaeser, Edward L., Bruce I. Sacerdote, and Jose A. Scheinkman. 2003. The social multiplier. *Journal of the European Economic Association* 1 (2–3): 345–53.

Goldin, Claudia, and Lawrence Katz. 2002. The power of the pill: Oral contraceptives and women's career and marriage decisions. *Journal of Political Economy* 110 (4): 730–70.

Harcourt, Bernard E., and Jens Ludwig. 2006. Broken windows: New evidence from New York City and a five-city social experiment. *University of Chicago Law Review* 73 (1): 271–320.

Harrison, Paige M., and Allan J. Beck. 2007. Prisoners in 2005. Bureau of Justice Statistics Bulletin. http://www.ojp.usdoj.gov/bjs/abstract/p05.htm.

Katz, Lawrence, Steven D. Levitt, and Ellen Shustorovich. 2003. Prison conditions, capital punishment, and deterrence. *American Law and Economics Review* 5 (2): 318–43.

Kelling, George L., and William H. Sousa Jr. 2001. Do police matter? An analysis of New York City's police reforms. Manhattan Institute Civic Report no. 22. www.manhattan-institute.org/html/cr_22.htm.

Kennedy, David M., Anthony Braga, Anne M. Piehl, and Elin J. Waring. 2001. Reducing gun violence: The Boston Gun Project's Operation Ceasefire. Washington, DC: National Institute of Justice.

Kleinknecht, William, and Jonathan Schuppe. 2006. Getting away with murder. *Newark Star-Ledger,* January 29, 30, and 31. www.nj.com/news/murder.

Levitt, Steven D. 1996. The effect of prison population size on crime rates: Evidence from prison overcrowding litigation. *Quarterly Journal of Economics* 111 (2): 319–51.

———. 1998. Why do increased arrest rates appear to reduce crime: Deterrence, incapacitation, or measurement error? *Economic Inquiry* 36 (3): 353–72.

———. 2002. Using electoral cycles in police hiring to estimate the effects of police on crime: Reply. *American Economic Review* 92 (4): 1244–50.

———. 2004. Understanding why crime fell in the 1990s: Four factors that explain the decline and six that do not. *Journal of Economic Perspectives* 18 (1): 163–90.

Levitt, Steven D., and Sudhir Venkatesh. 2000. An economic analysis of a drug-selling gang's finances. *Quarterly Journal of Economics* 115 (3): 755–89.

Marvell, Thomas, and Carlisle Moody. 1994. Prison population and crime reduction. *Journal of Quantitative Criminology* 10:109–39.

———. 1997. The impact of prison growth on homicide. *Homicide Studies* 1 (3): 205–33.

Minino, Arialdi, Robert N. Anderson, Lois A. Fingerhut, Manon A. Boudreault, and Margaret Warner. 2006. Deaths: Injuries, 2002. National Vital Statistics Reports no. 54 (10). National Center for Health Statistics, Centers for Disease Control and Prevention. www.cdc.gov/nchs.deaths.htm.

Miron, Jeffrey A. 1999. Violence and U.S. prohibitions on drugs and alcohol. *American Law and Economics Review* 1:78–114.

———. 2001. Violence, guns, and drugs: A cross-country analysis. *Journal of Law and Economics* 44 (2): 615–34.

O'Flaherty, Brendan. 1998. Why repeated criminal opportunities matter: A dynamic stochastic analysis of criminal decision-making. *Journal of Law, Economics, and Organization* 14 (2): 232–55.

O'Flaherty, Brendan, and Rajiv Sethi. 2008. Peaceable kingdoms and war zones: Preemption, ballistics and murder in Newark. Columbia University, Department of Economics, Working Paper no. 0708-02.

———. 2010. Witness intimidation. *Journal of Legal Studies,* forthcoming.

Piehl, Anne M., Suzanne J. Cooper, Anthony Braga, and David M. Kennedy. 2003.

Testing for structural breaks in the evaluation of programs. *Review of Economics and Statistics* 85:550–58.

Raphael, Steven, and Jens Ludwig. 2003. Prison sentence enhancements: The case of Project Exile. In Evaluating gun policy: Effects on crime and violence, ed. Jens Ludwig and Philip J. Cook, 251–76. Washington, DC: Brookings Institution Press.

Raphael, Steven, and Michael Stoll. 2004. The effect of prison releases on regional crime rates. *Brookings-Wharton Papers on Urban Affairs* 5:207–55.

Raphael, Steven, and Rudolf Winter-Ebmer. 2001. Identifying the effect of unemployment on crime. *Journal of Law and Economics* 44 (1): 259–84.

Rasmusen, Eric. 1996. Stigma and self-fulfilling expectations of criminality. *Journal of Law and Economics* 39:519–43.

Rosenfeld, Richard, Robert Fornango, and Eric Baumer. 2005. Did ceasefire, compstat, and exile reduce homicide? *Criminology and Public Policy* 4 (3): 419–50.

Sah, Raaj. 1991. Social osmosis and patterns of crime. *Journal of Political Economy* 99 (6): 169–217.

Schelling, Thomas C. 1960. *The strategy of conflict.* Cambridge, MA: Harvard University Press.

Schrag, Joel, and Suzanne Scotchmer. 1997. The self-reinforcing nature of crime. *International Review of Law and Economics* 17 (3): 325–35.

Swersey, Arthur J. 1980. A greater intent to kill: The changing pattern of homicide in Harlem and New York City. Yale University School of Management. Unpublished Manuscript.

Wilson, James Q., and George Kelling. 1982. Broken windows. *Atlantic Monthly* 249 (3): 29–38.

Zimring, Franklin. 1972. The medium is the message: Firearm caliber as a determinant of death from assault. *Journal of Legal Studies* 1 (1): 97–123.

Zimring, Franklin, and Gordon Hawkins. 1995. *Incapacitation and the restraint of crime.* New York: Oxford University Press.

Comment   Guillermo Cruces

Introduction

O'Flaherty and Sethi's study "Peaceable Kingdoms and War Zones: Preemption, Ballistics, and Murder in Newark" is a work of extensive breadth that makes a valuable contribution by incorporating game-theoretic social interactions to the economics of murder. Starting from recent evidence on an increasing trend in murders in Newark and other urban areas in New Jersey at the time of a generalized fall in aggregate U.S. trends, the paper turns to a detailed decomposition of gun discharge episodes, unearthing a puzzling stylized fact: murders rose much faster than shootings in Newark. The authors develop a game-theoretical model to explain this increase in lethality and to account for the differing New Jersey and U.S. trends simul-

Guillermo Cruces is deputy director of the Center for Distributive, Labor, and Social Studies (CEDLAS) at the Universidad Nacional de La Plata.

taneously. The chapter then relates the model and its implications to the most relevant empirical studies in the economics of crime literature and discusses most (though not all, as argued in the following pages) of the likely causes (or "changes in fundamentals") that might account for the diverging Newark trend. Finally, the authors turn to three well-known murder deterrence initiatives and to other policy measures that might revert the local trend.

This comment focuses first on O'Flaherty and Sethi's main contributions. It then turns to a few topics not covered in the chapter, mainly related to the potential role that organized crime might have played both within the model and regarding the Newark murder trend. Finally, based on the document's results and on these topics, the final paragraphs suggest some possibilities for further research.

The Paper's Contributions

This paper's main contributions stem from the introduction of "economic complexity" (in Durlauf's sense) in a model of murder and from the ensuing comparison of the model's theoretical, empirical, and policy implications with those from more conventional approaches.

The stylized facts that motivate the theoretical model are the Newark's murder rate trends above the national average and the increased lethality in the city's shooting incidents. This model constitutes the first contribution of the paper. While many existing economic approaches to murder use single-actor analysis or incorporate interactions as peer effects, this chapter develops a game theoretic setting where two players interact in a shooting incident and where the level of lethality is endogenous. The key factors in the model are the presence of a preemptive motive for murders, the role played by equilibrium expectations, and the presence of a "social-multipliers" effect that implies a higher level of murder with respect to a single-actor model. The game-theoretic setting gives the model a series of interesting characteristics, such as the presence of threshold levels and tipping points in murder and lethality rates and multiple equilibriums and irreversibilities. Communities with large social multipliers and high levels of murder are classified as "war zones," and the presence of nonlinearities implies that even small changes in fundamentals might turn "peaceable kingdoms" into "war zones."

The second contribution of the chapter is the discussion of the existing evidence on murder and its determinants in the light of the model's implications. The insight is that the standard, single-actor approach might lead to nonlinearity prediction biases: while current estimates might capture the average effect, they might miss out cases of high "socially multiplied" levels of murder, such as Newark. The chapter does not develop its own empirical estimations, but the authors discuss the effect of factors (such as indicators of law enforcement, guns, and illicit drugs) on murder rates in Newark and other cities in New Jersey by extrapolating the elasticities from other relevant studies in the economics of crime literature. They find support for the types of effects they model for New Jersey from the upper and lower bounds implied from existing estimates. Finally, the document also discusses the policy alternatives to reduce murder in a multiple equilibrium setting.

Organized Crime and the Model: From Two to Many

The plausibility of a social-multiplier effect in murders provides support for incorporating game-theoretic considerations into the analysis of murder, as O'Flaherty and Sethi do in their model. The "wars" and "kingdoms" in the document title, however, imply the presence of some sort of collective action among the criminals—kingdoms require kings, and wars require armies. The model developed in the chapter is akin to the confrontation between two individuals in a state of nature—criminals as wolves for other criminals, rather than knights fighting wars for their kings.

A general comment is that just as the extension from a single actor to two players proved worthwhile, the modeling (or at least the discussion) of the role of organized crime might give the model a more realistic feeling and might also result in a wider array of predictions.

An extended theoretical model could incorporate issues such as the discipline within criminal organizations as a deterrent for murder (some sort of "Leviathan effect"), or such as competition between organizations (of which "wars" would be a manifestation). Fully incorporating these aspects into the model is certainly demanding and probably beyond the scope of the chapter. Moreover, the chapter's model is probably a good approximation of the one-to-one interaction between two criminals, be it between two "mob soldiers" or between two "independent wolves."

The implications of organized crime, however, can still be informally discussed within the chapter's theoretical setting—like the authors did with the brief discussion of a dynamic extension of the model—or, better still, considered as plausible sources of change for the model's exogenous parameters. One of the most obvious ways to introduce an element of criminal collective action is through the comparative static exercises. The chapter stresses the decline in the effectiveness of the criminal justice system, but the change in a, shifting the cost distribution $F(\gamma,a)$, might originate in the actions of a criminal organization that routinely needs to order executions (increasing gains) or that lowers the costs of murder (hiring lawyers or enforcing silence codes). Confrontations between gangs for the control of territory might also shift the cost functions or increase the availability of more lethal weaponry, resulting in temporary "war zones."

The chapter discusses a few aspects of the collective organization of criminals, such as the effect of witness intimidation on arrest and conviction rates, but the confrontations are modeled mostly as a private interaction between two individuals. While this section argued that the theoretical model might gain by discussing organized crime, the most important implications are related to the chapter's interpretations of facts, predictions, and policy implications, covered in the following paragraphs.

Organized Crime as a Fundamental:
Empirical Results and Policy Implications

The chapter's section on "What happened in Newark?" is remarkable by its attempt to reconcile the preemption model with a variety of phenomena for which secondary data is available, such as arrest rates, prison population, and drug prices, but also for others with no direct sources of information, such as guns and police figures. HBO original series stereotypes notwithstanding, it is likely that organized crime, or at least its lack of organization, played a role in the increase in murder in Newark and other New Jersey cities. Even if data on criminal organizations is not easy to come by, there might be at least some anecdotal evidence, like the author's references to the disarray of the Newark police department or to the prosecutor's office's "flagrant reputation for failing to win convictions."

Besides the brief mention of witness intimidation, which is usually a collective task, the chapter mentions other evidence that, at the least, suggests the presence of criminal organizations. For instance, the lower (and falling) levels of illicit drug markup in the prices of illicit drugs signal the presence of reduced competition in South Jersey. Murder might be part of the collateral damage in a process of shake-out and consolidation in illicit drug trade that involves armed confrontations between gangs (just as layoffs and bankruptcies for legal businesses). Such a process could have an impact in some of the relevant parameters of the theoretical model, such as the costs and gains from murder and the availability of lethal weapons.

The inclusion of organized crime in the discussion could give a new interpretation to some of the provided evidence, such as the "gang related" shootings. It could also result in other implications for the model. A tacit agreement where the authorities trade a partial blind eye for peace and quiet in the streets is more likely to arise with a strong leadership within criminals. Organized crime leaders might also have an incentive to curb an outbreak of violence (and, thus, act as a Leviathan) if the violence's visibility hurts business, turning war zones into peaceable kingdoms where law enforcing agencies fail. Even the record forty days with no murders in early 2008, a period that should have seen six to eleven murders, according to table 9.4's historical rates, might be the result of a truce between warring gangs.

It is still entirely possible that organized crime had no role in the Newark murder and lethality rates. The examples in this section, however, intended to show that the issue could merit some discussion.

Further Research

The presence of multiple equilibriums and nonlinearities in the determinants of murder rates is probably the most important implication of the chapter's game-theoretic approach. A possibility for further research is to go beyond the detailed extrapolation of elasticities from other studies to the Newark data and attempt to test the implications of the model with larger data sets. The identification of multiple equilibriums and social interactions in econometrics is far from obvious, but other implications might be easier to test. For instance, the existing empirical work might be extended by means of quantile regression techniques, providing further evidence on nonlinearities in the effects of relevant variables on murder rates and, ultimately, strengthening the case for the chapter's theoretical model.

Crime Displacement and Police Interventions
Evidence from London's "Operation Theseus"

Mirko Draca, Stephen Machin, and Robert Witt

10.1 Introduction

Falling crime rates in the United States (and some other countries) since the late 1980s have prompted an extensive discussion of the determinants of crime (see Levitt [2004] and Freeman [1999] for a summary). The role of police in reducing crime has been a part of this discussion, and a series of contributions have sought to estimate the causal impact of police and crime in various settings.[1] This literature in economics has mainly examined the direct effects of police on crime, that is, the impact of additional police resources or interventions on intended crime reduction outcomes.

The indirect effects of police interventions have received less attention. Such indirect effects would occur in cases where an intervention changes the relative costs of different types of criminal activity. For example, if a change in relative costs is large enough, a crime reduction achieved in terms of the intended outcome may be offset by an increase in crime for another related outcome. Most simply, this would occur in cases where crimes are

Mirko Draca is a research economist and a PhD student in the Department of Economics at University College London. Stephen Machin is professor of economics at University College London, and director of the Centre for the Economics of Education and research director at the Centre for Economic Performance, both at London School of Economics. Robert Witt is head of the department and reader in economics at the University of Surrey.

We would like to thank Trevor Adams, Jay Gohil, Paul Leppard, and Carol McDonald at the Metropolitan Police and Gerry Weston at Transport for London for assistance with the data used in this study. Part of this chapter uses results from Draca, Machin, and Witt (2008) and extends the empirical analysis in a number of directions. Any errors are our own.

1. A long, but not exhaustive, list of papers trying to identify a causal impact of police on crime includes Levitt (1997, 2002), McCrary (2002), Corman and Mocan (2000), Di Tella and Schargrodsky (2004), Klick and Taborrak (2005), Evans and Owen (2007), and Machin and Marie (2009).

differentiated by time and location, thereby creating the possibility of temporal or spatial displacement in criminal activity.

The issue of displacement has been considered much more in criminology than economics. Braga (2001) provides a review of five studies in experimental criminology that focused on potential spatial displacement effects across a diverse set of crime reduction programs. These studies encompassed drug, gun, and general crime interventions and used research designs similar to those employed by empirical economists. There was minimal evidence of spatial displacement across a number of potential outcome variables (including actual crimes committed and service call-outs to police). Overall, these findings are in line with the conclusions of previous surveys of the criminology literature on displacement such as Hessling (1994) and Sherman and Weisburd (1995).

The recent paper by Jacob, Lefgren, and Moretti (2007) provides the most comprehensive discussion of displacement issues in the economics literature. This paper focuses on the dynamics of criminal behaviour and uses weather shocks as a source of exogenous variation to evaluate the intertemporal structure of criminal activity. Following this strategy, Jacob, Lefgren, and Moretti (2007) *do* find evidence of intertemporal shifts in criminal activity, estimating that a 10 percent increase in violent crime in a given week is followed by 2.6 percent reduction in the week after. Similarly, they estimate a 10 percent increase in property crime was followed by a 2 percent fall in the following week. In their simple dynamic model, the property crime effect works through an income effect, while the violent crime result is due to the diminishing marginal utility of violence (i.e., an offender may "settle a score" one week and derive less utility from using violence in the next week). This is particularly interesting in that it opens up the mechanisms underpinning crime displacement, that is, the specific costs and benefits faced by criminals when making decisions about criminal activity.

Braga (2001) provides a review of the "hot spot" policing strategies covered in the criminology literature that are relevant to the issue of crime displacement. They discuss risk-focused policing strategies, that is, attempts to target particular high-crime areas with additional police resources. These resources included actions such as tailored "problem-oriented" policing responses, patrol programs, and actions based on crackdowns or raids. The nine main studies they focus on cover the cities of Minneapolis, Jersey City (United States), St Louis, Kansas City, Houston, and Beenleigh (in Brisbane, Australia). Among these, five studies consider possible displacement effects, typically by looking at crime in closely adjacent areas (including the block-level). However, none of these studies were able to uncover systematic displacement effects; for example, while one St. Louis drug market study did find displacement effects in one location, it found no effects in two other areas.

In this chapter, we contribute to this topic by considering the displacement effects of a large-scale police intervention that occurred in London in 2005 following the terror attacks that hit the city in July of that year. In contrast to the Jacob, Lefgren, and Moretti (2007) study, the change in the relative costs of crime that we consider is based explicitly on a policy intervention. This policy intervention—stylishly dubbed "Operation Theseus" by the London Metropolitan Police—was implemented as part of a general security response to the terrorist attacks that occurred in London during July 2005. The intervention lasted six weeks and involved a major, highly visible police deployment that was geographically concentrated in five central London boroughs. As our paper on the direct crime effects (Draca, Machin, and Witt 2008) establishes, the intervention had a clear, direct impact on crime in the boroughs "treated" by the police deployment. The 34 percent increase in police in these boroughs was accompanied by a 13 percent fall in susceptible crimes.[2] Furthermore, this fall in crime was not due to other observable and unobservable shocks associated with the terrorist attacks (for example, change in transport usage patterns after the attacks that could have shifted the supply of potential victims for crime).

Our contribution in this chapter is not only to present evidence on the direct connections between crime and police, but also to investigate the indirect effects through potential displacement. We test for spatial displacement of crime from the treated boroughs into neighboring comparison group boroughs and for intertemporal displacement of crimes within the treatment group by looking at crime patterns in the immediate aftermath of the policy-on period. Despite the clear and well-identified direct effects of the policy intervention, we are unable to find evidence of significant displacement. This suggests that—at least at the geographical level we are considering here—crime displacement effects do not offset the direct effects of police interventions.

The rest of the chapter is structured as follows. In section 10.2, we discuss the issue of crime modeling with respect to the direct and indirect effects of increased police presence and the big increase in police deployment in London induced by Operation Theseus. Section 10.3 presents our empirical models of the direct and indirect effects on crime following the increased police presence. Section 10.4 concludes.

10.2   Crime, Police, and Displacement

In this section, we provide a more detailed discussion of crime displacement and give a short overview of the policy intervention at the center of our analysis. Our paper on the crime and police relation before and after the July

---

2. "Susceptible crimes" in this case are all those crimes that would have been plausibly affected by the public deterrence effects of street-level police deployment. These include all crimes in the major categories of Theft and Handling, Violence and Sexual Offences, and Robbery. See Draca, Machin, and Witt (2008) for more details.

2005 terror attacks (Draca, Machin, and Witt 2008) discusses the estimation and interpretation of the direct effects of this intervention in much more detail and formally analyzes the intervention as a quasi-experiment.

10.2.1   Crime and Police

In line with the empirical strategy we adopt in the following, we discuss modeling issues on the determinants of crime using areas (in our case London boroughs) as the unit of analysis. Consider a general description of an area-level crime function:

$$(1) \qquad\qquad C_{jt} = C(X_{jt}, P_{jt}, \mu_j, \tau_t, \upsilon_{jk}),$$

where C_{jt} is crime in area j at time t, X_{jt} is a vector of relevant area characteristics for determining crime, and P_{jt} is the level of police resources. The final three terms are μ_j (fixed unobserved area characteristics), τ_t (common time shocks across areas), and υ_{jk} (seasonal shocks specific to the area with k indexing the season).

A regression analogue of equation (1) can then be written as:

$$(2) \qquad\qquad C_{jt} = \alpha + \delta P_{jt} + \lambda X_{jt} + \mu_j + \tau_t + \upsilon_{jk} + u_{jt},$$

where the terms are defined as before, and u_{jt} is a stochastic error. As is well known, crime is highly persistent over time, and so it is natural to seasonally difference equation (2) to give:

$$(3) \qquad\qquad \Delta_k C_{jt} = \alpha + \delta\Delta_k P_{jt} + \lambda\Delta_k X_{jt} + \Delta_k \tau_t + \Delta_k \varepsilon_{jt},$$

where Δ is the differencing operator, with k indexing the order of the seasonal differencing. Note that the $\Delta_k \tau_t$ difference term can now be interpreted as the year-on-year change in factors that are common across all of the areas.

This estimating equation is useful for characterizing both the direct and indirect crime effects of an increased in police presence, P_{jt}.

1. Direct effects: The direct effects of an increase in police presence are clear, and the parameter δ gives the direct impact of police on crime. If the crime and police variables are specified in logarithms, δ is the elasticity of crime with respect to police. The difficult empirical issue in estimating equation (3) is to ensure the causality runs from police to crime (and not vice versa). In the following, we not only review estimated elasticities from studies that adopt instrumental variable (IV) strategies to try and ensure that δ picks up the causal impact of police on crime, but also present our own IV estimates using the July 2005 terror attacks of London to identify the crime-police relation.

2. Indirect effects: The indirect effects are more complex because they rely on displacement of some kind in response to an increased police presence. We consider two possibilities. The first is spatial displacement. As will be made clear in the following, we identify the impact of police on crime

by considering what happened to crime in areas where a sizable increase in police presence occurred as compared to areas where this did not happen. If criminals choose to relocate their criminal activities from the first to the second set of areas, then spatial displacement will occur. The second possibility is temporal displacement. In this case, criminals will still engage in crime in the same areas but will shift their activities to a different time period when the increased police presence does not occur. Thus, temporal displacement will occur if this dynamic notion of criminal behavior applies.

Of course, if these indirect effects do occur, then δ will not accurately measure the crime-police relation. Note, however, that if crime rises in an adjacent comparison group area because of spatial displacement, we are likely to be underestimating the direct impact of police on crime. That is, by (indirectly) increasing crime in a comparison area, the displacement effect will reduce the empirically measured effect of police on crime. In contrast, temporal displacement is likely to impart an upward bias on the direct estimate of police on crime. In this case, the temporal displacement effect causes an "extra" fall in crime during the policy-on period. This extra fall will then be offset by an increase in crime in subsequent periods when the policy is switched off. Empirically, this offsetting effect could become evident as a significant increase in crime for a treated area in the wake of the policy-on period. It is, therefore, important to consider possible indirect effects that occur through displacement in evaluating and interpreting a given estimate of δ.

10.2.2   Operation Theseus and the July 2005 Terror Attacks

In practical terms, the δ parameter is estimated by a difference-in-difference strategy centered on a group of London boroughs treated by a heavy police deployment. This deployment occurred in the six weeks following the terrorist attack of July 7, 2005. This attack involved the detonation of three bombs on London Underground train carriages near the tube stations of Russell Square (in the borough of Camden), Liverpool Street (in Tower Hamlets), and Edgware Road (in Kensington and Chelsea). A fourth bomb was detonated on a bus in Tavistock Square, Bloomsbury (in Camden). A second wave of attacks occurred two weeks later on July 21, 2005, and consisted of four unsuccessful attempts at detonating bombs on trains near the underground stations of Shepherds Bush (Kensington and Chelsea), the Oval (Lambeth); Warren Street (Westminster), and on a bus in Bethnal Green (Tower Hamlets). Despite the failure of the bombs to explode, this second wave of attacks caused much turmoil in London. There was a large manhunt to find the four men who escaped after the unsuccessful July 21 attacks, and all of them were captured by July 29, 2005.

In response to these attacks, the London Metropolitan Police intensified their police patrols and greatly increased their public presence at transport nodes (particularly Tube stations) and other sites of public importance.

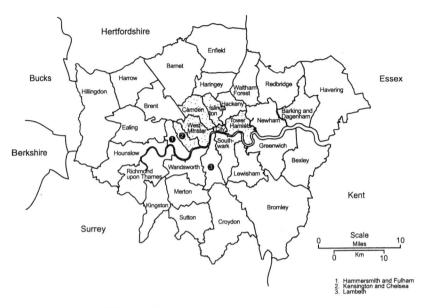

Fig. 10.1   A map of London boroughs

This extra deployment was achieved in various ways, including extending police overtime for approximately six weeks. Furthermore, the deployment was concentrated in the five boroughs of Westminster, Camden, Kensington and Chelsea, Tower Hamlets, and Islington (see figure 10.1 for a map). This deployment involved a 34 percent increase in police hours worked in these boroughs relative to the same period in the previous year.

Figure 10.2 plots police hours worked for this group of treated boroughs against all other London boroughs (the comparison group used in Draca, Machin, and Witt 2008). Also, in table 10.1, we report the changes in pre- and postpolicy levels of police and crime for different groups of boroughs. The striking thing to note from table 10.1 is the composition of the relative change in police hours for the treatment group. That is, police hours increased for the treatment group by 37.6 percent in year-on-year terms but stayed roughly constant across all of the remaining comparison boroughs. Furthermore, even when we break up the comparison group into smaller sets of boroughs (which is what we do to consider the possibility of spatial crime displacement), it is clear that the comparison boroughs did not suffer an absolute fall in police resources during Operation Theseus. This was made possible first by the increase in overtime hours worked across the Metropolitan Police and second by a reallocation of resources across boroughs. Specifically, extra hours worked in the comparison group boroughs were committed to a "central aid" policy, where officers assisted in the security operation underway in the treated boroughs.

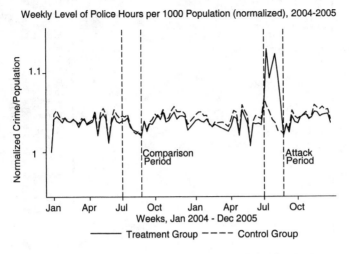

Fig. 10.2   **Police deployment, year-on-year changes 2004–2005, treatment versus comparison group**

As a result, the Metropolitan Police were able to avoid a situation where resources were allocated on a "zero-sum" basis, whereby the absolute levels of resources could have declined in the comparison group. This simplifies our framework in that it represents a much cleaner change in the relative costs of crime than would be the case if the comparison group was subject to absolute falls in police resources.

10.2.3   Data

Our main data comprises daily crime reports from the London Metropolitan Police Service (LMPS) covering the years 2004 to 2005. The daily reports are given at the ward level (641 wards across London) and aggregated to borough level at the weekly frequency. There are thirty-two London boroughs as shown on the map in figure 10.1.[3]

These boroughs correspond to the organizational units used by the LMPS, known as Borough Operational Command Units (BOCUs), apart from the case of Heathrow Airport, which represents a separate BOCU. Our final weekly panel, therefore, covers thirty-two London boroughs over two years, giving 3,328 observations. We use borough-level population estimates supplied by the Office of National Statistics (ONS) online database to normalize our counts of crime.

The police deployment data are reported only at the borough level and were provided under agreement with the LMPS. The underlying data source

---

3. Note that the City of London has its own police force, and so this small area is excluded from our analysis.

Table 10.1 Operation Theseus—year-on-year changes in police and crime

	Police deployment (hours worked per 1,000 population)			Crime rate (susceptible crimes per 1,000 population)		
	Pre-Period (1)	Post-Attack1 (2)	Difference (logs) (3)	Pre-Period (4)	Post-Attack1 (5)	Difference (logs) (6)
Treatment group						
Treatment group (5)[a]	169.46	242.29	0.376 (0.029)	3.30	2.89	-0.134 (0.030)
Comparison groups						
All comparison (27)	82.77	84.95	0.030 (0.013)	1.41	1.40	-0.004 (0.015)
Inner (8)	113.71	116.26	0.023 (0.015)	1.85	1.84	-0.008 (0.029)
Adjacent (7)	111.28	112.83	0.014 (0.015)	1.80	1.78	-0.003 (0.029)
Central (10)	121.86	123.75	0.015 (0.026)	1.99	1.93	-0.023 (0.045)
Outer (19)	69.79	71.81	0.033 (0.018)	1.22	1.22	-0.002 (0.019)
Difference-in-Difference (Treatment–All comparison)			0.346 (0.028)			-0.129 (0.031)

Notes: Treatment group is defined as boroughs of Westminster, Camden, Islington, Tower Hamlets, and Kensington and Chelsea. Inner London boroughs is defined following the Office of National Statistics classification as Westminster, Camden, Islington, Kensington and Chelsea, Tower Hamlets (treatment group), and Hackney, Hammersmith and Fulham, Haringey, Wandsworth, Lambeth, Lewisham, Southwark, and Newham (comparison group). Adjacent boroughs is defined as Brent, Hackney, Hammersmith and Fulham, Lambeth, Newham, Southwark, and Wandsworth. Central Ten boroughs is defined as Westminster, Camden, Islington, Kensington and Chelsea, Tower Hamlets (treatment group), and Brent, Hackney, Hammersmith and Fulham, Lambeth, and Southwark. Post-Attack1 represents the six weeks after July 7th 2005, while Pre-Period covers the equivalent weeks twelve months before. "Susceptible crimes" in this case are all those crimes that would have been plausibly affected by the public deterrence effects of street-level police deployment. These include all crimes in the major categories of Theft and Handling, Violence and Sexual Offences, and Robbery.

[a]Number of boroughs.

used to construct the data is known as CARM (Computer Aided Resource Management), the police service's human resource management system. The CARM database records hours worked by individual officers on a daily basis, and we aggregate this to the weekly, borough level. Furthermore, CARM also contains useful information on the allocation of hours worked by incident or police operation. Although hours worked are available according to officer rank, our main hours measure is based on total hours worked by all officers in the borough. We do, however, adjust for the reallocation effect, whereby officers were deployed into the treatment group during Operation Theseus in order to support security operations. As a supplement to this data, we also use daily data on tube journeys for all stations across the London boroughs. Again, this data (provided by Transport for London [TfL]) was aggregated up to the weekly, borough level. Finally, we also use data from the United Kingdom. Labour Force Survey (LFS) to provide information on area demographics and local labor market trends.

10.3   Empirical Models and Results

10.3.1   Estimating Direct and Indirect Effects

Before discussing the modeling of displacement, it is necessary to discuss the identification of δ, the parameter measuring impact of police on crime in equation (3). A straightforward ordinary least squares (OLS) estimate of this parameter will be affected by severe endogeneity bias because preexisting crime patterns influence the allocation of police. In Draca, Machin, and Witt (2008), we tackle this problem by using the structure of the Operation Theseus intervention to define an IV strategy. Specifically, we use the fact that the extra police deployment was concentrated in five central London boroughs to posit a treatment group of heavily affected boroughs, T_b. We then interact this with a "policy-on" term ($POST_t$) for the six-week duration of the intervention, estimating reduced form equations from police deployment and crime as follows:

$$(4) \qquad p_{bt} - p_{b(t-52)} = \alpha_1 + \beta_1 POST_t + \delta_1 (POST_t \cdot T_b) \\ + \lambda_1 [x_{bt} - x_{b(t-52)}] + [u_{1bt} - u_{1b(t-52)}]$$

$$(5) \quad c_{bt} - c_{b(t-52)} = \alpha_2 + \beta_2 POST_t + \delta_2 (POST_t \cdot T_b) + \lambda_2 [x_{bt} - x_{b(t-52)}] \\ + [u_{2bt} - u_{2b(t-52)}],$$

where lowercase letters denote logs, and the data is seasonally differenced across the same weeks of the year (represented by the $t - 52$ subscript in the differences).

The analogous structural equation for these reduced forms is

$$(6) \quad c_{bt} - c_{b(t-52)} = \alpha_3 + \beta_3 POST_t + \delta_3 [p_{bt} - p_{b(t-52)}] + \lambda_3 [x_{bt} - x_{b(t-52)}] \\ + [u_{3bt} - u_{3b(t-52)}].$$

The structural parameter δ_3, the causal impact of police on crime, is then recovered from the reduced forms as the ratio of the two reduced form coefficients $\delta_3 = \delta_2/\delta_1$.

Incorporating displacement into this estimating framework basically involves consideration of spatial and temporal effects. In the case of spatial displacement, we do this by defining different groups of boroughs immediately around the treatment group as pseudo-treatment groups that could have plausibly been subject to indirect effects. That is, as nearby boroughs, these groups would have been most vulnerable to the change in the relative levels of police between the treatment and comparison groups. We, therefore, interact a dummy for these various definitions of pseudo-treatment group with the six-week policy-on term in an extended reduced form for crime:

$$(7) \quad \Delta c_{b52} = \alpha_4 + \beta_4 POST_t + \delta_4(POST_t \cdot T_b) + \theta_{SD}(POST_t \cdot SD_b) + \lambda_4[x_{bt} - x_{b(t-52)}] + [u_{4bt} - u_{4b(t-52)}],$$

where SD_b is an indicator for whether a borough is part of the pseudo-treatment group that could be subject to indirect spatial displacement effects of the policy intervention.

In a similar fashion, we can test for intertemporal displacement by looking at whether crime rose significantly in treatment boroughs in the weeks after Operation Theseus was completed. To do so, we use the following equation:

$$(8) \quad \Delta c_{b52} = \alpha_5 + \beta_5 POST_t + \delta_5(POST_t \cdot T_b) + \theta_{TD}(TD_t \cdot T_b) + \lambda_5[x_{bt} - x_{b(t-52)}] + [u_{5bt} - u_{5b(t-52)}],$$

where TD_t is a dummy variable measuring the weeks after the operation that can be used to look for possible temporal displacement in individual weeks in the postpolicy period when police deployment fell back to preattack levels.

10.3.2 Descriptive Statistics

Table 10.1 shows some descriptive statistics on crime and police before and after the terror attacks. It shows a sharp rise in police deployment in the treatment groups in the six weeks following the first round of terror attacks (a 38 percent increase in hours worked per 1,000 population, rising from 169.46 to 242.29). In the full comparison group of twenty-seven boroughs, there was barely any change (going from 82.77 to 84.95). At the same time, crime fell significantly in the five treatment boroughs (by around 13 percent), while there was no change in the comparison boroughs. Thus, crime fell significantly in the treatment group relative to the control group (by 12.9 percent in the difference-in-difference given in the final row of the table).

For exploring possible spatial displacement effects, the table also shows what happened to crime and police for three groups of possible pseudo-treatment boroughs—a group for all of Inner London (as per the definition given by the Office of National Statistics, labelled "Inner"); a group of all those boroughs bordering the treatment group ("Adjacent"); and the five boroughs closest to the treatment group ("Central"). These are the different definitions of SD_b from equation (7) that we consider in our empirical analysis. The unconditional preperiod and postperiod statistics for these different groups are given in table 10.1. As we have already noted, in terms of police hours, there was very little change for any of our proposed pseudo-treatment boroughs. Similarly, these unconditional statistics do not show any evidence of the increase in crime that would be expected if the police intervention was displacing criminal activity from the treatment group into nearby boroughs.

10.3.3   Estimates of the Direct Impacts of Police on Crime

We report the main reduced form OLS and structural IV results corresponding to the direct effect of police on crime in table 10.2. We specify two $T \cdot$ Post-Attack terms that correspond first to the six-week policy-on period after July 7, 2005, and then second to the remaining postpolicy period in

Table 10.2   **Direct crime effects of Operation Theseus**

| | Reduced forms | | OLS | IV |
| | Police | Crime | | |
	(1)	(2)	(3)	(4)
$T \cdot$ Post-Attack1	0.342***	−0.131***		
	(0.028)	(0.030)		
$T \cdot$ Post-Attack2	0.001	−0.035		
	(0.010)	(0.030)		
ln(Police Deployment)			−0.031	0.382***
			(0.050)	(0.089)
Controls	Yes	Yes	Yes	Yes
No. of boroughs	32	32	32	32
No. of observations	1,664	1,664	1,664	1,664

Source: See Draca, Machin, and Witt (2008) for a more detailed set of results.

Notes: All specifications include week-fixed effects. Clustered standard errors in parentheses. Boroughs weighted by population. Weeks defined in a Thursday–Wednesday interval throughout to ensure a clean pre- and postsplit in the attack weeks. $T \cdot$ Post-Attack is defined as interaction of treatment group with a dummy variable for the postperiod. $T \cdot$ Post-Attack1 is defined as interaction of treatment group with a deployment "policy" dummy for weeks one–six following the July 7, 2005 attack. $T \cdot$ Post-Attack2 is defined as treatment group interaction for all weeks subsequent to the main Operation Theseus deployment. Treatment group defined as boroughs of Westminster, Camden, Islington, Tower Hamlets, and Kensington and Chelsea. Police deployment defined as total weekly hours worked by all police staff at borough-level. Controls based on Quarterly Labour Force Survey (QLFS) data and include borough unemployment rate, employment rate, males under twenty-five as proportion of population, and whites as proportion of population (following QLFS ethnic definitions). OLS = ordinary least squares; IV = instrumental variable.

***Significant at the 1 percent level.

the second half of 2005. The second term is, therefore, useful for detecting any persistent effects of the police deployment. The first two columns show the reduced form for police deployment and crime. The key term here is T • Post-Attack1, which represents the treatment • policy-on interaction for Operation Theseus. The coefficients here show that police deployment increased by 34.1 percent and crime fell by 13.1 percent in the treatment group during the policy-on period. Furthermore, there is no evidence of a persistent effect of the deployment (i.e., the T • Post-Attack2 coefficient is statistically indistinguishable from zero) for either crime or police.

The final two columns of table 10.2 show the results for the OLS and IV specifications that correspond to these reduced forms. Note that the OLS specification in column (3) is specified in differences, yielding a negative insignificant coefficient. This reflects the fact that, outside of our Operation Theseus policy window, there is minimal time series variation in police on a year-on-year basis. As reported in Draca, Machin, and Witt (2008), the levels version of this model shows a significant, positive coefficient (with an estimate 0.73 [0.053]). The final column in table 10.2 gives the IV estimate. This elasticity indicates that a 10 percent increase in police reduces crime by approximately 3.8 percent.

10.3.4   Estimates of the Indirect Impact of Crime— Spatial Displacement

The results using different control groups to explore possible spatial displacement are reported in table 10.3. The possible displacement effects for the six-week period during Operation Theseus are reported in first row as Area • Post-Attack1, where Area is a dummy variable for each our pseudo-treatment SD_b definitions. In the second row, we interact the Area dummy with a time dummy for all the weeks after Operation Theseus from late August until the end of 2005. This is done to test for potential long-term persistence effects. Similarly, the direct effects of the intervention are given in the rows labeled T • Post-Attack1 and T • Post-Attack2. It is clear from these conditional estimates that there are no significant, positive displacement effects—in fact, the coefficients are estimated to be slightly negative.

10.3.5   Estimates of the Indirect Impact of Crime— Temporal Displacement

The fact that the timing of the police increases and crime falls go hand in hand is in line with the idea that temporal displacement did not occur. In table 10.2, there is a sharp rise in police deployment in the six weeks after the first round of attacks (as shown by the significant positive coefficient on T • Post-Attack1), which then falls back to preattack levels for the rest of 2005 (as shown by the insignificant coefficient on T • Post-Attack1). The same is true of crime where the estimated coefficient on T • Post-Attack1 is significant and negative, yet the estimated coefficient on T • Post-Attack2 is insignificantly different from zero.

Table 10.3   Spatial displacement effects of Operation Theseus

	Inner (1)	Adjacent (2)	Central (3)
Area • Post-Attack1	−0.007	−0.001	−0.027
	(0.033)	(0.032)	(0.043)
Area • Post-Attack2	0.011	−0.007	−0.029
	(0.024)	(0.021)	(0.021)
T • Post-Attack1	−0.133	−0.132	−0.138
	(0.032)	(0.032)	(0.031)
T • Post-Attack2	−0.031	−0.037	−0.041
	(0.031)	(0.031)	(0.030)
Controls	Yes	Yes	Yes
No. of boroughs	32	32	32
No. of observations	1,664	1,664	1,664

Notes: Standard errors clustered by borough in parentheses. All regressions include week-fixed effects. Boroughs weighted by population. Weeks defined in a Thursday–Wednesday interval throughout to ensure a clean pre- and postsplit in the attack weeks. T • Post-Attack is defined as interaction of treatment group with a dummy variable for the postperiod. T • Post-Attack1 is defined as interaction of treatment group with a deployment "policy" dummy for weeks one–six following the July 7, 2005 attack. T • Post-Attack2 is defined as treatment group interaction for all weeks subsequent to the main Operation Theseus deployment. Area • Post-Attack1 and Area • Post-Attack2 are dummies for the pseudo-treatment boroughs interacted with the Post-Attack time dummies. Definitions of these areas are given in the notes to table 10.1. Controls based on Quarterly Labour Force Survey (QLFS) data and include borough unemployment rate, employment rate, males under twenty-five as proportion of population, and whites as proportion of population (following QLFS ethnic definitions).

The common timing of police increases and crime falls thus seems inconsistent with temporal displacement by criminals. This is considered in more detail in Table 10.4. In this table, we estimate the treatment group and week interaction for every week for the eight weeks following the end of Operation Theseus. This is effectively a placebo test for potential "policy" effects outside of the six-week period of the intervention. Following the intertemporal displacement hypothesis, a postpolicy rebound or "smoothing" response by criminals would be evident in the weeks after Operation Theseus. However, there is no evidence that crime increased significantly in year-on-year terms for the weeks after the policy was switched off. In fact, the coefficients are consistently negative, probably reflecting the slight downward trend for crime in the treatment group. This is in contrast to the direct effects during the policy-on period, which are significant for each week of the intervention.

10.3.6   Comparison of Estimated Effects With Those in the Literature

Therefore, it seems that our estimated direct effects are not contaminated by spatial or temporal displacement. Moreover, the magnitudes of our casual estimates are similar to the small number of causal estimates found

Table 10.4   Temporal displacement effects in the post Operation Theseus period

Weeks after Operation Theseus	Coefficient	Standard error
+1	−0.040	0.061
+2	−0.041	0.045
+3	−0.090	0.030
+4	−0.106	0.060
+5	−0.085	0.045
+6	−0.067	0.078
+7	−0.211	0.039
+8	−0.039	0.033

Notes: Controls and boroughs included follow those for table 10.2. This table reports the results for $T \cdot$ Week placebo policies for the eight weeks following the end of Operation Theseus. The full set of $T \cdot$ week coefficients for all weeks are shown graphically in Draca, Machin, and Witt (2008).

in the literature. They are also estimated much more precisely in statistical terms because of the very sharp discontinuity in police deployment that occurred.

Table 10.5 reports estimates from the other causal studies we know of. For example, Levitt's (1997) study found elasticities in the −0.43 to −0.50 range, while Corman and Mocan (2000) estimated an average elasticity of −0.45 across different types of offences. The papers based upon terror attacks (Di Tella and Schargrodsky [2004] and Klick and Tabarrok 2005) report elasticities in this range. Our results are certainly qualitatively similar, with our preferred result being −0.38. This coincidence of estimates in very different contexts is strongly supportive of the external validity of these studies.

10.4   Conclusions

In this chapter, we have presented causal estimates of the impact of police on crime and tested for possible spatial and intertemporal displacement effects in the context of a major police intervention in London from July to August 2005. This intervention had clear direct effects on crime in the areas heavily treated by a highly visible police deployment. The structure of the intervention also induced a very clean change in the relative costs of crime—police deployment levels in the comparison group boroughs were held constant, thereby avoiding the possibility that crime could have fallen due to an absolute fall in police. However, our tests of spatial and intertemporal displacement deliver an emphatic null result. At least at the level of aggregation we consider here (weekly, borough-level), the Operation Theseus intervention did not generate significant indirect displacement effects in addition to its direct crime reducing effects.

As this last comment implies, our results do not rule out the possibility that displacement effects may have had a role at a more disaggregated level.

ble 10.5   **Instrumental variable (IV) estimates of the police-crime relationship**

~~udy~~	IV strategy	Estimates
~~evitt~~ (1997)	Using timing of gubernatorial elections as an instrument for police expenditure and hiring.	Violent crime: IV estimates of –1.0 compared to ordinary least squares estimates of –0.3 (approximate elasticities). Property crime: IV estimates of –0.4 compared to ordinary least squares estimates of –0.2 (approximate elasticities).
~~C~~orman and Mocan (2000)	Uses a long thirty-year monthly time series on crime and the number of police officers in New York. Impact of police estimated by using lagged values.	Elasticity of –0.5 for robbery and –0.4 for burglary (approximate).
~~D~~i Tella and Schargrodsky (2004)	Used deployments around potential terrorist targets in Buenos Aires as a source of exogenous variation in police presence.	Elasticity of –0.33 with an estimate of –0.17 using the most conservative assumptions.
Klick and Tabarrok (2005)	Use changes in terror alert levels in Washington to infer a variation in police deployment.	Authors estimate a 15% fall in crime in high terror alert periods. Provide an estimate of the police crime elasticity as –0.3 (approximate).

Our tests for spatial displacement are effectively tests for between-borough displacement. We are unable to test for within-borough displacement arising from the allocation of police inside the treatment group boroughs. For example, less heavily treated parts of the treatment boroughs may experienced increases in crime relative to more heavily treated areas. However, as we point out in Draca, Machin, and Witt (2008), this would lead to a downward bias on our estimates of the direct effects of the intervention.

References

Braga, A. 2001. The effects of hot spots policing on crime. *Annals of the American Academy of Political and Social Sciences* 578:104–25.

Corman, H., and H. Mocan. 2000. A time series analysis of crime, deterrence, and drug abuse. *American Economic Review* 87:270–90.

Di Tella, R., and E. Schargrodsky. 2004. Do police reduce crime? Estimate using the allocation of police forces after a terrorist attack. *American Economic Review* 94:115–33.

Draca, M., S. Machin, and R. Witt. 2008. Panic on the streets of London: Police, crime, and the July 2005 terror attacks. CEP Discussion Paper no. 852. London: Centre for Economic Performance.

Evans, W., and E. Owens. 2007. COPS and crime. *Journal of Public Economics* 91: 181–201.

Freeman, R. 1999. The economics of crime. In *Handbook of labor economics,* ed. O. Ashenfelter and D. Card. Amsterdam: North Holland.

Hessling, R. 1994. Displacement: A review of the empirical literature. In *Crime Prevention Studies 3.* Monsey, NY: Criminal Justice Press.

Jacob, B., L. Lefgren, and E. Moretti. 2007. The dynamics of criminal behavior: Evidence from weather shocks. *Journal of Human Resources* 42:489–527.

Klick, J., and A. Tabarrok. 2005. Using terror alert levels to estimate the effect of police on crime. *Journal of Law and Economics* 48:267–79.

Levitt, S. 1997. Using electoral cycles in police hiring to estimate the effect of police on crime. *American Economic Review* 87:270–90.

———. 2002. Using electoral cycles in police hiring to estimate the effects of police on crime: Reply. *American Economic Review* 92:1244–50.

———. 2004. Understanding why crime fell in the 1990s: Four factors that explain the decline and six that do not. *Journal of Economic Perspectives* 18 (1): 163–90.

Machin, S., and O. Marie. 2009. Crime and police resources: The street crime initiative. *Journal of the European Economic Association,* forthcoming.

McCrary, J. 2002. Using electoral cycles in police hiring to estimate the effects of police on crime: Comment. *American Economic Review* 92:1236–43.

Sherman, L., and D. Weisburd. 1995. General deterrent effects of police patrols in crime "hot spots": A randomized control trial. *Justice Quarterly* 12:625–48.

Comment   Catherine Rodriguez

The objective of the chapter "Crime Displacement and Police Interventions: Evidence from London's 'Operation Theseus'" is to present evidence on the casual impact of police presence on crime rates and investigate its indirect effects through potential crime displacement. Using weekly data of crime and police force in London for the period between January 1, 2004, to December 31, 2005, the authors find an elasticity of crime with respect to police of approximately –0.3. In contrast with this clear direct effect, the authors do not find any evidence of significant spatial or intertemporal displacement in crime during or after the intervention took place.

Without a doubt, the question that the authors are interested in is of extreme importance. Previous work, such as Levitt (1997), Di Tella and Schargrodsky (2004), and Klick and Taborrak (2005), have established the direct effect of police force in crime reduction. However, as the authors men-

Catherine Rodriguez is assistant professor of economics at the Universidad de los Andes.

tion, less attention has been given to the potential indirect effects these policies might bring. Understanding the possible indirect effects that increases in police deployment could bring to criminal behavior is important in practical terms. If there is indeed criminal displacement, either temporal or spatial, the effectiveness of transitory deterrence interventions previously found in the literature could be very limited, and its application should hence be carefully evaluated.

The classical and most difficult problem to solve in studies of the effect of deterrence measures on crime is the endogeneity between both variables. In order to tackle with it, the authors follow the idea of previous work in which terrorist attacks allow the emergence of a quasi-experiment. Specifically, they used the fact that after the July 2005 London terrorist attacks, the police force in the center of the city increased by more than 30 percent for a consecutive period of six weeks. Such an increase, referred to by the police force as Operation Theseus, can be cataloged as an exogenous change in police force that was not related to the crime rate in the area. Moreover, as explained by the authors, this change in deployment was achieved using extra hours of work and, hence, no reduction of police force in other sectors of the city was necessary. It is precisely this last aspect of the policy that allows the authors to study any displacement effect.

Under such a scenario, the authors employ an instrumental variable (IV) estimation methodology that directly tries to identify the casual impact of the number of police deployed on crime rates. In the first stage, they estimate changes in police deployment using Operation Theseus as the instrumental variable. This clear and powerful exogenous variation of police force allows the authors in the second stage to estimate an elasticity of crime of –0.3. To analyze the possible displacement effects, the authors define different dummy variables measuring either time or location. Specifically, to analyze spatial displacement, the authors use as pseudo-treatment boroughs those immediately around the actual treated ones. To analyze intertemporal displacement, they define two treatment periods: one during the six weeks of operation Theseus and the second one with the remaining weeks of 2005 after the operation took place. In none of these alternative specifications are the authors able to reject the hypothesis that there are no significant spatial or intertemporal displacement effects of crime caused by Operation Theseus.

I believe the article clearly provides further evidence on the causal relationship of police on crime rates. It uses a clever idea of a quasi-experiment, is very well written, and, indeed, convinces the reader on the issues dealt. Furthermore, as previously mentioned, it deals with a question that has been understudied in the economics literature. However, there are some small comments that should be kept in mind related to the estimations presented and future research that, in my opinion, could in principle be a very interesting agenda.

The first comment relates to the policy implications of the study. From the IV estimates, we find that a 10 percent increase in police force could reduce crime rates by almost 3 percent. This effect is large and, hence, provides further evidence in favor of the convenience of having larger police forces in cities suffering from high crime rates. In addition, no evidence is found on possible negative effects on crime displacement and, hence, the estimate of elasticity previously mentioned should be accurate. However, it is important to have a cost-benefit analysis of these six weeks. Before any policy decision is taken, it is imperative to understand whether the costs associated with a bigger police force are compensated by the reduction in crime. This is probably not a difficult exercise to carry out, and it is certainly a very informative one.

The second comment relates to the spatial displacement analysis. The authors implicitly assume that displacement will occur only in adjacent boroughs but will not occur in further away places. It is reasonable to assume just the opposite. Given that a greater amount of policemen were deployed in central London, thieves, burglars, and other criminals would rather move to further apart areas that are relatively less protected than to displace their criminal activities to adjacent areas. It would be interesting to see whether any difference in the coefficients is obtained using as pseudo-treatment boroughs from outer London instead of using only boroughs located in the center of the city as it is done in the present chapter.

A similar suggestion can be raised with the temporal displacement of crime exercises. As mentioned, the authors define two treatment periods. The first one is the six weeks in which Operation Theseus was in place, while the second one is encompassed by the remaining weeks of 2005. It would be interesting to have a third alternative, namely the six weeks immediately after Operation Theseus was in place. Even though there was no change in police deployment compared to the previous year, the reduction in police force during these six weeks must have been evident for citizens and, hence, a change in criminal behavior could have taken place. This exercise could also shed light on an alternative view in which there is an inertial behavior of crime.

The last comment is related to the type of crimes analyzed by the authors in this and in their companion paper.[1] In the present paper, the analysis evolves around what the authors call "susceptible crimes." Although it is explained in more detail in Draka, Machin, and Witt (2008), according to the authors, this group is made up by violence and sexual offenses, theft, and robbery. Nonsusceptible crimes, on the other hand, are burglary and criminal damage. The results in their first paper show that while police deployment could indeed reduce the incidence of "susceptible crimes," it had no effect on burglary or criminal damage. Unfortunately, in this displacement

---

1. See Draca, Machin, and Witt (2008).

paper, the authors do not present any evidence on the possibility of different types of crime displacement among boroughs. Is it the case that after the increase in police deployment in the treated areas, different types of crimes increased in other areas? It would be very interesting to see this exercise in the future.

Moreover, I believe that an alternative analysis among the different types of crimes will not demand such an ad hoc division between them. In Draca, Machin, and Witt (2008), the authors' main argument to justify the division between susceptible and nonsusceptible crimes is that burglary and criminal damage are more prevalent in residential areas or frequently occur at night. In my opinion, it is difficult to foresee why a burglar will not be deterred if more police are visible while a rapist (that one would think are precisely the crimes that occur at night) or common thief will be. Moreover, the results in the first paper suggest that crimes against people were affected, while crimes against property were not. This actually could go against what the authors would like to prove in their first paper with respect to the nonexistence of any uncorrelated shocks after the attacks took place. The number of houses or amount of property did not change, and no effect was found there. The number of people traveling in the Tube in central London was reduced, and crimes against people also were reduced.

Perhaps a much cleaner division to study whether displacement in the types of crime took place would be to compare the effect on crimes that occur during the day versus those that took place at night, irrespective of their type. Probably during the day not only is the higher security more evident but also the vision of policemen is higher. At night, neither the criminals nor the policemen can see each other and, hence, it will be expected that the crime rates cannot be reduced as much. I believe that such an analysis of types of crimes committed will greatly enrich what already is an excellent chapter and will show the reader a third possibility of displacement that is often studied in the criminologist literature as stated by Jacob, Lefgren, and Moretti (2007).

References

Di Tella, R., and E. Schargrodsky. 2004. Do police reduce crime? Estimate using the allocation of police forces after a terrorist attack. *American Economic Review* 94:115–33.

Draca, M., S. Machin, and R. Witt. 2008. Panic on the streets of London: Police, crime, and the July 2005 terror attacks. CEP Discussion Paper no. 852. London: Centre for Economic Performance.

Jacob, B., L. Lefgren, and E. Moretti. 2007. The dynamics of criminal behavior: Evidence from weather shocks. *Journal of Human Resources* 42:489–527.

Klick, J., and A. Tabarrok. 2005. Using terror alert levels to estimate the effect of police on crime. *Journal of Law and Economics* 48:267–79.

Levitt, S. 1997. Using electoral cycles in police hiring to estimate the effect of police on crime. *American Economic Review* 87:270–90.

11

The Impact of Incentives on Human Behavior
Can We Make It Disappear?
The Case of the Death Penalty

Naci Mocan and Kaj Gittings

11.1 Introduction

Economists are interested in the investigation of human behavior and how individuals respond to prices and incentives. Economic theory, which demonstrates an inverse relationship between the price of a commodity and its consumption, suggests that an increase in the price or cost of a behavior leads to a reduction in the intensity of that behavior. Therefore, as economic analysis of consumer behavior is applicable to any commodity ranging from apples to cars, it is also applicable to any type of human behavior, ranging from drunk driving to sexual activity to marital dissolution. Based on economic theory, an immense amount of empirical research has investigated the extent to which individuals alter their behavior in response to increases in the relevant "prices" that may impact that behavior.

11.1.1 Rationality and Reaction to Incentives

One common argument made by noneconomists against the economic approach to human behavior is that people are not *rational enough* to behave according to the predictions of economic theory when it comes to behaviors such as smoking, consumption of alcohol and illicit drugs, sexual activity, and crime. However, an enormous empirical literature in economics has

Naci Mocan holds the Ourso Distinguished Chair of Economics at Louisiana State University, and is a research associate of the National Bureau of Economic Research. Kaj Gittings is assistant professor of economics at Louisiana State University.

We thank Paul Mahler and Weijia Wu for excellent research assistance and Rafael Di Tella, Ted Joyce, Michael Grossman, Steve Medema, Laura Argys, Erdal Tekin, the referees, the editors, and the participants of the NBER-LICIP Inter-American Seminar on Economics in Buenos Aires, Argentina, for helpful comments and suggestions.

demonstrated that even these behaviors are responsive to prices and incentives. For example, consumption of cigarettes declines when cigarette prices rise (e.g., Becker, Grossman, and Murphy 1994; Yurekli and Zhang 2000; Gruber, Sen, and Stabile 2003), alcohol consumption is curtailed when alcohol prices are increased (e.g., Farrell, Manning, and Finch 2003; Manning, Blumberg, and Moulton 1995), drug use responds to variations in drug prices (e.g., Van Ours 1995; Saffer and Chaloupka 1999; Grossman 2005), pregnancies and childbearing are influenced by state and federal policies that alter the costs (e.g., Mellor 1998; Lundberg and Plotnick 1995), and the timing of births within a year is responsive to the tax benefit of having a child (Dickert-Conlin and Chandra 1999). Such results hold true even in subpopulations such as adolescents, who are thought to be present-oriented and less rational (e.g., Pacula et al. 2001; Gruber and Zinman 2001; Grossman and Chaloupka 1998; Grossman et al. 1994; Lundberg and Plotnick 1990), and among individuals with mental health problems (Tekin, Mocan, and Liang, forthcoming; Saffer and Dave 2005). In a different vein, research in experimental economics has demonstrated that individuals respond to changes in prices as predicted by economic theory, and even children behave rationally when modifying their behavior in response to variations in prices (Harbaugh, Krause, and Berry 2001).

The same results are obtained from analyses of the response of criminal activity to the relevant costs and benefits. The pioneering work of Becker (1968) indicated that criminal activity should decline as the "price" of such activity increases. Empirical analyses testing the economic model of crime have demonstrated that illicit behavior indeed responds to incentives and sanctions. For example, Jacob and Levitt (2003) showed that incentives for high test scores motivate teachers and administrators to cheat on standardized tests in Chicago public schools. Corman and Mocan (2000, 2005) and DiTella and Schargrodsky (2004) demonstrated that increased arrests and more police officers reduce crime. Levitt (1998a) showed that juvenile crime goes down when punishment gets stiffer. Grogger (1998) and Mocan and Rees (2005) found that the extent of criminal involvement among high school students is influenced by both economic conditions and deterrence. Corman and Mocan (2005) and Hansen and Machin (2002) showed that criminal activity reacts to increases in the minimum wage. Similarly, it has been shown that prison crowding, which generates early release of prisoners, has a significant impact on crime rates (Levitt 1996).

One specific subanalysis in this domain has received significant attention. Specifically, the extent to which murder rates respond to deterrence was first investigated theoretically and empirically by Ehrlich (1973, 1975, 1977a), who found a deterrent effect of capital punishment. Some analysts questioned the robustness of the results (Hoenack and Weiler 1980; Passell and Taylor 1977), and Ehrlich and others responded to these criticisms (Ehrlich 1977b; Ehrlich and Mark 1977; Ehrlich and Brower 1987; Ehrlich and Liu

1999). In a recent article, Donohue and Wolfers (2005) focused on a number of recent papers that reported a deterrent effect of death penalty on murder and stated that the findings of these papers were not robust. The purpose of this paper is to provide a new and detailed analysis of the impact of leaving death row (executions, commutations, and other removals from death row) on state murder rates. Specifically, we make various attempts to eliminate the deterrent effect of capital punishment and investigate if and under what conditions one succeeds in eliminating the impact of leaving death row on the murder rate.

As we demonstrate in detail in the following, the signaling effect of leaving death row and its impact on murder is robust. Although the impact of executions sometimes disappears when one estimates specifications, which are inconsistent with theory, the impact of commutations remains significant even in those models. Furthermore, as summarized in table 11.13 and detailed in the chapter, in many cases the deterrence results *do not* disappear even under many specifications that have been tried out in the literature that have no theoretical foundation.

11.2   Data and the Empirical Model

The data set used in the chapter is the same one as employed by Mocan and Gittings (2003) and Donohue and Wolfers (2006). One distinguishing feature of the data set is that it contains the entire history of death sentences between 1977 and 1997, including the exact month of removal from death row and the reason for it (execution, commutation, etc.), for each death row inmate. The data on state-level crimes, arrests, prison population, prison deaths, and other state characteristics such as the unemployment rate, urbanization rate, racial composition of the state, and other attributes are compiled from various sources (see Mocan and Gittings 2003, 474–76).

The investigation of the impact of deterrence on murder is carried out by estimating models of the following form:

(1) $$M_{it} = \mathbf{D}_{it-1} \alpha + \mathbf{X}_{it}\beta + \mu_i + \eta_t + \psi_{it} + \varepsilon_{it},$$

where M_{it} is the murder rate in state i and year t. The vector $\mathbf{X}$ contains state characteristics that may be correlated with criminal activity, including the unemployment rate, real per capita income, the proportion of the state population in the following age groups: twenty to thirty-four, thirty-five to forty-four, forty-five to fifty-four and fifty-five and over, the proportion of the state population in urban areas, the proportion that is black, the infant mortality rate, the party affiliation of the governor, and the legal drinking age in the state. Theoretical and empirical justification for the inclusion of these variables can be found in Levitt (1998a) and Lott and Mustard (1997). Following Levitt (1998a) and Katz, Levitt, and Shustorovich (2003), we also control for the number of prisoners per violent crime and the prison death rate (a measure of prison conditions) as two additional measures of deterrence.

The variable μ_i represents unobserved state-specific characteristics that impact the murder rate, which are controlled for by state-fixed effects, η_t stands for common year effects, and the models also include state-specific time trends represented by ψ_{it}. To control for the impact of the 1995 Oklahoma City bombing, a dummy variable is included that takes the value of one in Oklahoma in 1995 and zero elsewhere.

11.2.1   Measurement of Risks (Increase and Decrease in the Cost of Murder)

The vector D represents deterrence variables and includes the probability of apprehension, the probability of sentencing given apprehension, as well as various probabilities pertaining to leaving death row, conditional on sentencing. It also includes the incarceration rate and the prison death rate. Note that execution is not the only outcome for prisoners on death row. During the period of 1977 to 1997 (the time period analyzed in this paper), 17 percent of inmates who completed their duration on death row were executed, while the other 83 percent left for other reasons (e.g., commutation of the sentence, sentence or conviction being overturned, sentence being found unconstitutional). This information allows for an investigation as to how the murder rate reacts to an increase in the price of crime (executions) as well as a decrease in the price of crime (commutation and all removals other than executions and deaths).

From a theoretical point of view, it is important to carefully consider the timing of events. The probability of apprehension is a measure of the risk of getting caught, given that a murder is committed. Because the unit of analysis is state-year, this probability is measured as the proportion of murders cleared by an arrest in a particular state and year; that is, $ARRATE_t = (AR_t/MUR_t)$, where AR_t is the number of murder arrests in a state in year t (state subscript is dropped for ease of exposition), and MUR_t stands for the number of murders in year t. The second risk variable is the probability of receiving a death sentence given that a murder arrest took place. After a person is arrested for murder, he or she does not automatically end up on death row; instead, a trial takes place in which not all defendants are found guilty nor do they all receive a capital sentence. Therefore, one can calculate the probability of being found guilty and sentenced to death, conditional on being arrested for murder. The average length of time between the date of a murder arrest and the date on which an inmate is sentenced to death is more than one year.[1] Thus, the risk of receiving the death sentence is defined as the number of death sentences handed out in a year divided

---

1. For example, a person who is arrested in October 1990, is likely to receive a death sentence after February 1992.

by the number of murder arrests two years prior. That is, $SENTRATE_t = (SENT_t/AR_{t-2})$, where $SENT_t$ represents the number of death sentences handed out in year t.

Following Mocan and Gittings (2003), three death penalty–related deterrence variables are created. When constructing the capital punishment variables, it is useful to realize that if a person receives the death sentence, he or she is not executed instantly; instead, it has been demonstrated that the average duration from sentencing to execution (across states) is about six years during the period studied in this paper (Bedau 1997; Dezhbakhsh, Rubin, and Shepherd 2003; Mocan and Gittings 2003; Argys and Mocan 2004). As was done in Mocan and Gittings (2003), this information suggests that the risk of execution should be calculated as the number of executions divided by the proper cohort of death sentences six years earlier; that is, $EXEC_t/SENT_{t-6}$. Also, about 83 percent of the inmates are removed from death row for reasons other than execution. One such reason is commutation, where the inmate is granted clemency and the sentence is changed to a prison term, typically life. Because commutation implies a reduced risk of death and, therefore, a reduced cost of committing murder, an increase in the probability of commutations should theoretically increase the murder rate. The same argument is true for all removals from death row (other than executions and other deaths while on death row). Figure 11.7 displays the average duration on death row by execution, commutation, and other removals from death row and shows that the proper cohort to use in calculating the risk of commutation and risk of removal is about the same as that for executions.[2]

Not all previous research has considered the relevant cohorts when calculating these risk variables. For example, Donohue and Wolfers (2005) employ the data and methods of Mocan and Gittings (2003), but they create these variables as the ratio of executions (or removals) in a given year to the number of death sentences *in that same year*, that is, as $(EXEC_t/SENT_t)$ or $(REMOVE_t/SENT_t)$. These variables have no real meaning because the numerator and denominator of the ratio have no connection to each other: employing the ratio of executions in year t to the death sentences in year t incorrectly assumes that execution of each inmate takes place in the same year of sentencing.

Although calculating the risks this way is not sensible, it would be reasonable to ask if the results were sensitive to variations in their proper measurement. Specifically, we consider variations in the probability of execution, the probability of commutation, and the probability of removal from death row in three different dimensions and investigate if these variations

---

2. Note that the duration on death row for removals other than execution is less than that for executions and approximately five years, on average. For this reason, Mocan and Gittings (2003) used the sentencing cohort five years ago in models that include removals; that is, $(EXEC_t/SENT_{t-5})$, or $(REMOVE_t/SENT_{t-5})$.

make the deterrence results disappear. We deviate from the existing analyses of Mocan and Gittings (2003), who used $EXEC_t/SENT_{t-6}$, and Donohue and Wolfers (2005), who used $EXEC_t/SENT_t$, and vary the sentencing cohort of the risk variables. For this exercise, we calculate the risks of execution, commutation and removals as $(EXEC_t/SENT_{t-5})$, $(COMM_t/SENT_{t-5})$, $(REMOVE_t/SENT_{t-5})$, assuming a five-year wait on death row, and $(EXEC_t/SENT_{t-4})$, $(COMM_t/SENT_{t-4})$, $(REMOVE_t/SENT_{t-4})$, assuming a four-year wait.[3]

The preceding discussion concerns variations in the denominator of the risk variable, but proper measurement of the numerator is important as well. If executions, commutations, or removals from death row send signals to potential criminals, then the timing of the signal needs to be addressed. An advantage of these data is the availability of the date of each execution and removal, which enables one to create execution, commutation, and removal measures that are consistent with theory. Mocan and Gittings (2003) considered a monthly adjustment to the capital punishment events where executions, commutations, and removals are prorated based on the month in which they occurred. For example, an execution that took place in January of 1980 can have an impact on the murder rate for the full year of 1980. However, if the execution took place in November 1980, it will have a trivial impact on the 1980 murder rate. Rather, the impact of this November execution on murder will primarily be felt in 1981. Thus, this November execution counts as 2/12 of an execution for 1980 and 10/12 of an execution for 1981. The same algorithms are applied for commutations, and removals. We call these the first measure of executions, commutations, and removals (EXEC, COMM, REMOVE). This is the measure employed by Mocan and Gittings (2003) and also by Donohue and Wolfers (2005).

The second dimension to vary the measurement of the risk variables is through the numerator. We consider a means of allocating the capital punishment events that uses a coarser algorithm than described in the preceding: if an execution took place within the first three quarters of a year, we attributed that execution to the same year. If the execution took place in the last quarter of a year (October to December), we attributed that execution to the following year under the assumption that the relative impact on

---

3. The issue here is how potential criminals measure risks. Assume that the true risk of execution conditional upon sentencing is 0.20. Specifically, assume that in a given state, each year ten people receive the death sentence, they stay on death row for four years, and at the end of the fourth year, two of them get executed. Thus, in each year, the risk of execution is, $(EXEC_t/SENT_{t-4}) = 2/10$. Now assume that in one particular year, the number of death sentences goes down to five. Would the criminal believe that the risk of execution doubled this year because only five people got sentenced this year instead of the usual ten (the thesis by Donohue and Wolfers 2005), or would the criminal's expected risk of execution given sentencing not change if the criminal knows that executions today pertain to sentences in the past (more closely estimating the true risk)? If criminals are utilizing information to form expectations about the true risk, the latter more likely approximates the behavior.

murders would be felt in the following year. The same was done for removals and commutations. We name these the second measures of executions, commutations, and removals (EXEC2, COMM2, and REMOVE2).[4]

The third dimension in which we vary the risk measures is by experimenting with the wide range of other denominators to calculate the risk of leaving death row. Some of these measures have been used previously in the literature (e.g., executions per state population, executions per prison population), while others have not, such as the total number of inmates on death row. Despite the fact that the measurement of these particular risk variables is inherently flawed, we incorporate them into the analysis to further examine the robustness of the results. Beyond measurement issues associated with the risk probabilities, we push the robustness check further by estimating these models across different samples (e.g., dropping various states) and using alternative weighting schemes.

Note that the models include a number of state-specific variables, ranging from the governor's party affiliation to the unemployment rate to socioeconomic controls that aim to capture time varying factors that may impact the homicide rate in the state. Also included are state-specific time trends (in addition to the year-fixed effects and state-fixed effects) to capture the impact of residual time varying unobservables. In addition to the homicide arrest rate, sentencing rate, and the execution, commutation, and removal rates that are in the models, it would be desirable to include additional measures of the severity of punishment, such as median time served for murder in each state and year. Although there is some information based on prison releases, these data are spotty and, therefore, not feasible to use. However, as was done in Mocan and Gittings (2003), the models we estimate also include prisoners per violent crime and the prison death rate as additional controls for the certainty and severity of punishment.

Donohue and Wolfers (2005) claim that the deterrence results reported in Mocan and Gittings (2003) disappear when coding errors are corrected, and they put forth two issues. The first issue pertains to dropping those observations where the denominator of the risk variable (SENT) is zero. The second issue is the lag length in the models, but in this regard, they simply estimate a different specification than Mocan and Gittings (2003).[5] While the first issue changes the sample slightly, this adjustment alone has no meaningful impact on the results. Changing the model specification (which is not a coding error correction), implemented by Donohue and Wolfers (2005), alters the significance of the execution coefficient, but not its magnitude. Their specification decision reduces the sample size (which they object elsewhere), diminishes the statistical power by definition and, thus, the statistical signifi-

---

4. In the following sensitivity tests, we also employ other measures, including raw *counts* of executions and commutations as pure signals to criminals.

5. See note 2 and panel B of table 6 in Donohue and Wolfers (2005).

cance of the execution coefficient. However, even this model alteration does not eliminate the significance of the commutations and removals from death row (see panel B, table 6 of Donohue and Wolfers 2005).

We estimate each specification using the exact same data set and the exact same programming code written by Donohue and Wolfers (2005) that addresses the division by zero issue. This allows us to produce a transparent picture as to how the murder rate reacts to alterations in two key deterrence variables: the risk of execution and the risk or commutation (or removal from death row), keeping *all else the same* in the specification.

11.3 Results

We estimate various versions of equation (1). Following Corman and Mocan (2000), Levitt (1998a), Katz, Levitt, and Shistorovich (2003), and Mocan and Gittings (2003), the deterrence variables are lagged by one year to minimize the concerns of simultaneity. For example, if the risk variable is $(EXEC_t/SENT_{t-5})$, its lagged value is employed in the regressions (i.e., $[EXEC_t/SENT_{t-5}]_{-1} = [EXEC_{t-1}/SENT_{t-6}]$). The models are estimated by weighted least squares, where the weights are state's share in the U.S. population. Later in the paper, we report and discuss results obtained without weighting. Robust standard errors, which are clustered at the state level, are reported in parentheses under the coefficients. In the interest of space, only the coefficients and standard errors pertaining to executions, commutations, and removals are reported.

Table 11.1 displays the results where the first measures of execution, commutation, and removal are employed. The top panel of table 11.1 measures the relevant risks as $(EXEC_t/SENT_{t-5})$, $(COMM_t/SENT_{t-5})$, $(REMOVE_t/SENT_{t-5})$. That is, it calculates the rates of execution, commutation, and removal per death sentences imposed five years earlier (assuming that the average duration on death row is five years). The models presented in the middle panel of table 11.1 are identical, except, the average duration on death row is assumed to be four years. Thus, the variables are calculated as $(EXEC_t/SENT_{t-4})$, $(COMM_t/SENT_{t-4})$, and $(REMOVE_t/SENT_{t-4})$.[6]

A number of aspects of the results in table 11.1 are noteworthy. First, the point estimates are very robust between specifications reported in the top two panels. Second, the execution rate has a negative and statistically significant impact on the murder rate. Third, the commutation and removal rates have positive impacts on the murder rate. Fourth, these results are consistent

---

6. Mocan and Gittings (2003) employed risk variables that take the average duration on death row as six years (denominator SENT lagged six years) in models for executions and commutations. Because the time between sentencing and REMOVE from death row is about five years, they employed SENT lagged five years in the denominator when the model included removals. Dohonue and Wolfers (2006), on the other hand, prefer zero lags of SENT in the denominator (as we replicated in the bottom panel of table 11.1).

Table 11.1 **Determinants of the murder rate: the first measure of execution, commutation, and removal**

	Duration on death row: 5 years				
$EXEC_t/SENT_{t-5})_{-1}$	−0.0056**			−0.0058**	−0.0066**
	(0.0027)			(0.0028)	(0.0029)
$COMM_t/SENT_{t-5})_{-1}$		0.0065		0.0070	
		(0.0047)		(0.0046)	
$REMOVE_t/SENT_{t-5})_{-1}$			0.0024***		0.0027***
			(0.0008)		(0.0009)
n	734	743	691	733	688
	Duration on death row: 4 years				
$(EXEC_t/SENT_{t-4})_{-1}$	−0.0054**			−0.0055**	−0.0047**
	(0.0022)			(0.0022)	(0.0021)
$(COMM_t/SENT_{t-4})_{-1}$		0.0036*		0.0038**	
		(0.0021)		(0.0019)	
$(REMOVE_t/SENT_{t-4})_{-1}$			0.0004		0.0005
			(0.0007)		(0.0007)
n	785	790	744	781	741
	Duration on death row: 0 years; time between arrest and death sentence: 0 years[a]				
$(EXEC_t/SENT_t)_{-1}$	0.0003			0.0001	0.0001
	(0.0014)			(0.0013)	(0.0014)
$(COMM_t/SENT_t)_{-1}$		0.0041***		0.0041***	
		(0.0013)		(0.0013)	
$(REMOVE_t/SENT_t)_{-1}$			0.0002		0.0002
			(0.0003)		(0.0003)
n	986	984	921	977	918

Notes: See section 11.2 for the explanation of the measurement of variables. Each model includes the following variables: murder arrest rate, sentencing rate, unemployment rate, real per capita income, proportion of the state population, in the following age groups: twenty to thirty-four, thirty-five to forty-four, forty-five to fifty-four, and fifty-five and over, proportion of the state population in urban areas, proportion that is black, infant mortality rate, legal drinking age in the state, number of prisoners per violent crime, and prison death rate. Also included in each model are state-fixed effects, a time trend, state-specific time trends, a dummy variable to control for the impact of the 1995 Oklahoma City bombing, and a dummy variable to indicate if the governor is a Republican. Robust and clustered standard errors are in parentheses.

[a]Specification estimated by Donohue and Wolfers (2006).

***Statistical significance at the 1 percent level or better.

**Statistical significance between 5 and 1 percent.

*Statistical significance between 10 and 5 percent.

with the specifications reported in Mocan and Gittings (2003), despite utilizing different sentencing cohorts as the denominator.

The bottom panel of table 11.1 displays the results of the model estimated by Donohue and Wolfers (2005) using the same data. In this specification, the execution, commutation, and removal rates are calculated by dividing executions, commutations, and removals in a year to the number of death sentences *in that same year.* Thus, it is assumed that the duration on death row is less than one year. Similarly, in this specification, the sentencing rate

Table 11.2   **Determinants of the murder rate: the second measure of execution, commutation, and removal**

	Duration on death row: 5 years				
$(EXEC2_t/SENT_{t-5})_{-1}$	−0.0058***			−0.0062***	−0.0073***
	(0.0020)			(0.0022)	(0.0022)
$(COMM2_t/SENT_{t-5})_{-1}$		0.0044		0.0056	
		(0.0047)		(0.0040)	
$(REMOVE2_t/SENT_{t-5})_{-1}$			0.0018***		0.0021***
			(0.0007)		(0.0007)
n	737	743	712	736	709
	Duration on death row: 4 years				
$(EXEC2_t/SENT_{t-4})_{-1}$	−0.0069*			−0.0070**	−0.0063*
	(0.0035)			(0.0035)	(0.0033)
$(COMM2_t/SENT_{t-4})_{-1}$		0.0034*		0.0036**	
		(0.0019)		(0.0016)	
$(REMOVE2_t/SENT_{t-4})_{-1}$			0.0002		0.0005
			(0.0008)		(0.0007)
n	785	792	761	783	758
	Duration on death row: 0 years; time between arrest and death sentence: 0 years[a]				
$(EXEC2_t/SENT_t)_{-1}$	−0.0002			−0.0001	−0.00004
	(0.0020)			(0.0019)	(0.0019)
$(COMM2_t/SENT_t)_{-1}$		0.0039***		0.0039***	
		(0.0010)		(0.0001)	
$(REMOVE2_t/SENT_t)_{-1}$			−0.0002		−0.0002
			(0.0006)		(0.0006)
n	989	990	952	984	949

Note: See table 11.1 notes.

is calculated as the ratio of death sentences in a year to murder arrests *in that same year,* assuming that the time length from arrest-to-trial-to-sentencing is also less than one year. Consequently, measuring the risk variables this way allows the execution result disappear, but the misspecification cannot eliminate the impact of commutations on the murder rate.[7]

Table 11.2 reports results obtained from models where the executions,

7. Note that the equation on page 816 of Donohue and Wolfers (2005) includes a variable called Pardons(t–1)/DeathSentences(t–7). Donohue and Wolfers (2005) write that Mocan and Gittings (2003) estimate that particular regression although Mocan and Gittings (2003) do not employ pardons in their paper. Similarly, table 6 of Donohue and Wolfers (2005 contains specifications in which a variable named "Pardons" is included, and a discussion is provided about pardons. For example, Donohue and Wolfers (2005) state on page 818 that "the two related measures of the porosity of the death sentence now yield sharply different results, with the *pardon rate* [emphasis added] robustly and positively associated with homicide . . ." Mocan and Gittings (2003) employ commutations in their regressions, not pardons. Commutations and pardons are two different events. A pardon, which is an extremely rare event, invalidates the guilt the punishment of the inmate. In fact, the official death row data we are using from the Bureau of Justice Statistics do not even identify a "pardon" as a type of removal from death row, unlike a sentence being commuted. A commutation reduces the severity of punishment; it is clemency, in which the sentence is reduced, typically to life in prison.

commutations, and removals are measured using the second set of variables that allocates events by the quarter in which they occur as described in section 11.2. In other words, the only difference between results reported in table 11.1 and table 11.2 is the measurement of the numerator of the execution, commutation, and removal rates. Once again, the impact of the execution rates does not disappear, unless one estimates the specification promoted by Donohue and Wolfers (2005). And, even in that case, similar to table 11.1, the impact of the commutation rate on the murder rate remains positive and statistically significant.

11.3.1 All Executions Are in Texas!

It can be argued that California and Texas are interesting states that contain potentially useful information for establishing the deterrent effect of the death penalty, and it could be that the deterrence results in the literature may be sensitive to exclusion of Texas and California from the analysis.[8] Table 11.3 is comparable to the top two panels in tables 11.1 and 11.2 with one difference: Texas and California are omitted from the models. As the table demonstrates, the impact of executions and commutations or removals are still significant when Texas and California are omitted from analysis.[9]

11.3.2 The Importance of the Denominator Once Again

Why is it the case that omitting Texas does not make the results disappear despite the fact that Texas executes a disproportionately large number of death row inmates? One explanation is that it is incorrect to focus on execution counts (to be included as an explanatory variable) when the correct measure is not the *number* of executions, but the *risk of the execution*. Despite the fact that a particular state has a large number of executions, the execution risk may not be high if the cohort of inmates that was sentenced to death is also large. Put differently, the number of executions needs to be adjusted by the appropriate denominator to obtain an actual measure of risk.

Table 11.4 summarizes the number of executions, commutation, and removals from death row between 1977 and 1997 for selected states; it also presents the average execution risk in each state during that period. The first measure is the number of executions in year t divided by the number of death sentences four years earlier. The second measure deflates the number of executions by death sentences five years prior. The third measure displayed in the table is a measure of risk previously used in the literature: the number of executions divided by prison population ($EXEC_t/PRISON_t$), and the fourth measure is the number of executions deflated by the number of inmates on death row in the same year ($EXEC_t/ROW_t$). While Texas executes

---

8. See Donahue and Wolfers (2005, 826).
9. We also omitted Texas and California individually. In neither case could we make the results disappear. See Mocan and Gittings (2006, 38–39).

Table 11.3   **Determinants of the murder rate (excluding Texas and California)**

	The first measure of executions, commutations, and removals				
	Duration on death row: 5 years				
$(EXEC_t/SENT_{t-5})_{-1}$	−0.0029			−0.0030**	−0.0041*
	(0.0019)			(0.0020)	(0.0023)
$(COMM_t/SENT_{t-5})_{-1}$		0.0048		0.0051	
		(0.0043)		(0.0042)	
$(REMOVE_t/SENT_{t-5})_{-1}$			0.0024***		0.0026***
			(0.0008)		(0.0009)
n	704	713	662	703	659
	Duration on death row: 4 years				
$(EXEC_t/SENT_{t-4})_{-1}$	−0.0041**			−0.0042**	−0.0036*
	(0.0019)			(0.0019)	(0.0018)
$(COMM_t/SENT_{t-4})_{-1}$		0.0042***		0.0043**	
		(0.0011)		(0.0019)	
$(REMOVE_t/SENT_{t-4})_{-1}$			0.0007		0.0008
			(0.0007)		(0.0007)
n	753	758	713	749	710
	The second measure of executions, commutations, and removals				
	Duration on death row: 5 years				
$(EXEC2_t/SENT_{t-4})_{-1}$	−0.0039**			−0.0042**	−0.0054***
	(0.0016)			(0.0017)	(0.0019)
$(COMM2_t/SENT_{t-4})_{-1}$		0.0037		0.0046	
		(0.0040)		(0.0034)	
$(REMOVE2_t/SENT_{t-4})_{-1}$			0.0018***		0.0020***
			(0.0006)		(0.0007)
n	707	713	682	706	679
	Duration on death row: 4 years				
$(EXEC2_t/SENT_{t-4})_{-1}$	−0.0055			−0.0056*	−0.0051
	(0.0034)			(0.0033)	(0.0031)
$(COMM2_t/SENT_{t-4})_{-1}$		0.0039***		0.0040***	
		(0.0011)		(0.0010)	
$(REMOVE2_t/SENT_{t-4})_{-1}$			0.0004		0.0006
			(0.0008)		(0.0007)
n	753	760	730	751	727

Note: See table 11.1 notes.

a large number of inmates annually, it is not the highest ranked state by any of these measures of execution risk. It is ranked fourth or fifth, depending on the risk measure, behind Virginia, Arkansas, and Louisiana. Missouri is generally ranked as the fifth. Therefore, the attempts to make the deterrence results disappear might be more productive if one were to omit high risk states rather than states with large absolute counts of executions.

Table 11.5 presents the results obtained from models when Virginia is dropped. Mocan and Gittings (2006) report the results when Arkansas or

Table 11.4 **Execution risk by state**

State	No. of exits from death row			Execution risk				Execution risk ranking			
	Executions	Commutations	Removals	$\frac{EXEC_t}{SENT_{t-4}}$	$\frac{EXEC_t}{SENT_{t-5}}$	$\frac{EXEC_t}{PRISON_t}$	$\frac{EXEC_t}{ROW_t}$	$\frac{EXEC_t}{SENT_{t-4}}$	$\frac{EXEC_t}{SENT_{t-5}}$	$\frac{EXEC_t}{PRISON_t}$	$\frac{EXEC_t}{ROW_t}$
Alabama	16	1	130	0.116	0.099	0.072	0.009	8	8	7	8
Arkansas	16	1	46	0.49	0.327	0.157	0.031	2	2	3	3
Georgia	22	6	150	0.136	0.127	0.057	0.012	7	7	8	7
Louisiana	24	2	78	0.345	0.315	0.226	0.056	3	3	1	2
Missouri	29	1	30	0.301	0.245	0.114	0.023	5	6	5	5
Nevada	6	3	32	0.079	0.08	0.072	0.007	10	9	6	9
Oklahoma	9	1	95	0.082	0.074	0.053	0.005	9	10	9	12
South Carolina	13	3	49	0.28	0.31	0.05	0.014	6	4	10	6
Texas	144	44	166	0.307	0.304	0.135	0.026	4	5	4	4
Virginia	46	5	15	0.612	0.652	0.162	0.059	1	1	2	1

Notes: PRISON is the total number of prisoners in the state. ROW is the number of death row inmates. The numbers in the execution risk columns are average annual values for the states.

Table 11.5   **Determinants of the murder rate (excluding Virginia)**

	The first measure of execution, commutation, and removal				
	Duration on death row: 5 years				
$(EXEC_t/SENT_{t-5})_{-1}$	–0.0066*			–0.0068*	–0.0084**
	(0.0035)			(0.0037)	(0.0036)
$(COMM_t/SENT_{t-5})_{-1}$		0.0087**		0.0091**	
		(0.0038)		(0.0039)	
$(REMOVE_t/SENT_{t-5})_{-1}$			0.0025***		0.0029***
			(0.0008)		(0.0010)
n	719	728	676	718	673
	Duration on death row: 4 years				
$(EXEC_t/SENT_{t-4})_{-1}$	–0.0052**			–0.0052**	–0.0045*
	(0.0025)			(0.0025)	(0.0024)
$(COMM_t/SENT_{t-4})_{-1}$		0.0044***		0.0045***	
		(0.0016)		(0.0015)	
$(REMOVE_t/SENT_{t-4})_{-1}$			0.0004		0.0005
			(0.0007)		(0.0007)
n	769	774	728	765	725

	The second measure of execution, commutation, and removal				
	Duration on death row: 5 years				
$(EXEC2_t/SENT_{t-5})_{-1}$	–0.0063**			–0.0061**	–0.0083***
	(0.0026)			(0.0026)	(0.0024)
$(COMM2_t/SENT_{t-5})_{-1}$		0.0083***		0.0083***	
		(0.0030)		(0.0031)	
$(REMOVE2_t/SENT_{t-5})_{-1}$			0.0019***		0.0023***
			(0.0007)		(0.0008)
n	722	728	697	721	694
	Duration on death row: 4 years				
$(EXEC2_t/SENT_{t-4})_{-1}$	–0.0066			–0.0067	–0.0060
	(0.0040)			(0.0040)	(0.0037)
$(COMM2_t/SENT_{t-4})_{-1}$		0.0043***		0.0044***	
		(0.0013)		(0.0012)	
$(REMOVE2_t/SENT_{t-4})_{-1}$			0.0003		0.0005
			(0.0008)		(0.0007)
n	769	776	745	767	742

Note: See table 11.1 notes.

Louisiana are dropped, respectively. In each case, dropping these states does not influence the results. That is, even when we remove the high-risk execution states from the analysis, the results are still robust. This may not be all that surprising as the coefficients are estimated through within state variation when including state-fixed effects.

This analysis shows that attempts to make the deterrence results disappear are ineffective. Even if one estimates an unusual specification that takes the numerator and denominator of the risk variables contemporaneously (in the bottom panels of table 11.1 and table 11.2), the estimated impact of executions becomes statistically insignificant, but the positive impact of commutations on the murder rate *does not disappear.*

11.4   The Impact of Death Penalty Laws

Donohue and Wolfers (2005) argued that the murder rates were *higher* in Kansas and New Hampshire after these states adopted the death penalty, were lower in New York and New Jersey after their adoption of the death penalty, and that murder rates *declined* in Massachusetts and Rhode Island after these states abolished the death penalty. We estimated various models in an effort to substantiate this statement. Because they indicate the impact of the death penalty laws are estimated separately for each of the mentioned states while controlling for the same variables as in the main specification, we estimated models separately for Kansas, New Hampshire, New York, New Jersey, Massachusetts, and Rhode Island.

For each state, a dummy variable is created that takes the value of one if the death penalty is legal and zero otherwise. Kansas legalized the death penalty in 1994. New Hampshire legalized it in 1991. Legalization took place in 1982 and 1995 for New Jersey and New York, respectively. Massachusetts and Rhode Island abolished the death penalty in 1984.[10] Because the sample runs from 1977 to 1997, estimating regressions for each state separately is complicated by a degrees-of-freedom problem. The results are summarized in table 11.6. The reported coefficients pertain to a lagged dummy variable indicating the legality of the death penalty.[11]

As the table shows, inclusion or exclusion of control variables has no substantial impact on the estimated coefficients of legal death penalty indicator. In these regressions, the coefficient of the death penalty indicator is not statistically different from zero in Rhode Island and New York. It is negative and significant in New Hampshire and New Jersey. In Kansas and Massachusetts, the coefficients are always negative and significant in one specification for each state.

As an alternative method to investigate the impact of each state's death penalty laws, we performed an interrupted time series analysis. To investigate

10. Massachusetts abolished the death penalty in October 1984. Thus, 1985 is the first year with no death penalty in Massachusetts in the data since abolishment took place. Similarly, 1985 is the first full year where the death penalty is illegal in Rhode Island.

11. The complete set of results can be found in Mocan and Gittings (2006). The number of control variables differs between the specifications to investigate the sensitivity. The sentencing rate could only be included in the regressions for New Jersey because there is no variation in the number of death sentences in the five other states. Similarly, the drinking age cannot be included in the models.

Table 11.6   **The impact of the death penalty on the murder rate**

State	(1)	(2)	(3)	(4)	(5)
	The coefficient of Death Penalty Legal ($t-1$)				
Kansas	−0.0214	−0.0044	−0.0007	−0.008*	−0.0011
	(0.0220)	(0.0183)	(0.0061)	(0.0040)	(0.0033)
New Hampshire	−0.0226	−0.0253**	−0.0125	−0.0206**	−0.0213**
	(0.0119)	(0.0099)	(0.0105)	(0.0080)	(0.0078)
Massachusetts	−0.0055	−0.0059	−0.0082*	−0.0075	−0.0066
	(0.0060)	(0.0048)	(0.0045)	(0.0065)	(0.0051)
Rhode Island	−0.0087	−0.0051	−0.0043	−0.0034	−0.0063
	(0.0046)	(0.0096)	(0.0070)	(0.0076)	(0.0067)
New York	0.0087	0.0165	0.0113	0.0119	0.0145
	(0.0183)	(0.0122)	(0.0125)	(0.0108)	(0.0194)
New Jersey	−0.0101	−0.009*	−0.0085***	−0.0132**	−0.0132**
	(0.0140)	(0.0037)	(0.0017)	(0.0036)	(0.0030)

Notes: Each cell reports the coefficient (standard error) of Death Penalty Legal ($t-1$) variable in the murder rate regressions for the corresponding state. This variable takes the value of 1 if death penalty is legal in the state and zero otherwise. Models in column (1) include murder arrest rate ($t-1$), sentencing rate, prisoners per violent crime ($t-1$), prison death rate ($t-1$), percent black, Republican governor, unemployment rate, per capita income, infant mortality rate, urbanization, percent aged twenty–thirty-four, percent aged thirty-five–forty-four, percent aged forty-five–fifty-four, percent aged fifty-five+, and time trend. Models in column (2) omit the unemployment rate, infant mortality rate, and urbanization. Models in column (3) omit the unemployment rate, infant mortality rate, urbanization, murder arrest rate ($t-1$), sentencing rate, prisoners per violent crime ($t-1$), and prison death rate ($t-1$). Models in column (4) omit percent black, Republican governor, unemployment rate, infant mortality rate, urbanization, percent aged twenty–thirty-four, percent aged thirty-five–forty-four, percent aged forty-five–fifty-four, and percent aged fifty-five+. Models in column (5) omit prison death rate ($t-1$), percent black, Republican governor, unemployment rate, per capita income, infant mortality rate, urbanization, percent aged twenty–thirty-four, percent aged thirty-five–forty-four, percent aged forty-five–fifty-four, and percent aged fifty-five+. Robust and clustered standard errors in parentheses.
***Statistical significance at the 1 percent level or better.
**Statistical significance between 5 and 1 percent.
*Statistical significance between 10 and 5 percent.

if the enactment or abolishment of the death penalty in a state has altered the behavior of the murder rate in that state over time, time series dynamics of the murder rate of each state can be modeled separately, and intervention variables can be added to investigate if the change in the death penalty law in that state in a particular year has altered the time series dynamics of the murder rate in that state. Following Mocan and Topyan (1993), Mocan (1994), and Harvey and Durbin (1986), let M_t stand for the murder rate in a particular state in year t. The dynamics of M_t over time can be expressed by equation (2), where μ_t represents slowly-evolving trend component of the murder rate, Ω_t stands for the cycle-component, and ε_t is regular random component.

(2)
$$M_t = \mu_t + \Omega_t + \varepsilon_t$$

The trend in the murder rate, μ_t, is determined by its level and the slope in each time period, which can be written in general as random walks as in equation (3).

(3)
$$\mu_t = \mu_{t-1} + \beta_{t-1} + \eta_t$$
$$\beta_t = \beta_{t-1} + \xi_t$$

A flexible method to model the cyclical behavior of the murder rate, represented by Ω in equation (2), is to assume a stochastic trigonometric process, which is depicted by equation (4).

(4)
$$\Omega_t = \rho \cos \lambda_c \Omega_{t-1} + \rho \sin \lambda_c \Omega^*_{t-1} + \tau_t$$
$$\Omega^*_t = -\rho \sin \lambda_c \Omega_{t-1} + \rho \cos \lambda_c \Omega^*_{t-1} + \tau_t^*,$$

where ρ is a damping factor with $0 \le \rho \le 1$, λ_c is the frequency of the cycle in radians, and τ_t and τ_t^* are independently, identically distributed disturbances with mean zero and variance σ_τ^2.

The model can be extended by adding an intervention variable to investigate the impact of an event that took place in period k. The immediate pulse effect of the intervention can be modeled by employing the variable ω_t defined as $\omega_t = 0$ if $t \ne k$, and $\omega_t = 1$ if $t = k$. If the intervention shifts the level of the variable, then the intervention variable ω_t is defined as $\omega_t = 0$ if $t \ne k$, and $\omega_t = 1$ if $t \ge k$, and $\mu_t = \mu_{t-1} + \beta_{t-1} + \delta \omega_t + \eta_t$.

We estimated the model, depicted by equations (2) to (4) by including the intervention variables. The models are first estimated from 1977 forward to be consistent with the time period used in the earlier analyses. The estimated trend values (depicted by the dashed lines) along with actual data are displayed in figures 11.1 to 11.6.

The solid lines in figures 11.1 and 11.2 present the time series behavior of the murder rates in Kansas and New Hampshire since 1960. These states legalized the death penalty in 1994 and in 1991, respectively. Although it was asserted by Donohue and Wolfers (2005) that the murder rate went up in these states after the legalization, figures 11.1 and 11.2 show that the opposite is the case. It was also claimed that the murder rates went down in the states of New York and New Jersey after legalization (figures 11.3 and 11.4) and that murder rates fell in Massachusetts and Rhode Island (presented in figures 11.5 and 11.6) due to the abolishment of the death penalty. The evidence in figures 11.3 and 11.4 indeed indicate that murder rates fell in New York and New Jersey after these states legalized death penalty. Figure 11.5 shows that there was an increase in the level of the murder rate in Massachusetts after this state abolished the death penalty followed by a drop in 1997, but it is uncertain whether this drop in 1997 can be attributed to the change in law twelve years prior. In the case of Rhode Island (figure 11.6), the

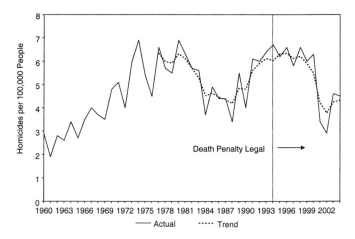

Fig. 11.1   Kansas murder rate and fitted trend

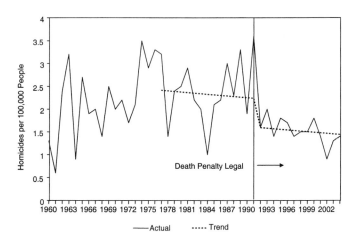

Fig. 11.2   New Hampshire murder rate and fitted trend

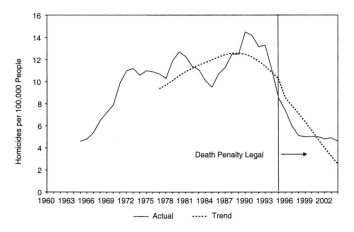

Fig. 11.3   New York murder rate and fitted trend

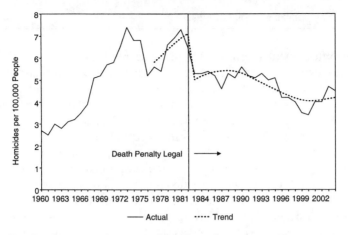

Fig. 11.4   New Jersey murder rate and fitted trend

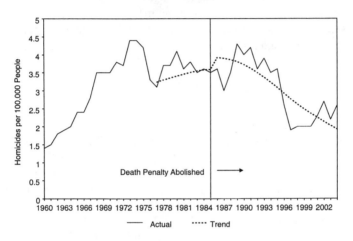

Fig. 11.5   Massachusetts murder rate and fitted trend

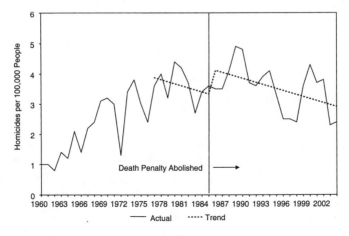

Fig. 11.6   Rhode Island murder rate and fitted trend

murder rate is fluctuating around a quadratic trend, and the level of the murder rate seems to have increased, rather than decreased, after the abolition.

As can be seen, in the four states that adopted the death penalty, the murder rate went down. In the two states that abolished the death penalty, on the other hand, the level of the murder rate has increased.[12]

As another set of analyses, we estimated the models starting in 1960, except for New York, where the data are available starting in 1965. This allowed us to investigate the impact of the adoption of the death penalty in South Dakota (in 1979), New Mexico (in 1979), and in Oregon (in 1978). Furthermore, we also jointly investigated the impact of the 1972 Supreme Court moratorium after the Furman decision.[13] In each case, the Furman decision is associated with an increase in the level of the murder rate. Consistent with the dynamics presented in figures 11.1 to 11.6, adoption of the death penalty generated declines in the murder trends, and abolition in Massachusetts and Rhode Island is associated with immediate increases in the murder rate although long-run trends in these series generated subsequent declines.[14]

11.4.1   Death Penalty Laws: Panel Data

In this section, we investigate whether the existence of the death penalty in a state has a separate impact on the murder rate in addition to the risks associated with being on the death row. To that end, we estimated the same models as those presented in tables 11.1 and 11.2, but we added a dichotomous indicator if death penalty is legal in a given state in a particular year. Furthermore, we interacted this dummy variable with the execution rate, commutation rate, and removal rate variables.

The results are displayed in tables 11.7 and 11.8, where the two alternative measures of execution, commutation, and removal risks are employed, except in column (1), which includes only the death penalty legality variable. In each case, models are estimated with 4 and 5 lags of the death sentences in

---

12. Although the death penalty was legal during the period before 1984 in Massachusetts, the 1970s and 1980s witnessed a series of legislation and judicial rulings regarding the death penalty. Identifying these time intervals and considering interventions associated with them did not alter the picture depicted in figure 11.5. The same, to a lesser degree, is true for Rhode Island, where the death penalty was reenacted in 1977, but in 1979 the Rhode Island Supreme Court issued the opinion of the violation of the prohibitions of the 8th amendment of the U.S. Constitution (Rhode Island Secretary of State Web site). Adding this potential intervention did not alter the picture depicted in figure 11.6.

13. In 1972, in case of *Furman v. the state of Georgia,* the Supreme Court of the United States struck down federal and state laws that allowed wide discretion that resulted in arbitrary and capricious application of the death penalty. As a result, executions were halted, and inmates had their death sentences lifted. Starting in mid-1970s, many states reacted by adopting new legislation to address the issues raised by the Supreme Court (see Mocan and Gittings [2003] for additional details).

14. These graphs, which are not reported in the interest of space, can be seen in Mocan and Gittings (2006).

Table 11.7 Determinants of the murder rate: Models with deterrence variables and the death penalty indicator—the first measure of execution, commutation, and removal

| | SENT$_{t-4}$ | | | SENT$_{t-5}$ | |
	(1)	(2)	(3)	(4)	(5)
Death Penalty Legal (−1)	−0.0152**	−0.0148**	−0.0123**	−0.0135**	−0.0116**
	(0.0063)	(0.0060)	(0.0056)	(0.0064)	(0.0056)
Murder Arrest Rate (−1)	−0.0009	−0.0019	−0.0020	−0.0028	−0.0021
	(0.0032)	(0.0026)	(0.0024)	(0.0026)	(0.0026)
Sentencing Rate (−1)	−0.0026	0.0093	0.0112	−0.0105	−0.0171
	(0.0216)	(0.0222)	(0.0236)	(0.0198)	(0.0198)
Prisoners per Violent Crime (−1)	−0.0401***	−0.0397***	−0.0378***	−0.0391***	−0.0375***
	(0.0087)	(0.0083)	(0.0085)	(0.0086)	(0.0087)
Death Penalty Legal (−1) × Execution Rate (−1)		−0.0056**	−0.0050**	−0.0061**	−0.0069**
		(0.0022)	(0.0020)	(0.0028)	(0.0029)
Death Penalty Legal (−1) × Commutation Rate (−1)		0.0038**		0.0067	
		(0.0019)		(0.0046)	
Death Penalty Legal (−1) × Removal Rate (−1)			0.0005		0.0028***
			(0.0007)		(0.0009)
n	894	781	741	733	688

Notes: The column headings SENT$_{t-4}$ and SENT$_{t-5}$ mean that execution, commutation, and removal rates are calculated by deflating EXEC$_t$, COMM$_t$, and RE-MOVE$_t$ by SENT$_{t-4}$ or SENT$_{t-5}$. Each model includes the following variables: murder arrest rate, sentencing rate, unemployment rate, real per capita income, proportion of the state population in the following age groups: twenty–thirty-four, thirty-five–forty-four, forty-five–fifty-four, and fifty-five and over, proportion of the state population in urban areas, proportion which is black, infant mortality rate, legal drinking age in the state, number of prisoners per violent crime, and prison death rate. Also included in each model are state-fixed effects, a time trend, state-specific time trends, a dummy variable to control for the impact of the 1995 Oklahoma City bombing, and a dummy variable to indicate the governor is a Republican. Robust and clustered standard errors are in parentheses.

***Statistical significance at the 1 percent level or better.

**Statistical significance between 5 and 1 percent.

*Statistical significance between 10 and 5 percent.

Table 11.8   Determinants of the murder rate: Models with deterrence variables and the death penalty indicator—the second measure of execution, commutation, and removal

	SENT_{t-4}			SENT_{t-5}	
	(1)	(2)	(3)	(4)	(5)
Death Penalty Legal (–1)	-0.0152**	-0.0147**	-0.0126**	-0.0136**	-0.0131**
	(0.0063)	(0.0060)	(0.0056)	(0.0064)	(0.0057)
Murder Arrest Rate (–1)	-0.0009	-0.0018	-0.0028	-0.0029	-0.0028
	(0.0032)	(0.0026)	(0.0028)	(0.0026)	(0.0028)
Sentencing Rate (–1)	-0.0026	0.0092	0.0121	-0.0069	-0.0105
	(0.0216)	(0.0222)	(0.0237)	(0.0209)	(0.0199)
Prisoners per Violent Crime (–1)	-0.0401***	-0.0398***	-0.0387***	-0.0399***	-0.0388***
	(0.0087)	(0.0082)	(0.0082)	(0.0085)	(0.0085)
Death Penalty Legal (–1) × Execution Rate (–1)		-0.0070**	-0.0064*	-0.0064***	-0.0075***
		(0.0035)	(0.0032)	(0.0021)	(0.0022)
Death Penalty Legal (–1) × Commutation Rate (–1)		0.0036**		0.0054	
		(0.0016)		(0.0040)	
Death Penalty Legal (–1) × REMOVE Rate (–1)			0.0005		0.0022***
			(0.0007)		(0.0007)
n	894	783	758	736	709

Note: See table 11.7 notes.

the denominator of the risk variables as before. The results demonstrate that the existence of the death penalty in a state has a negative and statistically significant impact on the murder rate. In addition, the execution rate has a negative impact on the murder rate, and commutations and removals have a positive impact, although not always statistically significant.

11.5   The Denominator of the Risk Variables Again

Individuals do not exit the death row in the same year as they received the death sentence. To make the point more visible, the average duration on death row is calculated each year for those inmates who are removed that year and plotted in figure 11.7 by the reason of exit. As can be inferred, individuals who were commuted, executed, or otherwise removed from death row had spent an average of about six years on death row. On the other hand, those who were executed or commuted in 1997 had completed about eleven years on death row. Given this picture, one can use time varying durations on death row to calculate the risks of execution, commutation, or removals. For example, the execution risk in year 1981 can be calculated as the number of executions in 1981 divided by the number of death sentences in 1980 (because the duration on death row was one year in 1981). On the other hand, the risk of execution in 1990 can be measured as the number of executions in 1990 divided by the number of death sentences in 1982 (because the average duration on death row for those who were executed in 1990 was eight years. See figure 11.7). More generally, the execution, commutation, and removal rates are calculated as $(EXEC_t/SENT_{t-i})$, $(COMM_t/SENT_{t-j})$, and $(REMOVE_t/SENT_{t-k})$, where i, j, and k are average durations on death row for spells ending in year t for executions, commutations, and removals,

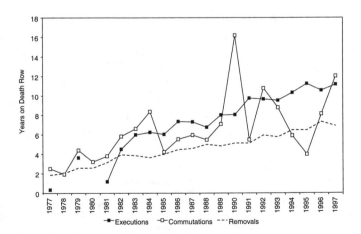

Fig. 11.7   Duration on death row from sentencing to exit

Table 11.9   **Determinants of the murder rate with time varying durations on death row**

The first measure of execution, commutation, and removal					
$(EXEC_i/SENT_{t-i})_{-1}$	−0.0058*			−0.0058*	−0.0055*
	(0.0031)			(0.0034)	(0.0029)
$(COMM_i/SENT_{t-j})_{-1}$		0.0014		0.0009	
		(0.0064)		(0.0067)	
$(REMOVE_i/SENT_{t-k})_{-1}$			0.0003		0.0001
			(0.0008)		(0.0008)
n	830	642	784	629	773
The second measure of execution, commutation, and removal					
$(EXEC2_i/SENT_{t-j})_{-1}$	−0.0049*			−0.0050	−0.0049*
	(0.0026)			(0.0032)	(0.0027)
$(COMM2_i/SENT_{t-j})_{-1}$		0.0009		0.0004	
		(0.0054)		(0.0059)	
$(REMOVE2_i/SENT_{t-k})_{-1}$			0.0007		0.0006
			(0.0007)		(0.0007)
n	833	643	806	632	797

Notes: See table 11.1 notes. i, j, and k are average durations on death row for spells ending in year t for executions, commutations and removals, respectively. For more details see section 11.5.

respectively. Calculating the risks this way produced the results displayed in table 11.9. Once again, we are unsuccessful in eliminating the impact of the execution risk on the murder rate.[15]

Some researchers calculated the execution risk as the number of executions in a year divided by the number of prisoners in that state in that year (e.g., Katz, Levitt, and Shustorovich 2003). This calculation assumes that every prisoner in state correctional facilities is at risk of being executed. This assumption has no validity as about 99.7 percent of the inmates in state prisons are incarcerated for noncapital offenses, and, therefore, they are not at risk of being executed. The difference is not simply a matter of scaling. The number of total prisoners to the number of death row inmates is not a constant proportion over time or across states.[16] Nevertheless, the results that use the total number of prisoners as the denominator is provided in table 11.10. Although this inaccurate measure makes the impact of commutations disappear, it cannot make the impact of executions go away.

A more appropriate way of calculating the risk of execution would be to

15. Another extreme is to uniformly increase the lag length of the denominator. For example, when lag-length seven is imposed, the same results are obtained, but not surprisingly, sample size and the statistical significance is reduced.

16. For example, in 1997, there were a total of 1,127,686 inmates in state prisons, and there were 3,328 death row inmates. The number of total prisoners was 1,316,302 in 2004, and the number of people on death row was 3,314 in the same year.

Table 11.10   **Determinants of the murder rate: Deterrence variables deflated by total prisoners**

The first measure of execution, commutation, and removal deflated by total prisoners/1,000					
XEC$_t$/PRIS$_t)_{-1}$	−0.0258**			−0.0255**	−0.0257**
	(0.0101)			(0.0102)	(0.0101)
COMM$_t$/PRIS$_t)_{-1}$		0.0085		0.0075	
		(0.0077)		(0.0083)	
REMOVE$_t$/PRIS$_t)_{-1}$			0.0007		0.0006
			(0.0008)		(0.0008)
	894	894	894	894	894
The second measure of execution, commutation, and removal deflated by total prisoners/1,000					
EXEC2$_t$/PRIS$_t)_{-1}$	−0.0208**			−0.0206**	−0.0208**
	(0.0083)			(0.0083)	(0.0083)
COMM2$_t$/PRIS$_t)_{-1}$		0.0065		0.0056	
		(0.0067)		(0.0073)	
REMOVE2$_t$/PRIS$_t)_{-1}$			0.0003		0.0028
			(0.0007)		(0.0007)
	894	894	894	894	894

Notes: See table 11.1 notes. PRIS = prisoners per 1,000 population.

use the ratio of executions to the number of inmates on death row rather than deflating by the prison population in the state, although this measure is still inappropriate because a particular death row inmate is not at risk of execution if he just entered death row. Nevertheless, deflating by the stock of death row inmates is much more reasonable than deflating by total prisoners. Results obtained from this exercise are reported in table 11.11. Once again, executions have a negative impact on the murder rate in the state, and commutations are positively related to murder.

Two other denominators are promoted as deflators to the number of executions. For example, Donohue and Wolfers (2005, 815) write "A very simple alternative that avoids this scaling issue is measuring executions per 100,000 residents." They also write: "Another alternative scaling—and perhaps the one most directly suggested by the economic model of crime—is to analyze the ratio of the number of executions to the (lagged) homicide rate" (815). Although it is evident that these suggested measures are poor indicators of the relevant risks, we estimated the models with these denominators as well. The first panel of table 11.12 displays the results when the annual count of executions, commutations, and removals are deflated by state population, and the second panel presents the results when they are deflated by lagged homicide rate. The raw counts of executions, commutations and removals are denoted by #EX, #C, and #R, respectively.

Note that the dependent variable for the analysis is the murder rate, which is measured as murders deflated by population; thus, deflating executions by the state population means that population enters into the denominator of

Table 11.11   Determinants of the murder rate: Determinance variables deflated by death row inmates

The first measure of execution, commutation, and removal deflated by death row inmates					
$(EXEC_t/ROW_t)_{-1}$	−0.0465*			−0.0463*	−0.046
	(0.0277)			(0.0276)	(0.028
$(COMM_t/ROW_t)_{-1}$		0.0098***		0.0097***	
		(0.0014)		(0.0015)	
$(REMOVE_t/ROW_t)_{-1}$			−0.0026		−0.002
			(0.0062)		(0.006
n	894	894	890	894	890
The second measure of execution, commutation, and removal deflated by death row inmates					
$(EXEC2_t/ROW_t)_{-1}$	−0.0501*			−0.0500*	−0.0485
	(0.0287)			(0.0285)	(0.0298
$(COMM2_t/ROW_t)_{-1}$		0.0084***		0.0083***	
		(0.0017)		(0.0017)	
$(REMOVE2_t/ROW_t)_{-1}$			−0.0043		−0.0039
			(0.0051)		(0.0052
n	894	894	893	894	893

Notes: See table 11.1 notes. ROW = the number of death row inmates.

both the dependent and independent variables, inducing a positive bias in the estimated coefficient of the execution rate. Nevertheless, the coefficient of the execution rate remains negative and significant. Because the dependent variable of the analysis is the murder rate, to use the murder rate as the deflator of executions is not meaningful either.[17] However, as the second panel of table 11.12 demonstrates, using the lagged murder rate as the denominator did not make the results disappear.

What happens to the results if we go to the extreme and use the number of executions, commutations, and removals as measures of risk, without deflating by anything? Here, the level of executions, commutations, and removals are considered as appropriate signals to individuals, rather than the rates at which they occur (as defined by the correct denominator). Though we do not agree that this is the correct specification, the bottom panel of table 11.12 shows that even this modification does not eliminate the impact of prices on human behavior. Although the coefficients of commutations and removals are statistically insignificant, the coefficient of execution *remains significant even in this model.*

17. Donohue and Wolfers seem to recognize this and write that in their analysis they employ the lagged homicide rate as the deflator (Donohue and Wolfers 2005, footnote 63). However, if the homicide rate has any path-dependence, such as a simple AR(1) model, using the lagged-dependent variable in the denominator of the independent variable does not avoid a bias, and it creates a strange specification.

Table 11.12   **Determinants of the murder rate deflated by population and lagged murder rate**

The raw count of executions, commutations, and removals deflated by population/100,000

$\#EX_t/POP_t)_{-1}$	−0.055*			−0.0055*	−0.0051*
	(0.0281)			(0.028)	(0.0028)
$\#C_t/POP_t)_{-1}$		0.0099		0.0011	
		(0.0212)		(0.020)	
$\#R_t/POP_t)_{-1}$			0.0037		0.0037
			(0.0061)		(0.0063)
	894	894	894	894	894

The raw count of executions, commutations, and removals deflated by lagged murder rate × 1,000

$\#EX_t/MURDER_{(t-1)})_{-1}$	−0.0543**			−0.0542**	−0.0543**
	(0.0251)			(0.0022)	(0.0021)
$\#C_t/MURDER_{(t-1)})_{-1}$		−0.0120		−0.0098	
		(0.0254)		(0.0252)	
$\#R_t/MURDER_{(t-1)})_{-1}$			−0.0004		0.0001
			(0.0122)		(0.0127)
n	894	894	894	894	894

The raw counts of executions, commutations and removals as risk variables (no deflator: denominator = 1)

$\#EX_{t-1}$	−0.0007***			−0.0007***	−0.0007***
	(0.0002)			(0.0002)	(0.0002)
$\#C_{t-1}$		−0.00008		−0.00009	
		(0.0002)		(0.0002)	
$\#R_{t-1}$			0.00004		0.00005
			(0.0001)		(0.0001)
n	894	894	894	894	894

Notes: See table 11.1 notes. $\#EX_t$ = the raw counts of executions; $\#C_t$ = the raw counts of commutations; $\#R_t$ = the raw counts of death row removals; POP = the population in the state; MURDER = the murder rate.

11.6   Further Attempts to Make the Results Disappear

The risk measures employed in this paper are calculated such that if there is an execution in a given state in a given year, but if it so happens that no individual received a capital sentence five years prior, then the risk ($EXEC_t/SENT_{t-5}$) is set to missing because the denominator is zero. On the other hand, in cases where nobody was sentenced and nobody was executed, the execution risk was taken as zero.

One can adopt an algorithm where observations are dropped from the data when the corresponding executions and death sentences are both zero. This algorithm assumes that the risks cannot be calculated in situations when they should be zero, such as the cases where there is no legal death penalty. Even so, and despite the fact that this algorithm eliminates about half of the legitimate observations, the impact of the death penalty on the murder rate remains as shown in tables 11.13 and 11.14.

Table 11.13   Determinants of the murder rate: Alternative deflators for deterrence variables

	Duration on death row: 5 years				
$(EXEC_t/SENT_{t-5})_{-1}$	−0.0043			−0.0045‡	−0.0061**
	(0.0027)			(0.0029)	(0.0026)
$(COMM_t/SENT_{t-5})_{-1}$		0.0057		0.0061	
		(0.0050)		(0.0050)	
$(REMOVE_t/SENT_{t-5})_{-1}$			0.0022**		0.0025**
			(0.0008)		(0.0009)
n	398	398	398	398	398
	Duration on death row: 4 years				
$(EXEC_t/SENT_{t-4})_{-1}$	−0.0053**			−0.0053**	−0.0054**
	(0.0022)			(0.0022)	(0.0021)
$(COMM_t/SENT_{t-4})_{-1}$		0.0018		0.0019	
		(0.0025)		(0.0023)	
$(REMOVE_t/SENT_{t-4})_{-1}$			0.0002		0.0003
			(0.0006)		(0.0006)
n	426	426	426	426	426
	Donohue III and Wolfers specification—duration on death row: 0 years; time between arrest and death sentence: 0 years				
$(EXEC_t/SENT_t)_{-1}$	0.00004			−0.0001	−0.0001
	(0.0012)			(0.0012)	(0.0013)
$(COMM_t/SENT_t)_{-1}$		0.0034*		0.0034*	
		(0.0019)		(0.0013)	
$(REMOVE_t/SENT_t)_{-1}$			0.0004		0.0004
			(0.0003)		(0.0003)
n	543	543	543	543	543

Notes: See table 11.1 notes. Observations are dropped when numerator = 0 and denominator = 0 when calculating the risk variable. Double dagger (‡) indicates p-value = 0.115.

It may be possible that the deterrent impact of the death penalty that exists in states with large populations such as New York and New Jersey exerts disproportionate influence in a population-weighted regression and overwhelms the no-deterrence result that would have been obtained in regressions with no weighting.[18] To investigate if the results are driven by this hypothesis, we take the models presented in tables 11.1 and 11.2 and reestimate them without population weights.[19] In models where the duration of death row is taken as five years, the results are actually stronger with the coefficients of the commutation rate being statistically significant. In the models where the duration of death row is taken as four years, the execution rate is insignificant, but the removal rate becomes significant when it was insignificant in the weighted regression displayed in tables 11.1 and

18. This hypothesis is developed by Donohue and Wolfers (2005, footnote 50).
19. The results, which are not reported in the interest of space, can be found in Mocan and Gittings (2006, 60–61).

Table 11.14   **Determinants of the murder rate dropping observations where risk is not well defined: the second measure of execution, commutation, and removal**

	Duration on death row: 5 years				
EXEC2$_t$/SENT$_{t-5}$)$_{-1}$	−0.0052**			−0.0058**	−0.0068***
	(0.0022)			(0.0023)	(0.0024)
COMM2$_t$/SENT$_{t-5}$)$_{-1}$		0.0041		0.0054	
		(0.0045)		(0.0037)	
REMOVE2$_t$/SENT$_{t-5}$)$_{-1}$			0.0017**		0.0020***
			(0.0006)		(0.0007)
	398	398	398	398	398
	Duration on death row: 4 years				
EXEC2$_t$/SENT$_{t-4}$)$_{-1}$	−0.0069*			−0.0069*	−0.0071**
	(0.0035)			(0.0036)	(0.0034)
COMM2$_t$/SENT$_{t-4}$)$_{-1}$		0.0019		0.0021	
		(0.0021)		(0.0019)	
REMOVE2$_t$/SENT$_{t-4}$)$_{-1}$			0.00002		0.0003
			(0.0007)		(0.0006)
n	426	426	426	426	426
Donohue III and Wolfers specification—duration on death row: 0 years; time between arrest and death sentence: 0 years					
(EXEC2$_t$/SENT$_t$)$_{-1}$	−0.0006			−0.0007	−0.00005
	(0.0020)			(0.0020)	(0.0019)
(COMM2$_t$/SENT$_t$)$_{-1}$		0.0034**		0.0034**	
		(0.0013)		(0.0013)	
(REMOVE2$_t$/SENT$_t$)$_{-1}$			−0.0005		−0.0005
			(0.0005)		(0.0005)
n	543	543	543	543	543

Note: See table 11.13 notes.

11.2. Finally, the results of the regression estimated by Donohue and Wolfers (2005) using contemporaneous numerators and denominators remain unchanged whether the regressions are weighted.

In table 11.15 we present the results obtained from the models that exclude New York and New Jersey and estimate the models without weighting. As can be seen, the impact of leaving the death row on the murder rate cannot be eliminated by dropping New York and New Jersey from the analysis and running the regressions with no weighting. The same conclusion is obtained when we ran the models displayed in tables 11.3 to 11.8 with no weights. Thus, the results are not an artifact of weighting.[20]

20. Dezhbakhsh and Rubin (2007) conduct extensive analyses on similar issues as well as others to investigate the sensitivity of deterrence results to model specification.

Table 11.15   Determinants of the murder rate (excluding New York and New Jersey): unweighted regressions

	The first measure of execution, commutation, and removal				
	Duration on death row: 5 years				
$(EXEC_t/SENT_{t-5})_{-1}$	−0.0043**			−0.0044**	−0.0056**
	(0.0022)			(0.0021)	(0.0025)
$(COMM_t/SENT_{t-5})_{-1}$		0.0077***		0.0079***	
		(0.0022)		(0.0021)	
$(REMOVE_t/SENT_{t-5})_{-1}$			0.0027***		0.0030***
			(0.0008)		(0.0009)
n	704	713	665	703	662
	Duration on death row: 4 years				
$(EXEC_t/SENT_{t-4})_{-1}$	−0.0038			−0.0036	−0.0033*
	(0.0023)			(0.0023)	(0.0022)
$(COMM_t/SENT_{t-4})_{-1}$		0.0050***		0.0049***	
		(0.0007)		(0.0007)	
$(REMOVE_t/SENT_{t-4})_{-1}$			0.0017**		0.0018**
			(0.0008)		(0.0008)
n	753	758	716	749	713
	The second measure of execution, commutation, and removal				
	Duration on death row: 5 years				
$(EXEC_t/SENT_{t-5})_{-1}$	−0.0044**			−0.0046**	−0.0054**
	(0.0022)			(0.0022)	(0.0027)
$(COMM_t/SENT_{t-5})_{-1}$		0.0064**		0.0068***	
		(0.0026)		(0.0022)	
$(REMOVE_t/SENT_{t-5})_{-1}$			0.0019***		0.0021***
			(0.0006)		(0.0007)
n	707	713	685	706	682
	Duration on death row: 4 years				
$(EXEC_t/SENT_{t-4})_{-1}$	−0.0048			−0.0048	−0.0049
	(0.0038)			(0.0038)	(0.0036)
$(COMM_t/SENT_{t-4})_{-1}$		0.0046***		0.0045***	
		(0.0008)		(0.0009)	
$(REMOVE_t/SENT_{t-4})_{-1}$			0.0013*		0.0015**
			(0.0007)		(0.0007)
n	753	760	732	751	729

Note: See table 11.1 notes.

11.7   Ph.D. Economists versus Criminals

In his Nobel lecture, Gary Becker (1992, 42) described his inspiration for modeling economic behavior of crime as follows:

> I began to think about crime in the 1960s after driving to Columbia University for an oral examination of a student in economic theory. I was late and had to decide quickly whether to put the car in a parking lot or risk

getting a ticket for parking illegally on the street. I calculated the likelihood of getting a ticket, the size of the penalty, and the cost of putting the car in a lot. I decided it paid to take the risk and park on the street. (I did not get a ticket.)

As I walked the few blocks to the examination room, it occurred to me that the city authorities had probably gone through a similar analysis. The frequency of their inspection of parked vehicles and the size of the penalty imposed on violators should depend on their estimates of the type of calculations potential violators like me would make.

One standard objection to economic analysis of crime is whether potential criminals are as astute as PhD economists to evaluate these probabilities accurately. This objection is invalid so long as the researcher believes that empirical research should be conceptually consistent with the underlying theory. If one assumes a priori that individuals are incapable of calculating the risks as they are defined by theory, then there is no room to conduct proper empirical research. For example, if one rejects the theoretically proper measure of the execution risk as executions within a cohort of death row inmates in a given year divided by death sentences handed out to that cohort in some earlier year (because one believes that potential criminals do not observe either the executions or the death sentences), then one ought to claim that they cannot observe and evaluate other variables either, including the arrest rates, the size of the police force, or police spending. Thus, there would be no need to conduct research investigating whether people react to deterrence, under the belief that people could not evaluate variations in deterrence risks to begin with.

Furthermore, attempts to justify the use of inappropriate variables based on the claim that individuals cannot observe, measure, or determine the values of decision parameters will produce peculiar analyses that cannot be defended theoretically.[21] For example, if the theory indicates that the real wages should matter in a particular context, it would be silly to suggest the use of nominal wages in a regression (instead of real wages) on the grounds that people cannot observe and predict accurately the level of the consumer price index. If the theory indicates that the accident risk in a state is best measured by the number of accidents per vehicle miles traveled, it would be incorrect to promote deflating accidents by other measures, such as the

---

21. In general, the manner in which individuals use information to determine the values of decision variables and whether these calculations are unbiased estimates of the true values has been investigated in a variety of context ranging from financial analysts (Keane and Runkle 1998) to parents as child care consumers (Mocan 2007). In the context of criminal activity, it has been acknowledged that the media coverage of the death penalty provides strong signals for potential criminals. For example, some papers investigated if media coverage of executions itself is a deterrent to murder (Bailey 1990; Stack 1987; Phillips 1980). Rincke and Traxler (2009) show that information on law enforcement is transmitted through word of mouth, which serves as a significant deterrent.

square miles of the state or the number of car dealerships, on the grounds that vehicle miles traveled is difficult to observe.

It should be noted that the deterrence results are robust even to the use of measures that are inconsistent with theory. A summary of the findings is provided in table 11.16, which displays the results obtained from estimating various versions of equation (1) along with the description of the measurement of the execution, commutation, and removal rates in each specification. The table displays results that are obtained from specifications where the key variables (execution, commutation, and removal risks) are measured as dictated by theory. The table also presents results from the models where they are measured incorrectly. Examples are the specifications where executions, commutations, and removals are deflated by lagged murder rate, by population; where the raw count of executions, commutations, and removals are used; or the specifications promoted by Donohue and Wolfers (2005, reported in rows [5] and [6] of table 11.16). As the table demonstrates, the results are remarkably stable even across models that substantially deviate from theory.

11.8   Conclusion and Discussion

Do people respond to incentives? An economist's answer to this question is a resounding "yes," not only because economic theory indicates that incentives matter, but also because an enormous empirical literature shows that they do. An especially confusing dimension for noneconomists is the behavior of individuals in such domains as the consumption of addictive substances, sexual activity, and criminal behavior. In the case of criminal behavior, noneconomists frequently express the belief that human beings are not rational enough to make calculated decisions about the costs and benefits of engaging in crime and that criminal activity cannot be altered by incentives. Of course, personal beliefs should not determine the answers to scientific questions. Rather, answers should be provided by careful and objective scientific inquiry.

In the economic approach to crime, decades of empirical research has demonstrated that potential criminals indeed respond to incentives. It has been documented that improved labor market conditions reduce the extent of criminal activity (recent examples include Grogger 1998; Freeman and Rodgers 2000; Gould et al. 2002), and criminal activity reacts to deterrence (e.g., Ehrlich 1975; Levitt 1998b; Kessler and Levitt 1999; Corman and Mocan 2000; Mustard 2003; Corman and Mocan 2005). For example, Levitt (1998b) shows that deterrence is empirically more important than incapacitation in explaining crime and that increases in arrest rates deter criminal activity. Kessler and Levitt (1999) show that Proposition 8 in California, which introduced sentence enhancements for certain crimes, reduced eligible crimes by 4 percent in the year following its passage and 8 percent

Table 11.16 Summary of the results

A	B	(A/B)	Execution rate	Commutation rate	Removal rate
		Risk Measures in the Analysis (A/B)	Impact on the murder rate of the:		
First measures of executions, commutations, and removals	Death sentences handed out 5 years prior (duration on death row = 5 years)	$(EXEC_t/SENT_{t-5})$, $(COMM_t/SENT_{t-5})$, $(REMOVE_t/SENT_{t-5})$	−*	+	+*
	Death sentences handed out 4 years prior (duration on death row = 4 years)	$(EXEC_t/SENT_{t-4})$, $(COMM_t/SENT_{t-4})$, $(REMOVE_t/SENT_{t-4})$	−*	+*	+
Second measures of executions, commutations, and removals	Death sentences handed out 5 years prior (duration on death row = 5 years)	$(EXEC2_t/SENT_{t-5})$, $(COMM2_t/SENT_{t-5})$, $(REMOVE2_t/SENT_{t-5})$	−*	+	+*
	Death sentences handed out 4 years prior (duration on death row = 4 years)	$(EXEC2_t/SENT_{t-4})$, $(COMM2_t/SENT_{t-4})$, $(REMOVE2_t/SENT_{t-4})$	−*	+*	+
First measures of executions, commutations, and removals (D-III and W specification)	Death sentences handed out the same year (duration on death row = 0 years)	$(EXEC_t/SENT_t)$, $(COMM_t/SENT_t)$, $(REMOVE_t/SENT_t)$	−	+*	+
Second measures of executions, commutations, and removals (D-III and W specification)	Death sentences handed out the same year (duration on death row = 0 years)	$(EXEC2_t/SENT_t)$, $(COMM2_t/SENT_t)$, $(REMOVE2_t/SENT_t)$	−	+*	+
First or second measures of executions, commutations, and removals	Death sentences handed out i, j, or k years prior for spells ending in year t (duration on death row = changes by year)	$(EXEC_t/SENT_{t-j})$, $(COMM_t/SENT_{t-j})$, $(REMOVE_t/SENT_{t-k})$	−*	+	+
First measures of executions, commutations, and removals	Death row inmates (ROW)	$(EXEC_t/ROW_t)$, $(COMM_t/ROW_t)$, $(REMOVE_t/ROW_t)$	−*	+*	−
Second measures of executions, commutations, and removals	Death row inmates (ROW)	$(EXEC2_t/ROW_t)$, $(COMM2_t/ROW_t)$, $(REMOVE2_t/ROW_t)$	−*	+*	−
First measures of executions, commutations, and removals	Total prisoners (PRIS)	$(EXEC_t/PRIS_t)$, $(COMM_t/PRIS_t)$, $(REMOVE_t/PRIS_t)$	−*	+	+

(continued)

Table 11.16 (continued)

A	B	Risk Measures in the Analysis (A/B) (A/B)	Impact on the murder rate of the: Execution rate	Commutation rate	Removal rate
Second measures of executions, commutations, and removals	Total prisoners (PRIS)	$(EXEC2_t/PRIS_t)$, $(COMM2_t/PRIS_t)$, $(REMOVE2_t/PRIS_t)$	–*	+	+
The raw count of executions (#EX), commutations (#C), removals (#R)	Population (POP)	$(\#EX_t/POP_t)$, $(\#C_t/POP_t)$, $(\#R_t/POP_t)$	–*	+	+
	Lagged murder rate (MURDER)	$(\#EX_t/MURDER_{t-1})$, $(\#C_t/MURDER_{t-1})$, $(\#R_t/MURDER_{t-1})$	–*	–	+
		$(\#EX_t)$, $(\#C_t)$, $(\#R_t)$	–*	–	+*
First measures of executions, commutations, and removals (unweighted regression)	Death sentences handed out 5 years prior (duration on death row = 5 years)	$(EXEC_t/SENT_{t-5})$, $(COMM_t/SENT_{t-5})$, $(REMOVE_t/SENT_{t-5})$	–*	+*	+*
	Death sentences handed out 4 years prior (duration on death row = 4 years)	$(EXEC_t/SENT_{t-4})$, $(COMM_t/SENT_{t-4})$, $(REMOVE_t/SENT_{t-4})$	–	+*	+*
Second measures of executions, commutations, and removals (unweighted regression)	Death sentences handed out 5 years prior (duration on death row = 5 years)	$(EXEC2_t/SENT_{t-5})$, $(COMM2_t/SENT_{t-5})$, $(REMOVE2_t/SENT_{t-5})$	–*	+*	+*
	Death sentences handed out 4 years prior (duration on death row = 4 years)	$(EXEC2_t/SENT_{t-4})$, $(COMM2_t/SENT_{t-4})$, $(REMOVE2_t/SENT_{t-4})$	–	+*	+
First measures of executions, commutations, and removals	Death sentences handed out 7 years prior (duration on death row = 7 years)	$(EXEC_t/SENT_{t-7})$, $(COMM_t/SENT_{t-7})$, $(REMOVE_t/SENT_{t-7})$	–	+	+
Second measures of executions, commutations, and removals	Death sentences handed out 7 years prior (duration on death row = 7 years)	$(EXEC2_t/SENT_{t-7})$, $(COMM2_t/SENT_{t-7})$, $(REMOVE2_t/SENT_{t-7})$	–	+	–

Notes: + (–) indicates that the coefficient is positive (negative) in at least two of the three regressions pertinent to that specification. * indicates that the coefficient is statistically significant in at least two of the three specifications. The details are reported in various tables in the paper. Note that a number of specifications summarized in this table are inconsistent with theory. They are estimated and reported here as part of sensitivity analysis. Note also that this table is not an exhaustive summary of the models estimated in the paper. Other models, which are not reported in the interest of space in this table, are consistent with the results displayed here. Those results are presented in previous tables.

three years after the passage, providing strong evidence that crime rates react to the severity of punishment. In an analysis of the relationship between crime and punishment for juveniles, Levitt (1998a) finds that changes in relative punishment between juveniles and adults explain 60 percent of the differential growth rates in juvenile and adult crime, and that abrupt changes in criminal involvement with the transition from juvenile to adult courts indicate that individuals do respond to the expected punishment (as economic theory suggests). Corman and Mocan (2005, 2000) and Di Tella and Schargrodsky (2004) show that criminal activity responds to variations in arrests and the size of the police force.

As discussed in the introduction, the signal provided by leaving death row is no different from any other change in expected punishment. That is, an execution is a signal of an increase in expected punishment, and a commutation represents a decrease in expected punishment. However, it is sometimes claimed that because executions are infrequent events, they cannot possibly be a strong enough signals to alter the behavior of people. Yet the same analysts have no difficulty in believing that a prospective criminal observes correctly and accurately the extent of the increase in the number of arrests, and coupled with the information about the level of crime, he calculates the enhanced risk of getting caught, and changes his behavior. Similarly, the suggestion that if the local authority hires twenty new police officers, the associated increase in the risk of getting caught by this move is properly evaluated by potential criminals does not raise objections. Even prison deaths are believed to provide signals to people who are not in prison. Katz, Levitt, and Shustorovich (2003) find that the death rate in prisons constitutes deterrence, and an increase in prison deaths has a negative impact on crime rates. It is very difficult to argue that an increase in prison deaths would be a signal of deterrence, but an increase in the executions would not.

Clearly, analysts' personal beliefs regarding what should and should not constitute a strong signal are irrelevant. Whether police, arrests, prison deaths, executions, or commutations provide signals to people about the extent of expected punishment is an empirical question. In this chapter, we estimate a large number of models in an effort to make the relationship between murder rates and death penalty related outcomes (executions, commutations, and removals) disappear. We change the measurement of the risk variables by altering the numerator and the denominator of the variables in a variety of ways (see table 11.16 for a summary); we also investigate how the results change when we exclude various states from the analysis. The basic results are insensitive to these and a variety of other specification tests performed in the chapter.

It is understandable that the death penalty evokes strong feelings that could be due to political, ideological, religious, or other personal beliefs. It could also be because of the fear that a scientific paper that identifies a deterrent effect could be taken as an endorsement or justification of the death penalty. This fear seems to be powerful especially when there are recent efforts to abolish the death penalty in the United States, while some other countries, such as Mexico, are entertaining the possibility of introducing the death penalty. However, such fears should not be relevant for any scientific research. This point is highlighted by Mocan and Gittings (2003) and Katz, Levitt, and Shustorovich (2003). For example, Katz, Levitt, and Shustorovich (2003) find that the death rate among prisoners (a proxy for prison conditions) deters crime and state the obvious that this finding does not suggest that the society should increase the death rate of the prisoners by worsening the prison conditions to reduce the crime rate. Similarly, Mocan and Gittings (2003, 474) write that the fact that there exists a deterrent effect of capital punishment should not imply a position on death penalty. There are a number of significant issues surrounding the death penalty, ranging from potential racial discrimination in the imposition of the death penalty (Baldus et al. 1998) to discrimination regarding who is executed and who is commuted once the death penalty is received (Argys and Mocan 2004).

Given these concerns, it is critically important to preserve objectivity in scientific research on a subject matter in which opinions may have been formed without, or sometimes despite, the empirical evidence. This unfortunate phenomenon is described succinctly by Sunstein and Vermeule (2005), where they write in their reply to Donohue and Wolfers (2005):

> We cannot help but add that as new entrants into the death penalty debate, we are struck by the intensity of people's beliefs on the empirical issues, and the extent to which their empirical judgments seem to be driven by their moral commitments. Those who oppose the death penalty on moral grounds often seem entirely unwilling to consider apparent evidence of deterrence and are happy to dismiss such evidence whenever even modest questions are raised about it. Those who accept the death penalty on moral grounds often seem to accept the claim of deterrence whether or not good evidence has been provided on its behalf. (848)

In summary, the detailed analysis in this chapter demonstrates the deterrent effect of capital punishment. Yet this finding does not imply that capital punishment is good or bad, nor does it provide any judgment about whether capital punishment should be implemented or abolished. It is just a scientific finding that demonstrates that people react to incentives.

References

Argys, Laura M., and Naci H. Mocan. 2004. Who shall live and who shall die? An analysis of prisoners on death row in the United States. *Journal of Legal Studies* 33 (2): 255–92.

Bailey, William C. 1990. Murder, capital punishment, and television: Execution publicity and homicide rates. *American Sociological Review* 55 (5): 628–33.

Baldus, David C., George Woodworth, David Zuckerman, Neil Allan Weiner, and Barbara Broffit. 1998. Race discrimination and the death penalty in the post Furman Era: An empirical and legal overview with preliminary findings from Philadelphia. *Cornell Law Review* 83:1638–1770.

Becker, Gary S. 1968. Crime and punishment: An economics perspective. *Journal of Political Economy* 76:169–217.

———. 1992. Nobel lecture. http://nobelprize.org/nobel_prizes/economics/laureates/1992/becker-lecture.html.

Becker, Gary, Michael Grossman, and Kevin Murphy. 1994. An empirical analysis of cigarette addiction. *American Economic Review* 81:396–418.

Bedau, Hugo A. 1997. *The death penalty in America: Current controversies.* New York: Oxford University Press.

Corman, Hope, and Naci H. Mocan. 2000. A time-series analysis of crime, deterrence, and drug abuse in New York City. *American Economic Review* 90: 584–604.

———. 2005. Carrots, sticks, and broken windows. *Journal of Law and Economics* 48 (1): 235–66.

Dezhbakhsh, Hashem, and Paul H. Rubin. 2007. From the "econometrics of capital punishment" to the "capital punishment" of econometrics: On the use and abuse of sensitivity analysis. Emory University Law School Research Paper No. 07-21.

Dezhbakhsh, Hashem, Paul H. Rubin, and Joanna Shepherd. 2003. Does capital punishment have a deterrent effect? New evidence from post-moratorium panel data. *American Law and Economics Review* 5:344–76.

Dickert-Conlin, Stacey, and Amitabh Chandra. 1999. Taxes and the timing of births. *Journal of Political Economy* 107:161–77.

Di Tella, Rafael, and Ernesto Schargrodsky. 2004. Do police reduce crime? Estimates using the allocation of police forces after a terrorist attack. *American Economic Review* 94:115–33.

Donohue, John, and Justin Wolfers. 2005. Uses and abuses of empirical evidence in the death penalty debate. *Stanford Law Review* 58:791–846.

Ehrlich, Isaac. 1973. Participation in illegitimate activities: A theoretical and empirical investigation. *Journal of Political Economy* 81 (May–June): 521–65.

———. 1975. The deterrent effect of capital punishment: A question of life and death. *American Economic Review* 65:395–417.

———. 1977a. Capital punishment and deterrence: Some further thoughts and evidence. *Journal of Political Economy* 85:741–88.

———. 1977b. The deterrent effect of capital punishment: Reply. *American Economic Review* 67:452–58.

Ehrlich, Isaac, and George D. Brower. 1987. On the issue of causality in the economic model of crime and law enforcement: Some theoretical considerations and experimental evidence. *American Economic Review* 77:99–106.

Ehrlich, Isaac, and Zhiqiang Liu. 1999. Sensitivity analyses of the deterrence hypothesis: Let's keep the econ in econometrics. *Journal of Law and Economics* 17: 455–88.

Ehrlich, Isaac and Randall Mark. 1977. Fear of deterrence: A critical evaluation of the "Report of the Panel on Research on Deterrent and Incapacitative Effects." *Journal of Legal Studies* 6:293–316.

Farrell, Susan, Willard G. Manning, and Michael D. Finch. 2003. Alcohol dependence and the price of alcoholic beverages. *Journal of Health Economics* 22: 117–47.

Freeman, Richard B., and William M. Rodgers. 2000. Area economic conditions and the labor market outcomes of young men in the 1990s expansion. In *Prosperity for all? The economic boom and African Americans,* ed. Robert Cherry and William M. Rodgers, 50–87. New York: Russell Sage Foundation.

Gould, Eric D., Bruce A. Weinberg, and David B. Mustard. Crime rates and local labor market opportunities in the United States: 1979–1997. *Review of Economics and Statistics* 84:45–61.

Grogger, Jeffrey. 1998. Market wages and youth crime. *Journal of Labor Economics* 16:756–91.

Grossman, Michael. 2005. Individual behaviours and substance use: The role of price. In *Substance use: Individual behaviour, social interactions, markets and politics,* ed. Bjorn Lindgren and Michael Grossman, 15–39. Advances in Health Economics and Health Services Research, vol. 16. Amsterdam: Elsevier.

Grossman, Michael, and Frank Chaloupka. 1998. The demand for cocaine by young adults: A rational addiction approach. *Journal of Health Economics* 17: 427–74.

Grossman, Michael, Frank Chaloupka, Henry Saffer, and Adit Laixuthai. 1994. Effects of alcohol price policy on youth: A summary of economic research. *Journal of Research on Adolescence* 4:347–64.

Gruber, Jonathan, Anindya Sen, and Mark Stabile. 2003. Estimating price elasticities when there is smuggling: The sensitivity of smoking to price in Canada. *Journal of Health Economics* 22:821–42.

Gruber, Jonathan, and Jonathan Zinman. 2001. Youth smoking in the United States: Evidence and implications. In *Risky behavior among youths: An economic analysis,* ed. Jonathan Gruber, 69–120. Chicago: University of Chicago Press.

Hansen, Kirstine, and Stephen Machin. 2002. Spatial crime patterns and the introduction of the UK minimum wage. *Oxford Bulletin of Economics and Statistics* 64:677–97.

Harbaugh, William T., Kate Krause, and Timothy R. Berry. 2001. GARP for kids: On the development of rational choice behavior. *American Economic Review* 91 (5): 1539–45.

Harvey, Andrew, and James Durbin. 1986. The effect of seat belt legislation on British road causalities: A case study in structural time series modeling. *Journal of the Royal Statistical Society* 149:187–227.

Hoenack, Stephen A., and William C. Weiler. 1980. A structural model of murder behavior and the criminal justice system. *American Economic Review* 70:327–41.

Jacob, Brian A., and Steven D. Levitt. 2003. Rotten apples: An investigation of the prevelance and predictors of teacher cheating. *Quarterly Journal of Economics* 118:843–77.

Katz, Lawrence, Steven D. Levitt, and Ellen Shustorovich. 2003. Prison conditions, capital punishment, and deterrence. *American Law and Economics Review* 5: 318–43.

Keane, Michael P., and David E. Runkle. 1998. Are financial analysts' forecasts of corporate profits rational? *Journal of Political Economy* 106 (4): 768–805.

Kessler, Daniel P., and Steven D. Levitt. 1999. Using sentence enhancements to distinguish between deterrence and incapacitation. *Journal of Law and Economics* 42:343–63.

Levitt, Steven D. 1996. The effect of prison population size on crime rates: Evidence from prison overcrowding litigation. *Quarterly Journal of Economics* 111 (2): 319–51.

———. 1998a. Juvenile crime and punishment. *Journal of Political Economy* 106:1156–85.

———. 1998b. Why do increased arrest rates appear to reduce crime: Deterrence, incapacitation, or measurement error? *Economic Inquiry* 36:353–72.

Lott, John, and David Mustard. 1997. Crime, deterrence and right-to-carry concealed handguns. *Journal of Legal Studies* 26 (1): 1–68.

Lundberg, Shelly, and Robert D. Plotnick. 1990. Effects of state welfare, abortion and family planning policies on premarital childbearing among white adolescents. *Family Planning Perspectives* 22:251–75.

———. 1995. Adolescent premarital childbearing: Do economic incentives matter? *Journal of Labor Economics* 13:177–200.

Manning, Willard G., Linda Blumberg, and Lawrence H. Moulton. 1995. The demand for alcohol: The differential response to price. *Journal of Health Economics* 14:123–48.

Mellor, Jennifer M. 1998. The effect of family planning programs on the fertility of welfare recipients: Evidence from Medicaid claims. *Journal of Human Resources* 33:866–95.

Mocan, Naci. 1994. Is there a unit root in U.S. real GNP? A re-assessment. *Economics Letters* 45:23–31.

———. 2007. Can consumers detect lemons? An empirical investigation of information asymmetry in the market for child care. *Journal of Population Economics* 20 (4): 743–80.

Mocan, Naci, and Kaj R. Gittings. 2003. Getting off death row: Commuted sentences and the deterrent effect of capital punishment. *Journal of Law and Economics* 46:453–78.

———. 2006. The impact of incentives on human behavior: Can we make it disappear: The case of the death penalty. NBER Working Paper no. 12631. Cambridge, MA: National Bureau of Economic Research.

Mocan, Naci, and Daniel Rees. 2005. Economic conditions, deterrence and juvenile crime: Evidence from micro data. *American Law and Economics Review* 7: 319–49.

Mocan, Naci, and Kudret Topyan. 1993. Real wages over the business cycle: Evidence from a structural time-series model. *Oxford Bulletin of Economics and Statistics* 55:363–89.

Mustard, David B. 2003. Reexamining criminal behavior: The importance of omitted variable bias. *Review of Economics and Statistics* 85:205–11.

Pacula, Rosalie, Michael Grossman, Frank Chaloupka, Patrick O'Malley, Llyod Johnston, and Matthew Farrelly. 2001. Marijuana and youth. In *Risky behavior among youths: An economic analysis,* ed. Jonathan Gruber, 271–326. Chicago: University of Chicago Press.

Passell, Peter, and John Taylor. 1977. The deterrent effect of capital punishment: Another view. *American Economic Review* 67:445–51.

Phillips, David P. 1980. The deterrent effect of capital punishment: New evidence on an old controversy. *American Journal of Sociology* 86 (1): 139–48.

Rincke, Johannes, and Christian Traxler. 2009. Deterrence through word of mouth. MPI Collective Goods Preprint no. 2009/4. http://ssrn.com/abstract=1337458.

Saffer, Henry, and Frank Chaloupka. 1999. The demand for illicit drugs. *Economic Inquiry* 37:401–11.

Saffer, Henry, and Dhaval Dave. 2005. Mental illness and the demand for alcohol, cocaine and cigarettes. *Economic Inquiry* 43:229–46.

Stack, Steven. 1987. Publicized executions and homicide, 1950–1980. *American Sociological Review* 52 (4): 532–40.

Sunstein, Cass, and Adrian Vermeule. 2005. Deterring murder: A reply. *Stanford Law Review* 58:847–57.

Tekin, Erdal, Naci Mocan, and Lan Liang. Forthcoming. Do adolescents with emotional and behavioral problems respond to cigarette prices? *Southern Economic Journal,* forthcoming.

Van Ours, Jan. 1995. The price elasticity of hard drugs: The case of opium in the Dutch East Indies, 1923–1938. *Journal of Political Economy* 103:261–79.

Yurekli, Ayda A., and Ping Zhang. 2000. The impact of clean-air laws and cigarette smuggling on demand for cigarettes: An empirical model. *Journal of Health Economics* 9:159–70.

Comment   Lucía Quesada

The objective of the chapter is to show that the death penalty works as crime deterrent, specifically to show that potential murderers respond to incentives in such a way that when the probability of being executed increases, the homicide rate decreases.

This idea is based on an economic approach to crime in which the probability of being punished is interpreted as the "price" of crime. Thus, when its price increases, crime should decrease.

A model of individual decision making indicates that individual i commits a crime if his or her expected utility with crime is greater than his/her expected utility without crime:

$$EU_i(\text{crime}) > EU_i(\text{no crime})$$

Thus, the probability that a crime is committed by individual i is

$$\Pr_i(\text{crime}) = \Pr[EU_i(\text{crime}) > EU_i(\text{no crime})].$$

Hence, the determinants of the probability of committing a crime are the determinants of the expected utility with and without crime for individual i. Among these, the punishment and the probability of being punished are of interest for this chapter. Of course, an increase in any of those variables decreases the expected utility with crime, which implies, according to the theory, that it should also decrease the probability of committing a crime. This is the basic idea behind the economic theory of crime, which the authors intend to test empirically for the particular case of the death penalty.

The main question here is how to do the empirical work.

The probability of being punished that is used in the theoretical model of individual choice depends on individual characteristics like age, race, and income level and is an estimation individuals make based on available information like the existing law, the perceived efficiency of the judicial system, and maybe learning from own experience. Hence, the theoretical model is

Lucía Quesada is assistant professor of economics at Universidad Torcuato Di Tella.

consistent with subjective probabilities of being punished that individuals form.

The central question in this empirical literature is to understand which variables should be used as proxies of this subjective probability of punishment, especially when facing aggregate data.

The case of the death penalty, analyzed in this paper, is particularly controversial because, as the authors acknowledge, it evokes strong feelings due to political, ideological, religious, moral, and other personal beliefs. It is for this reason that a paper that deals with the death penalty as an incentive to potential criminals must be very rigorous in the way the variables are constructed so that it is clear that the results are independent of those feelings.

The debate is about the choice of the variables that should be used in the empirical work to measure the probability of being executed.

Mocan and Gittings in their 2003 paper use the execution rate, the commutation rate, and the removal rate as several proxies that affect the probability of being punished with the death penalty. They argue that for the homicide rate in period t, the relevant variable is executions in period $t-1$ over sentences in period $t-7$, with the argument that the average duration from sentencing to execution is about six years.

Donohue and Wolfers in their 2006 paper argue that any truly meaningful assessment a potential murderer makes is likely to be based upon the most recent information available to him or her and conclude that the relevant variable to explain the homicide rate in period t is executions in period $t-1$ over sentences in the same period.

It is a priori difficult to say that one measure is better than the other one because they are both proxies of what potential murderers interpret as the true probability of being executed.

Likewise, another possibility that is not considered by any of these papers is to think about potential criminals as forward looking individuals. What a criminal really cares about is the probability that he or she will be executed, which will happen, on average, eight years from the moment the crime is committed, according to the data presented on the chapter. So why not consider executions in period $t+8$ over sentences in period $t+2$? This would be like rational expectations, and it represents the "true" risk of being executed if I murder somebody in period t.

Or maybe potential criminals consider all the information available up to date t and not only the last point of observation. Maybe we want to consider an average of all past execution rates as our proxy or just use all the available lags or anything that takes into account all the information.

It could also be that none of those variables is a really good measure of what potential murderers perceive as their probability of being executed. The case of Texas may be interesting to illustrate this. Indeed, the authors show that the execution rate in Texas is not the largest in the United States. It actually ranks fourth in the author's sample. Yet before knowing the true data, one has the impression that the risk of being executed in Texas is far above other states. The reasons may be that Texas executes more convicted than other states or that cases in Texas have more publicity or things like these that make executions in Texas more visible. Thus, it seems that the objective ("true") probability of being executed is different from individuals' estimations of it.

My feeling is that the main problem of all this literature (not exclusive of this chapter) is that the choice of proxies is very subjective. Because the true data (subjective probabilities) are not available, one can build arguments to use virtually anything as a proxy. Hence, personal beliefs end up having a huge impact on the answer of the scientific question through the choice of the relevant proxy. In this respect, one thing that the authors do in this paper is to try with an enormous set of different variables to show that all measures that they (or others) have thought of give the same result, namely, that potential criminals respond to incentives. This is a plus of this chapter. However, it is still unexplained why all the variables that affect the probability of being executed are not significant, even in the estimations that, according to the authors, are consistent with the theoretical model. In particular, why is that the probability of being executed conditional on having received a death sentence is significant but the probability of receiving a commutation conditional on the death sentence is not? Maybe the reason is that for some people the idea of spending all of their lives in prison is almost as bad as being executed.

In any case, I doubt the most relevant question is whether the death penalty has deterrent effects. I believe in incentives, so I'm not surprised by the finding that the death penalty has a deterrent effect. I think the real contribution of all this empirical literature should be to help policymakers choose the best instruments (in a cost-benefit perspective) to deter crime. In this respect, I think a nice thing to do would be to compare the effect of the death penalty on the crime rate with the effect of other types of punishment, like life sentences without parole. This may be beyond the scope of this particular chapter, but it would surely contribute to the debate of the real issue at stake: what the most effective incentives are.

Does Arrest Deter Violence?
Comparing Experimental and Nonexperimental Evidence on Mandatory Arrest Laws

Radha Iyengar

12.1 Introduction

For two decades, there has been considerable debate in economics about the use and validity of experimental approaches in the development and design of public policy.[1] In criminology, there has been a marked increase in the use of randomized experiments, signaling a widespread acceptance of experiments as an effective means of determining policy-relevant parameters. Recently, a new set of papers in economics by Deaton (2009) and Imbens (2009), in addition to ongoing work by Heckman and coauthors (e.g., Heckman and Urzua 2009; Heckman, Urzua, and Vytlacil 2006) have revived the debate on the usefulness of experiments in estimating parameters of economic and policy importance in both first-world and developing-world contexts. The debate partitions empirical research into two broad categories: design-based studies (DBS), which focus on the empirical evaluation design, and theory-based studies (TBS), which focus on the underlying theory and fit new or existing estimates explicitly within that framework. Included in DBS are both experimental evaluations, such as randomized controlled trials (RCT) and field experiments, and nonexperimental evaluations focused on establishing causal relationships, such as difference-in-

Radha Iyengar is assistant professor of economics at London School of Economics, and a faculty research fellow of the National Bureau of Economic Research.

I am grateful to David Autor, Josh Angrist, Francine Blau, Rafael Di Tella, Faruk Gul, Hank Farber, Lawrence Katz, Steve Pischke, Jesse Rothstein, and participants at numerous seminars for helpful comments and insightful suggestions. Financial support from the Robert Wood Johnson Foundation is gratefully acknowledged. Any remaining errors are entirely my own.

1. Meyers (1992) provides useful overview on this debate. For additional details, see, for example, Ashenfelter and Card (1985), Lalonde (1986), Heckman and Robb (1985), Friedlander and Robins (1995).

difference estimators, matching methods, and instrumental variables. Much of the TBS literature uses "structural estimation" in which the parameters of an explicit theoretical model are identified by imposing restrictions across various parameters in a generalized method of moments or maximum likelihood framework. This set of studies can also include models of sample selections and usually require explicit assumptions on optimality, rational expectations/behavior, and parametric or functional form. In the context of crime research, most empirical research has fallen into the DBS category; the emphasis on experimental evidence combined with the importance of establishing causation makes this methodological debate critical in directing future of crime policy research. This study considers the conflict between DBS and TBS in the context of an important social experiment: arrest laws for spousal abuse.

The most prominent and arguably influential theory among crime scholarship is that of deterrence, which predicts that an increase in the cost of a crime will reduce participation in that crime. While there existed some simple theoretical models (e.g., Becker 1968; Ehrlich 1972) and some limited calibrated models (Flinn 1986), there was limited evidence on the efficacy of deterrence. To determine if any such significant deterrence effect existed, a prominent set of experiments funded by the National Institute of Justice tested the effect of increasing the probability of arrest on future incidences of spousal abuse (thus called the Spousal Assault Replication Program [SARP]). The initial experiment, run in 1981 in Minneapolis, Minnesota, suggested that arrests were effective at deterring future violence, reducing future violence by more than 50 percent.[2] These results were used to justify laws requiring the warrantless arrests of individuals police believe to be responsible for misdemeanor assault of an intimate partner. Recent quasi-experimental evidence using Federal Bureau of Investigation (FBI) homicide data (Iyengar 2009) finds that laws aimed at increasing arrests for spousal abuse appear to have increased intimate partner homicides. The apparent contradiction between the experimental and the nonexperimental results can be understood by placing the experimental results in the broader context of a behavioral model of spousal abuse. The distinction this simple model highlights is that the deterrence effect is a product of both the probability of arrest conditional on reporting and the probability of reporting conditional on assault. By measuring only one of these parameters, the experiment could not accurately extrapolate to the unconditional effect of increased penalty (i.e., increased probability of arrest) on future violent incidents.

These experiments and the subsequent nonexperimental evidence provide a stark example of a common situation where experimental evidence was

---

2. Subsequent replication produced what appeared to be a range of results from deterrence to escalation. However, a recent reanalysis of the six experiments suggests that in all cases, arrest reduced the probability of future violence. This will be discussed in detail in section 12.2.

necessary but not sufficient. It naturally begs the question: why do experiments occupy such an important place in policy debates when they are likely to be insufficient to answer the policy question? While there are a range of detailed and nuanced arguments on the relative efficacy of either experimental/DBS and TBS, the crux of the issue lies in the trade-off between internal and external validity.[3] The benefit of DBS is that they focus on identifying a parameter with great internal validity. This means that in experimental, quasi-experimental, or instrumental variable settings, we may obtain an unbiased estimate of the local average treatment effect (LATE) with minimal assumptions that are easier to test and to believe. The cost of this approach is that the parameter we estimate may not be parameter of interest. This is because we obtain the LATE rather than the average treatment effect (ATE). As its name suggests, the LATE is locally unbiased (or in the case of instrumental variables, consistent) for the group over whom the estimate is constructed.[4] Instrumental variables (IV) typically obtain the LATE because the estimation uses variation from only portion of the sample—in the language of IV, the compliant subpopulation (Angrist and Imbens 1995). Experimental studies will only obtain ATE if the sample under investigation is representative of the general population (or at least the population for whom the experimental results will be generalized).[5] Because most social experiments also rely on a voluntary subject population, by the same logic as IV, experiments with selected samples will tend to identify only the LATE, in this case local to the voluntary sample, rather than the average treatment effect (as in the case of a randomly selected sample).[6]

Theory-based studies, on the other hand, offer a detailed underlying

---

3. Following the definition in Burtless (1995), I define an "internally valid" estimate as an unbiased measure of a given treatment effect in the chosen sample. An "externally valid" estimate is a treatment-effect estimate that can be validly extended beyond the chosen sample to some other external group.

4. As Deaton (2009, 10) suggests, "this goes beyond . . . looking [at] an object where the light is strong enough to see; rather we have control over the light but choose to let it fall where it may." Of course, this is a bit extreme because the experimental parameters are not entirely separate from the desired parameter. As Imbens (2009, 6) notes, "even if simple average effects of these interventions are not directly answering questions about plausible economic policies, they are often closely related to the effects of such policies and therefore viewed as quantities of interest."

5. This point ignores noncompliance among the subject population after the start of the experiment. In the case of experimental noncompliance, two approaches are used. One uses the original assignment and compares the assigned treatment and assigned control groups, regardless of actual treatment status. This estimate is the intent-to-treat (ITT) estimate and may also be obtained in some quasi-experimental settings. The second approach is to use the assigned treatment as an instrument for actual treatment status. In this case, the experiment reverts to the IV case.

6. This is related to the point made by Heckman (1992) regarding experiments under the Job Training Partnership Act (JTPA). Experiments may not obtain the average treatment effect, even when properly administered, due to sample contamination—that is, the sample chosen is not the general population that would experience the treatment in the absence of the program.

framework for both analyzing and interpreting results. This allows studies to take observational and even experimentally obtained parameters and formally extrapolate the results to a wide range of settings. These studies also make explicit both the underlying behavioral mechanism that the policy or program affects and the assumptions necessary to apply the estimates to other settings. In this sense, the TBS design is built on the importance of external validity. The cost of such a method, however, is lack of transparency and credibility due to the often complex and detailed assumptions required for estimation. As such, these methods may lack the internal validity necessary to make policymakers and even other nonspecialists confident in the estimates obtained.

Thus, the trade-off, agreed upon by all sides, is as follows: when done properly, randomized experiments can precisely isolate the effect of a specific intervention—that is, experiments can estimate and statistically bound a targeted behavioral parameter. Unfortunately, there is no guarantee that the parameter estimated is of particular interest or relevant for a related policy. On the other hand, while structural estimates (and generally TBS) provide a framework for extrapolating results, the estimates obtained from these methods often lack internal validity and credibility.

Thus, the use of the spousal abuse arrest experimental results to justify policies that had perverse effects illustrates both the danger of treating the LATE as the ATE and the importance of having clear, credible information available to policymakers during the policy design. It is for this reason that this paper rejects the dichotomy between internally valid DBS and externally valid TBS as a false one. At the heart of the issue is a serious information problem regarding most behavioral outcomes related to desired policies. Thus, we require several components: a credible measure of the average effect of each behavioral parameter of interest;[7] an estimate of the relative magnitude of these multiple parameters; and the relationship between the distribution of treatment effects and relevant population characteristics. When considering the policy decision problem as a whole, we can see the issue is not the hierarchy of evidence based on methodological selection (although surely the quality of any particular study is important) but rather how to aggregate information from multiple sources.[8] Based on this insight, this study offers two contributions to the literature on the relative value of experimental, quasi-experimental, and structural estimates.

First, this article wishes to diverge with the general tendency on both sides to dismiss quasi-experimental methods as both atheoretical (relative

---

7. Note that in general an experimental "treatment effect" need not be the composite response parameter anticipated in a policy (we shall return to this point later).

8. A procedure suggested to aggregate experimental, quasi-experimental, and structural evidence is presented in section 6 of Imbens (2009). Imbens suggests that one may use experimental evidence to "pin down some combination of the structural parameters." It is in this spirit that this article suggests combining experimental and quasi-experimental evidence.

to structural estimates) and potentially biased (relative to experimental estimates). Indeed, all sides in the methodological debate seem to agree that "quasi-experimental" approaches are "second-best" alternatives to either extreme of structural estimation or experimental evaluations (e.g., Imbens 2009, 15; Deaton 2009, p 23). Actually, quasi-experimental studies play a critical role in bridging the gap between experimental and structural models; they provide the best possible means of measuring the relative magnitude of competing behavioral parameters conditional on a set of both observable and unobservable characteristics typically based on an underlying theory of economic or individual behavior. As always, there is a trade-off and, in particular, such evaluations require additional assumptions (as noted in Imbens 2009, 15). However, one might argue that these evaluations provide the only feasible means to test the full effects of a policy and, thus, provide greater, rather than less, external validity than randomized experiments. At the same time, the more simple, intuitive assumptions made by quasi-experimental methods provide a more transparent and credible estimates. Thus, quasi-experimental findings can more useful for informing policy decisions than comparable structural model–based estimates. This point is especially salient when applied to crime policy research where state-level variation in laws and procedures facilitates a wide range of DBS approaches. Crime researchers especially should ignore the value of quasi-experimental studies even in the presence of a wide range of potential experimental approaches.

Second, this article attempts to reconcile the two apparently oppositional methodological positions: DBS and TBS. If the goal is gathering sufficient and accurate information to inform policy decisions, then there is a great deal of room for agreement between the two camps. As Imbens (2009, 3) notes, "conditional on the question of interest being one for which randomized experiment is feasible, randomized experiments are superior to all other designs in terms of statistical reliability." This statement is almost indisputable, but that is largely because of the initial conditioning statement. At issue is that in many cases, the policy option cannot be perfectly replicated in an experiment. Rather, the experiment must be used to isolate some relevant behavioral parameter that we must than use to extrapolate. It is in this sense that as Deaton (2009, 4) notes a "randomized controlled trial has no special priority." Indeed, one may agree that RCT is the "gold standard" for obtaining internally valid estimate of some behavioral parameters, while noting that in general the experimental results themselves will be insufficient to answer the question of interest. As such, no matter how internally valid the estimate may be, it is of little value to the policy question under debate. Randomized control trials specifically and DBS more generally must be subject to the same external validity scrutiny as their TBS counterparts. This study illustrates that it is not always the case that "better LATE than nothing" if the LATE estimate provide misleading information to policymakers. In the end, these estimates are not useful and may even be counterproductive if assumptions regarding the applicability of the results are not made *explicit* and appropriate caution is not taken in interpreting and presenting these results.

In order to more precisely discuss these points, this article will present and discuss both the experimental and the nonexperimental evidence on spousal arrests. Section 12.2 discusses the experimental evaluations of arrest policy as an illustration for both the uses and limitations of experimental methods. Section 12.3 discusses the theoretical complexity in translating the spousal assault arrest experiment to an arrest policy. Section 12.4 discusses the use of quasi-experimental methods to resolve theoretical ambiguities and to contextualize evidence obtained experimentally. Section 12.5 returns to the broader debate, discusses issues the results from previous sections, and concludes.

12.2   Experimental Evaluations of Arrests for Spousal Abuse

The use of arrests for spousal abuse and, in particular, the laws which mandated arrests were premised on the results of a series of randomized experiments conducted by National Institute of Justice (NIJ). The experiments were carried out over a ten-year period, from 1981 to 1991, in six different cities with different police departments. The initial and most influential of these studies was the Minnesota Domestic Violence Experiment (MDVE).[9] The experiment was motivated by basic deterrence theory (suggesting that the increased penalty for a crime reduces the incidence of that crime), which was tested using an innovative design. This experiment, funded by the Minnesota Police Department, the Police Foundation, and the Department of Justice, was run by randomly assigning a police response to domestic violence calls (Sherman 1992). The objective was to determine if arrests were more effective at reducing future violence. Police applied one of three possible treatments: (a) advising and counseling the couple, (b) separating the individuals, or (c) arresting the suspect. Researchers then interviewed the victims shortly after police involvement and then followed up every two weeks for six months. The original results found that arresting the suspect resulted in substantially less future violence than did either advising or counseling (Sherman 1992). Indeed, the initially estimated effect sizes suggested that future violence was reduced by nearly 50 percent.[10]

The experiment, while excellently designed and extremely well done,

9. Evidence that MDVE was discussed when passing these laws can be found in Wanless (1996).

10. An in-depth evaluation of the results by Tauchen and Witte (1995) found that arrest resulted in significantly more deterrence than either advising or separating the couple, consistent with the original findings of the experiment. However, unlike the original findings, Tauchen and Witte use a dynamic setting that found that most of the deterrent effect of arrest occurs within two weeks of the initial arrest.

suffered from a standard experimental problem: compliance. As noted in Angrist (2006), officers deviated from their randomly assigned responses for largely one of three reasons: first, officers may have determined that it was inappropriate to advise or separate the couple because doing so may put the victim at risk. This was most often the case when the suspect attempted to assault the officer and when both parties were injured. Second, victims sometimes persistently demanded an arrest. Third, officers occasionally forgot to bring their report forms. When police were randomly assigned to arrest a suspect, they did so 98.9 percent of the time; when they were assigned to separate, they did so 77.8 percent of the time; and when they were assigned to counsel, they did so 72.8 percent of the time (Sherman and Berk 1984). When estimating using treatment assigned as an instrument (rather than estimating the intent-to-treat effect), the effect size appears even larger. Put differently, among compliers, the effect of arrest is nearly 80 percent reduction in recidivism. The direction of the bias gives us a great deal of information about noncompliers. Those who were arrested when assigned to a less severe police response were likely also subject to the "treatment" and may have reduced their violence dramatically. This dilutes the effect of the treatment group in the intent-to-treat measure resulting in larger IV estimates.

The MDVE was replicated by five other experiments over the next decade in Charlotte, North Carolina; Colorado Springs, Colorado; Metro-Dade County, Florida; Milwaukee, Minnesota; and Omaha, Nebraska. These replications were not exactly the same as the original experiment in two dimensions. First the precise treatments differed, though all assigned at least one "arrest" and one "nonarrest" police response. Table 12.1 reports the results from the randomized experiments. The most commonly held view is that the replications failed to show that arrest deterred and indeed provided some evidence of escalation. This does not appear to be the case in a simple comparison of means in which the only significant effects (Miami Dade survey, Omaha Police reports, and the original MDVE results) indicate that the arrest disposition reduced recidivism relative to any other alternative disposition.[11] An analysis of the pooled data from all six sites by Maxwell, Garner, and Fagan (2001) finds that "arresting batterers was consistently related to reduced subsequent aggression against female intimate partners." While not all the effect sizes were statistically significant, there did not appear to be any association between arresting the offender and escalation of violence against the victim.

Before turning to the limitations of these experiments, it is worth explicitly considering the value such estimates provide. First, prior to the results from the MDVE, there was a tendency for police to offer nonpunitive and "therapeutic" responses to spousal abuse. The MDVE provided clear and

---

11. For a detailed and thoughtful review of why these differences cannot well be interpreted given the data available, see Garner, Fagan, and Maxwell (1995).

Table 12.1   Estimated treatment effects from six experiments on spousal assault

Site	N initial (N final)	Experimental comparison	% noncompliers	Recidivism	
				Survey reports	Police reports
Minneapolis	314 (202)	1. Arrest 2. Advise 3. Separate	17.8	-0.131* (0.073)	-0.083*** (0.012)
Charlotte	686 (650)	1. Arrest 2. Advise/Separate 3. Issue citation for court appearance	13.2	-0.039 (0.056)	.026 (.031)
Colorado Springs	1,660 (1,658)	1. Arrest + protective order 2. Protective order + counseling 3. Protective order 4. Restore order at the scene	6.9	—	-0.001 (0.022)
Metro-Dade County	916 (907)	1. Arrest 2. Nonarrest	10.0	-0.139*** (0.047)	-0.015 (0.028)
Milwaukee	1,200 (927)	1. Short arrest 2. Overnight arrest 3. Warning that next instance will result in arrest	0.0	0.014 (0.036)	-0.005 (0.052)
Omaha[a]	577	1. Arrest 2. Separate 3. Mediate	2.7	-0.026 (0.033)	-0.080* (0.049)

Source: Garner, Fagan, and Maxwell (1995).

Notes: Differences calculated comparing arrest to nonarrest dispositions. All reported differences report *assigned* treatment. Estimates are calculated using reported "Recidivism" in each study. Treatment and control effect sizes are not adjusted for any covariates. Recidivism is defined as committing a new offense at least once in the six-month period after treatment. Raw effect sizes based on sample size and number of failures. Dashed cells indicate no information on specified variable available from site.

[a]The Omaha experiment actually consisted of two experiments, one in which offenders were arrested if present and the other issued an arrest warrant if the offender was not out. These are combined here with arrest warrant treated as the arrest disposition.

***Significant at the 1 percent level.

*Significant at the 10 percent level.

convincing evidence that such approaches were substantially less effective at reducing violence than if the abuser had been subjected to an arrest. The authors of the initial MDVE report were even able to separate the deterrence effect from a simple incapacitation effect. Because more than 40 percent of offenders were released within one day and over 85 percent were released within one week, there was very little incapacitation due to arrest and imprisonment. This finding was among the first clear tests of deterrence theory, and the behavioral parameter identified in this setting is of significant academic and policy import. Second, although less frequently discussed, the data from these studies also provided detailed information as to the importance of police response *relative* to other offender characteristics (such as prior criminal history, race, age, or employment status). Table 12.2 shows the set of covariates available in all six experiments, illustrating the rich individual level data obtained on a sample of calls to the police for domestic violence. It appears that the effect size from arrests is quite modest when compared to the effect of other factors, such as age or prior criminal record. This type of analysis helps contextualize the results from the experiment and provides some hints as to why it may be difficult to extrapolate from the data. Third, there appears to be some variation in the intensity of the treatment effect by demographic characteristics. While the average effect across the sites was statistically similar, the variation in the estimated effect of arrest on recidivism varied greatly. This was in part due to the different distribution of covariates in the control and treatment groups.

While the experimental evidence on arrests advanced our understanding of how batterers respond to arrest, there are several issues that make it difficult to generalize from even these well-conducted experiments.[12] First is the issue of sample contamination; this is the concern that the sample of individuals who are in the experiment are not the same as those who would be in place if a policy that increased the likelihood of arrest were implemented. In part, this is due to some of the sample restrictions from the experiments that excluded serious cases (i.e., felonies) as determined by the officer. In addition, officers may not have included cases they deemed to not be misdemeanor assault. The unknown true distribution of intimate partner abuse case severity and case type makes it difficult to sign the bias on this type of sample selection. In part, the sample is by construction different from the policy sample. The experimental designed ensured the initial reporting of an offense because the sample frame is based on domestic violence cases that request police presence. This means that all experimental results are the effect of arrest *conditional on reporting,* and this condition is quite meaningful in the case of domestic violence. The sample could not measure whether

---

12. The subsequent discussion should not be read as a criticism of the methodology of these experiments. Indeed, the initial MDVE and the five replications are among the most carefully run experiments in the crime literature.

Table 12.2   Characteristics of subjects from six experiments on spousal assault

	Minneapolis	Charlotte	Colorado Springs	Metro-Dade County	Milwaukee	Omaha
Number of subjects	205	638	1238	906	954	296
A. Incident assignment data						
Assigned to arrest (%)	29	33	26	51	68	34
Actually arrested (%)	43	40	28	60	68	34
Initial victim interview completion rates (%)	62	64	83	65	60	79
Final victim interview completion rates (%)	49	50	70	42	78	73
B. Suspect characteristics						
Age (average)	32	33	31	35	31	31
Employed (%)	40	77	87	71	47	78
Prior arrest (%)	59	31	43	12	62	65
Use of intoxicant (%)	61	54	59	31	29	59
Race/Ethnicity						
African American (%)	23	70	30	42	75	42
White (%)	58	28	54	36	20	51
Hispanic (%)	1	0	15	22	4	5
Asian/Native American/other (%)	18	2	1	0	1	3
Relationship with victim						
Married (%)	35	48	67	79	31	46
Separated or divorced (%)	3	2	5	5	1	1
Unmarried (%) (current or former)	47	50	28	16	68	52
Son, brother, roommate (%)	15					
C. Incident characteristics						
Misdemeanor (%)	98	97	37	100	100	100
Victim injured (%)	—	84	55	92	100	73

Sources: Minneapolis: Sherman and Berk (1984) and data provided by Angrist (2006); Charlotte, Colorado Springs, Metro-Dade County, Omaha: Maxwell, Garner, and Fagan (2001). Dashed cells indicate no information on specified variable available from site.

Notes: Differences calculated comparing arrest to nonarrest dispositions. All reported differences report *assigned* treatment. Categories are pooled when appropriate to facilitate comparability across studies. Omaha sample uses only the Offender-Present sample.

victims would be more or less likely to report to the police because it was based on an initial report.

Second is the issue of police cooperation. The departments chosen to conduct the experiments tended be those for whom compliance would be a minimal issue (Maxwell, Garner, and Fagan 2001). In addition, among the officers conducting experiment, most of the sample was collected by only a few officers.[13] This lends itself to ensuring high quality experimental design but not necessarily generalizability. In particular, the ways in which police may choose to avoid compliance must be explicitly considered when determining how to implement a policy to achieve the experimental results.

Finally, because of the relatively small number of cases, experiments will in general *not* identify the most serious, low-probability events. Serious injury and death are relatively rare occurrences but so undesirable that policies wish to avoid any increases in these high-cost outcomes.[14] Experimental results will in general lack the power to detect these low-probability events and even structural models may not be able to determine the realistic probability of such occurrences.[15]

Thus, the experimental results leave open several questions. First, given relatively similar average effects but differences in the variance of these effects across sites, can we generalize from arrests in these six sites to the efficacy of arrest relative to nonarrest in other locations? Second, if arrest, relative to other nonarrest police responses, reduces recidivism under experimental conditions, what is the effect of a policy that increases arrest? While the parameters estimated in the experiments are informative about both of these questions, they cannot answer them definitively without additional assumptions.

12.3   Arrest Laws and Criminal Behavior in a Repeat Interaction Setting

Although the experimental evidence from the six spousal assault experiment sites did not directly answer a policy questions, the experimental evidence on the efficacy of arrest encouraged many states to pass policies that encourage or require arrest of domestic abusers. These policies play a prominent role in the government's attempt to combat domestic violence.[16]

---

13. For example, in the MDVE, 9 percent of the officers produced 28 percent of the cases (Sherman and Berk 1984).

14. This statement should not suggest to the reader that intimate partner homicide is at acceptable levels. Indeed, women are more likely to be killed by a current or former intimate partner than anyone else. It is rather a statistical statement about the likelihood of observed intimate partner homicide given the total sample size.

15. A similar problem is discussed in the context of suicide due to antidepression drugs by Ludwig and Marcotte (2005).

16. For a detailed discussion of the emergence of these statutes, see Iyengar (2009). For a discussion on the role of the experimental evidence in influencing policy, see Maxwell, Garner, and Fagan (2001, 4–5).

Currently, twelve states and the District of Columbia have passed mandatory arrest laws. These laws requires police to arrest a suspect without a warrant if there is probable cause to suspect that an individual has committed some form of assault (either misdemeanor or felonious) against an intimate partner or family member. An additional ten states have recommended arrest laws, which specify arrest as recommended but not required when confronted with probable cause that an intimidate partner or familial assault has occurred. States in both of these groups are reported in table 12.3. These laws were implemented as an explicit strategy to increase the fraction of domestic violence cases in which police arrest the suspect. Many economists may immediately note that this is not a direct application of the experimental results.[17] However, this also represents a realistic setting in which experimental evidence, when it is the *only* source of information regarding a policy, may not produce the desired outcome.

To illustrate how mandatory arrest laws changed interactions between abusers and victims, consider how they changed the nature of interaction in the repeated setting of intimate partnerships. Mandatory arrest laws increase the cost of choosing violence. This effect is largely the reason why mandatory arrest laws were originally advocated. Ideally, this increase in cost would result in a situation where violence is never chosen. Unfortunately it is typically difficult to sustain such a situation, in particular because it requires victims to report whenever there is a violent incident. Because both anecdotal and sociological evidence suggest victims dislike reporting, many situations arise where batters are violent but victims do not report. Given then that reporting is uncertain, we cannot assume that violence is never chosen, and, as such, we will observe some level of violence.

Arrest laws also change the cost of reporting abuse to the police. The problem with this is that because abusers have more freedom in adjusting their behavior than do victims, this increased cost is borne almost entirely by the victims. To illustrate this, supposed mandatory arrest laws increase the utility to victims from reporting so that, all other things equal, reporting would be more desirable after the law change. In such a situation, an abuser could adjust the probability of violence if the victim does not report relative to the probability of violence if the victim does report. This essentially allows abusers to adjust the probability of each outcome to fully account for any utility gains from reporting to the victim. Similarly, suppose arrest laws decrease the utility to victims from reporting so that reporting is really a punishment strategy taken by the victim to induce better stream of behavior by the abuser in the future. In such a situation, an abuser can adjust the probability of violence if the victim reports such that any punishment strategy

17. Indeed, the authors of the original study note that mandating arrests may not be appropriate because of potential heterogeneity in offender responses (Sherman and Berk 1984, 270).

Table 12.3   **Mandatory arrest laws by state**

	Year passed	Code/Statute
Recommended arrest states		
AZ	1991	Ariz. Rev. Stat. Ann. §13-3601(B)
CA	1993	Cal. Penal Code §836(c)(1)
KS	2000	Kan. Stat. Ann. §22-2401(c)(2)
MS	1995	Miss. Code Ann. §99-3-7(3)(a)
MO	1989	Mo. Ann. Stat. §455.085(1)
NY	1994	N.Y. Crim. Proc. Law §140.10(4)
OH	1994	Ohio Rev. Code Ann. §2935.032(A)(1)(a)
SC	2002	S.C. Code Ann. §16-25-70(B)
Mandatory arrest states		
AK	1996	Alaska Stat. §18.65.530(a)
CO	1994	Colo. Rev. Stat. Ann. §18-6-803.6(1)
CT	1987	Conn. Gen. Stat. §46b-38b(a)
DC	1991	D.C. Code Ann. §16-1031(a)
IA	1990	Iowa Code §236.12(3)
ME	1995	Me. Rev. Stat. Ann. tit. 19-A, §4012(6)(D)
NV	1989	Nev. Rev. Stat. Ann. §171.137(1)
NJ	1991	N.J. Stat. Ann. §2C:25-21(a)
OR	2001	Or. Rev. Stat. §133.055(2)(a)
RI	2000	R.I. Gen. Laws §12-29-3(c)(1)
SD	1998	S.D. Codified Laws §23A-3-2.1
UT	2000	Utah Code Ann. §7-36-2.2(2)(a)
VA	2002	Va. Code Ann. §19.2-81.3(B)
WI	1996	Wis. Stat. Ann. §968.075(2)(a)
WA	1999	Wash. Rev. Code Ann. §10.31.100(2)

Source: http://www.westlaw.com.

Notes: Mandatory arrest states are defined as states where officers have no discretion as to whether to make a warrantless arrest when an intimate partner offense is reported. Recommended arrest states are defined as states where officers are instructed but not required to make a warrantless arrest when an intimate partner offense is reported. For specific information on coverage, see data appendix available on author's Web site (http://personal.lse.ac.uk/iyengarr/ma_appendix.pdf).

is unsustainable (i.e., reporting becomes too costly to make the utility gains from nonviolence in the future worth seeking).

Thus, the abuser can essentially be nicer to the victim if she does not report him after a violent incident, thus encouraging her not to report after violence (i.e., reducing the probability of violence conditional on not reporting). Indeed, this is often referred to by domestic violence advocates as the "honeymoon period," where abusers are extra attentive and loving. In addition, the abuser can take retributive action after reporting (i.e., increasing the probability of violence after reporting). Thus, the counterintuitive result of arrest policies for intimate partner violence is that they may indeed increase intimate partner violence because batters have a greater ability to determine the outcomes. Thus, the abusers are better able to shift the burden of arrest onto the victims, deterring reporting rather than deterring abuse.

To illustrate how changes in the level of homicides can be linked to the total number of abusive incidents, consider a model where with some small probability, p, domestic abuse escalates to murder. For n intimate partner incidents, the number of homicides in a jurisdiction is then pn. There are two main theories on potential responses that may result in increased homicides after arrest laws: reprisal (abuser response) and reporting (victim response). I will consider each in turn.

A different explanation for the response could be that abusers respond to arrest by punishing victims, and this increases intimate partner homicides. Suppose p increases because violence becomes more severe. This could occur if abusers are very angry when returning home after arrest and so more frequently commit violence against their partners. Thus, for a given n intimate partner incidents, the number of homicides pn increases. Note that if there is no deterrence effect, that is, n is constant, then, once again, the effect on the law is to increase violence. However, if there is a decrease in incidents (n declines), then the overall effect of mandating arrest is ambiguous. This response is consistent with evidence on victim fears. As discussed in the preceding, fear of reprisal is the most commonly cited reason for not reporting. To the extent that the fear is rational, this is consistent with the reprisal hypothesis. Moreover, when a victim leaves her relationship, she is at the greatest risk from her partner.[18] If arrest allows women to leave, then reprisal rates may increase. Evidence against this hypothesis comes from the experimental evidence, which found no significant increase in reprisal, though this may be because the abusers did not blame their victims for their subsequent arrest (instead blaming police officers).

While the experimental results may provide evidence against the reprisal hypothesis, the results are silent in the context of the reporting hypothesis. The reporting hypothesis suggests that victims are less willing to report an incident if their abuser will be arrested. Suppose that the probability of reporting given violence decreases after the passage of mandatory arrest laws. Because police presence, regardless of the police response, can disrupt a violent incident and prevent escalation to homicide, this failure to report to the police can increase the rate of intimate partner homicides. Thus, the victim's decision not to notify the police may increase p. This is not the overall effect of the law because the threat of arrest deters (as it did in the MDVE); then n, may decrease. In this case, the effect of the law on homicides is ambiguous. While arrest, conditional on reporting, deters violence, the unconditional effect of arrest on violence may be small or zero if victims substantially reduce their reporting.

Domestic violence victims may decide not to report for several reasons.

18. See Tjaden & Thoennes (2000).

First, there is a psychological and emotional component of intimate partner abuse that often generates victims who remain committed to their abuser and do not wish to send him to prison. Thus, the victim's guilt may increase her or his own costs of reporting as well as the abusers.[19] Second, if abusers are arrested but no further legal action is taken, they may return home within a day of their arrest and further terrorize their victim. In a nonexperimental evaluation of mandatory arrest as a policy, Lyon (1999) used a logistic model to compare the likelihood of arrest under mandatory arrest laws versus proarrest laws in two cities in Michigan. She found that once a victim calls the police to report an incident, she is significantly less likely to call again. She posits this was likely because police intervention in the form of an arrest resulted in retribution by the abuser, deterring future reporting.[20] Third, in many cases, arrest laws resulted in the victim also being arrested if there was evidence that she (or he) physically assaulted her (or his) partner. In many areas, women constitute nearly 20 percent of domestic violence arrests, a far higher percentage than the estimated proportion of female abusers.[21] Over half of these female arrestees can be identified as previous victims of intimate partner violence (Martin 1997). Anecdotal evidence from some battered women advocates suggests that these "dual arrests" are the most serious problem with mandatory arrest.[22] Dual arrests have serious implications for victims who are immigrants and may be deported if convicted of assault. In addition, those who have children face potential loss of custody during the arrest period. This latter response can be viewed as a method by police to avoid complying with the intentions of the mandatory arrest laws.

19. Recent research finds that many women do not perceive any benefit from mandatory arrest laws, no-drop policies, (requiring prosecution conditional on reporting) and mandatory medical reporting, and these laws may make them less willing to report in the future (Smith 2000).

20. Rennison (2000) found that fear of reprisal from the abuser was the most commonly cited cause for not reporting a domestic violence incident. This is a hotly contested claim. Mills (1998), based on research by Sherman and Berk (1984), claims that arrests actually increase reassaults. More recent work by Maxwell, Garner, and Fagan (2001) find that there is no significant change in the risk of assault.

21. For example, in Phoenix, Arizona, 18 percent of domestic violence arrests are women (http://www.azcasa.org). Women are thought to be abusers in less than 5 percent of intimate partner violence cases (Dobash et al. 1992). Though some work suggests there is a surprisingly high rate of female-on-male abuse (see Strauss and Geller 1980), this work is problematic and, for the most part, ignores the severity and context of the violence (see Blau 1998). This is particularly relevant in the case of intimate partner abuse. For example, suppose a husband spent years beating his wife severely. At the time of the survey, the husband shoved his wife, and she immediately threatened him with a knife. The conflict tactics scale (CTS) treats the wife's behavior as aggressive when it is, in context, clearly defensive. Moreover, the CTS fails to properly differentiate acts of violence that constitute severe abuse. When severity of abuse is considered, men typically have the higher rates of the most dangerous behaviors, such as firing a gun, repeating their violence more often, and doing more physical harm. For a greater discussion, see DeKeserdy and Schwartz (1998).

22. This statement is based on conversations with individuals at battered women's coalitions in New Jersey, Arizona, New York, California, Connecticut, and Illinois.

This, thus, represents a second way in which implementation of policies that encourage arrests may differ from experimental evaluations of arrest policies. All of these costs may result in an increased unwillingness to report abuse to the police.

Thus, there is a potential that the results of a policy to increase arrest are the exact opposite of those in the experiment, even when the experimental parameter is an unbiased estimate of the deterrence effect and is externally valid to groups outside the original sample. This can be explained by recognizing that the experimental results estimated the effect of an actual arrest conditional on reporting, while the estimates presented in this study estimate the unconditional effect of the certainty of arrest. The spousal abuse arrest experiments held constant the probability of reporting given violence because all cases in the experiment required an initial report of domestic abuse to the police. Thus, the spousal abuse arrest experiments estimated the effect of a decrease in batterer's utility, when they abuse and are reported, on their probability of choosing violence in the future. Unfortunately, if the victim also faces an increased cost from the increased penalty, then the overall effect of these laws on abuse is theoretically ambiguous (and empirically these laws appear to increase levels of abuse).

Finally, it is worth noting that heterogeneity in responses is especially important in this case. Even if most offenders respond to arrest by reducing future violence, the risk that some may respond to arrest by increasing the severity of violence (in the extreme, committing murder) highlights the importance of considering both the mean and the variance of the treatment effect. If, as in the case of domestic violence, substantial variance in response to treatment may result in very serious outcomes, then the local average treatment effect, as estimated by the experiment (which becomes local by the nonrandomness of sample selection), may be insufficient for policy-making purposes.

12.4 Estimates on the Effectiveness of Mandating Arrest

To test the effectiveness of mandatory arrest laws, I consider the effect of these laws on intimate partner abuse. This requires special attention to the total number of incidents of domestic violence, not simply the number of reported incidents, because the fraction of incidents that are reported to the police is potentially affected by this policy.[23] If I cannot observe unreported incidents, changes in the number of reported incidents and change in the total number of incidents (both reported and unreported) are observation-

23. The National Incident Based Reporting System (NIBRS), which does provide identification of the victim-offender relationships, is, therefore, ill-suited to the purposes of this study. Because the NIBRS solely comprises reported incidents, analysis of this data is not useful for measuring the true incidence of domestic violence.

ally equivalent.[24] In part, because I can observe victim-offender relationships, and in part because these crimes are almost perfectly reported, I use a measure of intimate partner homicides as a way to measure intimate partner abuse. Assuming that police intervention can reduce the probability of violence changes in the intimate partner homicide measure may provide insight into the impact of mandatory arrest laws on intimate partner violence.[25]

To construct a data set of intimate partner homicides, I use the FBI Uniform Crime Reports, Supplementary Homicide Reports (1976–2003), which provide data for all homicides that took place in the years 1976 to 2003 in all fifty states and the District of Columbia with additional descriptive variables about the victim, offender, and the nature of the crime (Federal Bureau of Investigation). I define an intimate partner homicide to include any homicide committed against a husband, wife, common-law husband, common-law wife, ex-husband, or ex-wife.[26] The data are constructed at the incident level with about 6.5 percent of the sample (36,442 observations) being intimate partner homicides.[27] I constructed a count of the number of relevant homicides by aggregating the incidents of intimate partner homicide, as defined in the preceding, in a given state for each year from 1976 until 2003. I also aggregated the number of intimate partner homicides by the race of the victim and offender and by sex of the victim and offender. Estimates are then scaled using census estimates for state population.[28]

A plot of the trend in various types of homicides before and after mandatory arrest laws suggests that these laws may have had a significant impact on intimate partner abuse. Figure 12.1 shows the rate of intimate partner and

24. An ideal data source for this type of analysis would be the National Crime Victimization Survey (NCVS) with state-level identifiers. Although previous researchers were able to access geo-coded versions of this data (see, for example, Farmer and Tiefenthaler 2003), recent changes in the administration and management of the NCVS make such access no longer possible. Some analysis using this data previously obtained suggests that mandatory arrest laws may reduce intimate partner violence but also reduce the number of cases that are reported in the system (Dugan 2003). Additional information about reasons why NCVS access is no longer possible is available upon request.

25. The linkage between misdemeanor assault prevalence and intimate partner homicide is well established. See, for example, Gwinn and O'Dell (1993). Moreover, the underlying causes are linked; see Mercy and Saltzman (1989).

26. The specific coverage of each law is reported in the legal appendix of Iyengar (2009). The distribution of samples across all groups is also described there.

27. There is some measurement error in the victim-offender relationship variable. About 1.25 percent of female victims reported as having a relationship to their offender that would imply she's a man and about .43 percent of male victims reported as having a relationship to their offender that would imply he's a woman. Together, these account for about 200 observations and less than 1 percent of the total sample. This is due to the classification of multiple homicides. In multiple victim homicides, the first victim-offender relationship is recorded for all of the victims. Because the selection of the "first" victim tends to be arbitrary, and this constitutes a very small fraction of the overall sample, these cases are excluded from analysis.

28. This scaling by population seems the appropriate deflater as arrest laws often apply to unmarried couples; however, the subsequent analysis has been repeated with a number of married couples with little qualitative effect on the coefficients.

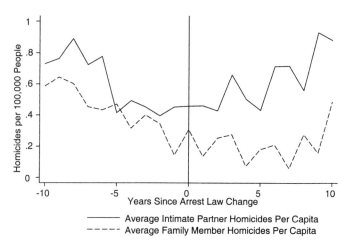

Fig. 12.1   Intimate partner and familial homicide rates in mandatory arrest law states

Notes: Means based on author's own calculations using Supplementary Homicide Reports 1976–2003. Intimate partner homicides include homicides of husbands, wives, ex-husbands, ex-wives, common-law husbands, and common-law wives. Mandatory arrest states are defined as states where officers have no discretion as to whether to make a warrantless arrest when an intimate partner offense is reported.

family homicide rates as a function of time since the arrest law change. There appears to be a discrete increase of about 0.4 intimate partner homicides per 100,000. There is only a small decline in the number of family violence homicides. In contrast, figure 12.2 shows that recommended arrest laws have relatively little effect on intimate partner or familial homicides.

Comparing intimate partner homicides in states with and without arrest laws before and after the passage of these laws, I estimate a linear regression of the impact of mandatory arrest laws on the number of intimate partner homicides per 100,000 inhabitants. Column (1) of table 12.4 reports some coefficients from this regression. The *mandatory arrest effect* variable is defined as 1 in states that passed mandatory arrest laws in the years after the law was passed. Similarly, *recommended arrest effect* variable equals 1 in states that passed recommended arrest laws in the years after the law was passed. The results suggest that mandatory arrest laws are responsible for an additional 0.8 murders per 100,000 people. This corresponds to a 54 percent increase in intimate partner homicides.

There does not appear to be a significant effect in recommended arrest law states. Although the coefficient is negative, it is measured relatively imprecisely. Estimates in columns (2) and (3) of table 12.4 include controls for some other state characteristics and crime rates. Because these laws are between the previous discretionary arrest system and the mandatory arrest, we might expect a smaller but positive effect on homicide rates. There are

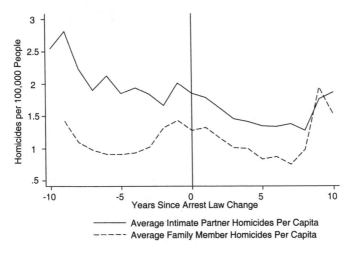

Fig. 12.2   Intimate partner and familial homicide rates in recommended arrest law states

Notes: Means based on author's own calculations using Supplementary Homicide Reports 1976–2003. Intimate partner homicides include homicides of husbands, wives, ex-husbands, ex-wives, common-law husbands, and common-law wives. Recommended arrest states are defined as states where officers are instructed, but not required, to make a warrantless arrest when an intimate partner offense is reported.

several reasons why this might not happen: first, if the arrest is perceived by abusers as discretionary, then they may not blame the victim for being arrested, reducing the reprisal rate. Second, because officers have discretion, victims may be more willing to call the police hoping to get an intermediate response. Finally, police themselves may not have changed their behavior much, opting to retain discretion and fill out paperwork rather than simply arresting.

There are several potential state-year factors that may be associated with both increased arrests and increased domestic violence. One important factor is the state crime rate, which may indicate how crime prone society is as well as the other crimes police must deal with. To measure the violent crime rate, I used the number of rape, robbery, and assault crime reports per 100,000 people from the FBI's Uniform Crime Reports. Column (2) of table 12.4 reports these results. Another concern might be state economic conditions that may increase domestic violence. I use average annual state unemployment rate derived from the Current Population Survey to control for this effect. There appears to be little effect of these limited covariates on the mandatory arrest law effect.

Column (3) of table 12.4 includes a more rich set of covariates including state-year level variables on demographics, economic conditions, and social policies. Because of racial differences in crime rates, I include some demographic controls (such as fraction of population that is black or white). I

Table 12.4 Difference-in-difference estimates of mandatory and recommended arrest laws

	(1)	(2)	(3)	(4)	(5)	(6)	(7)
	All intimate partner homicides per 100,000 inhabitants						
Dependent Variable Mean				1.48			
Mandatory arrest law effect	0.83**	0.81**	0.76**	1.15***	1.15***	1.10***	0.47
(=1 in MA law states after law change)	(0.33)	(0.33)	(0.34)	(0.40)	(0.41)	(0.39)	(0.30)
Recommended arrest law effect	−0.61	−0.66	−0.62	−0.31	−0.30	−0.36	−0.96*
(=1 in RA law states after law change)	(0.61)	(0.59)	(0.47)	(0.64)	(0.63)	(0.63)	(0.54)
Unemployment rate		0.01	0.04	0.019	0.019	0.02	0.02
		(0.07)	(0.09)	(0.07)	(0.07)	(0.07)	(0.07)
1 year postlaw change							0.23
							(0.27)
2 year postlaw change							0.14
							(0.31)
3 or more years postlaw change							0.41
							(0.42)
Estimation method	OLS	OLS	OLS	OLS	OLS	OLS	OLS
Controls for other violent crime rates[a]	No	Yes	Yes	Yes	Yes	Yes	Yes
Controls for unemployment rate[b]	No	Yes	Yes	Yes	Yes	Yes	Yes
State-year demographic variables[c]	No	No	Yes	Yes	Yes	Yes	Yes
State-year economic and social controls[d]	No	No	Yes	Yes	Yes	Yes	Yes

Linear trend	No	No	No	Yes	No	No
Quadratic trend	No	No	No	Yes	Yes	No
State-specific trend controls	No	No	Yes	Yes	Yes	Yes
Postlaw interaction effects	No	No	Yes	No	No	No
State-fixed effects	Yes	Yes	Yes	Yes	Yes	Yes
Year-fixed effects	Yes	Yes	Yes	Yes	Yes	Yes
R^2	0.6125	0.6127	0.6214	0.6275	0.6284	0.6252

(Final column: Linear trend No; Quadratic trend No; State-specific trend controls No; Postlaw interaction effects Yes; State-fixed effects Yes; Year-fixed effects Yes; R^2 0.6746)

Notes: All regressions include 992 observations. The dependent variable for each column is the column title per 100,000 inhabitants. Robust standard errors, clustered by state, are reported in parentheses. Intimate partner homicides include homicides of husbands, wives, ex-husbands, ex-wives, common-law husbands, and common-law wives. Mandatory arrest (MA) states are states that require an arrest conditional on a report of domestic violence. Recommended arrest (RA) states are states where officers are instructed but not required to make a warrantless arrest when an intimate partner offense is reported.

a Crime rate controls use FBI Uniform Crime reports for the number of crimes per 100,000 inhabitants. Indexed crimes included in the violent crime variable are murder, robbery, assault, and rape. Indexed crimes included in the nonviolent crime count are burglary, larceny, motor vehicle theft, and drug crimes.

b Unemployment estimates are based on the March *Current Population Survey.*

c State demographic controls are based on the March *Current Population Survey* and include variables for the fraction of the population that is black, white, and other race, as well as age composition indicating share of prison population that is aged fourteen–nineteen, twenty–forty-nine, and fifty or older.

d State economic control variables are based on the March *Current Population Survey* and include the variables log state personal income per capita, and female-to-male employment ratio. State social policy controls include max Aid to Families with Dependent Children/Temporary Assistance to Needy Families (AFDC/TANF) for a family of three, unilateral divorce laws indicators (based on classification in Stevenson and Wolfers 2006), and indicators for whether the state has the death penalty.

***Significant at the 1 percent level.

**Significant at the 5 percent level.

*Significant at the 10 percent level.

also include share of prison population in the state that is aged under twenty, twenty to thirty-five, thirty-six to forty-nine and fifty or older, which may be indicative of police behavior and crime enforcement levels in a given state. In addition to the unemployment rate used in the previous specification, I include economic covariates of crime, such as state-year average log personal income and male-female employment ratio. Finally, the state social policy controls that are related to crime generally include whether the state has the death penalty and the Aid to Families with Dependent Children/Temporary Assistance to Needy Families (AFDC/TANF) max for a family of three. I also included a control for when the state passed unilateral divorce laws based on Stevenson and Wolfers (2006). After including these covariates, the coefficient on the effect of mandatory arrest laws on intimate partner homicides shrinks to about 0.76, which is slightly smaller but similar in magnitude to the estimates from previous specification.

Because there was a significant secular trend in the domestic violence homicide rates, I estimated several specifications with trend variables. Column (4) reports the results when including a linear trend, and column (5) includes the results when including a quadratic trend. The inclusion of trend controls appears to increase the coefficient, suggesting that declining rates of intimate partner violence were inducing an underestimate of the full effect of the law. Column (6) reports the results from including state-specific linear trends. The coefficient is still larger than the estimates without a trend, consistent with the downward trend biasing the ordinary least squares (OLS) estimates.

To estimate the effect of the adoption of these laws over time, the specifications reported in column (7) include a time since law change interaction effect. Combined with the year-fixed effects, this both controls for any differences at a given point in time (year-fixed effect) as well as differences generated from the duration of the law (years since law change). The main effect of mandatory arrest laws corresponds to the effect of mandatory arrest laws in the initial year of passage. This effect is about half the size of previously estimated effect and insignificant. However, while the effect in the initial year is not significantly different than zero, the effect in the second year (the mandatory arrest law main effect plus the one-year postlaw change effect) is about 0.7 and is significant with a p-value of 0.02 (joint test statistics not reported in the table). The total law effect in later years is similarly significant (although the two-year postlaw effect is significant only at the 10 percent level), and there does not appear to be a significantly different effect of these laws over time. The effect does not appear to grow significantly over time (although there does appear to be a slight lag in the effect, which is to be expected). It is somewhat surprising that the effect of the law does not grow over time. There are several potential reasons why this may be the case. First is the annual nature of the data, which means that monthly growth over the first and second years may be missed and is aggregated into a single point estimate. Second, because the outcome variable is homicides, it may be less sensitive to the more subtle changes over time and, thus, is a relatively blunt outcome to measure the temporal diffusion of behavior. Finally, this is consistent with a reprisal story where the behavioral response is a one-time adoption immediately after the law change. If that is the case, and most police agencies adopted the law relatively rapidly, then we would not expect to see the effect grow over time.[29]

Because mandatory arrest laws were an important means by which domestic violence became represented and treated as a criminal justice issue (as compared to a family or community problem), we might be concerned that these laws will have a disparate impact on communities that have greater mistrust of the criminal justice system. In particular, some studies have shown that African American women may be especially reluctant to report crimes to the police, preferring instead to handle instances within their own communities.[30] To evaluate the effect on different subgroups of interest, columns (2), (3), and (4) of table 12.5 compare the effect of mandatory arrest laws on intimate partner homicides committed between white couples, African American couples, and Asian couples, respectively. The point estimate for white and blacks are similar although blacks have a larger increase in percentage terms (based on mean homicides rates reported in the first row of each column, whites have a base rate of 0.81 intimate partner homicides per 100,000, and blacks have a rate of 0.51 per 100,000). This provides some evidence that the negative effect of mandatory arrest laws is disproportionately strong in certain communities.

This is certainly consistent with some of the heterogeneity in the experimental evidence. For example, in Milwaukee, evidence suggested that African American men were more likely to escalate (rather than be deterred). In Dade County, experimental results suggested that unemployment increased the risk that the response was escalation rather than deterrence (Pate and

29. Thus far, little attention has been paid to the bias that unknown homicides might introduce into evidence. Underlying this is the assumption that it is less likely that family homicides are not likely to be unsolved as the offender would be a known individual (as opposed to a stranger-on-stranger crime in which the offender may be entirely unknown to the police). This assumption is not entirely accurate and, indeed, may produce some bias in measuring homicide rates (see Riedel 1999). However, a broad range of studies (e.g., Williams and Flewelling 1987; Pampel and Williams 2000) have suggested that family homicides need substantially less adjustment than intimate partner homicides, and, as such, this assumption may not be too harmful. For sensitivity analysis, see Iyengar (2009).

30. This point is highly contested. Evidence from the National Crime Victimization Survey suggests that African American women report intimate partner violence at higher rates than do their white or Asian counterparts (see, for example, Rennison 2002). However, surveys and outreach workers cite general mistrust of the police, mistreatment of the police, and concerns that reporting will send partners with criminal records back to prison as reasons why underreporting may be more prevalent in African American communities (see Hampton, Oliver, and Magarian 2003).

Table 12.5   Estimates of the effect of mandatory and recommended arrest laws on intimate partner homicides for various subgroups

	All intimate partner homicides per 100,000 inhabitants (1)	Intimate partner homicides with white victims and perpetrator (2)	Intimate partner homicides with black victims and perpetrators (3)	Intimate partner homicides with Asian victims and perpetrators (4)	Homicides of females by male intimate partners (5)	Homicides of males by female intimate partners (6)
Dependent variable mean	1.48	0.81	0.59	0.01	0.89	0.59
Mandatory arrest law effect	1.1525***	0.5080**	0.6208***	0.0144*	0.6023**	0.5502***
(=1 in MA law states after law change)	(0.4067)	(0.2339)	(0.1981)	(0.0077)	(0.2459)	(0.1863)
Recommended arrest law effect	−0.2960	−0.1225	−0.1342	0.0118	−0.0738	−0.2222
(=1 in RA law states after law change)	(0.6348)	(0.2785)	(0.3435)	(0.0124)	(0.3251)	(0.3270)
Unemployment rate	0.0196	0.0181	0.0066	−0.0000	0.0037	−0.0159
	(0.0741)	(0.0339)	(0.0403)	(0.0005)	(0.0366)	(0.0383)
Controls for other crime rates[a]	Yes	Yes	Yes	Yes	Yes	Yes
Controls for unemployment rate[b]	Yes	Yes	Yes	Yes	Yes	Yes
State-year demographic variables[c]	Yes	Yes	Yes	Yes	Yes	Yes
State-year economic and social controls[d]	Yes	Yes	Yes	Yes	Yes	Yes
State-fixed effects	Yes	Yes	Yes	Yes	Yes	Yes
Linear trend	Yes	Yes	Yes	Yes	Yes	Yes
Year-fixed effects	Yes	Yes	Yes	Yes	Yes	Yes
R^2	0.6284	0.6733	0.5643	0.4536	0.6448	0.5910

Note: See table 12.4 notes and footnotes.

Hamilton 1992). Given the differences in unemployment rates across subgroups, this is also consistent with observed differences in estimate effects. While the results appear to hold for all groups, the heterogeneity may be particularly prominent in the certain communities. If we believe that certain communities may be less willing to report to police, the reporting effect might be stronger in those communities. In this case, I find some evidence of this, which may suggest that reporting by victims could explain the rise in homicides. The larger (in percent terms) effect among blacks and Asians provides support for the reporting effect over the reprisal effect if aversion to the police in general makes the response of minority communities stronger than the response in white communities.

Thus far, I have given little attention to the question of fault when constructing these counts. This is relevant because the intimate partner homicide count used thus far likely includes some homicides that are eventually (but not initially) classified as self-defense or justifiable. While I cannot identify "self-defense" killings from murders, homicides of males by their female intimate partner may more closely approximate the subset of cases for which self-defense is a plausible future classification. Column (5) of table 12.5 presents estimate of intimate partner homicides with only female victims killed by male intimate partners. Column (6) presents estimates of intimate partner homicides committed against males by their female intimate partners. Intimate partner homicides of females increase about 50 percent, a similar percent increase to the main, unrestricted estimate (presented in column [1] of table 12.5). Similarly, homicides of males by their female intimate partners are significantly affected by mandatory arrest laws—in fact, the effect is larger in percent terms. Overall, these results are consistent with either a reporting or reprisal effect in response to the law change. Indeed, to the extent that police intervention facilitates some flight or escape by victims, murder of the abuser may be a substitute for other improved outside options. This evidence is consistent with studies that suggest that battered women who kill their husbands do so more often when they have fewer extralegal opportunities.[31]

In an effort to verify the difference-in-difference framework, I test the effect of mandatory arrest laws on various sets of uncovered homicides. If the difference-in-difference estimates find a significant effect of mandatory arrest laws on homicides between individuals who should be unaffected by domestic and family violence laws, then it is likely the differences identified in the preceding may be unrelated to the passage of these laws. For the purposes of these falsification tests, I define a class of homicides called "other homicides," which includes homicides committed against employees, employers,

---

31. See, for example, O'Keefe (1997). This is also consistent with evidence that finds female perpetrated abuse is affected not by criminal justice options but by outside extralegal resources (e.g., shelters). (See Browne and Williams 1989.)

friends, other known individuals, and strangers.[32] These homicides should be unaffected by mandatory arrest laws. I estimate two specifications, one with only state- and year-fixed effects and one with the full set of covariates described in the preceding. The results from these regressions are reported in table 12.6, columns (1) and (2). In both specifications, neither mandatory arrest laws nor recommended arrest laws have a significant effect on the homicide level of uncovered homicides. To more closely approximate the homicides of females, I also estimate these two specifications on a count of "other homicides," which have female victims. The results from these two regressions are reported in columns (3) and (4) of table 12.6, and again, there appears to be no significant effect of these laws on homicide rates. Finally, I test the effect of arrest laws on intimate and familial homicides that are uncovered by arrest laws. These include homicides committed by boyfriends, girlfriends, homosexual partners, and nonnuclear family relatives. Because the SHR data is from police reports, the distinction between cohabiting or common-law married partners is somewhat blurred. While some states do treat cohabiting and common-law married partners differently, the question of whether mandatory arrest laws are enforced in cases of cohabiting intimate partner violence is unclear, and to date, there does not appear any systematic evidence to answer the question. In the case of noncohabiting intimate partners, the law will only be enforced if these groups are specifically covered.[33] The results are reported in columns (5) and (6) of table 12.6. These results suggest that there is no significant effect of these laws on uncovered homicides, and the estimated effects are significantly smaller.[34]

12.5   Discussion and Concluding Remarks

Experimental evidence from the Minnesota Domestic Violence Experiment and replication at five other sites encouraged many states seeking better responses to the problem of domestic violence to pass laws requiring the arrest of individuals believed to abuse their spouses. An evaluation of these laws suggests that they have increased level of intimate partner homicide.

32. I have excluded homicides committed by individuals of "unknown relationship." While it is likely that these homicides were not committed by immediate family members or intimate partners, it is was not possible to estimate the subset of these homicides that would be covered, and, thus, all are excluded.

33. Including boyfriends and girlfriends in the intimate partner counts for states in which these groups are not explicitly covered does not significantly change the results. They remain a relatively small fraction of all intimate partner homicides, and while there does not seem to be a significant effect on this group, the results for common-law married, married, and formerly married couples are robust to their inclusion.

34. The Fisher test for equality between mandatory and recommended arrest law coefficients is rejected at the 0.02 level. The comparison is between specifications reported in column (6) of table 12.3 and column (6) of table 12.5.

Table 12.6   Falsification tests of difference-in-difference estimates of the effect of mandatory and recommended arrest laws

	"Other homicides" per 100,000 inhabitants		"Other homicides" with female victims		Intimate partner homicides uncovered by arrest laws	
	(1)	(2)	(3)	(4)	(5)	(6)
Dependent variable mean	10.37		1.41		0.73	
Mandatory arrest law effect	4.2531	3.9985	0.5064	0.4631	0.2929	0.2656
	(2.7014)	(2.6749)	(0.4168)	(0.4036)	(0.2103)	(0.2071)
Recommended arrest law effect	0.5980	0.2595	−0.2492	−0.3104	0.1237	0.0911
	(3.8689)	(3.8360)	(0.5675)	(0.5531)	(0.2128)	(0.2050)
		−0.1151		−0.0167		−0.0153
		(0.4438)		(0.0569)		(0.0233)
Controls for other crime rates[a]	No	Yes	No	Yes	No	Yes
Controls for unemployment rate[b]	No	Yes	No	Yes	No	Yes
State-year demographic variables[c]	No	Yes	No	Yes	No	Yes
State-year economic and social controls[d]	No	Yes	No	Yes	No	Yes
Linear trend	Yes	Yes	Yes	Yes	Yes	Yes
State-fixed effects	Yes	Yes	Yes	Yes	Yes	Yes
Year-fixed effects	Yes	Yes	Yes	Yes	Yes	Yes
R^2	0.6434	0.6454	0.6011	0.6050	0.6669	0.6710

Notes: All regressions include 994 observations. The dependent variable for each column is the column title per 100,000 inhabitants. Robust standard errors, clustered by state, are reported in parentheses. "Other homicides" include homicides committed against employees, employers, other (nonimmediate) family, friends, other known individuals, and strangers. Intimate partner homicides uncovered by law refers to relationships that are classified as intimate partner but were not specified in the state's arrest law statute. See Legal Appendix for detailed coverage by state. Mandatory arrest (MA) states are states which require an arrest conditional on a report of domestic violence. Recommended arrest (RA) states are states where officers are instructed but not required to make a warrantless arrest when an intimate partner offense is reported.

[a]Crime rate controls use FBI Uniform Crime reports for the number of crimes per 100,000 inhabitants. Indexed crimes included in the violent crime variable are murder, robbery, assault, and rape. Indexed crimes included in the nonviolent crime count are burglary, larceny, motor vehicle theft, and drug crimes.

[b]Unemployment estimates are based on the March *Current Population Survey*.

[c]State demographic controls are based on the March *Current Population Survey* and include variables for the fraction of the population that is black, white, and other race, as well as age composition indicating share of prison population that is aged fourteen–nineteen, twenty–forty-nine, and fifty or older.

[d]State economic control variables are based on the March *Current Population Survey* and include the variables log state personal income per capita, and female-to-male employment ratio. State social policy controls include max Aid to Families with Dependent Children/Temporary Assistance to Needy Families (AFDC/TANF) for a family of three, unilateral divorce laws indicators (based on classification in Stevenson and Wolfers 2006), and indicators for whether the state has the death penalty.

This may be because abusers escalate violence after arrest as retribution for their punishment or because abuse victims may be less likely to contact the police in the face of an increased likelihood the abuser will be arrested. While experimental evidence rejected the former theory (on retribution), it could not test the latter reporting theory. However, this failure to contact the police results in fewer interventions, risking an increased probability of escalating violence. The differences between the experimental and quasi-experimental results on arrests for spousal abuse thus raise three important issues related to the broader discussion on the value of design-based versus theory-based studies.

First, if the experimental conditions had been better replicated in the policy, would the experimental results have generalized? Put differently, if holding reporting fixed we could increase arrest rates, would violence decrease as predicted by experimental evidence. To test this, I considered the effect of mandatory arrest laws on homicides committed against members of the immediate family. Because mandatory arrest laws required the arrest of an abuser in a domestic situation, familial abuse was also covered by these laws. However, unlike for adults, children typically do not report their own physical abuse to police. Instead, abuse is usually detected by an outside adult (such as a teacher or a doctor).[35] In this case, the probability of reporting may not be affected by increased penalties for the abusers.[36] Under these conditions, a law mandating arrests may more closely replicate the experimental conditions and, therefore, probability of severe violence to children by family members. To test this further, I restrict attention to only homicides of school-aged children (i.e., age six to seventeen). It is likely that abuse of quite small children may rely more on the reporting by an individual within the household and thus be subject to the same transference of costs as direct victims of intimate partner violence. In contrast, school-aged children are likely to see teachers, doctors, and nurses on a regular basis. As such, heightened abuse of these children is mostly likely to generate an increased likelihood of third-party reporting.[37] Comparing states with and without mandatory arrest laws before and after the laws change, I find a nearly 75 percent reduction in homicides of these children.[38] These results are consistent with the model, suggesting that once arrest laws do not rely on reporting by the abused, these

35. More specifically, of the nearly 2.8 million child abuse cases reported to child protective services agencies in 2000, 56.1 percent of all reports were from law enforcement, educators, medical and mental health professionals, social services personnel, child care providers, and other mandated reporters. See U.S. Department of Health and Human Services, Administration on Children, Youth, and Families, *Child Maltreatment 2000*, (Washington, DC: U.S. Government Printing Office, 2002).

36. Actually, many professionals have legal requirements to report suspected abuse, which can compensate for any potential costs they might incur from reporting abusers in their community.

37. This mandated reported is believed to be related to the decline in familial homicides. For discussion of this trend, see Durose et al. (2005).

38. For detailed analysis, see Iyengar (2009). This specification controls for the full set of covariates included in table 12.4 as well as state- and year-fixed effects.

laws appear to function as predicted, reducing harm to victim by imposing costs on abuse. The effect size is quite similar to the IV estimates presented for the MDVE in Angrist (2006). This comparison suggests that perhaps the experimental results were inapplicable, but were insufficient to determine in what contexts the arrest may be an effective deterrence.

The second issue raised by the difference between the experimental and nonexperimental results highlights the concept stated succinctly by Deaton: "heterogeneity is *not* a technical problem" (2009, page 10). In particular, the concept of heterogeneity is intimately tied to the theory by which we extrapolate from experimental evidence. While understanding the mean effect is critical, determining the variance is crucial from determining how broadly effective a policy might be. In the case of arrest for spousal abuse, while intimate partner homicides may have increased, it is not certain that this corresponds to increased levels of intimate partner abuse. If the intimate partner homicides and intimate partner abuse are negatively correlated, then arrest laws may decrease abuse while increasing homicides. The theory of how arrests affect violence levels is thus critical in determining what to take away from both the experimental and the nonexperimental evidence. Understanding the nature of this heterogeneity is critical for determining how effective arrest policies may be. For example, if heterogeneity implies that low-level violence is deterred but for some small set of individuals, arrests increase escalation, leading to homicide, then a policy of more stringent lethality assessment and greater nonlegal resources for victims may be most appropriate. If, on the other hand, heterogeneity implies that violence and homicides increase for many victims, even if they decrease for others, encouraging arrest may not be an effective response to intimate partner violence. Thus, at the heart of the policy question is the extent to which the treatment population is heterogeneous, and that aspect is as important as accurately estimating the mean treatment effect. This argument should include the caveat that the reverse is true as well. That experimental studies may be limited in their ability to fully characterize the distribution of treatment effects does not undermine the value of what they can contribute: a credible, unbiased measure of the treatment effect—which is no small thing and also critical to policy decisions.

This leads to the final point highlighted by the experimental and nonexperimental results: the important role for quasi-experimental studies. It is clear that experimental evidence is both necessary and often insufficient for determining the full effect of many policies. In the case of violence, low probability but high-costs events like homicide are unlikely to be detected by small-sample experiments but critical for decision making by policymakers. A similar claim can be made about theory-based designs, which do not lend themselves naturally to transparency for policymakers. In addition, often theory alone can have ambiguous predictions of the overall effect of a policy. Quasi-experimental designs, especially those with transparent designs, have an important role to play, not as a second-best alternative, but as an important contribution to the overall information about the efficacy of a policy.

In conclusion, this article takes some issue with the debate that appears to force economists to take a stance on the primacy of either internal or external validity. In the end, such a distinction is not helpful because failure of either internal or external validity is problematic for both academics and policymakers. Instead of imposing a hierarchy of methods, I propose viewing the information provided by each method as complementary components to the knowledge necessary to make informed decisions about policy efficacy. I also wish to emphasize the point that in empirical research, humility is a virtue. There is a sad irony that a mandatory arrest law intended to deter abuse actually increases intimate partner homicides, which provides an important cautionary tale. Suggesting that implementing policies with *only* experimental evidence, absent theory and some confirming nonexperimental studies, may be not only ineffective but counterproductive, hurting the very people the policy seeks to help. Thus, rather than view experiments, quasi-experiments, or structural estimation as procedures at odds with each other, this paper highlights the value that an integrated approach, which explicitly links randomized controlled trials, quasi-experimental studies, and structural modeling, may provide to more fully understand the effects of a desired policy intervention.

References

Angrist, J. 2006. Instrumental variables methods in experimental criminological research: What, why and how. *Journal of Experimental Criminology* 2:23–44.

Angrist, J., and G. Imbens. 1995. Two staged least squares estimates of average causal effects in models with variable treatment intensity. *Journal of the American Statistical Association* 90 (430): 431–42.

Ashenfelter, O., and D. Card. 1985. Using the longitudinal structure of earnings to estimate the effect of training programs. *Review of Economics and Statistics* 67 (4): 648–60.

Becker, G. S. 1968. Crime and punishment: an economic approach. *Journal of Political Economy* 76 (2): 169–217.

Blau, F. D. 1998. Trends in the well-being of American women, 1970–1995. *Journal of Economic Literature* 36 (1): 112–65.

Browne, A., and K. Williams. 1989. Exploring the effect of resource availability and the likelihood of female-perpetrated homicides. *Law and Society Review* 23 (1): 75–94.

Burtless, G. 1995. The case for randomized field trials in economic and policy research. *Journal of Economic Perspectives* 9 (2): 63–84.

Buzawa, E. S., and C. G. Buzawa. 1996. *Domestic violence: The criminal justice response.* 2nd ed. Thousand Oaks, CA: Sage.

Deaton, A. 2009. Instruments for development: Randomization in the topics, and the search for the elusive keys to economic development. Paper presented at Keynes Lecture, British Academy, London.

DeKeserdy, W. D., and M. Schwartz. 1998. *Measuring the extent of woman abuse in intimate heterosexual relationships: a critique of the conflict tactics scales.* Harrisburg, PA: National Online Resource Center on Violence Against Women. Available at http://new.vawnet.org/assoc_files_vawnet/ar_ctscrit.pdf.

Dobash, R. P., E. E. Dobash, M. Wilson, and M. Daly. 1992. The myth of sexual symmetry in marital violence. *Social Problems* 391:71–91.

Dugan, L. 2003. Domestic violence legislation: Exploring its impact on the likelihood of domestic violence, police involvement, and arrest. *Criminology and Public Policy* 2:283.

Durose, M., C. Harlow, P. Langan, M. Motivans, R. Rantala, and E. Smith. 2005. Family violence statistics: Including statistics on strangers and acquaintances. Bureau of Justice Statistics Report no. NCJ 207846. Washington, DC: Bureau of Justice Statistics.

Ehrlich, I. 1972. The deterrent effect of criminal law enforcement. *Journal of Legal Studies* 1 (2): 259–276.

Farmer, A., and J. Tiefenthaler. 2003. Explaining the recent decline in domestic violence. *Contemporary Economic Policy* 21 (2): 158–72.

Federal Bureau of Investigation. 1999. *Uniform Crime Reports, Supplementary Homicides Reports 1976–1999.* Washington, DC: GPO.

Federal Bureau of Investigation. 1999. *Uniform Crime Reports, Offenses Known and Clearances 1965–1999.* Washington, DC: GPO.

Flinn, C. 1986. Dynamic models of criminal careers. In *Criminal careers and "career criminals."* Vol. 2, ed. A. Blumstein. Washington, DC: National Academy Press 356–79.

Friedlander, D., and P. K. Robins. 1995. Evaluating program evaluations: New evidence on commonly used nonexperimental methods. *American Economic Review* 85 (4): 923–37.

Garner, J., J. Fagan, and C. Maxwell. 1995. Published findings from the Spouse Assault Replication Program: A critical review. *Journal of Quantitative Criminology* 11 (1): 3–28.

Gwinn, C. G., and A. O'Dell. 1993. Stopping the violence: the role of the police officer and the prosecutor. *Western State University Law Review* 20:297–317.

Hampton, R., W. Oliver, and L. Magarian. 2003. Domestic violence in the African American community. *Violence Against Women* 9 (5): 533–57.

Heckman, J. J. 1992. Randomization and social policy evaluation. In *Evaluating welfare and training programs,* ed. C. F. Manski and I. Garvinkel. Cambridge MA: Harvard University Press, 207–30.

Heckman, J. J., and R. Robb. 1985. Alternative methods for evaluating the impact of interventions: An overview. *Journal of Econometrics* 30:239–67.

Heckman, J. J., and S. Urzua. 2009. Comparing IV with structural models: What simple IV can and cannot identify. NBER Working Paper no. 14706. Cambridge, MA: National Bureau of Economic Research.

Heckman, J. J., S. Urzua, and E. J. Vytlacil. 2006. Understanding instrumental variables in models with essential heterogeneity. *Review of Economic and Statistics* 88 (3):389–432.

Imbens, G. 2009. Better LATE than nothing: Some comments on Deaton (2009) and Heckman and Urzua (2009). NBER Working Paper no. 14896. Cambridge, MA: National Bureau of Economic Research.

Iyengar, R. 2009. Does the certainty of arrest reduce domestic violence: Evidence from mandatory and recommended arrest laws. *Journal of Public Economics* 93:85–98.

Lalonde, R. 1986. Evaluating the econometric evaluations of training programs with experimental data. *American Economic Review* 76 (4): 604–20.

Ludwig, J., and D. Marcotte. 2005. Anti-depressants, suicide and drug regulation. *Journal of Policy Analysis and Management* 24 (2): 249–72.

Lyon, A. D. 1999. Be careful what you wish for: An examination of arrest and prosecution patterns of domestic violence cases in two cities in Michigan. *Michigan Journal of Gender and Law* 5:272–97.

Martin, M. 1997. Double your trouble: Dual arrest in family violence. *Journal of Family Violence* 12 (2): 139–57.

Maxwell, C. D., J. H. Garner, and J. A. Fagan. 2001. The effects of arrest on intimate partner violence: New evidence from the Spouse Assault Replication Program. Research in Brief. NCJ 188199. Washington, DC: U.S. Dept. of Justice, National Institute of Justice.

Mercy, J. A., and L. E. Saltzman. 1989. Fatal violence among spouses in the United States. *American Journal of Public Health* 79 (5): 595–99.

Meyers, B. 1992. Natural and quasi-experimental in economics. *Journal of Business and Economic Statistics* 13 (2): 151–61. JBES Symposium on Program and Policy Evaluation (April 1995).

Mills, L. G. 1998. Mandatory arrest and prosecution policies for domestic violence: A critical literature review and the case for more research to test victim empowerment approaches. *Criminal Justice and Behavior* 25:306–18.

Neville, H. A., and A. O. Pugh. 1997. General and culture-specific factors influencing African American women's reporting patterns and perceived social support following sexual assault. An exploratory investigation. *Violence Against Women* 3 (4): 361–81.

O'Keefe, M. 1997. Incarcerated battered women: A comparison of battered women who killed their abusers and those incarcerated for other offenses. *Journal of Family Violence* 12 (1): 1–19.

Pampel, F. C., and K. R. Williams. 2000. Intimacy and homicide: Compensating for missing data in the SHR. *Criminology* 38 (2): 661–79.

Pate, A., and E. Hamilton. 1992. Formal and informal deterrents to domestic violence: The Dade County spouse assault experiment. *American Sociological Review* 57:691–97.

Pollak, R. A. 2004. An intergenerational model of domestic violence. *Journal of Population Economics*

Rennison, C. 2002. Rape and sexual assault: Reporting to police and medical attention 1992–2000. Washington, DC: Bureau of Justice Statistics.

Sherman, L. 1992. *Policing domestic violence.* New York: Free Press.

Sherman, L., and R. A. Berk. 1984. The specific deterrent effects of arrest for domestic assault. *American Sociological Review* 49 (1): 261–72.

Smith, A. 2000. It's my decision, isn't it? A research note on battered women's perceptions of mandatory intervention laws. *Violence Against Women* 6 (12): 1384–1402.

Stevenson, B., and J. Wolfers. 2006. Bargaining in the shadow of the law: Divorce laws and family distress. *Quarterly Journal of Economics* 121 (1): 267–88.

Strauss, M. A., and R. J. Gelles. 1980. *Behind closed doors: A survey of family violence in America.* New York: Double day.

Tauchen, H., and A. D. Witte. 1995. The dynamics of domestic violence. *American Economic Review* 85 (2): 414–18.

Tjaden, P., and N. Thoennes. 2000. *Extent, nature, and consequences of intimate partner violence: findings from the National Violence Against Women Survey.* Washington, DC: Dept. of Justice, National Institute of Justice.

Williams, K., and R. L. Flewelling. 1987. Family, acquaintance, and stranger homicide: Alternative procedures for rates calculations. *Criminology* 25 (3): 543–60.

Comment   Rafael Di Tella

This interesting chapter can be read as making two main points. First, it shows that mandatory arrest laws (MAL) in cases of domestic violence have been counterproductive on at least one dimension, namely the frequency of serious abuse cases. Second, it shows that the method used for evaluating alternative policies against crime that has become the golden standard in criminology (and economics), namely randomized evaluation, can be seriously misleading. While I appreciate that the first contribution is a good complement to other cautionary notes already raised regarding the correct interpretation of the Minnesota Domestic Violence Experiment (see, for example, Schmidt and Sherman 1993), I believe the second point could have important consequences for the way we approach the policy evaluation more generally.

Let me start with the first point raised in the chapter. It establishes that the moment when laws requesting the arrest of those accused of participating in domestic abuse is passed, average intimate homicides in the state (per capita) increases while that of family-member homicide falls. The effect is very large. And the difference-in-difference approach helps considerably in establishing the causal connection between the laws and the separation in the frequency of the two types of domestic abuse. Figure 12.1 illustrates well the main empirical result.

The suggested interpretation is this: mandatory arrest laws reduce reporting by the victim (because it is more "costly"), so it escalates to homicide more often. Familial homicide drops because there is more reporting. The difference is presumed to occur because reporting of familial violence is made by nonvictims (e.g., teachers, for whom the "cost" is lower, as they do not know—or are not attached to—the victimizer). This puts the focus on reporting, something for which we unfortunately get no data. One approach to investigate the proposed channel further would be to see if the response is particularly large in states with harsher punishments. There are differences in the severity of sentencing across states and over time (one example, of course, is the death penalty). This is particularly important with the appearance of three-strikes-and-you-are-out laws. A similar point suggests that groups that are incarcerated at higher rates might be more inclined to reduce reporting in response to MAL. Incidentally, the similarity in response rates across racial groups is perhaps troubling for those who believe both in the results of this paper and the presence of racial bias in the legal system. But these are relatively minor issues compared to the fact that the paper asks

Rafael Di Tella is the Joseph C. Wilson Professor of Business Administration at Harvard Business School, a research associate of the National Bureau of Economic Research, and a member of the Canadian Institute for Advanced Research.

us to think harder about theories of reporting, which is an important and understudied topic.

My second point is that the chapter raises an issue that far exceeds the issue of mandatory arrest laws. Indeed, I think it shows that randomized experiments, often by construction, can be misleading in the analysis of a large class of policies against crime because we can't be sure about the quantity of information in the hands of the public. For example, we typically want to look at incentives to reduce crime. But in order to study them, people must know about the different penalties they are faced with. But if the criminals know, then the public will know. And they may not be keen on allowing randomization of penalties. Thus, the paper suggests that there are limits to the use of randomized experiments in at least some important areas of crime.

As the author reminds us, mandatory arrest laws were passed in the United States in response to the results of the influential Minnesota Domestic Violence Experiment (MDVE). In it, the type of police intervention following the report of an incident was randomized (there were three groups: arrest for at least one night, arrest and immediate release, and simple warning plus reading of the rights of the victim). The study revealed large drops in domestic violence following arrest. Now, Iyengar's paper shows that it is wrong to extrapolate these results to justify MAL because they were obtained *conditional* on reporting. The public in general, and women in particular, were not informed of this experiment. A key point of the chapter is that this difference is significant because of behavioral differences that may arise in the relationship between the battered women and their abuser that may lead them to reduce reporting following an increase in punishment.

Now the question is whether we can avoid this problem in the future by designing better studies. I am pessimistic for one simple reason: I do not think that the lack of external validity in this dimension of the Minnesota experiment was the result of an avoidable mistake. It seems to me that it would have been impossible to communicate widely to women and other potential victims about the random nature of the program. And without such communication, incentives cannot really be studied. I know that randomization of the treatment is standard in the scientific evaluation of the effectiveness of medicines and that patients fully accept this. But it is also true that they voluntarily sign in to participate in such clinical trials. More important, we currently do not know much about the settings where the public will allow randomization of policies.

Public Reaction to Randomized Experiments

It is, of course, hard to know if the public holds such heterogeneous preferences over the domain over which it is appropriate to conduct scientific evaluation of policies through randomized trials. But given that it seems important for us to know where people actually accept randomization and where they do not, I have run a small scale survey asking high school students (fifteen to sixteen year olds) in Argentina the following two questions:

1. In the United States, there have been two recent studies. In one, in order to find out if a certain medicine was appropriate in fighting cancer, it had to be administered to only half of a group of patients (the other half receiving a placebo). In order to decide which half, the researchers threw a coin. Do you find this procedure acceptable?

Yes
No

2. In the other study (also in the United States), in order to find out if a certain punishment was appropriate in fighting crime, it had to be given to only half of a group of criminals (while the other half received a lower sentence as punishment). In order to decide which half, the researchers threw a coin. Do you find this procedure acceptable?

Yes
No

A sample of eighteen high school students were interviewed (one on one). The results are as follows:

Question 1: Yes = 14, No = 4
Question 2: Yes = 0, No = 18

Given the cheap design, the results are obviously just suggestive. Still, they show that it is indeed possible that the public supports the use of randomized experiments in some areas but not in others. One possible explanation for the differences observed here is that in the medical context it is a single agent decision problem. There is a procedure being considered and the person making the decision to engage in the trial bears all the potential costs. In the crime context, there are also victims (and these need to be consulted if their victimizers will be given less than fair sentences).[1]

In brief, my point is that the chapter shows that one of the most interesting and influential randomized experiments that we have available to inform the design of policy in the area of crime fails in some important way. And that the reason it fails is not because of a mistake that can easily be avoided in the future, but rather because experiments are not particularly useful in at least some areas in crime.[2] Indeed, it is useful to remember that experiments in medicine hope to uncover the effect of a medicine on a person. In contrast, in economics (and in criminology), we are often interested in the effect of affecting one person on the incentives that *other* people have for engaging in specific behaviors. And it is precisely the study of that "external" aspect that the public might refuse to study using randomized experiments.

1. Incidentally, this would favor retribution versus deterrence as positive theories of punishment, as in Di Tella and Dubra (2008).

2. For a good description of several important experimental projects in criminology, see Lawrence Sherman's Web page at the University of Pennsylvania.

References

Di Tella, Rafael, and Juan Dubra. 2008. Crime and punishment in the "American dream." *Journal of Public Economics* 92 (7): 1564–84.

Schmidt, Janell D., and Lawrence W. Sherman. 1993. Does arrest deter domestic violence? *American Behavioral Scientist* 36: 601–9.

Contributors

María Laura Alzúa
CEDLAS
Department of Economics, Faculty of
  Economic Science
Universidad Nacional de La Plata
Calle 6 entre 47 y 48
(1900) La Plata, Argentina

Andrés Borenstein
British Embassy
Dr. Luis Agote 2412
(1425) Buenos Aires, Argentina

Alfredo Canavese

Philip J. Cook
Sanford School of Public Policy
Duke University
Durham, NC 27708-0245

Guillermo Cruces
CEDLAS
Department of Economics, Faculty of
  Economic Science
Universidad Nacional de La Plata
Calle 6 entre 47 y 48
(1900) La Plata, Argentina

Rafael Di Tella
Harvard Business School
Soldiers Field
Boston, MA 02163

Angela K. Dills
Department of Economics
Wellesley College
106 Central Street
Wellesley, MA 02481

Mirko Draca
London School of Economics
Houghton Street
London WC2A 2AE, England

Sebastian Edwards
UCLA Anderson Graduate School of
  Business
110 Westwood Plaza, Suite C508
Box 951481
Los Angeles, CA 90095-1481

Sebastian Galiani
Department of Economics
Washington University in St. Louis
Campus Box 1208
St. Louis, MO 63130

Alejandro Gaviria
Department of Economics
Universidad de los Andes
Calle 19A No. 1-37 Este
12 Bogotá, Colombia

Kaj Gittings
Department of Economics
2114 Patrick F. Taylor Hall
Baton Rouge, LA 70803-6306

Ana María Ibáñez
Department of Economics
Universidad de los Andes
Calle 19A No. 1-37 Este
12 Bogotá, Colombia

Radha Iyengar
LSE Research Laboratory
Department of Economics and CEP
Houghton Street
London WC2A 2AE, England

Lucas Llach
Department of History and School of
    Government
Universidad Torcuato Di Tella
Miñones 2177
(1426) Buenos Aires, Argentina

Stephen Machin
Department of Economics
University College London
Gower Street
London WC1E 6BT, England

Carlos Medina
Banco de la República
Calle 50 No. 50-21
Medellín, Colombia

João M P De Mello
Department of Economics
Pontifical Catholic University of Rio
    de Janeiro
Rua Marquês de São Vicente,
    225-Gávea
22451-900 Rio de Janeiro, RJ Brazil

Jeffrey A. Miron
Department of Economics
Harvard University
Cambridge, MA 02138

Naci Mocan
Department of Economics
Louisiana State University
2119 Patrick F. Taylor Hall
Baton Rouge, LA 70803-6306

Leonardo Morales
Banco de la República
Calle 50 No. 50-21
Medellín, Colombia

Andrés Moya
Department of Agricultural and
    Resource Economics
University of California, Davis
One Shields Avenue
Davis, CA 95616

Joana Naritomi
The World Bank
1818 H Street, NW
Washington, DC 20433

Jairo Núñez
Department of Social Policy
Javeriana University
S.J. Bogotá, D.C. Colombia

Brendan O'Flaherty
Economics Department
Columbia University
827 International Affairs Building, MC
    3308
420 West 118th Street
New York, NY 10027

Rony Pshisva
Protego Mexico
Boulevard Manuel Ávila Camacho No.
    36 Piso 22
Col. Lomas de Chapultepec,
    Delegación Miguel
Hidalgo, México, Distrito Federal; C.P.
    11000

Juan Pantano
Department of Economics
Washington University in St. Louis
St. Louis, MO 63130-4899

Lucía Quesada
Department of Economics
Universidad Torcuato Di Tella
Sáenz Valiente 1010
(1428) Buenos Aires Argentina

Catherine Rodriguez
Department of Economics
Universidad de los Andes
Calle 19A No. 1-37 Este
12 Bogotá, Colombia

Lucas Ronconi
LICIP, Universidad Torcuato Di Tella
and CIPPEC
Saenz Valiente 1010
(1428) Buenos Aires, Argentina

Martín González Rozada
Business School
Universidad Torcuato Di Tella
Saenz Valiente 1010
(1428) Buenos Aires, Argentina

Ernesto Schargrodsky
Business School
Universidad Torcuato Di Tella
Saenz Valiente 1010
(1428) Buenos Aires, Argentina

Alexandre Schneider
Department of Education of São
    Paulo
Pc Br Homem de Melo
03423-010 São Paulo, SP Brazil

Rajiv Sethi
Department of Economics
Barnard College
Columbia University
3009 Broadway
New York, NY 10027

Rodrigo R. Soares
Department of Economics
Pontifical Catholic University of Rio
    de Janeiro
Rua Marquês de São Vicente,
    225-Gávea
22451-900 Rio de Janeiro, RJ Brazil

Gustavo A. Suarez
Board of Governors of the Federal
    Reserve System
20th Street and Constitution Avenue
Washington, DC 20551

Garrett Summers
1800 Defense Pentagon
Washington, DC 20301-1800

Edgar Villa
Department of Economics
Pontifica Universidad Javeriana
Calle 40 No. 6-23, Edificio Gabriel
    Giraldo
Bogotá, D.C. Colombia

Robert Witt
Department of Economics
The University of Surrey
Guildford, Surrey GU2 7XH, England

Author Index

Subject Index